Essays and Characters

LAMB TO THOMPSON

THE MACMILLAN COMPANY
NEW YORK · BOSTON · CHICAGO · DALLAS
ATLANTA · SAN FRANCISCO

MACMILLAN & CO., LIMITED
LONDON · BOMBAY · CALCUTTA
MELBOURNE

THE MACMILLAN COMPANY
OF CANADA, LIMITED
TORONTO

ESSAYS AND CHARACTERS

Lamb to Thompson

BY

ROBERT WITHINGTON, Ph.D.

*Professor of English Language and Literature,
Smith College*

NEW YORK

THE MACMILLAN COMPANY

1933

Set up and electrotyped.

Published September, 1933.

SET UP AND ELECTROTYPED BY T. MOREY & SON

· PRINTED IN THE UNITED STATES OF AMERICA ·

PREFACE

THE object of this collection, like that of the companion volume, *Essays and Characters: Montaigne to Goldsmith*, is to give a fairly representative selection of the more important essayists of the period covered by the book. Much prose was produced in the nineteenth century, and one cannot hope to include between two covers all the significant writing of the ten decades; I have, therefore, emphasized the informal essay, though I do add a few examples of the critical and the philosophical essay, if not too long or too formal. I need not remark that this is not an anthology of nineteenth-century prose, and that few readers will expect to find here the names of Carlyle, Macaulay, Newman, or even Arnold; their significant writings lie outside the field here represented.

No compiler of an anthology can hope to please everyone, and many colleagues will doubtless accuse me of sins, both of omission and commission. If I plead guilty to them, I can only trust that the virtues of this collection will outweigh its shortcomings. I have sought to bring together an adequate representation of few authors, rather than fragmentary selections from many, hoping that readers will be led to make the further acquaintance of these writers, as well as to enjoy the essays they find here.

A difference of practice in the various editions used as bases for the text, and my desire to keep, as closely as possible, to the original, account for the lack of a "standardization" commonly found in books of this kind. In a few passages, I have changed spelling or punctuation for the sake of clearness; I have silently corrected an occasional typographical error; but in general, I have tried to resist a strong temptation to introduce a colorless uniformity of the minutiæ which, like condiments, contribute to the flavor of style.

I am not burdening the text with notes—for I believe that the student will gain a more lasting benefit from the knowledge of reference-books which his effort to furnish his own notes must give him, than from the cursory reading of information furnished him without effort of his own. But I include the notes furnished by the authors themselves, and add a few explanatory comments at the back of the volume.

The term "essay" is not an easy one to define in brief, for many types of prose-writing are loosely classified under this head. If the reader wishes to try his hand at a definition, he will find here material on which to work. He should consider the relative importance of manner and matter; the part that style and mood play in his enjoyment of this kind of writing; the emphasis which can legitimately be placed on the revelation of personality; how far an essayist can try to persuade or convince his reader; how important the "lyrical" quality is; whether subjectivity is an essential element of all essays; whether an essayist must—or should not—preach; whether narration and description may be allowed in an essay, and, if so, to what extent. Ought an essayist to confine his efforts to amusing or entertaining the reader? does he stimulate thought? is he of interest to every age, or only to his contemporaries? Is there a close connection between the interpretation of life which an essayist may give, and that furnished by the dramatist or the novelist? and is this connection seen elsewhere than in the "character"? Does one, knowing Dickens, Thackeray, and George Eliot only from their novels, get a different light on them from their essays? or does one, through the essayist, catch glimpses of the novelist?

Back of all essays lies the suggestion of "trial," which is at the root of the word. An essay must exhaust neither the subject nor the reader. This is not saying that an essay may never be serious, and some essays are long; most effective essays, however, can be read by the average reader at one sitting. In general, an essay should leave a single impression—but there are exceptions (as in the case of Holmes, for example) to this generalization. In fact, one can find exceptions to most generalizations made about the essay, which is one of the delightful difficulties in formulating an adequate definition of the term. Perhaps it is not necessary that such a definition be formulated.

Even in objective essays, we can get an idea of the author's background by noting his allusions, the sources of his quotations, the matters to which he refers. His attitude toward life is shown by his manner of approaching his subject; his humor, his satire, his seriousness, his love of paradox, or his literalness, all throw light on his personality. Sometimes critical essays are subjective—and of course a subjective essay reveals the writer more clearly than one kept carefully objective. How far a revelation of personality is compatible with a sense of humor is an interesting question.

It may fairly be hoped that the essays printed in this volume will add to the pleasure and inspiration of the reader—for, like the poet, the dramatist, and the novelist, the essayist contributes to our understanding of human nature, and the deeper meaning of life. If he expresses his own personality or comments on the society about him; if he deals with ethical problems, or pictures the follies of his age—with the aim of correcting them; if his weapon is gentle satire or agreeable preaching, he gives us a sense of proportion. The Poet at the Breakfast Table could learn from everyone he met; everyone we meet can at least expound his point of view.

I wish to express my gratitude to Professor Chester N. Greenough, to Professor John C. Scammell, and to Professor A. C. Vaughan, for their advice and helpful criticism; to Dr. W. D. Howe and to Charles Scribner's Sons for their generous permission to print the essays of Stevenson, and to Wilfrid Meynell, Esq., for his kind permission to print those of Thompson; to Walter B. Briggs, Esq., and other officials of the Harvard University Library for their aid in procuring rare editions for collation; and to the Superintendent of the Reading Room of the Congressional Library at Washington for his help in various bibliographical details. I appreciate also the friendly encouragement of T. C. Morehouse, Esq., J. Alden Behnke, Esq., and Frederick T. Sutphen, Esq., of The Macmillan Company, who have recognized how much an attractive format adds to the joy of reading, and I am grateful for the assistance of the latter and Miss V. E. Smith, whose interest and expedition were invaluable while the volume was going through the press.

ROBERT WITHINGTON.

LITTLE COMPTON, RHODE ISLAND,
August, 1933.

CONTENTS

INTRODUCTION[1]

ONE is often tempted to wonder if, in their essence, humor and romance are not mutually exclusive qualities—incompatible, if not, indeed, antithetical; and if this be so, it seems paradoxical to think of romantic qualities in connection with a form of writing as humorous as the essay often is. Perhaps no more ridiculous figure can be found in our human comedy than the man who always takes himself seriously; it is only when we can laugh at ourselves—being in a ludicrous predicament—that we can lay claim to a sense of humor. Many who find it easy to laugh at their neighbors fall down on this final test of laughing at—or even with—themselves. The "practical joker" lacks, more often than he realizes, the sense of humor on which he prides himself; and the man intent on gaining a goal—be he reformer or lover—has neither time nor inclination to become objective.

The swain surprised on his knees before his mistress may laugh half-heartedly from embarrassment; it is rather his friends who will see the humor of the situation. Rare indeed is the earnest lover whose sense of detachment would allow him to view the scene through the eyes of his comrades, and so catch the fun of it; as a matter of fact, half the fun would be gone if he could do so. On the stage, the more we feel for the lovers, the less comedy do we find in the play; how much truer this is in "real life," particularly if we are one of the lovers ourselves! It is not by chance that there is so little humor in Malory, or in the romances from which he drew; our sympathy with these chivalric figures is so complete that we are blind to their absurdities. But romance withdraws before the humor, as well as the satire, of Cervantes.

Our use of the term "essay" is vague enough at best; but even if we limit it to its "true province,"—the "setting forth . . . of

---

[1] "Of the Romantic Essay," originally published in the *South Atlantic Quarterly*, July 1924. It is here reprinted with the permission of the editors of that periodical; a few typographical infelicities are silently corrected.

its author's moods, tastes, predilections, aversions, and all other reactions to experience," as Dr. Whitmore phrases it [1]—and exclude the "study," the "sketch," the "character," and the "portrait," we shall find plenty of room for humorous essays left. The term "romance," too, is capable of many interpretations; it means one thing to the schoolgirl, and another to the critic of literature,[2] but both of these meanings have a quality in common: and it is this quality which militates against humor.

Critics have found certain elements in that kind of writing which they term "romantic," and it might be well briefly to recall them. Broadly speaking, "romance" appeals to our emotions, rather than to our intellect; it expresses itself in an emphasis on that which is distant, in time or place; it deals with the supernatural, often, or with the melancholic; with mediæval ruins, with the uncanny, the eerie, the weird. It is essentially subjective. When Mark Twain takes a Connecticut Yankee to King Arthur's Court, he finds no longer the romantic Camelot of Malory—or even of Tennyson; Thomas Ingoldsby's ghosts are not romantic; the cowboy is not romantic to the Wyoming sheriff, though he may be to a New York urchin or to a French peasant. Within certain limits the boundary may shift: the trenches were much more romantic to those who never saw them than to those who did—so was the Civil War, or the Commune; but the subjective, lyric outpouring of a poet's soul can never be anything but romantic. It is this self-revelation which lyric poet and essayist share in common, that gives us our starting-point; subjectivity is an important element of the romantic spirit.[3]

From Montaigne on, essayists have voiced their moods in no argumentative or dogmatic way, but with an implicit—if not an expressed—tolerance of other people's moods and points of view. If essays are (as they have been called) "written monologues," or "personal letters addressed to the public," they are not propa-

---

[1] Charles E. Whitmore, "The Field of the Essay," in the *Publications of the Modern Language Association of America*, xxxvi, 4 (December 1921), pp. 551 ff.

[2] Cf. Greenough and Kittredge, *Words and Their Ways in English Speech* (Boston, 1901), pp. 380 f.

[3] "In a sense it is very true that the essay in the hands of such a writer as Lamb exemplifies the finest capacities of prose as a medium of self-expression precisely as lyric poetry expresses those of verse; but thereby an *Essay of Elia* and a pure lyric are as unlike as are the two media which they thus present at their most highly finished development; they are parallel, but unmistakably different." Whitmore, *art. cit.*

ganda, and aim neither to persuade nor to convince. Leaving out of account critical essays and such "non-exhaustive treatments" of historical, biographical, or even philosophical, topics (which Dr. Whitmore would call rather "studies" or "estimates"), as are sometimes included under this vaguely-used term, there remains a residuum of expository essay, condensing the writer's experience (Bacon) or discussing informally a point of manners or taste (Addison); and the essay which inverts or whimsically applies a normal expository process (as often in Addison or Lamb). Such is the classification of Whitmore. Not only does the personality of the writer tinge such essays with a romantic flavor (though in the case of Addison this is not common, as the "Spectator" is constantly objective), but the subject may often be romantic. Friendship, love—even marriage and single life—superstition, beauty, and adversity are among the subjects dealt with by Bacon; all of them are capable of romantic treatment, but when the point of view is not romantic (and Bacon's never was), the essay cannot be considered so. For, after all, the quality is determined not so much by the subject as by the treatment it receives; and Lord Verulam was too practical a man, too much guided by his head, to be considered in any sense romantic.

The following passage from Addison [1] illustrates how romantic material may be treated unromantically:

I was walking in this place last night between the hours of nine and ten, and could not but fancy it one of the most proper scenes in the world for a ghost to appear in. The ruins of the abbey are scattered up and down on every side, and half covered with ivy and elder-bushes, the harbours of several solitary birds which seldom make their appearance till the dusk of the evening. The place was formerly a church-yard, and has still several marks in it of graves and burying-places. There is such an echo among the old ruins and vaults, that if you stamp but a little louder than ordinary, you hear the sound repeated. At the same time the walk of elms, with the croaking of the ravens which from time to time are [sic] heard from the tops of them, looks exceedingly solemn and venerable. These objects naturally raise seriousness and attention; and when night heightens the awfulness of the place, and pours out her supernumerary horrors upon everything in it, I do not at all wonder that weak minds fill it with spectres and apparitions. . . . As I was walking in this solitude, where the

[1] "Spectator," 110 (6 July 1711).

dusk of the evening conspired with so many other occasions of terror, I observed a cow grazing not far from me, which an imagination that was apt to startle might easily have construed into a black horse without an head: and I dare say the poor footman lost his wits upon some such trivial occasion.

In an illuminating chapter on "Humor in Poetry," President Neilson points out "that in poetry of the romantic sort, and especially where the imagination is of the creative kind and works intensely, humor is often absent." [1] If a given stanza contains both humor and poetry, "when the humor comes in, the poetry goes out." But Dr. Neilson does observe a few cases of humor in combination with true imaginative poetry, and cites a passage from *Measure for Measure* to illustrate his contention that the mutual exclusion of humor and imaginative poetry is not always absolute. Their harmony is made possible, he notes, through the element of sympathy—in itself largely imaginative—which enriches the poetry and lifts it above the level of satire that merely stings. This sympathetic element in humor brings it into its familiar relation with pathos; and just as Dr. Neilson finds the best example of that rare combination of humor with true poetry in Shakespeare, so we may find the unusual combination of humor with true romantic feeling in Lamb. In both combinations the humor is delicate, sympathetic, closely related to pathos, if you will; but it is none the less humor.

As Dr. Neilson has shown, humor may be grim, pathetic, or merry. Such forms as irony or satire, directed as they are to the intellect, cannot, of course, be considered even remotely romantic. Summing up the relation of humor to various types of poetry, Dr. Neilson concludes: "In romantic poetry in general, poetry in which there is a marked predominance of imagination, we have found humor to be noticeably rare. . . . This has not been surprising. In real life everyone has observed the absence of humor in people of a strongly romantic tendency; and, in our own romantic moods, our flights into ideal realms are apt to be checked by the intrusion of even a momentary glimpse of ourselves as ludicrous. If it is difficult, as the philosophers have always said, to be in love

[1] William A. Neilson, *The Essentials of Poetry* (Houghton Mifflin, Boston, 1912), p. 247.

and to be wise, it is still more difficult to be a romantic lover and retain a sense of humor." It is needless to remark that the converse does not always hold: not everyone who lacks a sense of humor is necessarily in love.

What is true of romantic poetry is equally true of the romantic essay. When humor comes in, romance goes out; and if, in a given essay, both elements are found, those passages which are colored by the one lose the other. A lover may have a sense of humor—but he does not have it in his most lover-like moods. We are likely to think that once a person has a sense of humor, he has it for all time; and we are sometimes surprised when he fails to show it.

When we find the tender, romantic humor which is made up of sympathy and a delicate perception of the ludicrous, we are midway between the satiric and the sentimental. It is not easy to walk such a path without getting over toward one extreme or the other, and we should not wonder at finding few writers who can combine the two qualities in just the right degree. When we do find such a one, however, we find a master of letters. Literature of this kind can rise to no greater heights than it attains in the pages of Elia, when, for instance, he yearns toward the dim specks—poor blots—innocent blacknesses, the young Africans of our own growth—these almost clergy imps, who sport their cloth without assumption; and from their little pulpits (the tops of chimneys), in the nipping air of a December morning, preach a lesson of patience to mankind. Or when he considers the best of Sapors—in the dish, his second cradle, how meek he lieth!—wouldst thou have had this innocent grow up to the grossness and indocility which too often accompany maturer swinehood? Or when (tenderest of all), he talks to the John and Alice who were nothing; less than nothing, and dreams . . . and then wakes to find himself seated in his bachelor armchair, with the faithful Bridget unchanged by his side.

Such humor is like the happiness defined in a recent novel.[1] "Happiness to be realized needs faint perception of sadness as needs the egg the touch of salt to manifest its flavour. Flashes of entertainment may enliven the most wretched of us; but that's pleasure; that's not happiness. One comes to know the only true and ideal happiness is happiness tinctured with faintest, vaguest

[1] A. S. M. Hutchinson, *This Freedom* (Little, Brown), Book II, ch. iii.

hint of tears. It is peace; and who knows peace that has not come to it through storm . . . ?" The "flashes of entertainment" which are "pleasure" may be likened to wit, to satire; the happiness which is peace—which is "tinctured with faintest, vaguest hint of tears"—is the humor of the romantic essayist.

There are critics who scorn romanticism, in all of its manifestations, as if it were a plague; and undoubtedly if carried to excess it may become so. But all excesses are unhealthy, and the opposite extreme may be equally unwholesome. He who rules his life by intellect alone is no more pleasant to look upon than he whose imagination is "apt to startle," and turn a cow quietly grazing into a black horse without a head. *Medio tutissimus ibis* remains ever sound advice; but if one must have an extreme, remember Stevenson's "It is better to be a fool than to be dead." The coldness of Bacon may hide a geyser of emotion—for Bacon lived and suffered; but if it does, we do not feel it, and most of us are attracted to writers who show more sympathy and less objectivity. Can one get a better idea of Thackeray's personality—hidden in his novels—than by reading *The Roundabout Papers?* "I dare say," begins his essay on "Ogres," "the reader has remarked that the upright and independent vowel, which stands in the vowel-list between E and O, has formed the subject of the main part of these essays." Montaigne presented "a well-meaning Booke" to his reader; "I desire therein to be delineated in mine owne genuine, simple and ordinarie fashion, without contention, art or study, for it is my selfe I pourtray." If Lamb is less obviously personal, he works on our sympathies, and his appeal is none the less romantic. The Breakfast-Table Papers of Holmes combine—as do Thackeray's essays—humor with that quality we call romanticism; but the idyl on Boston Common and the story of Iris show the sympathetic delicate humor which fits the emotional appeal.

Laughter is a social emotion; we like to share our smiles, and for this reason we tell our stories to almost anyone who will listen to them—fellow-members of a club, or the stranger in the smoking-car. But we laugh best with our friends, as we laugh most heartily at those for whom we have little sympathy. No better distinction between romantic humor and its opposite can be drawn. At best, romantic humor is gentle; and when sympathy overflows upon us, our laughter fades.

No essay—in the true sense of the word—can be argumentative; indeed, no matter what his medium of expression, the artist should never argue. The observer, spectator, or whatever he may call himself, who stands outside his subject, looking at humanity objectively, may satirize manners and customs, but he cannot deal with subjects likely to arouse the antagonism of his readers or awaken his own bitterness. Tolerance, urbanity, humor, are the outstanding qualities of the objective essay; these may develop into sympathy, whimsicality, subjectivity. And when we find these qualities, we find romantic elements. *What* the subject is, is of minor importance; *how* it is dealt with, is what counts—the spirit of the essay gives it its classification. Often the qualities are felt rather than observed; sometimes each paragraph has its distinctive flavor, and the essay as a whole can hardly be classified—though it can be enjoyed. But if the essay is a "snapshot of a mood," why seek consistency?

One of the important characteristics of an essay is its style. To appreciate style, one has to use his intellect, it is true; but without analysis one can often feel a satisfaction in the way a writer expresses himself. When one is conscious of style, it is bad; for style is a window through which one looks at meaning, and one should never be aware of the glass. To deny romanticism any appeal to the intellect is, perhaps, unfair to romanticism; the approach to the intellect may, however, be made through the emotions; and when the emotions are aroused, the reader is not likely to analyze the means used to arouse them. If he becomes conscious of *tours de force*, his emotional response is weakened, and the romantic appeal of the essay is correspondingly lessened.

The romantic flavor of our essays can be traced back to Montaigne, whose chief aim was self-revelation. Bacon is the source of the objective essay—the handbook of conduct, which is in the back of the "Spectator's" mind, as he satirizes his contemporaries in an endeavor to improve their behavior. Steele is a more sympathetic critic than his associate; and it does not need Thackeray's portrait of him in *Henry Esmond* to make him more romantic—and more lovable—than Addison. That "classical" writer is at his best on his death-bed; and the gentle scorn with which Mr. Roundabout and the Professor regard the spectacle is romanticism's answer to the humbug. Says Thackeray: "I like these little tales and sportive exercises. I had begun a little print collection once. I had Addison in his night-gown in bed in at Holland House, requesting young Lord Warwick to remark how a Christian should die. . . ." "Addison," says Holmes, "gets up a *tableau* and utters an admirable sentiment,—or somebody makes up the posthumous dying epigram for him." [1]

For romanticism may preach and instruct—so long as it does so romantically; and romantic essayists may be permitted to sermonize occasionally, if they do not lose sympathy and tolerance in doing so. Propaganda kills romance, of all kinds; intolerance— that bane of the reformer—kills romance; but Mr. Roundabout, neither in nor out of his pulpit, professes to be bigger, or cleverer, or wiser, or better, than any of his congregation; and Holmes admits that he never met anyone who could not teach him something. When the moralizer turns satirist, he is in danger of losing his title of romanticist (and much of his charm), because he is losing his sympathy.

R. W.

---

[1] See Thackeray, "On a Hundred Years Hence," and Holmes, *The Professor at the Breakfast Table*, xii.

BIBLIOGRAPHICAL NOTE

THE history of the essay is adequately treated by Hugh Walker in *The English Essay and Essayists* (London, 1915). For an analysis of this form, see R. D. O'Leary, *The Essay* (New York, 1928). Short sketches of the history of the essay may be found in William F. Bryan and Ronald S. Crane, *The English Familiar Essay* (Boston, &c., 1916); George Carver, *Periodical Essays of the Eighteenth Century* (New York, 1930), and in Louis Wann, "The Development of the Essay in English," the Introduction to *Century Readings in the English Essay* (New York, 1926). Reading lists and bibliographical material are included in Professor Wann's volume, pp. 523–526; in Bryan and Crane, pp. 387–392; in Raymond W. Pence, *Essays by Present-Day Writers* (New York, 1924), pp. 353–360; Benjamin A. Heydrick, *Types of the Essay* (New York, 1921), pp. 367–373; for contemporary essays, see *The Reader's Guide to Periodical Literature*. Professor E. A. Walter, of the University of Michigan, has announced an *Essay Annual*, beginning in 1933, designed to interpret contemporary problems and events. For classification of essays, see Charles E. Whitmore, "The Field of the Essay," in *Publications of the Modern Language Association of America* for December, 1921 (xxxvi, 4), pp. 551–564.

Many of the authors here represented may be found in such accessible editions as the World's Classics, the Modern Student's Library, the Modern Reader's Library, the Everyman's Library, &c.

PERIODICAL PUBLICATION

The essays here reprinted were first published as follows:

LAMB. With the exception of "Valentine's Day" (*Examiner*, 14 and 15 February 1819; again in Leigh Hunt's *Indicator*, 14 February 1821), "The Genteel Style in Writing" (*New Monthly Magazine*, March 1826), and "Popular Fallacies" (*New Monthly Magazine*, January to September 1826), the essays appeared in the *London Magazine*, as indicated. "A Chapter on Ears" (March 1821); "A Quakers' Meeting" (April 1821); "The Old and the New Schoolmaster" (May 1821); "My Relations" (June 1821); "Mackery End, in Hertfordshire"

(July 1821); "Imperfect Sympathies" (August 1821); "Grace Before Meat" (November 1821); "Dream Children: A Reverie" (January 1822); "Distant Correspondents" (March 1822); "On the Artificial Comedy of the Last Century" (April 1822); "A Bachelor's Complaint of the Behaviour of Married People" (*Reflector*, no. 4 (1811); *London Magazine*, September 1822); "Old China" (March 1823); "Poor Relations" (May 1823); "The Convalescent" (July 1825). They were collected in *The Essays of Elia* (1823) and *The Last Essays of Elia* (1833).

HUNT. Unless otherwise noted, Hunt's essays appeared in the *Indicator*. "The Old Lady" (Round Table No. 45, in the *Examiner*, 29 September 1816); "The Maid-servant" (Round Table No. 46, in the *Examiner*, 20 October 1816); "Social Genealogy" (17 November 1819); "A Few Thoughts on Sleep" (12 January 1820); "Getting Up on Cold Mornings" (19 January 1820); "The Old Gentleman" (2 February 1820); "Walks Home by Night in Bad Weather. Watchmen" (*Companion*, 6 February 1820); "Deaths of Little Children" (5 April 1820); "Shaking Hands" (12 July 1820); "On the Talking of Nonsense" (13 December 1820); "Inexhaustibility of the Subject of Christmas" (*Monthly Repository*, December 1837).

HAZLITT. "On Nicknames" (*Edinburgh Magazine*, September 1818); "Thoughts on Taste" (*Edinburgh Magazine*, October 1818; July 1819); "Character of Cobbett" (*Table-Talk*, vi, 1821); "On Reading Old Books" (*London Magazine*, February 1821; *Plain Speaker*, xx); "On Living to One's-Self" (*Table-Talk*, x, 1821); "On Vulgarity and Affectation" (*Table-Talk*, xvi, 1821); "On Going a Journey" (*New Monthly Magazine*, January 1822; *Table-Talk*, xix); "On Familiar Style" (*Table-Talk*, xxiv, 1822); "Of Persons One Would Wish to Have Seen" (*New Monthly Magazine*, January 1826); "Of the Feeling of Immortality in Youth" (*Monthly Magazine*, March 1827); "On a Sun-Dial" (*New Monthly Magazine*, October 1827).

DE QUINCEY. "A Peripatetic Philosopher" (*London Magazine*, September 1823); "On the Knocking at the Gate in 'Macbeth'" (*London Magazine*, October 1823); "On Suicide" (*London Magazine*, November 1823); "William Hazlitt" (*Tait's Edinburgh Magazine*, December 1845); "Conversation" (*Tait's Edinburgh Magazine*, October 1847).

DICKENS. *The Sketches of Young Gentlemen* appeared in 1838; *The Sketches of Young Couples* in 1840. The contents of these volumes do not seem to have appeared in periodicals previously. "The Noble

Savage" was printed in *Household Words* (11 June 1853), and "Night Walks" and "A Plea for Total Abstinence" in *All the Year Round* (21 July 1860, and 5 June 1869).

THACKERAY. Essays published in the *Cornhill Magazine*, as indicated: "On a Lazy Idle Boy (January 1860); "Nil Nisi Bonum" (February 1860); "Tunbridge Toys" (September 1860); "On a Chalk-Mark on the Door" (April 1861); "On Being Found Out" (May 1861); "On a Hundred Years Hence" (June 1861); "Small-Beer Chronicle" (July 1861); "Ogres" (August 1861); "A Mississippi Bubble" (December 1861); "De Finibus" (August 1862); "On Some Carp at Sans Souci" (January 1863); "Autour de Mon Chapeau" (February 1863); "On a Medal of George the Fourth" (August 1863). The essays have been collected and are printed under the title of *The Roundabout Papers*, in Thackeray's collected works.

SMITH. The first six essays are taken from *Dreamthorp* (1863), and the last three from *Last Leaves* (1868). I can find no record of earlier periodical publication.

GEORGE ELIOT. The essays were not published in periodicals before they appeared in *The Impressions of Theophrastus Such* in 1879.

STEVENSON. "An Old Scots Gardener" (*Edinburgh University Magazine*, March 1871); "Ordered South" (*Macmillan's Magazine*, May 1874); "An Apology for Idlers" (*Cornhill Magazine*, July 1877); "Crabbed Age and Youth" (*Cornhill Magazine*, March 1878); "Æs Triplex" (*Cornhill Magazine*, April 1878); "El Dorado" (*London*, 11 May 1878); "The Foreigner at Home" (*Cornhill Magazine*, May 1882); "Old Mortality" (*Longman's Magazine*, May 1884); "A Gossip on a Novel of Dumas's" (*Memories and Portraits*, 1887). The essays were later collected and published in book-form, where they may be found in *Virginibus Puerisque* (1881) and *Memories and Portraits* (1887).

THOMPSON. In *Merry England*, as indicated, appeared "The Way of Imperfection" (November 1889); "The Fourth Order of Humanity" (December 1891); "A Renegade Poet on the Poet" (July 1892); and "Moestitiae Encomium" (October 1892). In *The Academy*, as indicated, appeared "Pope" (3 July 1897); "Bacon" (17 July 1897); "Don Quixote" (18 September 1897); "Goldsmith's Prose" (5 April 1902); and "The Poet's Poet" (12 September 1903).

Through the kindness of the Superintendent of the Reading Room of the Library of Congress, I obtained the information of the periodical publication of the essays. The Library has no set of *Merry England,* but the essays there published are recorded in the bibliography of George A. Beacock's *Francis Thompson, Versuch einer literarischen und metrischen Würdigung seiner poetischen Werke* (Marburg, 1912). Two introductory paragraphs, in the periodical version of "The Poet's Poet" are omitted in the volume of Thompson's collected essays on which this text is based.

Essays and Characters

LAMB TO THOMPSON

LAMB

CHARLES LAMB (*1775–1834*), *poet and essayist, long a clerk in the India House, was born in London, educated at Christ's Hospital ("the Blue Coat School") where he was a fellow-student of Coleridge's. On leaving school, he obtained a position in the India House, where he remained thirty years, retiring in 1825; he describes his feelings on this occasion in "The Superannuated Man." The sad story of his sister's insanity has often been told; his devotion to her was complete, and their collaboration on the "Tales from Shakespeare" (1807) was in part an attempt to occupy her. Poverty spurred him to contribute to the journals—he had written poems, a "prose romance," and a play with indifferent success—and he edited selections from the Elizabethan dramatists, which led to his recognition as a critic. His chief fame is due to the essays he contributed under the pen-name of "Elia" to the "London Magazine"; the first series was printed in a single volume in 1823, and later ones were collected under the title "The Last Essays of Elia" in 1833, the year before he died. His sister lived until 1847.*

Essentially a Londoner, Lamb had many friends among the chief literary figures of his day. He gathers the material for his essays from the happenings of his daily life, the people he knew, his memories of the past, transmuting them into papers of lasting charm by his humor, his sympathy, and his revelations of his own personality. It is hard to believe that he wrote more than a hundred years ago, and we return to the pages he has left us with renewed joy in his cheerful optimism without mawkishness, his sanity, his refusal to become embittered by his many trials.

LAMB

VALENTINE'S DAY

HAIL to thy returning festival, old Bishop Valentine! Great is thy name in the rubric, thou venerable Arch-flamen of Hymen! Immortal Go-between! who and what manner of person art thou? Art thou but a *name*, typifying the restless principle which impels poor humans to seek perfection in union? or wert thou indeed a mortal prelate, with thy tippet and thy rochet, thy apron on, and decent lawn sleeves? Mysterious personage! like unto thee, assuredly, there is no other mitred father in the calendar; not Jerome, nor Ambrose, nor Cyril; nor the consigner of undipt infants to eternal torments, Austin, whom all mothers hate; nor he who hated all mothers, Origen; nor Bishop Bull, nor Archbishop Parker, nor Whitgift. Thou comest attended with thousands and ten thousands of little Loves, and the air is

> Brush'd with the hiss of rustling wings.

Singing Cupids are thy choristers and thy precentors; and instead of the crosier, the mystical arrow is borne before thee.

In other words, this is the day on which those charming little missives, ycleped Valentines, cross and intercross each other at every street and turning. The weary and all for-spent twopenny postman sinks beneath a load of delicate embarrassments, not his own. It is scarcely credible to what an extent this ephemeral courtship is carried on in this loving town, to the great enrichment of porters, and detriment of knockers and bell-wires. In these little visual interpretations, no emblem is so common as the *heart*,— that little three-cornered exponent of all our hopes and fears,—the bestuck and bleeding heart; it is twisted and tortured into more allegories and affectations than an opera hat. What authority we have in history or mythology for placing the headquarters and metropolis of God Cupid in this anatomical seat rather than in any other, is not very clear; but we have got it, and it will serve as well as any other. Else we might easily imagine, upon some other system which might have prevailed for any thing which our pathology knows to the contrary, a lover addressing his mistress, in perfect simplicity of feeling, "Madam, my *liver* and fortune are entirely at your disposal;" or putting a delicate question, "Amanda, have you a *midriff* to bestow?" But custom has settled these things, and awarded the seat of sentiment to the aforesaid triangle, while its less fortunate neighbours wait at animal and anatomical distance.

Not many sounds in life, and I include all urban and all rural sounds, exceed in interest a *knock at the door*. It "gives a very echo to the throne where Hope is seated." But its issues seldom answer to this oracle within. It is so seldom that just the person we want to see comes. But of all the clamorous visitations the welcomest in expectation is the sound that ushers in, or seems to usher in, a Valentine. As the raven himself was hoarse that announced the fatal entrance of Duncan, so the knock of the postman on this day is light, airy, confident, and befitting one that bringeth good tidings. It is less mechanical than on other days; you will say, "That is not the post, I am sure." Visions of Love, of Cupids, of Hymens!—delightful eternal common-places, which "having been will always be;" which no school-boy nor schoolman can write away; having your irreversible throne in the fancy and affections—what are your transports, when the happy maiden, opening with careful finger, careful not to break the emblematic seal, bursts upon the sight of some well-designed allegory, some type, some youthful fancy, not without verses—

> Lovers all,
> A madrigal,

or some such device, not over abundant in sense—young Love disclaims it,—and not quite silly—something between wind and water, a chorus where the sheep might almost join the shepherd, as they did, or as I apprehend they did, in Arcadia.

All Valentines are not foolish; and I shall not easily forget thine, my kind friend (if I may have leave to call you so) E. B.—E. B. lived opposite a young maiden, whom he had often seen, unseen, from his parlour window in C—e-street. She was all joyousness and innocence, and just of an age to enjoy receiving a Valentine, and just of a temper to bear the disappointment of missing one with good humour. E. B. is an artist of no common powers; in the fancy parts of designing, perhaps inferior to none; his name is known at the bottom of many a well-executed vignette in the way of his profession, but no further; for E. B. is modest, and the world meets nobody half-way. E. B. meditated how he could repay this young maiden for many a favour which she had done him unknown; for when a kindly face greets us, though but passing by, and never knows us again, nor we it, we should feel it as an obligation; and E. B. did. This good artist set himself at work to please the damsel. It was just before Valentine's day three years since. He wrought, unseen and unsuspected, a wondrous work. We need not say it was on the finest gilt paper with borders—full, not of common hearts and heartless allegory, but all the prettiest stories of love from Ovid, and older poets than Ovid (for E. B. is a scholar). There was Pyramus and Thisbe, and be sure Dido was not forgot, nor Hero and Leander, and swans more than sang in Cayster, with mottos and fanciful devices, such as beseemed,—a work in short of magic. Iris dipt the woof. This on Valentine's eve he commended to the all-swallowing indiscriminate orifice—(O ignoble trust!)—of the common post; but the humble medium did its duty, and from his watchful stand, the next morning, he saw the cheerful messenger knock, and by and by the precious charge delivered. He saw, unseen, the happy girl unfold the Valentine, dance about, clap her hands, as one after one the pretty emblems unfolded themselves. She danced about, not with light love, or foolish expectations, for she had no lover; or, if she had, none she knew that could have created those bright images which delighted her. It was more like some fairy present; a God-send, as our familiarly pious ancestors termed a benefit received, where the benefactor was unknown. It would do her no harm. It would do her good for ever after. It is good to love the unknown. I only give this as a specimen of E. B. and his modest way of doing a concealed kindness.

Good-morrow to my Valentine, sings poor Ophelia; and no better wish, but with better auspices, we wish to all faithful lovers, who are not too wise to despise old legends, but are content to rank themselves humble diocesans of old Bishop Valentine, and his true church.

A CHAPTER ON EARS

I HAVE no ear.—

Mistake me not, reader,—nor imagine that I am by nature destitute of those exterior twin appendages, hanging ornaments, and (architecturally speaking) handsome volutes to the human capital. Better my mother had never borne me.—I am, I think, rather delicately than copiously provided with those conduits; and I feel no disposition to envy the mule for his plenty, or the mole for her exactness, in those ingenious labyrinthine inlets— those indispensable side-intelligencers.

Neither have I incurred or done anything to incur, with Defoe, that hideous disfigurement, which constrained him to draw upon assurance—to feel "quite unabashed," [1] and at ease upon that article. I was never, I thank my stars, in the pillory; nor, if I read them aright, is it within the compass of my destiny that I ever should be.

When therefore I say that I have no ear, you will understand me to mean—*for music.*—To say that this heart never melted at the concourse of sweet sounds, would be a foul self-libel.—"*Water parted from the sea*" never fails to move it strangely. So does "*In infancy.*" But they were used to be sung at her harpsichord (the old-fashioned instrument in vogue in those days) by a gentlewoman—the gentlest, sure, that ever merited the appellation— the sweetest—why should I hesitate to name Mrs. S——,[2] once the blooming Fanny Weatheral of the Temple—who had power to thrill the soul of Elia, small imp as he was, even in his long coats; and to make him glow, tremble, and blush with a passion, that not faintly indicated the day-spring of that absorbing sentiment, which was afterwards destined to overwhelm and subdue his nature quite, for Alice W——n.

I even think that *sentimentally* I am disposed to harmony. But *organically* I am incapable of a tune. I have been practising "*God save the King*" all my life; whistling and humming of it over to myself in solitary corners; and am not yet arrived, they tell me, within many quavers of it. Yet hath the loyalty of Elia never been impeached.

[1] "Earless on high stood, unabashed, Defoe."—*Dunciad.*
[2] Spinkes.

I am not without suspicion that I have an undeveloped faculty of music within me. For, thrumming, in my wild way, on my friend A.'s piano, the other morning, while he was engaged in an adjoining parlour,—on his return he was pleased to say, "*he thought it could not be the maid!*" On his first surprise at hearing the keys touched in somewhat an airy and masterful way, not dreaming of me, his suspicions had lighted on *Jenny*. But a grace, snatched from a superior refinement, soon convinced him that some being,— technically perhaps deficient, but higher informed from a principle common to all the fine arts,—had swayed the keys to a mood which Jenny, with all her (less-cultivated) enthusiasm, could never have elicited from them. I mention this as a proof of my friend's penetration, and not with any view of disparaging Jenny.

Scientifically I could never be made to understand (yet have I taken some pains) what a note in music is; or how one note should differ from another. Much less in voices can I distinguish a soprano from a tenor. Only sometimes the thorough bass I contrive to guess at, from its being supereminently harsh and disagreeable. I tremble, however, for my misapplication of the simplest terms of *that* which I disclaim. While I profess my ignorance, I scarce know what to *say* I am ignorant of. I hate, perhaps, by misnomers. *Sostenuto* and *adagio* stand in the like relation of obscurity to me; and *Sol, Fa, Mi, Re*, is as conjuring as *Baralipton*.

It is hard to stand alone—in an age like this,—(constituted to the quick and critical perception of all harmonious combinations, I verily believe, beyond all preceding ages, since Jubal stumbled upon the gamut)—to remain, as it were, singly unimpressible to the magic influences of an art, which is said to have such an especial stroke at soothing, elevating, and refining the passions.—Yet rather than break the candid current of my confessions, I must avow to you, that I have received a great deal more pain than pleasure from this so cried-up faculty.

I am constitutionally susceptible of noises. A carpenter's hammer, in a warm summer noon, will fret me into more than midsummer madness. But those unconnected, unset sounds are nothing to the measured malice of music. The ear is passive to those single strokes; willingly enduring stripes, while it hath no task to con. To music it cannot be passive. It will strive—mine at least will— 'spite of its inaptitude to thrid the maze; like an unskilled eye painfully poring upon hieroglyphics. I have sat through an Italian Opera, till, for sheer pain, and inexplicable anguish, I have rushed out into the noisiest places of the crowded streets, to solace myself with sounds, which I was not obliged to follow, and get rid of the distracting torment of endless, fruitless, barren attention! I take refuge in the unpretending assemblage of honest, common-life sounds;—and the purgatory of the Enraged Musician becomes my paradise.

I have sat at an Oratorio (that profanation of the purposes of the cheerful playhouse) watching the faces of the auditory in the pit (what a contrast to Hogarth's Laughing Audience!) immoveable, or affecting some faint emotion,—till (as some have said, that our occupations in the next world will be but a shadow of what delighted us in this) I have imagined myself in some cold Theatre in Hades, where some of the *forms* of the earthly one should be kept up, with none of the *enjoyment;* or like that—

> ———Party in a parlour,
> All silent, and all DAMNED:

Above all, those insufferable concertos, and pieces of music, as they are called, do plague and embitter my apprehension.—Words are something; but to be exposed to an endless battery of mere sounds; to be long a dying, to lie stretched upon a rack of roses; to keep up languor by unintermitted effort; to pile honey upon sugar, and sugar upon honey, to an interminable tedious sweetness; to fill up sound with feeling, and strain ideas to keep pace with it; to gaze on empty frames, and be forced to make the pictures for yourself; to read a book, *all stops*, and be obliged to supply the verbal matter; to invent extempore tragedies to answer to the vague gestures of an inexplicable rambling mime—these are faint shadows of what I have undergone from a series of the ablest-executed pieces of this empty *instrumental music.*

I deny not, that in the opening of a concert, I have experienced something vastly lulling and agreeable:—afterwards followeth the languor, and the oppression. Like that disappointing book in Patmos; or, like the comings on of melancholy, described by Burton, doth music make her first insinuating approaches:—"Most pleasant it is to such as are melancholy given, to walk alone in some solitary grove, betwixt wood and water, by some brook side, and to meditate upon some delightsome and pleasant subject, which shall affect him most, *amabilis insania,* and *mentis gratissimus error.* A most incomparable delight to build castles in the air, to go smiling to themselves, acting an infinite variety of parts, which they suppose, and strongly imagine, they act, or that they see done.—So delightsome these toys at first, they could spend whole days and nights without sleep, even whole years in such contemplations, and fantastical meditations, which are like so many dreams, and will hardly be drawn from them—winding and unwinding themselves as so many clocks, and still pleasing their humours, until at last the SCENE TURNS UPON A SUDDEN, and they being now habitated to such meditations, and solitary places, can endure no company, can think of nothing but harsh and distasteful subjects. Fear, sorrow, suspicion, *subrusticus pudor,* discontent, cares, and weariness of life, surprise them on a sudden, and they can think of nothing else: continually suspecting, no sooner are their eyes open, but this infernal plague of melancholy seizeth on them, and terrifies their souls, representing some dismal object to their minds; which now, by no means, no labour, no persuasions they can avoid, they cannot be rid of it, they cannot resist."

Something like this "SCENE-TURNING" I have experienced at the evening parties, at the house of my good Catholic friend *Nov*——; who, by the aid of a capital organ, himself the most finished of players, converts his drawing-room into a chapel, his week days into Sundays, and these latter into minor heavens.[1]

When my friend commences upon one of those solemn anthems which peradventure struck upon my heedless ear, rambling in the side aisles of the dim abbey, some five and thirty years since, waking a new sense and putting a soul of old religion into my young apprehension—(whether it be *that,* in which the psalmist, weary of the persecutions of bad men, wisheth to himself dove's wings— or *that other,* which, with a like measure of sobriety and pathos, inquireth by what means the young man shall best cleanse his mind)—a holy calm pervadeth me.—I am for the time

> ————rapt above earth,
> And possess joys not promised at my birth.

[1] I have been there, and still would go;
'Tis like a little heaven below.
—*Dr. Watts.*

But when this master of the spell, not content to have laid a soul prostrate, goes on, in his power, to inflict more bliss than lies in her capacity to receive,—impatient to overcome her "earthly" with his "heavenly,"—still pouring in, for protracted hours, fresh waves and fresh from the sea of sound, or from that inexhausted *German* ocean, above which, in triumphant progress, dolphin-seated, ride those Arions *Haydn* and *Mozart*, with their attendant tritons, *Bach, Beethoven*, and a countless tribe, whom to attempt to reckon up would but plunge me again in the deeps,—I stagger under the weight of harmony, reeling to and fro at my wit's end;—clouds, as of frankincense, oppress me—priests, altars, censers, dazzle before me—the genius of *his* religion hath me in her toils—a shadowy triple tiara invests the brow of my friend, late so naked, so ingenious—he is Pope,—and by him sits, like as in the anomaly of dreams, a she-Pope too,—tri-coroneted like himself!— I am converted, and yet a Protestant;—at once *malleus hereticorum*, and myself grand heresiarch: or three heresies centre in my person:—I am Marcion, Ebion, and Cerinthus—Gog and Magog— what not?—till the coming in of the friendly supper-tray dissipates the figment, and a draught of true Lutheran beer (in which chiefly my friend shows himself no bigot) at once reconciles me to the rationalities of a purer faith; and restores to me the genuine unterrifying aspects of my pleasant-countenanced host and hostess.

A QUAKERS' MEETING

Still-born Silence! thou that art
Flood-gate of the deeper heart!
Offspring of a heavenly kind!
Frost o' the mouth, and thaw o' the mind!
Secrecy's confidant, and he
Who makes religion mystery!
Admiration's speaking'st tongue!
Leave, thy desert shades among,
Reverend hermits' hallow'd cells,
Where retired devotion dwells!
With thy enthusiasms come,
Seize our tongues, and strike us dumb! [1]

READER, would'st thou know what true peace and quiet mean; would'st thou find a refuge from the noises and clamours of the multitude; would'st thou enjoy at once solitude and society; would'st thou possess the depth of thine own spirit in stillness, without being shut out from the consolatory faces of thy species; would'st thou be alone and yet accompanied; solitary, yet not desolate; singular, yet not without some to keep thee in countenance; a unit in aggregate; a simple in composite:— come with me into a Quakers' Meeting.

Dost thou love silence deep as that "before the winds were made"? go not out into the wilderness, descend not into the profundities of the earth; shut not up thy casements; nor pour wax into the little cells of thy ears, with little-faith'd self-mistrusting Ulysses.—Retire with me into a Quakers' Meeting.

For a man to refrain even from good words, and to hold his peace, it is commendable; but for a multitude it is great mastery.

What is the stillness of the desert, compared with this place? what the uncommunicating muteness of fishes?—here the goddess reigns and revels.—"Boreas, and Cesias, and Argestes loud," do not with their inter-confounding uproars more augment the brawl— nor the waves of the blown Baltic with their clubbed sounds— than their opposite (Silence her sacred self) is multiplied and rendered more intense by numbers, and by sympathy. She too hath her deeps, that call unto deeps. Negation itself hath a positive

[1] From "Poems of all sorts," by Richard Fleckno, 1653.

more and less; and closed eyes would seem to obscure the great obscurity of midnight.

There are wounds, which an imperfect solitude cannot heal. By imperfect I mean that which a man enjoyeth by himself. The perfect is that which he can sometimes attain in crowds, but nowhere so absolutely as in a Quakers' Meeting.—Those first hermits did certainly understand this principle, when they retired into Egyptian solitudes, not singly, but in shoals, to enjoy one another's want of conversation. The Carthusian is bound to his brethren by this agreeing spirit of incommunicativeness. In secular occasions, what so pleasant as to be reading a book through a long winter evening, with a friend sitting by—say, a wife—he, or she, too (if that be probable), reading another without interruption, or oral communication?—can there be no sympathy without the gabble of words?—away with this inhuman, shy, single, shade-and-cavern-haunting solitariness. Give me, Master Zimmerman, a sympathetic solitude.

To pace alone in the cloisters or side aisles of some cathedral, time-stricken;

> Or under hanging mountains,
> Or by the fall of fountains;

is but a vulgar luxury, compared with that which those enjoy, who come together for the purposes of more complete, abstracted solitude. This is the loneliness "to be felt."—The Abbey Church of Westminster hath nothing so solemn, so spirit-soothing, as the naked walls and benches of a Quakers' Meeting. Here are no tombs, no inscriptions.

> —sands, ignoble things,
> Dropt from the ruined sides of kings—

but here is something, which throws Antiquity herself into the fore-ground—SILENCE—eldest of things—language of old Night—primitive Discourser—to which the insolent decays of mouldering grandeur have but arrived by a violent, and, as we may say, unnatural progression.

> How reverend is the view of these hushed heads,
> Looking tranquillity!

Nothing-plotting, nought-caballing, unmischievous synod! con-vocation without intrigue! parliament without debate! what a lesson dost thou read to council, and to consistory!—if my pen treat of you lightly—as haply it will wander—yet my spirit hath gravely felt the wisdom of your custom, when, sitting among you in deepest peace, which some outwelling tears would rather con-firm than disturb, I have reverted to the times of your beginnings, and the sowings of the seed by Fox and Dewesbury.—I have wit-nessed that which brought before my eyes your heroic tranquillity, inflexible to the rude jests and serious violences of the insolent soldiery, republican or royalist, sent to molest you—for ye sate betwixt the fires of two persecutions, the out-cast and off-scower-ing of church and presbytery.—I have seen the reeling sea-ruffian, who had wandered into your receptacle with the avowed intention of disturbing your quiet, from the very spirit of the place receive in a moment a new heart, and presently sit among ye as a lamb amidst lambs. And I remembered Penn before his accusers, and Fox in the bail-dock, where he was lifted up in spirit, as he tells us, and "the Judge and the Jury became as dead men under his feet."

Reader, if you are not acquainted with it, I would recommend to you, above all church-narratives, to read Sewel's History of the Quakers. It is in folio, and is the abstract of the journals of Fox, and the primitive Friends. It is far more edifying and affecting than any thing you will read of Wesley and his colleagues. Here is nothing to stagger you, nothing to make you mistrust, no suspicion of alloy, no drop or dreg of the worldly or ambitious spirit. You will here read the true story of that much-injured, ridiculed man (who perhaps hath been a by-word in your mouth,)—James Nay-lor: what dreadful sufferings, with what patience, he endured even to the boring through his tongue with red-hot irons, without a murmur; and with what strength of mind, when the delusion he had fallen into, which they stigmatised for blasphemy, had given way to clearer thoughts, he could renounce his error, in a strain of the beautifullest humility, yet keep his first grounds, and be a Quaker still!—so different from the practice of your common con-verts from enthusiasm, who, when they apostatize, *apostatize all*, and think they can never get far enough from the society of their former errors, even to the renunciation of some saving truths, with which they had been mingled, not implicated.

Get the Writings of John Woolman by heart; and love the early Quakers.

How far the followers of these good men in our days have kept to the primitive spirit, or in what proportion they have substituted formality for it, the Judge of Spirits can alone determine. I have seen faces in their assemblies, upon which the dove sate visibly brooding. Others again I have watched, when my thoughts should have been better engaged, in which I could possibly detect nothing but a blank inanity. But quiet was in all, and the disposition to unanimity, and the absence of the fierce controversial workings.— If the spiritual pretensions of the Quakers have abated, at least they make few pretences. Hypocrites they certainly are not, in their preaching. It is seldom indeed that you shall see one get up amongst them to hold forth. Only now and then a trembling, female, generally *ancient*, voice is heard—you cannot guess from what part of the meeting it proceeds—with a low, buzzing, musical sound, laying out a few words which "she thought might suit the condition of some present," with a quaking diffidence, which leaves no possibility of supposing that anything of female vanity was mixed up, where the tones were so full of tenderness, and a restraining modesty.—The men, for what I have observed, speak seldomer.

Once only, and it was some years ago, I witnessed a sample of the old Foxian orgasm. It was a man of giant stature, who, as Wordsworth phrases it, might have danced "from head to foot equipt in iron mail." His frame was of iron too. But *he* was malleable. I saw him shake all over with the spirit—I dare not say, of delusion. The strivings of the outer man were unutterable— he seemed not to speak, but to be spoken from. I saw the strong man bowed down, and his knees to fail—his joints all seemed loosening—it was a figure to set off against Paul Preaching—the words he uttered were few, and sound—he was evidently resisting his will—keeping down his own word-wisdom with more mighty effort, than the world's orators strain for theirs. "He had been a WIT in his youth," he told us, with expressions of sober remorse. And it was not till long after the impression had begun to wear away, that I was enabled, with something like a smile, to recall the striking incongruity of the confession—understanding the term in its worldly acceptation—with the frame and physiognomy of the person before me. His brow would have scared away the Levities—the Jocos Risus-que—faster than the Loves fled the face of Dis at Enna.—By *wit*, even in his youth, I will be sworn he understood something far within the limits of an allowable liberty.

More frequently the Meeting is broken up without a word having been spoken. But the mind has been fed. You go away with a sermon, not made with hands. You have been in the milder caverns of Trophonius; or as in some den, where that fiercest and savagest of all wild creatures, the TONGUE, that unruly member, has strangely lain tied up and captive. You have bathed with stillness.—O when the spirit is sore fretted, even tired to sickness of the janglings, and nonsense-noises of the world, what a balm and a solace it is, to go and seat yourself, for a quiet half hour, upon some undisputed corner of a bench, among the gentle Quakers!

Their garb and stillness conjoined, present a uniformity, tranquil and herd-like—as in the pasture—"forty feeding like one."—

The very garments of a Quaker seem incapable of receiving a soil; and cleanliness in them to be something more than the absence of its contrary. Every Quakeress is a lily; and when they come up in bands to their Whitsun-conferences, whitening the easterly streets of the metropolis, from all parts of the United Kingdom, they show like troops of the Shining Ones.

THE OLD AND THE NEW SCHOOLMASTER

MY reading has been lamentably desultory and immethodical. Odd, out of the way, old English plays, and treatises, have supplied me with most of my notions, and ways of feeling. In everything that relates to *science*, I am a whole Encyclopædia behind the rest of the world. I should have scarcely cut a figure among the franklins, or country gentlemen, in King John's days. I know less geography than a school-boy of six weeks' standing. To me a map of old Ortelius is as authentic as Arrowsmith. I do not know whereabout Africa merges into Asia; whether Ethiopia lie in one or other of those great divisions; nor can form the remotest conjecture of the position of New South Wales, or Van Diemen's Land. Yet do I hold a correspondence with a very dear friend in the first-named of these two Terræ Incognitæ. I have no astronomy. I do not know where to look for the Bear, or Charles's Wain; the place of any star; or the name of any of them at sight. I guess at Venus only by her brightness—and if the sun on some portentous morn were to make his first appearance in the West, I verily believe, that, while all the world were gasping in apprehension about me, I alone should stand unterrified, from sheer incuriosity and want of observation. Of history and chronology I possess some vague points, such as one cannot help picking up in the course of miscellaneous study; but I never deliberately sat down to a chronicle, even of my own country. I have most dim apprehensions of the four great monarchies; and sometimes the Assyrian, sometimes the Persian, floats as *first* in my fancy. I make the widest conjectures concerning Egypt, and her shepherd kings. My friend *M.*, with great painstaking, got me to think I understood the first proposition in Euclid, but gave me over in despair at the second. I am entirely unacquainted with the modern languages; and, like a better man than myself, have "small Latin and less Greek." I am a stranger to the shapes and texture of the commonest trees, herbs, flowers—not from the circumstance of my being town-born—for I should have brought the same inobservant spirit into the world with me, had I first seen it "on Devon's leafy shores,"—and am no less at a loss among purely town-objects, tools, engines, mechanic processes.—Not that I affect ignorance—but my head has not many mansions, nor spacious; and I have been obliged to fill it with such cabinet curiosities as it can hold without aching. I sometimes wonder, how I have passed my probation with so little discredit in the world, as I have done, upon so meagre a stock. But the fact is, a man may do very well with a very little knowledge, and scarce be found out, in mixed company; everybody is so much more ready to produce his own, than to call for a display of your acquisitions. But in a *tête-à-tête* there is no shuffling. The truth will out. There is nothing which I dread so much, as the being left alone for a quarter of an hour with a sensible, well-informed man, that does not know me. I lately got into a dilemma of this sort.—

In one of my daily jaunts between Bishopsgate and Shacklewell, the coach stopped to take up a staid-looking gentleman, about the wrong side of thirty, who was giving his parting directions (while the steps were adjusting), in a tone of mild authority, to a tall youth, who seemed to be neither his clerk, his son, nor his servant, but something partaking of all three. The youth was dismissed, and we drove on. As we were the sole passengers, he naturally enough addressed his conversation to me; and we discussed the merits of the fare; the civility and punctuality of the driver; the circumstance of an opposition coach having been lately set up, with the probabilities of its success—to all which I was enabled to return pretty satisfactory answers, having been drilled into this kind of etiquette by some years' daily practice of riding to and fro in the stage aforesaid—when he suddenly alarmed me by a startling question, whether I had seen the show of prize cattle that morning in Smithfield? Now as I had not seen it, and do not greatly care for such sort of exhibitions, I was obliged to return a cold negative. He seemed a little mortified, as well as astonished, at my declaration, as (it appeared) he was just come fresh from the sight, and doubtless had hoped to compare notes on the subject. However, he assured me that I had lost a fine treat, as it far exceeded the show of last year. We were now approaching Norton Falgate, when the sight of some shop-goods *ticketed* freshened him up into a dissertation upon the cheapness of cottons this spring. I was now a little in heart, as the nature of my morning avocations had brought me into some sort of familiarity with the raw material; and I was surprised to find how eloquent I was becoming on the state of the India market—when, presently, he dashed my incipient vanity to the earth at once, by inquiring whether I had ever made any calculation as to the value of the rental of all the retail shops in London. Had he asked of me, what songs the Syrens sang, or what name Achilles assumed when he hid himself among women, I might, with Sir Thomas Browne, have hazarded a "wide solution." [1] My companion saw my embarrassment, and, the almshouses beyond Shoreditch just coming in view, with great goodnature and dexterity shifted his conversation to the subject of public charities; which led to the comparative merits of provision for the poor in past and present times, with observations on the old monastic institutions, and charitable orders;—but, finding me rather dimly impressed with some glimmering notions from old poetic associations, than strongly fortified with any speculations reducible to calculation on the subject, he gave the matter up; and, the country beginning to open more and more upon us, as

[1] Urn Burial.

we approached the turnpike at Kingsland (the destined termination of his journey), he put a home thrust upon me, in the most unfortunate position he could have chosen, by advancing some queries relative to the North Pole Expedition. While I was muttering out something about the Panorama of those strange regions (which I had actually seen), by way of parrying the question, the coach stopping relieved me from any further apprehensions. My companion getting out, left me in the comfortable possession of my ignorance; and I heard him, as he went off, putting questions to an outside passenger, who had alighted with him, regarding an epidemic disorder, that had been rife about Dalston; and which my friend assured him, had gone through five or six schools in that neighbourhood. The truth now flashed upon me, that my companion was a schoolmaster; and that the youth, whom he had parted from at our first acquaintance, must have been one of the bigger boys, or the usher.—He was evidently a kind-hearted man, who did not seem so much desirous of provoking discussion by the questions which he put, as of obtaining information at any rate. It did not appear that he took any interest, either, in such kind of inquiries, for their own sake; but that he was in some way bound to seek for knowledge. A greenish-coloured coat, which he had on, forbade me to surmise that he was a clergyman. The adventure gave birth to some reflections on the difference between persons of his profession in past and present times.

Rest to the squls of those fine old Pedagogues; the breed, long since extinct, of the Lilys, and the Linacres: who believing that all learning was contained in the languages which they taught, and despising every other acquirement as superficial and useless, came to their task as to a sport! Passing from infancy to age, they dreamed away all their days as in a grammar-school. Revolving in a perpetual cycle of declensions, conjugations, syntaxes, and prosodies; renewing constantly the occupations which had charmed their studious childhood; rehearsing continually the part of the past; life must have slipped from them at last like one day. They were always in their first garden, reaping harvests of their golden time, among their *Flori-* and their *Spici-legia;* in Arcadia still, but kings; the ferule of their sway not much harsher, but of like dignity with that mild sceptre attributed to king Basileus; the Greek and Latin, their stately Pamela and their Philoclea; with the occasional duncery of some untoward Tyro, serving for a refreshing interlude of a Mopsa, or a clown Damœtas!

With what a savour doth the Preface to Colet's, or (as it is sometimes called) Paul's Accidence, set forth! "To exhort every man to the learning of grammar, that intendeth to attain the understanding of the tongues, wherein is contained a great treasury of wisdom and knowledge, it would seem but vain and lost labour; for so much as it is known, that nothing can surely be ended, whose beginning is either feeble or faulty; and no building be perfect, whereas the foundation and ground-work is ready to fall, and unable to uphold the burden of the frame." How well doth this stately preamble (comparable to those which Milton commendeth as "having been the usage to prefix to some solemn law, then first promulgated by Solon, or Lycurgus") correspond with and illustrate that pious zeal for conformity, expressed in a succeeding clause, which would fence about grammar-rules with the severity of faith-articles!—"as for the diversity of grammars, it is well profitably taken away by the king majesties wisdom, who foreseeing the inconvenience, and favourably providing the remedie, caused one kind of grammar by sundry learned men to be diligently drawn, and so to be set out, only everywhere to be taught for the use of learners, and for the hurt in changing of schoolmaisters." What a *gusto* in that which follows: "wherein it is profitable that he can orderly decline his noun and his verb." *His* noun!

The fine dream is fading away fast; and the least concern of a teacher in the present day is to inculcate grammar-rules.

The modern schoolmaster is expected to know a little of every thing, because his pupil is required not to be entirely ignorant of any thing. He must be superficially, if I may so say, omniscient. He is to know something of pneumatics; of chemistry; of whatever is curious, or proper to excite the attention of the youthful mind; an insight into mechanics is desirable, with a touch of statistics; the quality of soils, &c., botany, the constitution of his country, *cum multis aliis*. You may get a notion of some part of his expected duties by consulting the famous Tractate on Education, addressed to Mr. Hartlib.

All these things—these, or the desire of them—he is expected to instil, not by set lessons from professors, which he may charge in the bill, but at school-intervals, as he walks the streets, or saunters through green fields (those natural instructors), with his pupils. The least part of what is expected from him, is to be done in school-hours. He must insinuate knowledge at the *mollia tempora fandi*. He must seize every occasion—the season of the year—the time of the day—a passing cloud—a rainbow—a waggon of hay—a regiment of soldiers going by—to inculcate something useful. He can receive no pleasure from a casual glimpse of Nature, but must catch at it as an object of instruction. He must interpret beauty into the picturesque. He cannot relish a beggar-man, or a gipsy, for thinking of the suitable improvement. Nothing comes to him, not spoiled by the sophisticating medium of moral uses. The Universe—that Great Book, as it has been called—is to him, indeed, to all intents and purposes, a book, out of which he is doomed to read tedious homilies to distasting school-boys.—Vacations themselves are none to him, he is only rather worse off than before; for commonly he has some intrusive upper-boy fastened upon him at such times; some cadet of a great family; some neglected lump of nobility, or gentry; that he must drag after him to the play, to the Panorama, to Mr. Bartley's Orrery, to the Panopticon, or into the country, to a friend's house, or to his favourite watering-place. Wherever he goes, this uneasy shadow attends him. A boy is at his board, and in his path, and in all his movements. He is boy-rid, sick of perpetual boy.

Boys are capital fellows in their own way, among their mates; but they are unwholesome companions for grown people. The restraint is felt no less on the one side, than on the other.—Even a child, that "plaything for an hour," tires *always*. The noises of children, playing their own fancies—as I now hearken to them by fits, sporting on the green before my window, while I am engaged in these grave speculations at my neat suburban retreat at Shackle-well—by distance made more sweet—inexpressibly take from the labour of my task. It is like writing to music. They seem to modulate my periods. They ought at least to do so—for in the voice of that tender age there is a kind of poetry, far unlike the harsh prose-accents of man's conversation.—I should but spoil their sport, and diminish my own sympathy for them, by mingling in their pastime.

I would not be domesticated all my days with a person of very superior capacity to my own—not, if I know myself at all, from any considerations of jealousy or self-comparison, for the occasional communion with such minds has constituted the fortune and felicity of my life—but the habit of too constant intercourse with spirits above you, instead of raising you, keeps you down. Too frequent doses of original thinking from others, restrain what lesser portion of that faculty you may possess of your own. You get entangled in another man's mind, even as you lose yourself in another man's grounds. You are walking with a tall varlet, whose strides out-pace yours to lassitude. The constant operation of such potent agency would reduce me, I am convinced, to imbecility. You may derive thoughts from others; your way of thinking, the mould in which your thoughts are cast, must be your own. Intellect may be imparted, but not each man's intellectual frame.—

As little as I should wish to be always thus dragged upwards, as little (or rather still less) is it desirable to be stunted downwards by your associates. The trumpet does not more stun you by its loudness, than a whisper teases you by its provoking inaudibility.

Why are we never quite at our ease in the presence of a schoolmaster?—because we are conscious that he is not quite at his ease in ours. He is awkward, and out of place, in the society of his equals. He comes like Gulliver from among his little people, and he cannot fit the stature of his understanding to yours. He cannot meet you on the square. He wants a point given him, like an indifferent whist-player. He is so used to teaching, that he wants to be teaching *you*. One of these professors, upon my complaining that these little sketches of mine were anything but methodical, and that I was unable to make them otherwise, kindly offered to instruct me in the method by which young gentlemen in *his* seminary were taught to compose English themes.—The jests of a schoolmaster are coarse, or thin. They do not *tell* out of school. He is under the restraint of a formal and didactive hypocrisy in company, as a clergyman is under a moral one. He can no more let his intellect loose in society, than the other can his inclinations.— He is forlorn among his co-evals; his juniors cannot be his friends.

"I take blame to myself," said a sensible man of this profession, writing to a friend respecting a youth who had quitted his school abruptly, "that your nephew was not more attached to me. But persons in my situation are more to be pitied, than can well be imagined. We are surrounded by young, and, consequently, ardently affectionate hearts, but *we* can never hope to share an atom of their affections. The relation of master and scholar forbids this. *How pleasing this must be to you, how I envy your feelings,* my friends will sometimes say to me, when they see young men whom I have educated, return after some years' absence from school, their eyes shining with pleasure, while they shake hands with their old master, bringing a present of game to me, or a toy to my wife, and thanking me in the warmest terms for my care of their education. A holiday is begged for the boys; the house is a scene of happiness; I, only, am sad at heart.—This fine-spirited and warmhearted youth, who fancies he repays his master with gratitude for the care of his boyish years—this young man—in the eight long years I watched over him with a parent's anxiety, never could repay me with one look of genuine feeling. He was proud, when I praised; he was submissive, when I reproved him; but he did never *love* me—and what he now mistakes for gratitude and kindness for me, is but the pleasant sensation, which all persons feel at revisiting the scene of their boyish hopes and fears; and the seeing on equal terms the man they were accustomed to look up to with reverence. My wife, too," this interesting correspondent goes on to say, "my once darling Anna, is the wife of a schoolmaster.—When I married her—knowing that the wife of a schoolmaster ought to be a busy notable creature, and fearing that my gentle Anna would ill supply the loss of my dear bustling mother, just then dead, who never sat still, was in every part of the house in a moment, and whom I was obliged sometimes to threaten to fasten down in a chair, to save her from fatiguing herself to death— I expressed my fears, that I was bringing her into a way of life unsuitable to her; and she, who loved me tenderly, promised for my sake to exert herself to perform the duties of her new situation. She promised, and she has kept her word. What wonders will not woman's love perform?—My house is managed with a propriety and decorum, unknown in other schools; my boys are well fed, look healthy, and have every proper accommodation; and all this performed with a careful economy, that never descends to meanness. But I have lost my gentle, *helpless* Anna!—When we sit down to enjoy an hour of repose after the fatigue of the day, I am compelled to listen to what have been her useful (and they are really useful) employments through the day, and what she proposes for her to-morrow's task. Her heart and her features are changed by the duties of her situation. To the boys, she never appears other than the *master's wife*, and she looks up to me as the *boys' master;* to whom all show of love and affection would be highly improper, and unbecoming the dignity of her situation and mine. Yet *this* my gratitude forbids me to hint to her. For my sake she submitted to be this altered creature, and can I reproach her for it?"—For the communication of this letter, I am indebted to my cousin Bridget.

MY RELATIONS

I AM arrived at that point of life, at which a man may account it a blessing, as it is a singularity, if he have either of his parents surviving. I have not that felicity—and sometimes think feelingly of a passage in Browne's Christian Morals, where he speaks of a man that hath lived sixty or seventy years in the world. "In such a compass of time," he says, "a man may have a close apprehension what it is to be forgotten, when he hath lived to find none who could remember his father, or scarcely the friends of his youth, and may sensibly see with what a face in no long time OBLIVION will look upon himself."

I had an aunt, a dear and good one. She was one whom single blessedness had soured to the world. She often used to say, that I was the only thing in it which she loved; and, when she thought I was quitting it, she grieved over me with mother's tears. A partiality quite so exclusive my reason cannot altogether approve. She was from morning till night poring over good books, and devotional exercises. Her favourite volumes were, Thomas à Kempis, in Stanhope's Translation; and a Roman Catholic Prayer Book, with the *matins* and *complines* regularly set down,—terms which I was at that time too young to understand. She persisted in reading them, although admonished daily concerning their Papistical tendency; and went to church every Sabbath, as a good Protestant should do. These were the only books she studied; though, I think, at one period of her life, she told me, she had read with great satisfaction the Adventures of an Unfortunate Young Nobleman. Finding the door of the chapel in Essex-street open one day—

it was in the infancy of that heresy—she went in, liked the sermon, and the manner of worship, and frequented it at intervals for some time after. She came not for doctrinal points, and never missed them. With some little asperities in her constitution, which I have above hinted at, she was a steadfast, friendly being, and a fine *old Christian*. She was a woman of strong sense, and a shrewd mind—extraordinary at a *repartee;* one of the few occasions of her breaking silence—else she did not much value wit. The only secular employment I remember to have seen her engaged in, was the splitting of French beans, and dropping them into a China basin of fair water. The odour of those tender vegetables to this day comes back upon my sense, redolent of soothing recollections. Certainly it is the most delicate of culinary operations.

Male aunts, as somebody calls them, I had none—to remember. By the uncle's side I may be said to have been born an orphan. Brother, or sister, I never had any—to know them. A sister, I think, that should have been Elizabeth, died in both our infancies. What a comfort, or what a care, may I not have missed in her!— But I have cousins, sprinkled about in Hertfordshire—besides *two*, with whom I have been all my life in habits of the closest intimacy, and whom I may term cousins *par excellence*. These are James and Bridget Elia. They are older than myself by twelve, and ten, years; and neither of them seems disposed, in matters of advice and guidance, to waive any of the prerogatives which primogeniture confers. May they continue still in the same mind; and when they shall be seventy-five, and seventy-three years old (I cannot spare them sooner), persist in treating me in my grand climacteric precisely as a stripling, or younger brother!

James is an inexplicable cousin. Nature hath her unities, which not every critic can penetrate; or, if we feel, we cannot explain them. The pen of Yorick, and of none since his, could have drawn J. E. entire—those fine Shandian lights and shades, which make up his story. I must limp after in my poor antithetical manner, as the fates have given me grace and talent. J. E. then—to the eye of a common observer at least—seemeth made up of contradictory principles.—The genuine child of impulse, the frigid philosopher of prudence—the phlegm of my cousin's doctrine is invariably at war with his temperament, which is high sanguine. With always some fire-new project in his brain, J. E. is the systematic opponent of innovation, and crier down of everything that has not stood the test of age and experiment. With a hundred fine notions chasing one another hourly in his fancy, he is startled at the least approach to the romantic in others; and, determined by his own sense in everything, commends *you* to the guidance of common sense on all occasions.—With a touch of the eccentric in all which he does, or says, he is only anxious that *you* should not commit yourself by doing anything absurd or singular. On my once letting slip at table, that I was not fond of a certain popular dish, he begged me at any rate not to *say* so—for the world would think me mad. He disguises a passionate fondness for works of high art (whereof he hath amassed a choice collection), under the pretext of buying only to sell again—that his enthusiasm may give no encouragement to yours. Yet, if it were so, why does that piece of tender, pastoral Domenichino hang still by his wall?— is the ball of his sight much more dear to him?—or what picture-dealer can talk like him?

Whereas mankind in general are observed to warp their speculative conclusions to the bent of their individual humours, *his* theories are sure to be in diametrical opposition to his constitution. He is courageous as Charles of Sweden, upon instinct; chary of his person, upon principle, as a travelling Quaker.—He has been preaching up to me, all my life, the doctrine of bowing to the great— the necessity of forms, and manner, to a man's getting on in the world. He himself never aims at either, that I can discover— and has a spirit, that would stand upright in the presence of the Cham of Tartary. It is pleasant to hear him discourse of patience— extolling it as the truest wisdom—and to see him during the last seven minutes that his dinner is getting ready. Nature never ran up in her haste a more restless piece of workmanship than when she moulded this impetuous cousin—and Art never turned out a more elaborate orator than he can display himself to be, upon his favourite topic of the advantages of quiet, and contentedness in the state, whatever it be, that we are placed in. He is triumphant on this theme, when he has you safe in one of those short stages that ply for the western road, in a very obstructing manner, at the foot of John Murray's street—where you get in when it is empty, and are expected to wait till the vehicle hath completed her just freight—a trying three quarters of an hour to some people. He wonders at your fidgetiness,—"where could we be better than we are, *thus sitting, thus consulting?*"—"prefers, for his part, a state of rest to locomotion,"—with an eye all the while upon the coachman—till at length, waxing out of all patience, at *your want of it*, he breaks out into a pathetic remonstrance at the fellow for detaining us so long over the time which he had professed, and declares peremptorily, that "the gentleman in the coach is determined to get out, if he does not drive on that instant."

Very quick at inventing an argument, or detecting a sophistry, he is incapable of attending *you* in any chain of arguing. Indeed he makes wild work with logic; and seems to jump at most admirable conclusions by some process, not at all akin to it. Consonantly enough to this, he hath been heard to deny, upon certain occasions, that there exists such a faculty at all in man as *reason;* and wondereth how man came first to have a conceit of it—enforcing his negation with all the might of *reasoning* he is master of. He has some speculative notions against laughter, and will maintain that laughing is not natural to *him*—when peradventure the next moment his lungs shall crow like Chanticleer. He says some of the best things in the world—and declareth that wit is his aversion. It was he who said, upon seeing the Eton boys at play in their grounds—*What a pity to think, that these fine ingenuous lads in a few years will all be changed into frivolous Members of Parliament!*

His youth was fiery, glowing, tempestuous—and in age he discovereth no symptom of cooling. This is that which I admire in him. I hate people who meet Time half-way. I am for no compromise with that inevitable spoiler. While he lives, J. E. will take his swing.—It does me good, as I walk towards the street of my daily avocation, on some fine May morning, to meet him marching in a quite opposite direction, with a jolly handsome presence, and shining sanguine face, that indicates some purchase in his eye—a Claude—or a Hobbima—for much of his enviable leisure is consumed at Christie's, and Phillips's—or where not, to pick up pictures, and such gauds. On these occasions he mostly stoppeth me, to read a short lecture on the advantages a person like me possesses above himself, in having his time occupied with business which he *must do*—assureth me that he often feels it hang heavy on his hands—wishes he had fewer holidays—and goes off— Westward Ho!—chanting a tune, to Pall Mall—perfectly convinced that he has convinced me—while I proceed in my opposite direction tuneless.

It is pleasant again to see this Professor of Indifference doing the honours of his new purchase, when he has fairly housed it. You must view it in every light, till *he* has found the best—placing it at this distance, and at that, but always suiting the focus of your sight to his own. You must spy at it through your fingers, to catch the aërial perspective—though you assure him that to you the landscape shows much more agreeable without that artifice. Wo be to the luckless wight, who does not only not respond to his rapture, but who should drop an unseasonable intimation of preferring one of his anterior bargains to the present!—The last is always his best hit—his "Cynthia of the minute." Alas! how many a mild Madonna have I known to *come in*—a Raphael!—keep its ascendency for a few brief moons—then, after certain intermedial degradations, from the front drawing-room to the back gallery, thence to the dark parlour,—adopted in turn by each of the Carracci, under successive lowering ascriptions of filiation, mildly breaking its fall—consigned to the oblivious lumber-room, *go out* at last a Lucca Giordano, or plain Carlo Maratti!—which things when I beheld—musing upon the chances and mutabilities of fate below, hath made me to reflect upon the altered condition of great personages, or that woful Queen of Richard the Second—

> ——set forth in pomp,
> She came adorned hither like sweet May.
> Sent back like Hollowmass or shortest day.

With great love for *you*, J. E. hath but a limited sympathy with what you feel or do. He lives in a world of his own, and makes slender guesses at what passes in your mind. He never pierces the marrow of your habits. He will tell an old established play-goer, that Mr. Such-a-one, of So-and-so (naming one of the theatres), is a very lively comedian—as a piece of news! He advertised me but the other day of some pleasant green lanes which he had found out for me, *knowing me to be a great walker*, in my own immediate vicinity—who have haunted the identical spot any time these twenty years!—He has not much respect for that class of feelings which goes by the name of sentimental. He applies the definition of real evil to bodily sufferings exclusively—and rejecteth all others as imaginary. He is affected by the sight, or the bare supposition, of a creature in pain, to a degree which I have never witnessed out of womankind. A constitutional acuteness to this class of sufferings may in part account for this. The animal tribe in particular he taketh under his especial protection. A broken-winded or spur-galled horse is sure to find an advocate in him. An overloaded ass is his client for ever. He is the apostle to the brute kind— the never-failing friend of those who have none to care for them. The contemplation of a lobster boiled, or eels skinned *alive*, will wring him so, that "all for pity he could die." It will take the savour from his palate, and the rest from his pillow, for days and nights. With the intense feeling of Thomas Clarkson, he wanted only the steadiness of pursuit, and unity of purpose, of that "true yoke-fellow with Time," to have effected as much for the *Animal*, as *he* hath done for the *Negro Creation*. But my uncontrollable cousin is but imperfectly formed for purposes which demand co-operation. He cannot wait. His amelioration-plans must be ripened in a day. For this reason he has cut but an equivocal figure in benevolent societies, and combinations for the alleviation of human sufferings. His zeal constantly makes him to outrun, and put out, his coadjutors. He thinks of relieving,—while they think of debating. He was black-balled out of a society for the Relief of * * * * *, because the fervour of his humanity toiled beyond the formal apprehension, and creeping processes, of his associates. I shall always consider this distinction as a patent of nobility in the Elia family!

Do I mention these seeming inconsistencies to smile at, or upbraid, my unique cousin? Marry, heaven, and all good manners, and the understanding that should be between kinsfolk, forbid!— With all the strangenesses of this *strangest of the Elias*—I would not have him in one jot or tittle other than he is; neither would I barter or exchange my wild kinsman for the most exact, regular, and every-way consistent kinsman breathing.

In my next, reader, I may perhaps give you some account of my cousin Bridget—if you are not already surfeited with cousins— and take you by the hand, if you are willing to go with us, on an excursion which we made a summer or two since, in search of *more cousins*—

Through the green plains of pleasant Hertfordshire.

MACKERY END, IN HERTFORDSHIRE

BRIDGET ELIA has been my housekeeper for many a long year. I have obligations to Bridget, extending beyond the period of memory. We house together, old bachelor and maid, in a sort of double singleness; with such tolerable comfort, upon the whole, that I, for one, find in myself no sort of disposition to go out upon the mountains, with the rash king's offspring, to bewail my celibacy. We agree pretty well in our tastes and habits—yet so, as "with a difference." We are generally in harmony, with occasional bickerings—as it should be among near relations. Our sympathies are rather understood, than expressed; and once, upon my dissembling a tone in my voice more kind than ordinary, my cousin burst into tears, and complained that I was altered. We are both great readers in different directions. While I am hanging over (for the thousandth time) some passage in old Burton, or one of his strange contemporaries, she is abstracted in some modern tale, or adventure, whereof our common reading-table is daily fed with assiduously fresh supplies. Narrative teazes me. I have little concern in the progress of events. She must have a story—well, ill, or indifferently told—so there be life stirring in it, and plenty of good or evil accidents. The fluctuations of fortune in fiction—and almost in real life—have ceased to interest, or operate but dully upon me. Out-of-the-way humours and opinions—heads with some diverting twist in them—the oddities of authorship please me most. My cousin has a native disrelish of any thing that sounds odd or bizarre. Nothing goes down with her, that is quaint, irregular, or out of the road of common sympathy. She "holds Nature more clever." I can pardon her blindness to the beautiful obliquities of the Religio Medici; but she must apoligise to me for certain disrespectful insinuations, which she has been pleased to throw out latterly, touching the intellectuals of a dear favourite of mine, of the last century but one—the thrice noble, chaste, and virtuous,—but again somewhat fantastical, and original-brain'd, generous Margaret Newcastle.

It has been the lot of my cousin, oftener perhaps than I could have wished, to have had for her associates and mine, free-thinkers —leaders, and disciples, of novel philosophies and systems; but she neither wrangles with, nor accepts, their opinions. That which was good and venerable to her, when a child, retains its authority over her mind still. She never juggles or plays tricks with her understanding.

We are both of us inclined to be a little too positive; and I have observed the result of our disputes to be almost uniformly this— that in matters of fact, dates, and circumstances, it turns out that I was in the right, and my cousin in the wrong. But where we have differed upon moral points; upon something proper to be done, or let alone; whatever heat of opposition, or steadiness of conviction, I set out with, I am sure always, in the long run, to be brought over to her way of thinking.

I must touch upon the foibles of my kinswoman with a gentle hand, for Bridget does not like to be told of her faults. She hath an awkward trick (to say no worse of it) of reading in company: at which times she will answer *yes* or *no* to a question, without fully understanding its purport—which is provoking, and derogatory in the highest degree to the dignity of the putter of the said question. Her presence of mind is equal to the most pressing trials of life, but will sometimes desert her upon trifling occasions. When the purpose requires it, and is a thing of moment, she can speak to it greatly; but in matters which are not stuff of the conscience, she hath been known sometimes to let slip a word less seasonably.

Her education in youth was not much attended to; and she happily missed all that train of female garniture, which passeth by the name of accomplishments. She was tumbled early, by accident or design, into a spacious closet of good old English reading, without much selection or prohibition, and browsed at will upon that fair and wholesome pasturage. Had I twenty girls, they should be brought up exactly in this fashion. I know not whether their chance in wedlock might not be diminished by it; but I can answer for it, that it makes (if the worst come to the worst) most incomparable old maids.

In a season of distress, she is the truest comforter; but in the teazing accidents, and minor perplexities, which do not call out the *will* to meet them, she sometimes maketh matters worse by an excess of participation. If she does not always divide your trouble, upon the pleasanter occasions of life she is sure always to treble your satisfaction. She is excellent to be at a play with, or upon a visit; but best, when she goes a journey with you.

We made an excursion together a few summers since, into Hertfordshire, to beat up the quarters of some of our less-known relations in that fine corn country.

The oldest thing I remember is Mackery End; or Mackarel End, as it is spelt, perhaps more properly, in some old maps of Hertfordshire; a farm-house,—delightfully situated within a gentle walk from Wheathampstead. I can just remember having been there, on a visit to a great-aunt, when I was a child, under the care of Bridget; who, as I have said, is older than myself by some ten years. I wish that I could throw into a heap the remainder of our joint existences, that we might share them in equal division. But that is impossible. The house was at that time in the occupation of a substantial yeoman, who had married my grandmother's sister. His name was Gladman. My grandmother was a Bruton, married to a Field. The Gladmans and the Brutons are still flourishing in that part of the county, but the Fields are almost extinct. More than forty years had elapsed since the visit I speak of; and, for the greater portion of that period, we had lost sight of the other two branches also. Who or what sort of persons inherited Mackery End—kindred or strange folk—we were afraid almost to conjecture, but determined some day to explore.

By somewhat a circuitous route, taking the noble park at Luton in our way from Saint Alban's, we arrived at the spot of our anxious curiosity about noon. The sight of the old farm-house, though every trace of it was effaced from my recollection, affected me with a pleasure which I had not experienced for many a year. For though *I* had forgotten it, *we* had never forgotten being there together, and we had been talking about Mackery End all our lives, till memory on my part became mocked with a phantom of itself, and I thought I knew the aspect of a place, which, when present, O how unlike it was to *that*, which I had conjured up so many times instead of it!

Still the air breathed balmily about it; the season was in the "heart of June," and I could say with the poet,

> But thou, that didst appear so fair
> To fond imagination,
> Dost rival in the light of day
> Her delicate creation!

Bridget's was more a waking bliss than mine, for she easily
remembered her old acquaintance again—some altered features, of
course, a little grudged at. At first, indeed, she was ready to disbelieve for joy; but the scene soon re-confirmed itself in her affections—and she traversed every out-post of the old mansion, to the
wood-house, the orchard, the place where the pigeon-house had
stood (house and birds were alike flown)—with a breathless impatience of recognition, which was more pardonable perhaps than
decorous at the age of fifty odd. But Bridget in some things is
behind her years.

The only thing left was to get into the house—and that was a
difficulty which to me singly would have been insurmountable; for
I am terribly shy in making myself known to strangers and out-of-
date kinsfolk. Love, stronger than scruple, winged my cousin in
without me; but she soon returned with a creature that might have
sat to a sculptor for the image of Welcome. It was the youngest of
the Gladmans; who, by marriage with a Bruton, had become mistress of the old mansion. A comely brood are the Brutons. Six of
them, females, were noted as the handsomest young women in
the county. But this adopted Bruton, in my mind, was better
than they all—more comely. She was born too late to have remembered me. She just recollected in early life to have had her
cousin Bridget once pointed out to her, climbing a style. But the
name of kindred, and of cousinship, was enough. Those slender
ties, that prove slight as gossamer in the rending atmosphere of
a metropolis, bind faster, as we found it, in hearty, homely, loving
Hertfordshire. In five minutes we were as thoroughly acquainted
as if we had been born and bred up together; were familiar, even to
the calling each other by our Christian names. So Christians should
call one another. To have seen Bridget, and her—it was like the
meeting of two scriptural cousins! There was a grace and dignity,
an amplitude of form and stature, answering to her mind, in this
farmer's wife, which would have shined in a palace—or so we
thought it. We were made welcome by husband and wife equally—
we, and our friend that was with us—I had almost forgotten him—
but B. F. will not so soon forget that meeting, if peradventure he
shall read this on the far distant shores where the Kangaroo haunts.
The fatted calf was made ready, or rather was already so, as if in
anticipation of our coming; and, after an appropriate glass of native

wine, never let me forget with what honest pride this hospitable cousin made us proceed to Wheathampstead, to introduce us (as some new-found rarity) to her mother and sister Gladmans, who did indeed know something more of us, at a time when she almost knew nothing.—With what corresponding kindness we were received by them also—how Bridget's memory, exalted by the occasion, warmed into a thousand half-obliterated recollections of things and persons, to my utter astonishment, and her own—and to the astoundment of B. F. who sat by, almost the only thing that was not a cousin there,—old effaced images of more than half-forgotten names and circumstances still crowding back upon her, as words written in lemon come out upon exposure to a friendly warmth,—when I forget all this, then may my country cousins forget me; and Bridget no more remember, that in the days of weakling infancy I was her tender charge—as I have been her care in foolish manhood since—in those pretty pastoral walks, long ago, about Mackery End, in Hertfordshire.

IMPERFECT SYMPATHIES

I am of a constitution so general, that it consorts and sympathizeth with all things; I have no antipathy, or rather idiosyncracy in any thing. Those national repugnancies do not touch me, nor do I behold with prejudice the French, Italian, Spaniard, or Dutch.—*Religio Medici*.

THAT the author of the Religio Medici, mounted upon the airy stilts of abstraction, conversant about notional and conjectural essences; in whose categories of Being the possible took the upper hand of the actual; should have overlooked the impertinent individualities of such poor concretions as mankind, is not much to be admired. It is rather to be wondered at, that in the genus of animals he should have condescended to distinguish that species at all. For myself—earth-bound and fettered to the scene of my activities,—

Standing on earth, not rapt above the sky,

I confess that I do feel the differences of mankind, national or individual, to an unhealthy excess. I can look with no indifferent eye upon things or persons. Whatever is, is to me a matter of taste or distaste; or when once it becomes indifferent, it begins to be disrelishing. I am, in plainer words, a bundle of prejudices—made up of likings and dislikings—the veriest thrall to sympathies, apathies, antipathies. In a certain sense, I hope it may be said of me that I am a lover of my species. I can feel for all indifferently, but I cannot feel towards all equally. The more purely-English word that expresses sympathy will better explain my meaning. I can be a friend to a worthy man, who upon another account cannot be my mate or *fellow*. I cannot *like* all people alike.[1]

I have been trying all my life to like Scotchmen, and am obliged to desist from the experiment in despair. They cannot like me—and in truth, I never knew one of that nation who attempted to do it. There is something more plain and ingenuous in their mode of proceeding. We know one another at first sight. There is an order of imperfect intellects (under which mine must be content to rank) which in its constitution is essentially anti-Caledonian. The owners of the sort of faculties I allude to, have minds rather suggestive than comprehensive. They have no pretences to much clearness or precision in their ideas, or in their manner of expressing them. Their intellectual wardrobe (to confess fairly) has few whole pieces in it. They are content with fragments and scattered pieces of Truth. She presents no full front to them—a feature or side-face at the most. Hints and glimpses, germs and crude essays at a system, is the utmost they pretend to. They beat up a little game peradventure—and leave it to knottier heads, more robust consti-

---

[1] I would be understood as confining myself to the subject of *imperfect sympathies*. To nations or classes of men there can be no direct *antipathy*. There may be individuals born and constellated so opposite to another individual nature, that the same sphere cannot hold them. I have met with my moral antipodes, and can believe the story of two persons meeting (who never saw one another before in their lives) and instantly fighting.

> ——We by proof find there should be
> 'Twixt man and man such an antipathy,
> That though he can show no just reason why
> For any former wrong or injury,
> Can neither find a blemish on his fame,
> Nor aught in face or feature justly blame,
> Can challenge or accuse him of no evil,
> Yet notwithstanding hates him as a devil.

The lines are from old Heywood's "Hierarchie of Angels," and he subjoins a curious story in confirmation, of a Spaniard who attempted to assassinate a King Ferdinand of Spain, and being put to the rack could give no other reason for the deed but an inveterate antipathy which he had taken to the first sight of the King.

> ——The cause which to that act compell'd him
> Was, he ne'er loved him since he first beheld him.

tutions, to run it down. The light that lights them is not steady and polar, but mutable and shifting: waxing, and again waning. Their conversation is accordingly. They will throw out a random word in or out of season, and be content to let it pass for what it is worth. They cannot speak always as if they were upon their oath—but must be understood, speaking or writing, with some abatement. They seldom wait to mature a proposition, but e'en bring it to market in the green ear. They delight to impart their defective discoveries as they arise, without waiting for their full developement. They are no systematizers, and would but err more by attempting it. Their minds, as I said before, are suggestive merely. The brain of a true Caledonian (if I am not mistaken) is constituted upon quite a different plan. His Minerva is born in panoply. You are never admitted to see his ideas in their growth—if, indeed, they do grow, and are not rather put together upon principles of clock-work. You never catch his mind in an undress. He never hints or suggests any thing, but unlades his stock of ideas in perfect order and completeness. He brings his total wealth into company, and gravely unpacks it. His riches are always about him. He never stoops to catch a glittering something in your presence, to share it with you, before he quite knows whether it be true touch or not. You cannot cry *halves* to any thing that he finds. He does not find, but bring. You never witness his first apprehension of a thing. His understanding is always at its meridian—you never see the first dawn, the early streaks.—He has no falterings of self-suspicion. Surmises, guesses, misgivings, half-intuitions, semi-consciousnesses, partial illuminations, dim instincts, embryo conceptions, have no place in his brain, or vocabulary. The twilight of dubiety never falls upon him. Is he orthodox—he has no doubts. Is he an infidel—he has none either. Between the affirmative and the negative there is no border-land with him. You cannot hover with him upon the confines of truth, or wander in the maze of a probable argument. He always keeps the path. You cannot make excursions with him—for he sets you right. His taste never fluctuates. His morality never abates. He cannot compromise, or understand middle actions. There can be but a right and a wrong. His conversation is as a book. His affirmations have the sanctity of an oath. You must speak upon the square with him. He stops a metaphor like a suspected person in an enemy's country.

"A healthy book!"—said one of his countrymen to me, who had ventured to give that appellation to John Buncle,—"did I catch rightly what you said? I have heard of a man in health, and of a healthy state of body, but I do not see how that epithet can be properly applied to a book." Above all, you must beware of indirect expressions before a Caledonian. Clap an extinguisher upon your irony, if you are unhappily blest with a vein of it. Remember you are upon your oath. I have a print of a graceful female after Leonardo da Vinci, which I was showing off to Mr. * * * *. After he had examined it minutely, I ventured to ask him how he liked MY BEAUTY (a foolish name it goes by among my friends)—when he very gravely assured me, that "he had considerable respect for my character and talents" (so he was pleased to say), "but had not given himself much thought about the degree of my personal pretensions." The misconception staggered me, but did not seem much to disconcert him.—Persons of this nation are particularly fond of affirming a truth—which nobody doubts. They do not so properly affirm, as annunciate it. They do indeed appear to have such a love of truth (as if, like virtue, it were valuable for itself) that all truth becomes equally valuable, whether the proposition that contains it be new or old, disputed, or such as is impossible to become a subject of disputation. I was present not long since at a party of North Britons, where a son of Burns was expected; and happened to drop a silly expression (in my South British way), that I wished it were the father instead of the son—when four of them started up at once to inform me, that "that was impossible, because he was dead." An impracticable wish, it seems, was more than they could conceive. Swift has hit off this part of their character, namely their love of truth, in his biting way, but with an illiberality that necessarily confines the passage to the margin.[1] The tediousness of these people is certainly provoking. I wonder if they ever tire one another!—In my early life I had a passionate fondness for the poetry of Burns. I have sometimes foolishly hoped

[1] There are some people who think they sufficiently acquit themselves, and entertain their company, with relating facts of no consequence, not at all out of the road of such common incidents as happen every day; and this I have observed more frequently among the Scots than any other nation, who are very careful not to omit the minutest circumstances of time or place; which kind of discourse, if it were not a little relieved by the uncouth terms and phrases, as well as accent and gesture peculiar to that country, would be hardly tolerable.—*Hints towards an Essay on Conversation.*

to ingratiate myself with his countrymen by expressing it. But I have always found that a true Scot resents your admiration of his compatriot, even more than he would your contempt of him. The latter he imputes to your "imperfect acquaintance with many of the words which he uses;" and the same objection makes it a presumption in you to suppose that you can admire him.—Thomson they seem to have forgotten. Smollett they have neither forgotten nor forgiven for his delineation of Rory and his companion, upon their first introduction to our metropolis.—Speak of Smollett as a great genius, and they will retort upon you Hume's History compared with *his* Continuation of it. What if the historian had continued Humphrey Clinker?

I have, in the abstract, no disrespect for Jews. They are a piece of stubborn antiquity, compared with which Stonehenge is in its nonage. They date beyond the pyramids. But I should not care to be in habits of familiar intercourse with any of that nation. I confess that I have not the nerves to enter their synagogues. Old prejudices cling about me. I cannot shake off the story of Hugh of Lincoln. Centuries of injury, contempt, and hate on the one side,—of cloaked revenge, dissimulation, and hate, on the other, between our and their fathers, must, and ought, to affect the blood of the children. I cannot believe it can run clear and kindly yet; or that a few fine words, such as candour, liberality, the light of a nineteenth century, can close up the breaches of so deadly a disunion. A Hebrew is nowhere congenial to me. He is least distasteful on 'Change—for the mercantile spirit levels all distinctions, as all are beauties in the dark. I boldly confess that I do not relish the approximation of Jew and Christian, which has become so fashionable. The reciprocal endearments have, to me, something hypocritical and unnatural in them. I do not like to see the Church and Synagogue kissing and congeeing in awkward postures of an affected civility. If *they* are converted, why do they not come over to us altogether? Why keep up a form of separation, when the life of it is fled? If they can sit with us at table, why do they keck at our cookery? I do not understand these half convertities. Jews christianizing—Christians judaizing—puzzle me. I like fish or flesh. A moderate Jew is a more confounding piece of anomaly than a wet Quaker. The spirit of the synagogue is essentially *separative.* B—— would have been more in keeping if he had abided by the faith of his forefathers. There is a fine scorn in his face, which nature meant to be of——Christians. The Hebrew spirit is strong in him, in spite of his proselytism. He cannot conquer the Shibboleth. How it breaks out, when he sings, "The Children of Israel passed through the Red Sea!" The auditors, for the moment, are as Egyptians to him, and he rides over our necks in triumph. There is no mistaking him.— B—— has a strong expression of sense in his countenance, and it is confirmed by his singing. The foundation of his vocal excellence is sense. He sings with understanding, as Kemble delivered dialogue. He would sing the Commandments, and give an appropriate character to each prohibition. His nation, in general, have not ever-sensible countenances. How should they?—but you seldom see a silly expression among them. Gain, and the pursuit of gain, sharpen a man's visage. I never heard of an idiot being born among them.—Some admire the Jewish female-physiognomy. I admire it—but with trembling. Jael had those full dark inscrutable eyes.

In the Negro countenance you will often meet with strong traits of benignity. I have felt yearnings of tenderness towards some of these faces—or rather masks—that have looked out kindly upon one in casual encounters in the streets and highways. I love what Fuller beautifully calls—these "images of God cut in ebony." But I should not like to associate with them, to share my meals and my good-nights with them—because they are black.

I love Quaker ways, and Quaker worship. I venerate the Quaker principles. It does me good for the rest of the day when I meet any of their people in my path. When I am ruffled or disturbed by any occurrence, the sight, or quiet voice of a Quaker, acts upon me as a ventilator, lightening the air, and taking off a load from the bosom. But I cannot like the Quakers (as Desdemona would say) "to live with them." I am all over sophisticated—with humours, fancies, craving hourly sympathy. I must have books, pictures, theatres, chit-chat, scandal, jokes, ambiguities, and a thousand whim-whams, which their simpler taste can do without. I should starve at their primitive banquet. My appetites are too high for the salads which (according to Evelyn) Eve dressed for the angel, my gusto too excited

To sit a guest with Daniel at his pulse.

The indirect answers which Quakers are often found to return to a question put to them may be explained, I think, without the vulgar assumption, that they are more given to evasion and equivocating than other people. They naturally look to their words more carefully, and are more cautious of committing themselves. They have a peculiar character to keep up on this head. They stand in a manner upon their veracity. A Quaker is by law exempted from taking an oath. The custom of resorting to an oath in extreme cases, sanctified as it is by all religious antiquity, is apt (it must be confessed) to introduce into the laxer sort of minds the notion of two kinds of truth—the one applicable to the solemn affairs of justice, and the other to the common proceedings of daily intercourse. As truth bound upon the conscience by an oath can be but truth, so in the common affirmations of the shop and the market-place a latitude is expected, and conceded upon questions wanting this solemn covenant. Something less than truth satisfies. It is common to hear a person say, "You do not expect me to speak as if I were upon my oath." Hence a great deal of incorrectness and inadvertency, short of falsehood, creeps into ordinary conversation; and a kind of secondary or laic-truth is tolerated, where clergy-truth—oath-truth, by the nature of the circumstances, is not required. A Quaker knows none of this distinction. His simple affirmation being received, upon the most sacred occasions, without any further test, stamps a value upon the words which he is to use upon the most indifferent topics of life. He looks to them, naturally, with more severity. You can have of him no more than his word. He knows, if he is caught tripping in a casual expression, he forfeits, for himself, at least, his claim to the invidious exemption. He knows that his syllables are weighed—and how far a consciousness of this particular watchfulness, exerted against a person, has a tendency to produce indirect answers, and a diverting of the question by honest means, might be illustrated, and the practice justified, by a more sacred example than is proper to be adduced upon this occasion. The admirable presence of mind, which is notorious in Quakers upon all contingencies, might be traced to this imposed self-watchfulness—if it did not seem rather an humble and secular scion of that old stock of religious constancy, which never bent or faltered, in the Primitive Friends, or gave way to the winds of persecution, to the violence of judge or ac-

cuser, under trials and racking examinations. "You will never
be the wiser, if I sit here answering your questions till midnight,"
said one of those upright Justicers to Penn, who had been putting
law-cases with a puzzling subtlety. "Thereafter as the answers
may be," retorted the Quaker. The astonishing composure of this
people is sometimes ludicrously displayed in lighter instances.—
I was travelling in a stage-coach with three male Quakers, buttoned
up in the straitest non-conformity of their sect. We stopped to
bait at Andover, where a meal, partly tea apparatus, partly supper, was set before us. My friends confined themselves to the tea-
table. I in my way took supper. When the landlady brought in
the bill, the eldest of my companions discovered that she had
charged for both meals. This was resisted. Mine hostess was very
clamorous and positive. Some mild arguments were used on the
part of the Quakers, for which the heated mind of the good lady
seemed by no means a fit recipient. The guard came in with his
usual peremptory notice. The Quakers pulled out their money,
and formally tendered it—so much for tea—I, in humble imitation, tendering mine—for the supper which I had taken. She
would not relax in her demand. So they all three quietly put
up their silver, as did myself, and marched out of the room,
the eldest and gravest going first, with myself closing up the
rear, who thought I could not do better than follow the example of such grave and warrantable personages. We got in.
The steps went up. The coach drove off. The murmurs of
mine hostess, not very indistinctly or ambiguously pronounced,
became after a time inaudible—and now my conscience, which
the whimsical scene had for a while suspended, beginning to
give some twitches, I waited, in the hope that some justification
would be offered by these serious persons for the seeming injustice of their conduct. To my great surprise, not a syllable
was dropped on the subject. They sate as mute as at a meeting. At length the eldest of them broke silence, by inquiring of
his next neighbour, "Hast thee heard how indigos go at the India
House?" and the question operated as a soporific on my moral
feeling as far as Exeter.

GRACE BEFORE MEAT

THE custom of saying grace at meals had, probably, its origin in the early times of the world, and the hunter-state of man, when dinners were precarious things, and a full meal was something more than a common blessing; when a belly-full was a windfall, and looked like a special providence. In the shouts and triumphal songs with which, after a season of sharp abstinence, a lucky booty of deer's or goat's flesh would naturally be ushered home, existed, perhaps, the germ of the modern grace. It is not otherwise easy to be understood, why the blessing of food—the act of eating—should have had a particular expression of thanksgiving annexed to it, distinct from that implied and silent gratitude .with which we are expected to enter upon the enjoyment of the many other various gifts and good things of existence.

I own that I am disposed to say grace upon twenty other occasions in the course of the day besides my dinner. I want a form for setting out upon a pleasant walk, for a moonlight ramble, for a friendly meeting, or a solved problem. Why have we none for books, those spiritual repasts—a grace before Milton—a grace before Shakespeare—a devotional exercise proper to be said before reading the Fairy Queen?—but, the received ritual having prescribed these forms to the solitary ceremony of manducation, I shall confine my observations to the experience which I have had of the grace, properly so called; commending my new scheme for extension to a niche in the grand philosophical, poetical, and perchance in part heretical, liturgy, now compiling by my friend Homo Humanus, for the use of a certain snug congregation of Utopian Rabelæsian Christians, no matter where assembled.

The form then of the benediction before eating has its beauty at a poor man's table, or at the simple and unprovocative repasts of children. It is here that the grace becomes exceedingly graceful. The indigent man, who hardly knows whether he shall have a meal the next day or not, sits down to his fare with a present sense of the blessing which can be but feebly acted by the rich, into whose minds the conception of wanting a dinner could never, but by some extreme theory, have entered. The proper end of food—the animal sustenance—is barely contemplated by them. The poor man's bread is his daily bread, literally his bread for the day. Their courses are perennial.

Again, the plainest diet seems the fittest to be preceded by the grace. That which is least stimulative to appetite, leaves the mind most free for foreign considerations. A man may feel thankful, heartily thankful, over a dish of plain mutton with turnips, and have leisure to reflect upon the ordinance and institution of eating; when he shall confess a perturbation of mind, inconsistent with the purposes of the grace, at the presence of venison or turtle. When I have sate (a *rarus hospes*) at rich men's tables, with the savoury soup and messes steaming up the nostrils, and moistening the lips of the guests with desire and a distracted choice, I have felt the introduction of that ceremony to be unseasonable. With the ravenous orgasm upon you, it seems impertinent to interpose a religious sentiment. It is a confusion of purpose to mutter out praises from a mouth that waters. The heats of epicurism put out the gentle flame of devotion. The incense which rises round is pagan, and the belly-god intercepts it for his own. The very excess of the provision beyond the needs, takes away all sense of proportion between the end and means. The giver is veiled by his gifts. You are startled at the injustice of returning thanks—for what?—for having too much, while so many starve. It is to praise the Gods amiss.

I have observed this awkwardness felt, scarce consciously perhaps, by the good man who says the grace. I have seen it in clergymen and others—a sort of shame—a sense of the co-presence of circumstances which unhallow the blessing. After a devotional tone put on for a few seconds, how rapidly the speaker will fall into his common voice, helping himself or his neighbour, as if to get rid of some uneasy sensation of hypocrisy. Not that the good man was a hypocrite, or was not most conscientious in the discharge of the duty; but he felt in his inmost mind the incompatibility of the scene and the viands before him with the exercise of a calm and rational gratitude.

I hear somebody exclaim,—Would you have Christians sit down at table, like hogs to their troughs, without remembering the Giver? —no—I would have them sit down as Christians, remembering the Giver, and less like hogs. Or if their appetites must run riot, and they must pamper themselves with delicacies for which east and west are ransacked, I would have them postpone their benediction to a fitter season, when appetite is laid; when the still small voice can be heard, and the reason of the grace returns—with temperate diet and restricted dishes. Gluttony and surfeiting are no proper occasions for thanksgiving. When Jeshurun waxed fat, we read that he kicked. Virgil knew the harpy-nature better, when he put into the mouth of Celæno any thing but a blessing. We may be gratefully sensible of the deliciousness of some kinds of food beyond others, though that is a meaner and inferior gratitude: but the proper object of the grace is sustenance, not relishes; daily bread, not delicacies; the means of life, and not the means of pampering the carcass. With what frame or composure, I wonder, can a city chaplain pronounce his benediction at some great Hall feast, when he knows that his last concluding pious word— and that, in all probability, the sacred name which he preaches— is but the signal for so many impatient harpies to commence their foul orgies, with as little sense of true thankfulness (which is temperance) as those Virgilian fowl! It is well if the good man himself does not feel his devotions a little clouded, those foggy sensuous steams mingling with and polluting the pure altar sacrifice.

The severest satire upon full tables and surfeits is the banquet which Satan, in the Paradise Regained, provides for a temptation in the wilderness:—

> A table richly spread in regal mode,
> With dishes piled, and meats of noblest sort
> And savour; beasts of chase, or fowl of game,
> In pastry built, or from the spit, or boiled,
> Gris-amber-steamed; all fish from sea or shore,
> Freshet or purling brook, for which was drained
> Pontus, and Lucrine bay, and Afric coast.

The Tempter, I warrant you, thought these cates would go down without the recommendatory preface of a benediction. They are like to be short graces where the devil plays the host.—I am afraid the poet wants his usual decorum in this place. Was he thinking of the old Roman luxury, or of a gaudy day at Cambridge? This was a temptation fitter for a Heliogabalus. The whole banquet is too civic and culinary, and the accompaniments altogether a profanation of that deep, abstracted, holy scene. The mighty artillery of sauces, which the cook-fiend conjures up, is out of pro-

portion to the simple wants and plain hunger of the guest. He
that disturbed him in his dreams, from his dreams might have been
taught better. To the temperate fantasies of the famished Son of
God, what sort of feasts presented themselves?—He dreamed indeed,

> ——— As appetite is wont to dream,
> Of meats and drinks, nature's refreshment sweet.

But what meats?—

> Him thought, he by the brook of Cherith stood,
> And saw the ravens with their horny beaks
> Food to Elijah bringing, even and morn;
> Though ravenous, taught to abstain from what they brought:
> He saw the prophet also how he fled
> Into the desert, and how there he slept
> Under a juniper; then how awaked
> He found his supper on the coals prepared,
> And by the angel was bid rise and eat,
> And ate the second time after repose,
> The strength whereof sufficed him forty days:
> Sometimes, that with Elijah he partook,
> Or as a guest with Daniel at his pulse.

Nothing in Milton is finelier fancied than these temperate dreams
of the divine Hungerer. To which of these two visionary banquets,
think you, would the introduction of what is called the grace have
been most fitting and pertinent?

Theoretically I am no enemy to graces; but practically I own
that (before meat especially) they seem to involve something awkward and unseasonable. Our appetites, of one or another kind,
are excellent spurs to our reason, which might otherwise but feebly
set about the great ends of preserving and continuing the species.
They are fit blessings to be contemplated at a distance with a becoming gratitude: but the moment of appetite (the judicious reader
will apprehend me) is, perhaps, the least fit season for that exercise. The Quakers, who go about their business, of every description, with more calmness than we, have more title to the use of
these benedictory prefaces. I have always admired their silent
grace, and the more because I have observed their applications
to the meat and drink following to be less passionate and sensual
than ours. They are neither gluttons nor wine-bibbers as a people.
They eat, as a horse bolts his chopt hay, with indifference, calmness, and cleanly circumstances. They neither grease nor slop

themselves. When I see a citizen in his bib and tucker, I cannot imagine it a surplice.

I am no Quaker at my food. I confess I am not indifferent to the kinds of it. Those unctuous morsels of deer's flesh were not made to be received with dispassionate services. I hate a man who swallows it affecting not to know what he is eating. I suspect his taste in higher matters. I shrink instinctively from one who professes to like minced veal. There is a physiognomical character in the tastes for food. C—— holds that a man cannot have a pure mind who refuses apple-dumplings. I am not certain but he is right. With the decay of my first innocence, I confess a less and less relish daily for these innocuous cates. The whole vegetable tribe have lost their gust with me. Only I stick to asparagus, which still seems to inspire gentle thoughts. I am impatient and querulous under culinary disappointments, as to come home at the dinner hour, for instance, expecting some savoury mess, and to find one quite tasteless and sapidless. Butter ill melted—that commonest of kitchen failures—puts me beside my tenour.—The author of the Rambler used to make inarticulate animal noises over a favourite food. Was this the music quite proper to be preceded by the grace? or would the pious man have done better to postpone his devotions to a season when the blessing might be contemplated with less perturbation? I quarrel with no man's tastes, nor would set my thin face against those excellent things, in their way, jollity and feasting. But as these exercises, however laudable, have little in them of grace or gracefulness, a man should be sure, before he ventures so to grace them, that while he is pretending his devotions otherwise, he is not secretly kissing his hand to some great fish—his Dagon—with a special consecration of no ark but the fat tureen before him. Graces are the sweet preluding strains to the banquets of angels and children: to the roots and severer repasts of the Chartreuse; to the slender, but not slenderly acknowledged, refection of the poor and humble man: but at the heaped-up boards of the pampered and the luxurious they become of dissonant mood, less timed and tuned to the occasion, methinks, than the noise of those better befitting organs would be, which children hear tales of, at Hog's Norton. We sit too long at our meals, or are too curious in the study of them, or too disordered in our application to them, or engross too great a portion of these good things (which should be common) to our share, to be able with any grace to say grace. To be thankful for what we grasp exceeding our proportion is to add hypocrisy to injustice. A lurking sense of this truth is what makes the performance of this duty so cold and spiritless a service at most tables. In houses where the grace is as indispensable as the napkin, who has not seen that never-settled question arise, as to *who shall say it;* while the good man of the house and the visitor clergyman, or some other guest belike of next authority from years or gravity, shall be bandying about the office between them as a matter of compliment, each of them not unwilling to shift the awkward burthen of an equivocal duty from his own shoulders?

I once drank tea in company with two Methodist divines of different persuasions, whom it was my fortune to introduce to each other for the first time that evening. Before the first cup was handed round, one of these reverend gentlemen put it to the other, with all due solemnity, whether he chose to *say any thing.* It seems it is the custom with some sectaries to put up a short prayer before this meal also. His reverend brother did not at first quite apprehend him, but upon an explanation, with little less importance he made answer, that it was not a custom known in his church: in which courteous evasion the other acquiescing for good manners' sake, or in compliance with a weak brother, the supplementary or tea-grace was waived altogether. With what spirit might not Lucian have painted two priests, of *his* religion, playing into each other's hands the compliment of performing or omitting a sacrifice,—the hungry God meantime, doubtful of his incense, with expectant nostrils hovering over the two flamens, and (as between two stools) going away in the end without his supper.

A short form upon these occasions is felt to want reverence; a long one, I am afraid, cannot escape the charge of impertinence. I do not quite approve of the epigrammatic conciseness with which that equivocal wag (but my pleasant school-fellow) C. V. L., when importuned for a grace, used to inquire, first slily leering down the table, "Is there no clergyman here?"—significantly adding, "Thank G——." Nor do I think our old form at school quite pertinent, where we were used to preface our bald bread and cheese suppers with a preamble, connecting with that humble blessing a recognition of benefits the most awful and overwhelming to the imagination which religion has to offer. *Non tunc illis erat locus.* I remember we were put to it to reconcile the phrase "good creatures," upon which the blessing rested, with the fare set before us, wilfully understanding that expression in a low and animal sense,—till some one recalled a legend, which told how in the golden days of Christ's, the young Hospitallers were wont to have smoking joints of roast meat upon their nightly boards, till some pious benefactor, commiserating the decencies, rather than the palates, of the children, commuted our flesh for garments, and gave us—*horresco referens*—trowsers instead of mutton.

DREAM CHILDREN: A REVERIE

CHILDREN love to listen to stories about their elders, when *they* were children; to stretch their imagination to the conception of a traditionary great-uncle, or grandame, whom they never saw. It was in this spirit that my little ones crept about me the other evening to hear about their great-grandmother Field, who lived in a great house in Norfolk (a hundred times bigger than that in which they and papa lived) which had been the scene—so at least it was generally believed in that part of the country—of the tragic incidents which they had lately become familiar with from the ballad of the Children in the Wood. Certain it is that the whole story of the children and their cruel uncle was to be seen fairly carved out in wood upon the chimney-piece of the great hall, the whole story down to the Robin Red-breasts, till a foolish rich person pulled it down to set up a marble one of modern invention in its stead, with no story upon it. Here Alice put out one of her dear mother's looks, too tender to be called upbraiding. Then I went on to say, how religious and how good their great-grandmother Field was, how beloved and respected by everybody, though she was not indeed the mistress of this great house, but had only the charge of it (and yet in some respects she might be said to be the mistress of it too) committed to her by the owner, who preferred living in a newer and more fashionable mansion which he had purchased somewhere in the adjoining county; but still she lived in it in a manner as if it had been her own, and kept up the dignity of the great house in a sort while she lived, which afterwards came to decay, and was nearly pulled down, and all its old ornaments stripped and carried away to the

owner's other house, where they were set up, and looked as awkward as if some one were to carry away the old tombs they had
seen lately at the Abbey, and stick them up in Lady C.'s tawdry
gilt drawing-room. Here John smiled, as much as to say, "that
would be foolish indeed." And then I told how, when she came to
die, her funeral was attended by a concourse of all the poor, and
some of the gentry too, of the neighbourhood for many miles
round, to show their respect for her memory, because she had
been such a good and religious woman; so good indeed that she
knew all the Psaltery by heart, ay, and a great part of the Testament besides. Here little Alice spread her hands. Then I told her
what a tall, upright, graceful person their great-grandmother Field
once was; and how in her youth she was esteemed the best dancer—
here Alice's little right foot played an involuntary movement, till,
upon my looking grave, it desisted—the best dancer, I was saying,
in the county, till a cruel disease, called a cancer, came, and bowed
her down with pain; but it could never bend her good spirits, or
make them stoop, but they were still upright, because she was so
good and religious. Then I told how she was used to sleep by
herself in a lone chamber of the great lone house; and how she
believed that an apparition of two infants was to be seen at midnight gliding up and down the great staircase near where she slept,
but she said "those innocents would do her no harm;" and how
frightened I used to be, though in those days I had my maid to
sleep with me, because I was never half so good or religious as she—
and yet I never saw the infants. Here John expanded all his eyebrows and tried to look courageous. Then I told how good she
was to all her grand-children, having us all to the great house in
the holy-days, where I in particular used to spend many hours by
myself, in gazing upon the old busts of the Twelve Cæsars, that
had been Emperors of Rome, till the old marble heads would seem
to live again, or I to be turned into marble with them; how I never
could be tired with roaming about that huge mansion, with its vast
empty rooms, with their worn-out hangings, fluttering tapestry,
and carved oaken panels, with the gilding almost rubbed out—
sometimes in the spacious old-fashioned gardens, which I had
almost to myself, unless when now and then a solitary gardening
man would cross me—and how the nectarines and peaches hung
upon the walls, without my ever offering to pluck them, because

they were forbidden fruit, unless now and then,—and because I had more pleasure in strolling about among the old melancholy-looking yew trees, or the firs, and picking up the red berries, and the fir apples, which were good for nothing but to look at—or in lying about upon the fresh grass with all the fine garden smells around me—or basking in the orangery, till I could almost fancy myself ripening too along with the oranges and the limes in that grateful warmth—or in watching the dace that darted to and fro in the fish-pond, at the bottom of the garden, with here and there a great sulky pike hanging midway down the water in silent state, as if it mocked at their impertinent friskings,—I had more pleasure in these busy-idle diversions than in all the sweet flavours of peaches, nectarines, oranges, and such-like common baits of children. Here John slyly deposited back upon the plate a bunch of grapes, which, not unobserved by Alice, he had meditated dividing with her, and both seemed willing to relinquish them for the present as irrelevant. Then in somewhat a more heightened tone, I told how, though their great-grandmother Field loved all her grand-children, yet in an especial manner she might be said to love their uncle, John L——, because he was so handsome and spirited a youth, and a king to the rest of us; and, instead of moping about in solitary corners, like some of us, he would mount the most mettlesome horse he could get, when but an imp no bigger than themselves, and make it carry him half over the county in a morning, and join the hunters when there were any out—and yet he loved the old great house and gardens too, but had too much spirit to be always pent up within their boundaries—and how their uncle grew up to man's estate as brave as he was handsome, to the admiration of every body, but of their great-grandmother Field most especially; and how he used to carry me upon his back when I was a lame-footed boy—for he was a good bit older than me—many a mile when I could not walk for pain;—and how in after life he became lame-footed too, and I did not always (I fear) make allowances enough for him when he was impatient and in pain, nor remember sufficiently how considerate he had been to me when I was lame-footed; and how when he died, though he had not been dead an hour, it seemed as if he had died a great while ago, such a distance there is betwixt life and death; and how I bore his death as I thought pretty well at first, but afterwards it haunted and

haunted me; and though I did not cry or take it to heart as some
do, and as I think he would have done if I had died, yet I missed
him all day long, and knew not till then how much I had loved
him. I missed his kindness, and I missed his crossness, and wished
him to be alive again, to be quarrelling with him (for we quar-
relled sometimes), rather than not have him again, and was as
uneasy without him, as he, their poor uncle, must have been
when the doctor took off his limb.—Here the children fell a-crying,
and asked if their little mourning which they had on was not for
uncle John, and they looked up, and prayed me not to go on about
their uncle, but to tell them some stories about their pretty dead
mother. Then I told how for seven long years, in hope sometimes,
sometimes in despair, yet persisting ever, I courted the fair Alice
W——n; and, as much as children could understand, I explained
to them what coyness, and difficulty, and denial, meant in maidens
—when suddenly turning to Alice, the soul of the first Alice looked
out at her eyes with such a reality of re-presentment, that I became
in doubt which of them stood there before me, or whose that
bright hair was; and while I stood gazing, both the children gradually grew fainter to my view, receding, and still receding, till
nothing at last but two mournful features were seen in the uttermost distance, which, without speech, strangely impressed upon
me the effects of speech: "We are not of Alice, nor of thee, nor are
we children at all. The children of Alice call Bartrum father. We
are nothing; less than nothing, and dreams. We are only what
might have been, and must wait upon the tedious shores of Lethe
millions of ages before we have existence, and a name"—and immediately awaking, I found myself quietly seated in my bachelor
arm-chair, where I had fallen asleep, with the faithful Bridget
unchanged by my side—but John L. (or James Elia) was gone for
ever.

DISTANT CORRESPONDENTS

In a Letter to B. F. Esq. at Sydney, New South Wales

MY DEAR F.—When I think how welcome the sight of a
letter from the world where you were born must be to
you in that strange one to which you have been transplanted, I feel some compunctious visitings at my long silence.
But, indeed, it is no easy effort to set about a correspondence at

our distance. The weary world of waters between us oppresses the imagination. It is difficult to conceive how a scrawl of mine should ever stretch across it. It is a sort of presumption to expect that one's thoughts should live so far. It is like writing for posterity; and reminds me of one of Mrs. Rowe's superscriptions, "Alcander to Strephon, in the shades." Cowley's Post-Angel is no more than would be expedient in such an intercourse. One drops a packet at Lombard-street, and in twenty-four hours a friend in Cumberland gets it as fresh as if it came in ice. It is only like whispering through a long trumpet. But suppose a tube let down from the moon, with yourself at one end, and *the man* at the other; it would be some balk to the spirit of conversation, if you knew that the dialogue exchanged with that interesting theosophist would take two or three revolutions of a higher luminary in its passage. Yet for aught I know, you may be some parasangs nigher that primitive idea—Plato's man—than we in England here have the honour to reckon ourselves.

Epistolary matter usually compriseth three topics; news, sentiment, and puns. In the latter, I include all non-serious subjects; or subjects serious in themselves, but treated after my fashion, non-seriously.—And first, for news. In them, the most desirable circumstance, I suppose, is that they shall be true. But what security can I have that what I now send you for truth shall not before you get it unaccountably turn into a lie? For instance, our mutual friend P. is at this present writing—*my Now*—in good health, and enjoys a fair share of worldly reputation. You are glad to hear it. This is natural and friendly. But at this present reading—*your Now*—he may possibly be in the Bench, or going to be hanged, which in reason ought to abate something of your transport (*i. e.*, at hearing he was well, &c.), or at least considerably to modify it. I am going to the play this evening, to have a laugh with Munden.—You have no theatre, I think you told me, in your land of d——d realities. You naturally lick your lips, and envy me my felicity. Think but a moment, and you will correct the hateful emotion. Why, it is Sunday morning with you, and 1823. This confusion of tenses, this grand solecism of *two presents*, is in a degree common to all postage. But if I sent you word to Bath or the Devises, that I was expecting the aforesaid treat this evening, though at the moment you received the intelligence my full feast of fun would be over, yet there would be for a day or two after, as you would well know, a smack, a relish left upon my mental palate, which would give rational encouragement for you to foster a portion at least of the disagreeable passion, which it was in part my intention to produce. But ten months hence your envy or your sympathy would be as useless as a passion spent upon the dead. Not only does truth, in these long intervals, un-essence herself, but (what is harder) one cannot venture a crude fiction for the fear that it may ripen into a truth upon the voyage. What a wild improbable banter I put upon you some three years since—— of Will Weatherall having married a servant-maid! I remember gravely consulting you how we were to receive her—for Will's wife was in no case to be rejected; and your no less serious replication in the matter; how tenderly you advised an abstemious introduction of literary topics before the lady, with a caution not to be too forward in bringing on the carpet matters more within the sphere of her intelligence; your deliberate judgment, or rather wise suspension of sentence, how far jacks, and spits, and mops, could with propriety be introduced as subjects; whether the conscious avoiding of all such matters in discourse would not have a worse look than the taking of them casually in our way; in what manner we should carry ourselves to our maid Becky, Mrs. William Weatherall being by; whether we show more delicacy, and a truer sense of respect for Will's wife, by treating Becky with our customary chiding before her, or by an unusual deferential civility paid to Becky as to a person of great worth, but thrown by the caprice of fate into a humble station. There were difficulties, I remember, on both sides, which you did me the favour to state with the precision of a lawyer, united to the tenderness of a friend. I laughed in my sleeve at your solemn pleadings, when lo! while I was valuing myself upon this flam put upon you in New South Wales, the devil in England, jealous possibly of any lie-children not his own, or working after my copy, has actually instigated our friend (not three days since) to the commission of a matrimony, which I had only conjured up for your diversion. William Weatherall has married Mrs. Cotterel's maid. But to take it in its truest sense, you will see, my dear F., that news from me must become history to you; which I neither profess to write, nor indeed care much for reading. No person, under a diviner, can with any prospect of veracity conduct a correspondence at such an arm's length. Two prophets, indeed, might thus interchange intelligence with effect; the epoch of the writer (Habakkuk) falling in with the true present time of the receiver (Daniel); but then we are no prophets.

Then as to sentiment. It fares little better with that. This kind of dish, above all, requires to be served up hot; or sent off in water-plates, that your friend may have it almost as warm as yourself. If it have time to cool, it is the most tasteless of all cold meats. I have often smiled at a conceit of the late Lord C. It seems that travelling somewhere about Geneva, he came to some pretty green spot, or nook, where a willow, or something, hung so fantastically and invitingly over a stream—was it?—or a rock?—no matter—but the stillness and the repose, after a weary journey 'tis likely, in a languid moment of his lordship's hot restless life, so took his fancy, that he could imagine no place so proper, in the event of his death, to lay his bones in. This was all very natural and excusable as a sentiment, and shows his character in a very pleasing light. But when from a passing sentiment it came to be an act; and when by a positive testamentary disposal, his remains were actually carried all that way from England; who was there, some desperate sentimentalists excepted, that did not ask the question, Why could not his lordship have found a spot as solitary, a nook as romantic, a tree as green and pendent, with a stream as emblematic to his purpose, in Surrey, in Dorset, or in Devon? Conceive the sentiment boarded up, freighted, entered at the Custom House (startling the tide-waiters with the novelty), hoisted into a ship. Conceive it pawed about and handled between the rude jests of tarpaulin ruffians—a thing of its delicate texture— the salt bilge wetting it till it became as vapid as a damaged lustring. Suppose it in material danger (mariners have some superstition about sentiments) of being tossed over in a fresh gale to some propitiatory shark (spirit of Saint Gothard, save us from a quietus so foreign to the deviser's purpose!) but it has happily evaded a fishy consummation. Trace it then to its lucky landing— at Lyons shall we say?—I have not the map before me—jostled upon four men's shoulders—baiting at this town—stopping to refresh at t'other village—waiting a passport here, a license there; the sanction of the magistracy in this district, the concurrence of the ecclesiastics in that canton; till at length it arrives at its destination, tired out and jaded, from a brisk sentiment, into a feature of silly pride or tawdry senseless affectation. How few sentiments, my dear F., I am afraid we can set down, in the sailor's phrase, as quite sea-worthy.

Lastly, as to the agreeable levities, which, though contemptible in bulk, are the twinkling corpuscula which should irradiate a right friendly epistle—your puns and small jests are, I apprehend, extremely circumscribed in their sphere of action. They are so far from a capacity of being packed up and sent beyond sea, they will scarce endure to be transported by hand from this room to the next. Their vigour is as the instant of their birth. Their nutriment for their brief existence is the intellectual atmosphere of the by-standers: or this last, is the fine slime of Nilus—the *melior lutus*,—whose maternal recipiency is as necessary as the *sol pater* to their equivocal generation. A pun hath a hearty kind of present ear-kissing smack with it; you can no more transmit it in its pristine flavour, than you can send a kiss.—Have you not tried in some instances to palm off a yesterday's pun upon a gentleman, and has it answered? Not but it was new to his hearing, but it did not seem to come new from you. It did not hitch in. It was like picking up at a village ale-house a two days old newspaper. You have not seen it before, but you resent the stale thing as an affront. This sort of merchandise above all requires a quick return. A pun, and its recognitory laugh, must be co-instantaneous. The one is the brisk lightning, the other the fierce thunder. A moment's interval, and the link is snapped. A pun is reflected from a friend's face as from a mirror. Who would consult his sweet visnomy, if the polished surface were two or three minutes (not to speak of twelve-months, my dear F.) in giving back its copy?

I cannot image to myself whereabout you are. When I try to fix it, Peter Wilkins's island comes across me. Sometimes you seem to be in the *Hades* of *Thieves*. I see Diogenes prying among you with his perpetual fruitless lantern. What must you be willing by this time to give for the sight of an honest man! You must almost have forgotten how *we* look. And tell me, what your Sydneyites do? are they th**v*ng all day long? Merciful heaven! what property can stand against such a depredation! The kangaroos—your Aborigines—do they keep their primitive simplicity un-Europe-tainted, with those little short fore-puds, looking like a lesson framed by nature to the pick-pocket! Marry, for diving into fobs they are rather lamely provided *a priori;* but if the hue and cry were once up, they would show as fair a pair of hind-shifters as the expertest loco-motor in the colony.—We hear the most improbable tales at this distance. Pray, is it true that the young Spartans among you are born with six fingers, which spoils their scanning?—It must look very odd; but use reconciles. For their scansion, it is less to be regretted, for if they take it into their heads to be poets, it is odds but they turn out, the greater part of them, vile plagiarists.—Is there much difference to see to between the son of a th**f, and the grandson? or where does the taint stop? Do you bleach in three or in four generations?—I have many questions to put, but ten Delphic voyages can be made in a shorter time than it will take to satisfy my scruples.—Do you grow your own hemp?—What is your staple trade, exclusive of the national profession, I mean? Your lock-smiths, I take it, are some of your great capitalists.

I am insensibly chatting to you as familiarly as when we used to exchange good-morrows out of our old contiguous windows, in pump-famed Hare-court in the Temple. Why did you ever leave that quiet corner?—Why did I?—with its complement of four poor elms, from whose smoke-dyed barks, the theme of jesting ruralists, I picked my first lady-birds! My heart is as dry as that spring sometimes proves in a thirsty August, when I revert to the space that is between us; a length of passage enough to render obsolete the phrases of our English letters before they can reach you. But while I talk, I think you hear me,—thoughts dallying with vain surmise—

> Aye me! while thee the seas and sounding shores
> Hold far away.

Come back, before I am grown into a very old man, so as you shall hardly know me. Come, before Bridget walks on crutches. Girls whom you left children have become sage matrons, while you are tarrying there. The blooming Miss W——r (you remember Sally W——r) called upon us yesterday, an aged crone. Folks, whom you knew, die off every year. Formerly, I thought that death was wearing out,—I stood ramparted about with so many healthy friends. The departure of J. W., two springs back corrected my delusion. Since then the old divorcer has been busy. If you do not make haste to return, there will be little left to greet you, of me, or mine.

ON THE ARTIFICIAL COMEDY OF THE LAST CENTURY

THE artificial Comedy, or Comedy of manners, is quite extinct on our stage. Congreve and Farquhar show their heads once in seven years only, to be exploded and put down instantly. The times cannot bear them. Is it for a few wild speeches, an occasional license of dialogue? I think not altogether. The business of their dramatic characters will not stand the moral test. We screw everything up to that. Idle gallantry in a fiction, a dream, the passing pageant of an evening, startles us in the same way as the alarming indications of profligacy in a son or ward in real life should startle a parent or guardian. We have no such middle emotions as dramatic interests left. We see a stage libertine playing his loose pranks of two hours' duration, and of no after consequence, with the severe eyes which inspect real vices with their bearings upon two worlds. We are spectators to a plot or intrigue (not reducible in life to the point of strict morality) and take it all for truth. We substitute a real for a dramatic person, and judge him accordingly. We try him in our courts, from which there is no appeal to the *dramatis personæ*, his peers. We have been spoiled with—not sentimental comedy—but a tyrant far more pernicious to our pleasures which has succeeded to it, the exclusive and all-devouring drama of common life; where the moral point is every thing; where, instead of the fictitious half-believed personages of the stage (the phantoms of old comedy) we recognise ourselves, our brothers, aunts, kinsfolk, allies, patrons, enemies,—the same as in life,—with an interest in what is going on so hearty and substantial, that we cannot afford our moral judgment, in its deepest and most vital results, to compromise or slumber for a moment. What is *there* transacting, by no modification is made to affect us in any other manner than the same events or characters would do in our relationships of life. We carry our fire-side concerns to the theatre with us. We do not go thither, like our ancestors, to escape from the pressure of reality, so much as to confirm our experience of it; to make assurance double, and take a bond of fate. We must live our toilsome lives twice over, as it was the mournful privilege of Ulysses to descend twice to the shades. All that neutral ground of character, which stood between vice and virtue; or which in fact was indifferent to neither, where neither properly was called in question; that happy breathing-place from the burthen of a perpetual moral questioning—the sanctuary and quiet Alsatia of hunted casuistry—is broken up and disfranchised, as injurious to the interests of society. The privileges of the place are taken away by law. We dare not dally with images, or names, of wrong. We bark like foolish dogs at shadows. We dread infection from the scenic representation of disorder; and fear a painted pustule. In our anxiety that our morality should not take cold, we wrap it up in a great blanket surtout of precaution against the breeze and sunshine.

I confess for myself that (with no great delinquencies to answer for) I am glad for a season to take an airing beyond the diocese of the strict conscience,—not to live always in the precincts of the law-courts,—but now and then, for a dream-while or so, to imagine a world with no meddling restrictions—to get into recesses, whither the hunter cannot follow me—

> ————Secret shades
> Of woody Ida's inmost grove,
> While yet there was no fear of Jove.

I come back to my cage and my restraint the fresher and more healthy for it. I wear my shackles more contentedly for having respired the breath of an imaginary freedom. I do not know how it is with others, but I feel the better always for the perusal of one of Congreve's—nay, why should I not add even of Wycherley's—comedies. I am the gayer at least for it; and I could never connect those sports of a witty fancy in any shape with any result to be drawn from them to imitation in real life. They are a world of themselves almost as much as fairy-land. Take one of their characters, male or female (with few exceptions they are alike), and place it in a modern play, and my virtuous indignation shall rise against the profligate wretch as warmly as the Catos of the pit could desire; because in a modern play I am to judge of the right and the wrong. The standard of *police* is the measure of *political justice.* The atmosphere will blight it; it cannot live here. It has got into a moral world, where it has no business, from which it must needs fall headlong; as dizzy, and incapable of making a stand, as a Swedenborgian bad spirit that has wandered unawares into the sphere of one of his Good Men, or Angels. But in its own world do we feel the creature is so very bad?—The Fainalls and the Mirabels, the Dorimants and the Lady Touchwoods, in their own sphere, do not offend my moral sense; in fact they do not appeal to it at all. They seem engaged in their proper element. They break through no laws, or conscientious restraints. They know of none. They have got out of Christendom into the land—what shall I call it?—of cuckoldry—the Utopia of gallantry, where pleasure is duty, and the manners perfect freedom. It is altogether a speculative scene of things, which has no reference whatever to the world that is. No good person can be justly offended as a spectator, because no good person suffers on the stage. Judged morally, every character in these plays—the few exceptions only are *mistakes*—is alike essentially vain and worthless. The great art of Congreve is especially shown in this, that he has entirely excluded from his scenes,—some little generosities in the part of Angelica perhaps excepted,—not only any thing like a faultless character, but any pretensions to goodness or good feelings whatsoever. Whether he did this designedly, or instinctively, the effect is as happy, as the design (if design) was bold. I used to wonder at the strange power which his Way of the World in particular possesses of interesting you all along in the pursuits of characters, for whom you absolutely care nothing—for you neither hate nor love his personages—and I think it is owing to this very indifference for any, that you endure the whole. He has spread a privation of moral light, I will call it, rather than by the ugly name of palpable darkness, over his creations; and his shadows flit before you without distinction or preference. Had he introduced a good character, a single gush of moral feeling, a revulsion of the judgment to actual life and actual duties, the impertinent Goshen would have only lighted to the discovery of deformities, which now are none, because we think them none.

Translated into real life, the characters of his, and his friend Wycherley's dramas, are profligates and strumpets,—the business of their brief existence, the undivided pursuit of lawless gallantry. No other spring of action, or possible motive of conduct, is recognised; principles which, universally acted upon, must reduce this frame of things to a chaos. But we do them wrong in so translating them. No such effects are produced in *their* world. When we are among them, we are amongst a chaotic people. We are not to judge them by our usages. No reverend institutions are insulted by their proceedings,—for they have none among them. No peace of families is violated,—for no family ties exist among them. No purity of the marriage bed is stained,—for none is supposed to have a being. No deep affections are disquieted,—no holy wedlock bands are snapped asunder,—for affection's depth and wedded faith are not of the growth of that soil. There is neither right nor wrong,—gratitude or its opposite,—claim or duty,—paternity or sonship. Of what consequence is it to Virtue, or how is she at all concerned about it, whether Sir Simon, or Dapperwit, steal away Miss Martha; or who is the father of Lord Froth's, or Sir Paul Pliant's, children?

The whole is a passing pageant, where we should sit as unconcerned at the issues, for life or death, as at a battle of the frogs and mice. But, like Don Quixote, we take part against the puppets, and quite as impertinently. We dare not contemplate an Atlantis, a scheme, out of which our coxcombical moral sense is for a little transitory ease excluded. We have not the courage to imagine a state of things for which there is neither reward nor punishment. We cling to the painful necessities of shame and blame. We would indict our very dreams.

Amidst the mortifying circumstances attendant upon growing old, it is something to have seen the School for Scandal in its glory. This comedy grew out of Congreve and Wycherley, but gathered some allays of the sentimental comedy which followed theirs. It is impossible that it should now be *acted*, though it continues, at long intervals, to be announced in the bills. Its hero, when Palmer played it at least, was Joseph Surface. When I remember the gay boldness, the graceful solemn plausibility, the measured step, the insinuating voice—to express it in a word—the downright *acted* villany of the part, so different from the pressure of conscious actual wickedness,—the hypocritical assumption of hypocrisy,—which made Jack so deservedly a favourite in that character, I must needs conclude the present generation of play-goers more virtuous than myself, or more dense. I freely confess that he divided the palm with me with his better brother; that, in fact, I liked him quite as well. Not but there are passages,—like that, for instance, where Joseph is made to refuse a pittance to a poor relation,—incongruities which Sheridan was forced upon by the attempt to join the artificial with the sentimental comedy, either of which must destroy the other—but over these obstructions Jack's manner floated him so lightly, that a refusal from him no more shocked you, than the easy compliance of Charles gave you in reality any pleasure; you got over the paltry question as quickly as you could, to get back into the regions of pure comedy, where no cold moral reigns. The highly artificial manner of Palmer in this character counteracted every disagreeable impression which you might have received from the contrast, supposing them real, between the two brothers. You did not believe in Joseph with the same faith with which you believed in Charles. The latter was a pleasant reality, the former a no less pleasant poetical foil to it. The comedy, I have said, is incongruous; a mixture of Congreve with sentimental incompatibilities; the gaiety upon the whole is buoyant; but it required the consummate art of Palmer to reconcile the discordant elements.

A player with Jack's talents, if we had one now, would not dare to do the part in the same manner. He would instinctively avoid every turn which might tend to unrealise, and so to make the character fascinating. He must take his cue from his spectators, who would expect a bad man and a good man as rigidly opposed to each other as the death-beds of those geniuses are contrasted in the prints, which I am sorry to say have disappeared from the windows of my old friend Carrington Bowles, of St. Paul's Churchyard memory—(an exhibition as venerable as the adjacent cathedral, and almost coeval) of the bad and good man at the hour of death; where the ghastly apprehensions of the former,—and truly the grim phantom with his reality of a toasting-fork is not to be despised,—so finely contrast with the meek complacent kissing of the rod,—taking it in like honey and butter,—with which the latter submits to the scythe of the gentle bleeder, Time, who wields his lancet with the apprehensive finger of a popular young ladies' surgeon. What flesh, like loving grass, would not covet to meet half-way the stroke of such a delicate mower?—John Palmer was twice an actor in this exquisite part. He was playing to you all the while that he was playing upon Sir Peter and his lady. You had the first intimation of a sentiment before it was on his lips. His altered voice was meant to you, and you were to suppose that his fictitious co-flutterers on the stage perceived nothing at all of it. What was it to you if that half-reality, the husband, was over-reached by the puppetry—or the thin thing (Lady Teazle's reputation) was persuaded it was dying of a plethory? The fortunes of Othello and Desdemona were not concerned in it. Poor Jack has passed from the stage in good time, that he did not live to this our age of seriousness. The pleasant old Teazle *King*, too, is gone in good time. His manner would scarce have passed current in our day. We must love or hate—acquit or condemn—censure or pity—exert our detestable coxcombry of moral judgment upon every thing. Joseph Surface, to go down now, must be a down-right revolting villain—no compromise—his first appearance must shock and give horror—his specious plausibilities, which the pleas-urable faculties of our fathers welcomed with such hearty greetings, knowing that no harm (dramatic harm even) could come, or was meant to come, of them, must inspire a cold and killing aversion. Charles (the real canting person of the scene—for the hypocrisy of Joseph has its ulterior legitimate ends, but his brother's profes-sions of a good heart centre in downright self-satisfaction) must be *loved*, and Joseph *hated*. To balance one disagreeable reality with another, Sir Peter Teazle must be no longer the comic idea of a fretful old bachelor bridegroom, whose teasings (while King acted it) were evidently as much played off at you, as they were meant to concern anybody on the stage,—he must be a real person, capable in law of sustaining an injury—a person towards whom duties are to be acknowledged—the genuine crim-con antagonist of the villanous seducer Joseph. To realise him more, his suffer-ings under his unfortunate match must have the downright pun-gency of life—must (or should) make you not mirthful but un-comfortable, just as the same predicament would move you in a neighbour or old friend. The delicious scenes which give the play its name and zest, must affect you in the same serious manner as if you heard the reputation of a dear female friend attacked in your real presence. Crabtree, and Sir Benjamin—those poor snakes that live but in the sunshine of your mirth—must be ripened by this hot-bed process of realization into asps or amphisbænas; and Mrs. Candour—O! frightful!—become a hooded serpent. Oh who that remembers Parsons and Dodd—the wasp and butterfly of the School for Scandal—in those two characters; and charming natural Miss Pope, the perfect gentlewoman as distinguished from the fine lady of comedy, in this latter part—would forego the true scenic delight—the escape from life—the oblivion of consequences—the holiday barring out of the pedant Reflection—those Saturnalia of two or three brief hours, well won from the world—to sit instead at one of our modern plays—to have his coward conscience (that forsooth must not be left for a moment) stimulated with perpetual appeals—dulled rather, and blunted, as a faculty without repose must be—and his moral vanity pampered with images of notional justice, notional beneficence, lives saved without the spectator's risk, and fortunes given away that cost the author nothing?

No piece was, perhaps, ever so completely cast in all its parts as this *manager's comedy.* Miss Farren had succeeded to Mrs. Abington in Lady Teazle; and Smith, the original Charles, had retired, when I first saw it. The rest of the characters, with very slight exceptions, remained. I remember it was then the fashion to cry down John Kemble, who took the part of Charles after Smith; but, I thought, very unjustly. Smith, I fancy, was more airy, and took the eye with a certain gaiety of person. He brought with him no sombre recollections of tragedy. He had not to expiate the fault of having pleased beforehand in lofty declamation. He had no sins of Hamlet or of Richard to atone for. His failure in these parts was a passport to success in one of so opposite a tendency. But, as far as I could judge, the weighty sense of Kemble made up for more personal incapacity than he had to answer for. His harshest tones in this part came steeped and dulcified in good humour. He made his defects a grace. His exact declamatory manner, as he managed it, only served to convey the points of his dialogue with more precision. It seemed to head the shafts to carry them deeper. Not one of his sparkling sentences was lost. I remember minutely how he delivered each in succession, and cannot by any effort imagine how any of them could be altered for the better. No man could deliver brilliant dialogue—the dialogue of Congreve or of Wycherley—because none understood it—half so well as John

Kemble. His Valentine, in Love for Love, was, to my recollection, faultless. He flagged sometimes in the intervals of tragic passion. He would slumber over the level parts of an heroic character. His Macbeth has been known to nod. But he always seemed to me to be particularly alive to pointed and witty dialogue. The relaxing levities of tragedy have not been touched by any since him—the playful court-bred spirit in which he condescended to the players in Hamlet—the sportive relief which he threw into the darker shades of Richard—disappeared with him. He had his sluggish moods, his torpors—but they were the halting-stones and resting-places of his tragedy—politic savings, and fetches of the breath—husbandry of the lungs, where nature pointed him to be an economist—rather, I think than errors of the judgment. They were, at worst, less painful than the eternal tormenting unappeasable vigilance,—the "lidless dragon eyes," of present fashionable tragedy.

A BACHELOR'S COMPLAINT OF THE BEHAVIOUR
OF MARRIED PEOPLE

AS a single man, I have spent a good deal of my time in noting down the infirmities of Married People, to console myself for those superior pleasures, which they tell me I have lost by remaining as I am.

I cannot say that the quarrels of men and their wives ever made any great impression upon me, or had much tendency to strengthen me in those anti-social resolutions which I took up long ago upon more substantial considerations. What oftenest offends me at the houses of married persons where I visit, is an error of quite a different description;—it is that they are too loving.

Not too loving neither: that does not explain my meaning. Besides, why should that offend me? The very act of separating themselves from the rest of the world, to have the fuller enjoyment of each other's society, implies that they prefer one another to all the world.

But what I complain of is, that they carry this preference so undisguisedly, they perk it up in the faces of us single people so shamelessly, you cannot be in their company a moment without being made to feel, by some indirect hint or open avowal, that *you* are not the object of this preference. Now there are some things which give no offence, while implied or taken for granted merely; but expressed, there is much offence in them. If a man were to accost the first homely-featured or plain-dressed young woman of his acquaintance, and tell her bluntly, that she was not handsome or rich enough for him, and he could not marry her, he would deserve to be kicked for his ill manners; yet no less is implied in the fact, that having access and opportunity of putting the question to her, he has never yet thought fit to do it. The young woman understands this as clearly as if it were put into words; but no reasonable young woman would think of making this the ground of a quarrel. Just as little right have a married couple to tell me by speeches, and looks that are scarce less plain than speeches, that I am not the happy man,—the lady's choice. It is enough that I know I am not: I do not want this perpetual reminding.

The display of superior knowledge or riches may be made sufficiently mortifying; but these admit of a palliative. The knowledge which is brought out to insult me, may accidentally improve me; and in the rich man's houses and pictures,—his parks and gardens, I have a temporary usufruct at least. But the display of married happiness has none of these palliatives: it is throughout pure, unrecompensed, unqualified insult.

Marriage by its best title is a monopoly, and not of the least invidious sort. It is the cunning of most possessors of any exclusive privilege to keep their advantage as much out of sight as possible, that their less favoured neighbours, seeing little of the benefit, may the less be disposed to question the right. But these married monopolists thrust the most obnoxious part of their patent into our faces.

Nothing is to me more distasteful than that entire complacency and satisfaction which beam in the countenances of a new-married couple,—in that of the lady particularly: it tells you, that her lot is disposed of in this world: that *you* can have no hopes of her. It is true, I have none: nor wishes either, perhaps: but this is one of the truths which ought, as I said before, to be taken for granted, not expressed.

The excessive airs which those people give themselves, founded on the ignorance of us unmarried people, would be more offensive if they were less irrational. We will allow them to understand the mysteries belonging to their own craft better than we, who have

not had the happiness to be made free of the company: but their
arrogance is not content within these limits. If a single person presume to offer his opinion in their presence, though upon the most
indifferent subject, he is immediately silenced as an incompetent
person. Nay, a young married lady of my acquaintance, who, the
best of the jest was, had not changed her condition above a fortnight before, in a question on which I had the misfortune to differ
from her, respecting the properest mode of breeding oysters for
the London market, had the assurance to ask with a sneer, how
such an old Bachelor as I could pretend to know anything about
such matters.

But what I have spoken of hitherto is nothing to the airs which
these creatures give themselves when they come, as they generally
do, to have children. When I consider how little of a rarity children are,—that every street and blind alley swarms with them,—
that the poorest people commonly have them in most abundance,—
that there are few marriages that are not blest with at least one of
these bargains,—how often they turn out ill, and defeat the fond
hopes of their parents, taking to vicious courses, which end in
poverty, disgrace, the gallows, &c.—I cannot for my life tell what
cause for pride there can possibly be in having them. If they were
young phœnixes, indeed, that were born but one in a year, there
might be a pretext. But when they are so common—

I do not advert to the insolent merit which they assume with
their husbands on these occasions. Let *them* look to that. But why
we, who are not their natural-born subjects, should be expected to
bring our spices, myrrh, and incense,—our tribute and homage of
admiration,—I do not see.

"Like as the arrows in the hand of the giant, even so are the
young children:" so says the excellent office in our Prayer-book
appointed for the churching of women. "Happy is the man that
hath his quiver full of them:" So say I; but then don't let him
discharge his quiver upon us that are weaponless;—let them be
arrows, but not to gall and stick us. I have generally observed
that these arrows are double-headed: they have two forks, to be
sure to hit with one or the other. As for instance, where you come
into a house which is full of children, if you happen to take no
notice of them (you are thinking of something else, perhaps, and
turn a deaf ear to their innocent caresses), you are set down as un-

tractable, morose, a hater of children. On the other hand, if you find them more than usually engaging,—if you are taken with their pretty manners, and set about in earnest to romp and play with them,—some pretext or other is sure to be found for sending them out of the room: they are too noisy or boisterous, or Mr. —— does not like children. With one or other of these forks the arrow is sure to hit you.

I could forgive their jealousy, and dispense with toying with their brats, if it gives them any pain; but I think it unreasonable to be called upon to *love* them, where I see no occasion,—to love a whole family, perhaps eight, nine, or ten, indiscriminately,—to love all the pretty dears, because children are so engaging.

I know there is a proverb, "Love me, love my dog:" that is not always so very practicable, particularly if the dog be set upon you to tease you or snap at you in sport. But a dog, or a lesser thing,—any inanimate substance, as a keep-sake, a watch or a ring, a tree, or the place where we last parted when my friend went away upon a long absence, I can make shift to love, because I love him, and any thing that reminds me of him; provided it be in its nature indifferent, and apt to receive whatever hue fancy can give it. But children have a real character and an essential being of themselves: they are amiable or unamiable *per se;* I must love or hate them as I see cause for either in their qualities. A child's nature is too serious a thing to admit of its being regarded as a mere appendage to another being, and to be loved or hated accordingly; they stand with me upon their own stock, as much as men and women do. O! but you will say, sure it is an attractive age,— there is something in the tender years of infancy that of itself charms us. That is the very reason why I am more nice about them. I know that a sweet child is the sweetest thing in nature, not even excepting the delicate creatures which bear them; but the prettier the kind of a thing is, the more desirable it is that it should be pretty of its kind. One daisy differs not much from another in glory; but a violet should look and smell the daintiest.— I was always rather squeamish in my women and children.

But this is not the worst: one must be admitted into their familiarity at least, before they can complain of inattention. It implies visits, and some kind of intercourse. But if the husband be a man with whom you have lived on a friendly footing before marriage,—if you do not come in on the wife's side,—if you did not sneak into the house in her train, but were an old friend in fast habits of intimacy before their courtship was so much as thought on,—look about you—your tenure is precarious—before a twelvemonth shall roll over your head, you shall find your old friend gradually grow cool and altered towards you, and at last seek opportunities of breaking with you. I have scarce a married friend of my acquaintance, upon whose firm faith I can rely, whose friendship did not commence *after the period of his marriage*. With some limitations they can endure that: but that the good man should have dared to enter into a solemn league of friendship in which they were not consulted, though it happened before they knew him,—before they that are now man and wife ever met,— this is intolerable to them. Every long friendship, every old authentic intimacy, must be brought into their office to be new stamped with their currency, as a sovereign Prince calls in the good old money that was coined in some reign before he was born or thought of, to be new marked and minted with the stamp of his authority, before he will let it pass current in the world. You may guess what luck generally befalls such a rusty piece of metal as I am in these *new mintings*.

Innumerable are the ways which they take to insult and worm you out of their husband's confidence. Laughing at all you say with a kind of wonder, as if you were a queer kind of fellow that said good things, *but an oddity*, is one of the ways;—they have a particular kind of stare for the purpose;—till at last the husband, who used to defer to your judgment, and would pass over some excrescences of understanding and manner for the sake of a general vein of observation (not quite vulgar) which he perceived in you, begins to suspect whether you are not altogether a humorist, —a fellow well enough to have consorted with in his bachelor days, but not quite so proper to be introduced to ladies. This may be called the staring way; and is that which has oftenest been put in practice against me.

Then there is the exaggerating way, or the way of irony: that is, where they find you an object of especial regard with their husband, who is not so easily to be shaken from the lasting attachment founded on esteem which he has conceived towards you; by never-qualified exaggerations to cry up all that you say or do, till the good man, who understands well enough that it is all done in compliment to him, grows weary of the debt of gratitude which is due to so much candour, and by relaxing a little on his part, and taking down a peg or two in his enthusiasm, sinks at length to that kindly level of moderate esteem—that "decent affection and complacent kindness" towards you, where she herself can join in sympathy with him without much stretch and violence to her sincerity.

Another way (for the ways they have to accomplish so desirable a purpose are infinite) is, with a kind of innocent simplicity, continually to mistake what it was which first made their husband fond of you. If an esteem for something excellent in your moral character was that which riveted the chain which she is to break, upon any imaginary discovery of a want of poignancy in your conversation, she will cry, "I thought, my dear, you described your friend, Mr. ——, as a great wit." If, on the other hand, it was for some supposed charm in your conversation that he first grew to like you, and was content for this to overlook some trifling irregularities in your moral deportment, upon the first notice of any of these she as readily exclaims, "This, my dear, is your good Mr. ——!" One good lady whom I took the liberty of expostulating with for not showing me quite so much respect as I thought due to her husband's old friend, had the candour to confess to me that she had often heard Mr. —— speak of me before marriage, and that she had conceived a great desire to be acquainted with me, but that the sight of me had very much disappointed her expectations; for, from her husband's representations of me, she had formed a notion that she was to see a fine, tall, officer-like looking man (I use her very words); the very reverse of which proved to be the truth. This was candid; and I had the civility not to ask her in return, how she came to pitch upon a standard of personal accomplishments for her husband's friends which differed so much from his own; for my friend's dimensions as near as possible approximate to mine; he standing five feet five in his shoes, in which I have the advantage of him by about half an inch; and he no more than myself exhibiting any indications of a martial character in his air or countenance.

These are some of the mortifications which I have encountered in the absurd attempt to visit at their houses. To enumerate them all would be a vain endeavour; I shall therefore just glance at the very common impropriety of which married ladies are guilty,—of treating us as if we were their husbands, and *vice versâ*. I mean, when they use us with familiarity, and their husbands with ceremony. *Testacea*, for instance, kept me the other night two or three hours beyond my usual time of supping, while she was fretting because Mr. —— did not come home, till the oysters were all spoiled, rather than she would be guilty of the impoliteness of touching one in his absence. This was reversing the point of good manners: for ceremony is an invention to take off the uneasy feeling which we derive from knowing ourselves to be less the object of love and esteem with a fellow-creature than some other person is. It endeavours to make up, by superior attentions in little points, for that invidious preference which it is forced to deny in the greater. Had *Testacea* kept the oysters back for me, and withstood her husband's importunities to go to supper, she would have acted according to the strict rules of propriety. I know no ceremony that ladies are bound to observe to their husbands, beyond the point of a modest behaviour and decorum: therefore I must protest against the vicarious gluttony of *Cerasia*, who at her own table sent away a dish of Morellas, which I was applying to with great good-will, to her husband at the other end of the table, and recommended a plate of less extraordinary gooseberries to my unwedded palate in their stead. Neither can I excuse the wanton affront of ——

But I am weary of stringing up all my married acquaintance by Roman denominations. Let them mend and change their manners, or I promise to record the full-length English of their names, to the terror of all such desperate offenders in future.

OLD CHINA

I HAVE an almost feminine partiality for old china. When I go to see any great house, I inquire for the china-closet, and next for the picture-gallery. I cannot defend the order of preference, but by saying that we have all some taste or other, of too ancient a date to admit of our remembering distinctly that it was an acquired one. I can call to mind the first play, and the first exhibition, that I was taken to; but I am not conscious of a time when china jars and saucers were introduced into my imagination.

I had no repugnance then—why should I now have?—to those little, lawless, azure-tinctured grotesques, that under the notion of men and women, float about, uncircumscribed by any element, in that world before perspective—a china tea-cup.

I like to see my old friends—whom distance cannot diminish—figuring up in the air (so they appear to our optics), yet on *terra firma* still—for so we must in courtesy interpret that speck of deeper blue, which the decorous artist, to prevent absurdity, had made to spring up beneath their sandals.

I love the men with women's faces, and the women, if possible, with still more womanish expressions.

Here is a young and courtly Mandarin, handing tea to a lady from a salver—two miles off. See how distance seems to set off respect! And here the same lady, or another—for likeness is identity on tea-cups—is stepping into a little fairy boat, moored on the hither side of this calm garden river, with a dainty mincing foot, which in a right angle of incidence (as angles go in our world) must infallibly land her in the midst of a flowery mead—a furlong off on the other side of the same strange stream!

Farther on—if far or near can be predicated of their world—see horses, trees, pagodas, dancing the hays.

Here—a cow and rabbit couchant, and co-extensive—so objects show, seen through the lucid atmosphere of fine Cathay.

I was pointing out to my cousin last evening, over our Hyson (which we are old-fashioned enough to drink unmixed still of an afternoon), some of these *speciosa miracula* upon a set of extraordinary old blue china (a recent purchase) which we were now for the first time using; and could not help remarking, how favourable circumstances had been to us of late years, that we could afford to please the eye sometimes with trifles of this sort—when a passing sentiment seemed to over-shade the brows of my companion. I am quick at detecting these summer clouds in Bridget.

"I wish the good old times would come again," she said, "when we were not quite so rich. I do not mean, that I want to be poor; but there was a middle state"—so she was pleased to ramble on,—"in which I am sure we were a great deal happier. A purchase is but a purchase, now that you have money enough and to spare.

Formerly it used to be a triumph. When we coveted a cheap luxury (and, O! how much ado I had to get you to consent in those times!)—we were used to have a debate two or three days before, and to weigh the *for* and *against*, and think what we might spare it out of, and what saving we could hit upon, that should be an equivalent. A thing was worth buying then, when we felt the money that we paid for it.

"Do you remember the brown suit, which you made to hang upon you, till all your friends cried shame upon you, it grew so thread-bare—and all because of that folio Beaumont and Fletcher, which you dragged home late at night from Barker's in Coventgarden? Do you remember how we eyed it for weeks before we could make up our minds to the purchase, and had not come to a determination till it was near ten o'clock of the Saturday night, when you set off from Islington, fearing you should be too late— and when the old bookseller with some grumbling opened his shop, and by the twinkling taper (for he was setting bedwards) lighted out the relic from his dusty treasures—and when you lugged it home, wishing it were twice as cumbersome—and when you presented it to me—and when we were exploring the perfectness of it (*collating*, you called it)—and while I was repairing some of the loose leaves with paste, which your impatience would not suffer to be left till day-break—was there no pleasure in being a poor man? or can those neat black clothes which you wear now, and are so careful to keep brushed, since we have become rich and finical— give you half the honest vanity with which you flaunted it about in that over-worn suit—your old corbeau—for four or five weeks longer than you should have done, to pacify your conscience for the mighty sum of fifteen—or sixteen shillings was it?—a great affair we thought it then—which you had lavished on the old folio. Now you can afford to buy any book that pleases you, but I do not see that you ever bring me home any nice old purchases now.

"When you came home with twenty apologies for laying out a less number of shillings upon that print after Lionardo, which we christened the 'Lady Blanch;' when you looked at the purchase, and thought of the money—and thought of the money, and looked again at the picture—was there no pleasure in being a poor man? Now, you have nothing to do but to walk into Colnaghi's, and buy a wilderness of Lionardos. Yet do you?

"Then, do you remember our pleasant walks to Enfield, and Potter's Bar, and Waltham, when we had a holyday—holydays, and all other fun, are gone, now we are rich—and the little hand-basket in which I used to deposit our day's fare of savoury cold lamb and salad—and how you would pry about at noon-tide for some decent house, where we might go in, and produce our store—only paying for the ale that you must call for—and speculate upon the looks of the landlady, and whether she was likely to allow us a table-cloth—and wish for such another honest hostess as Izaak Walton has described many a one on the pleasant banks of the Lea, when he went a-fishing—and sometimes they would prove obliging enough, and sometimes they would look grudgingly upon us—but we had cheerful looks still for one another, and would eat our plain food savourily, scarcely grudging Piscator his Trout Hall? Now—when we go out a day's pleasuring, which is seldom; moreover, we *ride* part of the way, and go into a fine inn, and order the best of dinners, never debating the expense—which, after all, never has half the relish of those chance country snaps, when we were at the mercy of uncertain usage, and a precarious welcome.

"You are too proud to see a play anywhere now but in the pit. Do you remember where it was we used to sit, when we saw the Battle of Hexham, and the Surrender of Calais, and Bannister and Mrs. Bland in the Children in the Wood—when we squeezed out our shillings a-piece to sit three or four times in a season in the one-shilling gallery—where you felt all the time that you ought not to have brought me—and more strongly I felt obligation to you for having brought me—and the pleasure was the better for a little shame—and when the curtain drew up, what cared we for our place in the house, or what mattered it where we were sitting, when our thoughts were with Rosalind in Arden, or with Viola at the Court of Illyria? You used to say, that the gallery was the best place of all for enjoying a play socially—that the relish of such exhibitions must be in proportion to the infrequency of going—that the company we met there, not being in general readers of plays, were obliged to attend the more, and did attend, to what was going on, on the stage—because a word lost would have been a chasm, which it was impossible for them to fill up. With such reflections we consoled our pride then—and I appeal to you, whether, as a woman, I met generally with less attention and accommodation, than I have done since in more expensive situations in the house? The getting in, indeed, and the crowding up those inconvenient staircases, was bad enough,—but there was still a law of civility to women recognised to quite as great an extent as we ever found in the other passages—and how a little difficulty over-come heightened the snug seat, and the play, afterwards! Now we can only pay our money, and walk in. You cannot see, you say, in the galleries now. I am sure we saw, and heard too, well enough then—but sight, and all, I think, is gone with our poverty.

"There was pleasure in eating strawberries, before they became quite common—in the first dish of peas, while they were yet dear—to have them for a nice supper, a treat. What treat can we have now? If we were to treat ourselves now—that is, to have dainties a little above our means, it would be selfish and wicked. It is the very little more that we allow ourselves beyond what the actual poor can get at, that makes what I call a treat—when two people living together, as we have done, now and then indulge themselves in a cheap luxury, which both like; while each apologises, and is willing to take both halves of the blame to his single share. I see no harm in people making much of themselves in that sense of the word. It may give them a hint how to make much of others. But now—what I mean by the word—we never do make much of ourselves. None but the poor can do it. I do not mean the veriest poor of all, but persons as we were, just above poverty.

"I know what you were going to say, that it is mighty pleasant at the end of the year to make all meet—and much ado we used to have every Thirty-first Night of December to account for our exceedings—many a long face did you make over your puzzled accounts, and in contriving to make it out how we had spent so much—or that we had not spent so much—or that it was impossible we should spend so much next year—and still we found our slender capital decreasing—but then, betwixt ways, and projects, and compromises of one sort or another, and talk of curtailing this charge, and doing without that for the future—and the hope that youth brings, and laughing spirits (in which you were never poor till now), we pocketed up our loss, and in conclusion, with 'lusty brimmers' (as you used to quote it out of *hearty cheerful Mr. Cotton*, as you called him), we used to welcome in the 'coming guest.'

Now we have no reckoning at all at the end of the old year—no flattering promises about the new year doing better for us."

Bridget is so sparing of her speech on most occasions, that when she gets into a rhetorical vein, I am careful how I interrupt it. I could not help, however, smiling at the phantom of wealth which her dear imagination had conjured up out of a clear income of poor —— hundred pounds a year. "It is true we were happier when we were poorer, but we were also younger, my cousin. I am afraid we must put up with the excess, for if we were to shake the superflux into the sea, we should not much mend ourselves. That we had much to struggle with, as we grew up together, we have reason to be most thankful. It strengthened, and knit our compact closer. We could never have been what we have been to each other, if we had always had the sufficiency which you now complain of. The resisting power—those natural dilations of the youthful spirit, which circumstances cannot straiten—with us are long since passed away. Competence to age is supplementary youth; a sorry supplement indeed, but I fear the best that is to be had. We must ride, where we formerly walked: live better, and lie softer—and shall be wise to do so—than we had means to do in those good old days you speak of. Yet could those days return—could you and I once more walk our thirty miles a day—could Bannister and Mrs. Bland again be young, and you and I be young to see them—could the good old one-shilling gallery days return—they are dreams, my cousin, now—but could you and I at this moment, instead of this quiet argument, by our well-carpeted fire-side, sitting on this luxurious sofa—be once more struggling up those inconvenient stair-cases, pushed about, and squeezed, and elbowed by the poorest rabble of poor gallery scramblers—could I once more hear those anxious shrieks of yours—and the delicious *Thank God, we are safe*, which always followed when the topmost stair, conquered, let in the first light of the whole cheerful theatre down beneath us—I know not the fathom line that ever touched a descent so deep as I would be willing to bury more wealth in than Crœsus had, or the great Jew R—— is supposed to have, to purchase it. And now do just look at that merry little Chinese waiter holding an umbrella, big enough for a bed-tester, over the head of that pretty insipid half Madonna-ish chit of a lady in that very blue summer-house."

POOR RELATIONS

A POOR Relation—is the most irrelevant thing in nature,
—a piece of impertinent correspondency,—an odious
approximation,—a haunting conscience,—a preposterous
shadow, lengthening in the noontide of your prosperity,—an unwelcome remembrancer,—a perpetually recurring mortification,—
a drain on your purse,—a more intolerable dun upon your pride,
—a drawback upon success,—a rebuke to your rising,—a stain
in your blood,—a blot on your scutcheon,—a rent in your garment,—a death's head at your banquet,—Agathocles' pot,—a
Mordecai in your gate,—a Lazarus at your door,—a lion in your
path,—a frog in your chamber,—a fly in your ointment,—a mote
in your eye,—a triumph to your enemy, an apology to your friends,
—the one thing not needful,—the hail in harvest,—the ounce of
sour in a pound of sweet.

He is known by his knock. Your heart telleth you "That is
Mr. ———." A rap, between familiarity and respect; that demands,
and, at the same time, seems to despair of, entertainment. He
entereth smiling, and—embarrassed. He holdeth out his hand to
you to shake, and—draweth it back again. He casually looketh in
about dinner time—when the table is full. He offereth to go away,
seeing you have company—but is induced to stay. He filleth a
chair, and your visitor's two children are accommodated at a side
table. He never cometh upon open days, when your wife says
with some complacency, "My dear, perhaps Mr. ——— will drop in
to-day." He remembereth birth-days—and professeth he is fortunate to have stumbled upon one. He declareth against fish, the
turbot being small—yet suffereth himself to be importuned into a
slice against his first resolution. He sticketh by the port—yet will
be prevailed upon to empty the remainder glass of claret, if a
stranger press it upon him. He is a puzzle to the servants, who are
fearful of being too obsequious, or not civil enough, to him. The
guests think "they have seen him before." Every one speculateth
upon his condition; and the most part take him to be—a tide waiter.
He calleth you by your Christian name, to imply that his other is
the same with your own. He is too familiar by half, yet you wish
he had less diffidence. With half the familiarity he might pass for
a casual dependent; with more boldness he would be in no danger

of being taken for what he is. He is too humble for a friend, yet taketh on him more state than befits a client. He is a worse guest than a country tenant, inasmuch as he bringeth up no rent—yet 'tis odds, from his garb and demeanour, that your guests take him for one. He is asked to make one at the whist table; refuseth on the score of poverty, and—resents being left out. When the company break up he proffereth to go for a coach—and lets the servant go. He recollects your grandfather; and will thrust in some mean, and quite unimportant anecdote of—the family. He knew it when it was not quite so flourishing as "he is blest in seeing it now." He reviveth past situations, to institute what he calleth— favourable comparisons. With a reflecting sort of congratulation, he will inquire the price of your furniture; and insults you with a special commendation of your window-curtains. He is of opinion that the urn is the more elegant shape, but, after all, there was something more comfortable about the old tea-kettle—which you must remember. He dare say you must find a great convenience in having a carriage of your own, and appealeth to your lady if it is not so. Inquireth if you have had your arms done on vellum yet; and did not know till lately, that such-and-such had been the crest of the family. His memory is unseasonable; his compliments perverse; his talk a trouble; his stay pertinacious; and when he goeth away, you dismiss his chair into a corner, as precipitately as possible, and feel fairly rid of two nuisances.

There is a worse evil under the sun, and that is—a female Poor Relation. You may do something with the other; you may pass him off tolerably well; but your indigent she-relative is hopeless. "He is an old humorist," you may say, "and affects to go threadbare. His circumstances are better than folks would take them to be. You are fond of having a Character at your table, and truly he is one." But in the indications of female poverty there can be no disguise. No woman dresses below herself from caprice. The truth must out without shuffling. "She is plainly related to the L——s; or what does she at their house?" She is, in all probability, your wife's cousin. Nine times out of ten, at least, this is the case. Her garb is something between a gentlewoman and a beggar, yet the former evidently predominates. She is most provokingly humble, and ostentatiously sensible to her inferiority. He may require to be repressed sometimes—*aliquando sufflaminandus erat*—but there is no raising her. You send her soup at dinner, and she begs to be helped—after the gentlemen. Mr. —— requests the honour of taking wine with her; she hesitates between Port and Madeira, and chooses the former—because he does. She calls the servant *Sir;* and insists on not troubling him to hold her plate. The housekeeper patronizes her. The children's governess takes upon her to correct her, when she has mistaken the piano for a harpsichord.

Richard Amlet, Esq., in the play, is a noticeable instance of the disadvantages to which this chimerical notion of *affinity constituting a claim to acquaintance,* may subject the spirit of a gentleman. A little foolish blood is all that is betwixt him and a lady of great estate. His stars are perpetually crossed by the malignant maternity of an old woman, who persists in calling him "her son Dick." But she has wherewithal in the end to recompense his indignities, and float him again upon the brilliant surface, under which it had been her seeming business and pleasure all along to sink him. All men, besides, are not of Dick's temperament. I knew an Amlet in real life, who, wanting Dick's buoyancy, sank indeed. Poor W—— was of my own standing at Christ's, a fine classic, and a youth of promise. If he had a blemish, it was too much pride; but its quality was inoffensive; it was not of that sort which hardens the heart, and serves to keep inferiors at a distance; it only sought to ward off derogation from itself. It was the principle of self-respect carried as far as it could go, without infringing upon that respect, which he would have every one else equally maintain for himself. He would have you to think alike with him on this topic. Many a quarrel have I had with him, when we were rather older boys, and our tallness made us more obnoxious to observation in the blue clothes, because I would not thread the alleys and blind ways of the town with him to elude notice, when we have been out together on a holiday in the streets of this sneering and prying metropolis. W—— went, sore with these notions, to Oxford, where the dignity and sweetness of a scholar's life, meeting with the alloy of a humble introduction, wrought in him a passionate devotion to the place, with a profound aversion from the society. The servitor's gown (worse than his school array) clung to him with Nessian venom. He thought himself ridiculous in a garb, under which Latimer must have walked erect; and in which Hooker, in his young days, possibly flaunted in a vein of no discommendable vanity. In the depths of college shades, or in his lonely chamber, the poor student shrunk from observation. He found shelter among books, which insult not; and studies, that ask no questions of a youth's finances. He was lord of his library, and seldom cared for looking out beyond his domains. The healing influence of studious pursuits was upon him, to soothe and to abstract. He was almost a healthy man; when the waywardness of his fate broke out against him with a second and worse malignity. The father of W—— had hitherto exercised the humble profession of house-painter at N——, near Oxford. A supposed interest with some of the heads of colleges had now induced him to take up his abode in that city, with the hope of being employed upon some public works which were talked of. From that moment I read in the countenance of the young man, the determination which at length tore him from academical pursuits for ever. To a person unacquainted with our Universities, the distance between the gownsmen and the townsmen, as they are called—the trading part of the latter especially—is carried to an excess that would appear harsh and incredible. The temperament of W——'s father was diametrically the reverse of his own. Old W—— was a little, busy, cringing tradesman, who, with his son upon his arm, would stand bowing and scraping, cap in hand, to any thing that wore the semblance of a gown—insensible to the winks and opener remonstrances of the young man, to whose chamber-fellow, or equal in standing, perhaps, he was thus obsequiously and gratuitously ducking. Such a state of things could not last. W—— must change the air of Oxford or be suffocated. He chose the former; and let the sturdy moralist, who strains the point of the filial duties as high as they can bear, censure the dereliction; he cannot estimate the struggle. I stood with W——, the last afternoon I ever saw him, under the eaves of his paternal dwelling. It was in the fine lane leading from the High-street to the back of * * * * college, where W—— kept his rooms. He seemed thoughtful, and more reconciled. I ventured to rally him—finding him in a better mood—upon a representation of the Artist Evangelist, which the old man, whose affairs were beginning to flourish, had caused to be set up in a splendid sort of frame over his really handsome shop, either as a token of prosperity, or badge of gratitude to his saint. W—— looked up at the Luke, and, like Satan, "knew his mounted sign—and fled." A letter on his father's table the next morning, announced that he had accepted a commission in a regiment about to embark for Portugal. He was among the first who perished before the walls of St. Sebastian.

I do not know how, upon a subject which I began with treating half seriously, I should have fallen upon a recital so eminently painful; but this theme of poor relationship is replete with so much matter for tragic as well as comic associations, that it is difficult to keep the account distinct without blending. The earliest impressions which I received on this matter, are certainly not attended with anything painful, or very humiliating, in the recalling. At my father's table (no very splendid one) was to be found, every Saturday, the mysterious figure of an aged gentleman, clothed in neat black, of a sad yet comely appearance. His deportment was of the essence of gravity; his words few or none; and I was not to make a noise in his presence. I had little inclination to have done so—for my cue was to admire in silence. A particular elbow chair was appropriated to him, which was in no case to be violated. A peculiar sort of sweet pudding, which appeared on no other occasion, distinguished the days of his coming. I used to think him a prodigiously rich man. All I could make out of him was, that he and my father had been schoolfellows a world ago at Lincoln, and that he came from the Mint. The Mint I knew to be a place where all the money was coined—and I thought he was the owner of all that money. Awful ideas of the Tower twined themselves about his presence. He seemed above human infirmities and passions. A sort of melancholy grandeur invested him. From some inexplicable doom I fancied him obliged to go about in an eternal suit of mourning; a captive—a stately being, let out of the Tower on Saturdays. Often have I wondered at the temerity of my father, who, in spite of an habitual general respect which we all in common manifested towards him, would venture now and then to stand up against him in some argument, touching their youthful days. The houses of the ancient city of Lincoln are divided (as most of my readers know) between the dwellers on the hill, and in the valley. This marked distinction formed an obvious division between the boys who lived above (however brought together in a common school) and the boys whose paternal residence was on the plain; a sufficient

cause of hostility in the code of these young Grotiuses. My father
had been a leading Mountaineer; and would still maintain the general superiority, in skill and hardihood, of the *Above Boys* (his own
faction) over the *Below Boys* (so were they called), of which party
his contemporary had been a chieftain. Many and hot were the
skirmishes on this topic—the only one upon which the old gentleman was ever brought out—and bad blood bred; even sometimes
almost to the recommencement (so I expected) of actual hostilities.
But my father, who scorned to insist upon advantages, generally
contrived to turn the conversation upon some adroit by-commen-
dation of the old Minster; in the general preference of which, before
all other cathedrals in the island, the dweller on the hill, and the
plain-born, could meet on a conciliating level, and lay down their
less important differences. Once only I saw the old gentleman
really ruffled, and I remembered with anguish the thought that
came over me: "Perhaps he will never come here again." He had
been pressed to take another plate of the viand, which I have already mentioned as the indispensable concomitant of his visits.
He had refused with a resistance amounting to rigour—when my
aunt, an old Lincolnian, but who had something of this, in common
with my cousin Bridget, that she would sometimes press civility
out of season—uttered the following memorable application—
"Do take another slice, Mr. Billet, for you do not get pudding every
day." The old gentleman said nothing at the time—but he took
occasion in the course of the evening, when some argument had
intervened between them, to utter with an emphasis which chilled
the company, and which chills me now as I write it—"Woman,
you are superannuated." John Billet did not survive long, after
the digesting of this affront; but he survived long enough to assure
me that peace was actually restored! and, if I remember aright,
another pudding was discreetly substituted in the place of that
which had occasioned the offence. He died at the Mint (Anno 1781)
where he had long held, what he accounted, a comfortable independence; and with five pounds, fourteen shillings, and a penny,
which were found in his escrutoire after his decease, left the world,
blessing God that he had enough to bury him, and that he had
never been obliged to any man for a sixpence. This was—a Poor
Relation.

THE CONVALESCENT

APRETTY severe fit of indisposition which, under the name of a nervous fever, has made a prisoner of me for some weeks past, and is but slowly leaving me, has reduced me to an incapacity of reflecting upon any topic foreign to itself. Expect no healthy conclusions from me this month, reader; I can offer you only sick men's dreams.

And truly the whole state of sickness is such; for what else is it but a magnificent dream for a man to lie a-bed, and draw day-light curtains about him; and, shutting out the sun, to induce a total oblivion of all the works which are going on under it? To become insensible to all the operations of life, except the beatings of one feeble pulse?

If there be a regal solitude, it is a sick-bed. How the patient lords it there! what caprices he acts without controul! how king-like he sways his pillow—tumbling, and tossing, and shifting, and lowering, and thumping, and flatting, and moulding it, to the ever-varying requisitions of his throbbing temples.

He changes *sides* oftener than a politician. Now he lies full length, then half-length, obliquely, transversely, head and feet quite across the bed; and none accuses him of tergiversation. Within the four curtains he is absolute. They are his Mare Clausum.

How sickness enlarges the dimensions of a man's self to himself! he is his own exclusive object. Supreme selfishness is inculcated upon him as his only duty. 'Tis the Two Tables of the Law to him. He has nothing to think of but how to get well. What passes out of doors, or within them, so he hear not the jarring of them, affects him not.

A little while ago he was greatly concerned in the event of a law-suit, which was to be the making or the marring of his dearest friend. He was to be seen trudging about upon this man's errand to fifty quarters of the town at once, jogging this witness, refreshing that solicitor. The cause was to come on yesterday. He is absolutely as indifferent to the decision as if it were a question to be tried at Pekin. Peradventure from some whispering, going on about the house, not intended for his hearing, he picks up enough to make him understand, that things went cross-grained in the

Court yesterday, and his friend is ruined. But the word "friend," and the word "ruin," disturb him no more than so much jargon. He is not to think of any thing but how to get better.

What a world of foreign cares are merged in that absorbing consideration!

He has put on the strong armour of sickness, he is wrapped in the callous hide of suffering; he keeps his sympathy, like some curious vintage, under trusty lock and key, for his own use only.

He lies pitying himself, honing and moaning to himself; he yearneth over himself; his bowels are even melted within him, to think what he suffers; he is not ashamed to weep over himself.

He is for ever plotting how to do some good to himself; studying little stratagems and artificial alleviations.

He makes the most of himself; dividing himself, by an allowable fiction, into as many distinct individuals, as he hath sore and sorrowing members. Sometimes he mediates—as of a thing apart from him—upon his poor aching head, and that dull pain which, dozing or waking, lay in it all the past night like a log, or palpable substance of pain, not to be removed without opening the very scull, as it seemed, to take it thence. Or he pities his long, clammy, attenuated fingers. He compassionates himself all over; and his bed is a very discipline of humanity, and tender heart.

He is his own sympathiser; and instinctively feels that none can so well perform that office for him. He cares for few spectators to his tragedy. Only that punctual face of the old nurse pleases him, that announces his broths, and his cordials. He likes it because it is so unmoved, and because he can pour forth his feverish ejaculations before it as unreservedly as to his bed-post.

To the world's business he is dead. He understands not what the callings and occupations of mortals are; only he has a glimmering conceit of some such thing, when the doctor makes his daily call: and even in the lines on that busy face he reads no multiplicity of patients, but solely conceives of himself as *the sick man*. To what other uneasy couch the good man is hastening, when he slips out of his chamber, folding up his thin douceur so carefully for fear of rustling—is no speculation which he can at present entertain. He thinks only of the regular return of the same phenomenon at the same hour to-morrow.

Household rumours touch him not. Some faint murmur, indicative of life going on within the house, soothes him, while he knows not distinctly what it is. He is not to know any thing, not to think of any thing. Servants gliding up or down the distant staircase, treading as upon velvet, gently keep his ear awake, so long as he troubles not himself further than with some feeble guess at their errands. Exacter knowledge would be a burthen to him: he can just endure the pressure of conjecture. He opens his eye faintly at the dull stroke of the muffled knocker, and closes it again without asking "who was it?" He is flattered by a general notion that inquiries are making after him, but he cares not to know the name of the inquirer. In the general stillness, and awful hush of the house, he lies in state, and feels his sovereignty.

To be sick is to enjoy monarchal prerogatives. Compare the silent tread, and quiet ministry, almost by the eye only, with which he is served—with the careless demeanour, the unceremonious goings in and out (slapping of doors, or leaving them open) of the very same attendants, when he is getting a little better—and you will confess, that from the bed of sickness (throne let me rather call it) to the elbow-chair of convalescence, is a fall from dignity, amounting to a deposition.

How convalescence shrinks a man back to his pristine stature! Where is now the space, which he occupied so lately, in his own, in the family's eye? The scene of his regalities, his sick room, which was his presence-chamber, where he lay and acted his despotic fancies—how is it reduced to a common bed-room! The trimness of the very bed has something petty and unmeaning about it. It is *made* every day. How unlike to that wavy, many-furrowed, oceanic surface, which it presented so short a time since, when to *make* it was a service not to be thought of at oftener than three or four day revolutions, when the patient was with pain and grief to be lifted for a little while out of it, to submit to the encroachments of unwelcome neatness, and decencies which his shaken frame deprecated; then to be lifted into it again, for another three or four days' respite, to flounder it out of shape again, while every fresh furrow was a historical record of some shifting posture, some uneasy turning, some seeking for a little ease; and the shrunken skin scarce told a truer story than the crumpled coverlid.

Hushed are those mysterious sighs—those groans—so much more awful, while we knew not from what caverns of vast hidden suffering they proceeded. The Lernean pangs are quenched. The riddle of sickness is solved; and Philoctetes is become an ordinary personage.

Perhaps some relic of the sick man's dream of greatness survives in the still lingering visitations of the medical attendant. But how is he, too, changed with everything else! Can this be he—this man of news—of chat—of anecdote—of everything but physic—can this be he, who so lately came between the patient and his cruel enemy, as on some solemn embassy from Nature, erecting herself into a high mediating party?—Pshaw! 'tis some old woman.

Farewell with him all that made sickness pompous—the spell that hushed the household—the desart-like stillness, felt throughout its inmost chambers—the mute attendance—the inquiry by looks—the still softer delicacies of self-attention—the sole and single eye of distemper alonely fixed upon itself—world-thoughts excluded—the man a world unto himself—his own theatre—

What a speck is he dwindled into!

In this flat swamp of convalescence, left by the ebb of sickness, yet far enough from the terra firma of established health, your note, dear Editor, reached me, requesting—an article. In Articulo Mortis, thought I; but it is something hard—and the quibble, wretched as it was, relieved me. The summons, unseasonable as it appeared, seemed to link me on again to the petty businesses of life, which I had lost sight of; a gentle call to activity, however trivial; a wholesome weaning from that preposterous dream of self-absorption—the puffy state of sickness—in which I confess to have lain so long, insensible to the magazines and monarchies of the world alike; to its laws, and to its literature. The hypochondriac flatus is subsiding; the acres, which in imagination I had spread over—for the sick man swells in the sole contemplation of his single sufferings, till he becomes a Tityus to himself—are wasting to a span; and for the giant of self-importance, which I was so lately, you have me once again in my natural pretensions—the lean and meagre figure of your insignificant Essayist.

THE GENTEEL STYLE IN WRITING

IT is an ordinary criticism, that my Lord Shaftesbury, and Sir William Temple, are models of the genteel style in writing. We should prefer saying—of the lordly, and the gentlemanly. Nothing can be more unlike, than the inflated finical rhapsodies of Shaftesbury, and the plain natural chit-chat of Temple. The man of rank is discernible in both writers; but in the one it is only insinuated gracefully, in the other it stands out offensively. The peer seems to have written with his coronet on, and his Earl's mantle before him; the commoner in his elbow-chair and undress.— What can be more pleasant than the way in which the retired statesman peeps out in his essays, penned by the latter in his delightful retreat at Shene? They scent of Nimeguen and the Hague. Scarce an authority is quoted under an ambassador. Don Francisco de Melo, a "Portugal Envoy in England," tells him it was frequent in his country for men, spent with age and other decays, so as they could not hope for above a year or two of life, to ship themselves away in a Brazil fleet, and after their arrival there to go on a great length, sometimes of twenty or thirty years, or more, by the force of that vigour they recovered with that remove. "Whether such an effect (Temple beautifully adds) might grow from the air, or the fruits of that climate, or by approaching nearer the sun, which is the fountain of light and heat, when their natural heat was so far decayed: or whether the piecing out of an old man's life were worth the pains; I cannot tell: perhaps the play is not worth the candle."—Monsieur Pompone, "French Ambassador in his (Sir William's) time at the Hague," certifies him, that in his life he had never heard of any man in France that arrived at a hundred years of age; a limitation of life which the old gentleman imputes to the excellence of their climate, giving them such a liveliness of temper and humour, as disposes them to more pleasures of all kinds than in other countries; and moralises upon the matter very sensibly. The "late Robert Earl of Leicester" furnishes him with a story of a Countess of Desmond, married out of England in Edward the Fourth's time, and who lived far in King James's reign. The "same noble person" gives him an account, how such a year, in the same reign, there went about the country a set of morrice-dancers, composed of ten men who danced, a

Maid Marian, and a tabor and pipe; and how these twelve, one
with another, made up twelve hundred years. "It was not so
much (says Temple) that so many in one small county (Hereford-
shire) should live to that age, as that they should be in vigour and
in humour to travel and to dance." Monsieur Zulichem, one of
his "colleagues at the Hague," informs him of a cure for the gout;
which is confirmed by another "Envoy," Monsieur Serinchamps,
in that town, who had tried it.—Old Prince Maurice of Nassau
recommends to him the use of hammocks in that complaint;
having been allured to sleep, while suffering under it himself, by
the "constant motion or swinging of those airy beds." Count
Egmont, and the Rhinegrave who "was killed last summer before
Maestricht," impart to him their experiences.

But the rank of the writer is never more innocently disclosed,
than where he takes for granted the compliments paid by foreigners
to his fruit-trees. For the taste and perfection of what we esteem
the best, he can truly say, that the French, who have eaten his
peaches and grapes at Shene in no very ill year, have generally
concluded that the last are as good as any they have eaten in France
on this side Fontainebleau; and the first as good as any they have
eaten in Gascony. Italians have agreed his white figs to be as good
as any of that sort in Italy, which is the earlier kind of white fig
there; for in the later kind and the blue, we cannot come near the
warm climates, no more than in the Frontignac or Muscat grape.
His orange-trees, too, are as large as any he saw when he was young
in France, except those of Fontainebleau, or what he had seen
since in the Low Countries; except some very old ones of the Prince
of Orange's. Of grapes he had the honour of bringing over four
sorts into England, which he enumerates, and supposes that they
are all by this time pretty common among some gardeners in his
neighbourhood, as well as several persons of quality; for he ever
thought all things of this kind "the commoner they are made the
better." The garden pedantry with which he asserts that 'tis to
little purpose to plant any of the best fruits, as peaches or grapes,
hardly, he doubts, beyond Northamptonshire at the furthest north-
wards; and praises the "Bishop of Munster at Cosevelt," for attempting nothing beyond cherries in that cold climate; is equally
pleasant and in character. "I may perhaps" (he thus ends his
sweet Garden Essay with a passage worthy of Cowley) "be allowed

to know something of this trade, since I have so long allowed myself to be good for nothing else, which few men will do, or enjoy
their gardens, without often looking abroad to see how other matters play, what motions in the state, and what invitations they
may hope for into other scenes. For my own part, as the country
life, and this part of it more particularly, were the inclination of
my youth itself, so they are the pleasure of my age; and I can truly
say that, among many great employments that have fallen to my
share, I have never asked or sought for any of them, but have
often endeavoured to escape from them, into 'the ease and freedom of a private scene, where a man may go his own way and his
own pace, in the common paths and circles of life. The measure
of choosing well is whether a man likes what he has chosen, which
I thank God has befallen me; and though among the follies of my
life, building and planting have not been the least, and have cost
me more than I have the confidence to own; yet they have been
fully recompensed by the sweetness and satisfaction of this retreat,
where, since my resolution taken of never entering again into any
public employments, I have passed five years without ever once
going to town, though I am almost in sight of it, and have a house
there always ready to receive me. Nor has this been any sort of
affectation, as some have thought it, but a mere want of desire
or humour to make so small a remove; for when I am in this corner,
I can truly say with Horace, *Me quoties reficit*, &c.

> " Me, when the cold Digentian stream revives,
>   What does my friend believe I think or ask?
>   Let me yet less possess, so I may live,
>   Whate'er of life remains, unto myself.
>   May I have books enough; and one year's store,
>   Not to depend upon each doubtful hour:
>   This is enough of mighty Jove to pray,
>   Who, as he pleases, gives and takes away."

The writings of Temple are, in general, after this easy copy.
On one occasion, indeed, his wit, which was mostly subordinate
to nature and tenderness, has seduced him into a string of felicitous antitheses; which, it is obvious to remark, have been a model
to Addison and succeeding essayists. "Who would not be covet-
ous, and with reason," he says, "if health could be purchased with
gold? who not ambitious, if it were at the command of power, or

restored by honour? but, alas! a white staff will not help gouty feet to walk better than a common cane; nor a blue riband bind up a wound so well as a fillet. The glitter of gold, or of diamonds, will but hurt sore eyes instead of curing them; and an aching head will be no more eased by wearing a crown, than a common night-cap." In a far better style, and more accordant with his own humour of plainness, are the concluding sentences of his "Discourse upon Poetry." Temple took a part in the controversy about the ancient and the modern learning; and, with that partiality so natural and so graceful in an old man, whose state engagements had left him little leisure to look into modern productions, while his retirement gave him occasion to look back upon the classic studies of his youth—decided in favour of the latter. "Certain it is," he says, "that, whether the fierceness of the Gothic humours, or noise of their perpetual wars, frighted it away, or that the unequal mixture of the modern languages would not bear it—the great heights and excellency both of poetry and music fell with the Roman learning and empire, and have never since recovered the admiration and applauses that before attended them. Yet, such as they are amongst us, they must be confessed to be the softest and the sweetest, the most general and most innocent amusements of common time and life. They still find room in the courts of princes, and the cottages of shepherds. They serve to revive and animate the dead calm of poor and idle lives, and to allay or divert the violent passions and perturbations of the greatest and the busiest men. And both these effects are of equal use to human life; for the mind of man is like the sea, which is neither agreeable to the beholder nor the voyager, in a calm or in a storm, but is so to both when a little agitated by gentle gales; and so the mind, when moved by soft and easy passions or affections. I know very well that many who pretend to be wise by the forms of being grave, are apt to despise both poetry and music, as toys and trifles too light for the use or entertainment of serious men. But whoever find themselves wholly insensible to their charms, would, I think, do well to keep their own counsel, for fear of reproaching their own temper, and bringing the goodness of their natures, if not their understandings, into question. While this world lasts, I doubt not but the pleasure and request of these two entertainments will do so too; and happy those that content themselves with these, or any other so easy and so innocent, and do not trouble the world or other men, because they cannot be quiet themselves, though nobody hurts them." "When all is done (he concludes), human life is at the greatest and the best but like a froward child, that must be played with, and humoured a little, to keep it quiet, till it falls asleep, and then the care is over."

POPULAR FALLACIES

I

THAT A BULLY IS ALWAYS A COWARD

THIS axiom contains a principle of compensation, which disposes us to admit the truth of it. But there is no safe trusting to dictionaries and definitions. We should more willingly fall in with this popular language, if we did not find *brutality* sometimes awkwardly coupled with *valour* in the same vocabulary. The comic writers, with their poetical justice, have contributed not a little to mislead us upon this point. To see a hectoring fellow exposed and beaten upon the stage, has something in it wonderfully diverting. Some people's share of animal spirits is notoriously low and defective. It has not strength to raise a vapour, or furnish out the wind of a tolerable bluster. These love to be told that huffing is no part of valour. The truest courage with them is that which is the least noisy and obtrusive. But confront one of these silent heroes with the swaggerer of real life, and his confidence in the theory quickly vanishes. Pretensions do not uniformly bespeak non-performance. A modest, inoffensive deportment does not necessarily imply valour; neither does the absence of it justify us in denying that quality. Hickman wanted modesty—we do not mean *him* of Clarissa—but who ever doubted his courage? Even the poets—upon whom this equitable distribution of qualities should be most binding—have thought it agreeable to nature to depart from the rule upon occasion. Harapha, in the "Agonistes," is indeed a bully upon the received notions. Milton has made him at once a blusterer, a giant, and a dastard. But Almanzor, in Dryden, talks of driving armies singly before him—and does it. Tom Brown had a shrewder insight into this kind of character than either of his predecessors. He divides the

palm more equably, and allows his hero a sort of dimidiate pre-
eminence:—"Bully Dawson kicked by half the town, and half
the town kicked by Bully Dawson." This was true distributive
justice.

III

THAT A MAN MUST NOT LAUGH AT HIS OWN JEST

THE severest exaction surely ever invented upon the self-
denial of poor human nature! This is to expect a gentleman
to give treat without partaking of it; to sit esurient at his
own table, and commend the flavour of his venison upon the absurd
strength of his never touching it himself. On the contrary, we
love to see a wag *taste* his own joke to his party; to watch a quirk,
or a merry conceit, flickering upon the lips some seconds before
the tongue is delivered of it. If it be good, fresh, and racy—begotten
of the occasion; if he that utters it never thought it before, he is
naturally the first to be tickled with it, and any suppression of
such complacence we hold to be churlish and insulting. What
does it seem to imply, but that your company is weak or foolish
to be moved by an image or a fancy, that shall stir you not at all,
or but faintly? This is exactly the humour of the fine gentleman
in Mandeville, who, while he dazzles his guests with the display of
some costly toy, affects himself to "see nothing considerable in it."

VI

THAT ENOUGH IS AS GOOD AS A FEAST

NOT a man, woman, or child, in ten miles round Guildhall,
who really believes this saying. The inventor of it did
not believe it himself. It was made in revenge by some
body, who was disappointed of a regale. It is a vile cold-scrag-of-
mutton sophism; a lie palmed upon the palate, which knows better
things. If nothing else could be said for a feast, this is sufficient—
that from the superflux there is usually something left for the
next day. Morally interpreted, it belongs to a class of proverbs,
which have a tendency to make us undervalue *money*. Of this
cast are those notable observations, that money is not health;
riches cannot purchase every thing: the metaphor which makes

gold to be mere muck, with the morality which traces fine clothing to the sheep's back, and denounces pearl as the unhandsome excretion of an oyster. Hence, too, the phrase which imputes dirt to acres—a sophistry so barefaced, that even the literal sense of it is true only in a wet season. This, and abundance of similar sage saws assuming to inculcate *content*, we verily believe to have been the invention of some cunning borrower, who had designs upon the purse of his wealthier neighbour, which he could only hope to carry by force of these verbal jugglings. Translate any one of these sayings out of the artful metonyme which envelopes it, and the trick is apparent. Goodly legs and shoulders of mutton, exhilarating cordials, books, pictures, the opportunities of seeing foreign countries, independence, heart's ease, a man's own time to himself, are not *muck*—however we may be pleased to scandalise with that appellation the faithful metal that provides them for us.

IX

THAT THE WORST PUNS ARE THE BEST

IF by worst be only meant the most far-fetched and startling, we agree to it. A pun is not bound by the laws which limit nicer wit. It is a pistol let off at the ear; not a feather to tickle the intellect. It is an antic which does not stand upon manners, but comes bounding into the presence, and does not show the less comic for being dragged in sometimes by the head and shoulders. What though it limp a little, or prove defective in one leg—all the better. A pun may easily be too curious and artificial. Who has not at one time or other been at a party of professors (himself perhaps an old offender in that line), where, after ringing a round of the most ingenious conceits, every man contributing his shot, and some there the most expert shooters of the day; after making a poor *word* run the gauntlet till it is ready to drop; after hunting and winding it through all the possible ambages of similar sounds; after squeezing, and hauling, and tugging at it, till the very milk of it will not yield a drop further,—suddenly some obscure, unthought-of fellow in a corner, who was never 'prentice to the trade, whom the company for very pity passed over, as we do by a known poor man when a money-subscription is going round, no one calling upon him for his quota—has all at once come out with something so whimsical, yet so pertinent; so brazen in its pretensions, yet so impossible to be denied; so exquisitely good, and so deplorably bad, at the same time,—that it has proved a Robin Hood's shot; any thing ulterior to that is despaired of; and the party breaks up, unanimously voting it to be the very worst (that is, best) pun of the evening. This species of wit is the better for not being perfect in all its parts. What it gains in completeness, it loses in naturalness. The more exactly it satisfies the critical, the less hold it has upon some other faculties. The puns which are most entertaining are those which will least bear an analysis. Of this kind is the following, recorded with a sort of stigma, in one of Swift's Miscellanies.

An Oxford scholar, meeting a porter who was carrying a hare through the streets, accosted him with this extraordinary question: "Prithee, friend, is that thy own hare, or a wig?"

There is no excusing this, and no resisting it. A man might blur ten sides of paper in attempting a defence of it against a critic who should be laughter-proof. The quibble in itself is not considerable. It is only a new turn given, by a little false pronunciation, to a very common, though not very courteous inquiry. Put by one gentleman to another at a dinner-party, it would have been vapid; to the mistress of the house, it would have shown much less wit than rudeness. We must take in the totality of time, place, and person; the pert look of the inquiring scholar, the desponding looks of the puzzled porter; the one stopping at leisure, the other hurrying on with his burthen; the innocent though rather abrupt tendency of the first member of the question, with the utter and inextricable irrelevancy of the second; the place—a public street, not favourable to frivolous investigations; the affrontive quality of the primitive inquiry (the common question) invidiously transferred to the derivative (the new turn given to it) in the implied satire; namely, that few of that tribe are expected to eat of the good things which they carry, they being in most countries considered rather as the temporary trustees than owners of such dainties,—which the fellow was beginning to understand; but then the *wig* again comes in, and he can make nothing of it: all put together constitute a picture: Hogarth could have made it intelligible on canvass.

Yet nine out of ten critics will pronounce this a very bad pun, because of the defectiveness in the concluding member, which is its very beauty, and constitutes the surprise. The same persons shall cry up for admirable the cold quibble from Virgil about the broken Cremona; [1] because it is made out in all its parts, and leaves nothing to the imagination. We venture to call it cold; because of thousands who have admired it, it would be difficult to find one who has heartily chuckled at it. As appealing to the judgment merely (setting the risible faculty aside), we must pronounce it a monument of curious felicity. But as some stories are said to be too good to be true, it may with equal truth be asserted of this bi-verbal allusion, that it is too good to be natural. One cannot help suspecting that the incident was invented to fit the line. It would have been better had it been less perfect. Like some Virgilian hemistichs, it has suffered by filling up. The *nimium Vicina* was enough in conscience; the *Cremonæ* afterwards loads it. It is in fact a double pun; and we have always observed that a superfœtation in this sort of wit is dangerous. When a man has said a good thing, it is seldom politic to follow it up. We do not care to be cheated a second time; or, perhaps, the mind of man (with reverence be it spoken) is not capacious enough to lodge two puns at a time. The impression, to be forcible, must be simultaneous and undivided.

XII

THAT HOME IS HOME THOUGH IT IS NEVER SO HOMELY

HOMES there are, we are sure, that are no homes: the home of the very poor man, and another which we shall speak to presently. Crowded places of cheap entertainment, and the benches of ale-houses, if they could speak, might bear mournful testimony to the first. To them the very poor man resorts for an image of the home, which he cannot find at home. For a starved grate, and a scanty firing, that is not enough to keep alive the natural heat in the fingers of so many shivering children with their mother, he finds in the depth of winter always a blazing hearth, and a hob to warm his pittance of beer by. Instead of the clamours of a wife, made gaunt by famishing, he meets with a cheerful attendance beyond the merits of the trifle which he can afford to spend. He has companions which his home denies him,

[1] Swift.

for the very poor man has no visiters. He can look into the goings on of the world, and speak a little to politics. At home there are no politics stirring, but the domestic. All interests, real or imaginary, all topics that should expand the mind of man, and connect him to a sympathy with general existence, are crushed in the absorbing considerations of food to be obtained for the family. Beyond the price of bread, news is senseless and impertinent. At home there is no larder. Here there is at least a show of plenty; and while he cooks his lean scrap of butcher's meat before the common bars, or munches his humbler cold viands, his relishing bread and cheese with an onion, in a corner, where no one reflects upon his poverty, he has a sight of the substantial joint providing for the landlord and his family. He takes an interest in the dressing of it; and while he assists in removing the trivet from the fire, he feels that there is such a thing as beef and cabbage, which he was beginning to forget at home. All this while he deserts his wife and children. But what wife, and what children? Prosperous men, who object to this desertion, image to themselves some clean contented family like that which they go home to. But look at the countenance of the poor wives who follow and persecute their good man to the door of the public house, which he is about to enter, when something like shame would restrain him, if stronger misery did not induce him to pass the threshold. That face, ground by want, in which every cheerful, every conversable lineament has been long effaced by misery,—is that a face to stay at home with? is it more a woman, or a wild cat? alas! it is the face of the wife of his youth, that once smiled upon him. It can smile no longer. What comforts can it share? what burthens can it lighten? Oh, 'tis a fine thing to talk of the humble meal shared together! But what if there be no bread in the cupboard? The innocent prattle of his children takes out the sting of a man's poverty. But the children of the very poor do not prattle. It is none of the least frightful features in that condition, that there is no childishness in its dwellings. Poor people, said a sensible old nurse to us once, do not bring up their children; they drag them up. The little careless darling of the wealthier nursery, in their hovel is transformed betimes into a premature reflecting person. No one has time to dandle it, no one thinks it worth while to coax it, to soothe it, to toss it up and down, to humour it. There is none to kiss away its tears. If it cries, it can only be beaten. It has been prettily said that "a babe is fed with milk and praise." But the ailment of this poor babe was thin, unnourishing; the return to its little baby-tricks, and efforts to engage attention, bitter ceaseless objurgation. It never had a toy, or knew what a coral meant. It grew up without the lullaby of nurses, it was a stranger to the patient fondle, the hushing caress, the attracting novelty, the costlier plaything, or the cheaper off-hand contrivance to divert the child; the prattled nonsense (best sense to it), the wise impertinencies, the wholesome lies, the apt story interposed, that puts a stop to present sufferings, and awakens the passion of young wonder. It was never sung to—no one ever told to it a tale of the nursery. It was dragged up, to live or to die as it happened. It had not young dreams. It broke at once into the iron realities of life. A child exists not for the very poor as any object of dalliance; it is only another mouth to be fed, a pair of little hands to be betimes inured to labour. It is the rival, till it can be the co-operator, for food with the parent. It is never his mirth, his diversion, his solace; it never makes him young again, with recalling his young times. The children of the very poor have no young times. It makes the very heart to bleed to overhear the casual street-talk between a poor woman and her little girl, a woman of the better sort of poor, in a condition rather above the squalid beings which we have been contemplating. It is not of toys, of nursery books, of summer holidays (fitting that age); of the promised sight, or play; of praised sufficiency at school. It is of mangling and clear-starching, of the price of coals, or of potatoes. The questions of the child, that should be the very outpourings of curiosity in idleness, are marked with forecast and melancholy providence. It has come to be a woman, before it was a child. It has learned to go to market; it chaffers, it haggles, it envies, it murmurs; it is knowing, acute, sharpened; it never prattles. Had we not reason to say, that the home of the very poor is no home?

There is yet another home, which we are constrained to deny to be one. It has a larder, which the home of the poor man wants; its fireside conveniences, of which the poor dream not. But with all this, it is no home. It is—the house of the man that is infested with many visiters. May we be branded for the veriest churl, if we deny our heart to the many noble-hearted friends that at times exchange their dwelling for our poor roof! It is not of guests that we complain, but of endless, purposeless visitants; droppers in, as they are called. We sometimes wonder from what sky they fall. It is the very error of the position of our lodging; its horoscopy was ill calculated, being just situate in a medium—a plaguy suburban mid-space—fitted to catch idlers from town or country. We are older than we were, and age is easily put out of its way. We have fewer sands in our glass to reckon upon, and we cannot brook to see them drop in endlessly succeeding impertinences. At our time of life, to be alone sometimes is as needful as sleep. It is the refreshing sleep of the day. The growing infirmities of age manifest themselves in nothing more strongly, than in an inveterate dislike of interruption. The thing which we are doing, we wish to be permitted to do. We have neither much knowledge nor devices; but there are fewer in the place to which we hasten. We are not willingly put out of our way, even at a game of ninepins. While youth was, we had vast reversions in time future; we are reduced to a present pittance, and obliged to economise in that article. We bleed away our moments now as hardly as our ducats. We cannot bear to have our thin wardrobe eaten and fretted into by moths. We are willing to barter our good time with a friend, who gives us in exchange his own. Herein is the distinction between the genuine guest and the visitant. This latter takes your good time, and gives you his bad in exchange. The guest is domestic to you as your good cat, or household bird; the visitant is your fly, that flaps in at your window, and out again, leaving nothing but a sense of disturbance, and victuals spoiled. The inferior functions of life begin to move heavily. We cannot concoct our food with interruptions. Our chief meal, to be nutritive, must be solitary. With difficulty we can eat before a guest; and never understood what the relish of public feasting meant. Meats have no sapor, nor digestion fair play, in a crowd. The unexpected coming in of a visitant stops the machine. There is a punctual generation who time their calls to the precise commencement of your dining-hour—not to eat—but to see you eat. Our knife and fork drop instinctively, and we feel that we have swallowed our latest morsel. Others again show their genius, as we have said, in knocking the moment you have just sat down to a book. They have a peculiar compassionate sneer, with which they "hope that they do not interrupt your studies." Though they flutter off the next moment, to carry their impertinences to the nearest student that they can call their friend, the tone of the book is spoiled; we shut the leaves, and, with Dante's lovers, read no more that day. It were well if the effect of intrusion were simply co-extensive with its presence; but it mars all the good hours afterwards. These scratches in appearance leave an orifice that closes not hastily. "It is a prostitution of the bravery of friendship," says worthy Bishop Taylor, "to spend it upon impertinent people, who are, it may be, loads to their families, but can never ease my loads." This is the secret of their gaddings, their visits, and morning calls. They too have homes, which are—no homes.

XIII

THAT YOU MUST LOVE ME AND LOVE MY DOG

"GOOD SIR, or madam, as it may be—we most willingly embrace the offer of your friendship. We have long known your excellent qualities. We have wished to have you nearer to us; to hold you within the very innermost fold of our heart. We can have no reserve towards a person of your open and noble nature. The frankness of your humour suits us exactly. We have been long looking for such a friend. Quick—let us disburthen our troubles into each other's bosom—let us make our single joys shine by reduplication.—But *yap, yap, yap!*—what is this confounded cur? he has fastened his tooth, which is none of the bluntest, just in the fleshy part of my leg."

"It is my dog, sir. You must love him for my sake. Here, Test—Test—Test!"

"But he has bitten me."

"Ay, that he is apt to do, till you are better acquainted with him. I have had him three years. He never bites me."

Yap, yap, yap!—"He is at it again."

"Oh, sir, you must not kick him. He does not like to be kicked. I expect my dog to be treated with all the respect due to myself."

"But do you always take him out with you, when you go a friendship-hunting?"

"Invariably. 'Tis the sweetest, prettiest, best-conditioned animal. I call him my *test*—the touchstone by which I try a friend.

No one can properly be said to love me, who does not love him."

"Excuse us, dear sir—or madam, aforesaid—if upon further consideration we are obliged to decline the otherwise invaluable offer of your friendship. We do not like dogs."

"Mighty well, sir—you know the conditions—you may have worse offers. Come along, Test."

The above dialogue is not so imaginary, but that, in the intercourse of life, we have had frequent occasions of breaking off an agreeable intimacy by reason of these canine appendages. They do not always come in the shape of dogs; they sometimes wear the more plausible and human character of kinsfolk, near acquaintances, my friend's friend, his partner, his wife, or his children. We could never yet form a friendship—not to speak of more delicate correspondences—however much to our taste, without the intervention of some third anomaly, some impertinent clog affixed to the relation—the understood *dog* in the proverb. The good things of life are not to be had singly, but come to us with a mixture; like a schoolboy's holiday, with a task affixed to the tail of it. What a delightful companion is * * * *, if he did not always bring his tall cousin with him! He seems to grow with him; like some of those double births which we remember to have read of with such wonder and delight in the old "Athenian Oracle," where Swift commenced author by writing Pindaric Odes (what a beginning for him!) upon Sir William Temple. There is the picture of the brother, with the little brother peeping out at his shoulder; a species of fraternity, which we have no name of kin close enough to comprehend. When * * * * comes, poking in his head and shoulders into your room, as if to feel his entry, you think, surely you have now got him to yourself—what a three hours' chat we shall have!—but, ever in the haunch of him, and before his diffident body is well disclosed in your apartment, appears the haunting shadow of the cousin, overpeering his modest kinsman, and sure to over-lay the expected good talk with his insufferable procerity of stature, and uncorresponding dwarfishness of observation. Misfortunes seldom come alone. 'Tis hard when a blessing comes accompanied. Cannot we like Sempronia, without sitting down to chess with her eternal brother? or know Sulpicia, without knowing all the round of her card-playing relations? must my friend's brethren of neces-

sity be mine also? must we be hand and glove with Dick Selby
the parson, or Jack Selby the calico-printer, because W. S., who is
neither, but a ripe wit and a critic, has the misfortune to claim a
common parentage with them? Let him lay down his brothers;
and 'tis odds but we will cast him in a pair of ours (we have a superflux) to balance the concession. Let F. H. lay down his garrulous
uncle; and Honorius dismiss his vapid wife, and superfluous establishment of six boys: things between boy and manhood—too ripe
for play, too raw for conversation—that come in, impudently staring his father's old friend out of countenance; and will neither aid,
nor let alone, the conference: that we may once more meet upon
equal terms, as we were wont to do in the disengaged state of bach-
elorhood.

It is well if your friend, or mistress, be content with these canicu-
lar probations. Few young ladies but in this sense keep a dog. But
while Rutilia hounds at you her tiger aunt; or Ruspina expects you
to cherish and fondle her viper sister, whom she has preposterously
taken into her bosom, to try stinging conclusions upon your constancy; they must not complain if the house be rather thin of
suitors. Scylla must have broken off many excellent matches in
her time, if she insisted upon all, that loved her, loving her dogs
also.

An excellent story to this moral is told of Merry, of Della Crus-
can memory. In tender youth he loved and courted a modest ap-
panage to the Opera—in truth, a dancer—who had won him by
the artless contrast between her manners and situation. She seemed
to him a native violet, that had been transplanted by some rude
accident into that exotic and artificial hotbed. Nor, in truth, was
she less genuine and sincere than she appeared to him. He wooed
and won this flower. Only for appearance' sake, and for due honour
to the bride's relations, she craved that she might have the attendance of her friends and kindred at the approaching solemnity.
The request was too amiable not to be conceded; and in this solicitude for conciliating the good-will of mere relations, he found a
presage of her superior attentions to himself, when the golden shaft
should have "killed the flock of all affections else." The morning
came: and at the Star and Garter, Richmond—the place appointed
for the breakfasting—accompanied with one English friend, he
impatiently awaited what reinforcements the bride should bring

to grace the ceremony. A rich muster she had made. They came in six coaches—the whole corps du ballet—French, Italian, men and women. Monsieur de B., the famous *pirouetter* of the day, led his fair spouse, but craggy, from the banks of the Seine. The Prima Donna had sent her excuse. But the first and second Buffa were there; and Signor Sc——, and Signora Ch——, and Madame V——, with a countless cavalcade besides of chorusers, figurantes, at the sight of whom Merry afterwards declared, that "then for the first time it struck him seriously, that he was about to marry— a dancer." But there was no help for it. Besides, it was her day; these were, in fact, her friends and kinsfolk. The assemblage, though whimsical, was all very natural. But when the bride— handing out of the last coach a still more extraordinary figure than the rest—presented to him as her *father*—the gentleman that was to *give her away*—no less a person than Signor Delpini himself— with a sort of pride, as much as to say, See what I have brought to do us honour!—the thought of so extraordinary a paternity quite overcame him; and slipping away under some pretence from the bride and her motley adherents, poor Merry took horse from the back yard to the nearest sea-coast, from which, shipping himself to America, he shortly after consoled himself with a more con-genial match in the person of Miss Brunton; relieved from his in-tended clown father, and a bevy of painted Buffas for bridesmaids.

XIV

THAT WE SHOULD RISE WITH THE LARK

AT what precise minute that little airy musician doffs his night gear, and prepares to tune up his unseasonable matins, we are not naturalists enough to determine. But for a mere human gentleman—that has no orchestra business to call him from his warm bed to such preposterous exercises— we take ten, or half after ten (eleven, of course, during this Christ-mas solstice), to be the very earliest hour at which he can begin to think of abandoning his pillow. To think of it, we say; for to do it in earnest requires another half hour's good consideration. Not but there are pretty sun-risings, as we are told, and such like gawds, abroad in the world, in summer time especially, some hours before what we have assigned; which a gentleman may see, as they say, only for getting up. But, having been tempted once or twice, in earlier life, to assist at those ceremonies, we confess our curiosity abated. We are no longer ambitious of being the sun's courtiers, to attend at his morning levees. We hold the good hours of the dawn too sacred to waste them upon such observances; which have in them, besides, something Pagan and Persic. To say truth, we never anticipated our usual hour, or got up with the sun (as 'tis called), to go on a journey, or upon a foolish whole day's pleasuring, but we suffered for it all the long hours after in listlessness and headaches; Nature herself sufficiently declaring her sense of our presumption, in aspiring to regulate our frail waking courses by the measures of that celestial and sleepless traveller. We deny not that there is something sprightly and vigorous, at the outset especially, in these break-of-day excursions. It is flattering to get the start of a lazy world; to conquer death by proxy in his image. But the seeds of sleep and mortality are in us; and we pay usually in strange qualms, before night falls, the penalty of the unnatural inversion. Therefore, while the busy part of mankind are fast huddling on their clothes, are already up and about their occupations, content to have swallowed their sleep by wholesale; we choose to linger a-bed, and digest our dreams. It is the very time to recombine the wandering images, which night in a confused mass presented; to snatch them from forgetfulness; to shape, and mould them. Some people have no good of their dreams. Like fast feeders, they gulp them too grossly, to taste them curiously. We love to chew the cud of a foregone vision; to collect the scattered rays of a brighter phantasm, or act over again, with firmer nerves, the sadder nocturnal tragedies; to drag into daylight a struggling and half-vanishing night-mare; to handle and examine the terrors, or the airy solaces. We have too much respect for these spiritual communications, to let them go so lightly. We are not so stupid, or so careless, as that Imperial forgetter of his dreams, that we should need a seer to remind us of the form of them. They seem to us to have as much significance as our waking concerns; or rather to import us more nearly, as more nearly we approach by years to the shadowy world, whither we are hastening. We have shaken hands with the world's business; we have done with it; we have discharged ourself of it. Why should we get up? we have neither suit to solicit, nor affairs to manage.

The drama has shut in upon us at the fourth act. We have nothing here to expect, but in a short time a sick bed, and a dismissal. We delight to anticipate death by such shadows as night affords. We are already half acquainted with ghosts. We were never much in the world. Disappointment early struck a dark veil between us and its dazzling illusions. Our spirits showed grey before our hairs. The mighty changes of the world already appear as but the vain stuff out of which dramas are composed. We have asked no more of life than what the mimic images in play-houses present us with. Even those types have waxed fainter. Our clock appears to have struck. We are SUPERANNUATED. In this dearth of mundane satisfaction, we contract politic alliances with shadows. It is good to have friends at court. The abstracted media of dreams seem no ill introduction to that spiritual presence, upon which, in no long time, we expect to be thrown. We are trying to know a little of the usages of that colony; to learn the language, and the faces we shall meet with there, that we may be the less awkward at our first coming among them. We willingly call a phantom our fellow, as knowing we shall soon be of their dark companionship. Therefore, we cherish dreams. We try to spell in them the alphabet of the invisible world; and think we know already, how it shall be with us. Those uncouth shapes, which, while we clung to flesh and blood, affrighted us, have become familiar. We feel attenuated into their meagre essences, and have given the hand of half-way approach to incorporeal being. We once thought life to be something; but it has unaccountably fallen from us before its time. Therefore we choose to dally with visions. The sun has no purposes of ours to light us to. Why should we get up?

HUNT

JAMES HENRY LEIGH HUNT (*1784–1859*), *journalist, essayist, critic, poet, was born at Southgate, Middlesex, attended the Christ's Hospital School (entering soon after Lamb and Coleridge had left); he did not go to college, but read much, and at an early age wrote poems in imitation of Spenser and Thomson. When in 1805 a brother founded the short-lived "News," Hunt wrote theatrical criticisms for the paper; he had previously contributed articles to the "Traveller" under the pseudonym "Mr. Town." In 1808, his brother started a weekly periodical, the "Examiner," of which Hunt became editor and leaderwriter; the liberal, non-partisan sheet became popular, and in the thirteen years during which he was connected with it, Hunt raised the tone of newspaper writing. Other journalistic ventures followed; the "Examiner" offending those in power, the brothers were prosecuted, but acquitted; in 1812, an attack on the Prince Regent resulted in a two-years' jail sentence and fine; Hunt edited the "Examiner" from his prison room. In 1819, he contributed some of his best essays to the "Indicator"; he visited Italy in 1821, and was away two years, contributing to periodicals during his absence, notably papers under the pen-name "Harry Honeycomb" to the "New Monthly Magazine." New journalistic ventures followed his return to London, and collections of his poems and essays were printed at intervals. He suffered from ill-health and poverty, received a royal grant, and a pension from the family of his friend Shelley; wrote his autobiography (1850), brought out other books and collections of his contributions to magazines; lost his wife two years before their fiftieth wedding anniversary, and died two years later.*

His essays bear no trace of his suffering, physical and financial; always cheerful, finding contentment in the little things of life, he remains optimistic. He believed in all that is good and beautiful, and got a simple joy from books, friends, and the blessings of every day. Courageous and humorous, he is at his best in the informal essays which show his essentially human character.

HUNT

THE OLD LADY

IF the Old Lady is a widow and lives alone, the manners of her condition and time of life are so much the more apparent. She generally dresses in plain silks, that make a gentle rustling as she moves about the silence of her room; and she wears a nice cap with a lace border, that comes under the chin. In a placket at her side is an old enamelled watch, unless it is locked up in a drawer of her toilet, for fear of accidents. Her waist is rather tight and trim than otherwise, as she had a fine one when young; and she is not sorry if you see a pair of her stockings on a table, that you may be aware of the neatness of her leg and foot. Contented with these and other evident indications of a good shape, and letting her young friends understand that she can afford to obscure it a little, she wears pockets, and uses them well too. In the one is her handkerchief, and any heavier matter that is not likely to come out with it, such as the change of a sixpence; in the other is a miscellaneous assortment, consisting of a pocket-book, a bunch of keys, a needle-case, a spectacle-case, crumbs of biscuit, a nutmeg and grater, a smelling-bottle, and, according to the season, an orange or apple, which after many days she draws out, warm and glossy, to give to some little child that has well behaved itself. She generally occupies two rooms, in the neatest condition possible. In the chamber is a bed with a white coverlet, built up high and round, to look well, and with curtains of a pastoral pattern, consisting alternately of large plants, and shepherds and shepherdesses. On the mantelpiece also are more shepherds and shepherdesses, with dot-eyed sheep at their feet, all in coloured ware: the man, perhaps, in a pink jacket and knots of ribbons at his knees and shoes, holding his crook lightly in one hand, and with the other at his breast, turning his toes out and looking tenderly at the shepherdess: the woman holding a crook also, and modestly returning his look, with a gipsy-hat jerked up behind, a very slender waist,

103

with petticoat and hips to counteract, and the petticoat pulled up through the pocket-holes in order to show the trimness of her ancles. But these patterns, of course, are various. The toilet is ancient, carved at the edges, and tied about with a snow-white drapery of muslin. Beside it are various boxes, mostly japan; and the set of drawers are exquisite things for a little girl to rummage, if ever little girl be so bold,—containing ribbons and laces of various kinds; linen smelling of lavender, of the flowers of which there is always dust in the corners; a heap of pocket-books for a series of years; and pieces of dress long gone by, such as head-fronts, stomachers, and flowered satin shoes, with enormous heels. The stock of letters are always under especial lock and key. So much for the bed-room. In the sitting-room is rather a spare assortment of shining old mahogany furniture, of carved arm-chairs equally old, with chintz draperies down to the ground; a folding or other screen, with Chinese figures, their round, little-eyed meek faces perking sideways; a stuffed bird, perhaps in a glass case (a living one is too much for her); a portrait of her husband over the mantel-piece, in a coat with frog-buttons, and a delicate frilled hand lightly inserted in the waistcoat; and opposite him on the wall, is a piece of embroidered literature, framed and glazed, containing some moral distich or maxim, worked in angular capital letters, with two trees or parrots below, in their proper colours; the whole concluding with an A B C and numerals, and the name of the fair industrious, expressing it to be "her work, Jan. 14, 1762." The rest of the furniture consists of a looking-glass with carved edges, perhaps a settee, a hassock for the feet, a mat for the little dog, and a small set of shelves, in which are the *Spectator* and *Guardian*, the *Turkish Spy*, a *Bible* and *Prayer Book*, *Young's Night Thoughts*, with a piece of lace in it to flatten, *Mrs. Rowe's Devout Exercises of the Heart*, *Mrs. Glasse's Cookery*, and perhaps *Sir Charles Grandison*, and *Clarissa*. *John Buncle* is in the closet among the pickles and preserves. The clock is on the landing-place between the two room doors, where it ticks audibly but quietly; and the landing-place, as well as the stairs, is carpeted to a nicety. The house is most in character, and properly coeval, if it is in a retired suburb, and strongly built, with wainscot rather than paper inside, and lockers in the windows. Before the windows also should be some quivering poplars. Here the Old Lady receives a few quiet visitors to tea, and perhaps an early game at cards: or you may see her going out on the same kind of visit herself, with a light umbrella running up into a stick and crooked ivory handle, and her little dog, equally famous for his love to her and captious antipathy to strangers. Her grand-children dislike him on holidays, and the boldest sometimes ventures to give him a sly kick under the table. When she returns at night, she appears, if the weather happens to be doubtful, in a calash; and her servant in pattens, follows half behind and half at her side, with a lantern.

Her opinions are not many nor new. She thinks the clergyman a nice man. The Duke of Wellington, in her opinion, is a very great man; but she has a secret preference for the Marquis of Granby. She thinks the young women of the present day too forward, and the men not respectful enough; but hopes her grand-children will be better; though she differs with her daughter in several points respecting their management. She sets little value on the new accomplishments; is a great though delicate connoisseur in butcher's meat and all sorts of housewifery: and if you mention waltzes, expatiates on the grace and fine breeding of the minuet. She longs to have seen one danced by Sir Charles Grandison, whom she almost considers as a real person. She likes a walk of a summer's evening, but avoids the new streets, canals, &c., and sometimes goes through the church-yard where her children and her husband lie buried, serious, but not melancholy. She has had three great epochs in her life:—her marriage—her having been at court to see the King and Queen and Royal Family,—and a compliment on her figure she once received, in passing, from Mr. Wilkes, whom she describes as a sad, loose man, but engaging. His plainness she thinks much exaggerated. If anything takes her at a distance from home, it is still the court; but she seldom stirs even for that. The last time but one that she went, was to see the Duke of Wirtemberg; and most probably for the last time of all, to see the Princess Charlotte and Prince Leopold. From this beatific vision she returned with the same admiration as ever for the fine comely appearance of the Duke of York and the rest of the family, and great delight at having had a near view of the Princess, whom she speaks of with smiling pomp and lifted mittens, clasping them as passionately as she can together, and calling her, in a sort of transport of mixed loyalty and self-love, a fine royal young creature, and "Daughter of England."

THE MAID–SERVANT [1]

MUST be considered as young, or else she has married the butcher, the butler, or her cousin, or has otherwise settled into a character distinct from her original one, so as to become what is properly called the domestic. The Maid-Servant, in her apparel, is either slovenly and fine by turns, and dirty always; or she is at all times neat and tight, and dressed according to her station. In the latter case, her ordinary dress is black stockings, a stuff gown, a cap, and a neck-handkerchief pinned corner-wise behind. If you want a pin, she feels about her, and has always one to give you. On Sundays and holidays, and perhaps of afternoons, she changes her black stockings for white, puts on a gown of a better texture and fine pattern, sets her cap and her curls jauntily, and lays aside the neck-handkerchief for a high-body, which, by the way, is not half so pretty.

The general furniture of her ordinary room, the kitchen, is not so much her own as her master's and mistress's, and need not be described: but in a drawer of the dresser or the table, in company with a duster and a pair of snuffers, may be found some of her property, such as a brass thimble, a pair of scissors, a thread-case, a piece of wax candle much wrinkled with the thread, an odd volume of Pamela, and perhaps a sixpenny play, such as George Barnwell or Southerne's *Oroonoko*. There is a piece of looking-glass in the window. The rest of her furniture is in the garret, where you may find a good looking-glass on the table; and in the window a Bible, a comb, and a piece of soap. Here stands also, under stout lock and key, the mighty mystery,—the box,—containing, among other things, her clothes, two or three song-books, consisting of nineteen for the penny; sundry Tragedies at a halfpenny the sheet; the *Whole Nature of Dreams Laid Open*, together with the *Fortune Teller* and the *Account of the Ghost of Mrs. Veal;* the *Story of the Beautiful Zoa* "who was cast away on a desart island, showing how," &c.; some half-crowns in a purse, including pieces of country-money; a silver penny wrapped up in cotton by

[1] In some respects, particularly of costume, this portrait must be understood of originals existing twenty or thirty years ago.

itself; a crooked sixpence, given her before she came to town, and the giver of which has either forgotten or been forgotten by her, she is not sure which;—two little enamel boxes, with looking-glass in the lids, one of them a fairing, the other "a Trifle from Margate"; and lastly, various letters, square and ragged, and directed in all sorts of spellings, chiefly with little letters for capitals. One of them, written by a girl who went to a day-school, is directed "Miss."

In her manners, the Maid-servant sometimes imitates her young mistress; she puts her hair in papers, cultivates a shape, and occasionally contrives to be out of spirits. But her own character and condition overcome all sophistications of this sort; her shape, fortified by the mop and scrubbing-brush, will make its way; and exercise keeps her healthy and cheerful. From the same cause her temper is good; though she gets into little heats when a stranger is over saucy, or when she is told not to go so heavily down stairs, or when some unthinking person goes up her wet stairs with dirty shoes,—or when she is called away often from dinner; neither does she much like to be seen scrubbing the street-door steps of a morning; and sometimes she catches herself saying, "Drat that butcher," but immediately adds, "God forgive me." The tradesmen indeed, with their compliments and arch looks, seldom give her cause to complain. The milkman bespeaks her good-humour for the day with "Come, pretty maids":—then follow the butcher, the baker, the oilman, &c., all with their several smirks and little loiterings; and when she goes to the shops herself, it is for her the grocer pulls down his string from its roller with more than ordinary whirl, and tosses his parcel into a tie.

Thus pass the mornings between working, and singing, and giggling, and grumbling, and being flattered. If she takes any pleasure unconnected with her office before the afternoon, it is when she runs up the area-steps or to the door to hear and purchase a new song, or to see a troop of soldiers go by; or when she happens to thrust her head out of a chamber window at the same time with a servant in the next house, when a dialogue infallibly ensues, stimulated by the imaginary obstacles between. If the Maid-servant is wise, the best part of her work is done by dinner-time; and nothing else is necessary to give perfect zest to the meal. She tells us what she thinks of it, when she calls it "a bit o' dinner."

There is the same sort of eloquence in her other phrase, "a cup o' tea"; but the old ones, and the washerwomen, beat her at that. After tea in great houses, she goes with the other servants to hot cockles, or What-are-my-thoughts-like, and tells Mr. John to "have done then"; or if there is a ball given that night, they throw open the doors, and make use of the music up stairs to dance by. In smaller houses, she receives the visit of her aforesaid cousin; and sits down alone, or with a fellow maid-servant, to work; talks of her young master or mistress and Mr. Ivins (Evans); or else she calls to mind her own friends in the country; where she thinks the cows and "all that" beautiful, now she is away. Meanwhile, if she is lazy, she snuffs the candle with her scissors; or if she has eaten more heartily than usual, she sighs double the usual number of times, and thinks that tender hearts were born to be unhappy.

Such being the Maid-servant's life in-doors, she scorns, when abroad, to be anything but a creature of sheer enjoyment. The Maid-servant, the sailor, and the school-boy, are the three beings that enjoy a holiday beyond all the rest of the world;—and all for the same reason,—because their inexperience, peculiarity of life, and habit of being with persons of circumstances or thoughts above them, give them all, in their way, a cast of the romantic. The most active of the money-getters is a vegetable compared with them. The Maid-servant, when she first goes to Vauxhall, thinks she is in heaven. A theatre is all pleasure to her, whatever is going forward, whether the play or the music, or the waiting which makes others impatient, or the munching of apples and gingerbread, which she and her party commence almost as soon as they have seated themselves. She prefers tragedy to comedy, because it is grander, and less like what she meets with in general; and because she thinks it more in earnest also, especially in the love-scenes. Her favourite play is *Alexander the Great, or the Rival Queens.* Another great delight is in going a shopping. She loves to look at the patterns in the windows, and the fine things labelled with those corpulent numerals of "only 7 *s.*"—"only 6 *s.* 6 *d.*" She has also, unless born and bred in London, been to see my Lord Mayor, the fine people coming out of Court, and the "beasties" in the Tower; and at all events she has been to Astley's and the Circus, from which she comes away equally smitten with the rider, and sore with laughing at the clown. But it is difficult to say what pleasure she enjoys most. One of the completest of all is the fair, where she walks through an endless round of noise, and toys, and gallant apprentices, and wonders. Here she is invited in by courteous well-dressed people, as if she were the mistress. Here also is the conjurer's booth, where the operator himself, a most stately and genteel person all in white, calls her Ma'am; and says to John by her side, in spite of his laced hat, "Be good enough, sir, to hand the card to the lady."

Ah! may her "cousin" turn out as true as he says he is; or may she get home soon enough and smiling enough to be as happy again next time.

SOCIAL GENEALOGY

IT is a curious and pleasant thing to consider, that a link of personal acquaintance can be traced up from the authors of our own times to those of Shakespeare, and to Shakespeare himself. Ovid, in recording his intimacy with Propertius and Horace, regrets that he had only seen Virgil. (*Trist.* Lib. IV, v. 51.) But still he thinks the sight of him worth remembering. And Pope, when a child, prevailed on some friends to take him to a coffee-house which Dryden frequented, merely to look at him; which he did, with great satisfaction. Now, such of us as have shaken hands with a living poet, might be able to reckon up a series of connecting shakes, to the very hand that wrote of Hamlet, and of Falstaff, and of Desdemona.

With some living poets, it is certain. There is Thomas Moore, for instance, who knew Sheridan. Sheridan knew Johnson, who was the friend of Savage, who knew Steele, who knew Pope. Pope was intimate with Congreve, and Congreve with Dryden. Dryden is said to have visited Milton. Milton is said to have known Davenant; and to have been saved by him from the revenge of the restored court, in return for having saved Davenant from the revenge of the Commonwealth. But if the link between Dryden and Milton, and Milton and Davenant, is somewhat apocryphal, or rather dependent on tradition (for Richardson the painter tells us the story from Pope, who had it from Betterton the actor, one of Davenant's company), it may be carried at once from Dryden to Davenant, with whom he was unquestionably intimate. Davenant then knew Hobbes, who knew Bacon, who knew Ben Jonson, who was intimate with Beaumont and Fletcher, Chapman, Donne, Drayton, Camden, Selden, Clarendon, Sidney, Raleigh, and perhaps all the great men of Elizabeth's and James's time, the greatest of them all undoubtedly. Thus have we a link of "beamy hands" from our own times up to Shakespeare.

In this friendly genealogy we have omitted the numerous side-branches or common friendships. It may be mentioned, however, in order not to omit Spenser, that Davenant resided some time in the family of Lord Brooke, the friend of Sir Philip Sidney. Spenser's intimacy with Sidney is mentioned by himself in a letter, still extant, to Gabriel Harvey.

We will now give the authorities for our intellectual pedigree. Sheridan is mentioned in Boswell as being admitted to the celebrated club of which Johnson, Goldsmith, and others were members. He had just written the *School for Scandal*, which made him the more welcome. Of Johnson's friendship with Savage (we cannot help beginning the sentence with his favourite leading preposition), the well-known Life is an interesting record. It is said that in the commencement of their friendship, they sometimes wandered together about London for want of a lodging—more likely for Savage's want of it, and Johnson's fear of offending him by offering a share of his own. But we do not remember how this circumstance is related by Boswell.

Savage's intimacy with Steele is recorded in a pleasant anecdote, which he told Johnson. Sir Richard once desired him, "with an air of the utmost importance," says his biographer, "to come very early to his house the next morning. Mr. Savage came as he had promised, found the chariot at the door, and Sir Richard waiting for him and ready to go out. What was intended, and whither they were to go, Savage could not conjecture, and was not willing to inquire, but immediately seated himself with Sir Richard. The coachman was ordered to drive, and they hurried with the utmost expedition to Hyde-park Corner, where they stopped at a petty tavern, and retired to a private room. Sir Richard then informed him that he intended to publish a pamphlet, and that he had desired him to come thither that he might write for him. They soon sat down to the work. Sir Richard dictated, and Savage wrote, till the dinner that had been ordered was put upon the table. Savage was surprised at the meanness of the entertainment, and after some hesitation, ventured to ask for wine, which Sir Richard, not without reluctance, ordered to be brought. They then finished their dinner, and proceeded in their pamphlet, which they concluded in the afternoon.

"Mr. Savage then imagined that his task was over, and expected that Sir Richard would call for the reckoning, and return home; but his expectations deceived him, for Sir Richard told him that he was without money, and that the pamphlet must be sold before the dinner could be paid for, and Savage was therefore obliged to go and offer their new production for sale for two guineas, which with some difficulty he obtained. Sir Richard then returned home, having retired that day only to avoid his creditors, and composed the pamphlet only to discharge his reckoning."

Steele's acquaintance with Pope, who wrote some papers for his *Guardian*, appears in the letters and other works of the wits of that time. Johnson supposes that it was his friendly interference, which attempted to bring Pope and Addison together after a jealous separation. Pope's friendship with Congreve appears also in his letters. He also dedicated the *Iliad* to Congreve, over the heads of peers and patrons. The dramatist, whose conversation most likely partook of the elegance and wit of his writings, and whose manners appear to have rendered him an universal favourite, had the honour, in his youth of attracting the respect and regard of Dryden. He was publicly hailed by him as his successor, and affectionately bequeathed the care of his laurels. Dryden did not know who had been looking at him in the coffee-house.

> Already I am worn with cares and age,
> And just abandoning th'ungrateful stage;
> Unprofitably kept at Heaven's expense,
> I live a rent-charge on his providence.
> But you, whom every Muse and Grace adorn,
> Whom I foresee to better fortune born,
> Be kind to my remains; and O, defend,
> Against your judgement, your departed friend!
> Let not th'insulting foe my fame pursue,
> But shade those laurels which descend to you.

Congreve did so, with great tenderness.

Dryden is reported to have asked Milton's permission to turn his *Paradise Lost* into a rhyming tragedy, which he called *The State of Innocence, or the Fall of Man;* a work, such as might be expected from such a mode of alteration. The venerable poet is said to have answered, "Ay, young man, you may tag my verses, if you will." Be the connexion, however, of Dryden with Milton, or of Milton with Davenant, as it may, Dryden wrote the alteration of Shakespeare's *Tempest*, as it is now perpetrated, in conjunction with Davenant. They were great hands, but they should not have touched the pure grandeur of Shakespeare. The intimacy of Davenant with Hobbes is to be seen by their correspondence prefixed to *Gondibert*. Hobbes was at one time secretary to Lord Bacon, a singularly illustrious instance of servant and master. Bacon also had Ben Jonson for a retainer in a similar capacity; and Jonson's link with the preceding writers could be easily supplied through the medium of Greville and Sidney, and indeed of many others of his contemporaries. Here then we arrive at Shakespeare, and feel the electric virtue of his hand. Their intimacy, dashed a little, perhaps, with jealousy on the part of Jonson, but maintained to the last by dint of the nobler part of him, and of Shakespeare's irresistible fineness of nature, is a thing as notorious as their fame. Fuller says: "Many were the wit-combates betwixt (Shakespeare) and Ben Jonson, which two I behold like a Spanish great galleon and an English man-of-war: Master Jonson (like the former) was built far higher in learning: solid, but slow in his performances. Shakespeare, with the English man-of-war, lesser in bulk, but lighter in sailing, could turn with all tides, tack about, and take advantage of all winds, by the quickness of his wit and invention." This is a happy simile, with the exception of what is insinuated about Jonson's greater solidity. But let Jonson show for himself the affection with which he regarded one, who did not irritate or trample down rivalry, but rose above it like the sun, and turned emulation to worship:—

> Soul of the age!
> Th'applause! delight! the wonder of our stage!
> My Shakespeare, rise! I will not lodge thee by
> Chaucer or Spenser, or bid Beaumont lie
> A little further, to make thee a room;
> Thou art a monument without a tomb;
> And art alive still, while thy book doth live,
> And we have wits to read, and praise to give.
> . . . . . .
> He was not of an age, but for all time.

A FEW THOUGHTS ON SLEEP

THIS is an article for the reader to think of, when he or she is warm in bed, a little before he goes to sleep, the clothes at his ear, and the wind moaning in some distant crevice. "Blessings," exclaimed Sancho, "on him that first invented sleep! It wraps a man all around like a cloak." It is a delicious moment certainly,—that of being well nestled in bed, and feeling that you shall drop gently to sleep. The good is to come, not past: the limbs have been just tired enough to render the remaining in one posture delightful: the labour of the day is done. A gentle failure of the perceptions comes creeping over one:—the spirit of consciousness disengages itself more and more, with slow and hushing degrees, like a mother detaching her hand from that of her sleeping child;—the mind seems to have a balmy lid closing over it, like the eye;—'tis closing;—'tis more closing;—'tis closed. The mysterious spirit has gone to take its airy rounds.

It is said that sleep is best before midnight: and Nature herself, with her darkness and chilling dews, informs us so. There is another reason for going to bed betimes: for it is universally acknowledged that lying late in the morning is a great shortener of life. At least, it is never found in company with longevity. It also tends to make people corpulent. But these matters belong rather to the subject of early rising, than of sleep.

Sleep at a late hour in the morning is not half so pleasant as the more timely one. It is sometimes however excusable, especially to a watchful or overworked head; neither can we deny the seducing merits of "t'other doze,"—the pleasing wilfulness of nestling in a new posture, when you know you ought to be up, like the rest of the house. But then you cut up the day and your sleep the next night.

In the course of the day, few people think of sleeping, except after dinner; and then it is often rather a hovering and nodding on the borders of sleep, than sleep itself. This is a privilege allowable, we think, to none but the old, or the sickly, or the very tired and careworn; and it should be well understood, before it is exercised in company. To escape into slumber from an argument; or to take it as an affair of course, only between you and your biliary duct; or to assent with involuntary nods to all that you have just been disputing, is not so well: much less, to sit nodding and tottering beside a lady; or to be in danger of dropping your head into the fruit-plate or your host's face; or of waking up, and saying "Just so," to the bark of a dog; or "Yes, Madam," to the black at your elbow.

Careworn people, however, might refresh themselves oftener with day-sleep than they do; if their bodily state is such as to dispose them to it. It is a mistake to suppose that all care is wakeful. People sometimes sleep, as well as wake, by reason of their sorrow. The difference seems to depend upon the nature of their temperament; though in the *most* excessive cases, sleep is perhaps Nature's never-failing relief, as swooning is upon the rack. A person with jaundice in his blood shall lie down and go to sleep at noon-day, when another of a different complexion shall find his eyes as uncloseable as a statue's, though he has had no sleep for nights together. Without meaning to lessen the dignity of suffering, which has quite enough to do with its waking hours, it is this that may often account for the profound sleeps enjoyed the night before hazardous battles, executions, and other demands upon an over-excited spirit.

The most complete and healthy sleep that can be taken in the day, is in summer-time, out in a field. There is perhaps no solitary sensation so exquisite as that of slumbering on the grass or hay, shaded from the hot sun by a tree, with the consciousness of a fresh but light air running through the wide atmosphere, and the sky stretching far overhead upon all sides. Earth, and heaven, and a placid humanity, seem to have the creation to themselves. There is nothing between the slumberer and the naked and glad innocence of Nature.

Next to this, but at a long interval, the most relishing snatch of slumber out of bed, is the one which a tired person takes before he retires for the night, while lingering in his sitting-room. The consciousness of being very sleepy and of having the power to go to bed immediately, gives great zest to the unwillingness to move. Sometimes he sits nodding in his chair; but the sudden and leaden jerks of the head to which a state of great sleepiness renders him liable, are generally too painful for so luxurious a moment; and he gets into a more legitimate posture, sitting sideways with his head on the chair-back, or throwing his legs up at once on another chair, and half reclining. It is curious, however, to find how long an inconvenient posture will be borne for the sake of this foretaste of repose. The worst of it is, that on going to bed, the charm sometimes vanishes; perhaps from the colder temperature of the chamber; for a fireside is a great opiate.

Speaking of the painful positions into which a sleepy lounger will get himself, it is amusing to think of the more fantastic attitudes that so often take place in bed. If we could add anything to the numberless things that have been said about sleep by the poets, it would be upon this point. Sleep never shows himself a greater leveller. A man in his waking moments may look as proud and self-possessed as he pleases. He may walk proudly, he may sit proudly, he may eat his dinner proudly; he may shave himself with an air of infinite superiority; in a word, he may show himself grand and absurd upon the most trifling occasions. But Sleep plays the petrifying magician. He arrests the proudest lord as well as the humblest clown in the most ridiculous postures: so that if you could draw a grandee from his bed without waking him, no limb-twisting fool in a pantomime should create wilder laughter. The toy with the string between its legs is hardly a posture-master more extravagant. Imagine a despot lifted up to the gaze of his valets, with his eyes shut, his mouth open, his left hand under his right ear, his other twisted and hanging helplessly before him like an idiot's, one knee lifted up, and the other leg stretched out, or both knees huddled up together;—what a scarecrow to lodge majestic power in!

But Sleep is kindly, even in his tricks; and the poets have treated him with proper reverence. According to the ancient mythologists, he had even one of the Graces to wife. He had a thousand sons, of whom the chief were Morpheus, or the Shaper; Icelos, or the Likely; Phantasus, the Fancy; and Phobetor, the Terror. His dwelling some writers place in a dull and darkling part of the earth; others, with a greater compliment, in heaven; and others, with another kind of propriety, by the sea-shore. There is a good description of it in Ovid; but in these abstracted tasks of poetry, the moderns outvie the ancients; and there is nobody who has built his bower for him so finely as Spenser. Archimago in the first book of the *Faerie Queene* (Canto I, st. 39), sends a little spirit down to Morpheus to fetch him a Dream:

> He, making speedy way through spersed ayre,
> And through the world of waters, wide and deepe,
> To Morpheus' house doth hastily repaire.
> Amid the bowels of the earth full steepe
> And low, where dawning day doth never peepe,
> His dwelling is. There, Tethys his wet bed
> Doth ever wash; and Cynthia still doth steepe
> In silver dew his ever-drouping hed,
> Whiles sad Night over him her mantle black doth spred.
>
> And more to lulle him in his slumber soft
> A trickling streame from high rocke tumbling downe,
> And ever-drizling raine upon the loft,
> Mixt with a murmuring winde, much like the soune
> Of swarming bees, did cast him in a swoune.
> No other noise, nor people's troublous cryes,
> As still are wont to annoy the walled towne,
> Might there be heard; but carelesse Quiet lyes,
> Wrapt in eternall silence, farre from enimyes.

Chaucer has drawn the cave of the same god with greater simplicity; but nothing can have a more deep and sullen effect than his cliffs and cold-running waters. It seems as real as an actual solitude, or some quaint old picture in a book of travels in Tartary. He is telling the story of Ceyx and Alcyone in the poem called his Dream. Juno tells a messenger to go to Morpheus and "bid him creep into the body" of the drowned king, to let his wife know the fatal event by his apparition.

> This messenger tooke leave, and went
> Upon his way; and never he stent
> Till he came to the dark valley,
> That stant betweene rockes twey.
> There never yet grew corne, ne gras,
> Ne tree, ne nought that aught was,
> Beast, ne man, ne naught else;
> Save that there were a few wells
> Came running fro the cliffs adowne,
> That made a deadly sleeping soune,
> And runnen downe right by a cave,
> That was under a rocke ygrave,
> Amid the valley, wonder-deepe.
> There these goddis lay asleepe,
> Morpheus and Eclympasteire,
> That was the god of Sleepis heire,
> That slept and did none other worke.

Where the credentials of this new son and heir, Eclympasteire, are
to be found, we know not; but he acts very much, it must be allowed, like an heir presumptive, in sleeping, and doing "none
other work."

We dare not trust ourselves with many quotations upon sleep
from the poets; they are so numerous as well as beautiful. We must
content ourselves with mentioning that our two most favourite
passages are one in the *Philoctetes* of Sophocles, admirable for its
contrast to a scene of terrible agony, which it closes; and the other
the following address in Beaumont and Fletcher's tragedy of
Valentinian, the hero of which is also a sufferer under bodily torment. He is in a chair, slumbering; and these most exquisite lines
are gently sung with music.

> Care-charming Sleep, thou easer of all woes,
> Brother to Death, sweetly thyself dispose
> On this afflicted prince. Fall like a cloud
> In gentle showers: give nothing that is loud
> Or painful to his slumbers: easy, light,
> And as a purling stream, thou son of Night,
> Pass by his troubled senses; sing his pain
> Like hollow murmuring wind, or silver rain:
> Into this prince, gently, oh gently slide;
> And kiss him into slumbers, like a bride.

How earnest and prayer-like are these pauses! How lightly sprinkled, and yet how deeply settling, like rain, the fancy! How quiet,
affectionate, and perfect the conclusion!

Sleep is most graceful in an infant; soundest, in one who has
been tired in the open air; completest, to the seaman after a hard
voyage; most welcome, to the mind haunted with one idea; most
touching to look at, in the parent that has wept; lightest, in the
playful child; proudest, in the bride adored.

GETTING UP ON COLD MORNINGS

AN Italian author,—Giulio Cordara, a Jesuit,—has written a
poem upon insects, which he begins by insisting, that
those troublesome and abominable little animals were
created for our annoyance, and that they were certainly not inhabitants of Paradise. We of the North may dispute this piece of
theology; but on the other hand, it is as clear as the snow on the

house-tops, that Adam was not under the necessity of shaving; and that when Eve walked out of her delicious bower, she did not step upon ice three inches thick.

Some people say it is a very easy thing to get up of a cold morning. You have only, they tell you, to take the resolution; and the thing is done. This may be very true; just as a boy at school has only to take a flogging, and the thing is over. But we have not at all made up our minds upon it; and we find it a very pleasant exercise to discuss the matter, candidly, before we get up. This at least is not idling, though it may be lying. It affords an excellent answer to those, who ask how lying in bed can be indulged in by a reasoning being,—a rational creature. How? Why with the argument calmly at work in one's head, and the clothes over one's shoulder. Oh—it is a fine way of spending a sensible, impartial half-hour.

If these people would be more charitable, they would get on with their argument better. But they are apt to reason so ill, and to assert so dogmatically, that one could wish to have them stand round one's bed of a bitter morning, and *lie* before their faces. They ought to hear both sides of the bed, the inside and out. If they cannot entertain themselves with their own thoughts for half an hour or so, it is not the fault of those who can.

Candid inquiries into one's decumbency, besides the greater or less privileges to be allowed a man in proportion to his ability of keeping early hours, the work given his faculties, &c., will at least concede their due merits to such representations as the following. In the first place, says the injured but calm appealer, I have been warm all night, and find my system in a state perfectly suitable to a warm-blooded animal. To get out of this state into the cold, besides the inharmonious and uncritical abruptness of the transition, is so unnatural to such a creature, that the poets, refining upon the tortures of the damned, make one of their greatest agonies consist in being suddenly transported from heat to cold,— from fire to ice. They are "haled" out of their "beds," says Milton, by "harpy-footed furies,"—fellows who come to call them.—On my first movement towards the anticipation of getting up, I find that such parts of the sheets and bolster, as are exposed to the air of the room, are stone cold. On opening my eyes, the first thing that meets them is my own breath rolling forth, as if in the open

air, like smoke out of a chimney. Think of this symptom. Then I
turn my eyes sideways and see the windows all frozen over. Think
of that. Then the servant comes in. "It is very cold this morning,
is it not?"—"Very cold, Sir."—"Very cold indeed, isn't it?"—
"Very cold indeed, Sir."—"More than usually so, isn't it, even for
this weather?" (Here the servant's wit and good-nature are put
to a considerable test, and the inquirer lies on thorns for the
answer.) "Why, Sir—I think it *is*." (Good creature! There is
not a better, or more truth-telling servant going.) "I must rise,
however—get me some warm water."—Here comes a fine interval
between the departure of the servant and the arrival of the hot
water; during which, of course, it is of "no use" to get up. The hot
water comes. "Is it quite hot?"—"Yes, Sir."—"Perhaps too hot
for shaving: I must wait a little?"—"No, Sir; it will just do."
(There is an over-nice propriety sometimes, an officious zeal of
virtue, a little troublesome.) "Oh—the shirt—you must air my
clean shirt;—linen gets very damp this weather."—"Yes, Sir."
Here another delicious five minutes. A knock at the door. "Oh,
the shirt—very well. My stockings—I think the stockings had
better be aired too."—"Very well, Sir."—Here another interval.
At length everything is ready, except myself. I now, continues
our incumbent (a happy word, by the bye, for a country vicar)—
I now cannot help thinking a good deal—who can?—upon the
unnecessary and villainous custom of shaving: it is a thing so
unmanly (here I nestle closer)—so effeminate (here I recoil from
an unlucky step into the colder part of the bed).—No wonder that
the Queen of France took part with the rebels against that degenerate King, her husband, who first affronted her smooth visage with
a face like her own. The Emperor Julian never showed the luxuri-
ancy of his genius to better advantage than in reviving the flowing
beard. Look at Cardinal Bembo's picture—at Michael Angelo's—
at Titian's—at Shakespeare's—at Fletcher's—at Spenser's—at
Chaucer's—at Alfred's—at Plato's—I could name a great man
for every tick of my watch. Look at the Turks, a grave and otiose
people.—Think of Haroun Al Raschid and Bed-ridden Hassan.—
Think of Wortley Montagu, the worthy son of his mother, a man
above the prejudice of his time.—Look at the Persian gentlemen,
whom one is ashamed of meeting about the suburbs, their dress
and appearance are so much finer than our own.—Lastly, think

of the razor itself—how totally opposed to every sensation of bed—how cold, how edgy, how hard! how utterly different from anything like the warm and circling amplitude, which

> Sweetly recommends itself
> Unto our gentle senses.

Add to this, benumbed fingers, which may help you to cut yourself, a quivering body, a frozen towel, and a ewer full of ice; and he that says there is nothing to oppose in all this, only shows, at any rate, that he has no merit in opposing it.

Thomson, the poet, who exclaims in his *Seasons*—

> Falsely luxurious! Will not man awake?

used to lie in bed till noon, because he said he had no motive in getting up. He could imagine the good of rising; but then he could also imagine the good of lying still; and his exclamation, it must be allowed, was made upon summer-time, not winter. We must proportion the argument to the individual character. A money-getter may be drawn out of his bed by three and fourpence; but this will not suffice for a student. A proud man may say, "What shall I think of myself, if I don't get up?" but the more humble one will be content to waive this prodigious notion of himself, out of respect to his kindly bed. The mechanical man shall get up without any ado at all; and so shall the barometer. An ingenious lier in bed will find hard matter of discussion even on the score of health and longevity. He will ask us for our proofs and precedents of the ill effects of lying later in cold weather; and sophisticate much on the advantages of an even temperature of body; of the natural propensity (pretty universal) to have one's way; and of the animals that roll themselves up, and sleep all the winter. As to longevity, he will ask whether the longest life is of necessity the best; and whether Holborn is the handsomest street in London.

THE OLD GENTLEMAN

OUR Old Gentleman, in order to be exclusively himself, must be either a widower or a bachelor. Suppose the former. We do not mention his precise age, which would be invidious:—nor whether he wears his own hair or a wig; which would be wanting in universality. If a wig, it is a compromise between the more modern scratch and the departed glory of the toupee. If his own hair, it is white, in spite of his favourite grandson, who used to get on the chair behind him, and pull the silver hairs out, ten years ago. If he is bald at top, the hair-dresser, hovering and breathing about him like a second youth, takes care to give the bald place as much powder as the covered; in order that he may convey to the sensorium within a pleasing indistinctness of idea respecting the exact limits of skin and hair. He is very clean and neat; and, in warm weather, is proud of opening his waistcoat half-way down, and letting so much of his frill be seen, in order to show his hardiness as well as taste. His watch and shirt-buttons are of the best; and he does not care if he has two rings on a finger. If his watch ever failed him at the club or coffee-house, he would take a walk every day to the nearest clock of good character, purely to keep it right. He has a cane at home, but seldom uses it, on finding it out of fashion with his elderly juniors. He has a small cocked hat for gala days, which he lifts higher from his head than the round one, when bowed to. In his pockets are two handkerchiefs (one for the neck at night-time), his spectacles, and his pocket-book. The pocket-book, among other things, contains a receipt for a cough, and some verses cut out of an odd sheet of an old magazine, on the lovely Duchess of A., beginning—

When beauteous Mira walks the plain.

He intends this for a common-place book which he keeps, consisting of passages in verse and prose, cut out of newspapers and magazines, and pasted in columns; some of them rather gay. His principal other books are Shakespeare's *Plays* and Milton's *Paradise Lost;* the *Spectator*, the *History of England;* the *Works* of Lady M. W. Montagu, Pope, and Churchill; Middleton's *Geography*, *The Gentleman's Magazine;* Sir John Sinclair on Longevity; several plays with portraits in character; *Account of Elizabeth Canning, Memoirs of George Ann Bellamy, Poetical Amusements at Bath-Easton*, Blair's *Works, Elegant Extracts; Junius* as originally published; a few pamphlets on the American War and Lord George Gordon, &c. and one on the French Revolution. In his sitting-rooms are some engravings from Hogarth and Sir Joshua; an engraved portrait of the Marquis of Granby; ditto of M. le Comte de

Grasse surrendering to Admiral Rodney; a humorous piece after Penny; and a portrait of himself, painted by Sir Joshua. His wife's portrait is in his chamber, looking upon his bed. She is a little girl, stepping forward with a smile, and a pointed toe, as if going to dance. He lost her when she was sixty.

The Old Gentleman is an early riser, because he intends to live at least twenty years longer. He continues to take tea for breakfast, in spite of what is said against its nervous effects; having been satisfied on that point some years ago by Dr. Johnson's criticism on Hanway, and a great liking for tea previously. His china cups and saucers have been broken since his wife's death, all but one, which is religiously kept for his use. He passes his morning in walking or riding, looking in at auctions, looking after his India bonds or some such money securities, furthering some subscription set on foot by his excellent friend Sir John, or cheapening a new old print for his portfolio. He also hears of the newspapers; not caring to see them till after dinner at the coffee-house. He may also cheapen a fish or so; the fishmonger soliciting his doubting eye as he passes, with a profound bow of recognition. He eats a pear before dinner.

His dinner at the coffee-house is served up to him at the accustomed hour, in the old accustomed way, and by the accustomed waiter. If William did not bring it, the fish would be sure to be stale, and the flesh new. He eats no tart; or if he ventures on a little, takes cheese with it. You might as soon attempt to persuade him out of his senses, as that cheese is not good for digestion. He takes port; and if he has drunk more than usual, and in a more private place, may be induced by some respectful inquiries respecting the old style of music, to sing a song composed by Mr. Oswald or Mr. Lampe, such as—

Chloe, by that borrowed kiss,

or

Come, gentle god of soft repose;

or his wife's favourite ballad beginning—

At Upton on the hill
There lived a happy pair.

Of course, no such exploit can take place in the coffee-room; but he will canvass the theory of that matter there with you, or discuss the weather, or the markets, or the theatres, or the merits of "my Lord North" or "my Lord Rockingham"; for he rarely says simply, lord; it is generally "my lord," trippingly and genteelly off the tongue. If alone after dinner, his great delight is the newspaper; which he prepares to read by wiping his spectacles, carefully adjusting them on his eyes, and drawing the candle close to him, so as to stand sideways betwixt his ocular aim and the small type. He then holds the paper at arm's length, and dropping his eyelids half down and his mouth half open, takes cognizance of the day's information. If he leaves off, it is only when the door is opened by a new-comer, or when he suspects somebody is over-anxious to get the paper out of his hand. On these occasions, he gives an important hem! or so; and resumes.

In the evening, our Old Gentleman is fond of going to the theatre, or of having a game of cards. If he enjoys the latter at his own house or lodgings, he likes to play with some friends whom he has known for many years; but an elderly stranger may be introduced, if quiet and scientific; and the privilege is extended to younger men of letters; who, if ill players, are good losers. Not that he is a miser; but to win money at cards is like proving his victory by getting the baggage; and to win of a younger man is a substitute for his not being able to beat him at rackets. He breaks up early, whether at home or abroad.

At the theatre, he likes a front row in the pit. He comes early, if he can do so without getting into a squeeze, and sits patiently waiting for the drawing up of the curtain, with his hands placidly lying one over the other on the top of his stick. He generously admires some of the best performers, but thinks them far inferior to Garrick, Woodward, and Clive. During splendid scenes, he is anxious that the little boy should see.

He has been induced to look in at Vauxhall again, but likes it still less than he did years back, and cannot bear it in comparison with Ranelagh. He thinks everything looks poor, flaring, and jaded. "Ah!" says he, with a sort of triumphant sigh, "Ranelagh was a noble place! Such taste, such elegance, such beauty! There was the Duchess of A., the finest woman in England, Sir; and Mrs. L., a mighty fine creature; and Lady Susan what's her name, that had that unfortunate affair with Sir Charles. Sir, they came swimming by you like the swans."

The Old Gentleman is very particular in having his slippers ready for him at the fire, when he comes home. He is also extremely choice in his snuff, and delights to get a fresh box-ful in Tavistock-street, in his way to the theatre. His box is a curiosity from India. He calls favourite young ladies by their Christian names, however slightly acquainted with them; and has a privilege of saluting all brides, mothers, and indeed every species of lady, on the least holiday occasion. If the husband, for instance, has met with a piece of luck, he instantly moves forward, and gravely kisses the wife on the cheek. The wife then says, "My niece, Sir, from the country"; and he kisses the niece. The niece, seeing her cousin biting her lips at the joke, says, "My cousin Harriet, Sir"; and he kisses the cousin. He "never recollects such weather," except during the "Great Frost," or when he rode down with "Jack Skrimshire to Newmarket." He grows young again in his little grand-children, especially the one which he thinks most like himself; which is the handsomest. Yet he likes best perhaps the one most resembling his wife; and will sit with him on his lap, holding his hand in silence, for a quarter of an hour together. He plays most tricks with the former, and makes him sneeze. He asks little boys in general who was the father of Zebedee's children. If his grand-sons are at school, he often goes to see them; and makes them blush by telling the master or the upper-scholars, that they are fine boys, and of a precocious genius. He is much struck when an old acquaintance dies, but adds that he lived too fast; and that poor Bob was a sad dog in his youth; "a very sad dog, Sir; mightily set upon a short life and a merry one."

When he gets very old indeed, he will sit for whole evenings, and say little or nothing; but informs you, that there is Mrs. Jones (the housekeeper),—"*She*'ll talk."

WALKS HOME BY NIGHT IN BAD WEATHER.
WATCHMEN

THE readers of these our lucubrations need not be informed that we keep no carriage. The consequence is, that being visitors of the theatre, and having some inconsiderate friends who grow pleasanter and pleasanter till one in the morning, we are great walkers home by night; and this has made us great acquaint-

ances of watchmen, moonlight, *mud*-light, and other accompaniments of that interesting hour. Luckily we are fond of a walk by
night. It does not always do us good; but that is not the fault of the
hour, but our own, who ought to be stouter; and therefore we extract what good we can out of our necessity, with becoming temper.
It is a remarkable thing in nature, and one of the good-naturedest
things we know of her, that the mere fact of looking about us, and
being conscious of what is going on, is its own reward, if we do
but notice it in good-humour. Nature is a great painter (and art
and society are among her works), to whose minutest touches the
mere fact of becoming alive is to enrich the stock of our enjoyments.

We confess there are points liable to cavil in a walk home by
night in February. Old umbrellas have their weak sides; and the
quantity of mud and rain may surmount the picturesque. Mistaking a soft piece of mud for hard, and so filling your shoe with
it, especially at setting out, must be acknowledged to be "aggravating." But then you ought to have boots. There are sights, indeed, in the streets of London, which can be rendered pleasant by
no philosophy; things too grave to be talked about in our present
paper; but we must premise, that our walk leads us out of town,
and through streets and suburbs of by no means the worst description. Even there we may be grieved if we will. The farther the
walk into the country, the more tiresome we may choose to find it;
and when we take it purely to oblige others, we must allow, as in
the case of a friend of ours, that generosity itself on two sick legs
may find limits to the notion of virtue being its own reward, and
reasonably "curse those comfortable people" who, by the lights
in their windows, are getting into their warm beds, and saying to
one another, "Bad thing to be out of doors to-night."

Supposing, then, that we are in a reasonable state of health and
comfort in other respects, we say that a walk home at night has its
merits, if you choose to meet with them. The worst part of it is
the setting out,—the closing of the door upon the kind faces that
part with you. But their words and looks, on the other hand, may
set you well off. We have known a word last us all the way home,
and a look make a dream of it. To a lover, for instance, no walk
can be bad. He sees but one face in the rain and darkness; the same
that he saw by the light in the warm room. This ever accompanies

him, looking in his eyes; and if the most pitiable and spoilt face in the world should come between them, startling him with the saddest mockery of love, he would treat it kindly for her sake. But this is a begging of the question. A lover does not walk. He is sensible neither to the pleasures nor pains of walking. He treads on air; and in the thick of all that seems inclement, has an avenue of light and velvet spread for him, like a sovereign prince.

To resume, then, like men of this world. The advantage of a late hour is, that everything is silent, and the people fast in their beds. This gives the whole world a tranquil appearance. Inanimate objects are no calmer than passions and cares now seem to be, all laid asleep. The human being is motionless as the house or the tree; sorrow is suspended; and you endeavour to think that love only is awake. Let not readers of true delicacy be alarmed, for we mean to touch profanely upon nothing that ought to be sacred; and as we are for thinking the best on these occasions, it is of the best love we think; love of no heartless order, and such only as ought to be awake with the stars.

As to cares, and curtain-lectures, and such-like abuses of the tranquillity of night, we call to mind, for their sakes, all the sayings of the poets and others, about "balmy sleep," and the soothing of hurt minds, and the weariness of sorrow, which drops into forgetfulness. The great majority are certainly "fast as a church" by the time we speak of; and for the rest, we are among the workers who have been sleepless for their advantage; so we take out our licence to forget them for the time being. The only thing that shall remind us of them is the red lamp, shining afar over the apothecary's door; which, while it does so, reminds us also that there is help for them to be had. I see him now, the pale blinker, suppressing the conscious injustice of his anger at being roused by the apprentice, and fumbling himself out of the house, in hoarseness and great-coat, resolved to make the sweetness of the Christmas bill indemnify him for the bitterness of the moment.

But we shall be getting too much into the interior of the houses. By this time the hackney-coaches have left all the stands—a good symptom of their having got their day's money. Crickets are heard, here and there, amidst the embers of some kitchen. A dog follows us. Will nothing make him "go along"? We dodge him in vain; we run; we stand and "hish!" at him, accompanying the prohibi-

tion with dehortatory gestures, and an imaginary picking up of a
stone. We turn again, and there he is, vexing our skirts. He even
forces us into an angry doubt whether he will not starve, if we do
not let him go home with us. Now if we could but lame him without being cruel; or if we were only an overseer, or a beadle, or a
dealer in dog-skin; or a political economist, to think dogs unnecessary. Oh! come; he has turned a corner; he is gone; we think we
see him trotting off at a distance, thin and muddy; and our heart
misgives us. But it was not our fault; we were not "hishing" at
the time. His departure was lucky, for he had got our enjoyments
into a dilemma; our "article" would not have known what to do
with him. These are the perplexities to which your sympathizers
are liable. We resume our way, independent and alone; for we have
no companion this time, except our never-to-be-forgotten and
ethereal companion, the reader. A real arm within another's puts
us out of the pale of walking that is to be made good. It is good
already. A fellow-pedestrian is company; is the party you have
left; you talk and laugh, and there is no longer anything to be
contended with. But alone, and in bad weather, and with a long
way to go, here is something for the temper and spirits to grapple
with and turn to account; and accordingly we are booted and buttoned up, an umbrella over our heads, the rain pelting upon it,
and the lamp-light shining in the gutters; "mud-shine," as an
artist of our acquaintance used to call it, with a gusto of reprobation. Now, walk cannot well be worse; and yet it shall be nothing
if you meet it heartily. There is a pleasure in overcoming obstacles;
mere action is something; imagination is more; and the spinning
of the blood, and vivacity of the mental endeavour, act well upon
one another, and gradually put you in a state of robust consciousness and triumph. Every time you set down your leg, you have a
respect for it. The umbrella is held in the hand like a roaring trophy.

We are now reaching the country: the fog and rain are over;
and we meet our old friends the watchmen, staid, heavy, indifferent, more coat than man, pondering, yet not pondering, old but
not reverend, immensely useless. No; useless they are not; for the
inmates of the houses think them otherwise, and in that imagination
they do good. We do not pity the watchmen as we used. Old age
often cares little for regular sleep. They could not be sleeping perhaps if they were in their beds; and certainly they would not be

earning. What sleep they get is perhaps sweeter in the watch-box, —a forbidden sweet; and they have a sense of importance, and a claim on the persons in-doors, which, together with the amplitude of their coating, and the possession of the box itself, make them feel themselves, not without reason, to be "somebody." They are peculiar and official. Tomkins is a cobbler as well as they; but then he is no watchman. He cannot speak to "things of night"; nor bid any man "stand in the King's name." He does not get fees and gratitude from the old, the infirm, and the drunken; nor "let gentlemen go"; nor is he "a parish-man." The churchwardens don't speak to him. If he put himself ever so much in the way of "the great plumber," he would not say "How do you find your-self, Tomkins?"—"An ancient and quiet watchman." Such he was in the time of Shakespeare, and such he is now. Ancient, because he cannot help it; and quiet, because he will not help it, if possible; his object being to procure quiet on all sides, his own in-cluded. For this reason he does not make too much noise in crying the hour, nor is offensively particular in his articulation. No man shall sleep the worse for him, out of a horrid sense of the word "three." The sound shall be three, four, or one, as suits their mu-tual convenience.

Yet characters are to be found even among watchmen. They are not all mere coat, and lump, and indifference. By the way, what do they think of in general? How do they vary the monotony of their ruminations from one to two, and from two to three, and so on? Are they comparing themselves with the unofficial cobbler; thinking of what they shall have for dinner to-morrow; or what they were about six years ago; or that their lot is the hardest in the world, as insipid old people are apt to think, for the pleasure of grumbling; or that it has some advantages nevertheless, besides fees; and that if they are not in bed, their wife is?

Of characters, or rather varieties among watchmen, we remem-ber several. One was a Dandy Watchman, who used to ply at the top of Oxford-street, next the park. We called him the dandy, on account of his utterance. He had a mincing way with it, pronounc-ing the *a* in the word "past" as it is in *hat*,—making a little pre-paratory hem before he spoke, and then bringing out his "păst ten" in a style of genteel indifference; as if, upon the whole, he was of that opinion.

Another was the Metallic Watchman, who paced the same street towards Hanover-square, and had a clang in his voice like a trumpet. He was a voice and nothing else; but any difference is something in a watchman.

A third, who cried the hour in Bedford-square, was remarkable in his calling for being abrupt and loud. There was a fashion among his tribe just come up at that time, of omitting the words "past" and "o'clock," and crying only the number of the hour. I know not whether a recollection I have of his performance one night is entire matter of fact, or whether any subsequent fancies of what might have taken place are mixed up with it; but my impression is, that as I was turning the corner into the square with a friend, and was in the midst of a discussion in which numbers were concerned, we were suddenly startled, as if in solution of it, by a brief and tremendous outcry of—ONE. This paragraph ought to have been at the bottom of the page, and the word printed abruptly round the corner.

A fourth watchman was a very singular phenomenon, a *Reading* Watchman. He had a book, which he read by the light of his lantern; and instead of a pleasant, gave you a very uncomfortable idea of him. It seemed cruel to pitch amidst so many discomforts and privations one who had imagination enough to wish to be relieved from them. Nothing but a sluggish vacuity befits a watchman.

But the oddest of all was the *Sliding* Watchman. Think of walking up a street in the depth of a frosty winter, with long ice in the gutters, and sleet over head, and then figure to yourself a sort of bale of a man in white coming sliding towards you with a lantern in one hand, and an umbrella over his head. It was the oddest mixture of luxury and hardship, of juvenility and old age! But this looked agreeable. Animal spirits carry everything before them; and our invincible friend seemed a watchman for Rabelais. Time was run at and butted by him like a goat. The slide seemed to bear him half through the night at once; he slipped from out of his box and his common-places at one rush of a merry thought, and seemed to say, "Everything's in imagination;—here goes the whole weight of my office."

But we approach our home. How still the trees! How deliciously asleep the country! How beautifully grim and nocturnal this

wooded avenue of ascent, against the cold white sky! The watchmen and patroles, which the careful citizens have planted in abundance within a mile of their doors, salute us with their "good
mornings";—not so welcome as we pretend; for we ought not to
be out so late; and it is one of the assumptions of these fatherly
old fellows to remind us of it. Some fowls, who have made a strange
roost in a tree, flutter as we pass them;—another pull up the hill,
unyielding; a few strides on a level; and *there* is the light in the
window, the eye of the warm soul of the house,—one's home.
How particular, and yet how universal, is that word; and how surely
does it deposit every one for himself in his own nest!

DEATHS OF LITTLE CHILDREN

A GRECIAN philosopher being asked why he wept for the
death of his son, since the sorrow was in vain, replied,
"I weep on that account." And his answer became his
wisdom. It is only for sophists to contend, that we, whose eyes
contain the fountains of tears, need never give way to them.
It would be unwise not to do so on some occasions. Sorrow unlocks them in her balmy moods. The first bursts may be bitter
and overwhelming; but the soil, on which they pour, would be
worse without them. They refresh the fever of the soul—the dry
misery which parches the countenance into furrows, and renders
us liable to our most terrible "flesh-quakes."

There are sorrows, it is true, so great, that to give them some of
the ordinary vents is to run a hazard of being overthrown. These
we must rather strengthen ourselves to resist, or bow quietly and
drily down, in order to let them pass over us, as the traveller does
the wind of the desert. But where we feel that tears would relieve
us, it is false philosophy to deny ourselves at least that first refreshment; and it is always false consolation to tell people that
because they cannot help a thing, they are not to mind it. The
true way is, to let them grapple with the unavoidable sorrow, and
try to win it into gentleness by a reasonable yielding. There are
griefs so gentle in their very nature, that it would be worse than
false heroism to refuse them a tear. Of this kind are the deaths of
infants. Particular circumstances may render it more or less ad-
visable to indulge in grief for the loss of a little child; but, in general,

parents should be no more advised to repress their first tears on such an occasion, than to repress their smiles towards a child surviving, or to indulge in any other sympathy. It is an appeal to the same gentle tenderness; and such appeals are never made in vain. The end of them is an acquittal from the harsher bonds of affliction—from the tying down of the spirit to one melancholy idea.

It is the nature of tears of this kind, however strongly they may gush forth, to run into quiet waters at last. We cannot easily, for the whole course of our lives, think with pain of any good and kind person whom we have lost. It is the divine nature of their qualities to conquer pain and death itself; to turn the memory of them into pleasure; to survive with a placid aspect in our imaginations. We are writing, at this moment just opposite a spot which contains the grave of one inexpressibly dear to us. We see from our window the trees about it, and the church spire. The green fields lie around. The clouds are travelling over-head, alternately taking away the sunshine and restoring it. The vernal winds, piping of the flowery summer-time, are nevertheless calling to mind the far-distant and dangerous ocean, which the heart that lies in that grave had many reasons to think of. And yet the sight of this spot does not give us pain. So far from it, it is the existence of that grave which doubles every charm of the spot; which links the pleasures of our childhood and manhood together; which puts a hushing tenderness in the winds, and a patient joy upon the landscape; which seems to unite heaven and earth, mortality and immortality, the grass of the tomb and the grass of the green field; and gives a more maternal aspect to the whole kindness of nature. It does not hinder gaiety itself. Happiness was what its tenant, through all her troubles, would have diffused. To diffuse happiness, and to enjoy it, is not only carrying on her wishes, but realising her hopes; and gaiety, freed from its only pollutions, malignity and want of sympathy, is but a child playing about the knees of its mother.

The remembered innocence and endearments of a child stand us in stead of virtues that have died older. Children have not exercised the voluntary offices of friendship; they have not chosen to be kind and good to us; nor stood by us, from conscious will, in the hour of adversity. But they have shared their pleasures and pains with us as well as they could; the interchange of good offices between us has, of necessity, been less mingled with the troubles of the world; the sorrow arising from their death is the only one which we can associate with their memories. These are happy thoughts that cannot die. Our loss may always render them pensive; but they will not always be painful. It is a part of the benignity of Nature that pain does not survive like pleasure, at any time, much less where the cause of it is an innocent one. The smile will remain reflected by memory, as the moon reflects the light upon us when the sun has gone into heaven.

When writers like ourselves quarrel with earthly pain (we mean writers of the same intentions, without implying, of course, anything about abilities or otherwise), they are misunderstood if they are supposed to quarrel with pains of every sort. This would be idle and effeminate. They do not pretend, indeed, that humanity might not wish, if it could, to be entirely free from pain; for it endeavours at all times to turn pain into pleasure: or at least to set off the one with the other, to make the former a zest and the latter a refreshment. The most unaffected dignity of suffering does this; and, if wise, acknowledges it. The greatest benevolence towards others, the most unselfish relish of their pleasures, even at its own expense, does but look to increasing the general stock of happiness, though content, if it could, to have its identity swallowed up in that splendid contemplation. We are far from meaning that this is to be called selfishness. We are far, indeed, from thinking so, or of so confounding words. But neither is it to be called pain when most unselfish, if disinterestedness be truly understood. The pain that is in it softens into pleasure, as the darker hue of the rainbow melts into the brighter. Yet even if a harsher line is to be drawn between the pain and pleasure of the most unselfish mind (and ill-health, for instance, may draw it), we should not quarrel with it if it contributed to the general mass of comfort, and were of a nature which general kindliness could not avoid. Made as we are, there are certain pains without which it would be difficult to conceive certain great and overbalancing pleasures. We may conceive it possible for beings to be made entirely happy; but in our composition something of pain seems to be a necessary ingredient, in order that the materials may turn to as fine account as possible, though our clay, in the course of ages and experience, may be refined more and more. We may get rid of the worst earth, though not of earth itself.

Now the liability to the loss of children—or rather what renders us sensible of it, the occasional loss itself—seems to be one of these necessary bitters thrown into the cup of humanity. We do not mean that every one must lose one of his children in order to enjoy the rest; or that every individual loss afflicts us in the same proportion. We allude to the deaths of infants in general. These might be as few as we could render them. But if none at all ever took place, we should regard every little child as a man or woman secured; and it will easily be conceived what a world of endearing cares and hopes this security would endanger. The very idea of infancy would lose its continuity with us. Girls and boys would be future men and women, not present children. They would have attained their full growth in our imaginations, and might as well have been men and women at once. On the other hand, those who have lost an infant, are never, as it were, without an infant child. They are the only persons who, in one sense, retain it always; and they furnish their neighbours with the same idea.[1] The other children grow up to manhood and womanhood, and suffer all the changes of mortality. This one alone is rendered an immortal child. Death has arrested it with his kindly harshness, and blessed it into an eternal image of youth and innocence.

Of such as these are the pleasantest shapes that visit our fancy and our hopes. They are the ever-smiling emblems of joy; the prettiest pages that wait upon imagination. Lastly, "Of these are the kingdom of heaven." Wherever there is a province of that benevolent and all-accessible empire, whether on earth or elsewhere, such are the gentle spirits that must inhabit it. To such simplicity, or the resemblance of it, must they come. Such must be the ready confidence of their hearts and creativeness of their fancy. And so ignorant must they be of the "knowledge of good and evil," losing their discernment of that self-created trouble, by enjoying the garden before them, and not being ashamed of what is kindly and innocent.

[1] "I sighed," said old Captain Bolton, "when I envied you the two bonnie children, but I sigh not now to call either the monk or the soldier mine own!"—*Monastery*, vol. iii, p. 341.

SHAKING HANDS

AMONG the first things which we remember noticing in the manners of people, were two errors in the custom of shaking hands. Some, we observed, grasped everybody's hand alike—with an equal fervour of grip. You would have thought that Jenkins was the best friend they had in the world; but on succeeding to the squeeze, though a slight acquaintance, you found it equally flattering to yourself; and on the appearance of somebody else (whose name, it turned out, the operator had forgotten), the crush was no less complimentary:—the face was as earnest, and beaming, the "glad to see you" was syllabical and sincere, and the shake as close, as long, and as rejoicing, as if the semi-unknown was a friend come home from the Deserts.

On the other hand, there would be a gentleman, now and then, as coy of his hand, as if he were a prude, or had a whitlow. It was in vain that your pretensions did not go beyond the "civil salute" of the ordinary shake; or that being introduced to him in a friendly manner, and expected to shake hands with the rest of the company, you could not in decency omit his. His fingers, half coming out and half retreating, seemed to think that you were going to do them a mischief; and when you got hold of them, the whole shake was on your side; the other hand did but proudly or pensively acquiesce—there was no knowing which; you had to sustain it, as you might a lady's in handing her to a seat; and it was an equal perplexity to know whether to shake or to let it go. The one seemed a violence done to the patient, the other an awkward responsibility brought upon yourself. You did not know, all the evening, whether you were not an object of dislike to the person; till, on the party's breaking up, you saw him behave like an equally ill-used gentleman to all who practised the same unthinking civility.

Both these errors, we think, might as well be avoided; but, of the two, we must say we prefer the former. If it does not look so much like particular sincerity, it looks more like general kindness; and if those two virtues are to be separated (which they assuredly need not be, if considered without spleen), the world can better afford to dispense with an unpleasant truth than a gratuitous humanity. Besides, it is more difficult to make sure of the one than to practise the other, and kindness itself is the best of all truths. As long as we are sure of that, we are sure of something, and of something pleasant. It is always the best end, if not in every instance the most logical means.

This manual shyness is sometimes attributed to modesty, but never, we suspect, with justice, unless it be that sort of modesty whose fear of committing itself is grounded in pride. Want of address is a better reason; but this particular instance of it would be grounded in the same feeling. It always implies a habit either of pride or mistrust. We have met with two really kind men who evinced this soreness of hand. Neither of them, perhaps, thought himself inferior to anybody about him, and both had good reason to think highly of themselves, but both had been sanguine men contradicted in their early hopes. There was a plot to meet the hand of one of them with a fish-slice, in order to show him the disadvantage to which he put his friends by that flat mode of salutation; but the conspirator had not the courage to do it. Whether he heard of the intention we know not, but shortly afterwards he took very kindly to a shake. The other was the only man of a warm set of politicians who remained true to his first hopes of mankind. He was impatient at the change in his companions, and at the folly and inattention of the rest; but though his manner became cold, his consistency remained warm, and this gave him a right to be as strange as he pleased.

ON THE TALKING OF NONSENSE

THERE is no greater mistake in the world than the looking upon every sort of nonsense as want of sense. Nonsense in the bad sense of the word, like certain suspicious ladies, is very fond of bestowing its own appellation,—particularly upon what renders other persons agreeable. But nonsense, in the good sense of the word, is a very sensible thing in its season; and is only confounded with the other by people of a shallow gravity, who cannot afford to joke.

These gentlemen live upon credit, and would not have it enquired into. They are perpetual beggars of the question. They are grave, not because they think, or feel the contrast of mirth, for then they would feel the mirth itself; but because gravity is their safest mode of behaviour. They must keep their minds sitting still, because they are incapable of a motion that is not awkward. They are waxen images among the living;—the deception is undone, if the others stir;—or hollow vessels covered up, which may be taken for full ones:—the collision of wits jars against them, and strikes out their hollowness.

In fact, the difference between nonsense not worth talking, and nonsense worth it, is simply this:—the former is the result of a want of ideas, the latter of a superabundance of them. This is remarkably exemplified by Swift's *Polite Conversation*, in which the dialogue, though intended to be a tissue of the greatest nonsense in request with shallow merriment, is in reality full of ideas, and many of them very humorous; but then they are all commonplace, and have been said so often, that the thing uppermost in your mind is the inability of the speakers to utter a sentence of their own;—they have no ideas at all. Many of the jokes and similes in that treatise are still the current coin of the shallow; though they are now pretty much confined to gossips of an inferior order, and the upper part of the lower classes.

On the other hand, the wildest rattling, as it is called, in which men of sense find entertainment, consists of nothing but a quick and original succession of ideas,—a finding as it were, of something in nothing,—a rapid turning of the hearer's mind to some new face of thought and sparkling imagery. The man of shallow gravity, besides an uneasy half-consciousness that he has nothing of the sort about him, is too dull of perception to see the delicate links between one thought and another; and he takes that for a mere chaos of laughing jargon, in which finer apprehensions perceive as much delightful association, as men of musical taste do in the most tricksome harmonies and accompaniments of Mozart or Beethoven. Between such gravity and such mirth, there is as much difference as between the driest and dreariest psalmody, and that exquisite laughing trio,—E voi ridete,—which is sung in *Cosi Fan Tutte*. A quaker's coat and a garden are not more dissimilar;—nor a death-bell, and the birds after a sunny shower.

It is on such occasions indeed that we enjoy the perfection of what is agreeable in humanity,—the harmony of mind and body,— intellect, and animal spirits. Accordingly the greatest geniuses appear to have been proficients in this kind of nonsense, and to have delighted in dwelling upon it, and attributing it to their favourites. Virgil is no joker, but Homer is; and there is the same difference between their heroes, Æneas and Achilles, the latter of whom is also a player on the harp. Venus, the most delightful of the goddesses, is Philommeides, the laughter-loving;—an epithet, by the bye, which might give a good hint to a number of very respectable ladies, "who love their lords," but who are too apt to let ladies less respectable run away with them. Horace represents Pleasantry as fluttering about Venus in company with Cupid,—

Quem *Jocus* circumvolat, et Cupido;

and these are followed by Youth, the enjoyer of animal spirits, and by Mercury, the god of persuasion. There is the same difference between Tasso and Ariosto as between Virgil and Homer; that is to say, the latter proves his greater genius by a completer and more various hold on the feelings, and has not only a fresher spirit of Nature about him, but a truer, because a happier; for the want of this enjoyment is at once a defect and a deterioration. It is more or less a disease of the blood;—a falling off from the pure and un-contradicted blithesomeness of childhood; a hampering of the mind with the altered nerves;—dust gathered in the watch, and perplexing our passing hours.

It may be thought a begging of the question to mention Anacreon, since he made an absolute business of mirth and enjoyment, and sat down systematically to laugh as well as to drink. But on that very account, perhaps, his case is still more in point; and Plato, one of the gravest, but not the shallowest, of philosophers, gave him the title of the Wise. The disciple of Socrates appears also to have been a great enjoyer of Aristophanes; and the divine Socrates himself was a wit and a joker.

But the divine Shakespeare;—the man to whom we go for everything, and are sure to find it, grave, melancholy, or merry,—what said he to this exquisite kind of nonsense? Perhaps next to his passion for detecting nature, and over-informing it with poetry, he took delight in pursuing a joke; and the lowest scenes of his in this way say more to men whose faculties are fresh about them, and who prefer enjoyment to criticism, than the most doting of commentators can find out. They are instances of his animal spirits, —of his sociality,—of his passion for giving and receiving pleasure, —of his enjoyment of something wiser than wisdom.

The greatest favourites of Shakespeare are made to resemble himself in this particular, Hamlet, Mercutio, Touchstone, Jaques, Richard the Third, and Falstaff, "inimitable Falstaff," are all men of wit and humour, modified according to their different temperaments or circumstances,—some from health and spirits, others from sociality, others from a contrast with their very melancholy. Indeed melancholy itself, with the profoundest intellects, will rarely be found to be anything else than a sickly temperament, induced or otherwise, preying in its turn upon the disappointed expectations of pleasure,—upon the contradiction of hopes, which this world is not made to realise, though (let us never forget) it is made, as they themselves prove, to suggest. Some of Shakespeare's characters, as Mercutio and Benedick, are almost entirely made up of wit and animal spirits; and delightful fellows they are; and ready, from their very taste, to perform the most serious and manly offices. Most of his women too have an abundance of natural vivacity. Desdemona herself is so pleasant of intercourse in every way, that upon the principle of the respectable mistakes above-mentioned, the Moor, when he grows jealous, is tempted to think it a proof of her want of honesty. But we must make Shakespeare speak for himself, or we shall not know how to be silent on this subject. What a description is that which he gives of a man of mirth,—or a mirth, too, which he has expressly stated to be within the limit of what is becoming? It is in *Love's Labour Lost:*—

> "A merrier man,
> Within the limit of becoming mirth,
> I never spent an hour's talk withall,
> His eye begets occasion for his wit:
> For every object that the one doth catch,
> The other turns to a mirth-moving jest;
> Which his fair tongue, conceit's expositor,
> Delivers in such apt and gracious words,
> That aged ears play truant at his tales,
> And younger hearings are quite ravished;
> So sweet and voluble is his discourse."

We have been led into these reflections, partly to introduce the conclusion of this article,—partly from being very fond of a joke ourselves, and so making our self-love as proud as possible,—and partly from having spent some most agreeable hours the other evening with a company, the members of which had all the right to be grave and disagreeable that rank and talent are supposed to confer, and yet from the very best sense or forgetfulness of both, were as lively and entertaining to each other as boys. Not one of them perhaps but had his cares,—one or two, of no ordinary description; but what then? These are the moments, if we can take advantage of them, when sorrows are shared, even unconsciously;—moments, when melancholy intermits her fever, and hope takes a leap into enjoyment;—when the pilgrim of life, if he cannot lay aside his burden, forgets it in meeting his fellows about a fountain; and soothes his weariness and his resolution with the sparkling sight, and the noise of the freshness.

To come to our anticlimax, for such we are afraid it must be called after all this grave sentiment and mention of authorities. The following dialogue is the substance of a joke (never meant for its present place) that was started the other day upon a late publication. The name of the book it is not necessary to mention, especially as it was pronounced to be one of the driest that had appeared for years. We cannot answer for the sentences being put to their proper speakers. The friends, whom we value most, happen to be great hunters in this way; and the reader may look upon the thing as a specimen of a joke run down, or of the sort of nonsense above mentioned; so that he will take due care how he professes not to relish it. We must also advertise him, that a proper quantity of giggling and laughter must be supposed to be interspersed, till towards the end it gradually becomes too great to go on with.

A. Did you ever see a such book?

B. Never, in all my life. It's as dry as a chip.

A. As a chip? A chip's a slice of orange to it.

B. Ay, or a wet sponge.

A. Or a cup in a currant tart.

B. Ah, ha; so it is. You feel as if you were fingering a brick-bat.

A. It makes you feel dust in the eyes.

B. It is impossible to shed a tear over it. The lachrymal organs are dried up.

A. If you shut it hastily, it is like clapping together a pair of fresh-cleaned gloves.

B. Before you have got far in it, you get up to look at your tongue in a glass.

A. It absolutely makes you thirsty.

B. Yes:—if you take it up at breakfast, you drink four cups instead of two.

A. At page 30 you call for beer.

B. They say it made a Reviewer take to drinking.

A. They have it lying on the table at inns to make you drink double. The landlord says, "A new book, Sir," and goes out to order two neguses.

B. It dries up everything so, it has ruined the draining business.

A. There is an Act of Parliament to forbid people's passing a vintner's with it in their pockets.

B. The Dutch subscribed for it to serve them instead of dykes.

INEXHAUSTIBILITY OF THE SUBJECT OF CHRISTMAS

SO many things have been said of late years about Christmas, that it is supposed by some there is no saying more. Oh they of little faith! What? do they suppose that everything has been said that *can* be said, about any one Christmas thing?

About beef, for instance?

About plum-pudding?

About mince-pie?

About holly?

About ivy?

About rosemary?

About mistletoe? (Good God! what an immense number of things remain to be said about mistletoe?)

About Christmas-eve?

About hunt-the-slipper?

About hot-cockles?

About blind-man's-buff?

About shoeing the wild-mare?

About thread-the-needle?

About he-can-do-little-that-can't-do-this?

About puss-in-the-corner?

About snapdragon?

About forfeits?

About Miss Smith?
About the bell-man?
About the waits?
About chilblains?
About carols?
About the fire?
About the block on it?
About school-boys?
About their mothers?
About Christmas-boxes?
About turkeys?
About Hogmany?
About goose-pie?
About mumming?
About saluting the apple-trees?
About brawn?
About plum-porridge?
About hobby-horse?
About hoppings?
About wakes?
About "Feed-the-dove"?
About hackins?
About yule-doughs?
About going-a-gooding?
About loaf-stealing?
About *julklaps?* (Who has exhausted that subject, we should like to know?)
About wad-shooting?
About elder-wine?
About pantomimes?
About cards?
About New-Year's day?
About gifts?
About wassail?
About twelfth-cake?
About king and queen?
About characters?
About eating too much?
About aldermen?

About the doctor?
About all being in the wrong?
About Charity?
About all being in the right?
About Faith, Hope, and Endeavour?
About the Greatest Plum-pudding for the Greatest Number?

Esto perpetua; that is, Faith, Hope, and Charity, and Endeavour; and plum-pudding enough, by-and-by, all the year round, for everybody that likes it. Why that should not be the case, we cannot see,—seeing that the earth is big, and human kind teachable, and God very good, and inciting us to do it.—Meantime, gravity apart, we ask anybody whether any of the above subjects are exhausted; and we inform everybody, that all the above customs still exist in some parts of our beloved country, however unintelligible they may have become in others.—But to give a specimen of the non-exhaustion of any one of their topics.

Beef, for example. Now we should like to know who has exhausted the subject of the fine old roast Christmas piece of beef,—from its original appearance in the meadows as part of the noble sultan of the herd, glorious old Taurus, the lord of the sturdy brow and ponderous agility, a sort of thunderbolt of a beast, well chosen by Jove to disguise in, one of Nature's most striking compounds of apparent heaviness and unencumbered activity,—up to its contribution to the noble Christmas dinner, smoking from the spit, and flanked by the outposts of Bacchus. John Bull (cannibalism apart) hails it like a sort of relation. He makes it part of his flesh and blood; glories in it; was named after it; has it served up, on solemn occasions, with music and a hymn, as it was the other day at the royal city dinner:—

> "Oh! the roast beef of old England;
> And oh! the old English roast beef."

"*And* oh!" observe; not merely "oh!" again; but "and" with it; as if, though the same piece of beef, it were also another;—another and the same;—cut, and come again;—making two of one, in order to express intensity and reduplication of satisfaction:—

> "Oh! the roast beef of old England;
> *And* oh! the old English roast beef."

We beg to assure the reader, that a whole essay might be written
on this single point of the Christmas dinner; and "shall we be told"
(as orators exclaim) "and this too in a British land," that the subject is "*exhausted*"! ! !

Then plum-pudding! What a word is that! how plump, and
plump again! How round, and repeated, and plenipotential!
(There are two *p's*, observe, in plenipotential, and so there are in
plum-pudding. We love an exquisite fitness,—a might and wealth
of adaptation.) Why, the whole round cheek of universal childhood
is in the idea of plum-pudding; ay, and the weight of manhood, and
the plenitude of the majesty of city dames. Wealth itself is sym-
bolised by the least of its fruity particles. "A plum" is a city fortune,—a million of money. He (the old boy, who has earned it)

> Put in his thumb,

videlicet, into his pocket,

> And pulls out a plum,
> And says what a "*good man*" am I.

Observe a little boy at a Christmas dinner, and his grandfather
opposite him. What a world of secret similarity there is between
them. How hope in one, and retrospection in the other, and
appetite in both, meet over the same ground of pudding, and understand it to a nicety. How the senior banters the little boy on his
third slice; and how the little boy thinks within himself that he
dines that day as well as the senior. How both look hot, and red,
and smiling, and juvenile. How the little boy is conscious of the
Christmas-box in his pocket (of which indeed the grandfather
jocosely puts him in mind); and how the grandfather is quite as
conscious of the plum, or part of a plum, or whatever fraction it
may be, in his own. How he incites the little boy to love money
and good dinners all his life; and how determined the little boy is
to abide by his advice,—with a secret addition in favour of holidays
and marbles,—to which there is an analogy, in the senior's mind,
on the side of trips to Hastings, and a game at whist. Finally, the
old gentleman sees his own face in the pretty smooth one of the
child; and if the child is not best pleased at his proclamation of the
likeness (in truth, is horrified at it, and thinks it a sort of madness), yet nice observers, who have lived long enough to see the

wonderful changes in people's faces from youth to age, probably discern the thing well enough; and feel a movement of pathos at their hearts, in considering the world of trouble and emotion that is the causer of the changes. *That* old man's face was once like that little boy's! *That* little boy's will be one day like that old man's! What a thought to make us all love and respect one another, if not for our fine qualities, yet, at least, for the trouble and sorrow which we all go through!

Ay, and joy too! for all people have their joys as well as troubles, at one time or another; most likely both together, or in constant alternation; and the greater part of troubles are not the worst things in the world, but only graver forms of the requisite motion of the universe, or workings towards a better condition of things, the greater or less violent according as we give them violence for violence, or respect them like awful but not ill-meaning gods, and entertain them with a rewarded patience.—Grave thoughts, you will say, for Christmas. But no season has a greater right to grave thoughts, in passing; and for that very reason, no season has a greater right to let them pass, and recur to more light ones.

So a noble and merry season to you, my masters; and may we meet, thick and threefold, many a time and oft in blithe yet most thoughtful pages. Fail not to call to mind, in the course of the 25th of this month, that the Divinest Heart that ever walked the earth was born on that day, and then smile and enjoy yourselves for the rest of it, for mirth is also of Heaven's making, and wondrous was the wine-drinking at Galilee.

HAZLITT

WILLIAM HAZLITT (1778–1830), *critic and essayist, was born at Maidstone; he accompanied his father to America (1783–1787); was educated at home until he entered a Unitarian college at Hackney to prepare himself for the ministry. He met Coleridge, and through him, Wordsworth; became much interested in philosophy and art, studying the latter at Paris for a while. Returning to London, he met the Lambs, Godwin, and other literary figures, wrote various political and philosophical essays, served as a reporter, contributed to the periodicals, gave lectures on literary subjects, many of which were later printed. In 1819, he contributed "Table-Talk" to the "London Magazine," and collected subsequently various volumes of essays for publication. In 1808, he had married Sarah Stoddart, but was not happy with her, and the couple was divorced in 1822; a strange love-affair resulted in "Liber Amoris," and a second marriage did not last long. His health gave way in 1827, and he died three years later.*

Quarrelsome, shy, selfish, and keen, he could not forget that he had been brought up a Dissenter. Frequently guided by his antipathies and prejudices, he is at his best in those essays which reveal his tastes.

HAZLITT

ON NICKNAMES

"Hæ nugæ in seria ducunt."

THIS is a more important subject than it seems at first sight. It is as serious in its results as it is contemptible in the means by which those results are brought about. Nicknames for the most part govern the world. The history of politics, of religion, of literature, of morals, and of private life, is too often little less than the history of nicknames. What are half the convulsions of the civilised world, the frequent overthrow of states and kingdoms, the shock and hostile encounter of mighty continents, the battles by sea and land, the intestine commotions, the feuds of the Vitelli and Orsini, of the Guelphs and Gibellines, the civil wars in England, and the League in France, the jealousies and heart-burnings of cabinets and councils, the uncharitable proscriptions of creeds and sects, Turk, Jew, Pagan, Papist and Puritan, Quaker and Methodist,—the persecutions and massacres, the burnings, tortures, imprisonments, and lingering deaths inflicted for a different profession of faith,—but so many illustrations of the power of this principle? Fox's Book of Martyrs, and Neale's History of the Puritans, are comments on the same text. The fires in Smithfield were fanned by nicknames, and a nickname set its seal on the unopened dungeons of the Holy Inquisition. Nicknames are the talismans and spells that collect and set in motion all the combustible part of men's passions and prejudices, which have hitherto played so much more successful a game, and done their work so much more effectually than reason, in all the grand concerns and petty details of human life, and do not yet seem tired of the task assigned them. Nicknames are the convenient portable tools by which they simplify the process of mischief, and get through their job with the least time and trouble. These worthless, unmeaning, irritating, envenomed words of re-

proach are the established signs by which the different compart-
ments of society are ticketed, labelled, and marked out for each
other's hatred and contempt. They are to be had, ready cut and
dry, of all sorts and sizes, wholesale and retail, for foreign exporta-
tion or home consumption, and for all occasions in life. "The
priest calls the lawyer a cheat, the lawyer beknaves the divine."
The Frenchman hates the Englishman because he is an Englishman,
and the Englishman hates the Frenchman for as good a reason.
The Whig hates the Tory, and the Tory the Whig. The Dissenter
hates the Church-of-England-man, and the Church-of-England-
man hates the Dissenter, as if they were of a different species,
because they have a different designation. The Mussulman calls
the worshipper of the Cross "Christian dog," spits in his face,
and kicks him from the pavement, by virtue of a nickname; and
the Papist retorts the indignity upon the Infidel and the Jew by
the same infallible rule of right. In France, they damn Shakespeare
in the lump, by calling him a *barbare;* and we talk of Racine's
verbiage with inexpressible contempt and self-complacency. Among
ourselves, an anti-Jacobin critic denounces a Jacobin poet and his
friends, at a venture, "as infidels and fugitives, who have left
their wives destitute, and their children fatherless"—whether they
have wives and children or not. The unenlightened savage makes
a meal of his enemy's flesh, after reproaching him with the name
of his tribe, because he is differently tattooed; and the literary
cannibal cuts up the character of his opponent by the help of a
nickname. The jest of all this is, that a party nickname is always
a relative term, and has its counter-sign, which has just the same
force and meaning, so that both must be perfectly ridiculous and
insignificant. A Whig implies a Tory; there must be "Malcontents"
as well as "Malignants"; Jacobins and Anti-Jacobins; French and
English. These sort of *noms des guerres* derive all their force from
their contraries. Take away the meaning of the one, and you take
the sting out of the other. They could not exist but upon the
strength of mutual and irreconcileable antipathies; there must be
no love lost between them. What is there in the names themselves
to give them a preference over each other? "Sound them, they do
become the mouth as well; weigh them, they are as heavy; conjure
with them, one will raise a spirit as soon as the other." If there
were not fools and madmen who hated both, there could not be

fools and madmen bigotted to either. I have heard an eminent
character boast that he had done more to produce the late war by
nicknaming Buonaparte "the Corsican," than all the state-papers
and documents on the subject put together. And yet Mr. Southey
asks triumphantly, "Is it to be supposed that it is England, *our*
England, to whom that war was owing?" As if, in a dispute between two countries, the conclusive argument which lies in the
pronoun *our*, belonged only to one of them. I like Shakespeare's
version of the matter better:

> "Hath Britain all the sun that shines? day, night,
> Are they not but in Britain? I' th' world's volume
> *Our* Britain seems as of it, but not in it;
> In a great pool a swan's nest. Prithee think
> There's livers out of Britain."

In all national disputes, it is common to appeal to the numbers on
your side as decisive on the point. If every body in England thought
the late war right, every body in France thought it wrong. There
were ten millions on one side of the question (or rather of the
water), and thirty millions on the other side. That's all. I remember
some one arguing, in justification of our ministers interfering on
that occasion, "That governments would not go to war for nothing;" to which I answered, Then they could not go to war at all,
for, at that rate, neither of them could be in the wrong, and yet
both of them must be in the right, which was absurd. The only
meaning of these vulgar nicknames and party-distinctions, where
they are urged most violently and confidently, is, that others differ
from you in some particular or other (whether it be opinion, dress,
clime, complexion), which you highly disapprove of, forgetting,
that, by the same rule, they have the very same right to be offended
at you because you differ from them. Those who have reason on
their side do not make the most obstinate and furious appeals to
prejudice and abusive language. I know but of one exception to
this general rule, and that is, where the things that excite disgust
are of such a kind that they cannot well be gone into without offence
to decency and good manners; but it is equally certain in this case,
that those who are most shocked at the things are not those who
are most forward to apply the names. A person will not be fond
of repeating a charge, or adverting to a subject, that inflicts a
wound on his own feelings, even for the sake of wounding the

feelings of another. A man should be very sure that he himself is not what he has always in his mouth. The greatest prudes have been often accounted the greatest hypocrites, and a satirist is at best but a suspicious character. The loudest and most unblushing invectives against vice and debauchery will as often proceed from a desire to inflame and pamper the passions of the writer, by raking into a nauseous subject, as from a wish to excite virtuous indignation against it in the public mind, or to reform the individual. To familiarise the mind to gross ideas is not the way to increase your own or the general repugnance to them. But, to return to the subject of nicknames.

The use of this figure of speech is, that it excites a strong idea without requiring any proof. It is a shorthand compendious mode of getting at a conclusion, and never troubling yourself or any body else with the formalities of reasoning or the dictates of common sense. It is superior to all evidence, for it does not rest upon any, and operates with the greatest force and certainty in proportion to the utter want of probability. Belief is only a strong impression, and the malignity or extravagance of the accusation passes for a proof of the crime. "Brevity is the soul of wit;" and of all eloquence a nickname is the most concise, and of all arguments the most unanswerable. It gives *carte blanche* to the imagination, throws the reins on the neck of the passions, and suspends the use of the understanding altogether. It does not stand upon ceremony, on the nice distinctions of right and wrong. It does not wait the slow processes of reason, or stop to unravel the web of sophistry. It takes every thing for granted that serves for nourishment for the spleen. It is instantaneous in its operations. There is nothing to interpose between the effect and it. It is passion without proof, and action without thought,—"the unbought grace of life, the cheap defence of nations." It does not, as Mr. Burke expresses it, "leave the will puzzled, undecided, and sceptical in the moment of action." It is a word and a blow.

> "Bring but a Scotsman frae his hill,
> Clap in his cheek a Highland gill,
> Say such is royal George's will,
>   And there's the foe,
> He has nae thought but how to kill
>   Twa at a blow."

The "No Popery" cry, raised a little while ago, let loose all the lurking spite and prejudice which had lain rankling in the proper receptacles for them for above a century, without any knowledge of the past history of the country which had given rise to them, or any reference to their connection with present circumstances; for the knowledge of the one would have prevented the possibility of their application to the other. Facts present a tangible and definite idea to the mind, a train of causes and consequences, accounting for each other, and leading to a positive conclusion— but no farther. But a nickname is tied down to no such limited service; it is a disposable force, that is almost always perverted to mischief. It clothes itself with all the terrors of uncertain abstraction, and there is no end of the abuse to which it is liable but the cunning of those who employ, or the credulity of those who are gulled by it. It is a reserve of the ignorance, bigotry, and intolerance of weak and vulgar minds, brought up where reason fails, and always ready, at a moment's warning, to be applied to any, the most absurd purposes. If you bring specific charges against a man, you thereby enable him to meet and repel them, if he thinks it worth his while; but a nickname baffles reply, by the very vagueness of the inferences from it, and gives increased activity to the confused, dim, and imperfect notions of dislike connected with it, from their having no settled ground to rest upon. The mind naturally irritates itself against an unknown object of fear or jealousy, and makes up for the blindness of its zeal by an excess of it. We are eager to indulge our hasty feelings to the utmost, lest, by stopping to examine, we should find that there is no excuse for them. The very consciousness of the injustice we may be doing another makes us only the more loud and bitter in our invectives against him. We keep down the admonitions of returning reason, by calling up a double portion of gratuitous and vulgar spite. The will may be said to act with most force *in vacuo;* the passions are the most ungovernable when they are blindfolded. That malignity is always the most implacable which is accompanied with a sense of weakness, because it is never satisfied of its own success or safety. A nickname carries the weight of the pride, the indolence, the cowardice, the ignorance, and the ill-nature of mankind on its side. It acts, by mechanical sympathy, on the nerves of society. Any one who is without character himself may make himself master of the reputation of another by the application of a nickname, as, if you do not mind soiling your fingers, you may always throw dirt on another. No matter how undeserved the imputation, it will stick; for, though it is sport to the bye-standers to see you bespattered, they will not stop to see you wipe out the stains. You are not heard in your own defence; it has no effect, it does not tell, excites no sensation, or it is only felt as a disappointment of their triumph over you. Their passions and prejudices are inflamed by the charge, "as rage with rage doth sympathise;" by vindicating yourself, you merely bring them back to common-sense, which is a very sober, mawkish state. *Give a dog a bad name, and hang him,* is a proverb. "A nickname is the heaviest stone that the devil can throw at a man." It is a bugbear to the imagination, and, though we do not believe it, it still haunts our apprehensions. Let a nickname be industriously applied to our dearest friend, and let us know that it is ever so false and malicious, yet it will answer its end; it connects the person's name and idea with an ugly association, you think of them with pain together, or it requires an effort of indignation or magnanimity on your part to disconnect them; it becomes an uneasy subject, a sore point, and you will sooner desert your friend, or join in the conspiracy against him, than be constantly forced to repel charges without truth or meaning, and have your penetration or character called in question by a rascal. Nay, such is the unaccountable construction of language and of the human mind, that the affixing the most innocent or praiseworthy appellation to any individual or set of individuals, *as a nickname*, has all the effect of the most opprobrious epithets. Thus the cant name "The Talents," was successfully applied as a stigma to the Whigs at one time; it held them up to ridicule, and made them obnoxious to public feeling, though it was notorious to every body that the Whig leaders were "the Talents," and that their adversaries nicknamed them so from real hatred and pretended derision. "The Party" is now substituted for "the Talents," since success has given their own set the monstrous affectation of being men of talents; and the poor Morning Chronicle is persecuted daily as the Party as it formerly stood the brunt (innocently enough) of all the abuse and sarcasms that were showered on the Talents. Call a man short by his Christian name, as Tom or Dick such a one, or by his profession (however respectable) as Canning pelted a noble lord with his left-off title of Doctor,—and you undo him for ever, if he has a reputation to lose. Such is the tenaciousness of spite and ill-nature, or the jealousy of public opinion, even this will be peg enough to hang doubtful innuendos, weighty dilemmas upon. "With so small a web as this will I catch so great a fly as Cassio." The public do not like to see their favourites treated with impertinent familiarity—it lowers the tone of admiration very speedily. It implies that some one stands in no great awe of their idol, and he perhaps may know as much about the matter as they do. It seems as if a man whose name, with some contemptuous abbreviation, is always dinned in the public ear, was distinguished by nothing else. By repeating a man's name in this manner you may soon make him sick of it, and of his life too. Mr. Southey has by this time, I should suppose, a tolerable surfeit of his title of Laureate! Children do not like to be *called out of their names*. It is questioning their personal identity. A writer, who has made his vocabulary rich in nicknames (the late Editor of the Times), thought he had made a great acquisition to his stock, when it was pretended at one time that Bonaparte's real name was not Napoleon but Nicholas. He congratulated himself on this discovery, as a standing jest and a lasting triumph. Yet there was nothing in the name to signify. Nicholas Poussin was an instance of a great man in the last age, and in our own times, have we not Nicholas Vansittart? The same writer has the merit of having carried this figure of speech as far as it would go. He fairly worried his readers into conviction by abuse and nicknames. People surrendered their judgments to escape the persecution of his style, and the disgust and indignation which his incessant violence and vulgarity excited, at last made you hate those who were the objects of it. *Causa causæ causa causati.* He made people sick of a subject by making them sick of his arguments. Yet he attributed the effect he produced to the eloquence of his phraseology and the force of his reasonings!

A parrot may be taught to call names; and if the person who keeps the parrot has a spite to his neighbours, he may give them a great deal of annoyance without much wit, either in the employer or the puppet. The insignificance of the instrument has nothing to do with the efficacy of the means. Hotspur would have had "a *starling* taught to repeat nothing but Mortimer," in the ears of his enemy. Nature, it is said, has given arms to all creatures the most proper to defend themselves, and annoy others: to the lowest she has given the use of nicknames.

There are some droll instances of the effect of proper names combined with circumstances. A young student had come up to London from Cambridge, and went in the evening and planted himself in the pit of the playhouse. He had not been seated long when, in one of the front boxes near him, he discovered one of his college tutors, with whom he felt an immediate and strong desire to claim acquaintance, and called out in a low and respectful voice, "Dr. Topping!" The appeal was, however, ineffectual. He then repeated in a louder tone, but still in an under key, so as not to excite the attention of any one but his friend, "Dr. Topping!" The Doctor took no notice. He then grew more impatient, and repeated "Dr. Topping, Dr. Topping!" two or three times pretty loud, to see whether the Doctor did not or would not hear him. Still the Doctor remained immovable. The joke began at length to get round, and one or two persons, as he continued his invocations of the Doctor's name, joined with him in them; these were reinforced by others calling out, "Dr. Topping! Dr. Topping!" on all sides, so that he could no longer avoid perceiving it, and at length the whole pit rose and roared, "Dr. Topping!" with loud and repeated cries, and the Doctor was forced to retire precipitately, frightened at the sound of his own name. There is sometimes an inconvenience in common as well as uncommon names. On the night that Garrick took his leave of the stage, an inveterate play-goer could not get a seat in any part of the house. At length he went up into the gallery, but found that equally full with the rest. In this extremity a thought struck him, and he called out as loud as he could, "Mr. Smith, you're wanted. Your wife's taken suddenly ill, and you must go home immediately." In an instant, half a dozen persons started up from different parts of the gallery to go out, and the gentleman took possession of the first place that offered. No doubt these persons would be disposed to quarrel with their names and their wives for some time after.

The calling people by their Christian or surnames is a proof of affection, as well as of hatred. They are generally the best good fellows with whom their friends take this sort of liberty. *Diminutives* are titles of endearment. Dr. Johnson's calling Goldsmith

"Goldy" did equal honour to both. It shewed the regard he had for him. This familiarity may perhaps imply a certain want of formal respect; but formal respect is not necessary to, if it is consistent with, cordial friendship. Titles of honour are the reverse of nicknames,—they convey the idea of respect as the others do of contempt, and equally mean little or nothing. Junius's motto, *Stat nominis umbra*, is a very significant one; it might be extended farther. A striking instance of the force of names, standing by themselves, is in the respect felt towards Michael Angelo in this country. We know nothing of him but his name. It is an abstraction of fame and greatness. Our admiration of him supports itself, and our idea of his superiority seems self-evident, because it is attached to his name only. Some of our artists seem trying to puff their names into reputation from an instinctive knowledge of this principle,—by talking incessantly of themselves and doing nothing. It is not, indeed, easy to deny the merit of the works—which they do *not* produce. Those which they have produced are very bad.

THOUGHTS ON TASTE

TASTE is nothing but sensibility to the different degrees and kinds of excellence in the works of art or nature. This definition will perhaps be disputed; for I am aware the general practice is to make it consist in a disposition to find fault. A French man or woman will in general conclude their account of Voltaire's denunciation of Shakespeare and Milton as barbarians, on the score of certain technical improprieties, with assuring you, that "he (Voltaire) had a great deal of taste." It is their phrase, *Il avait beaucoup de goût*. To which the proper answer is, that that might be; but that he did not shew it in this case; as the overlooking great and countless beauties, and being taken up only with petty or accidental blemishes, shews as little strength of understanding as it does refinement or elevation of taste. The French author, indeed, allows of Shakespeare, that "he had found a few pearls on his enormous dunghill." But there is neither truth nor proportion in this sentence, for his works are (to say the least),

> "Rich as the oozy bottom of the sea,
> With sunken wrack and sumless treasuries."

Genius is the power of producing excellence: taste is the power of perceiving the excellence thus produced in its several sorts and degrees, with all their force, refinement, distinctions, and connections. In other words, taste (as it relates to the productions of art) is strictly the power of being properly affected by works of genius. It is the proportioning admiration to power, pleasure to beauty: it is entire sympathy with the finest impulses of the imagination, not antipathy, not indifference to them. The eye of taste may be said to reflect the impressions of real genius, as the even mirror reflects the objects of nature in all their clearness and lustre, instead of distorting or diminishing them;

> "Or like a gate of steel,
> Fronting the sun, receives and renders back
> His figure and his heat."

To take a pride and pleasure in nothing but defects (and those perhaps of the most paltry, obvious, and mechanical kind)—in the disappointment and tarnishing of our faith in substantial excellence, in the proofs of weakness, not of power (and this where there are endless subjects to feed the mind with wonder and increased delight through years of patient thought and fond remembrance), is not a sign of uncommon refinement, but of unaccountable perversion of taste. So, in the case of Voltaire's hypercriticisms on Milton and Shakespeare, the most commonplace and prejudiced admirer of these authors knows, as well as Voltaire can tell him, that it is a fault to make a sea-port (we will say) in Bohemia, or to introduce artillery and gunpowder in the war in Heaven. This is common to Voltaire, and the merest English reader: there is nothing in it either way. But what he differs from us in, and, as it is supposed, greatly to his advantage, and to our infinite shame and mortification, is, that this is all that he perceives, or will hear of in Milton or Shakespeare, and that he either knows, or pretends to know, nothing of that prodigal waste, or studied accumulation of grandeur, truth, and beauty, which are to be found in each of these authors. Now, I cannot think, that, to be dull and insensible to so great and such various excellence,—to have no feeling in unison with it, no latent suspicion of the treasures hid beneath our feet, and which we trample upon with ignorant scorn, to be cut off, as by a judicial blindness, from that universe of thought and imagination that shifts its wondrous pageant before us, to turn aside from the throng and splendour of airy shapes that fancy weaves for our dazzled sight, and to strut and vapour over a little pettifogging blunder in geography or chronology, which a school-boy, or a village pedagogue, would be ashamed to insist upon, is any proof of the utmost perfection of taste, but the contrary. At this rate, it makes no difference whether Shakespeare wrote his works or not, or whether the critic, who "damns him into everlasting redemption" for a single slip of the pen, ever read them;—he is absolved from all knowledge, taste, or feeling, of the different excellencies, and inimitable creations of the poet's pen—from any sympathy with the wanderings and the fate of Imogen, the beauty and tenderness of Ophelia, the thoughtful abstraction of Hamlet; his soliloquy on life may never have given him a moment's pause, or touched his breast with one solitary reflection;—the Witches in Macbeth may "lay their choppy fingers upon their skinny lips" without making any alteration in his pulse,—and Lear's heart may break in vain for him;—he may hear no strange noises in Prospero's island,—and the moonlight that sleeps on beds of flowers, where fairies couch in the Midsummer Night's Dream, may never once have steeped his senses in repose. Nor will it avail Milton to "have built high towers in Heaven," nor to have brought down heaven upon earth, nor that he has made Satan rear his giant form before us, "majestic though in ruin," or decked the bridal-bed of Eve with beauty, or clothed her with innocence, "likest heaven," as she ministered to Adam, and his angel guest. Our critic knows nothing of all this, of beauty or sublimity, of thought or passion, breathed in sweet or solemn sounds, with all the magic of verse "in tones and numbers hit;" he lays his finger on the map, and shews you, that there is no sea-port for Shakespeare's weather-beaten travellers to land at in Bohemia, and takes out a list of mechanical inventions, and proves that gunpowder was not known till long after Milton's battle of the angels; and concludes, that every one who, after these profound and important discoveries, finds anything to admire in these two writers, is a person without taste, or any pretensions to it. By the same rule, a thorough-bred critic might prove that Homer was no poet, and the Odyssey a vulgar performance, because Ulysses makes a pun on the name of Noman. Or some other disciple of the

same literal school might easily set aside the whole merit of Racine's
Athalie, or Molière's École des Femmes, and pronounce these *chef-
d'œuvres* of art barbarous and Gothic, because the characters in
the first address one another (absurdly enough) as *Monsieur* and
Madame, and because the latter is written in rhyme, contrary to
all classical precedent. These little false measures of criticism may
be misapplied and retorted without end, and require to be eked
out by national antipathy or political prejudice to give them currency and weight. Thus it was in war-time that the author of the
"Friend" ventured to lump all the French tragedies together as a
smart collection of epigrams, and that the author of the "Excursion, a poem, being portion [1] of a larger poem, to be named the
Recluse," made bold to call Voltaire a dull prose-writer—with
impunity. Such pitiful quackery is a cheap way of setting up for
exclusive taste and wisdom, by pretending to despise what is most
generally admired, as if nothing could come up to or satisfy that
ideal standard of excellence, of which the person bears about the
select pattern in his own mind. "Not to admire any thing" is as
bad a test of wisdom as it is a rule for happiness. We sometimes
meet with individuals who have formed their whole character on
this maxim, and who ridiculously affect a decided and dogmatical
tone of superiority over others, from an uncommon degree both
of natural and artificial stupidity. They are blind to painting—
deaf to music—indifferent to poetry; and they triumph in the
catalogue of their defects as the fault of these arts, because they
have not sense enough to perceive their own want of perception.
To treat any art or science with contempt, is only to prove your
own incapacity and want of taste for it: to say that what has been
done best in any kind is good for nothing, is to say that the utmost
exertion of human ability is not equal to the lowest, for the produc-

---

[1] Why is the word *portion* here used, as if it were a portion of Scripture?

"Those strains that once did sweet in Zion glide,
He wales a *portion* with judicious care."
                    Cottar's Saturday Night.

Now, Mr. Wordsworth's poems, though not profane, yet neither are they sacred, to
deserve this solemn style, though some of his admirers have gone so far as to compare
them for primitive, patriarchal simplicity, to the historical parts of the Bible. Much has
been said of the merits and defects of this large poem, which is "portion of a larger;"—
perhaps Horace's rule has been a double bar to its success—*Non satis est pulchra poemata
esse, dulcia sunto.* The features of this author's muse want sweetness of expression as well
as regularity of outline.

tions of the lowest are worth something, except by comparison with what is better. When we hear persons exclaiming that the pictures at the Marquis of Stafford's or Mr. Angerstein's, or those at the British Gallery, are a heap of trash, we might tell them that they betray in this a want not of taste only, but of common sense, for that these collections contain some of the finest specimens of the greatest masters, and that *that* must be excellent in the productions of human art, beyond which human genius, in any age or country, has not been able to go. Ask these very fastidious critics what it is that they *do* like, and you will soon find, from tracing out the objects of their secret admiration, that their pretended disdain of first-rate excellence is owing either to ignorance of the last refinements of works of genius, or envy at the general admiration which they have called forth. I have known a furious Phillippic against the faults of shining talents and established reputation subside into complacent approbation of dull mediocrity, that neither tasked the kindred sensibility of its admirer beyond its natural inertness, nor touched his self-love with a consciousness of inferiority; and that, by never attempting original beauties, and never failing, gave no opportunity to intellectual ingratitude to be plausibly revenged for the pleasure or instruction it had reluctantly received. So there are judges who cannot abide Mr. Kean, and think Mr. Young an incomparable actor, for no other reason than because he never shocks them with an idea which they had not before. The only excuse for the over-delicacy and supercilious indifference here described, is when it arises from an intimate acquaintance with, and intense admiration of, other and higher degrees of perfection and genius. A person whose mind has been worked up to a lofty pitch of enthusiasm in this way, cannot perhaps condescend to notice, or be much delighted with inferior beauties; but then neither will he dwell upon, and be preposterously offended with, slight faults. So that the ultimate and only conclusive proof of taste is even here not indifference, but enthusiasm; and before a critic can give himself airs of superiority for what he despises, he must first lay himself open to reprisals, by telling us what he admires. There we may fairly join issue with him. Without this indispensable condition of all true taste, absolute stupidity must be more than on a par with the most exquisite refinement; and the most formidable drawcansir of all would be the most impenetrable blockhead. Thus, if we know that Voltaire's contempt of Shakespeare arose from his idolatry of Racine, this may excuse him in a national point of view; but he has no longer any advantage over us; and we must console ourselves as well as we can for Mr. Wordsworth's not allowing us to laugh at the wit of Voltaire, by laughing now and then at the only author whom he is known to understand and admire! [1]

THE SAME SUBJECT CONTINUED

INSTEAD of making a disposition to find fault a proof of taste, I would reverse the rule, and estimate every one's pretensions to taste by the degree of their sensibility to the highest and most various excellence. An indifference to less degrees of excellence is only excusable as it arises from a knowledge and admiration of higher ones; and a readiness in the detection of faults should pass for refinement only as it is owing to a quick sense and impatient love of beauties. In a word, fine taste consists in sympathy, not in antipathy; and the rejection of what is bad is only to be accounted a virtue when it implies a preference of and attachment to what is better.

There is a certain point, which may be considered as the highest point of perfection at which the human faculties can arrive in the conception and execution of certain things: to be able to reach this point in reality is the greatest proof of genius and power; and I imagine that the greatest proof of taste is given in being able to appreciate it when done. For instance, I have heard (and I can believe) that Madame Catalani's manner of singing "Hope told a flattering tale," was the perfection of singing; and I cannot conceive that it would have been the perfection of taste to have thought nothing at all of it. There was, I understand, a sort of fluttering of the voice and a breathless palpitation of the heart (like the ruffling of the feathers of the robin-redbreast), which completely gave back all the uneasy and thrilling voluptuousness of the sentiment; and I contend that the person on whom not a particle of

---

[1] A French teacher, in reading Titus and Berenice with an English pupil, used to exclaim, in raptures, at the best passages, "What have you in Shakespeare equal to this?" This showed that he had a taste for Racine, and a power of appreciating his beauties, though he might want an equal taste for Shakespeare.

this expression was lost (or would have been lost, if it had even been finer), into whom the tones of sweetness or tenderness sink deeper and deeper as they approach the farthest verge of ecstacy or agony, he who has an ear attuned to the trembling harmony, and a heart "pierceable" by pleasure's finest point, is the best judge of music,—not he who remains insensible to the matter himself, or, if you point it out to him, asks, "What of it?" I fancied that I had a triumph some time ago, over a critic and connoisseur of music, who thought little of the minuet in Don Giovanni; but the same person redeemed his pretensions to musical taste in my opinion by saying of some passage in Mozart, "This is a soliloquy equal to any in Hamlet." In hearing the accompaniment in the Messiah of angels' voices to the shepherds keeping watch at night, who has the most taste and delicacy, he who listens in silent rapture to the silver sounds, as they rise in sweetness and soften into distance, drawing the soul from earth to heaven, and making it partaker of the music of the spheres, or he who remains deaf to the summons, and remarks that it is an allegorical conceit? Which would Händel have been most pleased with, the man who was seen standing at the performance of the Coronation anthem in Westminster Abbey, with his face bathed in tears, and mingling "the drops which sacred joy had engendered" with that ocean of circling sound, or with him who sat with frigid, critical aspect, his heart untouched and his looks unaltered as the marble statue on the wall? [1] Again, if any one, in looking at Rembrandt's picture of Jacob's Dream, should not be struck with the solemn awe that surrounds it, and with the dazzling flights of angels' wings like steps of golden light, emanations of flame or spirit hovering between earth and sky, and should observe very wisely that Jacob was thrown in one corner of the picture like a bundle of clothes, without power, form, or motion, and should think this a defect, I should say that such a critic might possess great knowledge of the mechanical part of painting, but not an

[1] It is a fashion among the scientific or pedantic part of the musical world to decry Miss Stephens's singing as feeble and insipid. This it is to take things by their contraries. Her excellence does not lie in force or contrast, but in sweetness and simplicity. To give only one instance. Any person who does not feel the beauty of her singing the lines in Artaxerxes, "What was my pride is now my shame," &c., in which the notes seem to fall from her lips like languid drops from the bending flower, and her voice flutters and dies away with the expiring conflict of passion in her bosom, may console himself with the possession of other faculties, but assuredly he has no ear for music.

atom of feeling or imagination.[1] Or who is it that, in looking at the productions of Raphael or Titian, is the person of true taste? He who finds what there is, or he who finds what there is not in each? Not he who picks a petty vulgar quarrel with the colouring of Raphael or the drawing of Titian is the true critic and judicious spectator, but he who broods over the expression of the one till it takes possession of his soul, and who dwells on the tones and hues of the other till his eye is saturated with truth and beauty, for by this means he moulds his mind to the study and reception of what is most perfect in form and colour, instead of letting it remain empty, "swept and garnished," or rather a dull blank, with "knowledge at each entrance quite shut out." He who cavils at the want of drawing in Titian is not the most sensible to it in Raphael; instead of that, he only insists on his want of colouring. He who is offended at Raphael's hardness and monotony is not delighted with the soft, rich pencilling of Titian; he only takes care to find fault with him for wanting that which, if he possessed it in the highest degree, he would not admire or understand. And this is easy to be accounted for. First, such a critic has been told what to do, and follows his instructions. Secondly, to perceive the height of any excellence, it is necessary to have the most exquisite sense of that kind of excellence through all its gradations: to perceive the want of any excellence, it is merely necessary to have a negative or abstract notion of the thing, or perhaps only of the name. Or, in other words, any the most crude and mechanical idea of a given quality is a measure of positive deficiency, whereas none but the most refined idea of the same quality can be a standard of superlative merit. To distinguish the finest characteristics of Titian or Raphael, to go along with them in their imitation of Nature, is to be so far like them: to be occupied only with that in which they fell short of others, instead of that in which they soared above them, shows a vulgar, narrow capacity, insensible to any thing beyond mediocrity, and an ambition still more grovelling. To be

[1] There is a very striking and spirited picture of this subject by an ingenious living artist (Mr. Alston), in the present exhibition of the Royal Academy. The academic skill in it is admirable, and many of the forms are truly elegant and beautiful; but I may be permitted to add, that the scene (as he represents it) too much resembles the courtly designs of Vitruvius or Palladio, rather than "a temple not made with hands, eternal in the heavens"; and that the angels seem rather preparing to dance a minuet or grand ballet on the marble pavement which they tread, than descending the air in a dream of love, of hope, and gratitude.

dazzled by admiration of the greatest excellence, and of the highest works of genius, is natural to the best capacities, and the best natures; envy and dulness are most apt to detect minute blemishes and unavoidable inequalities, as we see the spots in the sun by having its rays blunted by mist or smoke. It may be asked, then, whether mere extravagance and enthusiasm are proofs of taste? And I answer, no, where they are without reason and knowledge. Mere sensibility is not true taste, but sensibility to real excellence is. To admire and be wrapt up in what is trifling or absurd, is a proof of nothing but ignorance or affectation: on the contrary, he who admires most what is most worthy of admiration (let his raptures or his eagerness to express them be what they may), shows himself neither extravagant nor "unwise." When Mr. Wordsworth once said that he could read the description of Satan in Milton,

> "Nor seem'd
> Less than archangel ruin'd, and the excess
> Of glory obscur'd,"

till he felt a certain faintness come over his mind from a sense of beauty and grandeur, I saw no extravagance in this, but the utmost truth of feeling. When the same author, or his friend Mr. Southey, says, that the Excursion is better worth preserving than the Paradise Lost, this appears to me, I confess, a great piece of impertinence, or an unwarrantable stretch of friendship. Nor do I think the preference given by certain celebrated reviewers, of Mr. Rogers's Human Life over Mr. Wordsworth's Lyrical Ballads, founded on the true principles of poetical justice; for something is, after all, better than nothing.

To hasten to a conclusion of these desultory observations. The highest taste is shown in habitual sensibility to the greatest beauties; the most general taste is shown in a perception of the greatest variety of excellence. Many people admire Milton, and as many admire Pope, while there are but few who have any relish for both. Almost all the disputes on this subject arise, not so much from false, as from confined taste. We suppose that only one thing can have merit; and that, if we allow it to any thing else, we deprive the favourite object of our critical faith of the honours due to it. We are generally right in what we approve ourselves; for liking proceeds from a certain conformity of objects to the taste; as we are generally wrong in condemning what others admire; for our dislike mostly proceeds from our want of taste for what pleases them. Our being totally senseless to what excites extreme delight in those who have as good a right to judge as we have, in all human probability implies a defect of faculty in us, rather than a limitation in the resources of nature or art. Those who are pleased with the fewest things, know the least; as those who are pleased with every thing, know nothing. Shakespeare makes Mrs. Quickly say of Falstaff, by a pleasant blunder, that "Carnation was a colour he could never abide." So there are persons who cannot like Claude, because he is not Salvator Rosa; some who cannot endure Rembrandt, and others who would not cross the street to see a Vandyke; one reader does not like the neatness of Junius, and another objects to the extravagance of Burke; and they are all right, if they expect to find in others what is only to be found in their favourite author or artist, but equally wrong if they mean to say, that each of those they would condemn by a narrow and arbitrary standard of taste, has not a peculiar and transcendent merit of his own. The question is not, whether *you* like a certain excellence (it is your own fault if you do not), but whether another possessed it in a very eminent degree. If he did not, who is there that possessed it in a greater—that ranks above him in that particular? Those who are accounted the best, are the best in their line. When we say that Rembrandt was a master of *chiaro-scuro*, for instance, we do not say that he joined to this the symmetry of the Greek statues, but we mean that we must go to him for the perfection of *chiaro-scuro*, and that a Greek statue has not *chiaro-scuro*. If any one objects to Junius's Letters, that they are a tissue of epigrams, we answer, Be it so; it is for that very reason that we admire them. Again, should any one find fault with Mr. Burke's writings as a collection of rhapsodies, the proper answer always would be, Who is there that has written finer rhapsodies? I know an admirer of Don Quixote who can see no merit in Gil Blas, and an admirer of Gil Blas who could never get through Don Quixote. I myself have great pleasure in reading both these works, and in that respect think I have an advantage over both these critics. It always struck me as a singular proof of good taste, good sense, and liberal thinking, in an old friend, who had Paine's Rights of Man and Burke's Reflections on the French Revolution, bound up in one volume, and who said, that, both together, they made a very good book. To agree with the greatest number of good judges, is to be in the right; and good judges are persons of natural sensibility and acquired knowledge.[1] On the other hand, it must be owned, there are critics whose praise is a libel, and whose recommendation of any work is enough to condemn it. Men of the greatest genius and originality are not always persons of the most liberal and unprejudiced taste; they have a strong bias to certain qualities themselves, are for reducing others to their own standard, and lie less open to the general impressions of things. This exclusive preference of their own peculiar excellencies to those of others, in writers whose merits have not been sufficiently understood or acknowledged by their contemporaries, chiefly because they were *not* common-place, may sometimes be seen mounting up to a degree of bigotry and intolerance, little short of insanity. There are some critics I have known who never allow an author any merit till all the world "cry out upon him," and others who never allow another merit that any one can discover but themselves. So there are connoisseurs who spend their lives and waste their breath in extolling sublime passages in obscure writers, and lovers who choose their mistresses for their ugly faces. This is not taste, but affectation. What is popular is not necessarily vulgar; and that which we try to rescue from fatal obscurity, had in general much better remain in it.

THE SAME SUBJECT CONTINUED

TASTE relates to that which, either in the objects of nature, or the imitation of them or the Fine Arts in general is calculated to give pleasure. Now, to know what is calculated to give pleasure, the way is to enquire what does give pleasure: so that taste is, after all, much more a matter of fact and less of theory than might be imagined. We may hence determine another point, *viz.*—whether there is any universal or exclusive standard

---

[1] I apprehend that natural is of more importance than acquired sensibility. Thus, any one, without having been at an opera, may judge of opera dancing, only from having seen (with judicious eyes) a stag bound across a lawn, or a tree wave its branches in the air. In all, the general principles of motion are the same.

of taste, since this is to enquire, in other words, whether there is any one thing that pleases all the world alike, or whether there is only one thing that pleases anybody, both which questions carry their own answers with them. Still it does not follow, because there is no dogmatic or bigoted standard of taste, like a formula of faith, which whoever does not believe without doubt he shall be damned everlastingly, that there is no standard of taste whatever, that is to say, that certain things are not more apt to please than others, that some do not please more generally, that there are not others that give most pleasure to those who have studied the subject, that one nation is most susceptible of a particular kind of beauty, and another of another, according to their characters, &c. It would be a difficult attempt to force all these into one general rule or system, and yet equally so to deny that they are absolutely capricious, and without any foundation or principle whatever. There are, doubtless, books for children that we discard as we grow up; yet, what are the majority of mankind, or even readers, but grown children? If put to the vote of all the milliners' girls in London, Old Mortality, or even Heart of Midlothian, would not carry the day (or, at least, not very triumphantly) over a common Minerva-press novel; and I will hazard another opinion, that no woman ever liked Burke. Mr. Pratt, on the contrary, said that he had to "boast of many learned and beautiful suffrages." [1] It is not, then, solely from the greatest number of voices, but from the opinion of the greatest number of well-informed minds, that we can establish, if not an absolute standard, at least a comparative scale, of taste. Certainly, it can hardly be doubted that the greater the number of persons of strong natural sensibility or love for any art, and who have paid the closest attention to it, who agree in their admiration of any work of art, the higher do its pretensions rise to classical taste and intrinsic beauty. In this way, as the opinion of a thousand good judges may outweigh that of nearly all the rest of the world, so there may be one individual among them whose opinion may outweigh that of the other nine hundred and ninety-nine; that is, one of a still stronger and more refined perception of beauty than all the rest, and to whose opinion that of the others and of the world at large would approximate and be conformed, as their taste or perception of what was pleasing be-

[1] In answer to a criticism by Mr. Godwin on his poem called *Sympathy*.

came stronger and more confirmed by exercise and proper objects to call it forth. Thus, if we were still to insist on an universal standard of taste, it must be that, not which *does*, but which *would* please universally, supposing all men to have paid an equal attention to any subject and to have an equal relish for it, which can only be guessed at by the imperfect and yet more than casual agreement among those who have done so from choice and feeling. Taste is nothing but an enlarged capacity for receiving pleasure from works of imagination, &c. It is time, however, to apply this rule. There is, for instance, a much greater number of habitual readers and playgoers in France, who are devoted admirers of Racine or Molière than there are in England of Shakespeare: does Shakespeare's fame rest, then, on a less broad and solid foundation than that of either of the others? I think not, supposing that the class of judges to whom Shakespeare's excellences appeal are a higher, more independent, and more original court of criticism, and that their suffrages are quite as unanimous (though not so numerous) in the one case as in the other. A simile or a sentiment is not the worse in common opinion for being somewhat superficial and hackneyed, but it is the worse in poetry. The perfection of *commonplace* is that which would unite the greatest number of suffrages, if there were not a tribunal above *commonplace*. For instance, in Shakespeare's description of flowers, primroses are mentioned—

> "That come before the swallow dares, and take
> The winds of March with beauty:"

Now, I do not know that this expression is translatable into French, or intelligible to the common reader of either nation, but raise the scale of fancy, passion, and observation of nature to a certain point, and I will be bold to say that there will be no scruple entertained whether this single metaphor does not contain more poetry of the kind than is to be found in all Racine. As no Frenchman could write it, so I believe no Frenchman could understand it. We cannot take this insensibility on their part as a mark of our superiority, for we have plenty of persons among ourselves in the same predicament, but not the wisest or most refined, and to these the appeal is fair from the many—"and fit audience find, though few." So I think it requires a higher degree of taste to judge of

Titian's portraits than Raphael's scripture pieces: not that I think more highly of the former than the latter, but the world and connoisseurs in general think there is no comparison (from the dignity of the subject), whereas I think it difficult to decide which are the finest. Here again we have a commonplace, a preconception, the moulds of the judgment preoccupied by certain assumptions of degrees and classes of excellence, instead of judging from the true and genuine impressions of things. Men of genius, or those who can produce excellence would be the best judges of it—poets of poetry, painters of painting, &c.—but that persons of original and strong powers of mind are too much disposed to refer every thing to their own peculiar bias, and are comparatively indifferent to merely passive impressions. On the other hand, it is wholly wrong to oppose taste to genius, for genius in works of art is nothing but the power of producing what is beautiful (which, however, implies the intimate sense of it), though this is something very different from mere negative or formal beauties, which have as little to do with taste as genius.

I have, in a former essay, ascertained one principle of taste or excellence in the arts of imitation, where it was shown that objects of sense are not as it were simple and self-evident propositions, but admit of endless analysis and the most subtle investigation. We do not see nature with our eyes, but with our understandings and our hearts. To suppose that we see the whole of any object, merely by looking at it, is a vulgar error: we fancy that we do, because we are, of course, conscious of no more than we see in it, but this circle of our knowledge enlarges with further acquaintance and study, and we then perceive that what we perhaps barely distinguished in the gross, or regarded as a dull blank, is full of beauty, meaning, and curious details. He sees most of nature who understands its language best, or connects one thing with the greatest number of other things. Expression is the key to the human countenance, and unfolds a thousand imperceptible distinctions. How, then, should every one be a judge of pictures, when so few are of faces? A merely ignorant spectator, walking through a gallery of pictures, no more distinguishes the finest than your dog would, if he was to accompany you. Do not even the most experienced dispute on the preference, and shall the most ignorant decide? A vulgar connoisseur would even prefer a Denner to a Titian, because there is more of merely curious and specific detail. We may hence account for another circumstance, why things please in the imitation which do not in reality. If we saw the whole of any thing, or if the object in nature were merely one thing, this could not be the case. But the fact is, that in the imitation, or in the scientific study of any object, we come to an analysis of the details or some other abstract view of the subject which we had overlooked in a cursory examination, and these may be beautiful or curious, though the object in the gross is disgusting, or connected with disagreeable or uninteresting associations. Thus, in a picture of *still life*, as a shell or a marble chimney-piece, the stains or the gradations of colour may be delicate, and subjects for a new and careful imitation, though the *tout ensemble* has not, like a living face, the highest beauty of intelligence and expression. Here lie and here return the true effects and triumphs of art. It is not in making the eye a microscope, but in making it the interpreter and organ of all that can touch the soul and the affections, that the perfection of fine art is shown. Taste, then, does not place in the first rank of merit what merely proves difficulty or gratifies curiosity, unless it is combined with excellence and sentiment, or the pleasures of imagination and the moral sense. In this case the pleasure is more than doubled, where not only the imitation but the thing imitated, is fine in itself. Hence the preference given to Italian over Dutch pictures.

In respect to the imitation of nature, I would further observe that I think Sir Joshua Reynolds was wrong in making the grandeur of the design depend on the omission of the details, or the want of finishing. This seems also to proceed on the supposition that there cannot be two views of nature, but that the details are opposed to and inconsistent with an attention to general effect. Now this is evidently false, since the two things are undoubtedly combined by nature. For instance, the grandeur of design or character in the arch of an eyebrow is not injured or destroyed in reality by the hair-lines of which it is composed. Nor is the general form or outline of the eyebrow altered in the imitation, whether you make it one rude mass or descend into the minutiæ of the parts, which are arranged in such a manner as to produce the arched form and give the particular expression. So the general form of a nose, say an aquiline one, is not affected, whether I paint a wart which may happen to be on it or not, and so of the outline and proportions of the whole face. That is, general effect is consistent with individual details, and though these are not necessary to it, yet they often assist it, and always confirm the sense of verisimilitude. The most finished paintings, it is true, are not the grandest in effect; but neither is it true that the greatest daubs are the most sublime in character and composition. The best painters have combined an eye to the whole with careful finishing, and as there is a medium in all things, so the rule here seems to be not to go on *ad infinitum* with the details, but to stop when the time and labour necessary seem, in the judgment of the artist, to exceed the benefit produced.

Beauty does not consist in a medium, but in gradation or harmony. It has been the fashion of late to pretend to refer everything to association of ideas (and it is difficult to answer this appeal, since association, by its nature, mixes up with everything), but as Hartley has himself observed, who carried this principle to the utmost extent, and might be supposed to understand its limits, association implies something to be associated, and if there is a pleasing association, there must be first something naturally pleasing from which the secondary satisfaction is reflected, or to which it is conjoined. The chirping of a sparrow is as much a rural and domestic sound as the notes of the robin or the thrush, but it does not serve as a point to link other interests to because it wants beauty in itself; and, on the other hand, the song of the nightingale draws more attention to itself as a piece of music, and conveys less sentiment than the simple note of the cuckoo, which, from its solitary singularity, acts as the warning voice of time. Those who deny that there is a natural and pleasing softness arising from harmony or gradation, might as well affirm that sudden and abrupt transitions do not make our impressions more distinct as that they do not make them more harsh and violent. Beauty consists in gradation of colours or symmetry of form (conformity): strength or sublimity arises from the sense of power, and is aided by contrast. The ludicrous is the incoherent, arising, not from a conflicting power, but from weakness or the inability of any habitual impulse to sustain itself. The *ideal* is not confined to creation, but takes place in imitation, where a thing is subjected to one view, as all the parts of a face to the same expression. Invention is only feigning according to nature, or with a certain proportion between causes and effects. Poetry is infusing the same spirit into a number of things, or bathing them all as it were, in the same overflowing sense of delight (making the language also soft and musical), as the same torch kindles a number of lamps. I think invention is chiefly confined to poetry and words or ideas, and has little place in painting or concrete imagery, where the want of truth, or of the actual object, soon spoils the effect and force of the representation. Indeed, I think all genius is, in a great measure, national and local, arising out of times and circumstances, and being sustained at its full height by these alone, and that originality is not a deviation from, but a recurrence to nature. Rules and models destroy genius and art; and the excess of the artificial in the end cures itself, for it in time becomes so uniform and vapid as to be altogether contemptible, and to seek *perforce* some other outlet or purchase for the mind to take hold of.

The metaphysical theory above premised will account not only for the difficulty of imitating nature, but for the excellence of various masters, and the diversity and popularity of different styles. If the truth of sense and nature were one, there could be but one mode of representing it, more or less correct. But nature contains an infinite variety of parts, with their relations and significations, and different artists take these, and altogether do not give the whole. Thus Titian coloured, Raphael designed, Rubens gave the florid hue and motions, Rembrandt *chiaro-scuro*, &c.; but none of these reached perfection in their several departments, much less with reference to the whole circumference of art. It is ridiculous to suppose there is but one standard or one style. One artist looks at objects with as different an eye from another, as he does from the mathematician. It is erroneous to tie down individual genius to ideal models. Each person should do that, not which is best in itself, even supposing this could be known, but that which he can do best, which he will find out if left to himself. Spenser could not have written *Paradise Lost*, nor Milton the *Faërie Queene*. Those who aim at faultless regularity will only produce mediocrity, and no one ever approaches perfection except by stealth, and unknown to themselves. Did Correggio know what he had done when he had painted the "St. Jerome"—or Rembrandt when he made the sketch of "Jacob's Dream"? Oh, no! Those who are conscious of their powers never do anything.

CHARACTER OF COBBETT

PEOPLE have about as substantial an idea of Cobbett as they have of Cribb. His blows are as hard, and he himself is as impenetrable. One has no notion of him as making use of a fine pen, but a great mutton-fist; his style stuns his readers, and he "fillips the ear of the public with a three-man beetle." He is too much for any single newspaper antagonist; "lays waste" a city orator or Member of Parliament, and bears hard upon the government itself. He is a kind of *fourth estate* in the politics of the country. He is not only unquestionably the most powerful political writer of the present day, but one of the best writers in the language. He speaks and thinks plain, broad, downright English. He might be said to have the clearness of Swift, the naturalness of Defoe, and the picturesque satirical description of Mandeville; if all such comparisons were not impertinent. A really great and original writer is like nobody but himself. In one sense, Sterne was not a wit, nor Shakespeare a poet. It is easy to describe second-rate talents, because they fall into a class, and enlist under a standard; but first-rate powers defy calculation or comparison, and can be defined only by themselves. They are *sui generis*, and make the class to which they belong. I have tried half a dozen times to describe Burke's style without ever succeeding;—its severe extravagance; its literal boldness; its matter-of-fact hyperboles; its running away with a subject, and from it at the same time—but there is no making it out, for there is no example of the same thing any where else. We have no common measure to refer to; and his qualities contradict even themselves.

Cobbett is not so difficult. He has been compared to Paine; and so far it is true there are no two writers who come more into juxtaposition from the nature of their subjects, from the internal resources on which they draw, and from the popular effect of their writings and their adaptation (though that is a bad word in the present case) to the capacity of every reader. But still if we turn to a volume of Paine's (his Common Sense or Rights of Man), we are struck (not to say somewhat refreshed) by the difference. Paine is a much more sententious writer than Cobbett. You cannot open a page in any of his best and earlier works without meeting with some maxim, some antithetical and memorable saying, which is a sort of starting-place for the argument, and the goal to which it returns. There is not a single *bon-mot*, a single sentence in Cobbett that has ever been quoted again. If any thing is ever quoted from him, it is an epithet of abuse or a nickname. He is an excellent hand at invention in that way, and has "damnable iteration" in him. What could be better than his pestering Erskine year after year with his second title of Baron Clackmannan? He is rather too fond of such phrases as *the Sons and Daughters of Corruption*. Paine affected to reduce things to first principles, to announce self-evident truths. Cobbett troubles himself about little but the details and local circumstances. The first appeared to have made up his mind beforehand to certain opinions, and to try to find the most compendious and pointed expresssions for them: his successor appears to have no clue, no fixed or leading principles, nor ever to have thought on a question till he sits down to write about it; but then there seems no end of his matters of fact and raw materials, which are brought out in all their strength and sharpness from not having been squared or frittered down or vamped up to suit a theory—he goes on with his descriptions and illustrations as if he would never come to a stop; they have all the force of novelty with all the familiarity of old acquaintance; his knowledge grows out of the subject, and his style is that of a man who has an absolute intuition of what he is talking about, and never thinks of any thing else. He deals in premises and speaks to evidence—the coming to a conclusion and summing up (which was Paine's *forte*) lies in a smaller compass. The one could not compose an elementary treatise on politics to become a manual for the popular reader; nor could the other in all probability have kept up a weekly journal for the same number of years with the same spirit, interest, and untired perseverance. Paine's writings are a sort of introduction to political arithmetic on a new plan: Cobbett keeps a day-book, and makes an entry at full of all the occurrences and troublesome questions that start up throughout the year. Cobbett, with vast industry, vast information, and the utmost power of making what he says intelligible, never seems to get at the beginning or come to the end of any question: Paine, in a few short sentences, seems by his peremptory manner "to clear it from all controversy, past, present, and to come." Paine takes a bird's-eye view of things. Cobbett sticks close to them, inspects the component parts, and keeps fast hold of the smallest advantages they afford him. Or, if I might here be indulged in a pastoral allusion, Paine tries to enclose his ideas in a fold for security and repose; Cobbett lets *his* pour out upon the plain like a flock of sheep to feet and batten. Cobbett is a pleasanter writer for those to read who do not agree with him; for he is less dogmatical, goes more into the common grounds of fact and argument to which all appeal, is more desultory and various, and appears less to be driving at a previous conclusion than urged on by the force of present conviction. He is therefore tolerated by all parties, though he has made himself by turns obnoxious to all; and even those he abuses read him. The Reformers read him when he was a Tory, and the Tories read him now that he is a Reformer. He must, I think, however, be *caviare* to the Whigs.[1]

If he is less metaphysical and poetical than his celebrated prototype, he is more picturesque and dramatic. His episodes, which are numerous as they are pertinent, are striking, interesting, full of life and *naïveté*, minute, double measure running over, but never tedious—*nunquam sufflaminandus erat*. He is one of those writers who can never tire us, not even of himself; and the reason is, he is always "full of matter." He never runs to lees, never gives us the vapid leavings of himself, is never "weary, stale, and unprofitable," but always setting out afresh on his journey, clearing away some old nuisance, and turning up new mould. His egotism is delightful, for there is no affectation in it. He does not talk of himself for lack of something to write about, but because some circumstance that has happened to himself is the best possible illustration of the subject, and he is not the man to shrink from giving the best possible illustration of the subject from a squeamish delicacy. He likes both himself and his subject too well. He does not put himself before it, and say,—"admire me first"—but places us in the same situation with himself, and makes us see all that he does. There is no blindman's-buff, no conscious hints, no awkward ventriloquism, no testimonies of applause, no abstract, senseless self-complacency, no smuggled admiration of his own person by proxy: it is all plain and above-board. He writes himself plain William Cobbett, strips himself quite as naked as any body would wish—

[1] The late Lord Thurlow used to say that Cobbett was the only writer that deserved the name of a political reasoner.

in a word, his egotism is full of individuality, and has room for very little vanity in it. We feel delighted, rub our hands, and draw our chair to the fire, when we come to a passage of this sort: we know it will be something new and good, manly and simple, not the same insipid story of self over again. We sit down at table with the writer, but it is to a course of rich viands, flesh, fish, and wild-fowl, and not to a nominal entertainment, like that given by the Barmecide in the Arabian Nights, who put off his visitors with calling for a number of exquisite things that never appeared, and with the honour of his company. Mr. Cobbett is not a *make-believe* writer. His worst enemy can not say that of him. Still less is he a vulgar one. He must be a puny, commonplace critic indeed, who thinks him so. How fine were the graphical descriptions he sent us from America: what a Transatlantic flavour, what a native *gusto*, what a fine *sauce-piquante* of contempt they were seasoned with! If he had sat down to look at himself in the glass, instead of looking about him like Adam in Paradise, he would not have got up these articles in so capital a style. What a noble account of his first breakfast after his arrival in America! It might serve for a month. There is no scene on the stage more amusing. How well he paints the gold and scarlet plumage of the American birds, only to lament more pathetically the want of the wild wood-notes of his native land! The groves of the Ohio that had just fallen beneath the axe's stroke "live in his description," and the turnips that he transplanted from Botley "look green" in prose! How well at another time he describes the poor sheep that had got the tick, and had tumbled down in the agonies of death! It is a portrait in the manner of Bewick, with the strength, the simplicity, and feeling of that great naturalist. What havoc he makes, when he pleases, of the curls of Dr. Parr's wig and of the Whig consistency of Mr. ——! His Grammar too is as entertaining as a story-book. He is too hard upon the style of others, and not enough (sometimes) on his own.

As a political partisan no one can stand against him. With his brandished club, like Giant Despair in the Pilgrim's Progress, he knocks out their brains; and not only no individual, but no corrupt system could hold out against his powerful and repeated attacks, but with the same weapon, swung round like a flail, with which he levels his antagonists, he lays his friends low, and puts his own party *hors de combat*. This is a bad propensity, and a worse principle in political tactics, though a common one. If his blows were straightforward and steadily directed to the same object, no unpopular Minister could live before him; instead of which he lays about right and left, impartially and remorselessly, makes a clear stage, has all the ring to himself, and then runs out of it, just when he should stand his ground. He throws his head into his adversary's stomach, and takes away from him all inclination for the fight, hits fair or foul, strikes at every thing, and as you come up to his aid or stand ready to pursue his advantage, trips up your heels or lays you sprawling, and pummels you when down as much to his heart's content as ever the Yanguesian carriers belaboured Rosinante with their pack-staves. *"He has the back-trick simply the best of any man in Illyria."* He pays off both scores of old friendship and new-acquired enmity in a breath, in one perpetual volley, one raking fire of "arrowy sleet" shot from his pen. However his own reputation or the cause may suffer in consequence, he cares not one pin about that, so that he disables all who oppose, or who pretend to help him. In fact, he cannot bear success of any kind, not even of his own views or party; and if any principle were likely to become popular, would turn round against it to shew his power in shouldering it on one side. In short, wherever power is, there is he against it: he naturally butts at all obstacles, as unicorns are attracted to oak trees, and feels his own strength only by resistance to the opinions and wishes of the rest of the world. To sail with the stream, to agree with the company, is not his humour. If he could bring about a Reform in Parliament, the odds are that he would instantly fall foul of and try to mar his own handy-work; and he quarrels with his own creatures as soon as he has written them into a little vogue—and a prison. I do not think this is vanity or fickleness so much as a pugnacious disposition, that must have an antagonistic power to contend with, and only finds itself at ease in systematic opposition. If it were not for this, the high towers and rotten places of the world would fall before the battering-ram of his hardheaded reasoning; but if he once found them tottering, he would apply his strength to prop them up, and disappoint the expectations of his followers. He cannot agree to any thing established, nor to set up any thing else in its stead. While it is established, he presses hard against it, because it presses upon him, at least in imagination. Let it crumble under his grasp, and the motive to resistance is gone. He then requires some other grievance to set his face against. His principle is repulsion, his nature contradiction: he is made up of mere antipathies, an Ishmaelite indeed without a fellow. He is always playing at *hunt-the-slipper* in politics. He turns round upon whoever is next him. The way to wean him from any opinion, and make him conceive an intolerable hatred against it, would be to place somebody near him who was perpetually dinning it in his ears. When he is in England, he does nothing but abuse the Boroughmongers and laugh at the whole system: when he is in America he grows impatient of freedom and a republic. If he had stayed there a little longer, he would have become a loyal and a loving subject of His Majesty King George IV. He lampooned the French Revolution when it was hailed as the dawn of liberty by millions: by the time it was brought into almost universal ill-odour by some means or other (partly no doubt by himself), he had turned, with one or two or three others, staunch Buonapartist. He is always of the militant, not of the triumphant party: so far he bears a gallant show of magnanimity; but his gallantry is hardly of the right stamp. It wants principle: for though he is not servile or mercenary, he is the victim of self-will. He must pull down and pull in pieces: it is not in his disposition to do otherwise. It is a pity; for with his great talents he might do great things, if he would go right forward to any useful object, make thorough-stitch-work of any question, or join hand and heart with any principle. He changes his opinions as he does his friends, and much on the same account. He has no comfort in fixed principles: as soon as anything is settled in his own mind, he quarrels with it. He has no satisfaction but in the chase after truth, runs a question down, worries and kills it, then quits it like vermin, and starts some new game, to lead him a new dance, and give him a fresh breathing through bog and brake, with the rabble yelping at his heels, and the leaders perpetually at fault. This he calls sport-royal. He thinks it as good as cudgel-playing or single-stick, or anything else that has life in it. He likes the cut and thrust, the falls, bruises, and dry blows of an argument: as to any good or useful results that may come of the amicable settling of it, any one is welcome to them for him. The amusement is over when the matter is once fairly decided.

There is another point of view in which this may be put. I

might say that Mr. Cobbett is a very honest man with a total want of principle, and I might explain this paradox thus:—I mean that he is, I think, in downright earnest in what he says, in the part he takes at the time; but in taking that part, he is led entirely by headstrong obstinacy, caprice, novelty, pique, or personal motive of some sort, and not by a stedfast regard for truth, or habitual anxiety for what is right uppermost in his mind. He is not a fee'd, time-serving, shuffling advocate (no man could write as he does who did not believe himself sincere)—but his understanding is the dupe and slave of his momentary, violent, and irritable humours. He does not adopt an opinion "deliberately or for money;" yet his conscience is at the mercy of the first provocation he receives, of the first whim he takes in his head: he sees things through the medium of heat and passion, not with reference to any general principles, and his whole system of thinking is deranged by the first object that strikes his fancy or sours his temper.—One cause of this phenomenon is perhaps his want of a regular education. He is a self-taught man, and has the faults as well as excellences of that class of persons in their most striking and glaring excess. It must be acknowledged that the editor of the Political Register (the *two penny trash*, as it was called, till a bill passed the House to raise the price to sixpence) is not "the gentleman and scholar:" though he has qualities that, with a little better management, would be worth (to the public) both those titles. For want of knowing what has been discovered before him, he has not certain general landmarks to refer to, or a general standard of thought to apply to individual cases. He relies on his own acuteness and the immediate evidence, without being acquainted with the comparative anatomy or philosophical structure of opinion. He does not view things on a large scale or at the horizon (dim and airy enough perhaps)— but as they affect himself, close, palpable, tangible. Whatever he finds out, is his own, and he only knows what he finds out. He is in the constant hurry and fever of gestation: his brain teems incessantly with some fresh project. Every new light is the birth of a new system, the dawn of a new world to him. He is continually outstripping and overreaching himself. The last opinion is the only true one. He is wiser to-day then he was yesterday. Why should he not be wiser to-morrow than he was to-day?—Men of a learned education are not so sharp-witted as clever men without it; but they know the balance of the human intellect better; if they are more stupid, they are more steady; and are less liable to be led astray by their own sagacity and the overweening petulance of hard-earned and late-acquired wisdom. They do not fall in love with every meretricious extravagance at first sight, or mistake an old battered hypothesis for a vestal, because they are new to the ways of this old world. They do not seize upon it as a prize, but are safe from gross imposition by being as wise and no wiser than those who went before them.

Paine said on some occasion, "What I have written, I have written"—as rendering any farther declaration of his principles unnecessary. Not so Mr. Cobbett. What he has written is no rule to him what he is to write. He learns something every day, and every week he takes the field to maintain the opinions of the last six days against friend or foe. I doubt whether this outrageous inconsistency, this headstrong fickleness, this understood want of all rule and method, does not enable him to go on with the spirit, vigour, and variety that he does. He is not pledged to repeat himself. Every new Register is a kind of new Prospectus. He blesses himself from all ties and shackles on his understanding; he has no mortgages on his brain; his notions are free and unincumbered. If he was put in trammels, he might become a vile hack like so many more. But he gives himself "ample scope and verge enough." He takes both sides of a question, and maintains one as sturdily as the other. If nobody else can argue against him, he is a very good match for himself. He writes better in favour of Reform than anybody else; he used to write better against it. Wherever he is, there is the tug of war, the weight of the argument, the strength of abuse. He is not like a man in danger of being *bed-rid* in his faculties—He tosses and tumbles about his unwieldy bulk, and when he is tired of lying on one side, relieves himself by turning on the other. His shifting his point of view from time to time not merely adds variety and greater compass to his topics (so that the Political Register is an armoury and magazine for all the materials and weapons of political warfare), but it gives a greater zest and liveliness to his manner of treating them. Mr. Cobbett takes nothing for granted as what he has proved before; he does not write a book of reference. We see his ideas in their first concoction, fermenting and overflowing with the ebullitions of a lively conception. We look

on at the actual process, and are put in immediate possession of
the grounds and materials on which he forms his sanguine, unset-
tled conclusions. He does not give us samples of reasoning, but the
whole solid mass, refuse and all.

> " —He pours out all as plain
> As downright Shipper or as old Montaigne."

This is one cause of the clearness and force of his writings. An argument does not stop to stagnate and muddle in his brain, but passes
at once to his paper. His ideas are served up, like pancakes, hot
and hot. Fresh theories give him fresh courage. He is like a young
and lusty bridegroom that divorces a favourite speculation every
morning, and marries a new one every night. He is not wedded to
his notions, not he. He has not one Mrs. Cobbett among all his
opinions. He makes the most of the last thought that has come in
his way, seizes fast hold of it, rumples it about in all directions with
rough strong hands, has his wicked will of it, takes a surfeit, and
throws it away.—Our author's changing his opinions for new ones
is not so wonderful; what is more remarkable is his facility in forgetting his old ones. He does not pretend to consistency (like
Mr. Coleridge); he frankly disavows all connection with himself.
He feels no personal responsibility in this way, and cuts a friend
or principle with the same decided indifference that Antipholis of
Ephesus cuts Ægeon of Syracuse. It is a hollow thing. The only
time he ever grew romantic was in bringing over the relics of
Mr. Thomas Paine with him from America to go a progress with
them through the disaffected districts. Scarce had he landed in
Liverpool when he left the bones of a great man to shift for themselves; and no sooner did he arrive in London than he made a
speech to disclaim all participation in the political and theological
sentiments of his late idol, and to place the whole stock of his
admiration and enthusiasm towards him to the account of his
financial speculations, and of his having predicted the fate of paper-
money. If he had erected a little gold statue to him, it might have
proved the sincerity of this assertion: but to make a martyr and
a patron saint of a man, and to dig up "his canonised bones" in
order to expose them as objects of devotion to the rabble's gaze,
asks something that has more life and spirit in it, more mind and
vivifying soul, than has to do with any calculation of pounds,

shillings, and pence! The fact is, he *ratted* from his own project.
He found the thing not so ripe as he had expected. His heart failed
him: his enthusiasm fled, and he made his retractation. His
admiration is short-lived: his contempt only is rooted, and his
resentment lasting.—The above was only one instance of his building too much on practical *data*. He has an ill habit of prophesying,
and goes on, though still deceived. The art of prophesying does not
suit Mr. Cobbett's style. He has a knack of fixing names and times
and places. According to him, the Reformed Parliament was to
meet in March 1818—it did not, and we heard no more of the matter. When his predictions fail, he takes no further notice of them,
but applies himself to new ones—like the country-people who turn
to see what weather there is in the almanac for the next week,
though it has been out in its reckoning every day of the last.

Mr. Cobbett is great in attack, not in defence: he cannot fight
an up-hill battle. He will not bear the least punishing. If any one
turns upon him (which few people like to do) he immediately turns
tail. Like an overgrown school-boy, he is so used to have it all his
own way, that he cannot submit to any thing like competition or a
struggle for the mastery; he must lay on all the blows, and take
none. He is bullying and cowardly; a Big Ben in politics, who will
fall upon others and crush them by his weight, but is not prepared
for resistance, and is soon staggered by a few smart blows. Whenever he has been set upon, he has slunk out of the controversy.
The Edinburgh Review made (what is called) a dead set at him
some years ago, to which he only retorted by an eulogy on the
superior neatness of an English kitchen-garden to a Scotch one.
I remember going one day into a bookseller's shop in Fleet-street
to ask for the Review; and on my expressing my opinion to a
young Scotchman, who stood behind the counter, that Mr. Cobbett might hit as hard in his reply, the North Briton said with
some alarm,—"But you don't think, Sir, Mr. Cobbett will be able
to injure the Scottish nation?" I said I could not speak to that
point, but I thought he was very well able to defend himself. He,
however, did not, but has borne a grudge to the Edinburgh Review
ever since, which he hates worse than the Quarterly. I cannot say
I do.[1]

---

[1] Mr. Cobbett speaks almost as well as he writes. The only time I ever saw him
he seemed to me a very pleasant man—easy of access, affable, clear-headed, simple and

ON READING OLD BOOKS

I HATE to read new books. There are twenty or thirty volumes that I have read over and over again, and these are the only ones that I have any desire ever to read at all. It was a long time before I could bring myself to sit down to the Tales of My Landlord, but now that author's works have made a considerable addition to my scanty library. I am told that some of Lady Morgan's are good, and have been recommended to look into Anastasius; but I have not yet ventured upon that task. A lady, the other day, could not refrain from expressing her surprise to a friend, who said he had been reading Delphine:—she asked,—If it had not been published some time back? Women judge of books as they do of fashions or complexions, which are admired only "in their newest gloss." That is not my way. I am not one of those who trouble the circulating libraries much, or pester the booksellers for mail-coach copies of standard periodical publications. I cannot say that I am greatly addicted to black-letter, but I profess myself well versed in the marble bindings of Andrew Millar, in the middle of the last century; nor does my taste revolt at Thurloe's State Papers, in Russia leather; or an ample impression of Sir William Temple's Essays, with a portrait after Sir Godfrey Kneller in front. I do not think altogether the worse of a book for having survived the author a generation or two. I have more confidence in the dead than the living. Contemporary writers may generally be divided into two classes—one's friends or one's foes. Of the first we are compelled to think too well, and of the last we are disposed to think too ill, to receive much genuine pleasure from the perusal, or to judge fairly of the merits of either. One candidate for literary fame, who happens to be of our acquaintance, writes finely, and like a man of genius; but unfortunately has a foolish face, which spoils a delicate passage:—another inspires us with the highest respect for his personal talents and character, but does not quite come up

mild in his manner, deliberate and unruffled in his speech, though some of his expressions were not very qualified. His figure is tall and portly. He has a good, sensible face—rather full, with little grey eyes, a hard, square forehead, a ruddy complexion, with hair grey or powdered; and had on a scarlet broadcloth waistcoat with the flaps of the pockets hanging down, as was the custom for gentlemen-farmers in the last century, or as we see it in the pictures of Members of Parliament in the reign of George I. I certainly did not think less favourably of him for seeing him.

to our expectations in print. All these contradictions and petty details interrupt the calm current of our reflections. If you want to know what any of the authors were who lived before our time, and are still objects of anxious inquiry, you have only to look into their works. But the dust and smoke and noise of modern literature have nothing in common with the pure, silent air of immortality.

When I take up a work that I have read before (the oftener the better) I know what I have to expect. The satisfaction is not lessened by being anticipated. When the entertainment is altogether new, I sit down to it as I should to a strange dish,—turn and pick out a bit here and there, and am in doubt what to think of the composition. There is a want of confidence and security to second appetite. New-fangled books are also like made-dishes in this respect, that they are generally little else than hashes and *rifaccimentos* of what has been served up entire and in a more natural state at other times. Besides, in thus turning to a well-known author, there is not only an assurance that my time will not be thrown away, or my palate nauseated with the most insipid or vilest trash, —but I shake hands with, and look an old, tried, and valued friend in the face,—compare notes, and chat the hours away. It is true, we form dear friendships with such ideal guests—dearer, alas! and more lasting, than those with our most intimate acquaintance. In reading a book which is an old favourite with me (say the first novel I ever read) I not only have the pleasure of imagination and of a critical relish of the work, but the pleasures of memory added to it. It recalls the same feelings and associations which I had in first reading it, and which I can never have again in any other way. Standard productions of this kind are links in the chain of our conscious being. They bind together the different scattered divisions of our personal identity. They are landmarks and guides in our journey through life. They are pegs and loops on which we can hang up, or from which we can take down, at pleasure, the wardrobe of a moral imagination, the relics of our best affections, the tokens and records of our happiest hours. They are "for thoughts and for remembrance!" They are like Fortunatus's Wishing-Cap— they give us the best riches—those of Fancy; and transport us, not over half the globe, but (which is better) over half our lives, at a word's notice!

My father Shandy solaced himself with Bruscambille. Give me

for this purpose a volume of Peregrine Pickle or Tom Jones. Open either of them any where—at the Memoirs of Lady Vane, or the adventures at the masquerade with Lady Bellaston, or the disputes between Thwackum and Square, or the escape of Molly Seagrim, or the incident of Sophia and her muff, or the edifying prolixity of her aunt's lecture—and there I find the same delightful, busy, bustling scene as ever, and feel myself the same as when I was first introduced into the midst of it. Nay, sometimes the sight of an odd volume of these good old English authors on a stall, or the name lettered on the back among others on the shelves of a library, answers the purpose, revives the whole train of ideas, and sets "the puppets dallying." Twenty years are struck off the list, and I am a child again. A sage philosopher, who was not a very wise man, said, that he should like very well to be young again, if he could take his experience along with him. This ingenious person did not seem to be aware, by the gravity of his remark, that the great advantage of being young is to be without this weight of experience, which he would fain place upon the shoulders of youth, and which never comes too late with years. Oh! what a privilege to be able to let this hump, like Christian's burthen, drop from off one's back, and transport one's self, by the help of a little musty duodecimo, to the time when "ignorance was bliss," and when we first got a peep at the raree-show of the world, through the glass of fiction—gazing at mankind, as we do at wild beasts in a menagerie, through the bars of their cages,—or at curiosities in a museum, that we must not touch! For myself, not only are the old ideas of the contents of the work brought back to my mind in all their vividness, but the old associations of the faces and persons of those I then knew, as they were in their life-time—the place where I sat to read the volume, the day when I got it, the feeling of the air, the fields, the sky—return, and all my early impressions with them. This is better to me—those places, those times, those persons, and those feelings that come across me as I retrace the story and devour the page, are to me better far than the wet sheets of the last new novel from the Ballantyne press, to say nothing of the Minerva press in Leadenhall-street. It is like visiting the scenes of early youth. I think of the time "when I was in my father's house, and my path ran down with butter and honey,"—when I was a little, thoughtless child, and had no other wish or care but to con my daily task, and be happy!—Tom Jones, I remember, was the first work that broke the spell. It came down in numbers once a fortnight, in Cooke's pocket-edition, embellished with cuts. I had hitherto read only in school-books, and a tiresome ecclesiastical history (with the exception of Mrs. Radcliffe's Romance of the Forest): but this had a different relish with it,—"sweet in the mouth," though not "bitter in the belly." It smacked of the world I lived in, and in which I was to live—and shewed me groups, "gay creatures" not "of the element," but of the earth; not "living in the clouds," but travelling the same road that I did;—some that had passed on before me, and others that might soon overtake me. My heart had palpitated at the thoughts of a boarding-school ball, or gala-day at Midsummer or Christmas: but the world I had found in Cooke's edition of the British Novelists was to me a dance through life, a perpetual gala-day. The sixpenny numbers of this work regularly contrived to leave off just in the middle of a sentence, and in the nick of a story, where Tom Jones discovers Square behind the blanket; or where Parson Adams, in the inextricable confusion of events, very undesignedly gets to bed to Mrs. Slip-slop. Let me caution the reader against this impression of Joseph Andrews; for there is a picture of Fanny in it which he should not set his heart on, lest he should never meet with any thing like it; or if he should, it would, perhaps, be better for him that he had not. It was just like ————— ————! With what eagerness I used to look forward to the next number, and open the prints! Ah! never again shall I feel the enthusiastic delight with which I gazed at the figures, and anticipated the story and adventures of Major Bath and Commodore Trunnion, of Trim and my Uncle Toby, of Don Quixote and Sancho and Dapple, of Gil Blas and Dame Lorenza Sephora, of Laura and the fair Lucretia, whose lips open and shut like buds of roses. To what nameless ideas did they give rise,—with what airy delights I filled up the outlines, as I hung in silence over the page!—Let me still recall them, that they may breathe fresh life into me, and that I may live that birthday of thought and romantic pleasure over again! Talk of the *ideal!* This is the only true ideal—the heavenly tints of Fancy reflected in the bubbles that float upon the spring-tide of human life.

> "Oh! Memory! shield me from the world's poor strife,
> And give those scenes thine everlasting life!"

The paradox with which I set out is, I hope, less startling than it was; the reader will, by this time, have been let into my secret. Much about the same time, or I believe rather earlier, I took a particular satisfaction in reading Chubb's Tracts, and I often think I will get them again to wade through. There is high gusto of polemical divinity in them; and you fancy that you hear a club of shoemakers at Salisbury, debating a disputable text from one of St. Paul's Epistles in a workmanlike style, with equal shrewdness and pertinacity. I cannot say much for my metaphysical studies, into which I launched shortly after with great ardour, so as to make a toil of pleasure. I was presently entangled in the briars and thorns of subtle distinctions,—of "fate, free-will, fore-knowledge absolute," though I cannot add that "in their wandering mazes I found no end"; for I did arrive at some very satisfactory and potent conclusions; nor will I go so far, however ungrateful the subject might seem, as to exclaim with Marlowe's Faustus—"Would I had never seen Wittenberg, never read book"—that is, never studied such authors as Hartley, Hume, Berkeley, &c. Locke's Essay on the Human Understanding is, however, a work from which I never derived either pleasure or profit; and Hobbes, dry and powerful as he is, I did not read till long afterwards. I read a few poets, which did not much hit my taste,—for I would have the reader understand, I am deficient in the faculty of imagination; but I fell early upon French romances and philosophy, and devoured them tooth-and-nail. Many a dainty repast have I made of the New Éloïse;—the description of the kiss; the excursion on the water; the letter of St. Preux, recalling the time of their first loves; and the account of Julia's death; these I read over and over again with unspeakable delight and wonder. Some years after, when I met with this work again, I found I had lost nearly my whole relish for it (except some few parts) and was, I remember, very much mortified with the change in my taste, which I sought to attribute to the smallness and gilt edges of the edition I had bought, and its being perfumed with rose-leaves. Nothing could exceed the gravity, the solemnity with which I carried home and read the Dedication to the Social Contract, with some other pieces of the same author, which I had picked up at a stall in a coarse leathern cover. Of the Confessions I have spoken elsewhere, and may repeat what I have said—"Sweet is the dew of their memory, and pleasant the balm of their recollection!" Their beauties are not "scattered like stray-gifts o'er the earth," but sown thick on the page, rich and rare. I wish I had never read the Emilius, or read it with less implicit faith. I had no occasion to pamper my natural aversion to affectation or pretence, by romantic and artificial means. I had better have formed myself on the model of Sir Fopling Flutter. There is a class of persons whose virtues and most shining qualities sink in, and are concealed by, an absorbent ground of modesty and reserve; and such a one I do, without vanity, profess myself.[1] Now these are the very persons who are likely to attach themselves to the character of Emilius, and of whom it is sure to be the bane. This dull, phlegmatic, retiring humour is not in a fair way to be corrected, but confirmed and rendered desperate, by being in that work held up as an object of imitation, as an example of simplicity and magnanimity—by coming upon us with all the recommendations of novelty, surprise, and superiority to the prejudices of the world—by being stuck upon a pedestal, made amiable, dazzling, a *leurre de dupe!* The reliance on solid worth which it inculcates, the preference of sober truth to gaudy tinsel, hangs like a mill-stone round the neck of the imagination—"a load to sink a navy"—impedes our progress, and blocks up every prospect in life. A man, to get on, to be successful, conspicuous, applauded, should not retire upon the centre of his conscious resources, but be always at the circumference of appearances. He must envelop himself in a halo of mystery—he must ride in an equipage of opinion—he must walk with a train of self-conceit following him—he must not strip himself to a buff-jerkin, to the doublet and hose of his real merits, but must surround himself with a *cortège* of prejudices, like the signs of the Zodiac—he must seem any thing but what he is, and then he may pass for any thing he pleases. The world love to be amused by hollow professions, to be deceived by flattering appearances, to live in a state of hallucination; and can forgive every thing but the plain, downright, simple honest truth—such as we see it chalked out in the character of Emilius.—To return from this digression, which is a little out of place here.

[1] Nearly the same sentiment was wittily and happily expressed by a friend, who had some lottery puffs, which he had been employed to write, returned on his hands for their too great severity of thought and classical terseness of style, and who observed on that occasion, that "Modest merit never can succeed!"

Books have in a great measure lost their power over me; nor can I revive the same interest in them as formerly. I perceive when a thing is good, rather than feel it. It is true,

"Marcian Colonna is a dainty book;"

and the reading of Mr. Keats's Eve of Saint Agnes lately made me regret that I was not young again. The beautiful and tender images there conjured up, "come like shadows—so depart." The "tiger-moth's wings," which he has spread over his rich poetic blazonry, just flit across my fancy; the gorgeous twilight window which he has painted over again in his verse, to me "blushes" almost in vain "with blood of queens and kings." I know how I should have felt at one time in reading such passages; and that is all. The sharp luscious flavour, the fine *aroma* is fled, and nothing but the stalk, the bran, the husk of literature is left. If any one were to ask me what I read now, I might answer with my Lord Hamlet in the play—"Words, words, words."—"What is the matter?"—"*Nothing!*"—They have scarce a meaning. But it was not always so. There was a time when to my thinking, every word was a flower or a pearl, like those which dropped from the mouth of the little peasant-girl in the Fairy tale, or like those that fall from the great preacher in the Caledonian Chapel! I drank of the stream of knowledge that tempted, but did not mock my lips, as of the river of life, freely. How eagerly I slaked my thirst of German sentiment, "as the hart that panteth for the water-springs"; how I bathed and revelled, and added my floods of tears to Goëthe's Sorrows of Werter, and to Schiller's Robbers—

"Giving my stock of more to that which had too much!"

I read, and assented with all my soul to Coleridge's fine Sonnet, beginning—

"Schiller! that hour I would have wish'd to die,
If through the shuddering midnight I had sent,
From the dark dungeon of the tow'r time-rent,
That fearful voice, a famish'd father's cry!"

I believe I may date my insight into the mysteries of poetry from the commencement of my acquaintance with the authors of the Lyrical Ballads; at least, my discrimination of the higher sorts—not my predilection for such writers as Goldsmith or Pope: nor do I imagine they will say I got my liking for the Novelists, or the comic writers,—for the characters of Valentine, Tattle, or Miss Prue, from them. If so, I must have got from them what they never had themselves. In points where poetic diction and conception are concerned, I may be at a loss, and liable to be imposed upon: but in forming an estimate of passages relating to common life and manners, I cannot think I am a plagiarist from any man. I there "know my cue without a prompter." I may say of such studies—*Intus et in cute.* I am just able to admire those literal touches of observation and description, which persons of loftier pretensions over-look and despise. I think I comprehend something of the characteristic part of Shakespeare; and in him indeed, all is characteristic, even the nonsense and poetry. I believe it was the celebrated Sir Humphry Davy who used to say, that Shakespeare was rather a metaphysician than a poet. At any rate, it was not ill said. I wish that I had sooner known the dramatic writers contemporary with Shakespeare; for in looking them over about a year ago, I almost revived my old passion for reading, and my old delight in books, though they were very nearly new to me. The Periodical Essayists I read long ago. The Spectator I liked extremely: but the Tatler took my fancy most. I read the others soon after, the Rambler, the Adventurer, the World, the Connoisseur: I was not sorry to get to the end of them, and have no desire to go regularly through them again. I consider myself a thorough adept in Richardson. I like the longest of his novels best, and think no part of them tedious; nor should I ask to have any thing better to do than to read them from beginning to end, to take them up when I chose, and lay them down when I was tired, in some old family mansion in the country, till every word and syllable relating to the bright Clarissa, the divine Clementina, the beautiful Pamela, "with every trick and line of their sweet favour," were once more "graven in my heart's tables." [1] I have a sneaking

[1] During the peace of Amiens, a young English officer, of the name of Lovelace, was presented at Buonaparte's levee. Instead of the usual question, "Where have you served, Sir?" the First Consul immediately addressed him, "I perceive your name, Sir, is the same as that of the hero of Richardson's Romance!" Here was a Consul. The young man's uncle, who was called Lovelace, told me this anecdote while we were stop-

kindness for Mackenzie's Julia de Roubigné—for the deserted mansion, and straggling gilliflowers on the mouldering garden-wall; and still more for his Man of Feeling; not that it is better, nor so good; but at the time I read it, I sometimes thought of the heroine, Miss Walton, and of Miss —— together, and "that ligament, fine as it was, was never broken!"—One of the poets that I have always read with most pleasure, and can wander about in for ever with a sort of voluptuous indolence, is Spenser; and I like Chaucer even better. The only writer among the Italians I can pretend to any knowledge of, is Boccaccio, and of him I cannot express half my admiration. His story of the Hawk I could read and think of from day to day, just as I would look at a picture of Titian's!—

I remember, as long ago as the year 1798, going to a neighbouring town (Shrewsbury, where Farquahar has laid the plot of his Recruiting Officer) and bringing home with me, "at one proud swoop," a copy of Milton's Paradise Lost, and another of Burke's Reflections on the French Revolution—both of which I have still; and I still recollect, when I see the covers, the pleasure with which I dipped into them as I returned with my double prize. I was set up for one while. That time is past "with all its giddy raptures": but I am still anxious to preserve its memory, "embalmed with odours."—With respect to the first of these works, I would be permitted to remark here in passing, that it is a sufficient answer to the German criticism which has since been started against the character of Satan (*viz.* that it is not one of disgusting deformity, or pure, defecated malice) to say that Milton has there drawn, not the abstract principle of evil, not a devil incarnate, but a fallen angel. This is the scriptural account, and the poet has followed it. We may safely retain such passages as that well-known one—

> ——"His form had not yet lost
> All her original brightness; nor appear'd
> Less than archangel ruin'd; and the excess
> Of glory obscur'd"——

for the theory, which is opposed to them, "falls flat upon the grunsel edge, and shames its worshippers." Let us hear no more

ping together at Calais. I had also been thinking that his was the same name as that of the hero of Richardson's Romance. This is one of my reasons for liking Buonaparte.

then of this monkish cant, and bigotted outcry for the restoration of the horns and tail of the devil!—Again, as to the other work, Burke's Reflections, I took a particular pride and pleasure in it, and read it to myself and others for months afterwards. I had reason for my prejudice in favour of this author. To understand an adversary is some praise: to admire him is more. I thought I did both: I knew I did one. From the first time I ever cast my eyes on any thing of Burke's (which was an extract from his Letter to a Noble Lord in a three-times a week paper, The St. James's Chronicle, in 1796), I said to myself, "This is true eloquence: this is a man pouring out his mind on paper." All other style seemed to me pedantic and impertinent. Dr. Johnson's was walking on stilts; and even Junius's (who at that time was a favourite with me) with all his terseness, shrunk up into little antithetic points and well-trimmed sentences. But Burke's style was forked and playful as the lightning, crested like the serpent. He delivered plain things on a plain ground; but when he rose, there was no end of his flights and circumgyrations—and in this very Letter, "he, like an eagle in a dove-cot, fluttered *his* Volscians" (the Duke of Bedford and the Earl of Lauderdale) [1] "in Corioli." I did not care for his doctrines. I was then, and am still, proof against their contagion; but I admired the author, and was considered as not a very staunch partisan of the opposite side, though I thought myself that an abstract proposition was one thing—a masterly transition, a brilliant metaphor, another. I conceived too that he might be wrong in his main argument, and yet deliver fifty truths in arriving at a false conclusion. I remember Coleridge assuring me, as a poetical and political set-off to my sceptical admiration, that Wordsworth had written an Essay on Marriage, which, for manly thought and nervous expression, he deemed incomparably superior. As I had not, at that time, seen any specimens of Mr. Wordsworth's prose style, I could not venture my doubts on the subject. If there are greater prose-writers than Burke, they either lie out of my course of study, or are beyond my sphere of comprehension. I am too old to be a convert to a new mythology of genius. The niches are occupied, the tables are full. If such is still my admiration of this man's misapplied powers, what must it have been at a

---

[1] He is there called "Citizen Lauderdale." Is this the present Earl?

time when I myself was in vain trying, year after year, to write a single Essay, nay, a single page or sentence; when I regarded the wonders of his pen with the longing eyes of one who was dumb and a changeling; and when, to be able to convey the slightest conception of my meaning to others in words, was the height of an almost hopeless ambition! But I never measured others' excellencies by my own defects: though a sense of my own incapacity, and of the steep, impassable ascent from me to them, made me regard them with greater awe and fondness. I have thus run through most of my early studies and favourite authors, some of whom I have since criticised more at large. Whether those observations will survive me, I neither know nor do I much care: but to the works themselves, "worthy of all acceptation," and to the feelings they have always excited in me since I could distinguish a meaning in language, nothing shall ever prevent me from looking back with gratitude and triumph. To have lived in the cultivation of an intimacy with such works, and to have familiarly relished such names, is not to have lived quite in vain.

There are other authors whom I have never read, and yet whom I have frequently had a great desire to read, from some circumstance relating to them. Among these is Lord Clarendon's History of the Grand Rebellion, after which I have a hankering, from hearing it spoken of by good judges—from my interest in the events, and knowledge of the characters from other sources, and from having seen fine portraits of most of them. I like to read a well-penned character, and Clarendon is said to have been a master in this way. I should like to read Froissart's Chronicles, Hollingshed and Stowe, and Fuller's Worthies. I intend, whenever I can, to read Beaumont and Fletcher all through. There are fifty-two of their plays, and I have only read a dozen or fourteen of them. A Wife for a Month, and Thierry and Theodoret, are, I am told, delicious, and I can believe it. I should like to read the speeches in Thucydides, and Guicciardini's History of Florence, and Don Quixote in the original. I have often thought of reading the Loves of Persiles and Sigismunda, and the Galatea of the same author. But I somehow reserve them like "another Yarrow." I should also like to read the last new novel (if I could be sure it was so) of the author of Waverley:—no one would be more glad than I to find it the best!—

ON LIVING TO ONE'S–SELF [1]

"Remote, unfriended, melancholy, slow,
Or by the lazy Scheldt or wandering Po."

I NEVER was in a better place or humour than I am at present for writing on this subject. I have a partridge getting ready for my supper, my fire is blazing on the hearth, the air is mild for the season of the year, I have had but a slight fit of indigestion to-day (the only thing that makes me abhor myself), I have three hours good before me, and therefore I will attempt it. It is as well to do it at once as to have it to do for a week to come.

If the writing on this subject is no easy task, the thing itself is a harder one. It asks a troublesome effort to ensure the admiration of others: it is a still greater one to be satisfied with one's own thoughts. As I look from the window at the wide bare heath before me, and through the misty moon-light air see the woods that wave over the top of Winterslow,

"While Heav'n's chancel-vault is blind with sleet,"

my mind takes its flight through too long a series of years, supported only by the patience of thought and secret yearnings after truth and good, for me to be at a loss to understand the feeling I intend to write about; but I do not know that this will enable me to convey it more agreeably to the reader.

Lady G., in a letter to Miss Harriet Byron, assures her that "her brother Sir Charles lived to himself": and Lady L. soon after (for Richardson was never tired of a good thing) repeats the same observation; to which Miss Byron frequently returns in her answers to both sisters—"For you know Sir Charles lives to himself," till at length it passes into a proverb among the fair correspondents. This is not, however, an example of what I understand by *living to one's-self*, for Sir Charles Grandison was indeed always thinking of himself; but by this phrase I mean never thinking at all about one's-self, any more than if there was no such person in existence. The character I speak of is as little of an egotist as possible: Richardson's great favourite was as much of one as possible.

[1] Written at Winterslow Hut, January 18–19, 1821.

Some satirical critic has represented him in Elysium "bowing over the *faded* hand of Lady Grandison" (Miss Byron that was)—he ought to have been represented bowing over his own hand, for he never admired any one but himself, and was the god of his own idolatry. Neither do I call it living to one's-self to retire into a desert (like the saints and martyrs of old) to be devoured by wild beasts, nor to descend into a cave to be considered as a hermit, nor to get to the top of a pillar or rock to do fanatic penance and be seen of all men. What I mean by living to one's-self is living in the world, as in it, not of it: it is as if no one knew there was such a person, and you wished no one to know it: it is to be a silent spectator of the mighty scene of things, not an object of attention or curiosity in it; to take a thoughtful, anxious interest in what is passing in the world, but not to feel the slightest inclination to make or meddle with it. It is such a life as a pure spirit might be supposed to lead, and such an interest as it might take in the affairs of men, calm, contemplative, passive, distant, touched with pity for their sorrows, smiling at their follies without bitterness, sharing their affections, but not troubled by their passions, not seeking their notice, nor once dreamt of by them. He who lives wisely to himself and to his own heart, looks at the busy world through the loop-holes of retreat, and does not want to mingle in the fray. "He hears the tumult, and is still." He is not able to mend it, nor willing to mar it. He sees enough in the universe to interest him without putting himself forward to try what he can do to fix the eyes of the universe upon him. Vain the attempt! He reads the clouds, he looks at the stars, he watches the return of the seasons, the falling leaves of autumn, the perfumed breath of spring, starts with delight at the note of a thrush in a copse near him, sits by the fire, listens to the moaning of the wind, pores upon a book, or discourses the freezing hours away, or melts down hours to minutes in pleasing thought. All this while he is taken up with other things, forgetting himself. He relishes an author's style without thinking of turning author. He is fond of looking at a print from an old picture in the room, without teasing himself to copy it. He does not fret himself to death with trying to be what he is not, or to do what he cannot. He hardly knows what he is capable of, and is not in the least concerned whether he shall ever make a figure in the world. He feels the truth of the lines—

> "The man whose eye is ever on himself,
>   Doth look one, the least of nature's works;
>   One who might move the wise man to that scorn
>   Which wisdom holds unlawful ever."—

He looks out of himself at the wide extended prospect of nature, and takes an interest beyond his narrow pretensions in general humanity. He is free as air, and independent as the wind. Woe be to him when he first begins to think what others say of him. While a man is contented with himself and his own resources, all is well. When he undertakes to play a part on the stage, and to persuade the world to think more about him than they do about themselves, he is got into a track where he will find nothing but briars and thorns, vexation and disappointment. I can speak a little to this point. For many years of my life I did nothing but think. I had nothing else to do but solve some knotty point, or dip in some abstruse author, or look at the sky, or wander by the pebbled seaside—

> "To see the children sporting on the shore,
>   And hear the mighty waters rolling evermore."

I cared for nothing, I wanted nothing. I took my time to consider whatever occurred to me, and was in no hurry to give a sophistical answer to a question—there was no printer's devil waiting for me. I used to write a page or two perhaps in half a year; and remember laughing heartily at the celebrated experimentalist Nicholson, who told me that in twenty years he had written as much as would make three hundred octavo volumes. If I was not a great author, I could read with ever fresh delight, "never ending, still beginning," and had no occasion to write a criticism when I had done. If I could not paint like Claude, I could admire "the witchery of the soft blue sky" as I walked out, and was satisfied with the pleasure it gave me. If I was dull, it gave me little concern: if I was lively, I indulged my spirits. I wished well to the world, and believed as favourably of it as I could. I was like a stranger in a foreign land, at which I looked with wonder, curiosity, and delight, without expecting to be an object of attention in return. I had no relations to the state, no duty to perform, no ties to bind me to others: I had neither friend nor mistress, wife or child. I lived in a world of contemplation, and not of action.

This sort of dreaming existence is the best. He who quits it to go in search of realities generally barters repose for repeated disappointments and vain regrets. His time, thoughts, and feelings are no longer at his own disposal. From that instant he does not survey the objects of nature as they are in themselves, but looks asquint at them to see whether he cannot make them the instruments of his ambition, interest, or pleasure; for a candid, undesigning, undisguised simplicity of character, his views become jaundiced, sinister, and double: he takes no farther interest in the great changes of the world but as he has a paltry share in producing them: instead of opening his senses, his understanding, and his heart to the resplendent fabric of the universe, he holds a crooked mirror before his face, in which he may admire his own person and pretensions, and just glance his eye aside to see whether others are not admiring him too. He no more exists in the impression which "the fair variety of things" makes upon him, softened and subdued by habitual contemplation, but in the feverish sense of his own upstart self-importance. By aiming to fix, he is become the slave of opinion. He is a tool, a part of a machine that never stands still, and is sick and giddy with the ceaseless motion. He has no satisfaction but in the reflection of his own image in the public gaze— but in the repetition of his own name in the public ear. He himself is mixed up with and spoils everything. I wonder Buonaparte was not tired of the N. N.'s stuck all over the Louvre and throughout France. Goldsmith (as we all know) when in Holland went out into a balcony with some handsome Englishwomen, and on their being applauded by the spectators, turned round and said peevishly, "There are places where I also am admired." He could not give the craving appetite of an author's vanity one day's respite. I have seen a celebrated talker of our own time turn pale and go out of the room when a showy-looking girl has come into it, who for a moment divided the attention of his hearers.—Infinite are the mortifications of the bare attempt to emerge from obscurity; numberless the failures; and greater and more galling still the vicissitudes and tormenting accompaniments of success—

> "Whose top to climb
> Is certain falling, or so slippery, that
> The fear's as bad as falling."

"Would to God," exclaimed Oliver Cromwell, when he was at any time thwarted by the Parliament, "that I had remained by my wood-side to tend a flock of sheep, rather than have been thrust on such a government as this!" When Buonaparte got into his carriage to proceed on his Russian expedition, carelessly twirling his glove, and singing the air,—"Malbrook to the war is going,"— he did not think of the tumble he has got since, the shock of which no one could have stood but himself. We see and hear chiefly of the favourites of Fortune and the Muse, of great generals, of first-rate actors, of celebrated poets. These are at the head; we are struck with the glittering eminence on which they stand, and long to set out on the same tempting career:—not thinking how many discontented half-pay lieutenants are in vain seeking promotion all their lives, and obliged to put up with "the insolence of office, and the spurns which patient merit of the unworthy takes"; how many half-starved strolling-players are doomed to penury and tattered robes in country-places, dreaming to the last of a London engagement; how many wretched daubers shiver and shake in the ague-fit of alternate hopes and fears, waste and pine away in the atrophy of genius, or else turn drawing-masters, picture-cleaners, or newspaper critics; how many hapless poets have sighed out their souls to the Muse in vain, without ever getting their effusions farther known than the Poet's-Corner of a country newspaper, and looked and looked with grudging, wistful eyes at the envious horizon that bounded their provincial fame!—Suppose an actor, for instance, "after the heart-aches and the thousand natural pangs that flesh is heir to," *does* get at the top of his profession, he can no longer bear a rival near the throne; to be second or only equal to another, is to be nothing: he starts at the prospect of a successor, and retains the mimic sceptre with a convulsive grasp: perhaps as he is about to seize the first place which he has long had in his eye, an unsuspected competitor steps in before him, and carries off the prize, leaving him to commence his irksome toil again: he is in a state of alarm at every appearance or rumour of the appearance of a new actor: "a mouse that takes up its lodg-ing in a cat's ear" [1] has a mansion of peace to him: he dreads every hint of an objection, and least of all, can forgive praise mingled with censure: to doubt is to insult, to discriminate is to degrade: he dare hardly look into a criticism unless some one has *tasted* it for him, to see that there is no offence in it: if he does not draw

[1] Webster's Duchess of Malfy.

crowded houses every night, he can neither eat nor sleep; or if all these terrible inflictions are removed, and he can "eat his meal in peace," he then becomes surfeited with applause and dissatisfied with his profession: he wants to be something else, to be distinguished as an author, a collector, a classical scholar, a man of sense and information, and weighs every word he utters, and half retracts it before he utters it, lest if he were to make the smallest slip of the tongue, it should get buzzed abroad that *Mr. ——— was only clever as an actor!* If ever there was a man who did not derive more pain than pleasure from his vanity, that man, says Rousseau, was no other than a fool. A country-gentleman near Taunton spent his whole life in making some hundreds of wretched copies of second-rate pictures, which were bought up at his death by a neighbouring Baronet, to whom

> "Some demon whisper'd, L———, have a taste!"

A little Wilson in an obscure corner escaped the man of *virtù*, and was carried off by a Bristol picture-dealer for three guineas, while the muddled copies of the owner of the mansion (with the frames) fetched thirty, forty, sixty, a hundred ducats a piece. A friend of mine found a very fine Canaletti in a state of strange disfigurement, with the upper part of the sky smeared over and fantastically variegated with English clouds; and on enquiring of the person to whom it belonged whether something had not been done to it, received for answer "that a gentleman, a great artist in the neighbourhood, had retouched some parts of it." What infatuation! Yet this candidate for the honours of the pencil might probably have made a jovial fox-hunter or respectable justice of the peace, if he could only have stuck to what nature and fortune intended him for. Miss ——— can by no means be persuaded to quit the boards of the theatre at ———, a little country town in the West of England. Her salary has been abridged, her person ridiculed, her acting laughed at; nothing will serve—she is determined to be an actress, and scorns to return to her former business as a milliner. Shall I go on? An actor in the same company was visited by the apothecary of the place in an ague-fit, who, on asking his landlady as to his way of life, was told that the poor gentleman was very quiet and gave little trouble, that he generally had a plate of mashed potatoes for his dinner, and lay in bed most of his time, repeating his part. A young couple, every way amiable and deserving, were to have been married, and a benefit-play was bespoke by the officers of the regiment quartered there, to defray the expense of a license and of the wedding-ring, but the profits of the night did not amount to the necessary sum, and they have, I fear, "virgined it e'er since"! Oh for the pencil of Hogarth or Wilkie to give a view of the comic strength of the company at ——, drawn up in battle-array in the Clandestine Marriage, with a *coup d'œil* of the pit, boxes, and gallery, to cure for ever the love of the *ideal*, and the desire to shine and make holiday in the eyes of others, instead of retiring within ourselves and keeping our wishes and our thoughts at home!

Even in the common affairs of life, in love, friendship, and marriage, how little security have we when we trust our happiness in the hands of others! Most of the friends I have seen have turned out the bitterest enemies, or cold, uncomfortable acquaintance. Old companions are like meats served up too often, that lose their relish and their wholesomeness. He who looks at beauty to admire, to adore it, who reads of its wondrous power in novels, in poems, or in plays, is not unwise; but let no man fall in love, for from that moment he is "the baby of a girl." I like very well to repeat such lines as these in the play of Mirandola—

> —"With what a waving air she goes
> Along the corridor. How like a fawn!
> Yet statelier. Hark! No sound, however soft,
> Nor gentlest echo telleth when she treads,
> But every motion of her shape doth seem
> Hallowed by silence"——

but however beautiful the description, defend me from meeting with the original!

> "The fly that sips treacle
> Is lost in the sweets;
> So he that tastes woman
> Ruin meets."

The song is Gay's, not mine, and a bitter-sweet it is.—How few out of the infinite number of those that marry and are given in marriage, wed with those they would prefer to all the world; nay, how far the greater proportion are joined together by mere motives of convenience, accident, recommendation of friends, or indeed not unfrequently by the very fear of the event, by repugnance and

a sort of fatal fascination: yet the tie is for life, not to be shaken
off but with disgrace or death: a man no longer lives to himself,
but is a body (as well as mind) chained to another, in spite of
himself—

> "Like life and death in disproportion met."

So Milton (perhaps from his own experience) makes Adam exclaim in the vehemence of his despair,

> "For either
> He never shall find out fit mate, but such
> As some misfortune brings him or mistake;
> Or whom he wishes most shall seldom gain
> Through her perverseness, but shall see her gain'd
> By a far worse; or if she love, withheld
> By parents; or his happiest choice too late
> Shall meet, already link'd and wedlock-bound
> To a fell adversary, his hate and shame;
> Which infinite calamity shall cause
> To human life, and household peace confound."

If love at first sight were mutual, or to be conciliated by kind offices;
if the fondest affection were not so often repaid and chilled by
indifference and scorn; if so many lovers both before and since the
madman in Don Quixote had not "worshipped a statue, hunted
the wind, cried aloud to the desert"; if friendship were lasting; if
merit were renown, and renown were health, riches, and long life;
or if the homage of the world were paid to conscious worth and
the true aspirations after excellence, instead of its gaudy signs and
outward trappings;—then indeed I might be of opinion that it is
better to live to others than one's-self; but as the case stands, I
incline to the negative side of the question.[1] —

> "I have not loved the world, nor the world me;
> I have not flattered its rank breath, nor bow'd
> To its idolatries a patient knee—
> Nor coin'd my cheek to smiles—nor cried aloud
> In worship of an echo; in the crowd

---

[1] Shenstone and Gray were two men, one of whom pretended to live to himself, and
the other really did so. Gray shrunk from the public gaze (he did not even like his portrait to be prefixed to his works) into his own thoughts and indolent musings; Shenstone
affected privacy that he might be sought out by the world; the one courted retirement
in order to enjoy leisure and repose, as the other coquetted with it, merely to be interrupted with the importunity of visitors and the flatteries of absent friends.

They could not deem me one of such; I stood
Among them, but not of them; in a shroud
Of thoughts which were not their thoughts, and still could,
Had I not filed my mind which thus itself subdued.

" I have not loved the world, nor the world me—
But let us part fair foes; I do believe,
Though I have found them not, that there may be
Words which are things—hopes which will not deceive,
And virtues which are merciful nor weave
Snares for the failing: I would also deem
O'er others' griefs that some sincerely grieve;
That two, or one, are almost what they seem—
That goodness is no name, and happiness no dream."

Sweet verse embalms the spirit of sour misanthropy: but woe betide the ignoble prose-writer who should thus dare to compare notes with the world, or tax it roundly with imposture.

If I had sufficient provocation to rail at the public, as Ben Jonson did at the audience in the Prologues to his plays, I think I should do it in good set terms, nearly as follows:—There is not a more mean, stupid, dastardly, pitiful, selfish, spiteful, envious, ungrateful animal than the Public. It is the greatest of cowards, for it is afraid of itself. From its unwieldy, overgrown dimensions, it dreads the least opposition to it, and shakes like isinglass at the touch of a finger. It starts at its own shadow, like the man in the Hartz mountains, and trembles at the mention of its own name. It has a lion's mouth, the heart of a hare, with ears erect and sleepless eyes. It stands "listening its fears." It is so in awe of its own opinion, that it never dares to form any, but catches up the first idle rumour, lest it should be behind-hand in its judgment, and echoes it till it is deafened with the sound of its own voice. The idea of what the public will think prevents the public from ever thinking at all, and acts as a spell on the exercise of private judgment, so that in short the public ear is at the mercy of the first impudent pretender who chooses to fill it with noisy assertions, or false surmises, or secret whispers. What is said by one is heard by all; the supposition that a thing is known to all the world makes all the world believe it, and the hollow repetition of a vague report drowns the "still, small voice" of reason. We may believe or know that what is said is not true: but we know or fancy that others believe it—we dare not contradict or are too indolent to dispute with them, and therefore give up our internal, and, as we think, our solitary conviction to a sound without substance, without proof, and often without meaning. Nay more, we may believe and know not only that a thing is false, but that others believe and know it to be so, that they are quite as much in the secret of the imposture as we are, that they see the puppets at work, the nature of the machinery, and yet if any one has the art or power to get the management of it, he shall keep possession of the public ear by virtue of a cant-phrase or nickname; and, by dint of effrontery and perseverance, make all the world believe and repeat what all the world know to be false. The ear is quicker than the judgment. We know that certain things are said; by that circumstance alone, we know that they produce a certain effect on the imagination of others, and we conform to their prejudices by mechanical sympathy, and for want of sufficient spirit to differ with them. So far then is public opinion from resting on a broad and solid basis, as the aggregate of thought and feeling in a community, that it is slight and shallow and variable to the last degree—the bubble of the moment—so that we may safely say the public is the dupe of public opinion, not its parent. The public is pusillanimous and cowardly, because it is weak. It knows itself to be a great dunce, and that it has no opinions but upon suggestion. Yet it is unwilling to appear in leading-strings, and would have it thought that its decisions are as wise as they are weighty. It is hasty in taking up its favourites, more hasty in laying them aside, lest it should be supposed deficient in sagacity in either case. It is generally divided into two strong parties, each of which will allow neither common sense nor common honesty to the other side. It reads the Edinburgh and Quarterly Reviews, and believes them both—or if there is a doubt, malice turns the scale. Taylor and Hessey told me that they had sold nearly two editions of the Characters of Shakespeare's Plays in about three months, but that after the Quarterly review of them came out, they never sold another copy. The public, enlightened as they are, must have known the meaning of that attack as well as those who made it. It was not ignorance then, but cowardice, that led them to give up their own opinion. A crew of mischievous critics at Edinburgh having affixed the epithet of the *Cockney School* to one or two writers born in the metropolis, all the people in London became afraid of looking into

their works, lest they too should be convicted of cockneyism. Oh
brave public! This epithet proved too much for one of the writers
in question, and stuck like a barbed arrow in his heart. Poor
Keats! What was sport to the town was death to him. Young,
sensitive, delicate, he was like

> "A bud bit by an envious worm,
> Ere he could spread his sweet leaves to the air
> Or dedicate his beauty to the sun "—

and unable to endure the miscreant cry and idiot laugh, withdrew
to sigh his last breath in foreign climes.—The public is as envious
and ungrateful as it is ignorant, stupid, and pigeon-livered—

> "A huge-sized monster of ingratitudes."

It reads, it admires, it extols, only because it is the fashion, not
from any love of the subject or the man. It cries you up or runs
you down out of mere caprice and levity. If you have pleased it,
it is jealous of its own involuntary acknowledgment of merit, and
seizes the first opportunity, the first shabby pretext, to pick a
quarrel with you, and be quits once more. Every petty caviller
is erected into a judge, every tale-bearer is implicitly believed.
Every little low paltry creature that gaped and wondered, only
because others did so, is glad to find you (as he thinks) on a level
with himself. An author is not then, after all, a being of another
order. Public admiration is forced, and goes against the grain.
Public obloquy is cordial and sincere: every individual feels his
own importance in it. They give you up bound hand and foot into
the power of your accusers. To attempt to defend yourself is a
high crime and misdemeanour, a contempt of court, an extreme
piece of impertinence. Or, if you prove every charge unfounded,
they never think of retracting their error, or making you amends.
It would be a compromise of their dignity; they consider themselves as the party injured, and resent your innocence as an imputation on their judgment. The celebrated Bub Doddington, when
out of favour at court, said "he would not *justify* before his sovereign: it was for Majesty to be displeased, and for him to believe
himself in the wrong!" The public are not quite so modest. People
already begin to talk of the Scotch Novels as overrated. How
then can common authors be supposed to keep their heads long
above water? As a general rule, all those who live by the public

starve, and are made a bye-word and a standing jest into the bargain. Posterity is no better (not a bit more enlightened or more liberal), except that you are no longer in their power, and that the voice of common fame saves them the trouble of deciding on your claims. The public now are the posterity of Milton and Shakespeare. Our posterity will be the living public of a future generation. When a man is dead, they put money in his coffin, erect monuments to his memory, and celebrate the anniversary of his birthday in set speeches. Would they take any notice of him if he were living? No!—I was complaining of this to a Scotchman who had been attending a dinner and a subscription to raise a monument to Burns. He replied, he would sooner subscribe twenty pounds to his monument than have given it him while living; so that if the poet were to come to life again, he would treat him just as he was treated in fact. This was an honest Scotchman. What *he* said, the rest would do.

Enough: my soul, turn from them, and let me try to regain the obscurity and quiet that I love, "far from the madding strife," in some sequestered corner of my own, or in some far-distant land! In the latter case, I might carry with me as a consolation the passage in Bolingbroke's Reflections on Exile, in which he describes in glowing colours the resources which a man may always find within himself, and of which the world cannot deprive him:—

"Believe me, the providence of God has established such an order in the world, that of all which belongs to us the least valuable parts can alone fall under the will of others. Whatever is best is safest; lies out of the reach of human power; can neither be given nor taken away. Such is this great and beautiful work of nature, the world. Such is the mind of man, which contemplates and admires the world whereof it makes the noblest part. These are inseparably ours, and as long as we remain in one we shall enjoy the other. Let us march therefore intrepidly wherever we are led by the course of human accidents. Wherever they lead us, on what coast soever we are thrown by them, we shall not find ourselves absolutely strangers. We shall feel the same revolution of seasons, and the same sun and moon [1] will guide the course of our

---

[1] Plut. of Banishment. He compares those who cannot live out of their own country to the simple people who fancied the moon of Athens was a finer moon than that of Corinth,
—*Labentem cœlo quæ ducitis annum.*
—Virg. *Georg.*

year. The same azure vault, bespangled with stars, will be every where spread over our heads. There is no part of the world from whence we may not admire those planets which roll, like ours, in different orbits round the same central sun; from whence we may not discover an object still more stupendous, that army of fixed stars hung up in the immense space of the universe, innumerable suns whose beams enlighten and cherish the unknown worlds which roll around them; and whilst I am ravished by such contemplations as these, whilst my soul is thus raised up to heaven, it imports me little what ground I tread upon."

ON VULGARITY AND AFFECTATION

FEW subjects are more nearly allied than these two—vulgarity and affectation. It may be said of them truly that "thin partitions do their bounds divide." There cannot be a surer proof of a low origin or of an innate meanness of disposition than to be always talking and thinking of being genteel. One must feel a strong tendency to that which one is always trying to avoid: whenever we pretend, on all occasions, a mighty contempt for any thing, it is a pretty clear sign that we feel ourselves very nearly on a level with it. Of the two classes of people, I hardly know which is to be regarded with most distaste, the vulgar aping the genteel, or the genteel constantly sneering at and endeavouring to distinguish themselves from the vulgar. These two sets of persons are always thinking of one another; the lower of the higher with envy, the more fortunate of their less happy neighbours with contempt. They are habitually placed in opposition to each other; jostle in their pretensions at every turn; and the same objects and train of thought (only reversed by the relative situation of either party) occupy their whole time and attention. The one are straining every nerve, and outraging common sense, to be thought genteel; the others have no other object or idea in their heads than *not* to be thought vulgar. This is but poor spite; a very pitiful style of ambition. To be merely not that which one heartily despises, is a very humble claim to superiority: to despise what one really is, is still worse. Most of the characters in Miss Burney's novels—the Branghtons, the Smiths, the Dubsters, the Cecilias, the Delvilles, &c. are well met in this respect, and much of a piece: the one half are trying not to be taken for themselves, and the other half not to be taken for the first. They neither of them have any pretensions of their own, or real standard of worth. "A feather will turn the scale of their avoirdupois"; though the fair authoress was not aware of the metaphysical identity of her principal and subordinate characters. Affectation is the master-key to both.

Gentility is only a more select and artificial kind of vulgarity. It cannot exist but by a sort of borrowed distinction. It plumes itself up and revels in the homely pretensions of the mass of mankind. It judges of the worth of every thing by name, fashion, and opinion; and hence, from the conscious absence of real qualities or sincere satisfaction in itself, it builds its supercilious and fantastic conceit on the wretchedness and wants of others. Violent antipathies are always suspicious, and betray a secret affinity. The difference between the "Great Vulgar and the Small" is mostly in outward circumstances. The coxcomb criticises the dress of the clown, as the pedant cavils at the bad grammar of the illiterate, or the prude is shocked at the back-slidings of her frail acquaintance. Those who have the fewest resources in themselves, naturally seek the food of their self-love elsewhere. The most ignorant people find most to laugh at in strangers: scandal and satire prevail most in country-places; and a propensity to ridicule every the slightest or most palpable deviation from what we happen to approve, ceases with the progress of common sense and decency.[1] True worth does not exult in the faults and deficiencies of others; as true refinement turns away from grossness and deformity, instead of being tempted to indulge in an unmanly triumph over it. Raphael would not faint away at the daubing of a sign-post, nor Homer hold his head the higher for being in the company of a Grub-street bard. Real power, real excellence, does not seek for a foil in imperfection; nor fear contamination from coming in contact

---

[1] "If an European, when he has cut off his beard and put false hair on his head, or bound up his own natural hair in regular hard knots, as unlike nature as he can possibly make it; and after having rendered them immovable by the help of the fat of hogs, has covered the whole with flour, laid on by a machine with the utmost regularity; if when thus attired he issues forth, and meets with a Cherokee Indian, who has bestowed as much time at his toilet, and laid on with equal care and attention his yellow and red oker on particular parts of his forehead or cheeks, as he judges most becoming; whoever of these two despises the other for this attention to the fashion of his country, whichever first feels himself provoked to laugh, is the barbarian."—Sir Joshua Reynolds's *Discourses*, vol. i. pp. 231, 232.

with that which is coarse and homely. It reposes on itself, and is equally free from spleen and affectation. But the spirit of gentility is the mere essence of spleen and affectation;—of affected delight in its own *would-be* qualifications, and of ineffable disdain poured out upon the involuntary blunders or accidental disadvantages of those whom it chooses to treat as its inferiors.—Thus a fashionable Miss titters till she is ready to burst her sides at the uncouth shape of a bonnet, or the abrupt drop of a courtesy (such as Jeanie Deans would make) in a country-girl who comes to be hired by her Mamma as a servant:—yet to shew how little foundation there is for this hysterical expression of her extreme good opinion of herself and contempt for the untutored rustic, she would herself the next day be delighted with the very same shaped bonnet if brought her by a French milliner and told it was all the fashion, and in a week's time will become quite familiar with the maid, and chatter with her (upon equal terms) about caps and ribbons and lace by the hour together. There is no difference between them but that of situation in the kitchen or in the parlour: let circumstances bring them together, and they fit like hand and glove. It is like mistress, like maid. Their talk, their thoughts, their dreams, their likings and dislikes are the same. The mistress's head runs continually on dress and finery, so does the maid's: the young lady longs to ride in a coach and six, so does the maid, if she could; Miss forms a *beau idéal* of a lover with black eyes and rosy cheeks, which does not differ from that of her attendant; both like a smart man, the one the footman and the other his master, for the same reason: both like handsome furniture and fine houses; both apply the terms, *shocking* and *disagreeable*, to the same things and persons: both have a great notion of balls, plays, treats, song-books, and love-tales: both like a wedding or a christening, and both would give their little fingers to see a coronation—with this difference, that the one has a chance of getting a seat at it, and the other is dying of envy that she has not.—Indeed, this last is a ceremony that delights equally the greatest monarch and the meanest of his subjects, the vilest of the rabble. Yet this, which is the height of gentility and consummation of external distinction and splendour, is, I should say, a vulgar ceremony. For what degree of refinement, of capacity, of virtue is required in the individual who is so distinguished, or is necessary to his enjoying this idle and imposing parade of his person? Is he delighted with the state-coach and gilded pannels? So is the poorest wretch that gazes at it. Is he struck with the spirit, the beauty, and symmetry of the eight cream-coloured horses? There is not one of the immense multitude, who flock to see the sight from town or country, St. Giles's or Whitechapel, young or old, rich or poor, gentle or simple, who does not agree to admire the same object. Is he delighted with the yeomen of the guard, the military escort, the groups of ladies, the badges of sovereign power, the kingly crown, the marshal's truncheon and the judge's robe, the array that precedes and follows him, the crowded streets, the windows hung with eager looks? So are the mob, for they "have eyes and see them!" There is no one faculty of mind or body, natural or acquired, essential to the principal figure in this procession, more than is common to the meanest and most despised attendant on it. A wax-work figure would answer the same purpose: a Lord Mayor of London has as much tinsel to be proud of. I would rather have a king do something that no one else has the power or magnanimity to do, or say something that no one else has the wisdom to say, or look more handsome, more thoughtful, or benign than any one else in his dominions. But I see nothing to raise one's idea of him in his being made a shew of: if the pageant would do as well without the man, the man would do as well without the pageant! Kings have been declared to be "lovers of low company"; and this maxim, besides the reason sometimes assigned for it, *viz.* that they meet with less opposition to their wills from such persons, will I suspect be found to turn at last on the consideration I am here stating, that they also meet with more sympathy in their tastes. The most ignorant and thoughtless have the greatest admiration of the baubles, the outward symbols of pomp and power, the sound and shew, which are the habitual delight and mighty prerogative of kings. The stupidest slave worships the gaudiest tyrant. The same gross motives appeal to the same gross capacities, flatter the pride of the superior, and excite the servility of the dependent: whereas a higher reach of moral and intellectual refinement might seek in vain for higher proofs of internal worth and inherent majesty in the object of its idolatry, and not finding the divinity lodged within, the unreasonable expectation raised would probably end in mortification on both sides!—There is little to distinguish a king from his subjects but the rabble's shout—if he loses that, and is reduced to the forlorn hope of gaining the suffrages of the wise and good, he is of all men the most miserable.—But enough of this.

"I like it," says Miss Branghton [1] in Evelina (meaning the Opera) "because it is not vulgar." That is, she likes it, not because there is anything to like in it, but because other people are prevented from liking or knowing any thing about it. Janus Weathercock, Esq., laugheth to scorn and spitefully entreateth and hugely condemneth my dramatic criticisms in the London Magazine, for a like reason. I must therefore make an example of him *in terrorem* to all such hypercritics. He finds fault with me and calls my taste vulgar, because I go to Sadler's Wells ("a place he has heard of"—O Lord, Sir!)—because I notice the Miss Dennetts, "great favourites with the Whitechapel orders"—praise Miss Valancy, "a bouncing Columbine at Ashley's and them there places, as his barber informs him" (has he no way of establishing himself in his own good opinion but by triumphing over his barber's bad English?)—and finally, because I recognised the existence of the Cobourg and the Surrey theatres, at the names of which he cries "Faugh" with great significance, as if he had some personal disgust at them, and yet he would be supposed never to have entered them. It is not his cue as a well-bred critic. *C'est beau ça.* Now this appears to me a very crude, unmeaning, indiscriminate, wholesale, and vulgar way of thinking. It is prejudicing things in the lump, by names and places and classes, instead of judging of them by what they are in themselves, by their real qualities and shades of distinction. There is no selection, truth, or delicacy in such a mode of proceeding. It is affecting ignorance, and making it a title to wisdom. It is a vapid assumption of superiority. It is exceeding impertinence. It is rank coxcombry. It is nothing in the world else. To condemn because the multitude admire is as essentially vulgar as to admire because they admire. There is no exercise of taste or judgment in either case: both are equally repugnant to good sense, and of the two I should prefer the good-natured side. I would as soon agree with my barber as differ from him: and why should I make a point of

---

[1] This name was originally spelt Braughton in the manuscript, and was altered to Branghton by a mistake of the printer. Branghton, however, was thought a good name for the occasion, and was suffered to stand. "Dip it in the ocean," as Sterne's barber says of the buckle, "and it will stand!"

reversing the sentence of the Whitechapel orders? Or how can it affect my opinion of the merits of an actor at the Cobourg or the Surrey theatres, that these theatres are in or out of the Bills of Mortality? This is an easy, short-hand way of judging, as gross as it is mechanical. It is not a difficult matter to settle questions of taste by consulting the map of London, or to prove your liberality by geographical distinctions. Janus jumbles things together strangely. If he had seen Mr. Kean in a provincial theatre, at Exeter or Taunton, he would have thought it vulgar to admire him: but when he had been stamped in London, Janus would no doubt shew his discernment and the subtlety of his tact for the display of character and passion, by not being behind the fashion. The Miss Dennetts are "little unformed girls," for no other reason than because they danced at one of the Minor Theatres: let them but come out on the Opera boards, and let the beauty and fashion of the season greet them with a fairy shower of delighted applause, and they would outshine Milanie "with the foot of fire." His gorge rises at the mention of a certain quarter of the town: whatever passes current in another, he "swallows total grist unsifted, husks and all." This is not taste, but folly. At this rate, the hackney-coachman who drives him, or his horse Contributor, whom he has introduced as a select personage to the vulgar reader, knows as much of the matter as he does.—In a word, the answer to all this in the first instance is to say what vulgarity is. Now its essence, I imagine, consists in taking manners, actions, words, opinions on trust from others, without examining one's own feelings or weighing the merits of the case. It is coarseness or shallowness of taste arising from want of individual refinement, together with the confidence and presumption inspired by example and numbers. It may be defined to be a prostitution of the mind or body to ape the more or less obvious defects of others, because by so doing we shall secure the suffrages of those we associate with. To affect a gesture, an opinion, a phrase, because it is the rage with a large number of persons, or to hold it in abhorrence because another set of persons very little, if at all, better informed, cry it down to distinguish themselves from the former, is in either case equal vulgarity and absurdity.—A thing is not vulgar merely because it is common. 'Tis common to breathe, to see, to feel, to live. Nothing is vulgar that is natural, spontaneous, unavoidable. Grossness is not vulgarity, ignorance is not vulgarity, awkwardness is not vulgarity: but all these become vulgar when they are affected and shewn off on the authority of others, or to fall in with *the fashion* or the company we keep. Caliban is coarse enough, but surely he is not vulgar. We might as well spurn the clod under our feet, and call it vulgar. Cobbett is coarse enough, but he is not vulgar. He does not belong to the herd. Nothing real, nothing original, can be vulgar: but I should think an imitator of Cobbett a vulgar man. Emery's Yorkshireman is vulgar, because he is a Yorkshireman. It is the cant and gibberish, the cunning and low life of a particular district; it has "a stamp exclusive and provincial." He might "gabble most brutishly" and yet not fall under the letter of the definition; but "his speech bewrayeth him," his dialect (like the jargon of a Bond-street lounger) is the damning circumstance. If he were a mere blockhead, it would not signify: but he thinks himself a *knowing hand*, according to the notions and practices of those with whom he was brought up, and which he thinks *the go* every where. In a word, this character is not the offspring of untutored nature but of bad habits; it is made up of ignorance and conceit. It has a mixture of *slang* in it. All slang phrases are for the same reason vulgar; but there is nothing vulgar in the common English idiom. Simplicity is not vulgarity; but the looking to affectation of any sort for distinction is. A cockney is a vulgar character, whose imagination cannot wander beyond the suburbs of the metropolis: so is a fellow who is always thinking of the High-street, Edinburgh. We want a name for this last character. An opinion is vulgar that is stewed in the rank breath of the rabble: nor is it a bit purer or more refined for having passed through the well-cleansed teeth of a whole court. The inherent vulgarity is in having no other feeling on any subject than the crude, blind, headlong, gregarious notion acquired by sympathy with the mixed multitude or with a fastidious minority, who are just as insensible to the real truth, and as indifferent to every thing but their own frivolous and vexatious pretensions. The upper are not wiser than the lower orders, because they resolve to differ from them. The fashionable have the advantage of the unfashionable in nothing but the fashion. The true vulgar are the *servum pecus imitatorum*— the herd of pretenders to what they do not feel and to what is not natural to them, whether in high or low life. To belong to any

class, to move in any rank or sphere of life, is not a very exclusive
distinction or test of refinement. Refinement will in all classes be
the exception, not the rule; and the exception may fall out in one
class as well as another. A king is but an hereditary title. A nobleman is only one of the House of Peers. To be a knight or alderman is confessedly a vulgar thing. The king the other day made
Sir Walter Scott a baronet, but not all the power of the Three
Estates could make another Author of Waverley. Princes, heroes,
are often common-place people: Hamlet was not a vulgar character,
neither was Don Quixote. To be an author, to be a painter, is
nothing. It is a trick, it is a trade.

> "An author! 'tis a venerable name:
> How few deserve it, yet what numbers claim!"

Nay, to be a Member of the Royal Academy or a Fellow of the
Royal Society is but a vulgar distinction. But to be a Virgil, a
Milton, a Raphael, a Claude, is what fell to the lot of humanity but
once! I do not think *they* were vulgar people; though, for any
thing I know to the contrary, the first Lord of the Bed-chamber
may be a very vulgar man: for any thing I know to the contrary,
he may not be so.—Such are pretty much my notions of gentility
and vulgarity.

There is a well-dressed and an ill-dressed mob, both which I
hate. *Odi profanum vulgus, et arceo.* The vapid affectation of the
one to me is even more intolerable than the gross insolence and
brutality of the other. If a set of low-lived fellows are noisy, rude,
and boisterous to shew their disregard of the company, a set of
fashionable coxcombs are, to a nauseous degree, finical and effeminate to shew their thorough breeding. The one are governed by
their feelings, however coarse and misguided, which is something:
the others consult only appearances, which are nothing, either as a
test of happiness or virtue. Hogarth in his prints has trimmed
the balance of pretension between the downright blackguard and
the *soi-disant* fine gentleman unanswerably. It does not appear in
his moral demonstrations (whatever it may do in the genteel
letter-writing of Lord Chesterfield, or the chivalrous rhapsodies
of Burke) that vice by losing all its grossness loses half its evil.
It becomes more contemptible, not less disgusting. What is there
in common, for instance, between his beaux and belles, his rakes

and his coquettes, and the men and women, the true heroic and ideal characters in Raphael? But his people of fashion and quality are just upon a par with the low, the selfish, the *unideal* characters in the contrasted view of human life, and are often the very same characters, only changing places. If the lower ranks are actuated by envy and uncharitableness towards the upper, the latter have scarcely any feelings but of pride, contempt, and aversion to the lower. If the poor would pull down the rich to get at their good things, the rich would tread down the poor as in a wine-press, and squeeze the last shilling out of their pockets, and the last drop of blood out of their veins. If the headstrong self-will and unruly turbulence of a common ale-house are shocking, what shall we say to the studied insincerity, the insipid want of common sense, the callous insensibility of the drawing-room and *boudoir?* I would rather see the feelings of our common nature (for they are the same at bottom) expressed in the most naked and unqualified way, than see every feeling of our nature suppressed, stifled, hermetically sealed under the smooth, cold, glittering varnish of pretended refinement and conventional politeness. The one may be corrected by being better informed; the other is incorrigible, wilful, heartless depravity. I cannot describe the contempt and disgust I have felt at the tone of what would be thought good company, when I have witnessed the sleek, smiling, glossy, gratuitous assumption of superiority to every feeling of humanity, honesty, or principle, making part of the etiquette, the mental and moral *costume* of the table, and every profession of toleration or favour for the lower orders, that is, for the great mass of our fellow-creatures, treated as an indecorum and breach of the harmony of well-regulated society. In short, I prefer a bear-garden to the adder's den. Or, to put this case in its extremest point of view, I have more patience with men in a rude state of nature outraging the human form than I have with apes "making mops and mows" at the extravagances they have first provoked. I can endure the brutality (as it is termed) of mobs better than the inhumanity of courts. The violence of the one rages like a fire; the insidious policy of the other strikes like a pestilence, and is more fatal and inevitable. The slow poison of despotism is worse than the convulsive struggles of anarchy. "Of all evils," says Hume, "anarchy is the shortest lived." The one may "break out like a wild overthrow"; but the

other from its secret, sacred stand, operates unseen, and under-
mines the happiness of kingdoms for ages, lurks in the hollow cheek,
and stares you in the face in the ghastly eye of want and agony
and woe. It is dreadful to hear the noise and uproar of an infuri-
ated multitude stung by the sense of wrong, and maddened by
sympathy: it is more appalling to think of the smile answered by
other gracious smiles, of the whisper echoed by other assenting
whispers, which doom them first to despair and then to destruction.
Popular fury finds its counterpart in courtly servility. If every
outrage is to be apprehended from the one, every iniquity is deliberately sanctioned by the other, without regard to justice or
decency. The word of a king, "Go thou and do likewise," makes
the stoutest heart dumb: truth and honesty shrink before it.[1]
If there are watchwords for the rabble, have not the polite and
fashionable their hackneyed phrases, their fulsome, unmeaning
jargon as well? Both are to me anathema!

To return to the first question, as it regards individual and
private manners. There is a fine illustration of the effects of preposterous and affected gentility in the character of Gertrude, in
the old comedy of Eastward Hoe, written by Ben Jonson, Marston,
and Chapman in conjunction. This play is supposed to have given
rise to Hogarth's series of prints of the Idle and Industrious Apprentice; and there is something exceedingly Hogarthian in the
view both of vulgar and of genteel life here displayed. The character of Gertrude, in particular, the heroine of the piece, is inimitably drawn. The mixture of vanity and meanness, the internal
worthlessness, and external pretence, the rustic ignorance and fine
lady-like airs, the intoxication of novelty and infatuation of pride,
appear like a dream or romance, rather than any thing in real life.
Cinderella and her glass-slipper are common-place to it. She is
not, like Millamant (a century afterwards), the accomplished fine
lady, but a pretender to all the foppery and finery of the character.
It is the honeymoon with her ladyship, and her folly is at the full.
To be a wife, and the wife of a knight, are to her pleasures "worn in
their newest gloss," and nothing can exceed her raptures in the
contemplation of both parts of the dilemma. It is not familiarity,

---

[1] A lady of quality, in allusion to the gallantries of a reigning Prince, being told, "I
suppose it will be your turn next?" said, "No, I hope not; for you know it is impossible
to refuse!"

but novelty, that weds her to the court. She rises into the air of
gentility from the ground of a city life, and flutters about there
with all the fantastic delight of a butterfly that has just changed
its caterpillar state. The sound of My Lady intoxicates her with
delight, makes her giddy, and almost turns her brain. On the bare
strength of it she is ready to turn her father and mother out of
doors, and treats her brother and sister with infinite disdain and
judicial hardness of heart. With some speculators the modern
philosophy has deadened and distorted all the natural affections:
and before abstract ideas and the mischievous refinements of
literature were introduced, nothing was to be met with in the pri-
meval state of society but simplicity and pastoral innocence of
manners—

> "And all was conscience and tender heart."

This historical play gives the lie to the above theory pretty broadly,
yet delicately. Our heroine is as vain as she is ignorant, and as
unprincipled as she is both; and without an idea or wish of any
kind but that of adorning her person in the glass, and being called
and thought a lady, something superior to a citizen's wife.[1] She is

---

[1] "*Gertrude.* For the passion of patience, look if Sir Petronel approach. That sweet,
that fine, that delicate, that—for love's sake, tell me if he come. Oh, sister Mill, though
my father be a low-capt tradesman, yet I must be a lady, and I praise God my mother
must call me madam. Does he come? Off with this gown for shame's sake, off with this
gown! Let not my knight take me in the city cut, in any hand! Tear't! Pox on't (does
he come?), tear't off! *Thus while she sleeps, I sorrow for her sake.* (Sings.)

Mildred. Lord, sister, with what an immodest impatiency and disgraceful scorn do
you put off your city-tire! I am sorry to think you imagine to right yourself in wronging
that which hath made both you and us.

Ger. I tell you, I cannot endure it: I must be a lady: do you wear your quoiff with a
London licket! your stamel petticoat with two guards! the buffin gown with the tuft-
afitty cap and the velvet lace! I must be a lady, and I will be a lady. I like some humours
of the city dames well; to eat cherries only at an angel a pound; good: to dye rich scarlet
black; pretty: to line a grogram gown clean through with velvet; tolerable: their pure
linen, their smocks of three pound a smock, are to be borne withal; but your mincing
niceries, taffity pipkins, durance petticoats, and silver bodkins—God's my life! as I
shall be a lady, I cannot endure it.

Mil. Well, sister, those that scorn their nest oft fly with a sick wing.

Ger. Bow-bell! Alas! poor Mill, when I am a lady, I'll pray for thee yet i'faith; nay,
and I'll vouchsafe to call thee sister Mill still; for though thou art not like to be a lady as
I am, yet surely thou art a creature of God's making, and may'st peradventure be saved
as soon as I (does he come?). *And ever and anon she doubled in her song.*

Mil. Now (lady's my comfort), what a profane ape's here!

[*Enter Sir* Petronel Flash, *Mr.* Touchstone, *and Mrs.* Touchstone.]

Ger. Is my knight come? O the lord, my band! Sister, do my cheeks look well? **Give**

so bent on finery that she believes in miracles to obtain it, and expects the fairies to bring it her. She is quite above thinking of a settlement, jointure, or pin-money. She takes the will for the deed all through the piece, and is so besotted with this ignorant, vulgar notion of rank and title as a real thing that cannot be counterfeited, that she is the dupe of her own fine stratagems, and marries a gull, a dolt, a broken adventurer for an accomplished and brave gentle-

me a little box o' the ear, that I may seem to blush. Now, now! so, there, there! here he is! O my dearest delight! Lord, Lord! and how does my knight?

Touchstone. Fie, with more modesty.

Ger. Modesty! why, I am no citizen now. Modesty! am I not to be married? You're best to keep me modest, now I am to be a lady.

Sir Petronel. Boldness is a good fashion and court-like.

Ger. Aye, in a country lady I hope it is, as I shall be. And how chance ye came no sooner, knight?

Sir Pet. Faith, I was so entertained in the progress with one Count Epernoun, a Welch knight: we had a match at baloon too with my Lord Whackum for four crowns.

Ger. And when shall's be married, my knight?

Sir Pet. I am come now to consummate: and your father may call a poor knight son-in-law.

Mrs. Touchstone. Yes, that he is a knight: I know where he had money to pay the gentlemen usher and heralds their fees Aye, that he is a knight: and so might you have been too, if you had been aught else but an ass, as well as some of your neighbours. An I thought you would not ha' been knighted, as I am an honest woman, I would ha' dubbed you myself. I praise God, I have wherewithal. But as for you, daughter——

Ger. Aye, mother, I must be a lady to-morrow; and by your leave, mother (I speak it not without my duty, but only in the right of my husband), I must take place of you, mother.

Mrs. Touch. That you shall, lady-daughter; and have a coach as well as I.

Ger. Yes, mother; but my coach-horses must take the wall of your coach-horses.

Touch. Come, come, the day grows low; 'tis supper time: and, sir respect my daughter; she has refused for you wealthy and honest matches, known good men.

Ger. Body o' truth, citizens, citizens! Sweet knight, as soon as ever we are married, take me to thy mercy, out of this miserable city. Presently: carry me out of the scent of Newcastle coal and the hearing of Bow-bell, I beseech thee; down with me, for God's sake."—Act I. Scene i.

This dotage on sound and show seemed characteristic of that age (see *New Way to Pay Old Debts*, &c.)—as if in the grossness of sense, and the absence of all intellectual and abstract topics of thought and discourse (the thin, circulating medium of the present day) the mind was attracted without the power of resistance to the tinkling sound of its own name with a title added to it, and the image of its own person tricked out in old-fashioned finery. The effect, no doubt, was also more marked and striking from the contrast between the ordinary penury and poverty of the age and the first and more extravagant demonstrations of luxury and artificial refinement. Here is one more specimen.

"*Gertrude.* Good Lord, that there are no fairies now-a-days, Syn.

Syndefy. Why, madam?

Ger. To do miracles, and bring ladies money. Sure, if we lay in a cleanly house, they would haunt it, Synne? I'll try. I'll sweep the chamber soon at night, and set a dish of water o' the hearth. A fairy may come and bring a pearl or a diamond. We do not know, Synne: or there may be a pot of gold hid in the yard, if we had tools to dig for't. Why

man. Her meanness is equal to her folly and her pride (and nothing can be greater), yet she holds out on the strength of her original pretensions for a long time, and plays the upstart with decent and imposing consistency. Indeed, her infatuation and caprices are akin to the flighty perversity of a disordered imagination; and another turn of the wheel of good or evil fortune would have sent her to keep company with Hogarth's *Merveilleuses* in Bedlam, or with Dekker's group of coquettes in the same place. The other parts of the play are a dreary lee-shore, like Cuckold's Point on the coast of Essex, where the preconcerted ship-wreck takes place that winds up the catastrophe of the piece. But this is also characteristic of the age, and serves as a contrast to the airy and factitious character which is the principal figure in the plot. We had made but little progress from that point till Hogarth's time, if Hogarth is to be believed in his description of city manners. How wonderfully we have distanced it since!

Without going into this at length, there is one circumstance I would mention in which I think there has been a striking improvement in the family economy of modern times—and that is in the relation of mistresses and servants. After visits and finery, a married woman of the old school had nothing to do but to attend to her housewifery. She had no other resource, no other sense of power, but to harangue and lord it over her domestics. Modern book-education supplies the place of the old-fashioned system of kitchen persecution and eloquence. A well-bred woman now seldom goes into the kitchen to look after the servants:—formerly what was called a good manager, an exemplary mistress of a family, did nothing but hunt them from morning to night, from one year's end to another, without leaving them a moment's rest, peace, or comfort. Now a servant is left to do her work without this sus-

---

may not we two rise early i' the morning, Synne, afore anybody is up, and find a jewel i' the streets worth a hundred pounds? May not some great court-lady, as she comes from revels at midnight, look out of her coach, as 'tis running, and lose such a jewel, and we find it? ha!

Syn. They are pretty waking dreams, these.

Ger. Or may not some old usurer be drunk over-night with a bag of money, and leave it behind him on a stall? For God's sake, Syn, let's rise to-morrow by break of day, and see. I protest, la, if I had as much money as an alderman, I would scatter some on't i' the streets for poor ladies to find when their knights were laid up. And now I remember my song of the Golden Shower, why may not I have such a fortune? I'll sing it, and try what luck I shall have after it."—Act V. Scene i.

picious and tormenting interference and fault-finding at every step, and she does it all the better. The proverbs about the mistress's eye, &c. are no longer held for current. A woman from this habit, which at last became an uncontrollable passion, would scold her maids for fifty years together, and nothing could stop her: now the temptation to read the last new poem or novel, and the necessity of talking of it in the next company she goes into, prevent her—and the benefit to all parties is incalculable!

ON GOING A JOURNEY

ONE of the pleasantest things in the world is going a journey; but I like to go by myself. I can enjoy society in a room; but out of doors, nature is company enough for me. I am then never less alone than when alone.

"The fields his study, nature was his book."

I cannot see the wit of walking and talking at the same time. When I am in the country I wish to vegetate like the country. I am not for criticising hedge-rows and black cattle. I go out of town in order to forget the town and all that is in it. There are those who for this purpose go to watering-places, and carry the metropolis with them. I like more elbow-room and fewer incumbrances. I like solitude, when I give myself up to it, for the sake of solitude; nor do I ask for

——"a friend in my retreat,
Whom I may whisper solitude is sweet."

The soul of a journey is liberty, perfect liberty, to think, feel, do, just as one pleases. We go a journey chiefly to be free of all impediments and of all inconveniences; to leave ourselves behind, much more to get rid of others. It is because I want a little breathing-space to muse on indifferent matters, where Contemplation

" May plume her feathers and let grow her wings,
That in the various bustle of resort
Were all too ruffled, and sometimes impair'd."

that I absent myself from the town for awhile, without feeling at a loss the moment I am left by myself. Instead of a friend in a post-chaise or in a tilbury, to exchange good things with, and vary the same stale topics over again, for once let me have a truce with impertinence. Give me the clear blue sky over my head, and the green turf beneath my feet, a winding road before me, and a three hours' march to dinner—and then to thinking! It is hard if I cannot start some game on these lone heaths. I laugh, I run, I leap, I sing for joy. From the point of yonder rolling cloud, I plunge into my past being, and revel there, as the sun-burnt Indian plunges headlong into the wave that wafts him to his native shore. Then long-forgotten things, like "sunken wrack and sumless treasuries," burst upon my eager sight, and I begin to feel, think, and be myself again. Instead of an awkward silence, broken by attempts at wit or dull common-places, mine is that undisturbed silence of the heart which alone is perfect eloquence. No one likes puns, alliterations, antitheses, argument, and analysis better than I do; but I sometimes had rather be without them. "Leave, oh, leave me to my repose!" I have just now other business in hand, which would seem idle to you, but is with me "the very stuff o' the conscience." Is not this wild rose sweet without a comment? Does not this daisy leap to my heart, set in its coat of emerald? Yet if I were to explain to you the circumstance that has so endeared it to me, you would only smile. Had I not better then keep it to myself, and let it serve me to brood over, from here to yonder craggy point, and from thence onward to the far-distant horizon? I should be but bad company all that way, and therefore prefer being alone. I have heard it said that you may, when the moody fit comes on, walk or ride on by yourself, and indulge your reveries. But this looks like a breach of manners, a neglect of others, and you are thinking all the time that you ought to rejoin your party. "Out upon such half-faced fellowship," says I. I like to be either entirely to myself, or entirely at the disposal of others; to talk or be silent, to walk or sit still, to be sociable or solitary. I was pleased with an observation of Mr. Cobbett's, that "he thought it a bad French custom to drink our wine with our meals, and that an Englishman ought to do only one thing at a time." So I cannot talk and think, or indulge in melancholy musing and lively conversation by fits and starts. "Let me have a companion of my way," says Sterne, "were it but to remark how the shadows lengthen as the sun goes down." It is beautifully said: but in my opinion, this continual comparing of notes interferes with the involuntary impression of things upon the mind, and hurts the sentiment. If you only hint what you feel in a kind of dumb shew, it is insipid: if you have to explain it, it is making a toil of a pleasure. You cannot read the book of nature, without being perpetually put to the trouble of translating it for the benefit of others. I am for this synthetical method on a journey, in preference to the analytical. I am content to lay in a stock of ideas then, and to examine and anatomise them afterwards. I want to see my vague notions float like the down of the thistle before the breeze, and not to have them entangled in the briars and thorns of controversy. For once, I like to have it all my own way; and this is impossible unless you are alone, or in such company as I do not covet. I have no objection to argue a point with any one for twenty miles of measured road, but not for pleasure. If you remark the scent of a bean-field crossing the road, perhaps your fellow-traveller has no smell. If you point to a distant object, perhaps he is short-sighted, and has to take out his glass to look at it. There is a feeling in the air, a tone in the colour of a cloud, which hits your fancy, but the effect of which you are unable to account for. There is then no sympathy, but an uneasy craving after it, and a dissatisfaction which pursues you on the way, and in the end probably produces ill-humour. Now I never quarrel with myself, and take all my own conclusions for granted till I find it necessary to defend them against objections. It is not merely that you may not be of accord on the objects and circumstances that present themselves before you—they may recall a number of ideas, and lead to associations too delicate and refined, to be possibly communicated to others. Yet these I love to cherish, and sometimes still fondly clutch them, when I can escape from the throng to do so. To give way to our feelings before company, seems extravagance or affection; on the other hand, to have to unravel this mystery of our being at every turn, and to make others take an equal interest in it (otherwise the end is not answered), is a task to which few are competent. We must "give it an understanding, but no tongue." My old friend C——, however, could do both. He could go on in the most delightful explanatory way over hill and dale, a summer's day, and convert a landscape into a didactic poem or a Pindaric ode. "He talked far above singing." If I could so clothe my ideas in sounding and flowing words, I might perhaps wish to have some one with me to admire the swelling theme; or I could be more content, were it possible for me still to hear his echoing voice in the woods of All-Foxden. They had "that fine madness in them which our first poets had"; and if they could have been caught by some rare instrument, would have breathed such strains as the following:

> ——"Here be woods as green
> As any, air likewise as fresh and sweet
> As when smooth Zephyrus plays on the fleet
> Face of the curled stream, with flow'rs as many
> As the young spring gives, and as choice as any;
> Here be all new delights, cool streams and wells,
> Arbours o'ergrown with woodbine, caves and dells:
> Choose where thou wilt, while I sit by and sing,
> Or gather rushes to make many a ring
> For thy long fingers; tell thee tales of love,
> How the pale Phœbe, hunting in a grove,
> First saw the boy Endymion, from whose eyes
> She took eternal fire that never dies;
> How she convey'd him softly in a sleep,
> His temples bound with poppy, to the steep
> Head of old Latmos, where she stoops each night,
> Gilding the mountain with her brother's light,
> To kiss her sweetest."
> —Faithful Shepherdess.

Had I words and images at command like these, I would attempt to wake the thoughts that lie slumbering on golden ridges in the evening clouds: but at the sight of nature my fancy, poor as it is, droops and closes up its leaves, like flowers at sunset. I can make nothing out on the spot: I must have time to collect myself.

In general, a good thing spoils out-of-door prospects: it should be reserved for Table-talk. L—— is for this reason, I take it, the worst company in the world out of doors; because he is the best within. I grant, there is one subject on which it is pleasant to talk on a journey; and that is, what one shall have for supper when we get to our inn at night. The open air improves this sort of conversation or friendly altercation, by setting a keener edge on appetite. Every mile of the road heightens the flavour of the viands we expect at the end of it. How fine it is to enter some old town, walled and turreted, just at approach of nightfall, or to come to some straggling village, with the lights streaming through the surrounding gloom; and then, after inquiring for the best entertainment that the place affords, to "take one's ease at one's inn"! These eventful moments in our lives are in fact too precious, too full of solid, heartfelt happiness to be frittered and dribbled away in imperfect sympathy. I would have them all to myself, and drain them to the last drop: they will do to talk of or to write about afterwards. What a delicate speculation it is, after drinking whole goblets of tea,

> "The cups that cheer, but not inebriate"

and letting the fumes ascend into the brain, to sit considering what we shall have for supper—eggs and a rasher, a rabbit smothered in onions, or an excellent veal-cutlet! Sancho in such a situation once fixed upon cow-heel; and his choice, though he could not help it, is not to be disparaged. Then in the intervals of pictured scenery and Shandean contemplation, to catch the preparation and the stir in the kitchen. *Procul, O procul este profani!* These hours are sacred to silence and to musing, to be treasured up in the memory, and to feed the source of smiling thoughts hereafter. I would not waste them in idle talk; or if I must have the integrity of fancy broken in upon, I would rather it were by a stranger than a friend. A stranger takes his hue and character from the time and place; he is a part of the furniture and costume of an inn. If he is a Quaker, or from the West Riding of Yorkshire, so much the better. I do not even try to sympathise with him, and he *breaks no squares*. I associate nothing with my travelling companion but present objects and passing events. In his ignorance of me and my affairs, I in a manner forget myself. But a friend reminds one of other things, rips up old grievances, and destroys the abstraction of the scene. He comes in ungraciously between us and our imaginary character. Something is dropped in the course of conversation that gives a hint of your profession and pursuits; or from having some one with you that knows the less sublime portions of your history, it seems that other people do. You are no longer a citizen of the world: but your "unhoused free condition is put into circumspection and confine." The *incognito* of an inn is one of its striking privileges—"lord of one's-self, uncumbered with a name." Oh! it is great to shake off the trammels of the world and of public opinion—to lose our importunate, tormenting, everlasting personal identity in the elements of nature, and become the creature of the moment, clear of all ties—to hold to the universe only by a dish of sweet-breads, and to owe nothing but the score of the evening—and no longer seeking for applause and meeting with contempt, to be known by no other title than *the Gentleman in the parlour!* One may take one's choice of all characters in this romantic state of uncertainty as to one's real pretensions, and become indefinitely respectable and negatively right-worshipful. We baffle prejudice and disappoint conjecture; and from being so to others, begin to be objects of curiosity and wonder even to ourselves. We are no more those hackneyed common-places that we appear in the world: an inn restores us to the level of nature, and quits scores with society! I have certainly spent some enviable hours at inns—sometimes when I have been left entirely to myself, and have tried to solve some metaphysical problem, as once at Witham-common, where I found out the proof that likeness is not a case of the association of ideas—at other times, when there have been pictures in the room, as at St. Neot's (I think it was), where I first met with Gribelin's engravings of the Cartoons, into which I entered at once; and at a little inn on the borders of Wales, where there happened to be hanging some of Westall's drawings, which I compared triumphantly (for a theory that I had, not for the admired artist) with the figure of a girl who had ferried me over the Severn, standing up in a boat between me and the fading twilight—at other times I might mention luxuriating in books, with a peculiar interest in this way, as I remember sitting up half the night to read Paul and Virginia, which I picked up at an inn at Bridgewater, after being drenched in the rain all day; and at the same place I got through two volumes of Madame D'Arblay's Camilla. It was on the 10th of April, 1798, that I sat down to a volume of the New Eloise, at the inn at Llangollen, over a bottle of sherry and a cold chicken. The letter I chose was that in which St. Preux describes his feelings as he first caught a glimpse from the heights of the Jura of the Pays de Vaud, which I had brought with me as a *bonne bouche* to crown the evening with. It was my birthday, and I had for the first time come from a place in the neighbourhood to visit this delightful spot. The road to Llangollen turns off between Chirk and Wrexham; and on passing a certain point you come all at once upon the valley, which opens like an amphitheatre, broad, barren hills rising in majestic state on either side, with "green upland swells that echo to the bleat of flocks" below, and the river Dee babbling over its stony bed in the midst of them. The valley at this time "glittered green with sunny showers," and a budding ash-tree dipped its tender branches in the chiding stream. How proud, how glad I was to walk along the high road that commanded the delicious prospect, repeating the lines which I have just quoted from Mr. Coleridge's poems! But besides the prospect which opened beneath my feet, another also opened to my inward sight, a heavenly vision, on which were written, in letters large as Hope could make them, these four words, LIBERTY, GENIUS, LOVE, VIRTUE; which have since faded into the light of common day, or mock my idle gaze.

"The beautiful is vanished, and returns not."

Still I would return some time or other to this enchanted spot; but I would return to it alone. What other self could I find to share that influx of thoughts, of regret, and delight, the traces of which I could hardly conjure up to myself, so much have they been broken and defaced. I could stand on some tall rock, and overlook the precipice of years that separates me from what I then was. I was at that time going shortly to visit the poet whom I have above named. Where is he now? Not only I myself have changed; the world, which was then new to me, has become old and incorrigible. Yet will I turn to thee in thought, O sylvan Dee, as thou then wert, in joy, in youth and gladness; and thou shalt always be to me the river of Paradise, where I will drink of the waters of life freely!

There is hardly any thing that shews the shortsightedness or capriciousness of the imagination more than travelling does. With change of place we change our ideas; nay, our opinions and feelings. We can by an effort indeed transport ourselves to old and long-forgotten scenes, and then the picture of the mind revives again; but we forget those that we have just left. It seems that we can think but of one place at a time. The canvas of the fancy has only a certain extent, and if we paint one set of objects upon it, they immediately efface every other. We cannot enlarge our conceptions; we only shift our point of view. The landscape bares its bosom to the enraptured eye; we take our fill of it; and seem as if we could form no other image of beauty or grandeur. We pass on, and think no more of it: the horizon that shuts it from our sight also blots it from our memory like a dream. In travelling through a wild barren country, I can form no idea of a woody and cultivated one. It appears to me that all the world must be barren, like what I see of it. In the country we forget the town, and in town we despise the country. "Beyond Hyde Park," says Sir Fopling Flutter, "all is a desert." All that part of the map that we do not see before us is a blank. The world in our conceit of it is not much bigger than a nutshell. It is not one prospect expanded into another, county joined to county, kingdom to kingdom, lands to seas, making an image voluminous and vast;—the mind can form no larger idea of space than the eye can take in at a single glance. The rest is a name written on a map, a calculation of arithmetic. For instance, what is the true signification of that immense mass of territory and population, known by the name of China to us? An inch of pasteboard on a wooden globe, of no more account than a China orange! Things near us are seen of the size of life: things at a distance are diminished to the size of the understanding. We measure the universe by ourselves, and even comprehend the texture of our being only piece-meal. In this way, however, we remember an infinity of things and places. The mind is like a mechanical instrument that plays a great variety of tunes, but it must play them in succession. One idea recalls another, but it at the same time excludes all others. In trying to renew old recollections, we cannot as it were unfold the whole web of our existence; we must pick out the single threads. So in coming to a place where we have formerly lived, and with which we have intimate associations, every one must have found that the feeling grows more vivid the nearer we approach the spot, from the mere anticipation of the actual impression: we remember circumstances, feelings, persons, faces, names that we had not thought of for years; but for the time all the rest of the world is forgotten!—To return to the question I have quitted above.

I have no objection to go to see ruins, aqueducts, pictures, in company with a friend or a party, but rather the contrary, for the former reason reversed. They are intelligible matters, and will bear talking about. The sentiment here is not tacit, but communicable and overt. Salisbury Plain is barren of criticism, but Stonehenge will bear a discussion antiquarian, picturesque, and philosophical. In setting out on a party of pleasure, the first consideration always is where we shall go: in taking a solitary ramble, the question is what we shall meet with by the way. The mind

then is "its own place"; nor are we anxious to arrive at the end
of our journey. I can myself do the honours indifferently well to
works of art and curiosity. I once took a party to Oxford with
no mean *éclat*—shewed them that seat of the Muses at a distance,

"With glistering spires and pinnacles adorn'd"—

descanted on the learned air that breathes from the grassy quad-
rangles and stone walls of halls and colleges—was at home in the
Bodleian; and at Blenheim quite superseded the powdered Cicerone
that attended us, and that pointed in vain with his wand to common-place beauties in matchless pictures.—As another exception
to the above reasoning, I should not feel confident in venturing on
a journey in a foreign country without a companion. I should want
at intervals to hear the sound of my own language. There is an involuntary antipathy in the mind of an Englishman to foreign manners and notions that requires the assistance of social sympathy to
carry it off. As the distance from home increases, this relief, which
was at first a luxury, becomes a passion and an appetite. A person
would almost feel stifled to find himself in the deserts of Arabia
without friends and countrymen: there must be allowed to be
something in the view of Athens or old Rome that claims the
utterance of speech; and I own that the Pyramids are too mighty
for any single contemplation. In such situations, so opposite to
all one's ordinary train of ideas, one seems a species by one's-self,
a limb torn off from society, unless one can meet with instant fellowship and support.—Yet I did not feel this want or craving very
pressing once, when I first set my foot on the laughing shores of
France. Calais was peopled with novelty and delight. The confused, busy murmur of the place was like oil and wine poured into
my ears; nor did the mariners' hymn, which was sung from the top
of an old crazy vessel in the harbour, as the sun went down, send
an alien sound into my soul. I breathed the air of general humanity.
I walked over "the vine-covered hills and gay regions of France,"
erect and satisfied; for the image of man was not cast down and
chained to the foot of arbitrary thrones. I was at no loss for language, for that of all the great schools of painting was open to me.
The whole is vanished like a shade. Pictures, heroes, glory, freedom, all are fled: nothing remains but the Bourbons and the French
people!—There is undoubtedly a sensation in travelling into for-

eign parts that is to be had nowhere else: but it is more pleasing at the time than lasting. It is too remote from our habitual associations to be a common topic of discourse or reference, and, like a dream or another state of existence, does not piece into our daily modes of life. It is an animated but a momentary hallucination. It demands an effort to exchange our actual for our ideal identity; and to feel the pulse of our old transports revive very keenly, we must "jump" all our present comforts and connexions. Our romantic and itinerant character is not to be domesticated. Dr. Johnson remarked how little foreign travel added to the facilities of conversation in those who had been abroad. In fact, the time we have spent there is both delightful, and in one sense instructive; but it appears to be cut out of our substantial, downright existence, and never to join kindly on to it. We are not the same, but another, and perhaps more enviable individual, all the time we are out of our own country. We are lost to ourselves, as well as our friends. So the poet somewhat quaintly sings:

> "Out of my country and myself I go."

Those who wish to forget painful thoughts, do well to absent themselves for a while from the ties and objects that recall them: but we can be said only to fulfil our destiny in the place that gave us birth. I should on this account like well enough to spend the whole of my life in travelling abroad, if I could any where borrow another life to spend afterwards at home!

ON FAMILIAR STYLE

IT is not easy to write a familiar style. Many people mistake a familiar for a vulgar style, and suppose that to write without affectation is to write at random. On the contrary, there is nothing that requires more precision, and, if I may so say, purity of expression, than the style I am speaking of. It utterly rejects not only all unmeaning pomp, but all low, cant phrases, and loose, unconnected, *slipshod* allusions. It is not to take the first word that offers, but the best word in common use; it is not to throw words together in any combinations we please, but to follow and avail ourselves of the true idiom of the language. To write a genuine familiar or truly English style, is to write as any one would speak in common conversation, who had a thorough command and choice of words, or who could discourse with ease, force, and perspicuity, setting aside all pedantic and oratorical flourishes. Or to give another illustration, to write naturally is the same thing in regard to common conversation, as to read naturally is in regard to common speech. It does not follow that it is an easy thing to give the true accent and inflection to the words you utter, because you do not attempt to rise above the level of ordinary life and colloquial speaking. You do not assume, indeed, the solemnity of the pulpit, or the tone of stage-declamation: neither are you at liberty to gabble on at a venture, without emphasis or discretion, or to resort to vulgar dialect or clownish pronunciation. You must steer a middle course. You are tied down to a given and appropriate articulation, which is determined by the habitual associations between sense and sound, and which you can only hit by entering into the author's meaning, as you must find the proper words and style to express yourself by fixing your thoughts on the subject you have to write about. Any one may mouth out a passage with a theatrical cadence, or get upon stilts to tell his thoughts: but to write or speak with propriety and simplicity is a more difficult task. Thus it is easy to affect a pompous style, to use a word twice as big as the thing you want to express: it is not so easy to pitch upon the very word that exactly fits it. Out of eight or ten words equally common, equally intelligible, with nearly equal pretensions, it is a matter of some nicety and discrimination to pick out the very one the preferableness of which is scarcely perceptible, but decisive. The reason why I object to Dr. Johnson's style is that there is no discrimination, no selection, no variety in it. He uses none but "tall, opaque words," taken from the "first row of the rubric"—words with the greatest number of syllables, or Latin phrases with merely English terminations. If a fine style depended on this sort of arbitrary pretension, it would be fair to judge of an author's elegance by the measurement of his words and the substitution of foreign circumlocutions (with no precise associations) for the mother-tongue.[1] How simple is it to be dignified without ease, to be pompous without meaning! Surely it is but a mechanical rule for avoiding what

---

[1] I have heard of such a thing as an author who makes it a rule never to admit a monosyllable into his vapid verse. Yet the charm and sweetness of Marlowe's lines depended often on their being made up almost entirely of monosyllables.

is low, to be always pedantic and affected. It is clear you cannot use a vulgar English word if you never use a common English word at all. A fine tact is shewn in adhering to those which are perfectly common, and yet never falling into any expressions which are debased by disgusting circumstances, or which owe their signification and point to technical or professional allusions. A truly natural or familiar style can never be quaint or vulgar, for this reason, that it is of universal force and applicability, and that quaintness and vulgarity arise out of the immediate connexion of certain words with coarse and disagreeable, or with confined ideas. The last form what we understand by *cant* or *slang* phrases.—To give an example of what is not very clear in the general statement. I should say that the phrase *To cut with a knife*, or *To cut a piece of wood*, is perfectly free from vulgarity, because it is perfectly common: but to *cut an acquaintance* is not quite unexceptionable, because it is not perfectly common or intelligible, and has hardly yet escaped out of the limits of slang phraseology. I should hardly, therefore, use the word in this sense without putting it in italics as a license of expression, to be received *cum grano salis*. All provincial or bye-phrases come under the same mark of reprobation—all such as the writer transfers to the page from his fireside or a particular *coterie*, or that he invents for his own sole use and convenience. I conceive that words are like money, not the worse for being common, but that it is the stamp of custom alone that gives them circulation or value. I am fastidious in this respect, and would almost as soon coin the currency of the realm as counterfeit the King's English. I never invented or gave a new and unauthorised meaning to any word but one single one (the term *impersonal* applied to feelings), and that was in an abstruse metaphysical discussion to express a very difficult distinction. I have been (I know) loudly accused of revelling in vulgarisms and broken English. I cannot speak to that point: but so far I plead guilty to the determined use of acknowledged idioms and common elliptical expressions. I am not sure that the critics in question know the one from the other, that is, can distinguish any medium between formal pedantry and the most barbarous solecism. As an author, I endeavour to employ plain words and popular modes of construction, as, were I a chapman and dealer, I should common weights and measures.

The proper force of words lies not in the words themselves, but in their application. A word may be a fine-sounding word, of an unusual length, and very imposing from its learning and novelty, and yet in the connexion in which it is introduced, may be quite pointless and irrelevant. It is not pomp or pretension, but the adaptation of the expression to the idea, that clenches a writer's meaning:—as it is not the size or glossiness of the materials, but their being fitted each to its place, that gives strength to the arch; or as the pegs and nails are as necessary to the support of the building as the larger timbers, and more so than the mere shewy, unsubstantial ornaments. I hate any thing that occupies more space than it is worth. I hate to see a load of band-boxes go along the street, and I hate to see a parcel of big words without any thing in them. A person who does not deliberately dispose of all his thoughts alike in cumbrous draperies and flimsy disguises, may strike out twenty varieties of familiar every-day language, each coming somewhat nearer to the feeling he wants to convey, and at last not hit upon that particular and only one which may be said to be identical with the exact impression in his mind. This would seem to shew that Mr. Cobbett is hardly right in saying that the first word that occurs is always the best. It may be a very good one; and yet a better may present itself on reflection or from time to time. It should be suggested naturally, however, and spontaneously, from a fresh and lively conception of the subject. We seldom succeed by trying at improvement, or by merely substituting one word for another that we are not satisfied with, as we cannot recollect the name of a place or person by merely plaguing ourselves about it. We wander farther from the point by persisting in a wrong scent; but it starts up accidentally in the memory when we least expected it, by touching some link in the chain of previous association.

There are those who hoard up and make a cautious display of nothing but rich and rare phraseology;—ancient medals, obscure coins, and Spanish pieces of eight. They are very curious to inspect; but I myself would neither offer nor take them in the course of exchange. A sprinkling of archaisms is not amiss, but a tissue of obsolete expressions is more fit *for keep than wear*. I do not say I would not use any phrase that had been brought into fashion before the middle or the end of the last century; but I should be shy of using any that had not been employed by any approved author during the whole of that time. Words, like clothes, get old-fashioned, or mean and ridiculous, when they have been for some time laid aside. Mr. Lamb is the only imitator of old English style I can read with pleasure; and he is so thoroughly imbued with the spirit of his authors, that the idea of imitation is almost done away. There is an inward unction, a marrowy vein both in the thought and feeling, an intuition, deep and lively, of his subject, that carries off any quaintness or awkwardness arising from an antiquated style and dress. The matter is completely his own, though the manner is assumed. Perhaps his ideas are altogether so marked and individual, as to require their point and pungency to be neutralised by the affectation of a singular but traditional form of conveyance. Tricked out in the prevailing costume, they would probably seem more startling and out of the way. The old English authors, Burton, Fuller, Coryate, Sir Thomas Browne, are a kind of mediators between us and the more eccentric and whimsical modern, reconciling us to his peculiarities. I do not, however, know how far this is the case or not, till he condescends to write like one of us. I must confess that what I like best of his papers under the signature of Elia (still I do not presume, amidst such excellence, to decide what is most excellent) is the account of "Mrs. Battle's Opinions on Whist," which is also the most free from obsolete allusions and turns of expression—

"A well of native English undefiled."

To those acquainted with his admired prototypes, these Essays of the ingenious and highly gifted author have the same sort of charm and relish, that Erasmus's Colloquies or a fine piece of modern Latin have to the classical scholar. Certainly, I do not know any borrowed pencil that has more power or felicity of execution than the one of which I have here been speaking.

It is as easy to write a gaudy style without ideas, as it is to spread a pallet of shewy colours or to smear in a flaunting transparency. "What do you read?"—"Words, words, words."—"What is the matter?"—"*Nothing*," it might be answered. The florid style is the reverse of the familiar. The last is employed as an unvarnished medium to convey ideas; the first is resorted to as a spangled veil to conceal the want of them. When there is nothing to be set down but words, it costs little to have them fine. Look through the dictionary, and cull out a *florilegium*, rival the *tulippomania*. *Rouge* high enough, and never mind the natural complexion. The vulgar, who are not in the secret, will admire the look of preternatural health and vigour; and the fashionable, who regard only appearances, will be delighted with the imposition. Keep to your sounding generalities, your tinkling phrases, and all will be well. Swell out an unmeaning truism to a perfect tympany of style. A thought, a distinction is the rock on which all this brittle cargo of verbiage splits at once. Such writers have merely *verbal* imaginations, that retain nothing but words. Or their puny thoughts have dragon-wings, all green and gold. They soar far above the vulgar failing of the *Sermo humi obrepens*—their most ordinary speech is never short of an hyperbole, splendid, imposing, vague, incomprehensible, magniloquent, a cento of sounding common-places. If some of us, whose "ambition is more lowly," pry a little too narrowly into nooks and corners to pick up a number of "unconsidered trifles," they never once direct their eyes or lift their hands to seize on any but the most gorgeous, tarnished, thread-bare, patch-work set of phrases, the left-off finery of poetic extravagance, transmitted down through successive generations of barren pretenders. If they criticise actors and actresses, a huddled phantasmagoria of feathers, spangles, floods of light, and oceans of sound float before their morbid sense, which they paint in the style of Ancient Pistol. Not a glimpse can you get of the merits or defects of the performers: they are hidden in a profusion of barbarous epithets and wilful rhodomontade. Our hypercritics are not thinking of these little fantoccini beings—

"That strut and fret their hour upon the stage"—

but of tall phantoms of words, abstractions, *genera* and *species*, sweeping clauses, periods that unite the Poles, forced alliterations, astounding antitheses—

"And on their pens *Fustian* sits plumed."

If they describe kings and queens, it is an Eastern pageant. The Coronation at either House is nothing to it. We get at four repeated images—a curtain, a throne, a sceptre, and a footstool. These are with them the wardrobe of a lofty imagination; and they turn their servile strains to servile uses. Do we read a description of pictures? It is not a reflection of tones and hues which "nature's own sweet and cunning hand laid on," but piles of precious stones, rubies, pearls, emeralds, Golconda's mines, and all the blazonry of art. Such persons are in fact besotted with words, and their brains are turned with the glittering but empty and sterile phantoms of things. Personifications, capital letters, seas of sunbeams, visions of glory, shining inscriptions, the figures of a transparency, Britannia with her shield, or Hope leaning on an anchor, make up their stock-in-trade. They may be considered as *hieroglyphical* writers. Images stand out in their minds isolated and important merely in themselves, without any ground-work of feeling—there is no context in their imaginations. Words affect them in the same way, by the mere sound, that is, by their possible, not by their actual application to the subject in hand. They are fascinated by first appearances, and have no sense of consequences. Nothing more is meant by them than meets the ear: they understand or feel nothing more than meets their eye. The web and texture of the universe, and of the heart of man, is a mystery to them: they have no faculty that strikes a chord in unison with it. They cannot get beyond the daubings of fancy, the varnish of sentiment. Objects are not linked to feelings, words to things, but images revolve in splendid mockery, words represent themselves in their strange rhapsodies. The categories of such a mind are pride and ignorance—pride in outside shew, to which they sacrifice every thing, and ignorance of the true worth and hidden structure both of words and things. With a sovereign contempt for what is familiar and natural, they are the slaves of vulgar affectation—of a routine of high-flown phrases. Scorning to imitate realities, they are unable to invent any thing, to strike out one original idea. They are not copyists of nature, it is true; but they are the poorest of all plagiarists, the plagiarists of words. All is far-fetched, dear-bought, artificial, oriental in subject and allusion: all is mechanical, conventional, vapid, formal, pedantic in style and execution. They startle and confound the understanding of the reader, by the remoteness and obscurity of their illustrations: they soothe the ear by the monotony of the same everlasting round of circuitous metaphors. They are the *mock-school* in poetry and prose. They flounder about between fustian in expression, and bathos in sentiment. They tantalise the fancy, but never reach the head nor touch the heart. Their Temple of Fame is like a shadowy structure raised by Dulness to Vanity,

or like Cowper's description of the Empress of Russia's palace of
ice, "as worthless as in shew 'twas glittering"—

> "It smiled, and it was cold!"

OF PERSONS ONE WOULD WISH TO HAVE SEEN

B—— it was, I think, who suggested this subject, as well as
the defence of Guy Faux, which I urged him to execute.
As, however, he would undertake neither, I suppose I must
do both—a task for which he would have been much fitter, no less
from the temerity than the felicity of his pen—

> "Never so sure our rapture to create
> As when it touch'd the brink of all we hate."

Compared with him I shall, I fear, make but a common-place piece
of business of it; but I should be loth the idea was entirely lost,
and besides I may avail myself of some hints of his in the progress
of it. I am sometimes, I suspect, a better reporter of the ideas of
other people than expounder of my own. I pursue the one too far
into paradox or mysticism; the others I am not bound to follow
farther than I like, or than seems fair and reasonable.

On the question being started, A—— said, "I suppose the two
first persons you would choose to see would be the two greatest
names in English literature, Sir Isaac Newton and Mr. Locke?"
In this A——, as usual, reckoned without his host. Every one
burst out a laughing at the expression of B——'s face, in which
impatience was restrained by courtesy. "Yes, the greatest names,"
he stammered out hastily, "but they were not persons—not persons."—"Not persons?" said A——, looking wise and foolish at
the same time, afraid his triumph might be premature. "That is,"
rejoined B——, "not characters, you know. By Mr. Locke and
Sir Isaac Newton, you mean the Essay on the Human Understanding, and the Principia, which we have to this day. Beyond
their contents there is nothing personally interesting in the men.
But what we want to see any one *bodily* for, is when there is something peculiar, striking in the individuals, more than we can learn
from their writings, and yet are curious to know. I dare say Locke
and Newton were very like Kneller's portraits of them. But who
could paint Shakespeare?"—"Ay," retorted A——, "there it is;

then I suppose you would prefer seeing him and Milton instead?"
—"No," said B——, "neither. I have seen so much of Shakespeare
on the stage and on book-stalls, in frontispieces and on mantle-
pieces, that I am quite tired of the everlasting repetition: and as
to Milton's face, the impressions that have come down to us of it
I do not like; it is too starched and puritanical; and I should be
afraid of losing some of the manna of his poetry in the leaven of
his countenance and the precisian's band and gown."—"I shall
guess no more," said A——. "Who is it, then, you would like to
see 'in his habit as he lived,' if you had your choice of the whole
range of English literature?" B—— then named Sir Thomas
Browne and Fulke Greville, the friend of Sir Philip Sidney, as the
two worthies whom he should feel the greatest pleasure to encounter
on the floor of his apartment in their nightgown and slippers,
and to exchange friendly greeting with them. At this A——
laughed outright, and conceived B—— was jesting with him; but
as no one followed his example, he thought there might be something in it, and waited for an explanation in a state of whimsical
suspense. B—— then (as well as I can remember a conversation
that passed twenty years ago—how time slips!) went on as follows.
"The reason why I pitch upon these two authors is, that their
writings are riddles, and they themselves the most mysterious of
personages. They resemble the soothsayers of old, who dealt
in dark hints and doubtful oracles; and I should like to ask them
the meaning of what no mortal but themselves, I should suppose,
can fathom. There is Dr. Johnson, I have no curiosity, no strange
uncertainty about him: he and Boswell together have pretty well
let me into the secret of what passed through his mind. He and
other writers like him are sufficiently explicit: my friends, whose
repose I should be tempted to disturb (were it in my power), are
implicit, inextricable, inscrutable.

> 'And call up him who left half-told
> The story of Cambuscan bold.'

"When I look at that obscure but gorgeous prose-composition
(the Urn-burial) I seem to myself to look into a deep abyss, at the
bottom of which are hid pearls and rich treasure; or it is like a
stately labyrinth of doubt and withering speculation, and I would
invoke the spirit of the author to lead me through it. Besides,

who would not be curious to see the lineaments of a man who,
having himself been twice married, wished that mankind were
propagated like trees! As to Fulke Greville, he is like nothing but
one of his own 'Prologues spoken by the ghost of an old king of
Ormus,' a truly formidable and inviting personage: his style is
apocalyptical, cabalistical, a knot worthy of such an apparition
to untie; and for the unravelling a passage or two, I would stand
the brunt of an encounter with so portentous a commentator!"—
"I am afraid in that case," said A——, "that if the mystery were
once cleared up, the merit might be lost;"—and turning to me,
whispered a friendly apprehension, that while B—— continued to
admire these old crabbed authors, he would never become a popular
writer. Dr. Donne was mentioned as a writer of the same period,
with a very interesting countenance, whose history was singular,
and whose meaning was often quite as *uncomeatable*, without a
personal citation from the dead, as that of any of his contemporaries.
The volume was produced; and while some one was expatiating on
the exquisite simplicity and beauty of the portrait prefixed to the
old edition, A—— got hold of the poetry, and exclaiming, "What
have we here?" read the following:—

> " 'Here lies a She-Sun and a He-Moon there,
>   She gives the best light to his sphere,
>   Or each is both and all, and so
>   They unto one another nothing owe.' "

There was no resisting this, till B——, seizing the volume, turned
to the beautiful "Lines to his Mistress," dissuading her from
accompanying him abroad, and read them with suffused features
and a faltering tongue.

> " 'By our first strange and fatal interview,
>   By all desires which thereof did ensue,
>   By our long starving hopes, by that remorse
>   Which my words' masculine persuasive force
>   Begot in thee, and by the memory
>   Of hurts, which spies and rivals threaten'd me,
>   I calmly beg. But by thy father's wrath,
>   By all pains which want and divorcement hath,
>   I conjure thee; and all the oaths which I
>   And thou have sworn to seal joint constancy
>   Here I unswear, and overswear them thus,
>   Thou shalt not love by ways so dangerous.

Temper, oh fair Love! love's impetuous rage,
Be my true mistress still, not my feign'd Page;
I'll go, and, by thy kind leave, leave behind
Thee, only worthy to nurse in my mind.
Thirst to come back; oh, if thou die before,
My soul from other lands to thee shall soar.
Thy (else Almighty) beauty cannot move
Rage from the seas, nor thy love teach them love,
Nor tame wild Boreas' harshness; thou hast read
How roughly he in pieces shivered
Fair Orithea, whom he swore he lov'd.
Fall ill or good, 'tis madness to have prov'd
Dangers unurg'd: Feed on this flattery,
That absent lovers one with th' other be.
Dissemble nothing, not a boy; nor change
Thy body's habit, nor mind; be not strange
To thyself only. All will spy in thy face
A blushing, womanly, discovering grace.
Richly cloth'd apes are called apes, and as soon
Eclips'd as bright we call the moon the moon.
Men of France, changeable cameleons,
Spittles of diseases, shops of fashions,
Love's fuellers, and the rightest company
Of players, which upon the world's stage be,
Will quickly know thee. . . . O stay here! for thee
England is only a worthy gallery,
To walk in expectation; till from thence
Our greatest King call thee to his presence.
When I am gone, dream me some happiness,
Nor let thy looks our long hid love confess,
Nor praise, nor dispraise me; nor bless, nor curse
Openly love's force, nor in bed fright thy nurse
With midnight startings, crying out, Oh, oh,
Nurse, oh, my love is slain, I saw him go,
O'er the white Alps alone; I saw him, I,
Assail'd, fight, taken, stabb'd, bleed, fall, and die.
Augur me better chance, except dread Jove
Think it enough for me to have had thy love.' "

Some one then inquired of B—— if we could not see from the
window the Temple-walk in which Chaucer used to take his exercise; and on his name being put to the vote, I was pleased to find
that there was a general sensation in his favour in all but A——,
who said something about the ruggedness of the metre, and even
objected to the quaintness of the orthography. I was vexed at this
superficial gloss, pertinaciously reducing every thing to its own

trite level, and asked "if he did not think it would be worth while to scan the eye that had first greeted the Muse in that dim twilight and early dawn of English literature; to see the head, round which the visions of fancy must have played like gleams of inspiration or a sudden glory; to watch those lips that 'lisped in numbers, for the numbers came'—as by a miracle, or as if the dumb should speak? Nor was it alone that he had been the first to tune his native tongue (however imperfectly to modern ears); but he was himself a noble, manly character, standing before his age and striving to advance it; a pleasant humourist withal, who has not only handed down to us the living manners of his time, but had, no doubt, store of curious and quaint devices, and would make as hearty a companion as Mine Host of Tabard. His interview with Petrarch is fraught with interest. Yet I would rather have seen Chaucer in company with the author of the Decameron, and have heard them exchange their best stories together, the Squire's Tale against the Story of the Falcon, the Wife of Bath's Prologue against the Adventures of Friar Albert. How fine to see the high mysterious brow which learning then wore, relieved by the gay, familiar tone of men of the world, and by the courtesies of genius. Surely, the thoughts and feelings which passed through the minds of these great revivers of learning, these Cadmuses who sowed the teeth of letters, must have stamped an expression on their features, as different from the moderns as their books, and well worth the perusal. Dante," I continued, "is as interesting a person as his own Ugolino, one whose lineaments curiosity would as eagerly devour in order to penetrate his spirit, and the only one of the Italian poets I should care much to see. There is a fine portrait of Ariosto by no less a hand than Titian's; light, Moorish, spirited, but not answering our idea. The same artist's large colossal profile of Peter Aretine is the only likeness of the kind that has the effect of conversing with 'the mighty dead,' and this is truly spectral, ghastly, necromantic." B—— put it to me if I should like to see Spenser as well as Chaucer; and I answered without hesitation, "No; for that his beauties were ideal, visionary, not palpable or personal, and therefore connected with less curiosity about the man. His poetry was the essence of romance, a very halo round the bright orb of fancy; and the bringing in the individual might dissolve the charm. No tones of voice could come up to the mellifluous cadence of his verse; no form but of a winged angel could vie with the airy shapes he has described. He was (to our apprehensions) rather 'a creature of the element, that lived in the rainbow and played in the plighted clouds,' than an ordinary mortal. Or if he did appear, I should wish it to be as a mere vision, like one of his own pageants, and that he should pass by unquestioned like a dream or sound—

> " —— '*That* was Arion crown'd:
> So went he playing on the wat'ry plain!' "

Captain C. muttered something about Columbus, and M. C. hinted at the Wandering Jew; but the last was set aside as spurious, and the first made over to the New World.

"I should like," said Miss D——, "to have seen Pope talking with Patty Blount; and I *have* seen Goldsmith." Every one turned round to look at Miss D——, as if by so doing they too could get a sight of Goldsmith.

"Where," asked a harsh croaking voice, "was Dr. Johnson in the years 1745–6? He did not write anything that we know of, nor is there any account of him in Boswell during those two years. Was he in Scotland with the Pretender? He seems to have passed through the scenes in the Highlands in company with Boswell many years after 'with lack-lustre eye,' yet as if they were familiar to him, or associated in his mind with interests that he durst not explain. If so, it would be an additional reason for my liking him; and I would give something to have seen him seated in the tent with the youthful Majesty of Britain, and penning the Proclamation to all true subjects and adherents of the legitimate Government."

"I thought," said A——, turning short round upon B——, "that you of the Lake School did not like Pope?"—"Not like Pope! My dear sir, you must be under a mistake—I can read him over and over for ever!"—"Why certainly, the Essay on Man must be a masterpiece."—"It may be so, but I seldom look into it."— "Oh! then it's his Satires you admire?"—"No, not his Satires, but his friendly Epistles and his compliments."—"Compliments! I did not know he ever made any."—"The finest," said B——, "that were ever paid by the wit of man. Each of them is worth an estate for life—nay, is an immortality. There is that superb one to Lord Cornbury:

> " 'Despise low joys, low gains;
> Disdain whatever Cornbury disdains;
> Be virtuous, and be happy for your pains.' "

Was there ever more artful insinuation of idolatrous praise?
And then that noble apotheosis of his friend Lord Mansfield (however little deserved), when, speaking of the House of Lords, he
adds—

> " 'Conspicuous scene! another yet is nigh,
> (More silent far) where kings and poets lie;
> Where Murray (long enough his country's pride)
> Shall be no more than Tully or than Hyde!' "

And with what a fine turn of indignant flattery he addresses
Lord Bolingbroke—

> " 'Why rail they then, if but one wreath of mine,
> Oh! all accomplish'd St. John, deck thy shrine?' "

Or turn," continued B——, with a slight hectic on his cheek and
his eye glistening, "to his list of early friends:

> " 'But why then publish? Granville the polite,
> And knowing Walsh, would tell me I could write;
> Well-natured Garth inflamed with early praise,
> And Congreve loved and Swift endured my lays:
> The courtly Talbot, Somers, Sheffield read,
> Ev'n mitred Rochester would nod the head;
> And St. John's self (great Dryden's friend before)
> Received with open arms one poet more.
> Happy my studies, if by these approved!
> Happier their author, if by these beloved!
> From these the world will judge of men and books,
> Not from the Burnets, Oldmixons, and Cooks.' "

Here his voice totally failed him, and throwing down the book, he
said, "Do you think I would not wish to have been friends with
such a man as this?"

"What say you to Dryden?"—"He rather made a shew of
himself, and courted popularity in that lowest temple of Fame, a
coffee-house, so as in some measure to vulgarize one's idea of him.
Pope, on the contrary, reached the very *beau idéal* of what a poet's
life should be; and his fame while living seemed to be an emanation
from that which was to circle his name after death. He was so far
enviable (and one would feel proud to have witnessed the rare

spectacle in him) that he was almost the only poet and man of genius who met with his reward on this side of the tomb, who realized in friends, fortune, the esteem of the world, the most sanguine hopes of a youthful ambition, and who found that sort of patronage from the great during his lifetime which they would be thought anxious to bestow upon him after his death. Read Gay's verses to him on his supposed return from Greece, after his translation of Homer was finished, and say if you would not gladly join the bright procession that welcomed him home, or see it once more land at Whitehall-stairs."—"Still," said Miss D——, "I would rather have seen him talking with Patty Blount, or riding by in a coronet-coach with Lady Mary Wortley Montagu!"

E——, who was deep in a game of piquet at the other end of the room, whispered to M. C. to ask if Junius would not be a fit person to invoke from the dead. "Yes," said B——, "provided he would agree to lay aside his mask."

We were now at a stand for a short time, when Fielding was mentioned as a candidate: only one, however, seconded the proposition. "Richardson?"—"By all means, but only to look at him through the glass-door of his back-shop, hard at work upon one of his novels (the most extraordinary contrast that ever was presented between an author and his works), but not to let him come behind his counter lest he should want you to turn customer, nor to go upstairs with him, lest he should offer to read the first manuscript of Sir Charles Grandison, which was originally written in eight and twenty volumes octavo, or get out the letters of his female correspondents, to prove that Joseph Andrews was low."

There was but one statesman in the whole of English history that any one expressed the least desire to see—Oliver Cromwell, with his fine, frank, rough, pimply face, and wily policy;—and one enthusiast, John Bunyan, the immortal author of the Pilgrim's Progress. It seemed that if he came into the room, dreams would follow him, and that each person would nod under his golden cloud, "nigh-sphered in Heaven," a canopy as strange and stately as any in Homer.

Of all persons near our own time, Garrick's name was received with the greatest enthusiasm, who was proposed by J. F——. He presently superseded both Hogarth and Händel, who had been talked of, but then it was on condition that he should act in trag-

edy and comedy, in the play and the farce, Lear and Wildair and
Abel Drugger. What a *sight for sore eyes* that would be! Who would
not part with a year's income at least, almost with a year of his
natural life, to be present at it? Besides, as he could not act alone,
and recitations are unsatisfactory things, what a troop he must
bring with him—the silver-tongued Barry, and Quin, and Shuter
and Weston, and Mrs. Clive and Mrs. Pritchard, of whom I have
heard my father speak as so great a favourite when he was young!
This would indeed be a revival of the dead, the restoring of art;
and so much the more desirable, as such is the lurking scepticism
mingled with our overstrained admiration of past excellence, that
though we have the speeches of Burke, the portraits of Reynolds,
the writings of Goldsmith, and the conversation of Johnson, to
show what people could do at that period, and to confirm the universal testimony to the merits of Garrick; yet, as it was before
our time, we have our misgivings, as if he was probably after all
little better than a Bartlemy-fair actor, dressed out to play Macbeth
in a scarlet coat and laced cocked-hat. For one, I should like to
have seen and heard with my own eyes and ears. Certainly, by all
accounts, if any one was ever moved by the true histrionic *æstus*,
it was Garrick. When he followed the Ghost in Hamlet, he did not
drop the sword, as most actors do behind the scenes, but kept the
point raised the whole way round, so fully was he possessed with
the idea, or so anxious not to lose sight of his part for a moment.
Once at a splendid dinner-party at Lord ——'s, they suddenly
missed Garrick, and could not imagine what was become of him,
till they were drawn to the window by the convulsive screams and
peals of laughter of a young negro boy, who was rolling on the
ground in an ecstasy of delight to see Garrick mimicing a turkey-
cock in the court-yard, with his coat-tail stuck out behind, and in
a seeming flutter of feathered rage and pride. Of our party only
two persons present had seen the British Roscius; and they seemed
as willing as the rest to renew their acquaintance with their old
favourite.

We were interrupted in the hey-day and mid-career of this fanciful speculation, by a grumbler in a corner, who declared it was a
shame to make all this rout about a mere player and farce-writer,
to the neglect and exclusion of the fine old dramatists, the contemporaries and rivals of Shakespeare. B—— said he had anticipated

this objection when he had named the author of Mustapha and Alaham; and out of caprice insisted upon keeping him to represent the set, in preference to the wild hair-brained enthusiast Kit Marlowe; to the sexton of St. Ann's, Webster, with his melancholy yew-trees and death's-heads; to Dekker, who was but a garrulous proser; to the voluminous Heywood; and even to Beaumont and Fletcher, whom we might offend by complimenting the wrong author on their joint productions. Lord Brook, on the contrary, stood quite by himself, or in Cowley's words, was "a vast species alone." Some one hinted at the circumstance of his being a lord, which rather startled B——, but he said a *ghost* would perhaps dispense with strict etiquette, on being regularly addressed by his title. Ben Jonson divided our suffrages pretty equally. Some were afraid he would begin to traduce Shakespeare, who was not present to defend himself. "If he grows disagreeable," it was whispered aloud, "there is G—— can match him." At length, his romantic visit to Drummond of Hawthornden was mentioned, and turned the scale in his favour.

B—— inquired if there was any one that was hanged that I would choose to mention? And I answered, Eugene Aram.[1] The name of the "Admirable Crichton" was suddenly started as a splendid example of *waste* talents, so different from the generality of his countrymen. This choice was mightily approved by a North-Briton present, who declared himself descended from that prodigy of learning and accomplishment, and said he had family-plate in his possession as vouchers for the fact, with the initials A. C.— *Admirable Crichton!* H—— laughed or rather roared as heartily at this as I should think he has done for many years.

The last-named Mitre-courtier [2] then wished to know whether there were any metaphysicians to whom one might be tempted to apply the wizard spell? I replied, there were only six in modern times deserving the name—Hobbes, Berkeley, Butler, Hartley, Hume, Leibnitz; and perhaps Jonathan Edwards, a Massachusetts man.[3] As to the French, who talked fluently of having *created* this

---

[1] See Newgate Calendar for 1758.

[2] B —— at this time occupied chambers in Mitre-court, Fleet-street.

[3] Lord Bacon is not included in this list, nor do I know where he should come in. It is not easy to make room for him and his reputation together. This great and celebrated man in some of his works recommends it to pour a bottle of claret into the ground of a morning, and to stand over it, inhaling the perfumes. So he sometimes enriched the dry

science, there was not a title in any of their writings, that was not to be found literally in the authors I had mentioned. [Horne Tooke, who might have a claim to come in under the head of Grammar, was still living.] None of these names seemed to excite much interest, and I did not plead for the re-appearance of those who might be thought best fitted by the abstract nature of their studies for their present spiritual and disembodied state, and who, even while on this living stage, were nearly divested of common flesh and blood. As A—— with an uneasy fidgetty face was about to put some question about Mr. Locke and Dugald Stewart, he was prevented by M. C. who observed, "If J—— was here, he would undoubtedly be for having up those profound and redoubted scholiasts, Thomas Aquinas and Duns Scotus." I said this might be fair enough in him who had read or fancied he had read the original works, but I did not see how we could have any right to call up these authors to give an account of themselves in person, till we had looked into their writings.

By this time it should seem that some rumour of our whimsical deliberation had got wind, and had disturbed the *irritabile genus* in their shadowy abodes, for we received messages from several candidates that we had just been thinking of. Gray declined our invitation, though he had not yet been asked: Gay offered to come and bring in his hand the Duchess of Bolton, the original Polly: Steele and Addison left their cards as Captain Sentry and Sir Roger de Coverley: Swift came in and sat down without speaking a word, and quitted the room as abruptly: Otway and Chatterton were seen lingering on the opposite side of the Styx, but could not muster enough between them to pay Charon his fare: Thomson fell asleep in the boat, and was rowed back again—and Burns sent a low fellow, one John Barleycorn, an old companion of his who had conducted him to the other world, to say that he had during his lifetime been drawn out of his retirement as a shew, only to be made an exciseman of, and that he would rather remain where he was. He desired, however, to shake hands by his representative—the hand, thus held out, was in a burning fever, and shook prodigiously.

and barren soil of speculation with the fine aromatic spirit of his genius. His "Essays" and his "Advancement of Learning" are works of vast depth and scope of observation. The last, though it contains no positive discoveries, is a noble chart of human intellect, and a guide to all future inquirers.

The room was hung round with several portraits of eminent painters. While we were debating whether we should demand speech with these masters of mute eloquence, whose features were so familiar to us, it seemed that all at once they glided from their frames, and seated themselves at some little distance from us. There was Leonardo with his majestic beard and watchful eye, having a bust of Archimedes before him; next him was Raphael's graceful head turned round to the Fornarina; and on his other side was Lucretia Borgia, with calm, golden locks; Michael Angelo had placed the model of St. Peter's on the table before him; Corregio had an angel at his side; Titian was seated with his Mistress between himself and Giorgioni; Guido was accompanied by his own Aurora, who took a dice-box from him; Claude held a mirror in his hand; Rubens patted a beautiful panther (led in by a satyr) on the head; Vandyke appeared as his own Paris, and Rembrandt was hid under furs, gold chains and jewels, which Sir Joshua eyed closely, holding his hand so as to shade his forehead. Not a word was spoken; and as we rose to do them homage, they still presented the same surface to the view. Not being *bonâ-fide* representations of living people, we got rid of the splendid apparitions by signs and dumb shew. As soon as they had melted into thin air, there was a loud noise at the outer door, and we found it was Giotto, Cimabue, and Ghirlandaio, who had been raised from the dead by their earnest desire to see their illustrious successors—

"Whose names on earth
In Fame's eternal records live for aye!"

Finding them gone, they had no ambition to be seen after them, and mournfully withdrew. "Egad!" said B——, "those are the very fellows I should like to have had some talk with, to know how they could see to paint when all was dark around them."

"But shall we have nothing to say," interrogated G. J——, "to the Legend of Good Women?"—"Name, name, Mr. J——," cried H—— in a boisterous tone of friendly exultation, "name as many as you please, without reserve or fear of molestation!" J—— was perplexed between so many amiable recollections, that the name of the lady of his choice expired in a pensive whiff of his pipe; and B—— impatiently declared for the Duchess of Newcastle. Mrs. Hutchinson was no sooner mentioned, than she carried the day from the Duchess. We were the less solicitous on this subject of filling up the posthumous lists of Good Women, as there was already one in the room as good, as sensible, and in all respects as exemplary, as the best of them could be for their lives! "I should like vastly to have seen Ninon de l'Enclos," said that incomparable person; and this immediately put us in mind that we had neglected to pay honour due to our friends on the other side of the Channel: Voltaire, the patriarch of levity, and Rousseau, the father of sentiment, Montaigne and Rabelais (great in wisdom and in wit), Molière and that illustrious group that are collected round him (in the print of that subject) to hear him read his comedy of the Tartuffe at the house of Ninon; Racine, La Fontaine, Rochefoucault, St. Evremont, &c.

"There is one person," said a shrill, querulous voice, "I would rather see than all these—Don Quixote!"

"Come, come!" said H——; "I thought we should have no heroes, real or fabulous. What say you, Mr. B——? Are you for eking out your shadowy list with such names as Alexander, Julius Cæsar, Tamerlane, or Ghengis Khan?"—"Excuse me," said B——, "on the subject of characters in active life, plotters and disturbers of the world, I have a crotchet of my own, which I beg leave to reserve."—"No, no! come, out with your worthies!"—"What do you think of Guy Faux and Judas Iscariot?" H—— turned an eye upon him like a wild Indian, but cordial and full of smothered glee. "'Your most exquisite reason!'" was echoed on all sides; and A—— thought that B—— had now fairly entangled himself. "Why, I cannot but think," retorted he of the wistful countenance, "that Guy Faux, that poor fluttering annual scare-crow of straw and rags, is an ill-used gentleman. I would give something to see him sitting pale and emaciated, surrounded by his matches and his barrels of gunpowder, and expecting the moment that was to transport him to Paradise for his heroic self-devotion; but if I say any more, there is that fellow G—— will make something of it. And as to Judas Iscariot, my reason is different. I would fain see the face of him, who, having dipped his hand in the same dish with the Son of Man, could afterwards betray him. I have no conception of such a thing; nor have I ever seen any picture (not even Leonardo's very fine one) that gave me the least idea of it."— "You have said enough, Mr. B——, to justify your choice."

"'Oh! ever right, Menenius,—ever right!'"

"There is only one other person I can ever think of after this," continued H——; but without mentioning a name that once put on a semblance of mortality. "If Shakespeare was to come into the room, we should all rise up to meet him; but if that person was to come into it, we should all fall down and try to kiss the hem of his garment!"

As a lady present seemed now to get uneasy at the turn the conversation had taken, we rose up to go. The morning broke with that dim, dubious light by which Giotto, Cimabue, and Ghirlandaio must have seen to paint their earliest works; and we parted to meet again and renew similar topics at night, the next night, and the night after that, till that night overspread Europe which saw no dawn. The same event, in truth, broke up our little Congress that broke up the great one. But that was to meet again: our deliberations have never been resumed.

OF THE FEELING OF IMMORTALITY IN YOUTH

NO young man believes he shall ever die. It was a saying of my brother's, and a fine one. There is a feeling of Eternity in youth, which makes us amends for every thing. To be young is to be as one of the Immortal Gods. One half of time indeed is flown—the other half remains in store for us with all its countless treasures; for there is no line drawn, and we see no limit to our hopes and wishes. We make the coming age our own.——

"The vast, the unbounded prospect lies before us."

Death, old age, are words without a meaning, that pass by us like the idle air which we regard not. Others may have undergone, or may still be liable to them—we "bear a charmed life," which laughs to scorn all such sickly fancies. As in setting out on a delightful journey, we strain our eager gaze forward—

"Bidding the lovely scenes at distance hail,"—

and see no end to the landscape, new objects presenting themselves as we advance; so, in the commencement of life, we set no bounds to our inclinations, nor to the unrestricted opportunities of gratifying them. We have as yet found no obstacle, no disposition to flag;

and it seems that we can go on so for ever. We look round in a new world, full of life, and motion, and ceaseless progress; and feel in ourselves all the vigour and spirit to keep pace with it, and do not foresee from any present symptoms how we shall be left behind in the natural course of things, decline into old age, and drop into the grave. It is the simplicity, and as it were *abstractedness* of our feelings in youth, that (so to speak) identifies us with nature, and (our experience being slight and our passions strong) deludes us into a belief of being immortal like it. Our short-lived connection with existence, we fondly flatter ourselves, is an indissoluble and lasting union—a honey-moon that knows neither coldness, jar, nor separation. As infants smile and sleep, we are rocked in the cradle of our wayward fancies, and lulled into security by the roar of the universe around us—we quaff the cup of life with eager haste without draining it, instead of which it only overflows the more—objects press around us, filling the mind with their magnitude and with the throng of desires that wait upon them, so that we have no room for the thoughts of death. From that plenitude of our being, we cannot change all at once to dust and ashes, we cannot imagine "this sensible, warm motion, to become a kneaded clod"—we are too much dazzled by the brightness of the waking dream around us to look into the darkness of the tomb. We no more see our end than our beginning: the one is lost in oblivion and vacancy, as the other is hid from us by the crowd and hurry of approaching events. Or the grim shadow is seen lingering in the horizon, which we are doomed never to overtake, or whose last, faint, glimmering outline touches upon Heaven and translates us to the skies! Nor would the hold that life has taken of us permit us to detach our thoughts from present objects and pursuits, even if we would. What is there more opposed to health, than sickness; to strength and beauty, than decay and dissolution; to the active search of knowledge than mere oblivion? Or is there none of the usual advantage to bar the approach of Death, and mock his idle threats; Hope supplies their place, and draws a veil over the abrupt termination of all our cherished schemes. While the spirit of youth remains unimpaired, ere the "wine of life is drank up," we are like people intoxicated or in a fever, who are hurried away by the violence of their own sensations: it is only as present objects begin to pall upon the sense, as we have been disappointed in our favourite pursuits, cut off from our closest

ties, that passion loosens its hold upon the breast, that we by degrees become weaned from the world, and allow ourselves to contemplate, "as in a glass, darkly," the possibility of parting with it
for good. The example of others, the voice of experience, has no
effect upon us whatever. Casualties we must avoid: the slow and
deliberate advances of age we can play at *hide-and-seek* with. We
think ourselves too lusty and too nimble for that blear-eyed de-
crepid old gentleman to catch us. Like the foolish fat scullion, in
Sterne, when she hears that Master Bobby is dead, our only reflection is—"So am not I!" The idea of death, instead of staggering
our confidence, rather seems to strengthen and enhance our possession and our enjoyment of life. Others may fall around us like
leaves, or be mowed down like flowers by the scythe of Time:
these are but tropes and figures to the unreflecting ears and overweening presumption of youth. It is not till we see the flowers of
Love, Hope, and Joy, withering around us, and our own pleasures
cut up by the roots, that we bring the moral home to ourselves,
that we abate something of the wanton extravagance of our pretensions, or that the emptiness and dreariness of the prospect before
us reconciles us to the stillness of the grave!

> "Life! thou strange thing, that hast a power to feel
> Thou art, and to perceive that others are." [1]

Well might the poet begin his indignant invective against an art,
whose professed object is its destruction, with this animated
apostrophe to life. Life is indeed a strange gift, and its privileges
are most miraculous. Nor is it singular that when the splendid
boon is first granted us, our gratitude, our admiration, and our
delight should prevent us from reflecting on our own nothingness,
or from thinking it will ever be recalled. Our first and strongest
impressions are taken from the mighty scene that is opened to us,
and we very innocently transfer its durability as well as magnificence to ourselves. So newly found, we cannot make up our minds
to parting with it yet and at least put off that consideration to an
indefinite term. Like a clown at a fair, we are full of amazement
and rapture, and have no thoughts of going home, or that it will
soon be night. We know our existence only from external objects,
and we measure it by them. We can never be satisfied with gazing;

[1] Fawcett's ART OF WAR, a poem, 1794.

and nature will still want us to look on and applaud. Otherwise, the sumptuous entertainment, "the feast of reason and the flow of soul," to which they were invited, seems little better than a mockery and a cruel insult. We do not go from a play till the scene is ended, and the lights are ready to be extinguished. But the fair face of things still shines on; shall we be called away, before the curtain falls, or ere we have scarce had a glimpse of what is going on? Like children, our stepmother Nature holds us up to see the raree-show of the universe; and then, as if life were a burthen to support, lets us instantly down again. Yet in that short interval, what "brave sublunary things" does not the spectacle unfold; like a bubble, at one minute reflecting the universe, and the next, shook to air!—To see the golden sun and the azure sky, the outstretched ocean, to walk upon the green earth, and to be lord of a thousand creatures, to look down giddy precipices or over distant flowery vales, to see the world spread out under one's finger in a map, to bring the stars near, to view the smallest insects in a microscope, to read history, and witness the revolutions of empires and the succession of generations, to hear of the glory of Sidon and Tyre, of Babylon and Susa, as of a faded pageant, and to say all these were, and are now nothing, to think that we exist in such a point of time, and in such a corner of space, to be at once spectators and a part of the moving scene, to watch the return of the seasons, of spring and autumn, to hear

> —— "The stockdove plain amid the forest deep,
> That drowsy rustles to the sighing gale"——

to traverse desert wildernesses, to listen to the midnight choir, to visit lighted halls, or plunge into the dungeon's gloom, or sit in crowded theatres and see life itself mocked, to feel heat and cold, pleasure and pain, right and wrong, truth and falsehood, to study the works of art and refine the sense of beauty to agony, to worship fame and to dream of immortality, to have read Shakespeare and belong to the same species as Sir Isaac Newton; [1] to be and to do

[1] Lady Wortley Montagu says, in one of her letters, that "she would much rather be a rich *effendi*, with all his ignorance, than Sir Isaac Newton, with all his knowledge." This was not perhaps an impolitic choice, as she had a better chance of becoming one than the other, there being many rich effendis to one Sir Isaac Newton. The wish was not a very intellectual one. The same petulance of rank and sex breaks out everywhere in these "*Letters.*" She is constantly reducing the poets or philosophers who have the misfortune of her acquaintance, to the figure they might make at her Ladyship's levee or

all this, and then in a moment to be nothing, to have it all snatched from one like a juggler's ball or a phantasmagoria; there is something revolting and incredible to sense in the transition, and no wonder that, aided by youth and warm blood, and the flush of enthusiasm, the mind contrives for a long time to reject it with

toilette, not considering that the public mind does not sympathize with this process of a fastidious imagination. In the same spirit, she declares of Pope and Swift, that "had it not been for the *good-nature* of mankind, these two superior beings were entitled, by their birth and hereditary fortune, to be only a couple of link-boys." Gulliver's Travels, and the Rape of the Lock, go for nothing in this critical estimate, and the world raised the authors to the rank of superior beings, in spite of their disadvantages of birth and fortune, *out of pure good-nature!* So, again, she says of Richardson, that he had never got beyond the servants' hall, and was utterly unfit to describe the manners of people of quality; till, in the capricious workings of her vanity, she persuades herself that Clarissa is very like what she was at her age, and that Sir Thomas and Lady Grandison strongly resembled what she had heard of her mother and remembered of her father. It is one of the beauties and advantages of literature, that it is the means of abstracting the mind from the narrowness of local and personal prejudices, and of enabling us to judge of truth and excellence by their inherent merits alone. Woe be to the pen that would undo this fine illusion (the only reality), and teach us to regulate our notions of genius and virtue by the circumstances in which they happen to be placed! You would not expect a person whom you saw in a servants' hall, or behind a counter, to write Clarissa; but after he had written the work, to *pre-judge* it from the situation of the writer, is an unpardonable piece of injustice and folly. His merit could only be the greater from the contrast. If literature is an elegant accomplishment, which none but persons of birth and fashion should be allowed to excel in, or to exercise with advantage to the public, let them by all means take upon them the task of enlightening and refining mankind: if they decline this responsibility as too heavy for their shoulders, let those who do the drudgery in their stead, however inadequately, for want of their polite example, receive the meed that is their due, and not to be treated as low pretenders who have encroached on the province of their betters. Suppose Richardson to have been acquainted with the great man's steward, or valet, instead of the great man himself, I will venture to say that there was more difference between him who lived in an *ideal world*, and had the genius and felicity to open that world to others, and his friend the steward, than between the lacquey and the mere lord, or between those who lived in different rooms of the same house, who dined on the same luxuries at different tables, who rode outside or inside of the same coach, and were proud of wearing or of bestowing the same tawdry livery. If the lord is distinguished from his valet by any thing else, it is by education and talent, which he has in common with our author. But if the latter shews these in the highest degree, it is asked what are his pretensions? Not birth or fortune, for neither of these would enable him to write a Clarissa. One man is born with a title and estate, another with genius. That is sufficient; and we have no right to question the genius for want of *gentility*, unless the former ran in families, or could be bequeathed with a fortune, which is not the case. Were it so, the flowers of literature, like jewels and embroidery, would be confined to the fashionable circles; and there would be no pretenders to taste or elegance but those whose names were found in the court list. No one objects to Claude's Landscapes as the work of a pastrycook, or withholds from Raphael the epithet of *divine*, because his parents were not rich. This impertinence is confined to men of letters; the evidence of the senses baffles the envy and foppery of mankind. No quarter ought to be given to this *aristocratic* tone of criticism whenever it appears. People of quality are not contented with carrying all the external advantages for their own share, but would persuade you that all the in-

disdain and loathing as a monstrous and improbable fiction, like a monkey on a house-top, that is loath, amidst its fine discoveries and specious antics, to be tumbled head-long into the street, and crushed to atoms, the sport and laughter of the multitude!

The change, from the commencement to the close of life, appears like a fable, after it has taken place; how should we treat it otherwise than as a chimera before it has come to pass? There are some things that happened so long ago, places or persons we have formerly seen, of which such dim traces remain, we hardly know whether it was sleeping or waking they occurred; they are like dreams within the dream of life, a mist, a film before the eye of memory, which, as we try to recall them more distinctly, elude our notice altogether. It is but natural that the lone interval that we thus look back upon, should have appeared long and endless in prospect. There are others so distinct and fresh, they seem but of yesterday—their very vividness might be deemed a pledge of their permanence. Then, however far back our impressions may go, we find others still older (for our years are multiplied in youth); descriptions of scenes that we had read, and people before our time, Priam and the Trojan war; and even then, Nestor was old and dwelt delighted on his youth, and spoke of the race, of heroes that were no more;—what wonder that, seeing this long line of being pictured in our minds, and reviving as it were in us, we should give ourselves involuntary credit for an indeterminate period of existence? In the Cathedral at Peterborough there is a monument to Mary, Queen of Scots, at which I used to gaze when a boy, while the events of the period, all that had happened since, passed in

tellectual ones are packed up in the same bundle. Lord Byron was a later instance of this double and unwarrantable style of pretension—*monstrum ingens, biforme.* He could not endure a lord who was not a wit, nor a poet who was not a lord. Nobody but himself answered to his own standard of perfection. Mr. Moore carries a proxy in his pocket from some noble persons to estimate literary merit by the same rule. Lady Mary calls Fielding names, but she afterwards makes atonement by doing justice to his frank, free, hearty nature, where she says " his spirits gave him raptures with his cook-maid, and cheerfulness when he was starving in a garret, and his happy constitution made him forget every thing when he was placed before a venison-pasty or over a flask of champagne." She does not want shrewdness and spirit when her petulance and conceit do not get the better of her, and she has done ample and merited execution on Lord Bolingbroke. She is, however, very angry at the freedoms taken with the Great; *smells a rat* in this indiscriminate scribbling, and the familiarity of writers with the reading public; and inspired by her Turkish costume, foretells a French or English revolution as the consequence of transferring the patronage of letters from the *quality* to the mob, and of supposing that ordinary writers or readers can have any notions in common with their superiors.

review before me. If all this mass of feeling and imagination could be crowded into a moment's compass, what might not the whole of life be supposed to contain? We are heirs of the past; we count upon the future as our natural reversion. Besides, there are some of our early impressions so exquisitely tempered, it appears that they must always last—nothing can add to or take away from their sweetness and purity—the first breath of spring, the hyacinth dipped in the dew, the mild lustre of the evening-star, the rainbow after a storm—while we have the full enjoyment of these, we must be young; and what can ever alter us in this respect? Truth, friendship, love, books, are also proof against the canker of time; and while we live, but for them, we can never grow old. We take out a new lease of existence from the objects on which we set our affections, and become abstracted, impassive, immortal in them. We cannot conceive how certain sentiments should ever decay or grow cold in our breasts; and, consequently, to maintain them in their first youthful glow and vigour, the flame of life must continue to burn as bright as ever, or rather, they are the fuel that feed the sacred lamp, that kindle "the purple light of love," and spread a golden cloud around our heads! Again, we not only flourish and survive in our affections (in which we will not listen to the possibility of a change, any more than we foresee the wrinkles on the brow of a mistress), but we have a farther guarantee against the thoughts of death in our favourite studies and pursuits, and in their continual advance. Art we know is long; life, we feel, should be so too. We see no end of the difficulties we have to encounter: perfection is slow of attainment, and we must have time to accomplish it in. Rubens complained that when he had just learnt his art, he was snatched away from it: we trust we shall be more fortunate! A wrinkle in an old head takes whole days to finish it properly: but to catch "the Raphael grace, the Guido air," no limit should be put to our endeavours. What a prospect for the future! What a task we have entered upon! and shall we be arrested in the middle of it? We do not reckon our time thus employed lost, or our pains thrown away, or our progress slow—we do not droop or grow tired, but "gain new vigour at our endless task;"—and shall Time grudge us the opportunity to finish what we have auspiciously begun, and have formed a sort of compact with nature to achieve? The fame of the great names we look up to is also imperishable; and shall not we, who contemplate it with such intense yearnings, imbibe a portion of ethereal fire, the *divinæ particula auræ*, which nothing can extinguish? I remember to have looked at a print of Rembrandt for hours together, without being conscious of the flight of time, trying to resolve it into its component parts, to connect its strong and sharp gradations, to learn the secret of its reflected lights, and found neither satiety nor pause in the prosecution of my studies. The print over which I was poring would last long enough; why should the idea in my mind, which was finer, more impalpable, perish before it? At this, I redoubled the ardour of my pursuit, and by the very subtlety and refinement of my inquiries, seemed to bespeak for them an exemption from corruption and the rude grasp of Death.[1]

Objects, on our first acquaintance with them, have that singleness and integrity of impression that it seems as if nothing could destroy or obliterate them, so firmly are they stamped and rivetted on the brain. We repose on them with a sort of voluptuous indolence, in full faith and boundless confidence. We are absorbed in the present moment, or return to the same point—idling away a great deal of time in youth, thinking we have enough and to spare. There is often a local feeling in the air, which is as fixed as if it were of marble; we loiter in dim cloisters, losing ourselves in thought and in their glimmering arches; a winding road before us seems as long as the journey of life, and as full of events. Time and experience dissipate this illusion; and by reducing them to detail, circumscribe the limits of our expectations. It is only as the pageant of life passes by and the masques turn their backs upon us, that we see through the deception, or believe that the train will have an end. In many cases, the slow progress and monotonous texture of our lives, before we mingle with the world and are embroiled in its affairs, has a tendency to aid the same feeling. We have a difficulty, when left to ourselves, and without the resource of books or some more lively pursuit, to "beguile the slow and creeping hours of time," and argue that if it moves on always at this tedious snail's-pace, it can never come to an end. We are willing to skip over certain portions of it that separate us from favourite objects, that irritate ourselves at the unnecessary delay. The young are prodigal

[1] Is it not this that frequently keeps artists alive so long, *viz.* the constant occupation of their minds with vivid images, with little of the *wear-and-tear* of the body?

of life from a superabundance of it; the old are tenacious on the
same score, because they have little left, and cannot enjoy even
what remains of it.

For my part, I set out in life with the French Revolution, and
that event had considerable influence on my early feelings, as on
those of others. Youth was then doubly such. It was the dawn of
a new era, a new impulse had been given to men's minds, and the
sun of Liberty rose upon the sun of Life in the same day, and both
were proud to run their race together. Little did I dream, while my
first hopes and wishes went hand in hand with those of the human
race, that long before my eyes should close, that dawn would be
overcast, and set once more in the night of despotism—"total
eclipse!" Happy that I did not. I felt for years, and during the
best part of my existence, *heart-whole* in that cause, and triumphed
in the triumphs over the enemies of man! At that time, while the
fairest aspirations of the human mind seemed about to be realized,
ere the image of man was defaced and his breast mangled in scorn,
philosophy took a higher, poetry could afford a deeper range. At
that time, to read the "ROBBERS," was indeed delicious, and to hear

> "From the dungeon of the tower time-rent,
> That fearful voice, a famish'd father's cry,"

could be borne only amidst the fulness of hope, the crash of the
fall of the strong holds of power, and the exulting sounds of the
march of human freedom. What feelings the death-scene in Don
Carlos sent into the soul! In that headlong career of lofty enthusiasm, and the joyous opening of the prospects of the world
and our own, the thought of death crossing it, smote doubly cold
upon the mind; there was a stifling sense of oppression and con-
finement, an impatience of our present knowledge, a desire to grasp
the whole of our existence in one strong embrace, to sound the
mystery of life and death, and in order to put an end to the agony
of doubt and dread, to burst through our prison-house, and confront the King of Terrors in his grisly palace! . . . As I was writing out this passage, my miniature-picture when a child lay on the
mantle-piece, and I took it out of the case to look at it. I could
perceive few traces of myself in it; but there was the same placid
brow, the dimpled mouth, the same timid, inquisitive glance as
ever. But its careless smile did not seem to reproach me with hav-

ing become a recreant to the sentiments that were then sown in my mind, or with having written a sentence that could call up a blush in this image of ingenuous youth!

"That time is past with all its giddy raptures." Since the future was barred to my progress, I have turned for consolation to the past, gathering up the fragments of my early recollections, and putting them into a form that might live. It is thus, that when we find our personal and substantial identity vanishing from us, we strive to gain a reflected and substituted one in our thoughts: we do not like to perish wholly, and wish to bequeath our names at least to posterity. As long as we can keep alive our cherished thoughts and nearest interests in the minds of others, we do not appear to have retired altogether from the stage, we still occupy a place in the estimation of mankind, exercise a powerful influence over them, and it is only our bodies that are trampled into dust or dispersed to air. Our darling speculations still find favour and encouragement, and we make as good a figure in the eyes of our descendants, nay, perhaps, a better than we did in our life-time. This is one point gained; the demands of our self-love are so far satisfied. Besides, if by the proofs of intellectual superiority we survive ourselves in this world, by exemplary virtue or unblemished faith, we are taught to ensure an interest in another and a higher state of being, and to anticipate at the same time the applauses of men and angels.

"Even from the tomb the voice of nature cries;
Even in our ashes live their wonted fires."

As we advance in life, we acquire a keener sense of the value of time. Nothing else, indeed, seems of any consequence; and we become misers in this respect. We try to arrest its few last tottering steps, and to make it linger on the brink of the grave. We can never leave off wondering how that which has ever been should cease to be, and would still live on, that we may wonder at our own shadow, and when "all the life of life is flown," dwell on the retrospect of the past. This is accompanied by a mechanical tenaciousness of whatever we possess, by a distrust and a sense of fallacious hollowness in all we see. Instead of the full, pulpy feeling of youth, every thing is flat and insipid. The world is a painted witch, that puts us off with false shews and tempting appearances. The ease,

the jocund gaiety, the unsuspecting security of youth are fled:
nor can we, without flying in the face of common sense,

> "From the last dregs of life, hope to receive
> What its first sprightly runnings could not give."

If we can slip out of the world without notice or mischance, can
tamper with bodily infirmity, and frame our minds to the becoming composure of *still-life*, before we sink into total insensibility, it
is as much as we ought to expect. We do not in the regular course
of nature die all at once: we have mouldered away gradually long
before; faculty after faculty, attachment after attachment, we are
torn from ourselves piece-meal while living; year after year takes
something from us; and death only consigns the last remnant of
what we were to the grave. The revulsion is not so great, and a
quiet *euthanasia* is a winding-up of the plot, that is not out of
reason or nature.

That we should thus in a manner outlive ourselves, and dwindle
imperceptibly into nothing, is not surprising, when even in our
prime the strongest impressions leave so little traces of themselves
behind, and the last object is driven out by the succeeding one.
How little effect is produced on us at any time by the books we
have read, the scenes we have witnessed, the sufferings we have
gone through! Think only of the variety of feelings we experience
in reading an interesting romance, or being present at a fine play—
what beauty, what sublimity, what soothing, what heart-rending
emotions! You would suppose these would last for ever, or at least
subdue the mind to a correspondent tone and harmony—while
we turn over the page, while the scene is passing before us, it seems
as if nothing could ever after shake our resolution, that "treason
domestic, foreign levy, nothing could touch us farther!" The first
splash of mud we get, on entering the street, the first pettifogging
shop-keeper that cheats us out of two-pence, and the whole vanishes clean out of our remembrance, and we become the idle prey
of the most petty and annoying circumstances. The mind soars by
an effort to the grand and lofty: it is at home, in the grovelling,
the disagreeable, and the little. This happens in the height and
hey-day of our existence, when novelty gives a stronger impulse
to the blood and takes a faster hold of the brain, (I have known the
impression on coming out of a gallery of pictures then last half a

day)—as we grow old, we become more feeble and querulous, every object "reverbs its own hollowness," and both worlds are not enough to satisfy the peevish importunity and extravagant presumption of our desires! There are a few superior, happy beings, who are born with a temper exempt from every trifling annoyance. This spirit sits serene and smiling as in its native skies, and a divine harmony (whether heard or not) plays around them. This is to be at peace. Without this, it is in vain to fly into deserts, or to build a hermitage on the top of rocks, if regret and ill-humour follow us there: and with this, it is needless to make the experiment. The only true retirement is that of the heart; the only true leisure is the repose of the passions. To such persons it makes little difference whether they are young or old; and they die as they have lived, with graceful resignation.

ON A SUN–DIAL

"To carve out dials quaintly, point by point."
—SHAKESPEARE.

HORAS non numero nisi serenas—is the motto of a sun-dial near Venice. There is a softness and a harmony in the words and in the thought unparalleled. Of all conceits it is surely the most classical. "I count only the hours that are serene." What a bland and care-dispelling feeling! How the shadows seem to fade on the dial-plate as the sky lours, and time presents only a blank unless as its progress is marked by what is joyous, and all that is not happy sinks into oblivion! What a fine lesson is conveyed to the mind—to take no note of time but by its benefits, to watch only for the smiles and neglect the frowns of fate, to compose our lives of bright and gentle moments, turning always to the sunny side of things, and letting the rest slip from our imaginations, unheeded or forgotten! How different from the common art of self-tormenting! For myself, as I rode along the Brenta, while the sun shone hot upon its sluggish, slimy waves, my sensations were far from comfortable; but the reading this inscription on the side of a glaring wall in an instant restored me to myself; and still, whenever I think of or repeat it, it has the power of wafting me into the region of pure and blissful abstraction. I cannot help fancying it to be a legend of Popish superstition. Some monk of the dark ages must have invented and bequeathed it to us, who, loitering in trim gardens and watching the silent march of time, as his fruits ripened in the sun or his flowers scented the balmy air, felt a mild languor pervade his senses, and having little to do or to care for, determined (in imitation of his sun-dial) to efface that little from his thoughts or draw a veil over it, making of his life one long dream of quiet! *Horas non numero nisi serenas*—he might repeat, when the heavens were overcast and the gathering storm scattered the falling leaves, and turn to his books and wrap himself in his golden studies! Out of some mood of mind, indolent, elegant, thoughtful, this exquisite device (speaking volumes) must have originated.

Of the several modes of counting time, that by the sun-dial is perhaps the most apposite and striking, if not the most convenient or comprehensive. It does not obtrude its observations, though it "morals on the time," and, by its stationary character, forms a contrast to the most fleeting of all essences. It stands *sub dio*— under the marble air, and there is some connexion between the image of infinity and eternity. I should also like to have a sunflower growing near it with bees fluttering round.[1] It should be of iron to denote duration, and have a dull, leaden look. I hate a sun-dial made of wood, which is rather calculated to show the variations of the seasons, than the progress of time, slow, silent, imperceptible, chequered with light and shade. If our hours were all serene, we might probably take almost as little note of them, as the dial does of those that are clouded. It is the shadow thrown across, that gives us warning of their flight. Otherwise our impressions would take the same undistinguishable hue; we should scarce be conscious of our existence. Those who have had none of the cares of this life to harass and disturb them, have been obliged to have recourse to the hopes and fears of the next to enliven the prospect before them. Most of the methods for measuring the lapse of time have, I believe, been the contrivance of monks and religious recluses, who, finding time hang heavy on their hands, were at some pains to see how they got rid of it. The hour-glass is, I suspect, an older invention; and it is certainly the most defective of all. Its creep-

---

[1] Is this a verbal fallacy? Or in the close, retired, sheltered scene which I have imagined to myself, is not the sun-flower a natural accompaniment of the sun-dial?

ing sands are not indeed an unapt emblem of the minute, countless portions of our existence; and the manner in which they gradually slide through the hollow glass and diminish in number till not a single one is left, also illustrates the way in which our years slip from us by stealth: but as a mechanical invention, it is rather a hindrance than a help, for it requires to have the time, of which it pretends to count the precious moments, taken up in attention to itself, and in seeing that when one end of the glass is empty, we turn it round, in order that it may go on again, or else all our labour is lost, and we must wait for some other mode of ascertaining the time before we can recover our reckoning and proceed as before. The philosopher in his cell, the cottager at her spinning-wheel must, however, find an invaluable acquisition in this "companion of the lonely hour," as it has been called,[1] which not only serves to tell how the time goes, but to fill up its vacancies. What a treasure must not the little box seem to hold, as if it were a sacred deposit of the very grains and fleeting sands of life! What a business, in lieu of other more important avocations, to see it out to the last sand, and then to renew the process again on the instant, that there may not be the least flaw or error in the account! What a strong sense must be brought home to the mind of the value and irrecoverable nature of the time that is fled; what a thrilling, incessant consciousness of the slippery tenure by which we hold what remains of it! Our very existence must seem crumbling to atoms, and running down (without a miraculous reprieve) to the last fragment. "Dust to dust and ashes to ashes" is a text that might be fairly inscribed on an hour-glass: it is ordinarily associated with the scythe of Time and a Death's-head, as a *Memento mori;* and has, no doubt, furnished many a tacit hint to the apprehensive and visionary enthusiast in favour of a resurrection to another life!

The French give a different turn to things, less *sombre* and less edifying. A common and also a very pleasing ornament to a clock, in Paris, is a figure of Time seated in a boat which Cupid is rowing along, with the motto, *L'Amour fait passer le Tems*—which the wits again have travestied into *Le Tems fait passer L'Amour*. All this

[1] "Once more, companion of the lonely hour,
   I'll turn thee up again."
   —*Bloomfield's Poems—The Widow to her Hour-glass.*

is ingenious and well; but it wants sentiment. I like a people who have something that they love and something that they hate, and with whom every thing is not alike a matter of indifference or *pour passer le tems*. The French attach no importance to any thing, except for the moment; they are only thinking how they shall get rid of one sensation for another; all their ideas are *in transitu*. Every thing is detached, nothing is accumulated. It would be a million of years before a Frenchman would think of the *Horas non numero nisi serenas*. Its impassioned repose and *ideal* voluptuousness are as far from their breasts as the poetry of that line in Shakespeare—"How sweet the moonlight sleeps upon that bank!" They never arrive at the classical—or the romantic. They blow the bubbles of vanity, fashion, and pleasure; but they do not expand their perceptions into refinement, or strengthen them into solidity. Where there is nothing fine in the ground-work of the imagination, nothing fine in the superstructure can be produced. They are light, airy, fanciful (to give them their due)—but when they attempt to be serious (beyond mere good sense) they are either dull or extravagant. When the volatile salt has flown off, nothing but a *caput mortuum* remains. They have infinite crotchets and caprices with their clocks and watches, which seem made for any thing but to tell the hour—gold-repeaters, watches with metal covers, clocks with hands to count the seconds. There is no escaping from quackery and impertinence, even in our attempts to calculate the waste of time. The years gallop fast enough for me, without remarking every moment as it flies; and farther, I must say I dislike a watch (whether of French or English manufacture) that comes to me like a footpad with its face muffled, and does not present its clear, open aspect like a friend, and point with its finger to the time of day. All this opening and shutting of dull, heavy cases (under pretence that the glass-lid is liable to be broken, or lets in the dust or air and obstructs the movement of the watch), is not to husband time, but to give trouble. It is mere pomposity and self-importance, like consulting a mysterious oracle that one carries about with one in one's pocket, instead of asking a common question of an acquaintance or companion. There are two clocks which strike the hour in the room where I am. This I do not like. In the first place, I do not want to be reminded twice how the time goes (it is like the second tap of a saucy servant at your door when

perhaps you have no wish to get up): in the next place, it is starting a difference of opinion on the subject, and I am averse to every
appearance of wrangling and disputation. Time moves on the
same, whatever disparity there may be in our mode of keeping
count of it, like true fame in spite of the cavils and contradictions
of the critics. I am no friend to repeating watches. The only
pleasant association I have with them is the account given by
Rousseau of some French lady, who sat up reading the New Heloise
when it first came out, and ordering her maid to sound the repeater,
found it was too late to go to bed, and continued reading on till
morning. Yet how different is the interest excited by this story
from the account which Rousseau somewhere else gives of his sitting up with his father reading romances, when a boy, till they
were startled by the swallows twittering in their nests at day-break,
and the father cried out, half angry and ashamed—"*Allons, mon
fils; je suis plus enfant que toi!*" In general, I have heard repeating watches sounded in stage-coaches at night, when some fellow-
traveller suddenly awaking and wondering what was the hour,
another has very deliberately taken out his watch, and pressing
the spring, it has counted out the time; each petty stroke acting
like a sharp puncture on the ear, and informing me of the dreary
hours I had already passed, and of the more dreary ones I had to
wait till morning.

The great advantage, it is true, which clocks have over watches
and other dumb reckoners of time is, that for the most part they
strike the hour—that they are as it were the mouth-pieces of time;
that they not only point it to the eye, but impress it on the ear;
that they "lend it both an understanding and a tongue." Time
thus speaks to us in an audible and warning voice. Objects of
sight are easily distinguished by the sense, and suggest useful reflections to the mind; sounds, from their intermittent nature, and
perhaps other causes, appeal more to the imagination, and strike
upon the heart. But to do this, they must be unexpected and involuntary—there must be no trick in the case—they should not be
squeezed out with a finger and a thumb; there should be nothing
optional, personal in their occurrence; they should be like stern,
inflexible monitors, that nothing can prevent from discharging
their duty. Surely, if there is any thing with which we should not
mix up our vanity and self-consequence, it is with Time, the most

independent of all things. All the sublimity, all the superstition that hang upon this palpable mode of announcing its flight, are chiefly attached to this circumstance. Time would lose its abstracted character, if we kept it like a curiosity or a jack-in-a-box: its prophetic warnings would have no effect, if it obviously spoke only at our prompting, like a paltry ventriloquism. The clock that tells the coming, dreaded hour—the castle bell, that "with its brazen throat and iron tongue, sounds one unto the drowsy ear of night" —the curfew, "swinging slow with sullen roar" o'er wizard stream or fountain, are like a voice from other worlds, big with unknown events. The last sound, which is still kept up as an old custom in many parts of England, is a great favourite with me. I used to hear it when a boy. It tells a tale of other times. The days that are past, the generations that are gone, the tangled forest glades and hamlets brown of my native country, the woodsman's art, the Norman warrior armed for the battle or in his festive hall, the conqueror's iron rule and peasant's lamp extinguished, all start up at the clamorous peal, and fill my mind with fear and wonder. I confess, nothing at present interests me but what has been—the recollection of the impressions of my early life, or events long past, of which only the dim traces remain in a smouldering ruin or half-obsolete custom. That *things should be that are now no more*, creates in my mind the most unfeigned astonishment. I cannot solve the mystery of the past, nor exhaust my pleasure in it. The years, the generations to come, are nothing to me. We care no more about the world in the year 2300 than we do about one of the planets. Even George IV is better than the Earl of Windsor. We might as well make a voyage to the moon as think of stealing a march upon Time with impunity. *De non apparentibus et non existentibus eadem est ratio.* Those who are to come after us and push us from the stage seem like upstarts and pretenders, that may be said to exist *in vacuo*, we know not upon what, except as they are blown up with vain and self conceit by their patrons among the moderns. But the ancients are true and *bonâ-fide* people, to whom we are bound by aggregate knowledge and filial ties, and in whom seen by the mellow light of history we feel our own existence doubled and our pride consoled, as we ruminate on the vestiges of the past. The public in general, however, do not carry this speculative indifference about the future to what is to happen to themselves, or to the

part they are to act in the busy scene. For my own part, I do; and
the only wish I can form, or that ever prompts the passing sigh,
would be to live some of my years over again—they would be those
in which I enjoyed and suffered most!

The ticking of a clock in the night has nothing very interesting
nor very alarming in it, though superstition has magnified it into
an omen. In a state of vigilance or debility, it preys upon the spirits
like the persecution of a teazing pertinacious insect; and haunting
the imagination after it has ceased in reality, is converted into the
death-watch. Time is rendered vast by contemplating its minute
portions thus repeatedly and painfully urged upon its attention,
as the ocean in its immensity is composed of water-drops. A clock
striking with a clear and silver sound is a great relief in such circumstances, breaks the spell, and resembles a sylph-like and friendly
spirit in the room. Foreigners, with all their tricks and contrivances
upon clocks and time-pieces, are strangers to the sound of village-
bells, though perhaps a people that can dance may dispense with
them. They impart a pensive, wayward pleasure to the mind, and
are a kind of chronology of happy events, often serious in the
retrospect—births, marriages, and so forth. Coleridge calls them
"the poor man's only music." A village-spire in England peeping
from its cluster of trees is always associated in imagination with
this cheerful accompaniment, and may be expected to pour its
joyous tidings on the gale. In Catholic countries, you are stunned
with the everlasting tolling of bells to prayers or for the dead. In
the Apennines, and other wild and mountainous districts of Italy,
the little chapel-bell with its simple tinkling sound has a romantic
and charming effect. The Monks in former times appear to have
taken a pride in the construction of bells as well as churches; and
some of those of the great cathedrals abroad (as at Cologne and
Rouen) may be fairly said to be hoarse with counting the flight
of ages. The chimes in Holland are a nuisance. They dance in the
hours and the quarters. They leave no respite to the imagination.
Before one set has done ringing in your ears, another begins. You
do not know whether the hours move or stand still, go backwards
or forwards, so fantastical and perplexing are their accompaniments. Time is a more staid personage, and not so full of gambols.
It puts you in mind of a tune with variations, or of an embroidered
dress. Surely, nothing is more simple than time. His march is

straightforward; but we should have leisure allowed us to look back upon the distance we have come, and not be counting his steps every moment. Time in Holland is a foolish old fellow with all the antics of a youth, who "goes to church in a coranto, and lights his pipe in a cinque-pace." The chimes with us, on the contrary, as they come in every three or four hours, are like stages in the journey of the day. They give a fillip to the lazy, creeping hours, and relieve the lassitude of country-places. At noon, their desultory, trivial song is diffused through the hamlet with the odour of rashers of bacon; at the close of day they send the toil-worn sleepers to their beds. Their discontinuance would be a great loss to the thinking or unthinking public. Mr. Wordsworth has painted their effect on the mind when he makes his friend Matthew, in a fit of inspired dotage,

> " Sing those witty rhymes
> About the crazy old church-clock
> And the bewilder'd chimes."

The tolling of the bell for deaths and executions is a fearful summons, though, as it announces, not the advance of time but the approach of fate, it happily makes no part of our subject. Otherwise, the "sound of the bell" for Macheath's execution in the "Beggar's Opera," or for that of the Conspirators in "Venice Preserved," with the roll of the drum at a soldier's funeral, and a digression to that of my Uncle Toby, as it is so finely described by Sterne, would furnish ample topics to descant upon. If I were a moralist, I might disapprove the ringing in the new and ringing out the old year.

> " Why dance ye, mortals, o'er the grave of Time?"

St. Paul's bell tolls only for the death of our English kings, or a distinguished personage or two, with long intervals between.[1]

Those who have no artificial means of ascertaining the progress of time, are in general the most acute in discerning its immediate signs, and are most retentive of individual dates. The mechanical aids to knowledge are not sharpeners of the wits. The understanding of a savage is a kind of natural almanac, and more true

---

[1] Rousseau has admirably described the effect of bells on the imagination in a passage in the Confessions, beginning " *Le son des cloches m'a toujours singulièrement affecté,*" &c.

in its prognostication of the future. In his mind's eye he sees what has happened or what is likely to happen to him, "as in a map the voyager his course." Those who read the times and seasons in the aspect of the heavens and the configurations of the stars, who count by moons and know when the sun rises and sets, are by no means ignorant of their own affairs or of the common concatenation of events. People in such situations have not their faculties distracted by any multiplicity of inquiries beyond what befalls themselves, and the outward appearances that mark the change. There is, therefore, a simplicity and clearness in the knowledge they possess, which often puzzles the more learned. I am sometimes surprised at a shepherd-boy by the roadside, who sees nothing but the earth and sky, asking me the time of day—he ought to know so much better than any one how far the sun is above the horizon. I suppose he wants to ask a question of a passenger, or to see if he has a watch. Robinson Crusoe lost his reckoning in the monotony of his life and that bewildering dream of solitude, and was fain to have recourse to the notches in a piece of wood. What a diary was his! And how time must have spread its circuit round him, vast and pathless as the ocean!

For myself, I have never had a watch nor any other mode of keeping time in my possession, nor ever wish to learn how time goes. It is a sign I have had little to do, few avocations, few engagements. When I am in a town, I can hear the clock; and when I am in the country, I can listen to the silence. What I like best is to lie whole mornings on a sunny bank on Salisbury Plain, without any object before me, neither knowing nor caring how time passes, and thus "with light-winged toys of feathered Idleness" to melt down hours to moments. Perhaps some such thoughts as I have here set down float before me like motes before my half-shut eyes, or some vivid image of the past by forcible contrast rushes by me— "Diana and her fawn, and all the glories of the antique world;" then I start away to prevent the iron from entering into my soul, and let fall some tears into that stream of time which separates me farther and farther from all I once loved! At length I rouse myself from my reverie, and home to dinner, proud of killing time with thought, nay even without thinking. Somewhat of this idle humour I inherit from my father, though he had not the same freedom from *ennui*, for he was not a metaphysician; and there were stops and vacant intervals in his being which he did not know how to fill up. He used in these cases, and as an obvious resource, carefully to wind up his watch at night, and "with lack-lustre eye" more than once in the course of the day look to see what o'clock it was. Yet he had nothing else in his character in common with the elder Mr. Shandy. Were I to attempt a sketch of him, for my own or the reader's satisfaction, it would be after the following manner: ——but now I recollect, I have done something of the kind once before, and were I to resume the subject here, some bat or owl of a critic, with spectacled gravity, might swear I had stolen the whole of this Essay from myself—or (what is worse) from him! So I had better let it go as it is.

DE QUINCEY

THOMAS DE QUINCEY (*1785–1859*), *essayist and critic, was born in Manchester; he attended various schools, from the last of which he ran away, and rambled through the country, eventually drifting to the metropolis. Entering Oxford, he left without a degree; it was as a student that he began to take opium, at first to relieve a toothache. In 1807, he met Coleridge, Wordsworth, and Southey; soon afterwards, Lamb and other literary men in London. He settled in Grasmere in 1809; visited Edinburgh and London at intervals; fought the opium habit as it grew upon him. He contributed to periodicals, but his career may be said to have begun with the publication of "The Confessions of an English Opium Eater" in 1821. In 1828, he settled in Edinburgh, where his family later joined him; he wrote essays and criticisms, and one novel, "Klosterheim," which was not popular. His last years were occupied with editing his collected works.*

Chiefly known as a stylist, De Quincey tried to restore the traditions of eighteenth-century prose. Musical, a great conversationalist, a person of remarkable charm, he was not without his idiosyncracies and extravagances. His writings have a strong autobiographical element; they have also beauty, keenness, humor, pathos, and critical acumen.

DE QUINCEY

A PERIPATETIC PHILOSOPHER

HE was a man of very extraordinary genius. He has generally been treated by those who have spoken of him in print as a madman. But this is a mistake, and must have been founded chiefly on the titles of his books. He was a man of fervid mind, and of sublime aspirations: but he was no madman; or, if he was, then I say that it is so far desirable to be a madman. In 1798 or 1799, when I must have been about thirteen to fourteen years old, Walking Stewart was in Bath—where my family at that time resided. He frequented the pump-room, and I believe all public places—walking up and down, and dispersing his philosophic opinions to the right and the left, like a Grecian philosopher. The first time I saw him was at a concert in the Upper Rooms; he was pointed out to me by one of my party as a very eccentric man who had walked over the habitable globe. I remember that Madame Mara was at that moment singing; and Walking Stewart, who was a true lover of music (as I afterwards came to know), was hanging upon her notes like a bee upon a jessamine flower. His countenance was striking, and expressed the union of benignity with philosophic habits of thought. In such health had his pedestrian exercises preserved him, connected with his abstemious mode of living, that, though he must at that time have been considerably above forty, he did not look older than twenty-eight; at least the face which remained upon my recollection for some years was that of a young man. Nearly ten years afterwards I became acquainted with him. During the interval I had picked up one of his works in Bristol,— viz., his "Travels to discover the Source of Moral Motion," the second volume of which is entitled "The Apocalypse of Nature." I had been greatly impressed by the sound and original views which, in the first volume, he had taken of the national characters throughout Europe. In particular, he was the first, and, so far as I know,

268

the only, writer who had noticed the profound error of ascribing a phlegmatic character to the English nation. "English phlegm" is the constant expression of authors, when contrasting the English with the French. Now, the truth is that, beyond that of all other nations, it has a substratum of profound passion: and, if we are to recur to the old doctrine of temperaments, the English character must be classed, not under the *phlegmatic*, but under the *melancholic*, temperament, and the French under the *sanguine*. The character of a nation may be judged of, in this particular, by examining its idiomatic language. The French, in whom the lower forms of passion are constantly bubbling up from the shallow and superficial character of their feelings, have appropriated all the phrases of passion to the service of trivial and ordinary life: and hence they have no language of passion for the service of poetry, or of occasions really demanding it: for it has been already enfeebled by continual association with cases of an unimpassioned order. But a character of deeper passion has a perpetual standard in itself, by which, as by an instinct, it tries all cases, and rejects the language of passion as disproportionate and ludicrous where it is not fully justified. "Ah Heavens!" or "Oh my God!" are exclamations, with us, so exclusively reserved for cases of profound interest, that, on hearing a woman even (*i.e.*, a person of the sex most easily excited) utter such words, we look round, expecting to see her child in some situation of danger. But in France, "*Ah Ciel!*" and "*Oh mon Dieu!*" are uttered by every woman if a mouse does but run across the floor. The ignorant and the thoughtless, however, will continue to class the English character under the phlegmatic temperament, whilst the philosopher will perceive that it is the exact polar antithesis to a phlegmatic character. In this conclusion, though otherwise expressed and illustrated, Walking Stewart's view of the English character will be found to terminate: and his opinion is especially valuable—first, and chiefly, because he was a philosopher; secondly, because his acquaintance with man, civilised and uncivilised, under all national distinctions, was absolutely unrivalled. Meantime, this and others of his opinions were expressed in language that, if literally construed, would often appear insane or absurd. The truth is, his long intercourse with foreign nations had given something of a hybrid tincture to his diction; in some of his works, for instance, he uses the French word *hélas!* uniformly for the English *alas!* and apparently with no consciousness of his mistake. He had also this singularity about him, that he was everlastingly metaphysicising against metaphysics. To me, who was buried in metaphysical reveries from my earliest days, this was not likely to be an attraction, any more than the vicious structure of his diction was likely to please my scholar-like taste. All grounds of disgust, however, gave way before my sense of his powerful merits; and, as I have said, I sought his acquaintance.

Coming up to London from Oxford about 1807 or 1808, I made inquiries about him, and found that he usually read the papers at a coffee-room in Piccadilly: understanding that he was poor, it struck me that he might not wish to receive visits at his lodgings, and therefore I sought him at the coffee-room. Here I took the liberty of introducing myself to him. He received me courteously, and invited me to his rooms, which at that time were in Sherrard-street, Golden-square—a street already memorable to me. I was much struck with the eloquence of his conversation; and afterwards I found that Mr. Wordsworth, himself the most eloquent of men in conversation, had been equally struck, when he had met him at Paris between the years 1790 and 1792, during the early storms of the French Revolution. In Sherrard-street I visited him repeatedly, and took notes of the conversations I had with him on various subjects. These I must have somewhere or other; and I wish I could introduce them here, as they would interest the reader. Occasionally, in these conversations, as in his books, he introduced a few notices of his private history: in particular, I remember his telling me that in the East Indies he had been a prisoner of Hyder's; that he had escaped with some difficulty; and that, in the service of one of the native princes as secretary or interpreter, he had accumulated a small fortune. This must have been too small, I fear, at that time to allow him even a philosopher's comforts: for some part of it, invested in the French funds, had been confiscated. I was grieved to see a man of so much ability, of gentlemanly manners and refined habits, and with the infirmity of deafness, suffering under such obvious privations; and I once took the liberty, on a fit occasion presenting itself, of requesting that he would allow me to send him some books which he had been casually regretting that he did not possess—for I was at that time in the hey-day of my worldly prosperity. This offer, however, he declined with firmness and dignity, though not unkindly. And I now mention it because I have seen him charged in print with a selfish regard to his own pecuniary interest. On the contrary, he appeared to me a very liberal and generous man: and I well remember that, whilst on his own part he refused to accept of anything, he compelled me to receive as presents all the books which he published during my acquaintance with him. Two of these, corrected with his own hand—viz. the "Lyre of Apollo" and the "Sophiometer"—I have lately found amongst other books left in London; and others he forwarded to me in Westmoreland. In 1809 I saw him often. In the spring of that year, I happened to be in London; and, Mr. Wordsworth's tract on the Convention of Cintra being at that time in the printer's hands, I superintended the publication of it; and, at Wordsworth's request, I added a long note on Spanish affairs, which is printed in the Appendix. The opinions I expressed in this note on the Spanish character, at that time much calumniated on the retreat to Corunna, then fresh in the public mind—above all, the contempt I expressed for the superstition in respect to the French military prowess, a superstition so dishonouring to ourselves, and so mischievous in its results, which was then at its height, and which gave way, in fact, only to the campaigns of 1814 and 1815—fell in, as it happened, with Mr. Stewart's political creed in those points where at that time it met with most opposition. In 1812 it was, I think, that I saw him for the last time: and, by the way, on the day of my parting with him, I had an amusing proof, in my own experience, of that sort of ubiquity ascribed to him by a witty writer in the "London Magazine." I met him and shook hands with him under Somerset House, telling him that I should leave town that evening for Westmoreland. Thence I went by the very shortest road (*i. e.*, through Moor-street, Soho—for I am learned in many quarters of London), towards a point which necessarily led me through Tottenham-Court-road; I stopped nowhere, and walked fast; yet so it was that in Tottenham-Court-road I was not overtaken by (*that* was comprehensible), but overtook Walking Stewart. Certainly, as the above writer alleges, there must have been three Walking Stewarts in London. He seemed nowise surprised at this himself, but explained to me that somewhere or other in the neighbourhood of Tottenham-Court-road there was a little theatre, at which there was dancing, and occasionally good singing, between which and a neighbouring coffee-house he sometimes divided his evenings. Singing, it seems, he could hear in spite of his deafness. In this street I took my final leave of him; it turned out such; and, anticipating at the time that it would, I looked after his white hat at the moment it was disappearing, and exclaimed, "Farewell, thou half-crazy and most eloquent of men! I shall never see thy face again." At that moment, I did not intend to visit London again for some years; as it happened, I was there for a short time in 1814; and then I heard, to my great satisfaction, that Walking Stewart had recovered a considerable sum (about £14,000, I believe) from the East India Company; and, from the abstract given in the "London Magazine" of the memoir by his relation, I have since learned that he applied this money most wisely to the purchase of an annuity, and that he "persisted in living" too long for the peace of an annuity office. So fare all companies, East and West, and all annuity offices, that stand opposed in interest to philosophers! In 1814, however, to my great regret, I did not see him; for I was then taking a great deal of opium, and never could contrive to issue to the light of day soon enough for a morning-call upon a philosopher of such early hours; and in the evening I concluded he would be generally abroad, from what he had formerly communicated to me of his own habits. It seems, however, that he afterwards held *conversazioni* at his own rooms, and did not stir out to theatres quite so much. From a brother of mine, who at one time occupied rooms in the same house with him, I learned that, in other respects, he did not deviate in his prosperity from the philosophic tenor of his former life. He abated nothing of his peripatetic exercises; and repaired duly in the morning, as he had done in former years, to St. James's Park, where he sate in trance-like reverie amongst the cows, inhaling their balmy breath and pursuing his philosophic speculations. He had also purchased an organ, or more than one, with which he solaced his solitude, and beguiled himself of uneasy thoughts, if he ever had any.

The works of Walking Stewart must be read with some indulgence: the titles are generally too lofty and pretending, and somewhat extravagant; the composition is lax and unprecise, as I have before said; and the doctrines are occasionally very bold, incautiously stated, and too hardy and high-toned for the nervous effeminacy of many modern moralists. But Walking Stewart was a man who thought nobly of human nature: he wrote, therefore, at times in the spirit and with the indignation of an ancient prophet against the oppressors and destroyers of the time. In particular, I remember that, in one or more of the pamphlets which I received from him at Grasmere, he expressed himself in such terms on the subject of Tyrannicide (distinguishing the cases in which it was and was not lawful) as seemed to Wordsworth and myself every way worthy of a philosopher; but, from the way in which that subject was treated in the House of Commons, where it was at that time occasionally introduced, it was plain that his doctrine was not fitted for the luxurious and relaxed morals of the age. Like all men who think nobly of human nature, Walking Stewart thought of it hopefully. In some respects his hopes were wisely grounded; in others, they rested too much upon certain metaphysical speculations which are untenable, and which satisfied himself only, because his researches in that track had been purely self-originated and self-disciplined. He relied upon his own native strength of mind; but, in questions which the wisdom and philosophy of every age, building successively upon each other, have not been able to settle, no mind, however strong, is entitled to build wholly upon itself. In many things he shocked the religious sense—especially as it exists in unphilosophic minds: he held a sort of rude and unscientific Spinosism; and he expressed it coarsely, and in the way most likely to give offence. And indeed there can be no stronger proof of the utter obscurity in which his works have slumbered than that they should all have escaped prosecution. He also allowed himself to look too lightly and indulgently on the afflicting spectacle of female prostitution as it exists in London and in all great cities. This was the only point on which I was disposed to quarrel with him; for I could not but view it as a greater reproach to human nature than the slave-trade, or any sight of wretchedness that the sun looks down upon. I often told him so; and that I was at a loss to guess how a philosopher could allow himself to view it simply as part of the equipage of civil life, and not less reasonably making part of the establishment and furniture of a great city than police-offices, lamp-lighting, or newspapers. Waiving, however, this one instance of something like compliance with the brutal spirit of the world, on all other subjects he was eminently unworldly, child-like, simple-minded, and upright. He would flatter no man: even when addressing nations it is almost laughable to see how invariably he prefaces his counsels with such plain truths, uttered in a manner so offensive, as must have defeated his purpose, if it had otherwise any chance of being accomplished. For instance, in addressing America, he begins thus:—"People of America! since your separation from the mother-country, your moral character has degenerated in the energy of thought and sense; produced by the absence of your association and intercourse with British officers and merchants: you have no moral discernment to distinguish between the protective power of England and the destructive power of France." And his letter to the Irish nation opens in this agreeable and conciliatory manner:—"People of Ireland! I address you as a true philosopher of nature, foreseeing the perpetual misery your irreflective character, and total absence of moral discernment, are preparing for," &c. The second sentence begins thus:—"You are sacrilegiously arresting the arm of your parent kingdom, fighting the cause of man and nature, when the triumph of the fiend of French police-terror would be your own instant extirpation." And the letter closes thus:—"I see but one awful alternative—that Ireland will be a perpetual moral volcano, threatening the destruction of the world, if the education and instruction of thought and sense shall not be able to generate the faculty of moral discernment among a very numerous class of the population, who detest the civic calm as sailors the natural calm, and make civic rights on which they cannot reason a pretext for feuds which they delight in." As he spoke freely and boldly to others, so he spoke loftily of himself. At p. 313 of "The Harp of Apollo," on making a comparison of himself with Socrates (in which he naturally gives the preference to himself), he styles the "Harp," &c., "this unparalleled work of human energy." At p. 315, he calls it "this stupendous work"; and lower down, on the same page, he says, "I was turned out of school, at the age of fifteen, for a dunce or blockhead, because I would not stuff into my memory all the nonsense of erudition and learning; and, if future ages should discover the unparalleled energies of genius in this work, it will prove my most important doctrine—that the powers of the human mind must be developed in the education of thought and sense in the study of moral opinion, not arts and science." Again, at p. 225 of his

"Sophiometer," he says, "The paramount thought that dwells in my mind incessantly is a question I put to myself—whether, in the event of my personal dissolution by death, I have communicated all the discoveries my unique mind possesses in the great master-science of man and nature." In the next page, he determines that he *has*, with the exception of one truth—viz. "the latent energy, physical and moral, of human nature as existing in the British people." But here he was surely accusing himself without ground; for, to my knowledge, he has not failed, in any one of his numerous works, to insist upon this theme at least a billion of times. Another instance of his magnificent self-estimation is that in the title pages of several of his works he announces himself as "John Stewart, the only Man of Nature [1] that ever appeared in the world."

By this time I am afraid the reader begins to suspect that he was crazy: and certainly, when I consider every thing, he must have been crazy when the wind was at N. N. E.; for who but Walking Stewart ever dated his books by a computation drawn—not from the Creation, not from the Flood, not from Nabonassar, or *ab urbe conditâ*, not from the Hegira—but from themselves, from their own day of publication, as constituting the one great era in the history of man by the side of which all other eras were frivolous and impertinent? Thus, in a work of his, given to me in 1812 and probably published in that year, I find him incidentally recording of himself that he was at that time "arrived at the age of sixty-three, with a firm state of health acquired by temperance, and a peace of mind almost independent of the vices of mankind—because my knowledge of life has enabled me to place my happiness beyond the reach or contact of other men's follies and passions, by avoiding all family connexions, and all ambitious pursuits of profit, fame, or power." On reading this passage, I was anxious to ascertain its date; but this, on turning to the title-page, I found thus mysteriously expressed: "In the 7000th year of Astronomical History, and the first day of Intellectual Life or Moral World, from the era of this work." Another slight indication of craziness appeared in a notion which obstinately haunted his mind, that all

---

[1] In Bath he was surnamed "the Child of Nature"; which arose from his contrasting, on every occasion, the existing man of our present experience with the ideal or Stewartian man that might be expected to emerge in some myriads of ages—to which latter man he gave the name of the Child of Nature.

the kings and rulers of the earth would confederate in every age against his works, and would hunt them out for extermination as keenly as Herod did the innocents of Bethlehem. On this consideration, fearing that they might be intercepted by the long arms of these wicked princes before they could reach that remote Stewartian man or his precursor to whom they were mainly addressed, he recommended to all those who might be impressed with a sense of their importance to bury a copy or copies of each work, properly secured from damp, &c., at a depth of seven or eight feet below the surface of the earth, and on their death-beds to communicate the knowledge of this fact to some confidential friends, who, in their turn, were to send down the tradition to some discreet persons of the next generation; and thus, if the truth was not to be dispersed for many ages, yet the knowledge that here and there the truth lay buried on this and that continent, in secret spots on Mount Caucasus, in the sands of Biledulgerid, and in hiding-places amongst the forests of America, and was to rise again in some distant age, and to vegetate and fructify for the universal benefit of man,—this knowledge at least was to be whispered down from generation to generation; and, in defiance of a myriad of kings crusading against him, Walking Stewart was to stretch out the influence of his writings through a long series of λαμπαδοφόροι to that child of nature whom he saw dimly through a vista of many centuries. If this were madness, it seemed to me a somewhat sublime madness: and I assured him of my co-operation against the kings, promising that I would bury the "Harp of Apollo" in my own orchard in Grasmere at the foot of Mount Fairfield, that I would bury the "Apocalypse of Nature" in one of the coves of Helvellyn, and several other works in several other places best known to myself. He accepted my offer with gratitude; but he then made known to me that he relied on my assistance for a still more important service—which was this: in the lapse of that vast number of ages that would probably intervene between the present period and the period at which his works would have reached their destination, he feared that the English language might itself have mouldered away. "No!" I said, "*that* was not probable: considering its extensive diffusion, and that it was now transplanted into all the continents of our planet, I would back the English language against any other on earth." His own persuasion, however, was, that the Latin was destined to survive all other languages; it was to be the eternal as well as the universal language; and his desire was that I should translate his works, or some part of them, into that language.[1] This I promised; and I seriously designed at some leisure hour to translate into Latin a selection of passages which should embody an abstract of his philosophy. This would have been doing a service to all those who might wish to see a digest of his peculiar opinions cleared from the perplexities of his peculiar diction, and brought into a narrow compass from the great number of volumes through which they are at present dispersed. However, like many another plan of mine, it went unexecuted.

On the whole, if Walking Stewart were at all crazy, he was so in a way which did not affect his natural genius and eloquence—but rather exalted them. The old maxim, indeed, that "great wits to madness sure are near allied," the maxim of Dryden and the popular maxim, I have heard disputed by Mr. Coleridge and Mr. Wordsworth, who maintain that mad people are the dullest and most wearisome of all people. As a body, I believe they are so. But I must dissent from the authority of Messrs. Coleridge and Wordsworth so far as to distinguish. Where madness is connected, as it often is, with some miserable derangement of the stomach, liver, &c., and attacks the principle of pleasurable life, which is manifestly seated in the central organs of the body (i. e., in the stomach and the apparatus connected with it), there it cannot but lead to perpetual suffering and distraction of thought; and there the patient will be often tedious and incoherent. People who have not suffered from any great disturbance in those organs are little aware how indispensable to the process of thinking are the momentary influxes of pleasurable feeling from the regular goings on of life in its primary function; in fact, until the pleasure is withdrawn or obscured,

[1] I was not aware until the moment of writing this passage that Walking Stewart had publicly made this request three years after making it to myself. Opening the "Harp of Apollo," I have just now accidently stumbled on the following passage:—"This stupendous work is destined, I fear, to meet a worse fate than the aloe, which, as soon as it blossoms, loses its stalk. This first blossom of reason is threatened with the loss of both its stalk and its soil; for, if the revolutionary tyrant should triumph, he would destroy all the English books and energies of thought. I conjure my readers to translate this work into Latin, and to bury it in the ground, communicating on their death-beds only its place of concealment to men of nature."

From the title page of this work, by the way, I learn that "the 7000th year of Astronomical History" is taken from the Chinese tables, and coincides (as I had supposed) with the year 1812 of our computation.

most people are not aware that they *have* any pleasure from the due action of the great central machinery of the system: proceeding in uninterrupted continuance, the pleasure as much escapes the consciousness as the act of respiration; a child, in the happiest state of its existence, does not *know* that it is happy. And, generally, whatsoever is the level state of the hourly feeling is never put down by the unthinking (*i. e.*, by 99 out of 100) to the account of happiness: it is never put down with the positive sign, as equal to $+ x;$ but simply as $= 0$. And men first become aware that it *was* a positive quantity, when they have lost it (*i. e.*, fallen into $- x$). Meantime the genial pleasure from the vital processes, though not represented to the consciousness, is *immanent* in every act, impulse, motion, word, and thought: and a philosopher sees that the idiots are in a state of pleasure, though they cannot see it themselves. Now I say that, where this principle of pleasure is not attacked, madness is often little more than an enthusiasm highly exalted; the animal spirits are exuberant and in excess; and the madman becomes, if he be otherwise a man of ability and information, all the better as a companion. I have met with several such madmen; and I appeal to my brilliant friend, Professor W——, who is not a man to tolerate dulness in any quarter, and is himself the ideal of a delightful companion, whether he ever met a more amusing person than that madman who took a post-chaise with us from Penrith to Carlisle, long years ago, when he and I were hastening with the speed of fugitive felons to catch the Edinburgh mail. His fancy and his extravagance, and his furious attacks on Sir Isaac Newton, like Plato's suppers, refreshed us not only for that day, but whenever they recurred to us; and we were both grieved when we heard some time afterwards, from a Cambridge man, that he had met our clever friend in a stage-coach under the care of a brutal keeper.—Such a madness, if any, was the madness of Walking Stewart; his health was perfect; his spirits as light and ebullient as the spirits of a bird in springtime; and his mind unagitated by painful thoughts, and at peace with himself. Hence, if he was not an amusing companion, it was because the philosophic direction of his thoughts made him something more. Of anecdotes and matters of fact he was not communicative: of all that he had seen in the vast compass of his travels he rarely availed himself in conversation. I do not remember, at this moment, that he ever once alluded

to his own travels in his intercourse with me, except for the purpose
of weighing down, by a statement grounded on his own great personal experience, an opposite statement of many hasty and misjudging travellers which he thought injurious to human nature.
The statement was this—that, in all his countless rencounters
with uncivilised tribes, he had never met with any so ferocious and
brutal as to attack an unarmed and defenceless man, who was able
to make them understand that he threw himself upon their hospitality and forbearance.

On the whole, Walking Stewart was a sublime visionary. He
had seen and suffered much amongst men; yet not too much, or so
as to dull the genial tone of his sympathy with the sufferings of
others. His mind was a mirror of the sentient universe—the whole
mighty vision that had fleeted before his eyes in this world: the
armies of Hyder Ali and his son Tippoo, with oriental and barbaric
pageantry; the civic grandeur of England; the great deserts of
Asia and America; the vast capitals of Europe; London, with its
eternal agitations, the ceaseless ebb and flow of its "mighty heart;"
Paris, shaken by the fierce torments of revolutionary convulsions;
the silence of Lapland; and the solitary forests of Canada; with
the swarming life of the torrid zone; together with innumerable
recollections of individual joy and sorrow that he had participated
by sympathy; lay like a map beneath him, as if eternally co-present
to his view, so that, in the contemplation of the prodigious whole,
he had no leisure to separate the parts, or occupy his mind with
details. Hence came the monotony which the frivolous and the
desultory would have found in his conversation. I, however, who
by accidents of experience, am qualified to speak of him, must
pronounce him to have been a man of great genius, and, with reference to his conversation, of great eloquence. That these were not
better known and acknowledged was owing to two disadvantages—
one grounded in his imperfect education, the other in the peculiar
structure of his mind. The first was this: like the late Mr. Shelley,
he had a fine vague enthusiasm, and lofty aspirations, in connexion
with human nature generally and its hopes; and, like him, he strove
to give steadiness, a uniform direction, and an intelligible purpose
to these feelings, by fitting to them a scheme of philosophical
opinions. But unfortunately the philosophic system of both was
so far from supporting their own views, and the cravings of their

own enthusiasm, that, as in some points it was baseless, incoherent, or unintelligible, so in others it tended to moral results from which, if they had foreseen them, they would have been themselves the first to shrink, as contradictory to the very purposes in which their system had originated. Hence, in maintaining their own system they found themselves painfully entangled, at times, with tenets pernicious and degrading to human nature. These were the inevitable consequences of the $\pi\rho\hat{\omega}\tau o\nu$ $\psi\epsilon\hat{v}\delta o\varsigma$ in their speculations; but were naturally charged upon them, by those who looked carelessly into their books, as opinions which not merely for the sake of consistency they thought themselves bound to endure, but to which they gave the full weight of their sanction and patronage as to so many moving principles in their system. The other disadvantage under which Walking Stewart laboured was this: he was a man of genius, but not a man of talents; at least his genius was out of all proportion to his talents, and wanted an organ, as it were, for manifesting itself, so that his most original thoughts were delivered in a crude state, imperfect, obscure, half-developed, and not productible to a popular audience. He was partially aware of this himself; and, though he claims everywhere the faculty of profound intuition into human nature, yet with equal candour, he accuses himself of asinine stupidity, dulness, and want of talent. He was a disproportioned intellect, and so far a monster: and he must be added to the long list of original-minded men who have been looked down upon with pity and contempt by common-place men of talent, whose powers of mind, though a thousand times inferior, were yet more manageable, more self-interpreted, and ran in channels better suited to common uses and common understandings.

N. B. About the year 1812 I remember seeing in many of the print-shops a whole-length sketch in water-colours of Walking Stewart in his customary dress and attitude. This, as the only memorial (I presume) in that shape of a man whose memory I love, I should be very glad to possess; and therefore I take the liberty of publicly requesting as a particular favour from any reader of this article who may chance to remember such a sketch in any collection of prints offered for sale, that he would cause it to be sent to the Editor of the LONDON MAGAZINE, who will pay for it.

ON THE KNOCKING AT THE GATE IN "MACBETH"

FROM my boyish days I had always felt a great perplexity on one point in *Macbeth*. It was this:—The knocking at the gate which succeeds to the murder of Duncan produced to my feelings an effect for which I never could account. The effect was that it reflected back upon the murderer a peculiar awfulness and a depth of solemnity; yet, however obstinately I endeavoured with my understanding to comprehend this, for many years I never could see *why* it should produce such an effect.

Here I pause for one moment, to exhort the reader never to pay any attention to his understanding when it stands in opposition to any other faculty of his mind. The mere understanding, however useful and indispensable, is the meanest faculty in the human mind, and the most to be distrusted; and yet the great majority of people trust to nothing else,—which may do for ordinary life, but not for philosophical purposes. Of this, out of ten thousand instances that I might produce, I will cite one. Ask of any person whatsoever who is not previously prepared for the demand by a knowledge of perspective to draw in the rudest way the commonest appearance which depends upon the laws of that science,—as, for instance, to represent the effect of two walls standing at right angles to each other, or the appearance of the houses on each side of a street as seen by a person looking down the street from one extremity. Now, in all cases, unless the person has happened to observe in pictures how it is that artists produce these effects, he will be utterly unable to make the smallest approximation to it. Yet why? For he has actually seen the effect every day of his life. The reason is that he allows his understanding to overrule his eyes. His understanding, which includes no intuitive knowledge of the laws of vision, can furnish him with no reason why a line which is known and can be proved to be a horizontal line, should not *appear* a horizontal line: a line that made any angle with the perpendicular less than a right angle, would seem to him to indicate that his houses were all tumbling down together. Accordingly, he makes the line of his houses a horizontal line, and fails, of course, to produce the effect demanded. Here, then, is one instance out of many in which not only the understanding is allowed to overrule the

eyes, but where the understanding is positively allowed to obliterate the eyes, as it were; for not only does the man believe the evidence of his understanding in opposition to that of his eyes, but
(which is monstrous) the idiot is not aware that his eyes ever gave
such evidence. He does not know that he has seen (and therefore
quoad his consciousness has *not* seen) that which he *has* seen every
day of his life.

But to return from this digression. My understanding could
furnish no reason why the knocking at the gate in *Macbeth* should
produce any effect, direct or reflected. In fact, my understanding
said positively that it could *not* produce any effect. But I knew
better; I felt that it did; and I waited and clung to the problem
until further knowledge should enable me to solve it.—At length,
in 1812, Mr. Williams made his *début* on the stage of Ratcliffe
Highway, and executed those unparalleled murders which have
procured for him such a brilliant and undying reputation. On which
murders, by the way, I must observe that in one respect they have
had an ill effect, by making the connoisseur in murder very fastidious in his taste, and dissatisfied with any thing that has been since
done in that line. All other murders look pale by the deep crimson
of his; and, as an amateur once said to me in a querulous tone,
"There has been absolutely nothing *doing* since his time, or nothing that's worth speaking of." But this is wrong; for it is unreasonable to expect all men to be great artists, and born with the genius
of Mr. Williams. Now, it will be remembered that in the first of
these murders (that of the Marrs) the same incident (of a knocking
at the door soon after the work of extermination was complete)
did actually occur which the genius of Shakespeare had invented;
and all good judges, and the most eminent dilettanti, acknowledged
the felicity of Shakespeare's suggestion as soon as it was actually
realized. Here, then, was a fresh proof that I was right in relying
on my own feeling, in opposition to my understanding; and I
again set myself to study the problem. At length I solved it to my
own satisfaction; and my solution is this:—Murder, in ordinary
cases, where the sympathy is wholly directed to the case of the
murdered person, is an incident of coarse and vulgar horror; and
for this reason,—that it flings the interest exclusively upon the
natural but ignoble instinct by which we cleave to life: an instinct
which, as being indispensable to the primal law of self-preservation,

is the same in kind (though different in degree) amongst all living creatures. This instinct, therefore, because it annihilates all distinctions, and degrades the greatest of men to the level of "the poor beetle that we tread on," exhibits human nature in its most abject and humiliating attitude. Such an attitude would little suit the purposes of the poet. What then must he do? He must throw the interest on the murderer: our sympathy must be with *him;* (of course I mean a sympathy of comprehension, a sympathy by which we enter into his feelings, and are made to understand them, —not a sympathy of pity or approbation). [1] In the murdered person, all strife of thought, all flux and reflux of passion and of purpose, are crushed by one overwhelming panic; the fear of instant death smites him "with its petrific mace." But in the murderer, such a murderer as a poet will condescend to, there must be raging some great storm of passion,—jealousy, ambition, vengeance, hatred,—which will create a hell within him; and into this hell we are to look.

In *Macbeth*, for the sake of gratifying his own enormous and teeming faculty of creation, Shakespeare has introduced two murderers: and, as usual in his hands, they are remarkably discriminated: but,—though in Macbeth the strife of mind is greater than in his wife, the tiger spirit not so awake, and his feelings caught chiefly by contagion from her,—yet, as both were finally involved in the guilt of murder, the murderous mind of necessity is finally to be presumed in both. This was to be expressed; and on its own account, as well as to make it a more proportionable antagonist to the unoffending nature of their victim, "the gracious Duncan," and adequately to expound "the deep damnation of his taking off," this was to be expressed with peculiar energy. We were to be made to feel that the human nature,—*i. e.*, the divine nature of love and mercy, spread through the hearts of all creatures, and seldom utterly withdrawn from man,—was gone, vanished, extinct, and that the fiendish nature had taken its place. And, as this

---

[1] It seems almost ludicrous to guard and explain my use of a word in a situation where it should naturally explain itself. But it has become necessary to do so, in consequence of the unscholarlike use of the word sympathy, at present so general, by which, instead of taking it in its proper sense, as the act of reproducing in our minds the feelings of another, whether for hatred, indignation, love, pity, or approbation, it is made a mere synonyme of the word *pity;* and hence, instead of saying, "sympathy *with* another," many writers adopt the monstrous barbarism of "sympathy *for* another."

effect is marvellously accomplished in the *dialogues* and *soliloquies* themselves, so it is finally consummated by the expedient under consideration; and it is to this that I now solicit the reader's attention. If the reader has ever witnessed a wife, daughter, or sister in a fainting fit, he may chance to have observed that the most affecting moment in such a spectacle, is *that* in which a sigh and a stirring announce the recommencement of suspended life. Or, if the reader has ever been present in a vast metropolis on the day when some great national idol was carried in funeral pomp to his grave, and, chancing to walk near to the course through which it passed, has felt powerfully, in the silence and desertion of the streets, and in the stagnation of ordinary business, the deep interest which at that moment was possessing the heart of man,—if all at once he should hear the death-like stillness broken up by the sound of wheels rattling away from the scene, and making known that the transitory vision was dissolved, he will be aware that at no moment was his sense of the complete suspension and pause in ordinary human concerns so full and affecting as at that moment when the suspension ceases, and the goings-on of human life are suddenly resumed. All action in any direction is best expounded, measured, and made apprehensible, by reaction. Now, apply this to the case in *Macbeth*. Here, as I have said, the retiring of the human heart and the entrance of the fiendish heart was to be expressed and made sensible. Another world has stept in; and the murderers are taken out of the region of human things, human purposes, human desires. They are transfigured: Lady Macbeth is "unsexed"; Macbeth has forgot that he was born of woman; both are conformed to the image of devils; and the world of devils is suddenly revealed. But how shall this be conveyed and made palpable? In order that a new world may step in, this world must for a time disappear. The murderers and the murder must be insulated—cut off by an immeasurable gulf from the ordinary tide and succession of human affairs—locked up and sequestered in some deep recess: we must be made sensible that the world of ordinary life is suddenly arrested, laid asleep, tranced, racked into a dread armistice; time must be annihilated; relation to things without abolished; and all must pass self-withdrawn into a deep syncope and suspension of earthly passion. Hence it is that, when the deed is done, when the work of darkness is perfect, then the world of darkness passes away like a pageantry in the clouds: the knocking at the gate is heard, and it makes known audibly that the reaction has commenced; the human has made its reflux upon the fiendish; the pulses of life are beginning to beat again; and the re-establishment of the goings-on of the world in which we live first makes us profoundly sensible of the awful parenthesis that had suspended them.

O mighty poet! Thy works are not as those of other men, simply and merely great works of art, but are also like the phenomena of nature, like the sun and the sea, the stars and the flowers, like frost and snow, rain and dew, hail-storm and thunder, which are to be studied with entire submission of our own faculties, and in the perfect faith that in them there can be no too much or too little, nothing useless or inert, but that, the further we press in our discoveries, the more we shall see proofs of design and self-supporting arrangement where the careless eye had seen nothing but accident!

ON SUICIDE

IT is a remarkable proof of the inaccuracy with which most men read that Donne's *Biathanatos* has been supposed to countenance suicide; and those who reverence his name have thought themselves obliged to apologise for it by urging that it was written before he entered the Church. But Donne's purpose in this treatise was a pious one. Many authors had charged the martyrs of the Christian Church with suicide, on the principle that, if I put myself in the way of a mad bull, knowing that he will kill me, I am as much chargeable with an act of self-destruction as if I fling myself into a river. Several casuists had extended this principle even to the case of Jesus Christ; one instance of which, in a modern author, the reader may see noticed and condemned by Kant, in his *Religion innerhalb der Grenzen der blossen Vernunft;* and another of much earlier date (as far back as the 13th century, I think) in a commoner book—Voltaire's notes on the little treatise of Beccaria *Dei delitti e delle pene.* These statements tended to one of two results: either they unsanctified the characters of those who founded and nursed the Christian Church; or they sanctified suicide. By way of meeting them, Donne wrote his book: and, as the whole argument of his opponents turned upon a false definition of suicide (not explicitly stated, but assumed), he endeavoured to reconstitute the notion of what is essential to create an act of suicide. Simply to kill a man is not murder: *prima facie*, therefore, there is some sort of presumption that simply for a man to kill himself may not always be so: there is such a thing as simple homicide distinct from murder: there may, therefore, possibly be such a thing as self-homicide distinct from self-murder. There *may* be a ground for such a distinction, *ex analogia*. But, secondly, on examination, *is* there any ground for such a distinction? Donne affirms that there is; and, reviewing several eminent cases of spontaneous martyrdom, he endeavours to show that acts so motived and so circumstantiated will not come within the notion of suicide properly defined.

Meantime, may not this tend to the encouragement of suicide in general, and without discrimination of its species? No: Donne's arguments have no prospective reference or application; they are purely retrospective. The circumstances necessary to create an act of mere self-homicide can rarely concur except in a state of disordered society, and during the *cardinal* revolutions of human history: where, however, they *do* concur, there it will not be suicide. In fact, this is the natural and practical judgment of us all. We do not all agree on the particular cases which will justify self-destruction; but we all feel and involuntarily acknowledge (*implicitly* acknowledge in our admiration, though not explicitly in our words or in our principles) that there *are* such cases. There is no man who in his heart would not reverence a woman that chose to die rather than to be dishonoured; and, if we do not say that it is her duty to do so, *that* is because the moralist must condescend to the weakness and infirmities of human nature: mean and ignoble natures must not be taxed up to the level of noble ones. Again, with regard to the other sex, corporal punishment is its peculiar and *sexual* degradation; and, if ever the distinction of Donne can be applied safely to any case, it will be to the case of him who chooses to die rather than to submit to that ignominy. *At present*, however, there is but a dim and very confined sense, even amongst enlightened men (as we may see by the debates of Parliament), of the injury which is done to human nature by giving legal sanction to such brutalising acts; and therefore most men, in seeking to escape it, would be merely shrinking from a *personal* dishonour.

Corporal punishment is usually argued with a single reference to the case of him who suffers it; and, *so* argued, God knows that it is worthy of all abhorrence: but the weightiest argument against it is the foul indignity which is offered to our common nature lodged in the person of him on whom it is inflicted. *His* nature is *our* nature; and, supposing it possible that *he* were so far degraded as to be unsusceptible of any influences but those which address him through the brutal part of his nature, yet for the sake of ourselves,—no! not merely for ourselves or for the human race now existing, but for the sake of human nature, which transcends all existing participators of that nature,—we should remember that the evil of corporal punishment is not to be measured by the poor transitory criminal, whose memory and offence are soon to perish. These, in the sum of things, are as nothing: the injury which can be done him, and the injury which he can do, have so momentary an existence that they may be safely neglected; but the abiding injury is to the most august interest which for the mind of man can have any existence,—viz. to his own nature: to raise and dignify which, I am persuaded, is the first, last, and holiest command [1] which the conscience imposes on the philosophic moralist. In countries where the traveller has the pain of seeing human creatures performing the labours of brutes,[2] surely the sorrow which the spectacle moves, if a wise sorrow, will not be chiefly directed to the poor degraded individual,—too deeply degraded, probably, to be sensible of his own degradation,—but to the reflection of that man's nature as thus exhibited in a state of miserable abasement, and, what is worst of all, abasement proceeding from man himself.

[1] On which account I am the more struck by the ignoble argument of those statesmen who have contended in the House of Commons that such and such classes of men in this nation are not accessible to any loftier influences. Supposing that there were any truth in this assertion,—which is a libel not on this nation only, but on man in general,—surely it is the duty of lawgivers not to perpetuate by their institutions the evil which they find, but to presume and gradually to create a better spirit.

[2] Of which degradation let it never be forgotten that France but *thirty* years ago [*i. e.*, about 1793] presented as shocking cases as any country, even where slavery is tolerated. An eye-witness to the fact, who has since published it in print, told me that in France before the Revolution he had repeatedly seen a woman yoked with an ass to the plough, and the brutal ploughman applying his whip indifferently to either. English people to whom I have occasionally mentioned this as an exponent of the hollow refinement of manners in France have uniformly exclaimed—"*That* is more than I can believe"; and have taken it for granted that I had my information from some prejudiced Englishman. But who was my informer? A Frenchman, reader,—M. Simond,—and, though now by adoption an American citizen, yet still French in his heart and in all his prejudices.

Now, whenever this view of corporal punishment becomes general (as inevitably it will, under the influence of advancing civilisation), I say that Donne's principle will then become applicable to this case, and it will be the duty of a man to die rather than to suffer his own nature to be dishonoured in that way. But, so long as a man is not fully sensible of the dishonour, to him the dishonour, except as a personal one, does not wholly exist. In general, whenever a paramount interest of human nature is at stake, a suicide which maintains that interest is self-homicide; but, for a personal interest, it becomes self-murder. And into this principle Donne's may be resolved.

A doubt has been raised whether brute animals ever commit suicide. To me it is obvious that they do not, and cannot. Some years ago, however, there was a case reported in all the newspapers of an old ram who committed suicide (as it was alleged) in the presence of many witnesses. Not having any pistols or razors, he ran for a short distance, in order to aid the impetus of his descent, and leaped over a precipice, at the foot of which he was dashed to pieces. His motive to the "rash act," as the papers called it, was supposed to be mere *tædium vitæ*. But, for my part, I doubted the accuracy of the report. Not long after a case occurred in Westmoreland which strengthened my doubts. A fine young blood horse, who could have no possible reason for making away with himself, unless it were the high price of oats at that time, was found one morning dead in his field. The case was certainly a suspicious one; for he was lying by the side of a stone-wall, the upper part of which wall his skull had fractured, and which had returned the compliment by fracturing his skull. It was argued, therefore, that, in default of ponds, &c., he had deliberately hammered with his head against the wall: this, at first, seemed the only solution; and he was generally pronounced *felo de se*. However, a day or two brought the truth to light. The field lay upon the side of a hill; and, from a mountain which rose above it, a shepherd had witnessed the whole catastrophe, and gave evidence which vindicated the character of the horse. The day had been very windy; and the young creature, being in high spirits, and caring evidently as little for the corn question as for the bullion question, had raced about in all directions, and at length, descending too steep a part of the field, had been unable to check himself, and was projected by the impetus of his own descent like a battering ram against the wall.

Of human suicides, the most affecting I have ever seen recorded is one which I met with in a German book: this I shall repeat a little further on: the most calm and deliberate is the following, which is *said* to have occurred at Keswick, in Cumberland: but I must acknowledge that I never had an opportunity whilst staying at Keswick of verifying the statement.

A young man of studious turn, who is said to have resided near Penrith, was anxious to qualify himself for entering the Church, or for any other mode of life which might secure to him a reasonable portion of literary leisure. His family, however, thought that under the circumstances of his situation he would have a better chance for success in life as a tradesman; and they took the necessary steps for placing him as an apprentice at some shopkeeper's in Penrith. This he looked upon as an indignity, to which he was determined in no case to submit. And, accordingly, when he had ascertained that all opposition to the choice of his friends was useless, he walked over to the mountainous district of Keswick (about sixteen miles distant)—looked about him in order to select his ground—coolly walked up Lattrig (a dependency of Skiddaw),—made a pillow of sods,—laid himself down with his face looking up to the sky,—and in that posture was found dead, with the appearance of having died tranquilly.

WILLIAM HAZLITT [1]

THIS man, who would have drawn in the scales against a select vestry of Fosters, is for the present deeper in the world's oblivion than the man with whom I here connect his name. *That* seems puzzling. For, if Hazlitt were misanthropic, so was Foster; both as writers were splenetic and more than peevish; but Hazlitt requited his reader for the pain of travelling through so gloomy an atmosphere by the rich vegetation which his teeming intellect threw up as it moved along. The soil in *his* brain was of a volcanic fertility; whereas in Foster, as in some tenacious clay, if the life were deep, it was slow and sullen in its throes. The reason for at all speaking of them in connexion is that both were Essayists,—neither in fact writing anything of note *except* essays, moral

[1] "Gallery of Literary Portraits." By George Gilfillan.

or critical,—and both were bred at the feet of Dissenters. But how different were the results from that connexion! Foster turned it to a blessing, winning the jewel that is most of all to be coveted,— peace and the *fallentis semita vitæ*. Hazlitt, on the other hand, sailed wilfully away from this sheltering harbour of his father's profession,—for sheltering it might have proved to *him*, and *did* prove to his youth,—only to toss ever afterwards as a drifting wreck at the mercy of storms. Hazlitt was not one of those who *could* have illustrated the benefits of a connexion with a sect,— *i. e.*, with a small confederation hostile by position to a larger; for the hostility from without, in order to react, presumes a concord from within. Nor does *his* case impeach the correctness of what I have said on that subject in speaking of Foster. He owed no introduction to the Dissenters; but it was because he *would* owe none. The Ishmaelite, whose hand is against every man, yet smiles at the approach of a brother, and gives the salutation of "Peace be with you!" to the tribe of his father. But Hazlitt smiled upon no man, nor exchanged tokens of peace with the nearest of fraternities. Wieland, in his *Oberon*, says of a benign patriarch—

"His eye a smile on all creation beamed."

Travestied as to one word, the line would have described Hazlitt—

"His eye a scowl on all creation beamed."

This inveterate misanthropy was constitutional. Exasperated it certainly had been by accidents of life, by disappointments, by mortifications, by insults, and still more by having wilfully placed himself in collision from the first with all the interests that were in the sunshine of this world, and with all the persons that were then powerful in England; but my impression was, if I had a right to *have* any impression with regard to one whom I knew so slightly, that no change of position or of fortunes could have brought Hazlitt into reconciliation with the fashion of this world, or of this England, or "this now." It seemed to me that he hated those whom hollow custom obliged him to call his "friends" considerably more than those whom notorious differences of opinion entitled him to rank as his enemies. At least within the ring of politics this was so. Between those particular Whigs whom Literature had connected him with, and the whole gang of *us* Conservatives he showed the same difference in his mode of fencing and parrying, and even in his style of civilities, as between the domestic traitor, hiding a stiletto among his robes of peace, and the bold enemy who sends a trumpet before him, and rides up sword-in-hand against your gates. *Whatever is*—so much I conceive to have been a fundamental lemma for Hazlitt—*is wrong*. So much he thought it safe to postulate. *How* it was wrong might require an impracticable investigation: you might fail for a century to discover; but *that* it was wrong he nailed down as a point of faith that could stand out against all counter-presumptions from argument, or counter-evidences from experience. A friend of his it was,—a friend wishing to love him, and admiring him almost to extravagance,—who told me, in illustration of the dark, sinister gloom which sate forever upon Hazlitt's countenance and gestures, that involuntarily, when Hazlitt put his hand within his waistcoat (as a mere unconscious trick of habit), he himself felt a sudden recoil of fear, as from one who was searching for a hidden dagger. Like "a Moor of Malabar," as described in the *Faery Queen*, at intervals Hazlitt threw up his angry eyes, and dark locks, as if wishing to affront the sun, or to search the air for hostility. And the same friend, on another occasion, described the sort of feudal fidelity to his belligerent duties which in company seemed to animate Hazlitt, as though he were mounting guard on all the citadels of malignity, under some *sacramentum militare*, by the following trait,—that, if it had happened to Hazlitt to be called out of the room, or to be withdrawn for a moment from the current of the general conversation by a fit of abstraction, or by a private whisper to himself from some person sitting at his elbow, always, on resuming his place as a party to what might be called the public business of the company, he looked round him with a mixed air of suspicion and defiance, such as seemed to challenge everybody by some stern adjuration into revealing whether, during his own absence or inattention, anything had been said demanding condign punishment at his hands. "Has any man uttered or presumed to insinuate," he seemed to insist upon knowing, "during this *interregnum*, things that I ought to proceed against as treasonable to the interests which I defend?" He had the unresting irritability of Rousseau, but in a nobler shape; for Rousseau transfigured every possible act or design of his acquaintances into some personal relation to

himself. The vile act was obviously meant, as a child could understand, to injure the person of Rousseau, or his interests, or his
reputation. It was meant to wound his feelings, or to misrepresent
his acts calumniously, or secretly to supplant his footing. But, on the
contrary, Hazlitt viewed all personal affronts or casual slights towards himself as tending to something more general, and masquing,
under a pretended horror of Hazlitt the author, a real hatred,
deeper than it was always safe to avow, for those social interests
which he was reputed to defend. It was not Hazlitt whom the
wretches struck at; no, no; it was democracy, or it was freedom,
or it was Napoleon, whose shadow they saw in the rear of Hazlitt,—
and Napoleon, not for anything in him that might be really bad, but
in revenge of that consuming wrath against the thrones of Christendom for which, said Hazlitt, let us glorify his name eternally.

Yet Hazlitt, like other men, and perhaps with more bitterness
than other men, sought for love and for intervals of rest, in which
all anger might sleep, and enmity might be laid aside like a travelling dress after tumultuous journeys:—

> "Though the sea-horse on the ocean
> Own no dear domestic cave,
> Yet he slumbers without motion
> On the still and halcyon wave.
>
> If, on windy days, the raven
> Gambol like a dancing skiff,
> Not the less he loves his haven
> On the bosom of a cliff.
>
> If almost with eagle pinion
> O'er the Alps the chamois roam,
> Yet he has some small dominion,
> Which, no doubt, he calls his home."

But Hazlitt, restless as the sea-horse, as the raven, as the cham-
ois, found not their respites from storm; he sought, but sought in
vain. And for *him* the closing stanza of that little poem remained
true to his dying hour. In the person of the "Wandering Jew," *he*
might complain,—

> "Day and night my toils redouble:
> Never nearer to the goal,
> Night and day I feel the trouble
> Of the wanderer in my soul."

Domicile he had not round whose hearth his affections might gather; rest he had not for the sole of his burning foot. One chance of regaining some peace,—or a chance, as he trusted, for a time,—was torn from him at the moment of gathering its blossoms. He had been divorced from his wife,—not by the law of England, which would have argued criminality in *her*, but by Scottish law, satisfied with some proof of frailty in himself. Subsequently he became deeply fascinated by a young woman in no very elevated rank,—for she held some domestic office of superintendence in a boarding-house kept by her father,—but of interesting person, and endowed with strong intellectual sensibilities. She had encouraged Hazlitt; had gratified him by reading his works with intelligent sympathy; and, under what form of duplicity it is hard to say, had partly engaged her faith to Hazlitt as his future wife, whilst secretly she was holding a correspondence, too tender to be misinterpreted, with a gentleman resident in the same establishment. Suspicions were put aside for a time; but they returned, and gathered too thickly for Hazlitt's penetration to cheat itself any longer. Once and forever he resolved to satisfy himself. On a Sunday, fatal to him and his farewell hopes of domestic happiness, he had reason to believe that she, whom he now loved to excess, had made some appointment out-of-doors with his rival. It was in London; and through the crowds of London, Hazlitt followed her steps to the rendezvous. Fancying herself lost in the multitude that streamed through Lincolns-Inn-Fields, the treacherous young woman met her more favoured lover without alarm, and betrayed, too clearly for any further deception, the state of her affections by the tenderness of her manner. *There* went out the last light that threw a guiding ray over the storm-vexed course of Hazlitt. He was too much in earnest, and he had witnessed too much to be deceived or appeased. "I whistled her down the wind," was his own account of the catastrophe; but, in doing so, he had torn his own heart-strings, entangled with her "jesses." Neither did he, as others would have done, seek to disguise his misfortune. On the contrary, he cared not for the ridicule attached to such a situation amongst the unfeeling: the wrench within had been too profound to leave room for sensibility to the sneers outside. A fast friend of his at that time, and one who never ceased to be his apologist, described him to me as having become absolutely maniacal during the first pressure of this affliction. He went about proclaiming the case, and insisting on its details, to every stranger that would listen. He even published the whole story to the world, in his *Modern Pygmalion*. And people generally, who could not be aware of his feelings, or the way in which this treachery acted upon his mind as a ratification of all other treacheries and wrongs that he had suffered through life, laughed at him, or expressed disgust for him as too coarsely indelicate in making such disclosures. But there was no indelicacy in such an act of confidence,—growing, as it did, out of his lacerated heart. It was an explosion of frenzy. He threw out his clamorous anguish to the clouds, and to the winds, and to the air, caring not *who* might listen, *who* might sympathise, or *who* might sneer. Pity was no demand of his; laughter was no wrong: the sole necessity for *him* was to empty his overburdened spirit.

After this desolating experience, the exasperation of Hazlitt's political temper grew fiercer, darker, steadier. His *Life of Napoleon* was prosecuted subsequently to this, and perhaps under this remembrance, as a reservoir that might receive all the vast overflows of his wrath, much of which was not merely political, or in a spirit of bacchanalian partisanship, but was even morbidly anti-social. He hated, with all his heart, every institution of man, and all his pretensions. He loathed his own relation to the human race.

It was but on a few occasions that I ever met Mr. Hazlitt myself; and those occasions, or all but one, were some time subsequent to the case of female treachery which I have here described. Twice, I think, or it might be three times, we walked for a few miles together: it was in London, late at night, and after leaving a party. Though depressed by the spectacle of a mind always in agitation from the gloomier passions, I was yet amused by the pertinacity with which he clung, through bad reasons or no reasons, to any public slander floating against men in power or in the highest rank. No feather, or dowl of a feather, but was heavy enough for *him*. Amongst other instances of this willingness to be deluded by rumours, if they took a direction favourable to his own bias, Hazlitt had adopted the whole strength of popular hatred which for many years ran violently against the King of Hanover, at that time Duke of Cumberland. A dark calumny had arisen against this prince amongst the populace of London, as though he had been accessory to the death of his valet. This valet (Sellis) had in fact attempted to murder the prince; and all that can be said in palliation of his act is that he *believed* himself to have sustained, in the person of his beautiful wife, the heaviest dishonour incident to man. How that matter stood I pretend not to know; the attempt at murder was baffled, and the valet then destroyed himself with a razor. All this had been regularly sifted by a coroner's inquest; and I remarked to Hazlitt that the witnesses seemed to have been called indifferently from all quarters likely to have known the facts,—so that, if this inquest had failed to elicit the truth, we might with equal reason presume as much of all other inquests. From the verdict of a jury, except in very peculiar cases, no candid and temperate man will allow himself to believe any appeal sustainable; for, having the witnesses before them face to face, and hearing the *whole* of the evidence, a jury have always some means of forming a judgment which cannot be open to him who depends upon an abridged report. But on this subject Hazlitt would hear no reason. He said—"No; all the princely houses of Europe have the instinct of murder running in their blood;—they cherish it through their privilege of making war, which being wholesale murder, once having reconciled themselves to *that*, they think of retail murder, committed on you or me, as of no crime at all." Under this obstinate prejudice against the Duke, Hazlitt read everything that he did, or did *not* do, in a perverse spirit. And in one of these nightly walks he mentioned to me, as something quite worthy of a murderer, the following little trait of casuistry in the royal duke's distribution of courtesies. "I saw it myself," said Hazlitt, "so no coroner's jury can put me down." His Royal Highness had rooms in St. James's; and one day as he was issuing from the palace into Pall-Mall, Hazlitt happened to be immediately behind him: he could therefore watch his motions along the whole line of his progress. It is the custom in England, wheresoever the persons of the royal family are familiar to the public eye, as at Windsor, &c., that all passengers in the streets, on seeing them, walk bareheaded, or make some signal of dutiful respect. On this occasion all the men who met the prince took off their hats, the prince acknowledging every such obeisance by a separate bow. Pall-Mall being finished, and its whole harvest of royal salutations gathered in, next the Duke came to Cockspur-street. But here, and taking a station close to the crossing, which daily he beautified and polished with his broom,

stood a negro sweep. If human at all,—which some people doubted,
—he was pretty nearly as abject a representative of our human
family divine as can ever have existed. Still he was held to be a
man by the law of the land; which would have hanged any person,
gentle or simple, for cutting his throat. Law (it is certain) conceived him to be a man, however poor a one; though Medicine,
in an under-tone, muttered sometimes a demur to that opinion.
But here the sweep *was*, whether man or beast, standing humbly in
the path of royalty: vanish he would not; he was (as the *Times*
says of the Corn League) "a great fact," if rather a muddy one;
and, though, by his own confession (repeated one thousand times
a-day), both "a nigger" and a sweep ("Remember poor nigger,
your honour! remember poor sweep!"), yet the creature could
take off his rag of a hat, and earn the bow of a prince, as well as
any white native of St. James's. What was to be done? A great
case of conscience was on the point of being raised in the person of
a paralytic nigger; nay, possibly a state question,—Ought a son
of England,[1] could a son of England, descend from his majestic
pedestal to gild with the rays of his condescension such a grub,
such a very doubtful grub, as this? Total Pall-Mall was sagacious
of the coming crisis; judgment was going to be delivered; a precedent to be raised; and Pall-Mall stood still, with Hazlitt at its
head, to learn the issue. How if the black should be a Jacobin, and
(in the event of the duke's bowing) should have a bas-relief sculp-
tured on his tomb, exhibiting an English prince, and a German
king, as two separate personages in the act of worshipping his
broom? Luckily it was not the black's province to settle the case.
The Duke of Cumberland, seeing no counsel at hand to argue either
the *pro* or the *contra*, found himself obliged to settle the question
de plano; so, drawing out his purse, he kept his hat as rigidly settled
on his head as William Penn and Mead did before the Recorder of

---

[1] "*Son of England*":—*i. e.*, prince of the blood in the *direct*, and not in the collateral,
line. I mention this for the sake of some readers who may not be aware that this beautiful
formula, so well known in France, is often transferred by the French writers of memoirs
to our English princes, though little used amongst ourselves. Gaston, Duke of Orleans,
brother of Louis XIV., was "a *son* of France," as being a child of Louis XIII. But the
son of Gaston, namely, the Regent Duke of Orleans, was a *grandson* of France. The first
wife of Gaston, our Princess Henrietta, was called "*Fille* d'Angleterre," as being a daughter of Charles I. The Princess Charlotte, again, was a *daughter* of England; her present
majesty, a *grand-daughter* of England. But all these ladies collectively would be called,
on the French principle, the Children of England.

London. All Pall-Mall applauded: *contradicente* Gulielmo Hazlitt, and Hazlitt only. The black swore that the prince gave him half-a-crown; but whether he regarded this in the light of a godsend to his avarice or a shipwreck to his ambition—whether he was more thankful for the money gained, or angry for the honour lost—did not transpire. "No matter," said Hazlitt, "the black might be a fool; but I insist upon it that he was entitled to the bow, since all Pall-Mall had it before him; and that it was unprincely to refuse it." Either as a black or as a scavenger, Hazlitt held him "qualified" for sustaining a royal bow: as a black, was he not a specimen (if rather a damaged one) of the *homo sapiens* described by Linnæus? As a sweep, in possession (by whatever title) of a lucrative crossing, had he not a kind of estate in London? Was he not, said Hazlitt, a fellow-subject, capable of committing treason, and paying taxes into the treasury? Not perhaps in any direct shape, but indirect taxes most certainly on his tobacco, and even on his broom!

These things could not be denied. But still, when my turn came for speaking, I confessed frankly that (politics apart) my feeling in the case went along with the Duke's. The bow would not be so useful to the black as the half-crown: he could not possibly have both; for how could any man make a bow to a beggar when in the act of giving him half-a-crown? Then, on the other hand, this bow, so useless to the sweep, and (to speak by a vulgar adage) as superfluous as a side-pocket to a cow, would react upon the other bows distributed along the line of Pall-Mall, so as to neutralise them one and all. No honour could continue such in which a paralytic negro sweep was associated. This distinction, however, occurred to me, —that, if, instead of a prince and a subject, the royal dispenser of bows had been a king, he ought *not* to have excluded the black from participation; because, as the common father of his people, he ought not to know of any difference amongst those who are equally his children. And, in illustration of that opinion, I sketched a little scene which I had myself witnessed, and with great pleasure, upon occasion of a visit made to Drury Lane by George IV. when Regent. At another time I may tell it to the reader. Hazlitt, however, listened fretfully to me when praising the deportment and beautiful gestures of one conservative leader; though he had compelled *me* to hear the most disadvantageous comments on another.

As a lecturer, I do not know what Hazlitt was, having never had an opportunity of hearing him. Some qualities in his style of composition were calculated to assist the purposes of a lecturer, who must produce an effect oftentimes by independent sentences and paragraphs; who must glitter and surprise; who must turn round within the narrowest compass, and cannot rely upon any sort of attention that would cost an effort. Mr. Gilfillan says, that "he proved more popular than was expected by those who knew his uncompromising scorn of all those tricks and petty artifices which are frequently employed to pump up applause. His manner was somewhat abrupt and monotonous, but earnest and energetic." At the same time Mr. Gilfillan takes an occasion to express some opinions, which appear very just, upon the unfitness (generally speaking) of men whom he describes as "fiercely inspired" for this mode of display. The truth is that all genius implies originality, and sometimes uncontrollable singularity, in the habits of thinking, and in the modes of viewing as well as of estimating objects, whereas a miscellaneous audience is best conciliated by that sort of talent which reflects the average mind, which is not overweighted in any one direction, is not tempted into any extreme, and is able to preserve a steady, rope-dancer's equilibrium of posture upon themes where a man of genius is most apt to lose it.

It would be interesting to have a full and accurate list of Hazlitt's works, including, of course, his contributions to journals and encyclopædias. This last, as shorter and oftener springing from an *impromptu* effort, are more likely than his regular books to have been written with a pleasurable enthusiasm; and the writer's proportion of pleasure in such cases very often becomes the regulating law for his reader's. Amongst the philosophical works of Hazlitt, I do not observe that Mr. Gilfillan is aware of two that are likely to be specially interesting. One is an examination of David Hartley, at least as to his law of association. Thirty years ago I looked into it slightly; but my reverence for Hartley offended me with its tone; and afterwards, hearing that Coleridge challenged for his own most of what was important in the thoughts, I lost all interest in the essay. Hazlitt unavoidably, having heard Coleridge talk on this theme, must have approached it with a mind largely preoccupied as regarded the weak points in Hartley, and the particular tactics for assailing them. But still the great talents for speculative research which Hazlitt had from nature, without having given to them the benefit of much culture or much exercise, would justify our attentive examination of the work. It forms part of the volume which contains the *Essay on Human Action;* which volume, by the way, Mr. Gilfillan supposes to have won the special applause of Sir James Mackintosh, then in Bengal. This, if accurately stated, is creditable to Sir James's generosity; for in this particular volume it is that Hazlitt makes a pointed assault, in sneering terms, and very unnecessarily, upon Sir James as a lecturer at Lincoln's Inn.

The other little work unnoticed by Mr. Gilfillan is an examination (but under what title I cannot say) of Lindley Murray's English Grammar. This may seem, by its subject, a trifle; yet Hazlitt could hardly have had a motive for such an effort but in some philosophic perception of the ignorance betrayed by many grammars of our language, and continually by that of Lindley Murray,—which Lindley, by the way, though resident in England, was an American. There is great room for a useful display of philosophic subtlety in an English grammar, even though meant for schools. Hazlitt could not *but* have furnished something of value towards such a display. And, if (as I was once told) his book was suppressed, I imagine that this suppression must have been purchased by some powerful publisher interested in keeping up the current reputation of Murray.

"Strange stories," says Mr. Gilfillan, "are told about his [Hazlitt's] latter days, and his deathbed." I know not whether I properly understand Mr. Gilfillan. The stories which I myself have happened to hear were not so much "strange," since they arose naturally enough out of pecuniary embarrassments, as they were afflicting in the turn they took. Dramatically viewed, if a man were speaking of things so far removed from our own times and interests as to excuse that sort of language, the circumstances of Hazlitt's last hours might rivet the gaze of a critic as fitted harmoniously, with almost scenic art, to the whole tenor of his life,— fitted equally to rouse his wrath, to deepen his dejection, and in the hour of death to justify his misanthropy. But I have no wish to utter a word on things which I know only at second-hand, and cannot speak upon without risk of misstating facts or doing injustice to persons. I prefer closing this section with the words of Mr. Gilfillan:—

"Well says Bulwer that, of all the mental wrecks which have

occurred in our era, this was the most melancholy. Others may have been as unhappy in their domestic circumstances, and gone down steeper places of dissipation than he; but they had meanwhile the breath of popularity, if not of wealth and station, to give them a certain solace." What had Hazlitt of this nature? Mr. Gilfillan answers,—"Absolutely nothing to support and cheer him. With no hope, no fortune, no *status* in society, no certain popularity as a writer, no domestic peace, little sympathy from kindred spirits, little support from his political party, no moral management, no definite belief,—with great powers, and great passions within, and with a host of powerful enemies without,—it was his to enact one of the saddest tragedies on which the sun ever shone. Such is a faithful portraiture of an extraordinary man, whose restless intellect and stormy passions have now, for fifteen years, found that repose in the grave which was denied them above it." Mr. Gilfillan concludes with expressing his conviction, in which I desire to concur, that both enemies and friends will *now* join in admiration for the man. "Both will readily concede *now* that a subtle thinker, an eloquent writer, a lover of beauty and poetry, and man and truth, one of the best of critics, and not the worst of men, expired in William Hazlitt." *Requiescat in pace!*

CONVERSATION

AMONGST the arts connected with the *elegancies* of social life in a degree which nobody denies is the Art of Conversation; but in a degree which almost everybody denies, if one may judge by their neglect of its simple rules, this same art is not less connected with the *uses* of social life. Neither the luxury of conversation, nor the possible benefit of conversation, is to be found under that rude administration of it which generally prevails. Without an art, without some simple system of rules, gathered from experience of such contingencies as are most likely to mislead the practice when left to its own guidance, no act of man nor effort accomplishes its purposes in perfection. The sagacious Greek would not so much as drink a glass of wine amongst a few friends without a systematic art to guide him, and a regular form of polity to control him,—which art and which polity (begging Plato's pardon) were better than any of more ambitious aim in his

Republic. Every *symposium* had its set of rules, and rigorous they were; had its own *symposiarch* to govern it, and a tyrant he was. Elected democratically, he became, when once installed, an autocrat not less despotic than the King of Persia. Purposes still more slight and fugitive have been organized into arts. Taking soup gracefully, under the difficulties opposed to it by a dinner dress at that time fashionable, was reared into an art about forty-five years ago by a Frenchman who lectured upon it to ladies in London; and the most brilliant duchess of that day, viz. the Duchess of Devonshire, was amongst his best pupils. Spitting, if the reader will pardon the mention of so gross a fact, was shown to be a very difficult art, and publicly prelected upon, about the same time in the same great capital. The professors in this faculty were the hackney-coachmen; the pupils were gentlemen, who paid a guinea each for three lessons; the chief problem in this system of hydraulics being to throw the salivating column in a parabolic curve from the centre of Parliament-street, when driving four-in-hand, to the foot pavements, right and left, so as to alarm the consciences of guilty peripatetics on either side. The ultimate problem, which closed the *curriculum* of study, was held to lie in spitting round a corner; when *that* was mastered, the pupil was entitled to his doctor's degree. Endless are the purposes of man, merely festal or merely comic, and aiming but at the momentary life of a cloud, which have earned for themselves the distinction and apparatus of a separate art. Yet for conversation, the great paramount purpose of social meetings, no art exists or has been attempted.

That seems strange, but is not really so. A limited process submits readily to the limits of a technical system; but a process so unlimited as the interchange of thought seems to reject them. And, even if an art of conversation were less unlimited, the means of carrying such an art into practical effect amongst so vast a variety of minds seems wanting. Yet again, perhaps, after all, this may rest on a mistake. What we begin by misjudging is the particular phasis of conversation which brings it under the control of art and discipline. It is not in its relation to the intellect that conversation ever has been improved or *will* be improved primarily, but in its relation to manners. Has a man ever mixed with what in technical phrase is called "good company," meaning company in the highest degree polished,—company which (being or *not* being aristocratic as respects its composition) is aristocratic as respects the standard of its manners and usages? If he really *has*, and does not deceive himself from vanity or from pure inacquaintance with the world, in that case he must have remarked the large effect impressed upon the grace and upon the freedom of conversation by a few simple instincts of real good breeding. Good breeding— what is it? There is no need in this place to answer that question comprehensively; it is sufficient to say that it is made up chiefly of *negative* elements,—that it shows itself far less in what it prescribes than in what it forbids. Now, even under this limitation of the idea, the truth is that more will be done for the benefit of conversation by the simple magic of good manners (that is, chiefly by a system of forbearances), applied to the besetting vices of social intercourse, than ever *was* or *can* be done by all varieties of intellectual power assembled upon the same arena. Intellectual graces of the highest order may perish and confound each other when exercised in a spirit of ill-temper, or under the licence of bad manners; whereas very humble powers, when allowed to expand themselves colloquially in that genial freedom which is possible only under the most absolute confidence in the self-restraint of your collocutors, accomplish their purpose to a certainty if it be the ordinary purpose of liberal amusement, and have a chance of accomplishing it even when this purpose is the more ambitious one of communicating knowledge or exchanging new views upon truth.

In my own early years, having been formed by nature too exclusively and morbidly for solitary thinking, I observed nothing. Seeming to have eyes, in reality I saw nothing. But it is a matter of no very uncommon experience that, whilst the mere observers never became meditators, the mere meditators, on the other hand, may finally ripen into close observers. Strength of thinking, through long years, upon innumerable themes, will have the effect of disclosing a vast variety of questions, to which it soon becomes apparent that answers are lurking up and down the whole field of daily experience; and thus an external experience which was slighted in youth, because it was a dark cipher that could be read into no meaning, a key that answered to no lock, gradually becomes interesting as it is found to yield one solution after another to problems that have independently matured in the mind. Thus, for instance, upon the special functions of conversation, upon its powers, its laws, its ordinary diseases, and their appropriate remedies, in youth I never bestowed a thought or a care. I viewed it not as one amongst the gay ornamental arts of the intellect, but as one amongst the dull necessities of business. Loving solitude too much, I understood the capacities of colloquial intercourse too little. And thus it is, though not for *my* reason, that most people estimate the intellectual relations of conversation. Let these, however, be what they may, one thing seemed undeniable—that this world talked a great deal too much. It would be better for all parties if nine in every ten of the *winged words* flying about in this world (Homer's *epea pteroenta*) had their feathers clipped amongst men,—or even amongst women, who have a right to a larger allowance of words. Yet, as it was quite out of my power to persuade the world into any such self-denying reformation, it seemed equally out of the line of my duties to nourish any moral anxiety in that direction. *To talk* seemed to me at that time in the same category as *to sleep*,—not an accomplishment, but a base physical infirmity. As a moralist, I really was culpably careless upon the whole subject. I cared as little what absurdities men practised in their vast tennis-courts of conversation, where the ball is flying backwards and forwards to no purpose for ever, as what tricks Englishmen might play with their monstrous national debt. Yet at length what I disregarded on any principle of moral usefulness I came to make an object of the profoundest interest on principles of art. *Betting*, in like manner, and *wagering*,—which apparently had no moral value, and for that reason had been always slighted as inconsiderable arts (though, by the way, they always had one valuable use, viz. that of evading quarrels, since a bet summarily intercepts an altercation),—rose suddenly into a philosophic rank when, successively, Huygens, the Bernoullis, and De Moivre were led by the suggestion of these trivial practices amongst men to throw the light of a high mathematical analysis upon the whole doctrine of Chances.[1] Lord Bacon had been led to remark the capacities of conversation as an organ for sharpening one particular mode of intellectual power. Circumstances, on the other hand, led me into remarking the special capacities of conversation as an organ for absolutely creating another mode of

[1] Huygens, 1629–1695; James Bernoulli, 1654–1705; John Bernoulli, 1667–1748; De Moivre, 1667–1754.

power. Let a man have read, thought, studied, as much as he may, rarely will he reach his possible advantages as a *ready* man, unless he has exercised his powers much in conversation: that, I think, was Lord Bacon's idea. Now, this wise and useful remark points in a direction not objective, but subjective; that is, it does not promise any absolute extension to truth itself, but only some greater facilities to the man who expounds or diffuses the truth. Nothing will be done for truth objectively that would not at any rate be done; but subjectively it will be done with more fluency, and at less cost of exertion to the doer. On the contrary, my own growing reveries on the latent powers of conversation (which, though a thing that then I hated, yet challenged at times unavoidably my attention) pointed to an absolute birth of new insight into the truth itself as inseparable from the finer and more scientific exercise of the talking art. It would not be the brilliancy, the ease, or the adroitness of the expounder that would benefit, but the absolute interests of the thing expounded. A feeling dawned on me of a secret magic lurking in the peculiar life, velocities, and contagious ardour of conversation, quite separate from any which belonged to books,—arming a man with new forces, and not merely with a new dexterity in wielding the old ones. I felt (and in this I could not be mistaken, as too certainly it was a fact of my own experience) that in the electric kindling of life between two minds,—and far less from the kindling natural to conflict (though *that* also is something) than from the kindling through sympathy with the object discussed in its momentary coruscation of shifting phases,—there sometimes arise glimpses and shy revelations of affinity, suggestion, relation, analogy, that could not have been approached through any avenues of methodical study. Great organists find the same effect of inspiration, the same result of power creative and revealing, in the mere movement and velocity of their own voluntaries. Like the heavenly wheels of Milton, throwing off fiery flakes and bickering flames, these *impromptu* torrents of music create rapturous *fioriture*, beyond all capacity in the artist to register, or afterwards to imitate. The reader must be well aware that many philosophic instances exist where a change in the degree makes a change in the kind. Usually this is otherwise; the prevailing rule is that the principle subsists unaffected by any possible variation in the amount or degree of the force. But a large class of exceptions must have met the reader,—though, from want of a pencil, he has improperly omitted to write them down in his pocket-book,—cases, viz., where, upon passing beyond a certain point in the graduation, an alteration takes place suddenly in the *kind* of effect, a new direction is given to the power. Some illustration of this truth occurs in conversation, where a velocity in the movement of thought is made possible (and often natural) greater than ever can arise in methodical books, and where, *2dly*, approximations are more obvious and easily effected between things too remote for a steadier contemplation.

One remarkable evidence of a *specific* power lying hid in conversation may be seen in such writings as have moved by impulses most nearly resembling those of conversation,—for instance, in those of Edmund Burke. For one moment, reader, pause upon the spectacle of two contrasted intellects, Burke's and Johnson's: one an intellect essentially going forward, governed by the very necessity of growth, by the law of motion in advance; the latter essentially an intellect retrogressive, retrospective, and throwing itself back on its own steps. This original difference was aided accidentally in Burke by the tendencies of political partisanship,—which, both from moving amongst moving things and uncertainties, as compared with the more stationary aspects of moral philosophy, and also from its more fluctuating and fiery passions, must unavoidably reflect in greater life the tumultuary character of conversation. The result from these original differences of intellectual constitution, aided by these secondary differences of pursuit, is, that Dr. Johnson never, in any instance, GROWS a truth before your eyes whilst in the act of delivering it or moving towards it. All that he offers up to the end of the chapter he had when he began. But to Burke, such was the prodigious elasticity of his thinking, equally in his conversation and in his writings, the mere act of movement became the principle or cause of movement. Motion propagated motion, and life threw off life. The very violence of a projectile as thrown by *him* caused it to rebound in fresh forms, fresh angles, splintering, coruscating, which gave out thoughts as new (and as startling) to himself as they are to his reader. In this power, which might be illustrated largely from the writings of Burke, is seen something allied to the powers of a prophetic seer, who is compelled oftentimes into seeing things as unexpected by himself as by others. Now, in conversation, considered as to its *tendencies* and capacities, there sleeps an intermitting spring of such sudden revelation, showing much of the same general character,—a power putting on a character *essentially* differing from the character worn by the power of books.

If, then, in the *colloquial* commerce of thought there lurked a power not shared by other modes of that great commerce, a power separate and *sui generis*, next it was apparent that a great art must exist somewhere applicable to this power,—not in the Pyramids, or in the tombs of Thebes, but in the unwrought quarries of men's minds, so many and so dark. There was an art missing. If an art, then an artist was missing. If the art (as we say of foreign mails) were "due," then the artist was "due." How happened it that this great man never made his appearance? But perhaps he *had*. Many persons think Dr. Johnson the *exemplar* of conversational power. I think otherwise, for reasons which I shall soon explain; and far sooner I should look for such an *exemplar* in Burke. But neither Johnson nor Burke, however they might rank as *powers*, was the *artist* that I demanded. Burke valued not at all the reputation of a great performer in conversation; he scarcely contemplated the skill as having a real existence; and a man will never be an artist who does not value his art, or even recognise it as an object distinctly defined. Johnson, again, relied sturdily upon his natural powers for carrying him aggressively through all conversational occasions or difficulties that English society, from its known character and composition, could be supposed likely to bring forward, without caring for any art or system of rules that might give further effect to that power. If a man is strong enough to knock down ninety-nine in a hundred of all antagonists in spite of any advantages as to pugilistic science which they may possess over himself, he is not likely to care for the improbable case of a hundredth man appearing with strength equal to his own superadded to the utmost excess of that artificial skill which is wanting in himself. Against such a contingency it is not worth while going to the cost of a regular pugilistic training. Half a century might not bring up a case of actual call for its application. Or, if it did, for a single *extra* case of that nature there would always be a resource in the *extra* (and, strictly speaking, foul) arts of kicking, scratching, pinching, and tearing hair.

The conversational powers of Johnson were narrow in compass, however strong within their own essential limits. As a *conditio sine qua non*, he did not absolutely demand a *personal* contradictor by way of "stoker" to supply fuel and keep up his steam; but he demanded at least a *subject* teeming with elements of known contradictory opinion, whether linked to partisanship or not. His views of all things tended to negation, never to the positive and the creative. Hence may be explained a fact which cannot have escaped any keen observer of those huge Johnsonian *memorabilia* which we possess,—viz. that the gyration of his flight upon any one question that ever came before him was so exceedingly brief. There was no process, no evolution, no movement of self-conflict or preparation: a word, a distinction, a pointed antithesis, and, above all, a new abstraction of the logic involved in some popular fallacy, or doubt, or prejudice, or problem, formed the utmost of his efforts. He dissipated some casual perplexity that had gathered in the eddies of conversation, but he contributed nothing to any weightier interest; he unchoked a strangulated sewer in some blind alley, but what river is there that felt his cleansing power? There is no man that can cite any single error which Dr. Johnson unmasked, or any important truth which he expanded. Nor is this extraordinary. Dr. Johnson had not within himself the fountain of such power, having not a brooding or naturally philosophic intellect. Philosophy in any acquired sense he had none. How else could it have happened that upon David Hartley, upon David Hume, upon Voltaire, upon Rousseau,—the true or the false philosophy of his own day,—beyond a personal sneer, founded on some popular slander, he had nothing to say and said nothing? A new world was moulding itself in Dr. Johnson's meridian hours; new generations were ascending, and "other palms were won." Yet of all this the Doctor suspected nothing. Countrymen and contemporaries of the Doctor's, brilliant men, but (as many think) trifling men, such as Horace Walpole and Lord Chesterfield, already in the middle of that eighteenth century could read the signs of the great changes advancing. Already they started in horror from the portents which rose before them in Paris like the procession of regal phantoms before Macbeth, and have left in their letters records undeniable (such as now read like Cassandra prophecies) that already they had noticed tremors in the ground below their feet, and sounds in the air, running before the great convulsions under which Europe was destined to rock full thirty years later. Many instances during the last war showed us that in the frivolous dandy might often lurk the most fiery and accomplished of *aides-de-camp;* and these cases show that men in whom the world sees only elegant *roués*, sometimes from carelessness, sometimes from want of opening for display, conceal qualities of penetrating sagacity, and a learned spirit of observation, such as may be looked for vainly in persons of more solemn and academic pretension. But there was a greater defect in Dr. Johnson for purposes of conversation than merely want of eye for the social phenomena rising around him. He had no eye for such phenomena, because he had a somnolent want of interest in them; and why? Because he had little interest in man. Having no sympathy with human nature in its struggles, or faith in the progress of man, he could not be supposed to regard with much interest any forerunning symptoms of changes that to him were themselves indifferent. And the reason that he felt thus careless was the desponding taint in his blood. It is good to be of a melancholic temperament, as all the ancient physiologists held, but only if the melancholy is balanced by fiery aspiring qualities,—not when it gravitates essentially to the earth. Hence the drooping, desponding character, and the monotony, of the estimate which Dr. Johnson applied to life. We are all, in *his* view, miserable, scrofulous wretches; the "strumous diathesis" was developed in our flesh, or soon would be; and, but for his piety, —which was the best indication of some greatness latent within him,—he would have suggested to all mankind a nobler use for garters than any which regarded knees. In fact I believe that, but for his piety, he would not only have counselled hanging in general, but hanged himself in particular. Now, this gloomy temperament, not as an occasional but as a permanent state, is fatal to the power of brilliant conversation, in so far as that power rests upon raising a continual succession of topics, and not merely using with lifeless talent the topics offered by others. Man is the central interest about which revolve all the fleeting phenomena of life; these secondary interests demand the first; and, with the little knowledge about them which must follow from little care about them, there can be no salient fountain of conversational themes. "*Pectus,*" says Quintilian, "*id est quod disertum facit*":—*The heart* (and not the brain) *is that which makes a man eloquent*. From the heart, from an interest of love or hatred, of hope or care, springs all permanent eloquence; and the elastic spring of conversation is gone if the talker is a mere showy man of talent, pulling at an oar which he detests.

What an index might be drawn up of subjects interesting to human nature, and suggested by the events of the Johnsonian period, upon which the Doctor ought to have talked, and must have talked if his interest in man had been catholic, but on which the Doctor is not recorded to have uttered one word! Visiting Paris once in his whole life, he applied himself diligently to the measuring of—what? Of gilt mouldings and diapered panels! Yet books, it will be said, suggest topics as well as life and the moving sceneries of life; and surely Dr. Johnson had *this* fund to draw upon? No; for, though he had read much in a desultory way, he had studied nothing; [1] and without that sort of systematic reading, it is but a rare chance that books can be brought to bear effectually, and yet indirectly, upon conversation; whilst to make them directly and formally the subjects of discussion, presupposes either a learned audience, or, if the audience is not so, much pedantry and much arrogance in the talker.

The flight of our human hours, not really more rapid at any one moment than another, yet oftentimes to our feelings *seems* more rapid; and this flight startles us like guilty things with a more affecting *sense* of its rapidity when a distant church-clock strikes in the night-time, or when, upon some solemn summer evening, the sun's disc, after settling for a minute with farewell horizontal rays, suddenly drops out of sight. The record of our loss in such a case seems to us the first intimation of its possibility,—as if we could not be made sensible that the hours were perishable until it is announced to us that already they have perished. We feel a

---

[1] "*Had studied nothing*":—It may be doubted whether Dr. Johnson understood any one thing thoroughly except Latin; not that he understood even *that* with the elaborate and circumstantial accuracy required for the editing critically of a Latin classic. But, if he had less than *that*, he also had more: he *possessed* that language in a way that no extent of mere critical knowledge could confer. He wrote it genially, not as one translating into it painfully from English, but as one using it for his original organ of thinking. And in Latin verse he expressed himself at times with the energy and freedom of a Roman. With Greek his acquaintance was far more slender.

perplexity of distress when that which seems to us the cruellest of injuries, a robbery committed upon our dearest possession by the conspiracy of the world outside, seems also as in part a robbery sanctioned by our own collusion. The world, and the customs of the world, never cease to levy taxes upon our time: that is true, and so far the blame is not ours; but the particular *degree* in which we suffer by this robbery depends much upon the weakness with which we ourselves become parties to the wrong, or the energy with which we resist it. Resisting or not, however, we are doomed to suffer a bitter pang as often as the irrecoverable flight of our time is brought home with keenness to our hearts. The spectacle of a lady floating over the sea in a boat, and waking suddenly from sleep to find her magnificent ropes of pearl-necklace by some accident detached at one end from its fastenings, the loose string hanging down into the water, and pearl after pearl slipping off for ever into the abyss, brings before us the sadness of the case. That particular pearl which at the very moment is rolling off into the unsearchable deeps carries its own separate reproach to the lady's heart. But it is more deeply reproachful as the representative of so many others, uncounted pearls, that have already been swallowed up irrecoverably whilst she was yet sleeping, and of many beside that must follow before any remedy can be applied to what we may call this jewelly hæmorrhage. A constant hæmorrhage of the same kind is wasting our jewelly hours. A day has perished from our brief calendar of days: and *that* we could endure; but this day is no more than the reiteration of many other days,—days counted by thousands,—that have perished to the same extent and by the same unhappy means, viz. the evil usages of the world made effectual and ratified by our own *lâcheté*. Bitter is the upbraiding which we seem to hear from a secret monitor—"My friend, you make very free with your days: pray, how many do you expect to have? What is your rental, as regards the total harvest of days which this life is likely to yield?" Let us consider. Threescore years and ten produce a total sum of 25,550 days,—to say nothing of some seventeen or eighteen more that will be payable to you as a *bonus* on account of leap years. Now, out of this total, one-third must be deducted at a blow for a single item, viz. sleep. Next, on account of illness, of recreation, and the serious occupations spread over the surface of life, it will be little enough to deduct another third. Recollect also that twenty years will have gone from the earlier end of your life (viz. above seven thousand days) before you can have attained any skill or system, or any definite purpose in the distribution of your time. Lastly, for that single item which amongst the Roman armies was indicated by the technical phrase "*corpus curare*,"—tendance on the animal necessities, viz. eating, drinking, washing, bathing, and exercise,—deduct the smallest allowance consistent with propriety; and, upon summing up all these appropriations, you will not find so much as four thousand days left disposable for direct intellectual culture. Four thousand, or forty hundreds, will be a hundred forties: that is, according to the lax Hebrew method of indicating six weeks by the phrase of "forty days," you will have a hundred bills or drafts on Father Time, value six weeks each, as the whole period available for intellectual labour. A solid block of about eleven and a half continuous years is all that a long life will furnish for the development of what is most august in man's nature. After *that*, the night comes when no man can work; brain and arm will be alike unserviceable; or, if the life should be unusually extended, the vital powers will be drooping as regards all motions in advance.

Limited thus severely in his *direct* approaches to knowledge, and in his approaches to that which is a thousand times more important than knowledge, viz. the conduct and discipline of the knowing faculty, the more clamorous is the necessity that a wise man should turn to account any INDIRECT and supplementary means towards the same ends; and amongst these means a chief one by right and potentially is CONVERSATION. Even the primary means,— books, study, and meditation,—through errors from without and errors from within, are not *that* which they might be made. Too constantly, when reviewing his own efforts for improvement, a man has reason to say (indignantly, as one injured by others; penitentially, as contributing to this injury himself) "Much of my studies has been thrown away; many books which were useless, or worse than useless, I have read; many books which ought to have been read I have left unread: such is the sad necessity under the absence of all preconceived plan; and the proper road is first ascertained when the journey is drawing to its close." In a wilderness so vast as that of books, to go astray often and widely is pardonable, because it is inevitable; and, in proportion as the errors on this primary field of study have been great, it is important to have reaped some compensatory benefits on the secondary field of conversation. Books teach by one machinery, conversation by another; and, if these resources were trained into correspondence to their own separate ideals, they might become reciprocally the complements of each other. The false selection of books, for instance, might often be rectified at once by the frank collation of experiences which takes place in miscellaneous colloquial intercourse. But other and greater advantages belong to conversation for the effectual promotion of intellectual culture. Social discussion supplies the natural integration for the deficiencies of private and sequestered study. Simply to rehearse, simply to express in words amongst familiar friends, one's own intellectual perplexities, is oftentimes to clear them up. It is well known that the best means of learning is by teaching. The effort that is made for others is made eventually for ourselves; and the readiest method of illuminating obscure conceptions, or maturing such as are crude, lies in an earnest effort to make them apprehensible by others. Even this is but one amongst the functions fulfilled by conversation. Each separate individual in a company is likely to see any problem or idea under some difference of angle. Each may have some difference of views to contribute, derived either from a different course of reading, or a different tenor of reflection, or perhaps a different train of experience. The advantages of colloquial discussion are not only often commensurate in *degree* to those of study, but they recommend themselves also as being different in *kind;* they are special and *sui generis*. It must, therefore, be important that so great an organ of intellectual development should not be neutralized by mismanagement, as generally it is, or neglected through insensibility to its latent capacities. The importance of the subject should be measured by its relation to the interests of the intellect; and on this principle we do not scruple to think that, in reviewing our own experience of the causes most commonly at war with the free movement of conversation as it ought to be, we are in effect contributing hints for a new chapter in any future "Essay on the Improvement of the Mind." Watts's book under that title is really of little practical use; nor would it ever have been thought so had it not been patronized, in a spirit of partisanship, by a particular section of religious dissenters.

Wherever *that* happens, the fortune of a book is made; for the sectarian impulse creates a sensible current in favour of the book, and the general or neutral reader yields passively to the motion of the current without knowing or caring to know whence it is derived.

Our remarks must of necessity be cursory here, so that they will not need or permit much preparation; but one distinction which is likely to strike on some minds as to the two different purposes of conversation ought to be noticed, since otherwise it will seem doubtful whether we have not confounded them, or, secondly, if we have *not* confounded them, which of the two it is that our remarks contemplate. In speaking above of conversation, we have fixed our view on those uses of conversation which are ministerial to intellectual culture; but, in relation to the majority of men, conversation is far less valuable as an organ of intellectual culture than of social enjoyment. For one man interested in conversation as a means of advancing his studies, there are fifty men whose interest in conversation points exclusively to convivial pleasure. This, as being a more extensive function of conversation, is so far the more dignified function; whilst, on the other hand, such a purpose as direct mental improvement seems by its superior gravity to challenge the higher rank. Yet, in fact, even here the more general purpose of conversation takes precedence; for, when dedicated to the objects of festal delight, conversation rises by its tendency to the rank of a fine art. It is true that not one man in a million rises to any distinction in this art; nor, whatever France may conceit of herself, has any one nation, amongst other nations, a real precedency in this art. The artists are rare indeed; but still the art, as distinguished from the artist, may, by its difficulties, by the quality of its graces, and by the range of its possible brilliances, take rank as a *fine* art; or, at all events, according to its powers of execution, it tends to that rank; whereas the best order of conversation that is simply ministerial to a purpose of use cannot pretend to a higher name than that of a *mechanic* art. But these distinctions, though they would form the grounds of a separate treatment in a regular treatise on Conversation, may be practically neglected on this occasion, because the hints offered, by the generality of the terms in which they express themselves, may be applied indifferently to either class of conversation. The main diseases, indeed, which obstruct the healthy movement of conversation recur everywhere; and, alike whether the object be pleasure or profit in the free interchange of thought, almost universally that free interchange is obstructed in the very same way,—by the very same defect of any controlling principle for sustaining the general rights and interests of the company, and by the same vices of self-indulgent indolence, or of callous selfishness, or of insolent vanity, in the individual talkers.

Let us fall back on the recollections of our own experience. In the course of our life we have heard much of what was reputed to be the select conversation of the day, and we have heard many of those who figured at the moment as effective talkers; yet, in mere sincerity, and without a vestige of misanthropic retrospect, we must say that never once has it happened to us to come away from any display of that nature without intense disappointment; and it always appeared to us that this failure (which soon ceased to be a *disappointment*) was inevitable by a necessity of the case. For here lay the stress of the difficulty: almost all depends in most trials of skill upon the parity of those who are matched against each other. An ignorant person supposes that to an able disputant it must be an advantage to have a feeble opponent; whereas, on the contrary, it is ruin to him; for he cannot display his own powers but through something of a corresponding power in the resistance of his antagonist. A brilliant fencer is lost and confounded in playing with a novice; and the same thing takes place in playing at ball, or battledore, or in dancing, where a powerless partner does not enable you to shine the more, but reduces you to mere helplessness, and takes the wind altogether out of your sails. Now, if by some rare good luck the great talker, the protagonist, of the evening has been provided with a commensurate second, it is just possible that something like a brilliant "passage of arms" may be the result,—though much even in that case will depend on the chances of the moment for furnishing a fortunate theme, and even then, amongst the superior part of the company, a feeling of deep vulgarity and of mountebank display is inseparable from such an ostentatious duel of wit. On the other hand, supposing your great talker to be received like any other visitor, and turned loose upon the company, then he must do one of two things: either he will talk upon *outré* subjects specially tabooed to his own private use,—

in which case the great man has the air of a quack-doctor addressing a mob from a street stage; or else he will talk like ordinary
people upon popular topics,—in which case the company, out of
natural politeness, that they may not seem to be staring at him
as a lion, will hasten to meet him in the same style, the conversation will become general, the great man will seem reasonable and
well-bred, but at the same time, we grieve to say it, the great
man will have been extinguished by being drawn off from his exclusive ground. The dilemma, in short, is this:—If the great
talker attempts the plan of showing off by firing cannon-shot
when everybody else is content with musketry, then undoubtedly
he produces an impression, but at the expense of insulating himself
from the sympathies of the company, and standing aloof as a sort
of monster hired to play tricks of funambulism for the night. Yet,
again, if he contents himself with a musket like other people, then
for *us*, from whom he modestly hides his talent under a bushel, in
what respect is he different from the man who *has* no such talent?

> "If she be not fair to me,
>   What care I how fair she be?"

The reader, therefore, may take it, upon the *a priori* logic of this
dilemma, or upon the evidence of our own experience, that all
reputation for brilliant talking is a visionary thing, and rests upon
a sheer impossibility: viz. upon such a histrionic performance in
a state of insulation from the rest of the company as could not be
effected, even for a single time, without a rare and difficult collusion, and could not, even for that single time, be endurable to a
man of delicate and honourable sensibilities.

Yet surely Coleridge *had* such a reputation, and without needing
any collusion at all; for Coleridge, unless he could have all the talk,
would have none. But then this was not conversation. It was not
colloquium, or talking *with* the company, but *alloquium*, or talking
to the company, As Madame de Staël observed, Coleridge talked,
and *could* talk, only by monologue. Such a mode of systematic
trespass upon the conversational rights of a whole party gathered
together under pretence of amusement is fatal to every purpose of
social intercourse, whether that purpose be connected with direct
use and the service of the intellect, or with the general graces and
amenities of life. The result is the same under whatever impulse

such an outrage is practised; but the impulse is not always the same; it varies, and so far the criminal intention varies. In some people this gross excess takes its rise in pure arrogance. They are fully aware of their own intrusion upon the general privileges of the company; they are aware of the temper in which it is likely to be received; but they persist wilfully in the wrong, as a sort of homage levied compulsorily upon those who may wish to resist it, but hardly *can* do so without a violent interruption, wearing the same shape of indecorum as that which they resent. In most people, however, it is not arrogance which prompts this capital offence against social rights, but a blind selfishness, yielding passively to its own instincts, without being distinctly aware of the degree in which this self-indulgence trespasses on the rights of others. We see the same temper illustrated at times in travelling. A brutal person, as we are disposed at first to pronounce him, but more frequently one who yields unconsciously to a lethargy of selfishness, plants himself at the public fireplace, so as to exclude his fellow-travellers from all but a fraction of the warmth. Yet he does not do this in a spirit of wilful aggression upon others; he has but a glimmering suspicion of the odious shape which his own act assumes to others, for the luxurious torpor of self-indulgence has extended its mists to the energy and clearness of his perceptions. Meantime, Coleridge's habit of soliloquizing through a whole evening of four or five hours had its origin neither in arrogance nor in absolute selfishness. The fact was that he *could* not talk unless he were uninterrupted, and unless he were able to count upon this concession from the company. It was a silent contract between him and his hearers that nobody should speak but himself. If any man objected to this arrangement, why did he come? For, the custom of the place, the *lex loci*, being notorious, by coming at all he was understood to profess his allegiance to the autocrat who presided. It was not, therefore, by an insolent usurpation that Coleridge persisted in monology through his whole life, but in virtue of a concession from the kindness and respect of his friends. You could not be angry with him for using his privilege, for it was a privilege conferred by others, and a privilege which he was ready to resign as soon as any man demurred to it. But, though reconciled to it by these considerations, and by the ability with which he used it, you could not but feel that it worked ill for all parties. Himself it tempted oftentimes into pure garrulity of egotism, and the listeners it reduced to a state of debilitated sympathy or of absolute torpor. Prevented by the custom from putting questions, from proposing doubts, from asking for explanations, reacting by no mode of mental activity, and condemned also to the mental distress of hearing opinions or doctrines stream past them by flights which they must not arrest for a moment so as even to take a note of them, and which yet they could not often understand, or, seeming to understand, could not always approve, the audience sank at times into a listless condition of inanimate vacuity. To be acted upon for ever, but never to react, is fatal to the very powers by which sympathy must grow, or by which intelligent admiration can be evoked. For his own sake, it was Coleridge's interest to have forced his hearers into the active commerce of question and answer, of objection and demur. Not otherwise was it possible that even the attention could be kept from drooping, or the coherency and dependency of the arguments be forced into light.

The French rarely make a mistake of this nature. The graceful levity of the nation could not easily err in this direction, nor tolerate such deliration in the greatest of men. Not the gay temperament only of the French people, but the particular qualities of the French language,—which (however poor for the higher purposes of passion) is rich beyond all others for purposes of social intercourse, —prompt them to rapid and vivacious exchange of thought. Tediousness, therefore, above all other vices, finds no countenance or indulgence amongst the French, excepting always in two memorable cases: viz., first, the case of tragic dialogue on the stage, which is privileged to be tedious by usage and tradition; and, secondly, the case (authorised by the best usages in living society) of narrators or *raconteurs*. This is a shocking anomaly in the code of French good taste as applied to conversation. Of all the bores whom man in his folly hesitates to hang, and Heaven in its mysterious wisdom suffers to propagate their species, the most insufferable is the teller of "good stories,"—a nuisance that should be put down by cudgelling, a submersion in horse-ponds, or any mode of abatement, as summarily as men would combine to suffocate a vampire or a mad dog. This case excepted, however, the French have the keenest possible sense of all that is odious and all that is ludicrous in prosing, and universally have a horror of *des longueurs*. It is not strange, therefore, that Madame de Staël noticed little as extraordinary in Coleridge beyond this one capital monstrosity of unlimited soliloquy,—that being a peculiarity which she never could have witnessed in France; and, considering the burnish of her French tastes in all that concerned colloquial characteristics, it is creditable to her forbearance that she noticed even this rather as a memorable fact than as the inhuman fault which it was. On the other hand, Coleridge was not so forbearing as regarded the brilliant French lady. He spoke of her to ourselves as a very frivolous person, and in short summary terms that disdained to linger on a subject so inconsiderable. It is remarkable that Goethe and Schiller both conversed with Madame de Staël, like Coleridge, and both spoke of her afterwards in the same disparaging terms as Coleridge.   But it is equally remarkable that Baron *William* Humboldt, who was personally acquainted with all the four parties—Madame de Staël, Goethe, Schiller, and Coleridge—gave it as his opinion (in letters subsequently published) that the lady had been calumniated through a very ignoble cause,—viz. mere ignorance of the French language, or at least non-familiarity with the fluencies of *oral* French. Neither Goethe nor Schiller, though well acquainted with written French, had any command of it for purposes of *rapid* conversation; and Humboldt supposes that mere spite at the trouble which they found in limping after the lady so as to catch one thought that she uttered had been the true cause of their unfavourable sentence upon her. Not malice aforethought, so much as vindictive fury for the sufferings they had endured, accounted for their severity in the opinion of the diplomatic baron. He did not extend the same explanation to Coleridge's case,— because, though even then in habits of intercourse with Coleridge, he had not heard of *his* interview with the lady, nor of the results from that interview; else what was true of the two German wits was true *a fortiori* of Coleridge. The Germans at least *read* French, and talked it slowly, and occasionally understood it when talked by others; but Coleridge did none of these things. We are all of us well aware that Madame de Staël was *not* a trifler: nay, that she gave utterance at times to truths as worthy to be held oracular as any that were uttered by the three inspired wits,—all philosophers, and bound to truth, but all poets, and privileged to be wayward.

Thus we may collect from these anecdotes that people accustomed to colloquial despotism, and who wield a sceptre within a circle of their own, are no longer capable of impartial judgments, and do not accommodate themselves with patience, or even with justice, to the pretensions of rivals; and, were it only for this result of conversational tyranny, it calls clamorously for extinction by some combined action upon the part of society.

Is such a combination on the part of society possible as a sustained effort? We imagine that it *is* in these times, and will be more so in the times which are coming. Formerly the social meetings of men and women, except only in capital cities, were few; and even in such cities the infusion of female influence was not broad and powerful enough for the correction of those great aberrations from just ideals which disfigured social intercourse. But great changes are proceeding: were it only by the vast revolution in our *means* of intercourse, laying open every village to the contagion of social temptations, the world of Western Europe is tending more and more to a mode of living in public. Under such a law of life, conversation becomes a vital interest of every hour, that can no more suffer interruption from individual caprice or arrogance than the animal process of respiration from transient disturbances of health. Once, when travelling was rare, there was no fixed law for the usages of public rooms in inns or coffee-houses; the courtesy of individuals was the tenure by which men held their rights. If a morose person detained the newspaper for hours, there was no remedy. At present, according to the circumstances of the case, there are strict regulations which secure to each individual his own share of the common rights.

A corresponding change will gradually take place in the usages which regulate conversation. It will come to be considered an infringement of the general rights for any man to detain the conversation, or arrest its movement, for more than a short space of time, —which gradually will be more and more defined. This one curtailment of arrogant pretensions will lead to others. Egotism will no longer freeze the openings to intellectual discussions; and conversation will then become, what it never *has* been before, a powerful ally of education and generally of self-culture. The main diseases that besiege conversation at present are—1*st*, The want of *timing*. Those who are not recalled by a sense of courtesy and equity to the continual remembrance that, in appropriating too large a share of the conversation, they are committing a fraud upon their companions, are beyond all control of monitory hints or of reproof which does not take a direct and open shape of personal remonstrance; but this, where the purpose of the assembly is festive and convivial, bears too harsh an expression for most people's feelings. That objection, however, would not apply to any mode of admonition that was universally established. A public memento carries with it no personality. For instance, in the Roman law-courts, no advocate complained of the *clepsydra*, or water time-piece, which regulated the duration of his pleadings. Now, such a contrivance would not be impracticable at an after-dinner talk. To invert the clepsydra, when all the water had run out, would be an act open to any one of the guests, and liable to no misconstruction when this check was generally applied, and understood to be a simple expression of public defence, not of private rudeness or personality. The clepsydra ought to be filled with some brilliantly-coloured fluid, to be placed in the centre of the table, and with the capacity, at the very most, of the little minute-glasses used for regulating the boiling of eggs. It would obviously be insupportably tedious to turn the glass every two or three minutes; but to do so occasionally would avail as a sufficient memento to the company. 2*d*, Conversation suffers from the want of some discretional power lodged in an individual for controlling its movements. Very often it sinks into flats of insipidity through mere accident. Some trifle has turned its current upon ground where few of the company have anything to say: the commerce of thought languishes; and the consciousness that it *is* languishing about a narrow circle, "unde pedem proferre pudor vetat," operates for a general refrigeration of the company. Now, the ancient Greeks had an officer appointed over every convivial meeting, whose functions applied to all cases of doubt or interruption that could threaten the genial harmony, or, perhaps, the genial movement intellectually, of the company. We also have such officers,—presidents, vice-presidents, &c.; and we need only to extend their powers so that they may exercise over the movement of the conversation the beneficial influence of the Athenian *symposiarch*. At present the evil is that conversation has no authorized originator; it is servile to the accidents of the moment, and generally these accidents are merely verbal. Some word or some name is dropped casually in the course of an illustration; and *that* is allowed to suggest a topic, though neither interesting to the majority of the persons present, nor leading naturally into other collateral topics that are more so. Now, in such cases it will be the business of the symposiarch to restore the interest of the conversation, and to rekindle its animation, by recalling it from any tracks of dulness or sterility into which it may have rambled. The natural *excursiveness* of colloquial intercourse, its tendency to advance by subtle links of association, is one of its advantages; but mere *vagrancy* from positive acquiescence in the direction given to it by chance or by any verbal accident is amongst its worst diseases. The business of the symposiarch will be to watch these morbid tendencies, which are not the deviations of graceful freedom, but the distortions of imbecility and collapse. His business it will also be to derive occasions of discussion bearing a general and permanent interest from the fleeting events or the casual disputes of the day. His business again it will be to bring back a subject that has been imperfectly discussed, and has yielded but half of the interest which it promises, under the interruption of any accident which may have carried the thoughts of the company into less attractive channels. Lastly, it should be an express office of education to form a particular style, cleansed from *verbiage*, from elaborate parenthesis, and from circumlocution,[1] as the only style fitted for a purpose which is one of pure enjoyment, and where every moment used by the speaker is deducted from a public stock.

Many other suggestions for the improvement of conversation might be brought forward within ampler limits; and especially for that class of conversation which moves by discussion a whole code of regulations might be proposed that would equally promote the interests of the individual speakers and the public interests of the truth involved in the question discussed. Meantime nobody is more aware than we are that no style of conversation is more essentially vulgar than that which moves by disputation. This is the vice of the young and the inexperienced, but especially of those amongst them who are fresh from academic life. But discussion is not necessarily disputation; and the two orders of conversation—

[1] *Circumlocution* and *parenthesis* agree in this—that they keep the attention in a painful condition of suspense. But suspense is anxiety.

that, on the one hand, which contemplates an interest of knowledge and of the self-developing intellect; *that*, on the other hand, which forms one and the widest amongst the gay embellishments of life—will always advance together. Whatever there may remain of illiberal in the first (for, according to the remark of Burke, there is always something illiberal in the severer aspects of study until balanced by the influence of social amenities) will correct itself, or will tend to correct itself, by the model held up in the second; and thus the great organ of social intercourse by means of speech, which hitherto has done little for man, except through the channel of its ministrations to the direct *business* of daily necessities, will at length rise into a rivalship with books, and become fixed amongst the alliances of intellectual progress, not less than amongst the ornamental accomplishments of convivial life.

DICKENS

CHARLES DICKENS (*1812–1870*), *journalist, editor, novelist, was born at Portsea; after a childhood of hardships, he became a reporter, publishing his first article in 1833—a collection of sketches, written under the pen-name "Boz," was printed in 1836, the year of his marriage. The success of his first work of fiction—a collection of sketches rather than a novel in the limited sense of the word—encouraged him to continue in this field; to "Pickwick Papers" succeeded "Oliver Twist," which was followed by a long series of novels, many of which appeared in monthly numbers. In 1842, he paid his first visit to the United States, an account of which is preserved in "American Notes." He edited various magazines, gave many readings from his own works, and continued writing until his sudden death in 1870.*

Chiefly known for his novels, Dickens shows his powers of observation also in his shorter sketches, which are frequently based on people he has seen or experiences he has had. His sympathy is with the lower and middle classes rather than with the gentry; and if he draws caricatures sometimes, his people are recognizable human types. The propaganda which occasionally intrudes into his novels is less obvious in his sketches, but some of these are written rather to instruct than to amuse.

DICKENS

THE BASHFUL YOUNG GENTLEMAN

WE found ourselves seated at a small dinner party the other day, opposite a stranger of such singular appearance and manner, that he irresistibly attracted our attention.

This was a fresh-coloured young gentleman, with as good a promise of light whisker as one might wish to see, and possessed of a very velvet-like, soft-looking countenance. We do not use the latter term invidiously, but merely to denote a pair of smooth, plump, highly-coloured cheeks of capacious dimensions, and a mouth rather remarkable for the fresh hue of the lips than for any marked or striking expression it presented. His whole face was suffused with a crimson blush, and bore that downcast, timid, retiring look, which betokens a man ill at ease with himself.

There was nothing in these symptoms to attract more than a passing remark, but our attention had been originally drawn to the bashful young gentleman, on his first appearance in the drawing-room above-stairs, into which he was no sooner introduced, than making his way towards us who were standing in a window, and wholly neglecting several persons who warmly accosted him, he seized our hand with visible emotion, and pressed it with a convulsive grasp for a good couple of minutes, after which he dived in a nervous manner across the room, oversetting in his way a fine little girl of six years and a quarter old—and shrouding himself behind some hangings, was seen no more, until the eagle eye of the hostess detecting him in his concealment, on the announcement of dinner, he was requested to pair off with a lively single lady, of two or three and thirty.

This most flattering salutation from a perfect stranger, would have gratified us not a little as a token of his having held us in high respect, and for that reason been desirous of our acquaintance, if we had not suspected from the first, that the young gentleman, in making a desperate effort to get through the ceremony of introduction, had, in the bewilderment of his ideas, shaken hands with us at random. This impression was fully confirmed by the subsequent behaviour of the bashful young gentleman in question, which we noted particularly, with the view of ascertaining whether we were right in our conjecture.

The young gentleman seated himself at table with evident misgivings, and turning sharp round to pay attention to some observation of his loquacious neighbour, overset his bread. There was nothing very bad in this, and if he had had the presence of mind to let it go, and say nothing about it, nobody but the man who had laid the cloth would have been a bit the wiser; but the young gentleman, in various semi-successful attempts to prevent its fall, played with it a little, as gentlemen in the streets may be seen to do with their hats on a windy day, and then giving the roll a smart rap in his anxiety to catch it, knocked it with great adroitness into a tureen of white soup at some distance, to the unspeakable terror and disturbance of a very amiable bald gentleman, who was dispensing the contents. We thought the bashful young gentleman would have gone off in an apoplectic fit, consequent upon the violent rush of blood to his face at the occurrence of this catastrophe.

From this moment we perceived, in the phraseology of the fancy, that it was "all up" with the bashful young gentleman, and so indeed it was. Several benevolent persons endeavoured to relieve his embarrassment by taking wine with him, but finding that it only augmented his sufferings, and that after mingling sherry, champagne, hock, and moselle together, he applied the greater part of the mixture externally, instead of internally, they gradually dropped off, and left him to the exclusive care of the talkative lady, who not noting the wildness of his eye, firmly believed she had secured a listener. He broke a glass or two in the course of the meal, and disappeared shortly afterwards; it is inferred that he went away in some confusion, inasmuch as he left the house in another gentleman's coat, and the footman's hat.

This little incident led us to reflect upon the most prominent characteristics of bashful young gentlemen in the abstract; and as this portable volume will be the great text-book of young ladies in all future generations, we record them here for their guidance and behoof.

If the bashful young gentleman, in turning a street corner, chance to stumble suddenly upon two or three young ladies of his acquaintance, nothing can exceed his confusion and agitation. His first impulse is to make a great variety of bows, and dart past them, which he does until, observing that they wish to stop, but are uncertain whether to do so or not, he makes several feints of returning, which causes them to do the same; and at length, after a great quantity of unnecessary dodging and falling up against the other passengers, he returns and shakes hands most affectionately with all of them, in doing which he knocks out of their grasp sundry little parcels, which he hastily picks up, and returns very muddy and disordered. The chances are that the bashful young gentleman then observes it is very fine weather, and being reminded that it has only just left off raining for the first time these three days, he blushes very much, and smiles as if he had said a very good thing. The young lady who was most anxious to speak, here inquires, with an air of great commiseration, how his dear sister Harriet is to-day; to which the young gentleman, without the slightest consideration, replies with many thanks, that she is remarkably well. "Well, Mr. Hopkins!" cries the young lady, "why, we heard she was bled yesterday evening, and have been perfectly miserable about her." "Oh, ah," says the young gentleman, "so she was. Oh, she's very ill, very ill indeed." The young gentleman then shakes his head, and looks very desponding (he has been smiling perpetually up to this time), and after a short pause, gives his glove a great wrench at the wrist, and says, with a strong emphasis on the adjective, "*Good* morning, *good* morning." And making a great number of bows in acknowledgment of several little messages to his sister, walks backward a few paces, and comes with great violence against a lamp-post, knocking his hat off in the contact, which in his mental confusion and bodily pain he is going to walk away without, until a great roar from a carter attracts his attention, when he picks it up, and tries to smile cheerfully to the young ladies, who are looking back, and who, he has the satisfaction of seeing, are all laughing heartily.

At a quadrille party, the bashful young gentleman always remains as near the entrance of the room as possible, from which

position he smiles at the people he knows as they come in, and sometimes steps forward to shake hands with more intimate friends:
a process which on each repetition seems to turn him a deeper
scarlet than before. He declines dancing the first set or two,
observing, in a faint voice, that he would rather wait a little;
but at length is absolutely compelled to allow himself to be introduced to a partner, when he is led, in a great heat and blushing
furiously, across the room to a spot where half-a-dozen unknown
ladies are congregated together.

"Miss Lambert, let me introduce Mr. Hopkins for the next quadrille." Miss Lambert inclines her head graciously. Mr. Hopkins
bows, and his fair conductress disappears, leaving Mr. Hopkins,
as he too well knows, to make himself agreeable. The young lady
more than half expects that the bashful young gentleman will say
something, and the bashful young gentleman feeling this, seriously
thinks whether he has got anything to say, which, upon mature
reflection, he is rather disposed to conclude he has not, since
nothing occurs to him. Meanwhile, the young lady, after several
inspections of her *bouquet*, all made in the expectation that the
bashful young gentleman is going to talk, whispers her mama, who
is sitting next her, which whisper the bashful young gentleman
immediately suspects (and possibly with very good reason) must
be about *him*. In this comfortable condition he remains until it is
time to "stand up," when murmuring a "Will you allow me?"
he gives the young lady his arm, and after inquiring where she
will stand, and receiving a reply that she has no choice, conducts
her to the remotest corner of the quadrille, and making one attempt
at conversation, which turns out a desperate failure, preserves a
profound silence until it is all over, when he walks her twice round
the room, deposits her in her old seat, and retires in confusion.

A married bashful gentleman—for these bashful gentlemen *do*
get married sometimes; how it is ever brought about, is a mystery
to us—a married bashful gentleman either causes his wife to appear bold by contrast, or merges her proper importance in his own
insignificance. Bashful young gentlemen should be cured, or
avoided. They are never hopeless, and never will be, while female
beauty and attractions retain their influence, as any young lady
will find, who may think it worth while on this confident assurance
to take a patient in hand.

THE OUT–AND–OUT YOUNG GENTLEMAN

OUT–AND–OUT young gentlemen may be divided into two classes—those who have something to do, and those who have nothing. I shall commence with the former, because that species come more frequently under the notice of young ladies, whom it is our province to warn and to instruct.

The out-and-out young gentleman is usually no great dresser, his instructions to his tailor being all comprehended in the one general direction to "make that what's-a-name a regular bang-up sort of thing." For some years past, the favourite costume of the out-and-out young gentleman has been a rough pilot coat, with two gilt hooks and eyes to the velvet collar; buttons somewhat larger than crown-pieces; a black or fancy neckerchief, loosely tied; a wide-brimmed hat, with a low crown; tightish inexpressibles, and iron-shod boots. Out of doors he sometimes carries a large ash stick, but only on special occasions, for he prefers keeping his hands in his coat pockets. He smokes at all hours, of course, and swears considerably.

The out-and-out young gentleman is employed in a city counting-house or solicitor's office, in which he does as little as he possibly can: his chief places of resort are, the streets, the taverns, and the theatres. In the streets at evening time, out-and-out young gentlemen have a pleasant custom of walking six or eight abreast, thus driving females and other inoffensive persons into the road, which never fails to afford them the highest satisfaction, especially if there be any immediate danger of their being run over, which enhances the fun of the thing materially. In all places of public resort, the out-and-outers are careful to select each a seat to himself, upon which he lies at full length, and (if the weather be very dirty, but not in any other case) he lies with his knees up, and the soles of his boots planted firmly on the cushion, so that if any low fellow should ask him to make room for a lady, he takes ample revenge upon her dress, without going at all out of his way to do it. He always sits with his hat on, and flourishes his stick in the air while the play is proceeding, with a dignified contempt of the performance; if it be possible for one or two out-and-out young gentlemen to get up a little crowding in the passages, they are quite in their element, squeezing, pushing, whooping, and shouting

in the most humorous manner possible. If they can only succeed
in irritating the gentleman who has a family of daughters under
his charge, they are like to die with laughing, and boast of it
among their companions for a week afterwards, adding, that one
or two of them were "devilish fine girls," and that they really
thought the youngest would have fainted, which was the only
thing wanted to render the joke complete.

If the out-and-out young gentleman have a mother and sisters,
of course he treats them with becoming contempt, inasmuch as
they (poor things!) having no notion of life or gaiety, are far too
weak-spirited and moping for him. Sometimes, however, on a
birth-day or at Christmas time, he cannot very well help accompanying them to a party at some old friend's, with which view he
comes home when they have been dressed an hour or two, smelling
very strongly of tobacco and spirits, and after exchanging his rough
coat for some more suitable attire (in which however he loses
nothing of the out-and-outer), gets into the coach and grumbles
all the way at his own good-nature: his bitter reflections aggravated
by the recollection, that Tom Smith has taken the chair at a little
impromptu dinner at a fighting man's, and that a set-to was to
take place on a dining-table, between the fighting man and his
brother-in-law, which is probably "coming off" at that very
instant.

As the out-and-out young gentleman is by no means at his ease
in ladies' society, he shrinks into a corner of the drawing-room
when they reach the friend's, and unless one of his sisters is kind
enough to talk to him, remains there without being much troubled
by the attentions of other people, until he espies, lingering outside
the door, another gentleman, whom he at once knows, by his air
and manner (for there is a kind of free-masonry in the craft), to
be a brother out-and-outer, and towards whom he accordingly
makes his way. Conversation being soon opened by some casual
remark, the second out-and-outer confidentially informs the first,
that he is one of the rough sort and hates that kind of thing, only
he couldn't very well be off coming; to which the other replies,
that that's just his case—"and I'll tell you what," continues the
out-and-outer in a whisper, "I should like a glass of warm brandy
and water just now."—"Or a pint of stout and a pipe," suggests
the other out-and-outer.

The discovery is at once made that they are sympathetic souls; each of them says at the same moment, that he sees the other understands what's what: and they become fast friends at once, more especially when it appears, that the second out-and-outer is no other than a gentleman, long favourably known to his familiars as "Mr. Warmint Blake," who upon divers occasions, has distinguished himself in a manner that would not have disgraced the fighting man, and who—having been a pretty long time about town—had the honour of once shaking hands with the celebrated Mr. Thurtell himself.

At supper, these gentlemen greatly distinguish themselves, brightening up very much when the ladies leave the table, and proclaiming aloud their intention of beginning to spend the evening—a process which is generally understood to be satisfactorily performed, when a great deal of wine is drunk and a great deal of noise made, both of which feats the out-and-out young gentlemen execute to perfection. Having protracted their sitting until long after the host and the other guests have adjourned to the drawing-room, and finding that they have drained the decanters empty, they follow them thither, with complexions rather heightened, and faces rather bloated with wine; and the agitated lady of the house whispers her friends as they waltz together, to the great terror of the whole room, that "both Mr. Blake and Mr. Dummins are very nice sort of young men in their way, only they are eccentric persons, and unfortunately *rather too wild!*"

The remaining class of out-and-out young gentlemen is composed of persons, who, having no money of their own and a soul above earning any, enjoy similar pleasures, nobody knows how. These respectable gentlemen, without aiming quite so much at the out-and-out in external appearance, are distinguished by all the same amiable and attractive characteristics, in an equal or perhaps greater degree, and now and then find their way into society, through the medium of the other class of out-and-out young gentlemen, who will sometimes carry them home, and who usually pay their tavern bills. As they are equally gentlemanly, clever, witty, intelligent, wise, and well-bred, we need scarcely have recommended them to the peculiar consideration of the young ladies, if it were not that some of the gentle creatures whom we hold in such high respect, are perhaps a little too apt to confound a great many heavier terms with the light word eccentricity, which we beg them henceforth to take in a strictly Johnsonian sense, without any liberality or latitude of construction.

THE DOMESTIC YOUNG GENTLEMAN

LET us make a slight sketch of our amiable friend, Mr. Felix Nixon. We are strongly disposed to think, that if we put him in this place, he will answer our purpose without another word of comment.

Felix, then, is a young gentleman who lives at home with his mother, just within the twopenny-post office circle of three miles from St. Martin le Grand. He wears India-rubber goloshes when the weather is at all damp, and always has a silk handkerchief neatly folded up in the right-hand pocket of his great-coat, to tie over his mouth when he goes home at night; moreover, being rather near-sighted, he carries spectacles for particular occasions, and has a weakish tremulous voice, of which he makes great use, for he talks as much as any old lady breathing.

The two chief subjects of Felix's discourse, are himself and his mother, both of whom would appear to be very wonderful and interesting persons. As Felix and his mother are seldom apart in body, so Felix and his mother are scarcely ever separate in spirit. If you ask Felix how he finds himself to-day, he prefaces his reply with a long and minute bulletin of his mother's state of health; and the good lady in her turn, edifies her acquaintance with a circumstantial and alarming account, how he sneezed four times and coughed once after being out in the rain the other night, but having his feet promptly put into hot water, and his head into a flannel-something, which we will not describe more particularly than by this delicate allusion, was happily brought round by the next morning, and enabled to go to business as usual.

Our friend is not a very adventurous or hot-headed person, but he has passed through many dangers, as his mother can testify: there is one great story in particular, concerning a hackney coachman who wanted to overcharge him one night for bringing them home from the play, upon which Felix gave the aforesaid coachman a look which his mother thought would have crushed him to the earth, but which did not crush him quite, for he continued to

demand another sixpence, notwithstanding that Felix took out
his pocketbook, and, with the aid of a flat candle, pointed out the
fare in print, which the coachman obstinately disregarding, he
shut the street door with a slam which his mother shudders to
think of; and then, roused to the most appalling pitch of passion
by the coachman knocking a double knock to show that he was by
no means convinced, he broke with uncontrollable force from his
parent and the servant girl, and running into the street without
his hat, actually shook his fist at the coachman, and came back
again with a face as white, Mrs. Nixon says, looking about her for
a simile, as white as that ceiling. She never will forget his fury
that night, Never!

To this account Felix listens with a solemn face, occasionally
looking at you to see how it affects you, and when his mother has
made an end of it, adds that he looked at every coachman he met
for three weeks afterwards, in hopes that he might see the scoundrel;
whereupon Mrs. Nixon, with an exclamation of terror, requests to
know what he would have done to him if he *had* seen him, at which
Felix smiling darkly and clenching his right fist, she exclaims,
"Goodness gracious!" with a distracted air, and insists upon ex-
torting a promise that he never will on any account do anything
so rash, which her dutiful son—it being something more than three
years since the offence was committed—reluctantly concedes, and
his mother, shaking her head prophetically, fears with a sigh that
his spirit will lead him into something violent yet. The discourse
then, by an easy transition, turns upon the spirit which glows
within the bosom of Felix, upon which point Felix himself becomes
eloquent, and relates a thrilling anecdote of the time when he
used to sit up till two o'clock in the morning reading French, and
how his mother used to say, "Felix, you will make yourself ill, I
know you will;" and *he* used to say, "Mother, I don't care—I will
do it;" and how at last his mother privately procured a doctor to
come and see him, who declared, the moment he felt his pulse,
that if he had gone on reading one night more—only one night
more—he must have put a blister on each temple, and another
between his shoulders; and who, as it was, sat down upon the
instant, and writing a prescription for a blue pill, said it must
be taken immediately, or he wouldn't answer for the consequences. The recital of these and many other moving perils of the

like nature, constantly harrows up the feelings of Mr. Nixon's friends.

Mrs. Nixon has a tolerably extensive circle of female acquaintance, being a good-humoured, talkative, bustling little body, and to the unmarried girls among them she is constantly vaunting the virtues of her son, hinting that she will be a very happy person who wins him, but that they must mind their P's and Q's, for he is very particular, and terribly severe upon young ladies. At this last caution the young ladies resident in the same row, who happen to be spending the evening there, put their pocket-handkerchiefs before their mouths, and are troubled with a short cough; just then Felix knocks at the door, and his mother drawing the tea-table nearer the fire, calls out to him as he takes off his boots in the back parlour that he needn't mind coming in in his slippers, for there are only the two Miss Greys and Miss Thompson, and she is quite sure they will excuse *him*, and nodding to the two Miss Greys, she adds, in a whisper, that Julia Thompson is a great favourite with Felix, at which intelligence the short cough comes again, and Miss Thompson in particular is greatly troubled with it, till Felix coming in, very faint for want of his tea, changes the subject of discourse, and enables her to laugh out boldly and tell Amelia Grey not to be so foolish. Here they all three laugh, and Mrs. Nixon says they are giddy girls; in which stage of the proceedings, Felix, who has by this time refreshened himself with the grateful herb that "cheers but not inebriates," removes his cup from his countenance and says with a knowing smile, that all girls are; whereat his admiring mama pats him on the back and tells him not to be sly, which calls forth a general laugh from the young ladies, and another smile from Felix, who thinking he looks very sly indeed, is perfectly satisfied.

Tea being over, the young ladies resume their work, and Felix insists upon holding a skein of silk while Miss Thompson winds it on a card. This process having been performed to the satisfaction of all parties, he brings down his flute in compliance with a request from the youngest Miss Grey, and plays divers tunes out of a very small music-book till supper-time, when he is very facetious and talkative indeed. Finally, after half a tumberful of warm sherry and water, he gallantly puts on his goloshes over his slippers, and telling Miss Thompson's servant to run on first and get the door open, escorts that young lady to her house, five doors off: the Miss Greys who live in the next house but one stopping to peep with merry faces from their own door till he comes back again, when they call out "Very well, Mr. Felix," and trip into the passage with a laugh more musical than any flute that was ever played.

Felix is rather prim in his appearance, and perhaps a little priggish about his books and flute, and so forth, which have all their peculiar corners of peculiar shelves in his bed-room; indeed, all his female acquaintance (and they are good judges) have long ago set him down as a thorough old bachelor. He is a favourite with them however, in a certain way, as an honest, inoffensive, kind-hearted creature; and as his peculiarities harm nobody, not even himself, we are induced to hope that many who are not personally acquainted with him will take our good word in his behalf, and be content to leave him to a long continuance of his harmless existence.

THE POETICAL YOUNG GENTLEMAN

TIME was, and not very long ago either, when a singular epidemic raged among the young gentlemen, vast numbers of whom, under the influence of the malady, tore off their neckerchiefs, turned down their shirt collars, and exhibited themselves in the open streets with bare throats and dejected countenances, before the eyes of an astonished public. These were poetical young gentlemen. The custom was gradually found to be inconvenient, as involving the necessity of too much clean linen and too large washing bills, and these outward symptoms have consequently passed away; but we are disposed to think, notwithstanding, that the number of poetical young gentlemen is considerably on the increase.

We know a poetical young gentleman—a very poetical young gentleman. We do not mean to say that he is troubled with the gift of poesy in any remarkable degree, but his countenance is of a plaintive and melancholy cast, his manner is abstracted and bespeaks affliction of soul: he seldom has his hair cut, and often talks about being an outcast and wanting a kindred spirit; from which, as well as from many general observations in which he is wont to indulge, concerning mysterious impulses, and yearnings of the heart, and the supremacy of intellect gilding all earthly things with the glowing magic of immortal verse, it is clear to all his friends that he has been stricken poetical.

The favourite attitude of the poetical young gentleman is lounging on a sofa with his eyes fixed upon the ceiling, or sitting bolt upright in a high-backed chair, staring with very round eyes at the opposite wall. When he is in one of these positions, his mother, who is a worthy affectionate old soul, will give you a nudge to bespeak your attention without disturbing the abstracted one, and whisper, with a shake of the head, that John's imagination is at some extraordinary work or other, you may take her word for it. Hereupon John looks more fiercely intent upon vacancy than before, and suddenly snatching a pencil from his pocket, puts down three words, and a cross on the back of a card, sighs deeply, paces once or twice across the room, inflicts a most unmerciful slap upon his head, and walks moodily up to his dormitory.

The poetical young gentleman is apt to acquire peculiar notions of things too, which plain ordinary people, unblessed with a poetical obliquity of vision, would suppose to be rather distorted. For instance, when the sickening murder and mangling of a wretched woman was afforded delicious food wherewithal to gorge the insatiable curiosity of the public, our friend the poetical young gentleman was in ecstasies—not of disgust, but admiration. "Heavens!" cried the poetical young gentleman, "how grand; how great!" We ventured deferentially to inquire upon whom these epithets were bestowed: our humble thoughts oscillating between the police officer who found the criminal, and the lock-keeper who found the head. "Upon whom!" exclaimed the poetical young gentleman in a frenzy of poetry, "Upon whom should they be bestowed but upon the murderer!"—and thereupon it came out, in a fine torrent of eloquence, that the murderer was a great spirit, a bold creature full of daring and nerve, a man of dauntless heart and determined courage, and withal a great casuist and able reasoner, as was fully demonstrated in his philosophical colloquies with the great and noble of the land. We held our peace, and meekly signified our indisposition to controvert these opinions—firstly, because we were no match at quotation for the poetical young gentleman; and, secondly, because we felt it would be of little use our entering into any disputation, if we were: being perfectly convinced that the respectable and immortal hero in question is not the first and will not be the last hanged gentleman upon whom false sympathy or diseased curiosity will be plentifully expended.

This was a stern mystic flight of the poetical young gentleman. In his milder and softer moments he occasionally lays down his neckcloth, and pens stanzas, which sometimes find their way into a Lady's Magazine, or the "Poet's Corner" of some country news-paper; or which, in default of either vent for his genius, adorn the rainbow leaves of a lady's album. These are generally written upon some such occasions as contemplating the Bank of England by midnight, or beholding Saint Paul's in a snow storm; and when these gloomy objects fail to afford him inspiration, he pours forth his soul in a touching address to a violet, or a plaintive lament that he is no longer a child, but has gradually grown up.

The poetical young gentleman is fond of quoting passages from his favourite authors, who are all of the gloomy and desponding school. He has a great deal to say, too, about the world, and is much given to opining, especially if he has taken anything strong to drink, that there is nothing in it worth living for. He gives you to understand, however, that for the sake of society, he means to bear his part in the tiresome play, manfully resisting the gratifica-tion of his own strong desire to make a premature exit; and consoles himself with the reflection, that immortality has some chosen nook for himself and the other great spirits whom earth has chafed and wearied.

When the poetical young gentleman makes use of adjectives, they are all superlatives. Everything is of the grandest, greatest, noblest, mightiest, loftiest; or the lowest, meanest, obscurest, vilest, and most pitiful. He knows no medium: for enthusiasm is the soul of poetry; and who so enthusiastic as a poetical young gentleman? "Mr. Milkwash," says a young lady as she unlocks her album to receive the young gentleman's original impromptu contribution, "how very silent you are! I think you must be in love." "Love!" cries the poetical young gentleman, starting from his seat by the fire and terrifying the cat who scampers off at full speed, "Love! that burning consuming passion; that ardour of the soul, that fierce glowing of the heart. Love! The withering blighting influence of hope misplaced and affection slighted. Love did you say! Ha! ha! ha!"

With this, the poetical young gentleman laughs a laugh belonging only to poets and Mr. O. Smith of the Adelphi Theatre, and sits down, pen in hand, to throw off a page or two of verse in the biting, semi-atheistical demoniac style, which, like the poetical young gentleman himself, is full of sound and fury, signifying nothing.

THE FORMAL COUPLE

THE formal couple are the most prim, cold, immovable, and unsatisfactory people on the face of the earth. Their faces, voices, dress, house, furniture, walk, and manner, are all the essence of formality, unrelieved by one redeeming touch of frankness, heartiness, or nature.

Everything with the formal couple resolves itself into a matter of form. They don't call upon you on your account, but their own; not to see how you are, but to show how they are: it is not a ceremony to do honour to you, but to themselves,—not due to your position, but to theirs. If one of a friend's children die, the formal couple are as sure and punctual in sending to the house as the undertaker; if a friend's family be increased, the monthly nurse is not more attentive than they. The formal couple, in fact, joyfully seize all occasions of testifying their good-breeding and precise observance of the little usages of society; and for you, who are the means to this end, they care as much as a man does for the tailor who has enabled him to cut a figure, or a woman for the milliner who has assisted her to a conquest.

Having an extensive connexion among that kind of people who make acquaintances and eschew friends, the formal gentleman attends from time to time a great many funerals, to which he is formally invited, and to which he formally goes, as returning a call for the last time. Here his deportment is of the most faultless description; he knows the exact pitch of voice it is proper to assume, the sombre look he ought to wear, the melancholy tread which should be his gait for the day. He is perfectly acquainted with all the dreary courtesies to be observed in a mourning-coach; knows when to sigh, and when to hide his nose in the white handkerchief; and looks into the grave and shakes his head when the ceremony is concluded, with the sad formality of a mute.

"What kind of a funeral was it?" says the formal lady, when he returns home. "Oh!" replies the formal gentleman, "there never was such a gross and disgusting impropriety; there were no feathers." "No feathers!" cries the lady, as if on wings of black feathers dead people fly to Heaven, and, lacking them, they must of necessity go elsewhere. Her husband shakes his head; and further adds, that they had seed-cake instead of plum-cake, and that it was all white wine. "All white wine!" exclaims his wife. "Nothing but sherry and madeira," says the husband. "What! no port?" "Not a drop." No port, no plums, and no feathers! "You will recollect, my dear," says the formal lady, in a voice of stately reproof, "that when we first met this poor man who is now dead and gone, and he took that very strange course of addressing me at dinner without being previously introduced, I ventured to express my opinion that the family were quite ignorant of etiquette, and very imperfectly acquainted with the decencies of life. You have now had a good opportunity of judging for yourself, and all I have to say is, that I trust you will never go to a funeral *there* again." "My dear," replies the formal gentleman, "I never will." So the informal deceased is cut in his grave; and the formal couple, when they tell the story of the funeral, shake their heads, and wonder what some people's feelings *are* made of, and what their notions of propriety *can* be!

If the formal people have a family (which they sometimes have), they are not children, but little, pale, sour, sharp-nosed men and women; and so exquisitely brought up, that they might be very old dwarfs for anything that appeareth to the contrary. Indeed, they are so acquainted with forms and conventionalities, and conduct themselves with such strict decorum, that to see the little girl break a looking-glass in some wild outbreak, or the little boy kick his parents, would be to any visitor an unspeakable relief and consolation.

The formal couple are always sticklers for what is rigidly proper, and have a great readiness in detecting hidden impropriety of speech or thought, which by less scrupulous people would be wholly unsuspected. Thus, if they pay a visit to the theatre, they sit all night in a perfect agony lest anything improper or immoral should proceed from the stage; and if anything should happen to be said which admits of a double construction, they never fail to take it up directly, and to express by their looks the great outrage which their feelings have sustained. Perhaps this is their chief reason for absenting themselves almost entirely from places of public amusement. They go sometimes to the Exhibition of the Royal Academy; —but that is often more shocking than the stage itself, and the formal lady thinks that it really is high time Mr. Etty was prosecuted and made a public example of.

We made one at a christening party not long since, where there was amongst the guests a formal couple, who suffered the acutest torture from certain jokes, incidental to such an occasion, cut— and very likely dried also—by one of the godfathers; a red-faced elderly gentleman, who, being highly popular with the rest of the company, had it all his own way, and was in great spirits. It was at supper-time that this gentleman came out in full force. We— being of a grave and quiet demeanour—had been chosen to escort the formal lady down stairs, and, sitting beside her, had a favourable opportunity of observing her emotions.

We have a shrewd suspicion that, in the very beginning, and in the first blush—literally the first blush—of the matter, the formal lady had not felt quite certain whether the being present at such a ceremony, and encouraging, as it were, the public exhibition of a baby, was not an act involving some degree of indelicacy and impropriety; but certain we are, that when that baby's health was drunk, and allusions were made, by a grey-headed gentleman proposing it, to the time when he had dandled in his arms the young christian's mother,—certain we are that then the formal lady took the alarm, and recoiled from the old gentleman as from a hoary profligate. Still she bore it; she fanned herself with an indignant air, but still she bore it. A comic song was sung, involving a confession from some imaginary gentleman that he had kissed a female, and yet the formal lady bore it. But when at last, the health of the godfather before-mentioned being drunk, the godfather rose to return thanks, and in the course of his observations darkly hinted at babies yet unborn, and even contemplated the possibility of the subject of that festival having brothers and sisters, the formal lady could endure no more, but, bowing slightly round, and sweeping haughtily past the offender, left the room in tears, under the protection of the formal gentleman.

THE LOVING COUPLE

THERE cannot be a better practical illustration of the wise saw and ancient instance, that there may be too much of a good thing, than is presented by a loving couple. Undoubtedly it is meet and proper that two persons joined together in holy matrimony should be loving, and unquestionably it is pleasant to know and see that they are so; but there is a time for all things, and the couple who happen to be always in a loving state before company, are well nigh intolerable.

And in taking up this position we would have it distinctly understood that we do not seek alone the sympathy of bachelors, in whose objection to loving couples we recognise interested motives and personal considerations. We grant that to that unfortunate class of society there may be something very irritating, tantalising, and provoking, in being compelled to witness those gentle endearments and chaste interchanges which to loving couples are quite the ordinary business of life. But while we recognise the natural character of the prejudice to which these unhappy men are subject, we can neither receive their biassed evidence, nor address ourself to their inflamed and angered minds. Dispassionate experience is our only guide; and in these moral essays we seek no less to reform hymeneal offenders than to hold out a timely warning to all rising couples, and even to those who have not yet set forth upon their pilgrimage towards the matrimonial altar.

Let all couples, present or to come, therefore profit by the example of Mr. and Mrs. Leaver, themselves a loving couple in the first degree.

Mr. and Mrs. Leaver are pronounced by Mrs. Starling, a widow lady who lost her husband when she was young, and lost herself about the same time—for by her own count she has never since grown five years older—to be a perfect model of wedded felicity. "You would suppose," says the romantic lady, "that they were lovers only just now engaged. Never was such happiness! They are so tender, so affectionate, so attached to each other, so enamoured, that positively nothing can be more charming!"

"Augusta, my soul," says Mr. Leaver. "Augustus, my life," replies Mrs. Leaver. "Sing some little ballad, darling," quoth Mr. Leaver. "I couldn't, indeed, dearest," returns Mrs. Leaver.

"Do, my dove," says Mr. Leaver. "I couldn't possibly, my love," replies Mrs. Leaver; "and it's very naughty of you to ask me." "Naughty, darling!" cries Mr. Leaver. "Yes, very naughty, and very cruel," returns Mrs. Leaver, "for you know I have a sore throat, and that to sing would give me great pain. You're a monster, and I hate you. Go away!" Mrs. Leaver has said, "go away," because Mr. Leaver has tapped her under the chin: Mr. Leaver not doing as he is bid, but on the contrary, sitting down beside her, Mrs. Leaver slaps Mr. Leaver; and Mr. Leaver in return slaps Mrs. Leaver, and it being now time for all persons present to look the other way, they look the other way, and hear a still small sound as of kissing, at which Mrs. Starling is thoroughly enraptured, and whispers her neighbour that if all married couples were like that, what a heaven this earth would be!

The loving couple are at home when this occurs, and may be only three or four friends are present, but, unaccustomed to reserve upon this interesting point, they are pretty much the same abroad. Indeed, upon some occasions, such as a pic-nic or a water-party, their lovingness is even more developed, as we had an opportunity last summer of observing in person.

There was a great water-party made up to go to Twickenham and dine, and afterwards dance in an empty villa by the river side, hired expressly for the purpose. Mr. and Mrs. Leaver were of the company; and it was our fortune to have a seat in the same boat, which was an eight-oared galley, manned by amateurs, with a blue striped awning of the same pattern as their Guernsey shirts, and a dingy red flag of the same shade as the whiskers of the stroke oar. A coxswain being appointed, and all other matters adjusted, the eight gentlemen threw themselves into strong paroxysms, and pulled up with the tide, stimulated by the compassionate remarks of the ladies, who one and all exclaimed, that it seemed an immense exertion—as indeed it did. At first we raced the other boat, which came alongside in gallant style; but this being found an unpleasant amusement, as giving rise to a great quantity of splashing, and rendering the cold pies and other viands very moist, it was unanimously voted down, and we were suffered to shoot a-head, while the second boat followed ingloriously in our wake.

It was at this time that we first recognised Mr. Leaver. There were two firemen-watermen in the boat, lying by until somebody was exhausted; and one of them, who had taken upon himself the direction of affairs, was heard to cry in a gruff voice, "Pull away, number two,—give it her, number two,—take a long reach, number two,—now, number two, sir, think you're winning a boat." The greater part of the company had no doubt begun to wonder which of the striped Guernseys it might be that stood in need of such encouragement, when a stifled shriek from Mrs. Leaver confirmed the doubtful and informed the ignorant; and Mr. Leaver, still further disguised in a straw hat and no neckcloth, was observed to be in a fearful perspiration, and failing visibly. Nor was the general consternation diminished at this instant by the same gentleman, (in the performance of an accidental aquatic feat, termed "catching a crab") plunging suddenly backward, and displaying nothing of himself to the company, but two violently struggling legs. Mrs. Leaver shrieked again several times, and cried piteously— "Is he dead? Tell me the worst. Is he dead?"

Now, a moment's reflection might have convinced the loving wife, that unless her husband were endowed with some most surprising powers of muscular action, he never could be dead while he kicked so hard; but still Mrs. Leaver cried, "Is he dead? is he dead?" and still everybody else cried—"No, no, no," until such time as Mr. Leaver was replaced in a sitting posture, and his oar (which had been going through all kinds of wrong-headed performances on its own account) was once more put in his hand, by the exertions of the two firemen-watermen. Mrs. Leaver then exclaimed, "Augustus, my child, come to me;" and Mr. Leaver said, "Augusta, my love, compose yourself, I am not injured." But Mrs. Leaver cried again more piteously than before, "Augustus, my child, come to me;" and now the company generally, who seemed to be apprehensive that if Mr. Leaver remained where he was, he might contribute more than his proper share towards the drowning of the party, disinterestedly took part with Mrs. Leaver, and said he really ought to go, and that he was not strong enough for such violent exercise, and ought never to have undertaken it. Reluctantly, Mr. Leaver went, and laid himself down at Mrs. Leaver's feet, and Mrs. Leaver stooping over him, said, "Oh Augustus, how could you terrify me so?" and Mr. Leaver said, "Augusta, my sweet, I never meant to terrify you;" and Mrs. Leaver said, "You are faint, my dear;" and Mr. Leaver said, "I am rather so, my love;" and they were very loving indeed under Mrs. Leaver's veil, until at length Mr. Leaver came forth again, and pleasantly asked if he had not heard something said about bottled stout and sandwiches.

Mrs. Starling, who was one of the party, was perfectly delighted with this scene, and frequently murmured half-aside, "What a loving couple you are!" or, "How delightful it is to see man and wife so happy together!" To us she was quite poetical, (for we are a kind of cousins,) observing that hearts beating in unison like that made life a paradise of sweets; and that when kindred creatures were drawn together by sympathies so fine and delicate, what more than mortal happiness did not our souls partake! To all this we answered, "Certainly," or "Very true," or merely sighed, as the case might be. At every new act of the loving couple, the widow's admiration broke out afresh; and when Mrs. Leaver would not permit Mr. Leaver to keep his hat off, lest the sun should strike to his head, and give him a brain fever, Mrs. Starling actually shed tears, and said it reminded her of Adam and Eve.

The loving couple were thus loving all the way to Twickenham, but when we arrived there (by which time the amateur crew looked very thirsty and vicious) they were more playful than ever, for Mrs. Leaver threw stones at Mr. Leaver, and Mr. Leaver ran after Mrs. Leaver on the grass, in a most innocent and enchanting manner. At dinner, too, Mr. Leaver *would* steal Mrs. Leaver's tongue, and Mrs. Leaver *would* retaliate upon Mr. Leaver's fowl; and when Mrs. Leaver was going to take some lobster salad, Mr. Leaver wouldn't let her have any, saying that it made her ill, and she was always sorry for it afterwards, which afforded Mrs. Leaver an opportunity of pretending to be cross, and showing many other prettinesses. But this was merely the smiling surface of their loves, not the mighty depths of the stream, down to which the company, to say the truth, dived rather unexpectedly, from the following accident. It chanced that Mr. Leaver took upon himself to propose the bachelors who had first originated the notion of that entertainment, in doing which he affected to regret that he was no longer of their body himself, and pretended grievously to lament his fallen state. This Mrs. Leaver's feelings could not brook, even in jest, and consequently, exclaiming aloud, "He loves me not, he loves me not!" she fell in a very pitiable state into the arms of

Mrs. Starling, and, directly becoming insensible, was conveyed by that lady and her husband into another room. Presently Mr. Leaver came running back to know if there was a medical gentleman in company, and as there was, (in what company is there not?) both Mr. Leaver and the medical gentleman hurried away together.

The medical gentleman was the first who returned, and among his intimate friends he was observed to laugh and wink, and look as unmedical as might be; but when Mr. Leaver came back he was very solemn, and in answer to all inquiries, shook his head, and remarked that Augusta was far too sensitive to be trifled with—an opinion which the widow subsequently confirmed. Finding that she was in no imminent peril, however, the rest of the party betook themselves to dancing on the green, and very merry and happy they were, and a vast quantity of flirtation there was; the last circumstance being no doubt attributable, partly to the fineness of the weather, and partly to the locality, which is well-known to be favourable to all harmless recreations.

In the bustle of the scene, Mr. and Mrs. Leaver stole down to the boat, and disposed themselves under the awning, Mrs. Leaver reclining her head upon Mr. Leaver's shoulder, and Mr. Leaver grasping her hand with great fervour, and looking in her face from time to time with a melancholy and sympathetic aspect. The widow sat apart, feigning to be occupied with a book, but stealthily observing them from behind her fan; and the two firemen-watermen, smoking their pipes on the bank hard by, nudged each other, and grinned in enjoyment of the joke. Very few of the party missed the loving couple; and the few who did, heartily congratulated each other on their disappearance.

THE CONTRADICTORY COUPLE

ONE would suppose that two people who are to pass their whole lives together, and must necessarily be very often alone with each other, could find little pleasure in mutual contradiction; and yet what is more common than a contradictory couple?

The contradictory couple agree in nothing but contradiction. They return home from Mrs. Bluebottle's dinner-party, each in an opposite corner of the coach, and do not exchange a syllable until they have been seated for at least twenty minutes by the fire-side at home, when the gentleman, raising his eyes from the stove, all at once breaks silence:

"What a very extraordinary thing it is," says he, "that you *will* contradict, Charlotte?" "*I* contradict!" cries the lady, "but that's just like you." "What's like me?" says the gentleman sharply. "Saying that I contradict you," replies the lady. "Do you mean to say that you do *not* contradict me?" retorts the gentleman; "do you mean to say that you have not been contradicting me the whole of this day? Do you mean to tell me now, that you have not?" "I mean to tell you nothing of the kind," replies the lady quietly; "when you are wrong, of course I shall contradict you."

During this dialogue the gentleman has been taking his brandy-and-water on one side of the fire, and the lady, with her dressing-case on the table, has been curling her hair on the other. She now lets down her back hair, and proceeds to brush it; preserving at the same time an air of conscious rectitude and suffering virtue, which is intended to exasperate the gentleman—and does so.

"I do believe," he says, taking the spoon out of his glass, and tossing it on the table, "that of all the obstinate, positive, wrong-headed creatures that were ever born, you are the most so, Charlotte." "Certainly, certainly, have it your own way, pray. You see how much *I* contradict you," rejoins the lady. "Of course, you didn't contradict me at dinner-time—oh no, not you!" says the gentleman. "Yes I did," says the lady. "Oh, you did?" cries the gentleman; "you admit that?" "If you call that contradiction, I do," the lady answers; "and I say again, Edward, that when I know you are wrong, I will contradict you. I am not your slave." "Not my slave!" repeats the gentleman bitterly; "and you still mean to say that in the Blackburns' new house there are not more than fourteen doors, including the door of the wine-cellar!" "I mean to say," retorts the lady, beating time with her hair-brush on the palm of her hand, "that in that house there are fourteen doors and no more." "Well then—" cries the gentleman, rising in despair, and pacing the room with rapid strides. "By G——, this is enough to destroy a man's intellect, and drive him mad!"

By and by the gentleman comes-to a little, and passing his hand gloomily across his forehead, reseats himself in his former chair.

There is a long silence, and this time the lady begins. "I appealed to Mr. Jenkins, who sat next to me on the sofa in the drawing-room during tea—" "Morgan, you mean," interrupts the gentle-man. "I do not mean anything of the kind," answers the lady. "Now, by all that is aggravating and impossible to bear," cries the gentleman, clenching his hands and looking upwards in agony, "she is going to insist upon it that Morgan is Jenkins!" "Do you take me for a perfect fool?" exclaims the lady; "do you suppose I don't know the one from the other? Do you suppose I don't know that the man in the blue coat was Mr. Jenkins?" "Jenkins in a blue coat!" cries the gentleman with a groan; "Jenkins in a blue coat! a man who would suffer death rather than wear anything but brown!" "Do you dare to charge me with telling an untruth?" demands the lady, bursting into tears. "I charge you, ma'am," retorts the gentleman, starting up, "with being a monster of contradiction, a monster of aggravation, a— a— a— Jenkins in a blue coat! what have I done that I should be doomed to hear such statements!"

Expressing himself with great scorn and anguish, the gentleman takes up his candle and stalks off to bed, where feigning to be fast asleep when the lady comes up stairs drowned in tears, mur-muring lamentations over her hard fate and indistinct intentions of consulting her brothers, he undergoes the secret torture of hear-ing her exclaim between whiles, "I know there are only fourteen doors in the house, I know it was Mr. Jenkins, I know he had a blue coat on, and I would say it as positively as I do now, if they were the last words I had to speak!"

If the contradictory couple are blessed with children, they are not the less contradictory on that account. Master James and Miss Charlotte present themselves after dinner, and being in perfect good humour, and finding their parents in the same amiable state, augur from these appearances half a glass of wine a-piece and other extraordinary indulgences. But unfortunately, Master James, growing talkative upon such prospects, asks his mama how tall Mrs. Parsons is, and whether she is not six feet high; to which his mama replies, "Yes, she should think she was, for Mrs. Parsons is a very tall lady indeed; quite a giantess." "For Heaven's sake, Charlotte," cries her husband, "do not tell the child such pre-posterous nonsense. Six feet high!" "Well," replies the lady, "surely I may be permitted to have an opinion; my opinion is, that she is six feet high—at least six feet." "Now you know, Charlotte," retorts the gentleman sternly, "that that is *not* your opinion—that you have no such idea—and that you only say this for the sake of contradiction." "You are exceedingly polite," his wife replies; "to be wrong about such a paltry question as anybody's height, would be no great crime; but I say again, that I believe Mrs. Parsons to be six feet—more than six feet; nay, I believe you know her to be full six feet, and only say she is not, because I say she is." This taunt disposes the gentleman to become violent, but he checks himself, and is content to mutter, in a haughty tone, "Six feet—ha! ha! Mrs. Parsons six feet!" And the lady answers, "Yes, six feet. I am sure I am glad you are amused, and I'll say it again—six feet." Thus the subject gradually drops off, and the contradiction begins to be forgotten, when Master James, with some undefined notion of making himself agreeable, and putting things to rights again, unfortunately asks his mama what the moon's made of; which gives her occasion to say that he had better not ask her, for she is always wrong and never can be right; that he only exposes her to contradiction by asking any question of her; and that he had better ask his papa, who is infallible, and never can be wrong. Papa, smarting under this attack, gives a terrible pull at the bell, and says, that if the conversation is to proceed in this way, the children had better be removed. Removed they are, after a few tears and many struggles; and Pa, having looked at Ma sideways for a minute or two, with a baleful eye, draws his pocket-handkerchief over his face, and composes himself for his after-dinner nap.

The friends of the contradictory couple often deplore their frequent disputes, though they rather make light of them at the same time: observing, that there is no doubt they are very much attached to each other, and that they never quarrel except about trifles. But neither the friends of the contradictory couple, nor the contradictory couple themselves, reflect, that as the most stupendous objects in nature are but vast collections of minute particles, so the slightest and least considered trifles make up the sum of human happiness or misery.

THE COUPLE WHO DOTE UPON THEIR CHILDREN

THE couple who dote upon their children have usually a great many of them: six or eight at least. The children are either the healthiest in all the world, or the most unfortunate in existence. In either case, they are equally the theme of their doting parents, and equally a source of mental anguish and irritation to their doting parents' friends.

The couple who dote upon their children recognise no dates but those connected with their births, accidents, illnesses, or remarkable deeds. They keep a mental almanack with a vast number of Innocents' days, all in red letters. They recollect the last coronation, because on that day little Tom fell down the kitchen stairs; the anniversary of the Gunpowder Plot, because it was on the fifth of November that Ned asked whether wooden legs were made in heaven and cocked hats grew in gardens. Mrs. Whiffler will never cease to recollect the last day of the old year as long as she lives, for it was on that day that the baby had the four red spots on its nose which they took for measles: nor Christmas day, for twenty-one days after Christmas day the twins were born; nor Good Friday, for it was on a Good Friday that she was frightened by the donkey-cart when she was in the family way with Georgiana. The movable feasts have no motion for Mr. and Mrs. Whiffler, but remain pinned down tight and fast to the shoulders of some small child, from whom they can never be separated any more. Time was made, according to their creed, not for slaves but for girls and boys; the restless sands in his glass are but little children at play.

As we have already intimated, the children of this couple can know no medium. They are either prodigies of good health or prodigies of bad health; whatever they are, they must be prodigies. Mr. Whiffler must have to describe at his office such excruciating agonies constantly undergone by his eldest boy, as nobody else's eldest boy ever underwent; or he must be able to declare that there never was a child endowed with such amazing health, such an indomitable constitution, and such a cast-iron frame, as his child. His children must be, in some respect or other, above and beyond the children of all other people. To such an extent is this feeling pushed, that we were once slightly acquainted with a lady and gentleman who carried their heads so high and became so proud after their youngest child fell out of a two-pair-of-stairs window without hurting himself much, that the greater part of their friends were obliged to forego their acquaintance.

But perhaps this may be an extreme case, and one not justly entitled to be considered as a precedent of general application.

If a friend happen to dine in a friendly way with one of these couples who dote upon their children, it is nearly impossible for him to divert the conversation from their favourite topic. Everything reminds Mr. Whiffler of Ned, or Mrs. Whiffler of Mary Anne, or of the time before Ned was born, or the time before Mary Anne was thought of. The slightest remark, however harmless in itself, will awaken slumbering recollections of the twins. It is impossible to steer clear of them. They will come uppermost, let the poor man do what he may. Ned has been known to be lost sight of for half an hour, Dick has been forgotten, the name of Mary Anne has not been mentioned, but the twins will out. Nothing can keep down the twins.

"It's a very extraordinary thing, Saunders," says Mr. Whiffler to the visitor, "but—you have seen our little babies, the—the—twins?" The friend's heart sinks within him as he answers, "Oh, yes—often." "Your talking of the Pyramids," says Mr. Whiffler, quite as a matter of course, "reminds me of the twins. It's a very extraordinary thing about those babies—what colour should you say their eyes were?" "Upon my word," the friend stammers, "I hardly know how to answer"—the fact being, that except as the friend does not remember to have heard of any departure from the ordinary course of nature in the instance of these twins, they might have no eyes at all for aught he has observed to the contrary. "You wouldn't say they were red, I suppose?" says Mr. Whiffler. The friend hesitates, and rather thinks they are; but inferring from the expression of Mr. Whiffler's face that red is not the colour, smiles with some confidence, and says, "No, no! very different from that." "What should you say to blue?" says Mr. Whiffler. The friend glances at him, and, observing a different expression in his face, ventures to say, "I should say they *were* blue—a decided blue." "To be sure!" cries Mr. Whiffler, triumphantly, "I knew you would! But what should you say if I was to tell you that the boy's eyes are blue and the girl's hazel, eh?" "Impossible!"

exclaims the friend, not at all knowing why it should be impossible. "A fact, notwithstanding," cries Mr. Whiffler; "and let me tell you, Saunders, *that*'s not a common thing in twins, or a circumstance that'll happen every day."

In this dialogue Mrs. Whiffler, as being deeply responsible for the twins, their charms and singularities, has taken no share; but she now relates, in broken English, a witticism of little Dick's bearing upon the subject just discussed, which delights Mr. Whiffler beyond measure, and causes him to declare that he would have sworn that was Dick's if he had heard it anywhere. Then he requests that Mrs. Whiffler will tell Saunders what Tom said about mad bulls; and Mrs. Whiffler relating the anecdote, a discussion ensues upon the different character of Tom's wit and Dick's wit, from which it appears that Dick's humour is of a lively turn, while Tom's style is the dry and caustic. This discussion being enlivened by various illustrations, lasts a long time, and is only stopped by Mrs. Whiffler instructing the footman to ring the nursery bell, as the children were promised that they should come down and taste the pudding.

The friend turns pale when this order is given, and paler still when it is followed up by a great pattering on the staircase, (not unlike the sound of rain upon a skylight,) a violent bursting open of the dining-room door, and the tumultuous appearance of six small children, closely succeeded by a strong nursery-maid with a twin in each arm. As the whole eight are screaming, shouting, or kicking—some influenced by a ravenous appetite, some by a horror of the stranger, and some by a conflict of the two feelings—a pretty long space elapses before all their heads can be ranged round the table and anything like order restored; in bringing about which happy state of things both the nurse and footman are severely scratched. At length Mrs. Whiffler is heard to say, "Mr. Saunders, shall I give you some pudding?" A breathless silence ensues, and sixteen small eyes are fixed upon the guest in expectation of his reply. A wild shout of joy proclaims that he has said, "No, thank you." Spoons are waved in the air, legs appear above the table-cloth in uncontrollable ecstacy, and eighty short fingers dabble in damson syrup.

While the pudding is being disposed of, Mr. and Mrs. Whiffler look on with beaming countenances; and Mr. Whiffler nudging his friend Saunders, begs him take notice of Tom's eyes, or Dick's chin, or Ned's nose, or Mary Anne's hair, or Emily's figure, or little Bob's calves, or Fanny's mouth, or Cary's head, as the case may be. Whatever the attention of Mr. Saunders is called to, Mr. Saunders admires of course; though he is rather confused about the sex of the youngest branches and looks at the wrong children, turning to a girl when Mr. Whiffler directs his attention to a boy, and falling into raptures with a boy when he ought to be enchanted with a girl. Then the dessert comes, and there is a vast deal of scrambling after fruit, and sudden spirting forth of juice out of tight oranges into infant eyes, and much screeching and wailing in consequence. At length it becomes time for Mrs. Whiffler to retire, and all the children are by force of arms compelled to kiss and love Mr. Saunders before going up stairs, except Tom, who, lying on his back in the hall, proclaims that Mr. Saunders "is a naughty beast;" and Dick, who, having drunk his father's wine when he was looking another way, is found to be intoxicated and is carried out, very limp and helpless.

Mr. Whiffler and his friend are left alone together, but Mr. Whiffler's thoughts are still with his family, if his family are not with him. "Saunders," says he, after a short silence, "if you please, we'll drink Mrs. Whiffler and the children." Mr. Saunders feels this to be a reproach against himself for not proposing the same sentiment, and drinks it in some confusion. "Ah!" Mr. Whiffler sighs, "these children, Saunders, make one quite an old man." Mr. Saunders thinks that if they were his, they would make him a very old man; but he says nothing. "And yet," pursues Mr. Whiffler, "what can equal domestic happiness? what can equal the engaging ways of children? Saunders, why don't *you* get married?" Now, this is an embarrassing question, because Mr. Saunders has been thinking that if he had at any time entertained matrimonial designs, the revelation of that day would surely have routed them for ever. "I am glad, however," says Mr. Whiffler, "that you *are* a bachelor,—glad on one account, Saunders; a selfish one, I admit. Will you do Mrs. Whiffler and myself a favour?" Mr. Saunders is surprised—evidently surprised; but he replies, "with the greatest pleasure." "Then, will you, Saunders," says Mr. Whiffler, in an impressive manner, "will you cement and consolidate our friendship by coming into the family (so to speak) as a godfather?" "I shall be proud and delighted," replies Mr. Saunders: "which of the children is it? really, I thought they were all christened; or—" "Saunders," Mr. Whiffler interposes, "they *are* all christened; you are right. The fact is, that Mrs. Whiffler is—in short, we expect another." "Not a ninth!" cries the friend, all aghast at the idea. "Yes, Saunders," rejoins Mr. Whiffler solemnly, "a ninth. Did we drink Mrs. Whiffler's health? Let us drink it again, Saunders, and wish her well over it!"

Doctor Johnson used to tell a story of a man who had but one idea, which was a wrong one. The couple who dote upon their children are in the same predicament: at home or abroad, at all times, and in all places, their thoughts are bound up in this one subject, and have no sphere beyond. They relate the clever things their offspring say or do, and weary every company with their prolixity and absurdity. Mr. Whiffler takes a friend by the button at the street corner on a windy day to tell him a *bon mot* of his youngest boy's; and Mrs. Whiffler, calling to see a sick acquaintance, entertains her with a cheerful account of all her own past sufferings and present expectations. In such cases the sins of the fathers indeed descend upon the children; for people soon come to regard them as predestined little bores. The couple who dote upon their children cannot be said to be actuated by a general love for these engaging little people (which would be a great excuse); for they are apt to underrate and entertain a jealousy of any children but their own. If they examined their own hearts, they would, perhaps, find at the bottom of all this, more self-love and egotism than they think of. Self-love and egotism are bad qualities, of which the unrestrained exhibition, though it may be sometimes amusing, never fails to be wearisome and unpleasant. Couples who dote upon their children, are best avoided.

THE NICE LITTLE COUPLE

A CUSTOM once prevailed in old-fashioned circles, that when a lady or gentleman was unable to sing a song, he or she should enliven the company with a story. As we find ourself in the predicament of not being able to describe (to our own satisfaction) nice little couples in the abstract, we purpose telling in this place a little story about a nice little couple of our acquaintance.

Mr. and Mrs. Chirrup are the nice little couple in question. Mr. Chirrup has the smartness, and something of the brisk, quick manner of a small bird. Mrs. Chirrup is the prettiest of all little women, and has the prettiest little figure conceivable. She has the neatest little foot, and the softest little voice, and the pleasantest little smile, and the tidiest little curls, and the brightest little eyes, and the quietest little manner, and is, in short, altogether one of the most engaging of all little women, dead or alive. She is a condensation of all the domestic virtues,—a pocket edition of the young man's best companion,—a little woman at a very high pressure, with an amazing quantity of goodness and usefulness in an exceedingly small space. Little as she is, Mrs. Chirrup might furnish forth matter for the moral equipment of a score of house-wives, six feet high in their stockings—if, in the presence of ladies, we may be allowed the expression—and of corresponding robustness.

Nobody knows all this better than Mr. Chirrup, though he rather takes on that he don't. Accordingly he is very proud of his better-half, and evidently considers himself, as all other people consider him, rather fortunate in having her to wife. We say evidently, because Mr. Chirrup is a warm-hearted little fellow; and if you catch his eye when he has been slily glancing at Mrs. Chirrup in company, there is a certain complacent twinkle in it, accompanied, perhaps, by a half-expressed toss of the head, which as clearly indicates what has been passing in his mind as if he had put it into words, and shouted it out through a speaking-trumpet. Moreover, Mr. Chirrup has a particularly mild and bird-like manner of calling Mrs. Chirrup "my dear;" and—for he is of a jocose turn—of cutting little witticisms upon her, and making her the subject of various harmless pleasantries, which nobody enjoys more thoroughly than Mrs. Chirrup herself. Mr. Chirrup, too, now and then affects to deplore his bachelor-days, and to bemoan (with a marvellously contented and smirking face) the loss of his freedom, and the sorrow of his heart at having been taken captive by Mrs. Chirrup—all of which circumstances combine to show the secret triumph and satisfaction of Mr. Chirrup's soul.

We have already had occasion to observe that Mrs. Chirrup is an incomparable housewife. In all the arts of domestic arrangement and management, in all the mysteries of confectionary-making, pickling, and preserving, never was such a thorough adept as that

nice little body. She is, besides, a cunning worker in muslin and
fine linen, and a special hand at marketing to the very best advantage. But if there be one branch of housekeeping in which she
excels to an utterly unparalleled and unprecedented extent, it is
in the important one of carving. A roast goose is universally allowed to be the great stumbling-block in the way of young aspirants
to perfection in this department of science; many promising carvers,
beginning with legs of mutton, and preserving a good reputation
through fillets of veal, sirloins of beef, quarters of lamb, fowls,
and even ducks, have sunk before a roast goose, and lost caste and
character for ever. To Mrs. Chirrup the resolving a goose into its
smallest component parts is a pleasant pastime—a practical joke—
a thing to be done in a minute or so, without the smallest interruption to the conversation of the time. No handing the dish over to
an unfortunate man upon her right or left, no wild sharpening of
the knife, no hacking and sawing at an unruly joint, no noise, no
splash, no heat, no leaving off in despair; all is confidence and
cheerfulness. The dish is set upon the table, the cover is removed;
for an instant, and only an instant, you observe that Mrs. Chirrup's
attention is distracted; she smiles, but heareth not. You proceed
with your story; meanwhile the glittering knife is slowly upraised,
both Mrs. Chirrup's wrists are slightly but not ungracefully agitated, she compresses her lips for an instant, then breaks into a
smile, and all is over. The legs of the bird slide gently down into
a pool of gravy, the wings seem to melt from the body, the breast
separates into a row of juicy slices, the smaller and more complicated parts of his anatomy are perfectly developed, a cavern
of stuffing is revealed, and the goose is gone!

To dine with Mr. and Mrs. Chirrup is one of the pleasantest
things in the world. Mr. Chirrup has a bachelor friend, who lived
with him in his own days of single blessedness, and to whom he is
mightily attached. Contrary to the usual custom, this bachelor
friend is no less a friend of Mrs. Chirrup's, and, consequently,
whenever you dine with Mr. and Mrs. Chirrup, you meet the
bachelor friend. It would put any reasonably-conditioned mortal
into good humour to observe the unanimity which subsists between
these three; but there is a quiet welcome dimpling in Mrs. Chirrup's
face, a bustling hospitality oozing as it were out of the waistcoat-
pockets of Mr. Chirrup, and a patronising enjoyment of their

cordiality and satisfaction on the part of the bachelor friend, which is quite delightful. On these occasions Mr. Chirrup usually takes an opportunity of rallying the friend on being single, and the friend retorts upon Mr. Chirrup for being married, at which moments some single young ladies present are like to die of laughter; and we have more than once observed them bestow looks upon the friend, which convinces us that his position is by no means a safe one, as, indeed, we hold no bachelor's to be who visits married friends, and cracks jokes on wedlock, for certain it is that such men walk among traps and nets and pitfalls innumerable, and often find themselves down upon their knees at the altar rails, taking M. or N. for their wedded wives before they knew anything about the matter.

However, this is no business of Mr. Chirrup's, who talks, and laughs, and drinks his wine, and laughs again, and talks more, until it is time to repair to the drawing-room, where, coffee served over and over, Mrs. Chirrup prepares for a round game, by sorting the nicest possible little fish into the nicest possible little pools, and calling Mr. Chirrup to assist her, which Mr. Chirrup does. As they stand side by side, you find that Mr. Chirrup is the least possible shadow of a shade taller than Mrs. Chirrup, and that they are the neatest and best-matched little couple that can be, which the chances are ten to one against your observing with such effect at any other time, unless you see them in the street arm-in-arm, or meet them some rainy day trotting along under a very small umbrella. The round game (at which Mr. Chirrup is the merriest of the party) being done and over, in course of time a nice little tray appears, on which is a nice little supper; and when that is finished likewise, and you have said good night, you find yourself repeating a dozen times as you ride home, that there never was such a nice little couple as Mr. and Mrs. Chirrup.

Whether it is that pleasant qualities, being packed more closely in small bodies than in large, come more readily to hand than when they are diffused over a wider space, and have to be gathered together for use, we don't know, but, as a general rule,—strengthened like all other rules by its exceptions,—we hold that little people are sprightly and good-natured. The more sprightly and good-natured people we have, the better; therefore, let us wish well to all nice little couples, and hope that they may increase and multiply.

THE NOBLE SAVAGE

TO come to the point at once, I beg to say that I have not the least belief in the Noble Savage. I consider him a prodigious nuisance, and an enormous superstition. His calling rum fire-water, and me a pale face, wholly fail to reconcile me to him. I don't care what he calls me. I call him a savage, and I call a savage a something highly desirable to be civilised off the face of the earth. I think a mere gent (which I take to be the lowest form of civilisation) better than a howling, whistling, clucking, stamping, jumping, tearing savage. It is all one to me, whether he sticks a fish-bone through his visage, or bits of trees through the lobes of his ears, or birds' feathers in his head; whether he flattens his hair between two boards, or spreads his nose over the breadth of his face, or drags his lower lip down by great weights, or blackens his teeth, or knocks them out, or paints one cheek red and the other blue, or tattoos himself, or oils himself, or rubs his body with fat, or crimps it with knives. Yielding to whichsoever of these agreeable eccentricities, he is a savage—cruel, false, thievish, murderous; addicted more or less to grease, entrails, and beastly customs; a wild animal with the questionable gift of boasting; a conceited, tiresome, bloodthirsty, monotonous humbug.

Yet it is extraordinary to observe how some people will talk about him, as they talk about the good old times; how they will regret his disappearance, in the course of this world's development, from such and such lands where his absence is a blessed relief and an indispensable preparation for the sowing of the very first seeds of any influence that can exalt humanity; how, even with the evidence of himself before them, they will either be determined to believe, or will suffer themselves to be persuaded into believing, that he is something which their five senses tell them he is not.

There was Mr. Catlin, some few years ago, with his Ojibbeway Indians. Mr. Catlin was an energetic earnest man, who had lived among more tribes of Indians than I need reckon up here, and who had written a picturesque and glowing book about them. With his party of Indians squatting and spitting on the table before him, or dancing their miserable jigs after their own dreary manner, he called, in all good faith, upon his civilised audience to take notice of their symmetry and grace, their perfect limbs, and the exquisite expression of their pantomime; and his civilised audience, in all good faith, complied and admired. Whereas, as mere animals, they were wretched creatures, very low in the scale and very poorly formed; and as men and women possessing any power of truthful dramatic expression by means of action, they were no better than the chorus at an Italian Opera in England— and would have been worse if such a thing were possible.

Mine are no new views of the noble savage. The greatest writers on natural history found him out long ago. BUFFON knew what he was, and showed why he is the sulky tyrant that he is to his women, and how it happens (Heaven be praised!) that his race is spare in numbers. For evidence of the quality of his moral nature, pass himself for a moment and refer to his "faithful dog." Has he ever improved a dog, or attached a dog, since his nobility first ran wild in woods, and was brought down (at a very long shot) by POPE? Or does the animal that is the friend of man always degenerate in his low society?

It is not the miserable nature of the noble savage that is the new thing; it is the whimpering over him with maudlin admiration, and the affecting to regret him, and the drawing of any comparison of advantage between the blemishes of civilisation and the tenor of his swinish life. There may have been a change now and then in those diseased absurdities, but there is none in him.

Think of the Bushmen. Think of the two men and the two women who have been exhibited about England for some years. Are the majority of persons—who remember the horrid little leader of that party in his festering bundle of hides, with his filth and his antipathy to water, and his straddled legs, and his odious eyes shaded by his brutal hand, and his cry of "Qu-u-u-u-aaa!" (Bosjes-man for something desperately insulting I have no doubt)—con-scious of an affectionate yearning towards that noble savage, or is it idiosyncratic in me to abhor, detest, abominate, and abjure him? I have no reserve on this subject, and will frankly state that, setting aside that stage of the entertainment when he counter-feited the death of some creature he had shot, by laying his head on his hand and shaking his left leg—at which time I think it would have been justifiable homicide to slay him—I have never seen that group sleeping, smoking, and expectorating round their brazier, but I have sincerely desired that something might happen to the charcoal smouldering therein, which would cause the immediate suffocation of the whole of the noble strangers.

There is at present a party of Zulu Kaffirs exhibiting at the St. George's Gallery, Hyde Park Corner, London. These noble savages are represented in a most agreeable manner; they are seen in an elegant theatre, fitted with appropriate scenery of great beauty, and they are described in a very sensible and unpretending lecture, delivered with a modesty which is quite a pattern to all similar exponents. Though extremely ugly, they are much better shaped than such of their predecessors as I have referred to; and they are rather picturesque to the eye, though far from odoriferous to the nose. What a visitor left to his own interpretings and imaginings might suppose these noblemen to be about, when they give vent to that pantomimic expression which is quite settled to be the natural gift of the noble savage, I cannot possibly conceive; for it is so much too luminous for my personal civilisation that it conveys no idea to my mind beyond a general stamping, ramping, and raving, remarkable (as everything in savage life is) for its dire uniformity. But let us—with the interpreter's assistance, of which I for one stand so much in need—see what the noble savage does in Zulu Kaffirland.

The noble savage sets a king to reign over him, to whom he submits his life and limbs without a murmur or question, and whose whole life is passed chin deep in a lake of blood; but who, after killing incessantly, is in his turn killed by his relations and friends, the moment a gray hair appears on his head. All the noble savage's wars with his fellow-savages (and he takes no pleasure in anything else) are wars of extermination—which is the best thing I know of him, and the most comfortable to my mind when I look at him. He has no moral feelings of any kind, sort, or description; and his "mission" may be summed up as simply diabolical.

The ceremonies with which he faintly diversifies his life are, of course, of a kindred nature. If he wants a wife he appears before the kennel of the gentleman whom he has selected for his father-in-law, attended by a party of male friends of a very strong flavour, who screech and whistle and stamp an offer of so many cows for the young lady's hand. The chosen father-in-law—also supported by a high-flavoured party of male friends—screeches, whistles, and yells (being seated on the ground he can't stamp) that there never was such a daughter in the market as his daughter, and that

he must have six more cows. The son-in-law and his select circle
of backers screech, whistle, stamp, and yell in reply, that they will
give three more cows. The father-in-law (an old deluder, overpaid
at the beginning) accepts four, and rises to bind the bargain. The
whole party, the young lady included, then falling into epileptic
convulsions, and screeching, whistling, stamping, and yelling together—and nobody taking any notice of the young lady (whose
charms are not to be thought of without a shudder)—the noble
savage is considered married, and his friends make demoniacal
leaps at him by way of congratulation.

When the noble savage finds himself a little unwell, and mentions the circumstance to his friends, it is immediately perceived
that he is under the influence of witchcraft. A learned personage,
called an Imyanger or Witch Doctor, is immediately sent for to
Nooker the Umtargartie, or smell out the witch. The male inhabitants of the kraal being seated on the ground, the learned
doctor, got up like a grizzly bear, appears, and administers a dance
of a most terrific nature, during the exhibition of which remedy he
incessantly gnashes his teeth, and howls:—"I am the original
physician to Nooker the Umtargartie. Yow yow yow! No connexion with any other establishment. Till till till! All other Umtargarties are feigned Umtargarties, Boroo Boroo! but I perceive
here a genuine and real Umtargartie, Hoosh Hoosh Hoosh! in whose
blood I, the original Imyanger and Nookerer, Blizzerum Boo! will
wash these bear's claws of mine. O yow yow yow!" All this time the
learned physician is looking out among the attentive faces for some
unfortunate man who owes him a cow, or who has given him any
small offence, or against whom, without offence, he has conceived
a spite. Him he never fails to Nooker as the Umtargartie, and he
is instantly killed. In the absence of such an individual, the usual
practice is to Nooker the quietest and most gentlemanly person in
company. But the nookering is invariably followed on the spot by
the butchering.

Some of the noble savages in whom Mr. Catlin was so strongly
interested, and the diminution of whose numbers, by rum and
small-pox, greatly affected him, had a custom not unlike this,
though much more appalling and disgusting in its odious details.

The women being at work in the fields, hoeing the Indian corn,
and the noble savage being asleep in the shade, the chief has some-

times the condescension to come forth, and lighten the labour by looking at it. On these occasions he seats himself in his own savage chair, and is attended by his shield-bearer: who holds over his head a shield of cowhide—in shape like an immense mussel shell— fearfully and wonderfully, after the manner of a theatrical super- numerary. But lest the great man should forget his greatness in the contemplation of the humble works of agriculture, there sud- denly rushes in a poet, retained for the purpose, called a Praiser. This literary gentleman wears a leopard's head over his own, and a dress of tigers' tails; he has the appearance of having come ex- press on his hind legs from the Zoological Gardens; and he incon- tinently strikes up the chief's praises, plunging and tearing all the while. There is a frantic wickedness in this brute's manner of worry- ing the air, and gnashing out, "O what a delightful chief he is! O what a delicious quantity of blood he sheds! O how majestically he laps it up! O how charmingly cruel he is! O how he tears the flesh of his enemies and crunches the bones! O how like the tiger and the leopard and the wolf and the bear he is! O, row row row row, how fond I am of him!"—which might tempt the Society of Friends to charge at a hand-gallop into the Swartz-Kop location and exterminate the whole kraal.

When war is afoot among the noble savages—which is always— the chief holds a council to ascertain whether it is the opinion of his brothers and friends in general that the enemy shall be ex- terminated. On this occasion, after the performance of an Umse- beuza, or war song,—which is exactly like all the other songs,— the chief makes a speech to his brothers and friends, arranged in single file. No particular order is observed during the delivery of this address, but every gentleman who finds himself excited by the subject, instead of crying "Hear, hear!" as is the custom with us, darts from the rank and tramples out the life, or crushes the skull, or mashes the face, or scoops out the eyes, or breaks the limbs, or performs a whirlwind of atrocities on the body, of an imaginary enemy. Several gentlemen becoming thus excited at once, and pounding away without the least regard to the orator, that illustrious person is rather in the position of an orator in an Irish House of Commons. But, several of these scenes of savage life bear a strong generic resemblance to an Irish election, and I think would be extremely well received and understood at Cork.

In all these ceremonies the noble savage holds forth to the utmost possible extent about himself; from which (to turn him to some civilised account) we may learn, I think, that as Egotism is one of the most offensive and contemptible littlenesses a civilised man can exhibit, so it is really incompatible with the interchange of ideas; inasmuch as if we all talked about ourselves we should soon have no listeners, and must be all yelling and screeching at once on our own separate accounts; making society hideous. It is my opinion that if we retained in us anything of the noble savage, we could not get rid of it too soon. But the fact is clearly otherwise. Upon the wife and dowry question, substituting coin for cows, we have assuredly nothing of the Zulu Kaffir left. The endurance of despotism is one great distinguishing mark of a savage always. The improving world has quite got the better of that too. In like manner, Paris is a civilised city, and the Théâtre Français a highly civilised theatre; and we shall never hear, and never have heard in these later days (of course) of the Praiser *there*. No, no, civilised poets have better work to do. As to Nookering Umtargarties, there are no pretended Umtargarties in Europe, and no European Powers to Nooker them; that would be mere spydom, subornation, small malice, superstition, and false pretence. And as to private Umtargarties, are we not in the year eighteen hundred and fifty-three, with spirits rapping at our doors?

To include as I began. My position is, that if we have anything to learn from the Noble Savage, it is what to avoid. His virtues are a fable; his happiness is a delusion; his nobility, nonsense. We have no greater justification for being cruel to the miserable object, than for being cruel to a WILLIAM SHAKESPEARE or an ISAAC NEWTON; but he passes away before an immeasurably better and higher power than ever ran wild in any earthly woods, and the world will be all the better when his place knows him no more.

NIGHT WALKS

SOME years ago, a temporary inability to sleep, referable to a distressing impression, caused me to walk about the streets all night, for a series of several nights. The disorder might have taken a long time to conquer, if it had been faintly experimented on in bed; but it was soon defeated by the brisk treatment of getting up directly after lying down, and going out, and coming home tired at sunrise.

In the course of those nights, I finished my education in a fair amateur experience of houselessness. My principal object being to get through the night, the pursuit of it brought me into sympathetic relations with people who have no other object every night in the year.

The month was March, and the weather damp, cloudy, and cold. The sun not rising before half-past five, the night perspective looked sufficiently long at half-past twelve: which was about my time for confronting it.

The restlessness of a great city, and the way in which it tumbles and tosses before it can get to sleep, formed one of the first entertainments offered to the contemplation of us houseless people. It lasted about two hours. We lost a great deal of companionship when the late public-houses turned their lamps out, and when the potmen thrust the last brawling drunkards into the street; but stray vehicles and stray people going home were left us, after that. If we were very lucky, a policeman's rattle sprang and a fray turned up; but, in general, surprisingly little of this diversion was provided. Except in the Haymarket, which is the worst kept part of London, and about Kent-street in the Borough, and along a portion of the line of the Old Kent-road, the peace was seldom violently broken. But it was always the case that London, as if in imitation of individual citizens belonging to it, had expiring fits and starts of restlessness. After all seemed quiet, if one cab rattled by, half a dozen would surely follow; and Houselessness even observed that intoxicated people appeared to be magnetically attracted towards each other, so that we knew when we saw one drunken object staggering against the shutters of a shop, that another drunken object would probably stagger up before five minutes were out, to fraternise or fight with it. When we made a divergence from the regular species of drunkard, the thin-armed puff-faced leaden-lipped gin-drinker, and encountered a rarer specimen of a more decent appearance, fifty to one but that specimen was dressed in soiled mourning. As the street experience in the night, so the street experience in the day; the common folk who come unexpectedly into a little property, come unexpectedly into a deal of liquor.

At length these flickering sparks would die away, worn out— the last veritable sparks of waking life trailed from some late pieman or hot potato man—and London would sink to rest. And then the yearning of the houseless mind would be for any sign of company, any lighted place, any movement, anything suggestive of any one being up—nay, even so much as awake, for the houseless eye looked out for lights in windows.

Walking the streets under the pattering rain, Houselessness would walk and walk and walk, seeing nothing but the interminable tangle of streets, save at a corner, here and there, two policemen in conversation, or the sergeant or inspector looking after his men. Now and then in the night—but rarely—Houselessness would become aware of a furtive head peering out of a doorway a few yards before him, and, coming up with the head, would find a man standing bolt upright to keep within the doorway's shadow, and evidently intent upon no particular service to society. Under a kind of fascination, and in a ghostly silence suitable to the time, Houselessness and this gentleman would eye one another from head to foot, and so, without exchange of speech, part, mutually suspicious. Drip, drip, drip, from ledge and coping, splash from pipes and water-spouts, and by-and-by the houseless shadow would fall upon the stones that pave the way to Waterloo-bridge; it being in the houseless mind to have a halfpennyworth of excuse for saying "Good night" to the toll-keeper, and catching a glimpse of his fire. A good fire and a good great-coat and a good woollen neck-shawl, were comfortable things to see in conjunction with the toll-keeper; also his brisk wakefulness was excellent company when he rattled the change of halfpence down upon that metal table of his, like a man who defied the night, with all its sorrowful thoughts, and didn't care for the coming of dawn. There was need of encouragement on the threshold of the bridge, for the bridge was dreary. The chopped up murdered man, had not been lowered with a rope over the parapet when those nights were; he was alive, and slept then quietly enough most likely, and undisturbed by any dream of where he was to come. But the river had an awful look, the buildings on the banks were muffled in black shrouds, and the reflected lights seemed to originate deep in the water, as if the spectres of suicides were holding them to show where they went down. The wild moon and clouds were as restless as an evil conscience in a tumbled bed, and the very shadow of the immensity of London seemed to lie oppressively upon the river.

Between the bridge and the two great theatres, there was but the distance of a few hundred paces, so the theatres came next. Grim and black within, at night, those great dry Wells, and lonesome to imagine, with the rows of faces faded out, the lights extinguished, and the seats all empty. One would think that nothing in them knew itself at such a time but Yorick's skull. In one of my night walks, as the church steeples were shaking the March wind and rain with the strokes of Four, I passed the outer boundary of one of these great deserts, and entered it. With a dim lantern in my hand, I groped my well-known way to the stage and looked over the orchestra—which was like a great grave dug for a time of pestilence—into the void beyond. A dismal cavern of an immense aspect, with the chandelier gone dead like everything else, and nothing visible through mist and fog and space, but tiers of winding-sheets. The ground at my feet where, when last there, I had seen the peasantry of Naples dancing among the vines, reckless of the burning mountain which threatened to overwhelm them, was now in possession of a strong serpent of engine-hose, watchfully lying in wait for the serpent Fire, and ready to fly at it if it showed its forked tongue. A ghost of a watchman carrying a faint corpse-candle, haunted the distant upper gallery and flitted away. Retiring within the proscenium, and holding my light above my head towards the rolled-up curtain—green no more, but black as ebony—my sight lost itself in a gloomy vault, showing faint indications in it of a shipwreck of canvas and cordage. Methought I felt much as a diver might, at the bottom of the sea.

In those small hours when there was no movement in the streets, it afforded matter for reflection to take Newgate in the way, and, touching its rough stone, to think of the prisoners in their sleep, and then to glance in at the lodge over the spiked wicket, and see the fire and light of the watching turnkeys, on the white wall. Not an inappropriate time either to linger by that wicked little Debtor's Door—shutting tighter than any other door one ever saw—which has been Death's Door to so many. In the days of the uttering of forged one-pound notes by people tempted up from the country, how many hundreds of wretched creatures of both sexes—many quite innocent—swung out of a pitiless and inconsistent world, with the tower of yonder Christian church of Saint Sepulchre monstrously before their eyes! Is there any haunting of the Bank

Parlour by the remorseful souls of old directors, in the nights of these later days, I wonder, or is it as quiet as this degenerate Aceldama of an Old Bailey?

To walk on to the Bank, lamenting the good old times and bemoaning the present evil period, would be an easy next step, so I would take it, and would make my houseless circuit of the Bank, and give a thought to the treasure within; likewise to the guard of soldiers passing the night there, and nodding over the fire. Next, I went to Billingsgate, in some hope of market-people, but, it proving as yet too early, crossed London-bridge and got down by the water-side on the Surrey shore among the buildings of the great brewery. There was plenty going on at the brewery; and the reek, and the smell of grains, and the rattling of the plump dray horses at their mangers, were capital company. Quite refreshed by having mingled with this good society, I made a new start with a new heart, setting the old King's Bench prison before me for my next object, and resolving, when I should come to the wall, to think of poor Horace Kinch, and the Dry Rot in men.

A very curious disease the Dry Rot in men, and difficult to detect the beginning of. It had carried Horace Kinch inside the wall of the old King's Bench prison, and it had carried him out with his feet foremost. He was a likely man to look at, in the prime of life, well to do, as clever as he needed to be, and popular among many friends. He was suitably married, and had healthy and pretty children. But, like some fair-looking houses or fair-looking ships, he took the Dry Rot. The first strong external revelation of the Dry Rot in men, is a tendency to lurk and lounge; to be at street-corners without intelligible reason; to be going anywhere when met; to be about many places rather than at any; to do nothing tangible, but to have an intention of performing a variety of intangible duties to-morrow or the day after. When this manifestation of the disease is observed, the observer will usually connect it with a vague impression once formed or received, that the patient was living a little too hard. He will scarcely have had leisure to turn it over in his mind and form the terrible suspicion "Dry Rot," when he will notice a change for the worse in the patient's appearance: a certain slovenliness and deterioration, which is not poverty, nor dirt, nor intoxication, nor ill-health, but simply Dry Rot. To this, succeeds a smell as of strong waters, in

the morning; to that, a looseness respecting money; to that, a
stronger smell as of strong waters, at all times; to that, a looseness
respecting everything; to that, a trembling of the limbs, som-
nolency, misery, and crumbling to pieces. As it is in wood, so it
is in men. Dry Rot advances at a compound usury quite incalculable. A plank is found infected with it, and the whole structure is devoted. Thus it had been with the unhappy Horace
Kinch, lately buried by a small subscription. Those who knew
him had not nigh done saying, "So well off, so comfortably established, with such hope before him—and yet, it is feared, with a
slight touch of Dry Rot!" when lo! the man was all Dry Rot
and dust.

From the dead wall associated on those houseless nights with
this too common story, I chose next to wander by Bethlehem
Hospital; partly because it lay on my road round to Westminster;
partly, because I had a night-fancy in my head which could be
best pursued within sight of its walls and dome. And the fancy
was this: Are not the sane and the insane equal at night as the
sane lie a dreaming? Are not all of us outside this hospital, who
dream, more or less in the condition of those inside it, every night
of our lives? Are we not nightly persuaded, as they daily are,
that we associate preposterously with kings and queens, emperors
and empresses, and notabilities of all sorts? Do we not nightly
jumble events and personages and times and places, as these do
daily? Are we not sometimes troubled by our own sleeping inconsistencies, and do we not vexedly try to account for them or
excuse them, just as these do sometimes in respect of their waking
delusions? Said an afflicted man to me, when I was last in a hospital like this, "Sir, I can frequently fly." I was half ashamed to
reflect that so could I—by night. Said a woman to me on the
same occasion, "Queen Victoria frequently comes to dine with me,
and her Majesty and I dine off peaches and maccaroni in our night-
gowns, and his Royal Highness the Prince Consort does us the
honour to make a third on horseback in a Field-Marshal's uniform." Could I refrain from reddening with consciousness when I
remembered the amazing royal parties I myself had given (at
night), the unaccountable viands I had put on table, and my
extraordinary manner of conducting myself on those distinguished
occasions? I wonder that the great master who knew everything,

when he called Sleep the death of each day's life, did not call Dreams the insanity of each day's sanity.

By this time I had left the Hospital behind me, and was again setting towards the river; and in a short breathing space I was on Westminster-bridge, regaling my houseless eyes with the external walls of the British Parliament—the perfection of a stupendous institution, I know, and the admiration of all surrounding nations and succeeding ages, I do not doubt, but perhaps a little the better now and then for being pricked up to its work. Turning off into Old Palace-yard, the Courts of Law kept me company for a quarter of an hour; hinting in low whispers what numbers of people they were keeping awake, and how intensely wretched and horrible they were rendering the small hours to unfortunate suitors. Westminster Abbey was fine gloomy society for another quarter of an hour; suggesting a wonderful procession of its dead among the dark arches and pillars, each century more amazed by the century following it than by all the centuries going before. And indeed in those houseless night walks—which even included cemeteries where watchmen went round among the graves at stated times, and moved the tell-tale handle of an index which recorded that they had touched it at such an hour—it was a solemn consideration what enormous hosts of dead belong to one old great city, and how, if they were raised while the living slept, there would not be the space of a pin's point in all the streets and ways for the living to come out into. Not only that, but the vast armies of dead would overflow the hills and valleys beyond the city, and would stretch away all round it, God knows how far: seemingly, to the confines of the earth.

When a church clock strikes, on houseless ears in the dead of the night, it may be at first mistaken for company and hailed as such. But, as the spreading circles of vibration, which you may perceive at such a time with great clearness, go opening out, for ever and ever afterwards widening perhaps (as the philosopher has suggested) in eternal space, the mistake is rectified and the sense of loneliness is profounder. Once—it was after leaving the Abbey and turning my face north—I came to the great steps of Saint Martin's church as the clock was striking Three. Suddenly, a thing that in a moment more I should have trodden upon without seeing, rose up at my feet with a cry of loneliness and houselessness, struck out of it by the bell, the like of which I never heard. We then stood face to face looking at one another, frightened by one another. The creature was like a beetle-browed hair-lipped youth of twenty, and it had a loose bundle of rags on, which it held together with one of its hands. It shivered from head to foot, and its teeth chattered, and as it stared at me—persecutor, devil, ghost, whatever it thought me—it made with its whining mouth as if it were snapping at me, like a worried dog. Intending to give this ugly object money, I put out my hand to stay it—for it recoiled as it whined and snapped—and laid my hand upon its shoulder. Instantly, it twisted out of its garment, like the young man in the New Testament, and left me standing alone with its rags in my hands.

Covent-garden Market, when it was market morning, was wonderful company. The great waggons of cabbages, with growers' men and boys lying asleep under them, and with sharp dogs from market-garden neighbourhoods looking after the whole, were as good as a party. But one of the worst night sights I know in London, is to be found in the children who prowl about this place; who sleep in the baskets, fight for the offal, dart at any object they think they can lay their thieving hands on, dive under the carts and barrows, dodge the constables, and are perpetually making a blunt pattering on the pavement of the Piazza with the rain of their naked feet. A painful and unnatural result comes of the comparison one is forced to institute between the growth of corruption as displayed in the so much improved and cared for fruits of the earth, and the growth of corruption as displayed in these all uncared for (except inasmuch as ever-hunted) savages.

There was early coffee to be got about Covent-garden Market, and that was more company—warm company, too, which was better. Toast of a very substantial quality, was likewise procurable: though the towzled-headed man who made it, in an inner chamber within the coffee room, hadn't got his coat on yet, and was so heavy with sleep that in every interval of toast and coffee he went off anew behind the partition into complicated cross-roads of choke and snore, and lost his way directly. Into one of these establishments (among the earliest) near Bow-street, there came, one morning as I sat over my houseless cup, pondering where to go next, a man in a high and long snuff-coloured coat, and shoes, and, to the best of my belief, nothing else but a hat, who took out of his hat a large cold meat pudding; a meat pudding so large that it was a very tight fit, and brought the lining of the hat out with it. This mysterious man was known by his pudding, for, on his entering, the man of sleep brought him a pint of hot tea, a small loaf, and a large knife and fork and plate. Left to himself in his box, he stood the pudding on the bare table, and, instead of cutting it, stabbed it, over-hand, with the knife, like a mortal enemy; then took the knife out, wiped it on his sleeve, tore the pudding asunder with his fingers, and ate it all up. The remembrance of this man with the pudding remains with me as the remembrance of the most spectral person my houselessness encountered. Twice only was I in that establishment, and twice I saw him stalk in (as I should say, just out of bed, and presently going back to bed), take out his pudding, stab his pudding, wipe the dagger, and eat his pudding all up. He was a man whose figure promised cadaverousness, but who had an excessively red face, though shaped like a horse's. On the second occasion of my seeing him, he said huskily to the man of sleep, "Am I red to-night?" "You are," he uncompromisingly answered. "My mother," said the spectre, "was a red-faced woman that liked drink, and I looked at her hard when she laid in her coffin, and I took the complexion." Somehow, the pudding seemed an unwholesome pudding after that, and I put myself in its way no more.

When there was no market, or when I wanted variety, a railway terminus with the morning mails coming in, was remunerative company. But like most of the company to be had in this world, it lasted only a very short time. The station lamps would burst out ablaze, the porters would emerge from places of concealment, the cabs and trucks would rattle to their places (the post-office carts were already in theirs), and, finally, the bell would strike up, and the train would come banging in. But there were few passengers and little luggage, and everything scuttled away with the greatest expedition. The locomotive post-offices, with their great nets—as if they had been dragging the country for bodies—would fly open as to their doors, and would disgorge a smell of lamp, an exhausted clerk, a guard in a red coat, and their bags of letters; the engine would blow and heave and perspire, like an engine wiping its forehead and saying what a run it had had; and within ten minutes the lamps were out, and I was houseless and alone again.

But now, there were driven cattle on the high road near, wanting (as cattle always do) to turn into the midst of stone walls, and squeeze themselves through six inches' width of iron railing, and getting their heads down (also as cattle always do) for tossing-purchase at quite imaginary dogs, and giving themselves and every devoted creature associated with them a most extraordinary amount of unnecessary trouble. Now, too, the conscious gas began to grow pale with the knowledge that daylight was coming, and straggling work-people were already in the streets, and, as waking life had become extinguished with the last pieman's sparks, so it began to be rekindled with the fires of the first street corner breakfast-sellers. And so by faster and faster degrees, until the last degrees were very fast, the day came, and I was tired and could sleep. And it is not, as I used to think, going home at such times, the least wonderful thing in London, that in the real desert region of the night, the houseless wanderer is alone there. I knew well enough where to find Vice and Misfortune of all kinds, if I had chosen; but they were put out of sight, and my houselessness had many miles upon miles of streets in which it could, and did, have its own solitary way.

A PLEA FOR TOTAL ABSTINENCE

ONE day this last Whitsuntide, at precisely eleven o'clock in the forenoon, there suddenly rode into the field of view commanded by the windows of my lodging, an equestrian phenomenon. It was a fellow-creature on horseback, dressed in the absurdest manner. The fellow-creature wore high boots; some other (and much larger) fellow-creature's breeches, of a slack-baked doughy colour and a baggy form, a blue shirt whereof the skirt or tail was puffily tucked into the waistband of the said breeches, no coat, a red shoulder-belt, and a demi-semi-military scarlet hat with a feathered ornament in front, which to the uninstructed human vision, had the appearance of a moulting shuttlecock. I laid down the newspaper with which I had been occupied, and suveyed the fellow-man in question, with astonishment. Whether he had been sitting to any painter as a frontispiece for a

new edition of Sartor Resartus; whether "the husk or shell of him,"
as the esteemed Herr Teufelsdröckh might put it, were founded on
a jockey, on a circus, on General Garibaldi, on cheap porcelain,
on a toy-shop, on Guy Fawkes, on Wax-Work, on Gold Digging,
on Bedlam, or on all, were doubts that greatly exercised my mind.
Meanwhile my fellow-man stumbled and slided, excessively against
his will, on the slippery stones of my Covent Garden street, and
elicited shrieks from several sympathetic females, by convulsively
restraining himself from pitching over his horse's head. In the
very crisis of these evolutions, and indeed at the trying moment
when his charger's tail was in a tobacconist's shop, and his head
anywhere about town, this cavalier was joined by two similar portents, who, likewise stumbling and sliding, caused him to stumble
and slide the more distressingly. At length this Gilpinian trium-
virate effected a halt, and, looking northward, waved their three
right hands as commanding unseen troops to Up, guards! and at
'em. Hereupon a brazen band burst forth, which caused them to
be instantly bolted with to some remote spot of earth in the direction of the Surrey Hills.

Judging from these appearances that a procession was under
way, I threw up my window, and, craning out, had the satisfaction
of beholding it advancing along the street. It was a Tee-Total
procession, as I learnt from its banners, and was long enough to
consume twenty minutes in passing. There were a great number
of children in it, some of them so very young in their mothers'
arms as to be in the act of practically exemplifying their abstinence
from fermented liquors, and attachment to an unintoxicating drink,
while the procession defiled. The display was, on the whole, pleasant to see, as any good-humoured holiday assemblage of clean,
cheerful, and well-conducted people should be. It was bright with
ribbons, tinsel, and shoulder-belts, and abounded in flowers, as
if those latter trophies had come up in profusion under much water-
ing. The day being breezy, the insubordination of the large banners was very reprehensible. Each of these, being borne aloft on
two poles and stayed with some half dozen lines, was carried, as
polite books in the last century used to be written, by "various
hands," and the anxiety expressed in the upturned faces of those
officers—something between the anxiety attendant on the balanc-
ing art, and that inseparable from the pastime of kite flying, with

a touch of the angler's quality in landing his scaly prey—much impressed me. Suddenly, too, a banner would shiver in the wind, and go about in the most inconvenient manner. This always happened oftenest with such gorgeous standards as those representing a gentleman in black, corpulent with tea and water, in the laudable act of summarily reforming a family feeble and pinched with beer. The gentleman in black distended by wind would then conduct himself with the most unbecoming levity, while the beery family, growing beerier, would frantically try to tear themselves away from his ministration. Some of the inscriptions accompanying the banners were of a highly determined character, as "We never, never will give up the temperance cause:" with similar sound resolutions, rather suggestive to the profane mind of Mrs. Micawber's "I never will desert Mr. Micawber," and of Mr. Micawber's retort, "Really, my dear, I am not aware that you were ever required by any human being to do anything of the sort."

At intervals a gloom would fall on the passing members of the procession, for which I was at first unable to account. But this I discovered, after a little observation, to be occasioned by the coming on of the Executioners—the terrible official Beings who were to make the speeches bye-and-bye—who were distributed in open carriages at various points of the cavalcade. A dark cloud and a sensation of dampness, as from many wet blankets, invariably preceded the rolling on of the dreadful cars containing these Headsmen, and I noticed that the wretched people who closely followed them, and who were in a manner forced to contemplate their folded arms, complacent countenances, and threatening lips, were more overshadowed by the cloud and damp than those in front. Indeed, I perceived in some of these so moody an implacability towards the magnates of the scaffold, and so plain a desire to tear them limb from limb, that I would respectfully suggest to the managers the expediency of conveying the Executioners to the scene of their dismal labours by unfrequented ways, and in closely tilted carts, next Whitsuntide.

The Procession was composed of a series of smaller processions which had come together, each from its own metropolitan district. An infusion of Allegory became perceptible when patriotic Peckham advanced. So I judged, from the circumstance of Peckham's unfurling a silken banner that fanned Heaven and Earth with the words, "The Peckham Life Boat." No Boat being in attendance, though Life, in the likeness of "a gallant, gallant crew" in nautical uniform followed the flag, I was led to meditate on the fact that Peckham is described by Geographers as an inland settlement, with no larger or nearer shore-line than the towing-path of the Surrey Canal, on which stormy station I had been given to understand no Life Boat exists. Thus I deduced an allegorical meaning, and came to the conclusion that if patriotic Peckham picked a peck of pickled poetry, this *was* the peck of pickled poetry which patriotic Peckham picked.

I have observed that the aggregate Procession was on the whole pleasant to see. I made use of that qualified expression with a direct meaning which I will now explain. It involves the title of this paper, and a little fair trying of Tee-Totalism by its own tests.

There were many people on foot, and many people in vehicles of various kinds. The former were pleasant to see, and the latter were not pleasant to see: for the reason that I never, on any occasion or under any circumstances, have beheld heavier overloading of horses than in this public show. Unless the imposition of a great van laden with from ten to twenty people on a single horse be a moderate tasking of the poor creature, then the Temperate use of horses was immoderate and cruel. From the smallest and lightest horse to the largest and heaviest, there were many instances in which the beast of burden was so shamefully overladen, that the Society for the Prevention of Cruelty to Animals has frequently interposed in less gross cases.

Now, I have always held that there may be, and that there unquestionably is, such a thing as Use without Abuse, and that therefore the Total Abolitionists are irrational and wrong-headed. But the Procession completely converted me. For, so large a number of the people using draught-horses in it were so clearly unable to Use them without Abusing them, that I perceived Total Abstinence from Horseflesh to be the only remedy of which the case admitted. As it is all one to Tee-Totallers whether you take half a pint of beer or half a gallon, so it was all one here whether the beast of burden were a pony or a cart-horse. Indeed, my case had the special strength that the half-pint quadruped underwent as much suffering as the half-gallon quadruped. Moral: Total Asbtinence from Horseflesh through the whole length and breadth of the scale. This Pledge will be in course of administration to all Tee-Total processionists, not pedestrians, at the publishing office of ALL THE YEAR ROUND, on the first day of April, One Thousand Eight Hundred and Seventy.

Observe a point for consideration. This Procession comprised many persons, in their gigs, broughams, tax-carts, barouches, chaises, and what not, who were merciful to the dumb beasts that drew them, and did not overcharge their strength. What is to be done with those unoffending persons? I will not run amuck and vilify and defame them, as Tee-Total tracts and platforms would most assuredly do, if the question were one of drinking instead of driving; I merely ask what is to be done with them? The reply admits of no dispute whatever. Manifestly, in strict accordance with Tee-Total Doctrines, THEY must come in too, and take the Total Abstinence from Horseflesh Pledge. It is not pretended that those members of the Procession misused certain auxiliaries which in most countries and all ages have been bestowed upon man for his use, but it is undeniable that other members of the Procession did. Tee-Total mathematics demonstrate that the less includes the greater; that the guilty include the innocent, the blind the seeing, the deaf the hearing, the dumb the speaking, the drunken the sober. If any of the moderate users of draught-cattle in question should deem that there is any gentle violence done to their reason by these elements of logic, they are invited to come out of the Procession next Whitsuntide, and look at it from my window.

THACKERAY

WILLIAM MAKEPEACE THACKERAY (*1811–1863*), *novelist, editor, essayist, was born in Calcutta, and was sent to England at the age of six; brought up by relatives, he attended the Charterhouse School, went to Cambridge (where he shone rather socially than scholastically), leaving without a degree. After travelling on the Continent, he began the study of law, which he soon abandoned, trying his hand at editing. Losing his money, he turned to art—in which his delight was greater than his skill—and made some unsuccessful literary experiments. As Paris correspondent for London journals, he lived in France, returning to England after a year, to do hack-writing and a little illustration. After six years of married life, his wife became hopelessly ill (she lived until 1892); but he remained cheerful, enjoying his friends and his clubs, despite melancholy periods. When "Punch" was founded, in 1841, Thackeray became a contributor; his "Book of Snobs" made him famous. A long series of novels began with "Vanity Fair" (1847); he lectured (like Coleridge, Hazlitt, and Carlyle), and came to America in 1852—making a second tour in 1855—repeating his lectures in England and Scotland on his return. When the "Cornhill Magazine" was founded (in 1860), he became its first editor; resigning in 1862, he remained a contributor until his sudden death.*

Sympathetic with good, he attacked humbug of all kinds, both in novels and essays. Unfairly called cynical by some of his contemporaries, he resented the appellation; his essays reflect his humor, his kindliness, and a moral aim which can only be pleasantly received, for he includes himself in the congregation of the sinners he addresses with gentle satire.

THACKERAY

ON A LAZY IDLE BOY

I HAD occasion to pass a week in the autumn in the little old town of Coire or Chur, in the Grisons, where lies buried that very ancient British king, saint, and martyr, Lucius,[1] who founded the Church of Saint Peter, on Cornhill. Few people note the church nowadays, and fewer ever heard of the saint. In the cathedral at Chur, his statue appears surrounded by other sainted persons of his family. With tight red breeches, a Roman habit, a curly brown beard, and a neat little gilt crown and sceptre, he stands, a very comely and cheerful image: and, from what I may call his peculiar position with regard to Cornhill, I beheld this figure of Saint Lucius with more interest than I should have bestowed upon personages who, hierarchically, are, I dare say, his superiors.

The pretty little city stands, so to speak, at the end of the world— of the world of to-day, the world of rapid motion, and rushing railways, and the commerce and intercourse of men. From the northern gate, the iron road stretches away to Zürich, to Basle, to Paris, to home. From the old southern barriers, before which a little river rushes, and around which stretch the crumbling battlements of the ancient town, the road bears the slow diligence or lagging vetturino by the shallow Rhine, through the awful gorges of the Via Mala, and presently over the Splügen to the shores of Como.

I have seldom seen a place more quaint, pretty, calm, and pastoral than this remote little Chur. What need have the inhabitants of walls and ramparts, except to build summer-houses, to trail

---

[1] Stow quotes the inscription, still extant, "from the table fast chained in St. Peter's Church, Cornhill;" and says, "he was after some chronicle buried at London, and after some chronicle buried at Glowcester"—but, oh! these incorrect chroniclers! when Alban Butler, in the "Lives of the Saints," v. xii., and Murray's "Handbook," and the Sacristan at Chur, all say Lucius was killed there, and I saw his tomb with my own eyes!

vines, and hang clothes to dry on them? No enemies approach the great mouldering gates: only at morn and even the cows come lowing past them, the village maidens chatter merrily round the fountains, and babble like the ever-voluble stream that flows under the old walls. The schoolboys, with book and satchel, in smart uniforms, march up to the gymnasium, and return thence at their stated time. There is one coffee-house in the town, and I see one old gentleman goes to it. There are shops with no customers seemingly, and the lazy tradesmen look out of their little windows at the single stranger sauntering by. There is a stall with baskets of queer little black grapes and apples, and a pretty brisk trade with half-a-dozen urchins standing round. But, beyond this, there is scarce any talk or movement in the street. There's nobody at the book-shop. "If you will have the goodness to come again in an hour," says the banker, with his mouth full of dinner at one o'clock, "you can have the money." There is nobody at the hotel save the good landlady, the kind waiters, the brisk young cook who ministers to you. Nobody is in the Protestant church—(oh! strange sight, the two confessions are here at peace!)—nobody in the Catholic church: until the sacristan, from his snug abode in the cathedral close, espies the traveller eyeing the monsters and pillars before the old shark-toothed arch of his cathedral, and comes out (with a view to remuneration possibly) and opens the gate, and shows you the venerable church, and the queer old relics in the sacristy, and the ancient vestments (a black velvet cope, amongst other robes, as fresh as yesterday, and presented by that notorious "pervert," Henry of Navarre and France), and the statue of Saint Lucius who built Saint Peter's Church, on Cornhill.

What a quiet, kind, quaint, pleasant, pretty old town! Has it been asleep these hundreds and hundreds of years, and is the brisk young Prince of the Sidereal Realms in his screaming car drawn by his snorting steel elephant coming to waken it? Time was when there must have been life and bustle and commerce here. Those vast venerable walls were not made to keep out cows, but men-at-arms, led by fierce captains, who prowled about the gates, and robbed the traders as they passed in and out with their bales, their goods, their pack-horses and their wains. Is the place so dead that even the clergy of the different denominations can't quarrel? Why, seven or eight, or a dozen, or fifteen hundred years ago (they haven't the register at Saint Peter's up to that remote period—I dare say it was burnt in the fire of London)—a dozen hundred years ago, when there was some life in the town, Saint Lucius was stoned here on account of theological differences, after founding our church in Cornhill.

There was a sweet pretty river walk we used to take in the evening and mark the mountains round glooming with a deeper purple; the shades creeping up the golden walls; the river brawling, the cattle calling, the maids and chatterboxes round the fountains babbling and bawling; and several times in the course of our sober walks we overtook a lazy slouching boy, or hobbledehoy, with a rusty coat, and trousers not too long, and big feet trailing lazily one after the other, and large lazy hands dawdling from out the tight sleeves, and in the lazy hands a little book, which my lad held up to his face, and which I dare say so charmed and ravished him, that he was blind to the beautiful sights around him; unmindful, I would venture to lay any wager, of the lessons he had to learn for to-morrow; forgetful of mother waiting supper, and father preparing a scolding;—absorbed utterly and entirely in his book.

What was it that so fascinated the young student, as he stood by the river shore? Not the *pons asinorum*. What book so delighted him, and blinded him to all the rest of the world, so that he did not care to see the apple-woman with her fruit, or (more tempting still to sons of Eve) the pretty girls with their apple cheeks, who laughed and prattled round the fountain? What was the book? Do you suppose it was Livy, or the Greek grammar? No; it was a NOVEL that you were reading, you lazy, not very clean, good-for-nothing, sensible boy. It was D'Artagnan locking up General Monk in a box, or almost succeeding in keeping Charles the First's head on. It was the prisoner of the Château d'If cutting himself out of the sack fifty feet under water (I mention the novels I like best myself—novels without love or talking, or any of that sort of nonsense, but containing plenty of fighting, escaping, robbery, and rescuing)—cutting himself out of the sack and swimming to the island of Monte Cristo. O Dumas! O thou brave kind gallant old Alexandre! I hereby offer thee homage, and give thee thanks for many pleasant hours. I have read thee (being sick in bed) for thirteen hours of a happy day, and had the ladies of the house fighting for the volumes. Be assured that lazy boy was reading

Dumas (or I will go so far as to let the reader here pronounce the eulogium, or insert the name of his favourite author); and as for the anger, or, it may be, the verberations of his schoolmaster, or the remonstrances of his father, or the tender pleadings of his mother that he should not let the supper grow cold—I don't believe the scapegrace cared one fig. No! Figs are sweet, but fictions are sweeter.

Have you ever seen a score of white-bearded, white-robed warriors, or grave seniors of the city, seated at the gate of Jaffa or Beyrout, and listening to the story-teller reciting his marvels out of "Antar" or the "Arabian Nights"? I was once present when a young gentleman at table put a tart away from him, and said to his neighbour, the Younger Son (with rather a fatuous air), "I never eat sweets."

"Not eat sweets! and do you know why?" says T.

"Because I am past that kind of thing," says the young gentleman.

"Because you are a glutton and a sot!" cries the Elder (and Juvenis winces a little). "All people who have natural healthy appetites love sweets; all children, all women, all Eastern people, whose tastes are not corrupted by gluttony and strong drink." And a plateful of raspberries and cream disappeared before the philosopher.

You take the allegory? Novels are sweets. All people with healthy literary appetites love them—almost all women;—a vast number of clever hard-headed men. Why, one of the most learned physicians in England said to me only yesterday, "I have just read *So-and-so* for the second time" (naming one of Jones's exquisite fictions). Judges, bishops, chancellors, mathematicians, are notorious novel-readers; as well as young boys and sweet girls, and their kind tender mothers. Who has not read about Eldon, and how he cried over novels every night when he was not at whist?

As for that lazy naughty boy at Chur, I doubt whether *he* will like novels when he is thirty years of age. He is taking too great a glut of them now. He is eating jelly until he will be sick. He will know most plots by the time he is twenty, so that *he* will never be surprised when the Stranger turns out to be the rightful earl,— when the old waterman, throwing off his beggarly gabardine, shows his stars and the collars of his various orders, and clasping

Antonia to his bosom, proves himself to be the prince, her long-lost father. He will recognise the novelist's same characters, though they appear in red-heeled pumps and *ailes-de-pigeon*, or the garb of the nineteenth century. He will get weary of sweets, as boys of private schools grow (or used to grow, for I have done growing some little time myself, and the practice may have ended too)—as private schoolboys used to grow tired of the pudding before their mutton at dinner.

And pray what is the moral of this apologue? The moral I take to be this: the appetite for novels extending to the end of the world —far away in the frozen deep, the sailors reading them to one another during the endless night; far away under the Syrian stars, the solemn sheikhs and elders hearkening to the poet as he recites his tales; far away in the Indian camps, where the soldiers listen to ——'s tales, or ——'s, after the hot day's march; far away in little Chur yonder, where the lazy boy pores over the fond volume, and drinks it in with all his eyes;—the demand being what we know it is, the merchant must supply it as he will supply saddles and pale ale for Bombay or Calcutta.

But as surely as the cadet drinks too much pale ale, it will disagree with him; and so surely, dear youth, will too much of novels cloy on thee. I wonder, do novel-writers themselves read many novels? If you go into Gunter's, you don't see those charming young ladies (to whom I present my most respectful compliments) eating tarts and ices, but at the proper eventide they have good plain wholesome tea and bread-and-butter. Can anybody tell me does the author of the "Tale of Two Cities" read novels? does the author of the "Tower of London" devour romances? does the dashing "Harry Lorrequer" delight in "Plain or Ringlets" or "Sponge's Sporting Tour"? Does the veteran, from whose flowing pen we had the books which delighted our young days, "Darnley," and "Richelieu," and "Delorme," [1] relish the works of Alexandre the Great, and thrill over the "Three Musketeers"? Does the accomplished author of the "Caxtons" read the other tales in *Blackwood?* (For example, that ghost-story printed last August, and which, for my part, though I read it in the public reading-room

---

[1] By the way, what a strange fate is that which befell the veteran novelist! He was appointed Her Majesty's Consul-General in Venice, the only city in Europe where the famous "two cavaliers" cannot by any possibility be seen riding together.

at the "Pavilion" Hotel at Folkestone, I protest frightened me so that I scarce dared look out over my shoulder.) Does "Uncle Tom" admire "Adam Bede"? and does the author of the "Vicar of Wrexhill" laugh over the "Warden" and the "Three Clerks"? Dear youth of ingenuous countenance and ingenuous pudor! I make no doubt that the eminent parties above named all partake of novels in moderation—eat jellies—but mainly nourish themselves upon wholesome roast and boiled.

Here, dear youth aforesaid! our *Cornhill Magazine* owners strive to provide thee with fact as well as fiction; and though it does not become them to brag of their Ordinary, at least they invite thee to a table where thou shalt sit in good company. That story of the "Fox" [1] was written by one of the gallant seamen who sought for poor Franklin under the awful Arctic Night: that account of China [2] is told by the man of all the empire most likely to know of what he speaks: those pages regarding Volunteers [3] come from an honoured hand that has borne the sword in a hundred famous fields, and pointed the British guns in the greatest siege in the world.

Shall we point out others? We are fellow-travellers, and shall make acquaintance as the voyage proceeds. In the Atlantic steamers, on the first day out (and on high and holy-days subsequently), the jellies set down on table are richly ornamented; *medioque in fonte leporum* rise the American and British flags nobly emblazoned in tin. As the passengers remark this pleasing phenomenon, the Captain no doubt improves the occasion by expressing a hope, to his right and left, that the flag of Mr. Bull and his younger Brother may always float side by side in friendly emulation. Novels having been previously compared to jellies— here are two (one perhaps not entirely saccharine, and flavoured with an *amari aliquid* very distasteful to some palates)—two novels [4] under two flags, the one that ancient ensign which has hung before the well-known booth of "Vanity Fair"; the other that fresh and handsome standard which has lately been hoisted on "Barchester Towers." Pray, sir, or madam, to which dish will you be helped?

[1] "The Search for Sir John Franklin." (From the Private Journal of an Officer of the "Fox.")
[2] "The Chinese and the Outer Barbarians." By Sir John Bowring.
[3] "Our Volunteers." By Sir John Burgoyne.
[4] "Lovel the Widower" and "Framley Parsonage."

So have I seen my friends Captain Lang and Captain Comstock press their guests to partake of the fare on that memorable "First day out," when there is no man, I think, who sits down but asks a blessing on his voyage, and the good ship dips over the bar, and bounds away into the blue water.

NIL NISI BONUM

ALMOST the last words which Sir Walter spoke to Lockhart, his biographer, were, "Be a good man, my dear!" and with the last flicker of breath on his dying lips, he sighed a farewell to his family, and passed away blessing them.

Two men, famous, admired, beloved, have just left us, the Goldsmith and Gibbon of our time.[1] Ere a few weeks are over, many a critic's pen will be at work, reviewing their lives and passing judgment on their works. This is no review, or history, or criticism: only a word in testimony of respect and regard from a man of letters, who owes to his own professional labour the honour of becoming acquainted with these two eminent literary men. One was the first Ambassador whom the New World of Letters sent to the Old. He was born almost with the republic; the *pater patriæ* had laid his hand on the child's head. He bore Washington's name; he came amongst us bringing the kindest sympathy, the most artless smiling goodwill. His new country (which some people here might be disposed to regard rather superciliously) could send us, as he showed in his own person, a gentleman, who, though himself born in no very high sphere, was most finished, polished, easy, witty, quiet; and, socially, the equal of the most refined Europeans. If Irving's welcome in England was a kind one, was it not also gratefully remembered? If he ate our salt, did he not pay us with a thankful heart? Who can calculate the amount of friendliness and good feeling for our country which this writer's generous and untiring regard for us disseminated in his own? His books are read by millions [2] of his countrymen, whom he has taught to love England, and why to love her. It would have been easy to

---

[1] Washington Irving, died November 28, 1859; Lord Macaulay, died December 28, 1859.

[2] See his *Life* in the most remarkable *Dictionary of Authors*, published lately at Philadelphia by Mr. Allibone.

speak otherwise than he did: to inflame national rancours, which, at the time when he first became known as a public writer, war had just renewed: to cry down the old civilisation at the expense of the new: to point out our faults, arrogance, shortcomings, and give the republic to infer how much she was the parent state's superior. There are writers enough in the United States, honest and otherwise, who preach that kind of doctrine. But the good Irving, the peaceful, the friendly, had no place for bitterness in his heart, and no scheme but kindness. Received in England with extraordinary tenderness and friendship (Scott, Southey, Byron, a hundred others have borne witness to their liking for him), he was a messenger of goodwill and peace between his country and ours. "See, friends!" he seems to say, "these English are not so wicked, rapacious, callous, proud, as you have been taught to believe them. I went amongst them a humble man; won my way by my pen; and, when known, found every hand held out to me with kindliness and welcome. Scott is a great man, you acknowledge. Did not Scott's King of England give a gold medal to him, and another to me, your countryman, and a stranger?"

Tradition in the United States still fondly retains the history of the feasts and rejoicings which awaited Irving on his return to his native country from Europe. He had a national welcome; he stammered in his speeches, hid himself in confusion, and the people loved him all the better. He had worthily represented America in Europe. In that young community a man who brings home with him abundant European testimonials is still treated with respect (I have found American writers, of wide-world reputation, strangely solicitous about the opinions of quite obscure British critics, and elated or depressed by their judgments); and Irving went home medalled by the King, diplomatised by the University, crowned and honoured and admired. He had not in any way intrigued for his honours, he had fairly won them; and, in Irving's instance, as in others, the old country was glad and eager to pay them.

In America the love and regard for Irving was a national sentiment. Party wars are perpetually raging there, and are carried on by the press with a rancour and fierceness against individuals which exceeds British, almost Irish, virulence. It seemed to me, during a year's travel in the country, as if no one ever aimed a blow at

Irving.   All men held their hands from that harmless friendly peacemaker.   I had the good fortune to see him at New York, Philadelphia, Baltimore, and Washington,[1] and remarked how in every place he was honoured and welcome.   Every large city has its "Irving House."   The country takes pride in the fame of its men of letters.   The gate of his own charming little domain on the beautiful Hudson River was for ever swinging before visitors who came to him.   He shut out no one.[2]   I had seen many pictures of his house, and read descriptions of it, in both of which it was treated with a not unusual American exaggeration.   It was but a pretty little cabin of a place; the gentleman of the press who took notes of the place, whilst his kind old host was sleeping, might have visited the whole house in a couple of minutes.

And how came it that this house was so small, when Mr. Irving's books were sold by hundreds of thousands, nay, millions, when his profits were known to be large, and the habits of life of the good old bachelor were notoriously modest and simple?   He had loved once in his life.   The lady he loved died; and he, whom all the world loved, never sought to replace her.   I can't say how much the thought of that fidelity has touched me.   Does not the very cheerfulness of his after life add to the pathos of that untold story?   To grieve always was not in his nature: or, when he had his sorrow, to bring all the world in to condole with him and bemoan it.   Deep and quiet he lays the love of his heart, and buries it; and grass and flowers grow over the scarred ground in due time.

Irving had such a small house and such narrow rooms, because there was a great number of people to occupy them.   He could only afford to keep one old horse (which, lazy and aged as it was, managed once or twice to run away with that careless old horseman).   He could only afford to give plain sherry to that amiable

---

[1] At Washington, Mr. Irving came to a lecture given by the writer, which Mr. Fillmore and General Pierce, the President and President Elect, were also kind enough to attend together.   "Two Kings of Brentford smelling at one rose," says Irving, looking up with his good-humoured smile.

[2] Mr. Irving described to me, with that humour and good-humour which he always kept, how, amongst other visitors, a member of the British press who had carried his distinguished pen to America (where he employed it in vilifying his own country) came to Sunnyside, introduced himself to Irving, partook of his wine and luncheon, and in two days described Mr. Irving, his house, his nieces, his meal, and his manner of dozing afterwards, in a New York paper.   On another occasion, Irving said, laughing, "Two persons came to me, and one held me in conversation whilst the other miscreant took my portrait!"

British paragraph-monger from New York, who saw the patriarch asleep over his modest blameless cup, and fetched the public into his private chamber to look at him. Irving could only live very modestly, because the wifeless, childless man had a number of children to whom he was as a father. He had as many as nine nieces, I am told—I saw two of these ladies at his house—with all of whom the dear old man had shared the produce of his labour and genius.

"*Be a good man, my dear.*" One can't but think of these last words of the veteran Chief of Letters, who had tasted and tested the value of worldly success, admiration, prosperity. Was Irving not good, and of his works, was not his life the best part? In his family, gentle, generous, good-humoured, affectionate, self-denying: in society, a delightful example of complete gentlemanhood; quite unspoiled by prosperity; never obsequious to the great (or, worse still, to the base and mean, as some public men are forced to be in his and other countries); eager to acknowledge every contemporary's merit; always kind and affable to the young members of his calling; in his professional bargains and mercantile dealings delicately honest and grateful; one of the most charming masters of our lighter language; the constant friend to us and our nation; to men of letters doubly dear, not for his wit and genius merely, but as an exemplar of goodness, probity, and pure life:—I don't know what sort of testimonial will be raised to him in his own country, where generous and enthusiastic acknowledgment of American merit is never wanting; but Irving was in our service as well as theirs; and as they have placed a stone at Greenwich yonder in memory of that gallant young Bellot, who shared the perils and fate of some of our Arctic seamen, I would like to hear of some memorial raised by English writers and friends of letters in affectionate remembrance of the dear and good Washington Irving.

As for the other writer, whose departure many friends, some few most dearly-loved relatives, and multitudes of admiring readers deplore, our republic has already decreed his statue, and he must have known that he had earned this posthumous honour. He is not a poet and man of letters merely, but citizen, statesman, a great British worthy. Almost from the first moment when he appears, amongst boys, amongst college students, amongst men, he is marked, and takes rank as a great Englishman. All sorts of successes are easy to him: as a lad he goes down into the arena with others, and wins all the prizes to which he has a mind. A place in the senate is straightway offered to the young man. He takes his seat there; he speaks, when so minded, without party anger or intrigue, but not without party faith and a sort of heroic enthusiasm for his cause. Still he is poet and philosopher even more than orator. That he may have leisure and means to pursue his darling studies, he absents himself for a while, and accepts a richly-remunerative post in the East. As learned a man may live in a cottage or a college common-room; but it always seemed to me that ample means and recognised rank were Macaulay's as of right. Years ago there was a wretched outcry raised because Mr. Macaulay dated a letter from Windsor Castle, where he was staying. Immortal gods! Was this man not a fit guest for any palace in the world? or a fit companion for any man or woman in it? I dare say, after Austerlitz, the old K. K. Court officials and footmen sneered at Napoleon for dating from Schönbrunn. But that miserable "Windsor Castle" outcry is an echo out of fast-retreating old-world remembrances. The place of such a natural chief was amongst the first in the land; and that country is best, according to our British notion at least, where the man of eminence has the best chance of investing his genius and intellect.

If a company of giants were got together, very likely one or two of the mere six-feet-six people might be angry at the incontestable superiority of the very tallest of the party: and so I have heard some London wits, rather peevish at Macaulay's superiority, complain that he occupied too much of the talk, and so forth. Now that wonderful tongue is to speak no more, will not many a man grieve that he no longer has the chance to listen? To remember the talk is to wonder: to think not only of the treasures he had in his memory, but of the trifles he had stored there, and could produce with equal readiness. Almost on the last day I had the fortune to see him, a conversation happened suddenly to spring up about senior wranglers, and what they had done in after life. To the almost terror of the persons present, Macaulay began with the senior wrangler of 1801-2-3-4, and so on, giving the name of each, and relating his subsequent career and rise. Every man who has known him has his story regarding that astonishing memory. It may be that he was not ill-pleased that you should recognise it; but to those prodigious intellectual feats, which were so easy to him, who would grudge his tribute of homage? His talk was, in a word, admirable, and we admired it.

Of the notices which have appeared regarding Lord Macaulay, up to the day when the present lines are written (the 9th of January [1860]), the reader should not deny himself the pleasure of looking especially at two. It is a good sign of the times when such articles as these (I mean the articles in the *Times* and *Saturday Review*) appear in our public prints about our public men. They educate us, as it were, to admire rightly. An uninstructed person in a museum or at a concert may pass by without recognising a picture or a passage of music, which the connoisseur by his side may show him is a masterpiece of harmony, or a wonder of artistic skill. After reading these papers you like and respect more the person you have admired so much already. And so with regard to Macaulay's style there may be faults of course—what critic can't point them out? But for the nonce we are not talking about faults: we want to say *nil nisi bonum*. Well—take at hazard any three pages of the "Essays" or "History";—and, glimmering below the stream of the narrative, as it were, you, an average reader, see one, two, three, a half-score of allusions to other historic facts, characters, literature, poetry, with which you are acquainted. Why is this epithet used? Whence is that simile drawn? How does he manage, in two or three words, to paint an individual, or to indicate a landscape? Your neighbour, who has *his* reading, and his little stock of literature stowed away in his mind, shall detect more points, allusions, happy touches, indicating not only the prodigious memory and vast learning of this master, but the wonderful industry, the honest, humble, previous toil of this great scholar. He reads twenty books to write a sentence; he travels a hundred miles to make a line of description.

Many Londoners—not all—have seen the British Museum Library. I speak *à cœur ouvert*, and pray the kindly reader to bear with me. I have seen all sorts of domes of Peters and Pauls, Sophia, Pantheon,—what not?—and have been struck by none of them so much as by that catholic dome in Bloomsbury, under which our million volumes are housed. What peace, what love, what truth, what beauty, what happiness for all, what generous kindness for you and me, are here spread out! It seems to me one cannot sit down in that place without a heart full of grateful reverence. I

own to have said my grace at the table, and to have thanked
Heaven for this my English birthright, freely to partake of these
bountiful books, and to speak the truth I find there. Under the
dome which held Macaulay's brain, and from which his solemn
eyes looked out on the world but a fortnight since, what a vast,
brilliant, and wonderful store of learning was ranged! what strange
lore would he not fetch for you at your bidding! A volume of law,
or history, a book of poetry familiar or forgotten (except by himself
who forgot nothing), a novel ever so old, and he had it at hand.
I spoke to him once about "Clarissa." "Not read 'Clarissa'!"
he cried out. "If you have once thoroughly entered on 'Clarissa'
and are infected by it, you can't leave it. When I was in India I
passed one hot season at the hills, and there were the Governor-
General, and the Secretary of Government, and the Commander-
in-Chief and their wives. I had 'Clarissa' with me: and, as soon
as they began to read, the whole station was in a passion of excitement about Miss Harlowe and her misfortunes, and her scoun-
drelly Lovelace! The Governor's wife seized the book, and the
Secretary waited for it, and the Chief Justice could not read it for
tears!" He acted the whole scene: he paced up and down the
"Athenæum" library: I dare say he could have spoken pages of
the book—of that book, and of what countless piles of others!

In this little paper let us keep to the text of *nil nisi bonum*.
One paper I have read regarding Lord Macaulay says "he had no
heart." Why, a man's books may not always speak the truth,
but they speak his mind in spite of himself: and it seems to me
this man's heart is beating through every page he penned. He is
always in a storm of revolt and indignation against wrong, craft,
tyranny. How he cheers heroic resistance; how he backs and ap-
plauds freedom struggling for its own; how he hates scoundrels,
ever so victorious and successful; how he recognises genius, though
selfish villains possess it! The critic who says Macaulay had no
heart, might say that Johnson had none: and two men more generous, and more loving, and more hating, and more partial, and
more noble, do not live in our history. Those who knew Lord
Macaulay knew how admirably tender and generous,[1] and affec-

---

[1] Since the above was written, I have been informed that it has been found, on examining Lord Macaulay's papers, that he was in the habit of giving away *more than a fourth
part* of his annual income.

tionate he was. It was not his business to bring his family before the theatre footlights, and call for bouquets from the gallery as he wept over them.

If any young man of letters reads this little sermon—and to him, indeed, it is addressed—I would say to him, "Bear Scott's words in your mind, and '*be good, my dear.*'" Here are two literary men gone to their account, and, *laus Deo*, as far as we know, it is fair, and open, and clean. Here is no need of apologies for short-comings, or explanations of vices which would have been virtues but for unavoidable, &c. Here are two examples of men most differently gifted: each pursuing his calling; each speaking his truth as God bade him; each honest in his life; just and irreproach-able in his dealings; dear to his friends; honoured by his country; beloved at his fireside. It has been the fortunate lot of both to give incalculable happiness and delight to the world, which thanks them in return with an immense kindliness, respect, affection. It may not be our chance, brother scribe, to be endowed with such merit, or rewarded with such fame. But the rewards of these men are rewards paid to *our service*. We may not win the bâton or epaulettes; but God give us strength to guard the honour of the flag!

TUNBRIDGE TOYS

I WONDER whether those little silver pencil-cases with a movable almanack at the butt-end are still favourite imple-ments with boys, and whether pedlars still hawk them about the country? Are there pedlars and hawkers still, or are rustics and children grown too sharp to deal with them? Those pencil-cases, as far as my memory serves me, were not of much use. The screw, upon which the movable almanack turned, was constantly getting loose. The 1 of the table would work from its moorings, under Tuesday or Wednesday, as the case might be, and you would find, on examination, that Th. or W. was the $23\frac{1}{2}$ of the month (which was absurd on the face of the thing), and in a word your cherished pencil-case an utterly unreliable time-keeper. Nor was this a matter of wonder. Consider the position of a pencil-case in a boy's pocket. You had hardbake in it; marbles, kept in your purse when the money was all gone; your mother's purse, knitted so fondly and supplied with a little bit of gold, long since—prodigal little son!—scattered amongst the swine—I mean amongst brandy-balls, open tarts, three-cornered puffs, and similar abominations. You had a top and string; a knife; a piece of cobbler's wax; two or three bullets; a "Little Warbler"; and I, for my part, remember, for a considerable period, a brass-barrelled pocket-pistol (which would fire beautifully, for with it I shot off a button from Butt Major's jacket);—with all these things, and ever so many more, clinking and rattling in your pockets, and your hands, of course, keeping them in perpetual movement, how could you expect your movable almanack not to be twisted out of its place now and again—your pencil-case to be bent—your liquorice water not to leak out of your bottle over the cobbler's wax, your bull's eyes not to ram up the lock and barrel of your pistol, and so forth?

In the month of June, thirty-seven years ago, I bought one of those pencil-cases from a boy whom I shall call Hawker, and who was in my form. Is he dead? Is he a millionaire? Is he a bankrupt now? He was an immense screw at school, and I believe to this day that the value of the thing for which I owed and eventually paid three-and-sixpence, was in reality not one-and-nine.

I certainly enjoyed the case at first a good deal, and amused myself with twiddling round the movable calendar. But this pleasure wore off. The jewel, as I said, was not paid for, and Hawker, a large and violent boy, was exceedingly unpleasant as a creditor. His constant remark was, "When are you going to pay me that three-and-sixpence? What sneaks your relations must be! They come to see you. You go out to them on Saturdays and Sundays, and they never give you anything! Don't tell *me*, you little hum-bug!" and so forth. The truth is that my relations were respectable; but my parents were making a tour in Scotland; and my friends in London, whom I used to go and see, were most kind to me, cer-tainly, but somehow never tipped me. That term, of May to August 1823, passed in agonies, then, in consequence of my debt to Hawker. What was the pleasure of a calendar pencil-case in comparison with the doubt and torture of mind occasioned by the sense of the debt, and the constant reproach in that fellow's scowling eyes and gloomy coarse reminders? How was I to pay off such a debt out of sixpence a week? ludicrous! Why did not some one come to see me, and tip me? Ah! my dear sir, if you have any little friends at school, go and see them, and do the natural thing by them. You

won't miss the sovereign. You don't know what a blessing it will
be to them. Don't fancy they are too old—try 'em. And they
will remember you, and bless you in future days; and their gratitude shall accompany your dreary after life; and they shall meet
you kindly when thanks for kindness are scant. Oh mercy! shall I
ever forget that sovereign you gave me, Captain Bob? or the
agonies of being in debt to Hawker? In that very term, a relation
of mine was going to India. I actually was fetched from school in
order to take leave of him. I am afraid I told Hawker of this
circumstance. I own I speculated upon my friend's giving me a
pound. A pound? Pooh! A relation going to India, and deeply
affected at parting from his darling kinsman, might give five pounds
to the dear fellow! . . . There was Hawker when I came back—
of course there he was. As he looked in my scared face, his turned
livid with rage. He muttered curses, terrible from the lips of so
young a boy. My relation, about to cross the ocean to fill a lucrative appointment, asked me with much interest about my progress
at school, heard me construe a passage of Eutropius, the pleasing
Latin work on which I was then engaged; gave me a God bless
you, and sent me back to school; upon my word of honour, without
so much as a half-crown! It is all very well, my dear sir, to say
that boys contract habits of expecting tips from their parents'
friends, that they become avaricious, and so forth. Avaricious!
fudge! Boys contract habits of tart and toffee-eating, which they
do not carry into after life. On the contrary, I wish I *did* like 'em.
What raptures of pleasure one could have now for five shillings, if
one could but pick it off the pastry-cook's tray! No. If you have
any little friends at school, out with your half-crowns, my friend,
and impart to those little ones the little fleeting joys of their age.

Well, then. At the beginning of August 1823, Bartlemytide
holidays came, and I was to go to my parents, who were at Tunbridge Wells. My place in the coach was taken by my tutor's
servants—"Bolt-in-Tun," Fleet Street, seven o'clock in the morning, was the word. My tutor, the Reverend Edward P——, to
whom I hereby present my best compliments, had a parting interview with me: gave me my little account for my governor: the
remaining part of the coach-hire; five shillings for my own expenses;
and some five-and-twenty shillings on an old account which had
been overpaid, and was to be restored to my family.

Away I ran and paid Hawker his three-and-six. Ouf! what a weight it was off my mind! (He was a Norfolk boy, and used to go home from Mrs. Nelson's "Bell Inn," Aldgate—but that is not to the point.) The next morning, of course, we were an hour before the time. I and another boy shared a hackney-coach, two-and-six; porter for putting luggage on coach, threepence. I had no more money of my own left. Rasherwell, my companion, went into the "Bolt-in-Tun" coffee-room, and had a good breakfast. I couldn't: because, though I had five-and-twenty shillings of my parents' money, I had none of my own, you see.

I certainly intended to go without breakfast, and still remember how strongly I had that resolution in my mind. But there was that hour to wait. A beautiful August morning—I am very hungry. There is Rasherwell "tucking" away in the coffee-room. I pace the street, as sadly almost as if I had been coming to school, not going thence. I turn into a court by mere chance—I vow it was by mere chance—and there I see a coffee-shop with a placard in the window. "Coffee, Twopence, Round of buttered toast, Twopence." And here am I, hungry, penniless, with five-and-twenty shillings of my parents' money in my pocket.

What would you have done? You see I had had my money, and spent it in that pencil-case affair. The five-and-twenty shillings were a trust—by me to be handed over.

But then would my parents wish their only child to be actually without breakfast? Having this money and being so hungry, so *very* hungry, mightn't I take ever so little? Mightn't I at home eat as much as I chose?

Well, I went into the coffee-shop, and spent fourpence. I remember the taste of the coffee and toast to this day—a peculiar, muddy, not-sweet-enough, most fragrant coffee—a rich, rancid, yet not-buttered-enough, delicious toast. The waiter had nothing. At any rate, fourpence, I know, was the sum I spent. And the hunger appeased, I got on the coach a guilty being.

At the last stage,—what is its name? I have forgotten in seven-and-thirty years,—there is an inn with a little green and trees before it; and by the trees there is an open carriage. It is our carriage. Yes, there are Prince and Blucher, the horses; and my parents in the carriage. Oh! how I had been counting the days until this one came! Oh! how happy had I been to see them yesterday! But there was that fourpence. All the journey down the toast had choked me, and the coffee poisoned me.

I was in such a state of remorse about the fourpence, that I forgot the maternal joy and caresses, the tender paternal voice. I pulled out the twenty-four shillings and eightpence with a trembling hand.

"Here's your money," I gasp out, "which Mr. P—— owes you, all but fourpence. I owed three-and-sixpence to Hawker out of my money for a pencil-case, and I had none left, and I took fourpence of yours, and had some coffee at a shop."

I suppose I must have been choking whilst uttering this confession.

"My dear boy," says the governor, "why didn't you go and breakfast at the hotel?"

"He must be starved," says my mother.

I had confessed; I had been a prodigal; I had been taken back to my parents' arms again. It was not a very great crime as yet, or a very long career of prodigality; but don't we know that a boy who takes a pin which is not his own, will take a thousand pounds when occasion serves, bring his parents' grey heads with sorrow to the grave, and carry his own to the gallows? Witness the career of Dick Idle, upon whom our friend Mr. Sala has been discoursing. Dick only began by playing pitch-and-toss on a tombstone: playing fair, for what we know: and even for that sin he was promptly caned by the beadle. The bamboo was ineffectual to cane that reprobate's bad courses out of him. From pitch-and-toss he proceeded to manslaughter if necessary: to highway robbery; to Tyburn and the rope there. Ah! Heaven be thanked, my parents' heads are still above the grass, and mine still out of the noose.

As I looked up from my desk, I see Tunbridge Wells Common and the rocks, the strange familiar place which I remember forty years ago. Boys saunter over the green with stumps and cricket-bats. Other boys gallop by on the riding-master's hacks. I protest it is "Cramp, Riding Master," as it used to be in the reign of George IV., and that Centaur Cramp must be at least a hundred years old. Yonder comes a footman with a bundle of novels from the library. Are they as good as *our* novels? Oh! how delightful they were! Shades of Valancour, awful ghost of Manfroni, how I shudder at your appearance! Sweet image of Thaddeus of Warsaw, how often has this almost infantile hand tried to depict you in a

Polish cap and richly embroidered tights! And as for Corinthian Tom in light blue pantaloons and hessians, and Jerry Hawthorn from the country, can all the fashion, can all the splendour of real life which these eyes have subsequently beheld, can all the wit I have heard or read in later times, compare with your fashion, with your brilliancy, with your delightful grace, and sparkling vivacious rattle?

Who knows? They *may* have kept those very books at the library still—at the well-remembered library on the Pantiles, where they sell that delightful, useful Tunbridge ware. I will go and see. I wend my way to the Pantiles, the queer little old-world Pantiles, where, a hundred years since, so much good company came to take its pleasure. Is it possible, that in the past century, gentlefolks of the first rank (as I read lately in a lecture on George II. in the *Cornhill Magazine*) assembled here and entertained each other with gaming, dancing, fiddling, and tea? There are fiddlers, harpers, and trumpeters performing at this moment in a weak little old balcony, but where is the fine company? Where are the earls, duchesses, bishops, and magnificent embroidered gamesters? A half-dozen of children and their nurses are listening to the musicians; an old lady or two in a poke bonnet passes; and for the rest, I see but an uninteresting population of native tradesmen. As for the library, its window is full of pictures of burly theologians, and their works, sermons, apologues, and so forth. Can I go in and ask the young ladies at the counter for "Manfroni, or the One-handed Monk," and "Life in London, or the Adventures of Corinthian Tom, Jeremiah Hawthorn, Esquire, and their friend Bob Logic"?—absurd. I turn away abashed from the casement—from the Pantiles—no longer Pantiles—but Parade. I stroll over the Common and survey the beautiful purple hills around, twinkling with a thousand bright villas, which have sprung up over this charming ground since first I saw it. What an admirable scene of peace and plenty! What a delicious air breathes over the heath, blows the cloud-shadows across it, and murmurs through the full-clad trees! Can the world show a land fairer, richer, more cheerful? I see a portion of it when I look up from the window at which I write. But fair scene, green woods, bright terraces gleaming in sunshine, and purple clouds swollen with summer rain—nay, the very pages over which my head bends—disappear from before my eyes. They are looking backwards, back into forty years off, into a dark room, into a little house hard by on the Common here, in the Bartlemytide holidays. The parents have gone to town for two days: the house is all his own, his own and a grim old maid-servant's, and a little boy is seated at night in the lonely drawing-room, poring over "Manfroni, or the One-handed Monk," so frightened that he scarcely dares to turn round.

ON A CHALK–MARK ON THE DOOR

ON the door-post of the house of a friend of mine, a few inches above the lock, is a little chalk-mark, which some sportive boy in passing has probably scratched on the pillar. The door-steps, the lock, handle, and so forth, are kept decently enough; but this chalk-mark, I suppose some three inches out of the housemaid's beat, has already been on the door for more than a fortnight, and I wonder whether it will be there whilst this paper is being written, whilst it is at the printer's, and, in fine, until the month passes over? I wonder whether the servants in that house will read these remarks about the chalk-mark? That the *Cornhill Magazine* is taken in in that house I know. In fact I have seen it there. In fact I have read it there. In fact I have written it there. In a word, the house to which I allude is mine—the "editor's private residence," to which, in spite of prayers, en-treaties, commands, and threats, authors, and ladies especially, *will* send their communications, although they won't understand that they injure their own interests by so doing; for how is a man who has his own work to do, his own exquisite inventions to form and perfect—Maria to rescue from the unprincipled Earl—the atrocious General to confound in his own machinations—the angelic Dean to promote to a bishopric, and so forth—how is a man to do all this, under a hundred interruptions, and keep his nerves and temper in that just and equable state in which they ought to be when he comes to assume the critical office? As you will send here, ladies, I must tell you you have a much worse chance than if you forward your valuable articles to Cornhill. Here your papers arrive, at dinner-time, we will say. Do you suppose that is a pleasant period, and that we are to criticise you between the *ovum* and *malum*, between the soup and the dessert? I have touched, I think, on this subject before. I say again, if you want real justice shown you, don't send your papers to the private residence. At home, for instance, yesterday, having given strict orders that I was to receive nobody, "except on business," do you suppose a smiling young Scottish gentleman, who forced himself into my study, and there announced himself as agent of a Cattle-food Company, was received with pleasure? There, as I sat in my arm-chair, suppose he had proposed to draw a couple of my teeth, would I have been pleased? I could have throttled that agent. I dare say the whole of that day's work will be found tinged with a ferocious misanthropy, occasioned by my clever young friend's intrusion. Cattle-food indeed! As if beans, oats, warm mashes, and a ball, are to be pushed down a man's throat just as he is meditating on the great social problem, or (for I think it was my epic I was going to touch up) just as he was about to soar to the height of the empyrean!

Having got my cattle-agent out of the door, I resume my consideration of that little mark on the door-post, which is scored up as the text of the present little sermon; and which I hope will relate, not to chalk, nor to any of its special uses or abuses (such as milk, neck-powder, and the like), but to servants. Surely ours might remove that unseemly little mark. Suppose it were on my coat, might I not request its removal? I remember, when I was at school, a little careless boy, upon whose forehead an ink-mark remained, and was perfectly recognisable for three weeks after its first appearance. May I take any notice of this chalk-stain on the forehead of my house? Whose business is it to wash that forehead? and ought I to fetch a brush and a little hot water, and wash it off myself?

Yes. But that spot removed, why not come down at six, and wash the doorsteps? I dare say the early rising and exercise would do me a great deal of good. The housemaid, in that case, might lie in bed a little later, and have her tea and the morning paper brought to her in bed: then, of course, Thomas would expect to be helped about the boots and knives; cook about the saucepans, dishes, and what not; the lady's-maid would want somebody to take the curl-papers out of her hair, and get her bath ready. You should have a set of servants for the servants, and these under-servants should have slaves to wait on them. The king commands

the first lord in waiting to desire the second lord to intimate to
the gentleman usher to request the page of the ante-chamber to
entreat the groom of the stairs to implore John to ask the captain
of the buttons to desire the maid of the still-room to beg the housekeeper to give out a few more lumps of sugar, as His Majesty has
none for his coffee, which probably is getting cold during the nego-
tiation. In our little Brentfords we are all kings, more or less.
There are orders, gradations, hierarchies, everywhere. In your
house and mine there are mysteries unknown to us. I am not going
into the horrid old question of "followers." I don't mean cousins
from the country, love-stricken policemen, or gentlemen in mufti
from Knightsbridge Barracks; but people who have an occult
right on the premises; the uncovenanted servants of the house;
grey women who are seen at evening with baskets flitting about
area-railings; dingy shawls which drop you furtive curtseys in
your neighbourhood; demure little Jacks, who start up from behind
boxes in the pantry. Those outsiders wear Thomas's crest and
livery, and call him "Sir"; those silent women address the female
servants as "Mum," and curtsey before them, squaring their
arms over their wretched lean aprons. Then, again, those *servi
servorum* have dependants in the vast, silent, poverty-stricken
world outside your comfortable kitchen fire, in the world of darkness, and hunger, and miserable cold, and dank flagged cellars,
and huddled straw, and rags, in which pale children are swarming.
It may be your beer (which runs with great volubility) has a pipe
or two which communicates with those dark caverns where hopeless anguish pours the groan, and would scarce see light but for a
scrap or two of candle which has been whipped away from your
worship's kitchen. Not many years ago—I don't know whether
before or since that white mark was drawn on the door—a lady
occupied the confidential place of housemaid in this "private
residence," who brought a good character, who seemed to have a
cheerful temper, whom I used to hear clattering and bumping overhead or on the stairs long before daylight—there, I say, was poor
Camilla, scouring the plain, trundling, and brushing, and clattering
with her pans and brooms, and humming at her work. Well, she
had established a smuggling communication of beer over the area
frontier. This neat-handed Phyllis used to pack up the nicest
baskets of my provender, and convey them to somebody outside—

I believe, on my conscience, to some poor friend in distress. Camilla was consigned to her doom. She was sent back to her friends in the country: and when she was gone we heard of many of her faults. She expressed herself, when displeased, in language that I shall not repeat. As for the beer and meat, there was no mistake about them. But *après?* Can I have the heart to be very angry with that poor jade for helping another poorer jade out of my larder? On your honour and conscience, when you were a boy, and the apples looked temptingly over Farmer Quarringdon's hedge, did you never——? When there was a grand dinner at home, and you were sliding, with Master Bacon, up and down the stairs, and the dishes came out, did you ever do such a thing as just to——? Well, in many and many a respect servants are like children. They are under domination. They are subject to reproof, to ill-temper, to petty exactions and stupid tyrannies not seldom. They scheme, conspire, fawn, and are hypocrites. "Little boys should not loll on chairs." "Little girls should be seen, and not heard;" and so forth. Have we not almost all learnt these expressions of old foozles: and uttered them ourselves when in the square-toed state? The Eton master who was breaking a lance with our Paterfamilias of late, turned on Paterfamilias, saying, He knows not the nature and exquisite candour of well-bred English boys. Exquisite fiddlestick's end, Mr. Master! Do you mean for to go for to tell us that the relations between young gentlemen and their schoolmasters are entirely frank and cordial; that the lad is familiar with the man who can have him flogged; never shirks his exercises; never gets other boys to do his verses; never does other boys' verses; never breaks bounds; never tells fibs—I mean the fibs permitted by scholastic honour? Did I know of a boy who pretended to such a character, I would forbid my scapegraces to keep company with him. Did I know a schoolmaster who pretended to believe in the existence of many hundred such boys in one school at one time, I would set that man down as a baby in knowledge of the world. "Who was making that noise?" "I don't know, sir."—And he knows it was the boy next him in school. "Who was climbing over that wall?" "I don't know, sir."—And it is in the speaker's own trousers, very likely, the glass bottle-tops have left their cruel scars. And so with servants. "Who ate up the three pigeons which went down in the pigeon-pie at breakfast this morning?" "Oh dear me! sir, it was John, who went away last month!"—or, "I think it was Miss Mary's canary-bird, which got out of the cage, and is so fond of pigeons, it never can have enough of them." Yes, it *was* the canary-bird; and Eliza saw it; and Eliza is ready to vow she did. These statements are not true; but please don't call them lies. This is not lying; this is voting with your party. You *must* back your own side. The servants'-hall stands by the servants'-hall against the dining-room. The schoolboys don't tell tales of each other. They agree not to choose to know who has made the noise, who has broken the window, who has eaten up the pigeons, who has picked all the plovers' eggs out of the aspic, how it is that liqueur brandy of Gledstane's is in such porous glass bottles— and so forth. Suppose Brutus had a footman, who came and told him that the butler drank the curaçoa: which of these serv-ants would you dismiss?—the butler, perhaps, but the footman certainly.

No. If your plate and glass are beautifully bright, your bell quickly answered, and Thomas ready, neat, and good-humoured, you are not to expect absolute truth from him. The very obse-quiousness and perfection of his service prevents truth. He may be ever so unwell in mind or body, and he must go through his service—hand the shining plate, replenish the spotless glass, lay the glittering fork—never laugh when you yourself or your guests joke—be profoundly attentive, and yet look utterly impassive— exchange a few hurried curses at the door with that unseen slavey who ministers without, and with you be perfectly calm and polite. If you are ill, he will come twenty times in an hour to your bell; or leave the girl of his heart—his mother, who is going to America— his dearest friend, who has come to say farewell—his lunch, and his glass of beer just freshly poured out—any or all of these, if the door-bell rings, or the master calls out "THOMAS" from the hall. Do you suppose you can expect absolute candour from a man whom you may order to powder his hair? As between the Reverend Henry Holyshade and his pupil, the idea of entire unreserve is utter bosh: so the truth as between you and Jeames or Thomas, or Mary the housemaid, or Betty the cook, is relative, and not to be demanded on one side or the other. Why, respectful civility is itself a lie, which poor Jeames often has to utter or perform to many a swaggering vulgarian, who should black Jeames's boots, did Jeames wear them and not shoes. There is your little Tom, just ten, ordering the great, large, quiet, orderly young man about— shrieking calls for hot water—bullying Jeames because the boots are not varnished enough, or ordering him to go to the stables, and ask Jenkins why the deuce Tomkins hasn't brought his pony round—or what you will. There is mamma rapping the knuckles of Pincot the ladysmaid, and little Miss scolding Martha, who waits up five pair of stairs in the nursery. Little Miss, Tommy, papa, mamma, you all expect from Martha, from Pincot, from Jenkins, from Jeames, obsequious civility and willing service. My dear good people, you can't have truth too. Suppose you ask for your newspaper, and Jeames says, "I'm reading it, and jest beg not to be disturbed;" or suppose you ask for a can of water, and he remarks, "You great big 'ulking fellar, ain't you big enough to bring it hup yoursulf?" what would your feelings be? Now, if you made similar proposals or requests to Mr. Jones next door, this is the kind of answer Jones would give you. You get truth habitually from equals only; so my good Mr. Holyshade, don't talk to me about the habitual candour of the young Etonian of high birth, or I have my own opin- ion of *your* candour or discernment when you do. No. Tom Bowling is the soul of honour and has been true to Black-eyed Syousan since the last time they parted at Wapping Old Stairs; but do you suppose Tom is perfectly frank, familiar, and above-board in his conversation with Admiral Nelson, K. C. B.? There are secrets, prevarications, fibs, if you will, between Tom and the Admiral— between your crew and *their* captain. I know I hire a worthy, clean, agreeable, and conscientious male or female hypocrite, at so many guineas a year, to do so and so for me. Were he other than hypocrite I would send him about his business. Don't let my displeasure be too fierce with him for a fib or two on his own account.

Some dozen years ago, my family being absent in a distant part of the country, and my business detaining me in London, I re- mained in my own house with three servants on board wages. I used only to breakfast at home; and future ages will be inter- ested to know that this meal used to consist, at that period, of tea, a penny roll, a pat of butter, and, perhaps, an egg. My weekly bill used invariably to be about fifty shillings; so that as I never dined in the house, you see, my breakfast, consisting of the delicacies before mentioned, cost about seven shillings and threepence per diem. I must, therefore, have consumed daily—

	s.	d.
A quarter of a pound of tea (say)	1	3
A penny roll (say)	1	0
One pound of butter (say)	1	3
One pound of lump sugar	1	0
A new-laid egg	2	9

Which is the only possible way in which I can make out the sum.

Well, I fell ill while under this regimen, and had an illness which, but for a certain doctor, who was brought to me by a certain kind friend I had in those days, would, I think, have prevented the possibility of my telling this interesting anecdote now a dozen years after. Don't be frightened, my dear madam; it is not a horrid sentimental account of a malady you are coming to—only a question of grocery. This illness, I say, lasted some seventeen days, during which the servants were admirably attentive and kind; and poor John, especially, was up at all hours, watching night after night—amiable, cheerful, untiring, respectful, the very best of Johns and nurses.

Twice or thrice in the seventeen days I may have had a glass of *eau sucrée*—say half-a-dozen glasses of *eau sucrée*—certainly not more. Well, this admirable, watchful, cheerful, tender, affectionate John brought me in a little bill for seventeen pounds of sugar consumed during the illness—"Often 'ad sugar-and-water; always was a-callin' for it," says John, wagging his head quite gravely. You are dead, years and years ago, poor John—so patient, so friendly, so kind, so cheerful to the invalid in the fever. But confess, now, wherever you are, that seventeen pounds of sugar to make six glasses of *eau sucrée* was a *little* too strong, wasn't it, John? Ah, how frankly, how trustily, how bravely he lied, poor John! One evening, being at Brighton in the convalescence, I remember John's step was unsteady, his voice thick, his laugh queer —and having some quinine to give me, John brought the glass to me—not to my mouth, but struck me with it pretty smartly in the eye, which was not the way in which Doctor Elliotson had intended his prescription should be taken. Turning that eye upon him, I ventured to hint that my attendant had been drinking. Drinking! I never was more humiliated at the thought of my own injustice than at John's reply. "Drinking! Sulp me! I have had ony an 'alf-pint of beer with my dinner at one o'clock!" and he retreats, holding on by a chair. These are fibs, you see, appertaining to the situation. John is drunk. "*Sulp* him, he has only had an 'alf-pint of beer with his dinner six hours ago:" and none of his fellow-servants will say otherwise. Polly is smuggled on board ship. Who tells the lieutenant when he comes his rounds? Boys are playing cards in the bedroom. The outlying fag announces master coming—out go candles—cards popped into bed—boys sound asleep. Who had that light in the dormitory? Law bless you! the poor dear innocents are every one snoring. Every one snoring, and every snore is a lie told through the nose! Suppose one of your boys or mine is engaged in that awful crime, are we going to break our hearts about it? Come, come. We pull a long face, waggle a grave head, and chuckle within our waistcoats.

Between me and those fellow-creatures of mine who are sitting in the room below, how strange and wonderful is the partition! We meet at every hour of the daylight, and are indebted to each other for a hundred offices of duty and comfort of life; and we live together for years, and don't know each other. John's voice to me is quite different from John's voice when it addresses his mates below. If I met Hannah in the street with a bonnet on, I doubt whether I should know her. And all these good people with whom I may live for years and years, have cares, interests, dear friends and relatives, mayhap schemes, passions, longing hopes, tragedies of their own, from which a carpet and a few planks and beams utterly separate me. When we were at the seaside, and poor Ellen used to look so pale, and run after the postman's bell, and seize a letter in a great scrawling hand, and read it, and cry in a corner, how should we know that the poor little thing's heart was breaking? She fetched the water, and she smoothed the ribbons, and she laid out the dresses, and brought the early cup of tea in the morning just as if she had had no cares to keep her awake. Henry (who lived out of the house) was a servant of a friend of mine, who lived in chambers. There was a dinner one day, and Henry waited all through the dinner. The champagne was properly iced, the dinner was excellently served; every guest was attended to; the dinner disappeared; the dessert was set; the claret was in perfect order, carefully decanted, and more ready. And then Henry said, "If you please, sir, may I go home?" He had received word that his house was on fire; and having seen through his dinner, he wished to go and look after his children, and little sticks of furniture. Why, such a man's livery is a uniform of honour. The crest on his button is a badge of bravery.

Do you see—I imagine I do myself—in these little instances, a tinge of humour? Ellen's heart is breaking for handsome Jeames of Buckley Square, whose great legs are kneeling, and who has given a lock of his precious powdered head, to some other than Ellen. Henry is preparing the sauce for his master's wild-ducks while the engines are squirting over his own little nest and brood. Lift these figures up but a storey from the basement to the ground-floor, and the fun is gone. We may be *en pleine tragédie*. Ellen may breathe her last sigh in blank verse, calling down blessings upon James the profligate who deserts her. Henry is a hero, and epaulettes are on his shoulders. *Atqui sciebat*, &c.: whatever tortures are in store for him, he will be at his post of duty.

You concede, however, that there is a touch of humour in the two tragedies here mentioned. Why? Is it that the idea of persons in service is somehow ludicrous? Perhaps it is made more so in this country by the splendid appearance of the liveried domestics of great people. When you think that we dress in black ourselves, and put our fellow-creatures in green, pink or canary-coloured breeches; that we order them to plaster their hair with flour, having brushed that nonsense out of our own heads fifty years ago; that some of the most genteel and stately among us cause the men who drive their carriages to put on little albino wigs, and sit behind great nosegays—I say I suppose it is this heaping of gold lace, gaudy colours, blooming plushes, on honest John Trot, which makes the man absurd in our eyes, who need be nothing but a simple reputable citizen and indoor labourer. Suppose, my dear sir, that you yourself were suddenly desired to put on a full dress, or even undress, domestic uniform with our friend Jones's crest repeated in varied combinations of button on your front and back? Suppose, madam, your son were told, that he could not get out except in lower garments of carnation or amber-coloured plush—would you let him? . . . But, as you justly say, this is not the question, and besides it is a question fraught with danger, sir; and radicalism, sir; and subversion of the very foundations of the social fabric, sir. . . . Well, John, we won't enter on your great domestic question. Don't let us disport with Jeames's dangerous strength, and the edge-tools about his knife-board: but with Betty and Susan who wield the playful mop, and set on the simmering kettle. Surely you have heard Mrs. Toddles talking to Mrs. Doddles about their mutual maids. Miss Susan must have a silk gown, and Miss Betty must wear flowers under her bonnet when she goes to church if you please, and did you ever hear such impudence? The servant in many small establishments is a constant and endless theme of talk. What small wage, sleep, meal, what endless scouring, scolding, tramping on messages fall to that poor Susan's lot; what indignation at the little kindly passing word with the grocer's young man, the pot-boy, the chubby butcher! Where such things will end, my dear Mrs. Toddles, I don't know. What wages they will want next, my dear Mrs. Doddles, &c.

Here, dear ladies, is an advertisement which I cut out of the *Times* a few days since, expressly for you:—

"A LADY is desirous of obtaining a SITUATION for a very respectable young woman as HEAD KITCHEN-MAID under a man-cook. She has lived four years under a very good cook and housekeeper. Can make ice, and is an excellent baker. She will only take a place in a very good family, where she can have the opportunity of improving herself, and, if possible, staying for two years. Apply by letter to," &c. &c.

There, Mrs. Toddles, what do you think of that, and did you ever? Well, no, Mrs. Doddles. Upon my word now, Mrs. T., I don't think I ever did. A respectable young woman—as head kitchen-maid—under a man-cook, will only take a place in a very good family, where she can improve, and stay two years. Just note up the conditions, Mrs. Toddles, mum, if you please, mum, and *then* let us see:—

1. This young woman is to be HEAD kitchen-maid, that is to say, there is to be a chorus of kitchen-maids, of which Y. W. is to be chief.

2. She will only be situated under a man-cook. (A) Ought he to be a French cook; and (B), if so, would the lady desire him to be a Protestant?

3. She will only take a place in a *very good family*. How old ought the family to be, and what do you call good? that is the question. How long after the Conquest will do? Would a banker's family do, or is a baronet's good enough? Best say what rank in the peerage would be sufficiently high. But the lady does not say whether she would like a High Church or a Low

Church family. Ought there to be unmarried sons, and may they follow a profession? and please say how many daughters; and would the lady like them to be musical? And how many company dinners a week? Not too many, for fear of fatiguing the upper kitchen-maid; but sufficient, so as to keep the upper kitchen-maid's hand in. [*N. B.*—I think I can see a rather bewildered expression on the countenances of Mesdames Doddles and Toddles as I am prattling on in this easy bantering way.]

4. The head kitchen-maid wishes to stay for two years, and improve herself under the man-cook, and having of course sucked the brains (as the phrase is) from under the chef's nightcap, then the head kitchen-maid wishes to go.

And upon my word, Mrs. Toddles, mum, I will go and fetch the cab for her. The cab? Why not her Ladyship's own carriage and pair, and the head coachman to drive away the head kitchen-maid? You see she stipulates for everything—the time to come; the time to stay; the family she will be with; and as soon as she has improved herself enough, of course the upper kitchen-maid will step into the carriage and drive off.

Well, upon my word and conscience, if things are coming to *this* pass, Mrs. Toddles and Mrs. Doddles, mum, I think I will go up-stairs and get a basin and a sponge, and then downstairs and get some hot water; and then I will go and scrub that chalk-mark off my own door with my own hands.

It is wiped off, I declare! After ever so many weeks! Who has done it? It was just a little roundabout mark, you know, and it was there for days and weeks, before I ever thought it would be the text of a Roundabout Paper.

ON BEING FOUND OUT

AT the close (let us say) of Queen Anne's reign when I was a boy at a private and preparatory school for young gentlemen, I remember the wiseacre of a master ordering us all, one night, to march into a little garden at the back of the house, and thence to proceed one by one into a tool- or hen-house (I was but a tender little thing just put into short clothes, and can't exactly say whether the house was for tools or hens), and in that house to put our hands into a sack which stood on a bench, a candle burning beside it. I put my hand into the sack. My hand came out quite black. I went and joined the other boys in the schoolroom; and all their hands were black too.

By reason of my tender age (and there are some critics who, I hope, will be satisfied by my acknowledging that I am a hundred and fifty-six next birthday) I could not understand what was the meaning of this night excursion—this candle, this tool-house, this bag of soot. I think we little boys were taken out of our sleep to be brought to the ordeal. We came, then, and showed our little hands to the master; washed them or not—most probably, I should say, not—and so went bewildered back to bed.

Something had been stolen in the school that day; and Mr. Wiseacre having read in a book of an ingenious method of finding out a thief by making him put his hand into a sack (which, if guilty, the rogue would shirk from doing), all we boys were subjected to the trial. Goodness knows what the lost object was, or who stole it. We all had black hands to show to the master. And the thief, whoever he was, was not Found Out that time.

I wonder if the rascal is alive—an elderly scoundrel he must be by this time; and a hoary old hypocrite, to whom an old schoolfellow presents his kindest regards—parenthetically remarking what a dreadful place that private school was: cold, chilblains, bad dinners, not enough victuals, and caning awful!—Are you alive still, I say, you nameless villain, who escaped discovery on that day of crime? I hope you have escaped often since, old sinner. Ah, what a lucky thing it is, for you and me, my man, that we are *not* found out in all our peccadilloes; and that our backs can slip away from the master and the cane!

Just consider what life would be, if every rogue was found out, and flogged *coram populo!* What a butchery, what an indecency, what an endless swishing of the rod! Don't cry out about my misanthropy. My good friend Mealymouth, I will trouble you to tell me, do you go to church? When there, do you say, or do you not, that you are a miserable sinner? and saying so, do you believe or disbelieve it? If you are a M. S., don't you deserve correction, and aren't you grateful if you are to be let off? I say, again, what a blessed thing it is that we are not all found out!

Just picture to yourself everybody who does wrong being found out, and punished accordingly. Fancy all the boys in all the school being whipped; and then the assistants, and then the head master (Doctor Badford let us call him). Fancy the provost-marshal being tied up, having previously superintended the correction of the whole army. After the young gentlemen have had their turn for the faulty exercises, fancy Doctor Lincolnsinn being taken up for certain faults in *his* Essay and Review. After the clergyman has cried his peccavi, suppose we hoist up a Bishop, and give him a couple of dozen! (I see my Lord Bishop of Double-Gloucester sitting in a very uneasy posture on his right reverend bench.) After we have cast off the Bishop, what are we to say to the Minister who appointed him? My Lord Cinqwarden, it is painful to have to use personal correction to a boy of your age; but really . . . *Siste tandem, carnifex!* The butchery is too horrible. The hand drops powerless, appalled at the quantity of birch which it must cut and brandish. I am glad we are not all found out, I say again; and protest, my dear brethren, against our having our deserts.

To fancy all men found out and punished is bad enough; but imagine all women found out in the distinguished social circle in which you and I have the honour to move. Is it not a mercy that so many of these fair criminals remain unpunished and undiscovered? There is Mrs. Longbow, who is forever practising, and who shoots poisoned arrows, too; when you meet her you don't call her liar, and charge her with the wickedness she has done, and is doing. There is Mrs. Painter, who passes for a most respectable woman, and a model in society. There is no use in saying what you really know regarding her and her goings on. There is Diana Hunter—what a little haughty prude it is; and yet *we* know stories about her which are not altogether edifying. I say it is best, for the sake of the good, that the bad should not all be found out. You don't want your children to know the history of that lady in the next box, who is so handsome, and whom they admire so. Ah me! what would life be if we were all found out, and punished for all our faults? Jack Ketch would be in permanence; and then who would hang Jack Ketch?

They talk of murderers being pretty certainly found out. Psha! I have heard an authority awfully competent vow and declare that scores and hundreds of murders are committed, and nobody is the wiser. That terrible man mentioned one or two ways of committing murder, which he maintained were quite common, and were scarcely ever found out. A man, for instance, comes home to his wife, and . . . but I pause—I know that this Magazine has a very large circulation. Hundreds and hundreds of thousands—

why not say a million of people at once?—well, say a million read
it. And amongst these countless readers, I might be teaching some
monster how to make away with his wife without being found out,
some fiend of a woman how to destroy her dear husband. I will
not then tell this easy and simple way of murder, as communicated
to me by a most respectable party in the confidence of private
intercourse. Suppose some gentle reader were to try this most
simple and easy receipt—it seems to me almost infallible—and
come to grief in consequence, and be found out and hanged?
Should I ever pardon myself for having been the means of doing
injury to a single one of our esteemed subscribers? The prescription whereof I speak—that is to say, whereof I *don't* speak—shall
be buried in this bosom. No, I am a humane man. I am not one
of your Bluebeards to go and say to my wife, "My dear! I am going
away for a few days to Brighton. Here are all the keys of the house.
You may open every door and closet, except the one at the end of
the oak-room opposite the fireplace, with the little bronze Shakespeare on the mantelpiece (or what not)." I don't say this to a
woman—unless, to be sure, I want to get rid of her—because, after
such a caution, I know she'll peep into the closet. I say nothing
about the closet at all. I keep the key in my pocket, and a being
whom I love, but who, as I know, has many weaknesses, out of
harm's way. You toss up your head, dear angel, drub on the ground
with your lovely little feet, on the table with your sweet rosy
fingers, and cry, "Oh, sneerer! You don't know the depth of woman's feeling, the lofty scorn of all deceit, the entire absence of mean
curiosity in the sex, or never, never would you libel us so!" Ah,
Delia! dear dear Delia! It is because I fancy I *do* know something
about you (not all, mind—no, no; no man knows that)—Ah, my
bride, my ringdove, my rose, my poppet—choose, in fact, whatever name you like—bulbul of my grove, fountain of my desert,
sunshine of my darkling life, and joy of my dungeoned existence,
it is because I *do* know a little about you that I conclude to say
nothing of that private closet, and keep my key in my pocket.
You take away that closet-key then, and the house-key. You
lock Delia in. You keep her out of harm's way and gadding, and
so she never *can* be found out.

    And yet by little strange accidents and coincidences how we
are being found out every day. You remember that old story of

the Abbé Kakatoes, who told the company at supper one night how the first confession he ever received was—from a murderer let us say. Presently enters to supper the Marquis de Croquemitaine. "Palsambleu, abbé!" says the brilliant Marquis, taking a pinch of snuff, "are you here? Gentlemen and ladies! I was the Abbé's first penitent, and I made him a confession which I promise you astonished him."

To be sure how queerly things are found out! Here is an instance. Only the other day I was writing in these Roundabout Papers about a certain man, whom I facetiously called Baggs, and who had abused me to my friends, who of course told me. Shortly after that paper was published another friend—Sacks let us call him—scowls fiercely at me as I am sitting in perfect good-humour at the club, and passes on without speaking. A cut. A quarrel. Sacks thinks it is about him that I was writing: whereas, upon my honour and conscience, I never had him once in my mind, and was pointing my moral from quite another man. But don't you see, by this wrath of the guilty-conscienced Sacks, that he had been abusing me too? He has owned himself guilty, never having been accused. He has winced when nobody thought of hitting him. I did but put the cap out, and madly butting and chafing, behold my friend rushes to put his head into it! Never mind, Sacks, you are found out; but I bear you no malice, my man.

And yet to be found out, I know from my own experience, must be painful and odious, and cruelly mortifying to the inward vanity. Suppose I am a poltroon, let us say. With fierce moustache, loud talk, plentiful oaths, and an immense stick, I keep up nevertheless a character for courage. I swear fearfully at cabmen and women; brandish my bludgeon, and perhaps knock down a little man or two with it: brag of the images which I break at the shooting-gallery, and pass amongst my friends for a whiskery fire-eater, afraid of neither man nor dragon. Ah me! Suppose some brisk little chap steps up and gives me a caning in St. James's Street, with all the heads of my friends looking out of all the club windows. My reputation is gone. I frighten no man more. My nose is pulled by whipper-snappers, who jump up on a chair to reach it. I am found out. And in the days of my triumphs, when people were yet afraid of me, and were taken in by my swagger, I always knew that I was a lily-liver, and expected that I should be found out some day.

That certainty of being found out must haunt and depress many a bold braggadocio spirit. Let us say it is a clergyman, who can pump copious floods of tears out of his own eyes and those of his audience. He thinks to himself, "I am but a poor swindling chattering rogue. My bills are unpaid. I have jilted several women whom I have promised to marry. I don't know whether I believe what I preach, and I know I have stolen the very sermon over which I have been snivelling. Have they found me out?" says he, as his head drops down on the cushion.

Then your writer, poet, historian, novelist, or what not? The *Beacon* says that "Jones's work is one of the first order." The *Lamp* declares that "Jones's tragedy surpasses every work since the days of Him of Avon." The *Comet* asserts that "J.'s 'Life of Goody Two-shoes' is a κτῆμα ἐς ἀεί, a noble and enduring monument to the fame of that admirable Englishwoman," and so forth. But then Jones knows that he has lent the critic of the *Beacon* five pounds; that his publisher has a half-share in the *Lamp;* and that the *Comet* comes repeatedly to dine with him. It is all very well. Jones is immortal until he is found out; and then down comes the extinguisher, and the immortal is dead and buried. The idea (*dies iræ!*) of discovery must haunt many a man, and make him uneasy, as the trumpets are puffing in his triumph. Brown, who has a higher place than he deserves, cowers before Smith, who has found him out. What is a chorus of critics shouting "Bravo"?—a public clapping hands and flinging garlands? Brown knows that Smith has found him out. Puff, trumpets! Wave, banners! Huzza, boys, for the immortal Brown! "This is all very well," B. thinks (bowing the while, smiling, laying his hand to his heart); "but there stands Smith at the window: *he* has measured me; and some day the others will find me out too." It is a very curious sensation to sit by a man who has found you out, and who you know has found you out; or, *vice versâ*, to sit with a man whom *you* have found out. His talent? Bah! His virtue? We know a little story or two about his virtue, and he knows we know it. We are thinking over friend Robinson's antecedents, as we grin, bow, and talk; and we are both humbugs together. Robinson a good fellow, is he? You know how he behaved to Hicks? A good-natured man, is he? Pray do you remember that little story of Mrs. Robinson's black eye? How men have to work, to talk, to smile, to go to bed, and try to sleep, with this dread of being found out on their consciences! Bardolph, who has robbed a church, and Nym, who has taken a purse, go to their usual haunts, and smoke their pipes with their companions. Mr. Detective Bullseye appears, and says, "Oh, Bardolph, I want you about that there pyx business!" Mr. Bardolph knocks the ashes out of his pipe, puts out his hands to the little steel cuffs, and walks away quite meekly. He is found out. He must go. "Good-bye, Doll Tearsheet! Good-bye, Mrs. Quickly, ma'am!" The other gentlemen and ladies *de la société* look on and exchange mute adieux with the departing friends. And an assured time will come when the other gentlemen and ladies will be found out too.

What a wonderful and beautiful provision of nature it has been that, for the most part, our womankind are not endowed with the faculty of finding us out! *They* don't doubt, and probe, and weigh, and take your measure. Lay down this paper, my benevolent friend and reader, go into your drawing-room now, and utter a joke ever so old, and I wager sixpence the ladies there will all begin to laugh. Go to Brown's house, and tell Mrs. Brown and the young ladies what you think of him, and see what a welcome you will get! In like manner, let him come to your house, and tell *your* good lady his candid opinion of you, and fancy how she will receive him! Would you have your wife and children know you exactly for what you are, and esteem you precisely at your worth? If so, my friend, you will live in a dreary house, and you will have but a chilly fireside. Do you suppose the people round it don't see your homely face as under a glamour, and, as it were, with a halo of love round it? You don't fancy you *are*, as you seem to them? No such thing, my man. Put away that monstrous conceit, and be thankful that *they* have not found you out.

ON A HUNDRED YEARS HENCE

WHERE have I just read of a game played at a country house? The party assembles round a table with pens, ink, and paper. Some one narrates a tale containing more or less incidents and personages. Each person of the company then writes down, to the best of his memory and ability, the anecdote just narrated, and finally the papers are to be read out.

I do not say I should like to play often at this game, which might possibly be a tedious and lengthy pastime, not by any means so amusing as smoking a cigar in the conservatory; or even listening to the young ladies playing their piano-pieces; or to Hobbs and Nobbs lingering round the bottle and talking over the morning's run with the hounds; but surely it is a moral and ingenious sport. They say the variety of narratives is often very odd and amusing. The original story becomes so changed and distorted that at the end of all the statements you are puzzled to know where the truth is at all. As time is of small importance to the cheerful persons engaged in this sport, perhaps a good way of playing it would be to spread it over a couple of years. Let the people who played the game in '60 all meet and play it once more in '61, and each write his story over again. Then bring out your original and compare notes. Not only will the stories differ from each other, but the writers will probably differ from themselves. In the course of the year the incidents will grow or will dwindle strangely. The least authentic of the statements will be so lively or so malicious, or so neatly put, that it will appear most like the truth. I like these tales and sportive exercises. I had begun a little print collection once. I had Addison in his nightgown in bed at Holland House, requesting young Lord Warwick to remark how a Christian should die. I had Cambronne clutching his cocked hat, and uttering the immortal "La Garde meurt et ne se rend pas." I had the "Vengeur" going down, and all the crew hurraying like madmen. I had Alfred toasting the muffin; Curtius (Haydon) jumping into the gulf; with extracts from Napoleon's bulletins, and a fine authentic portrait of Baron Munchausen.

What man who has been before the public at all has not heard similar wonderful anecdotes regarding himself and his own history? In these humble essaykins I have taken leave to egotise. I cry out about the shoes which pinch me, and, as I fancy, more naturally and pathetically than if my neighbour's corns were trodden under foot. I prattle about the dish which I love, the wine which I like, the talk I heard yesterday—about Brown's absurd airs—Jones's ridiculous elation when he thinks he has caught me in a blunder (a part of the fun, you see, is that Jones will read this, and will perfectly well know that I mean him, and that we shall meet and grin at each other with entire politeness). This is not the highest kind of speculation, I confess, but it is a gossip which amuses some folks. A brisk and honest small-beer will refresh those who do not care for the frothy outpourings of heavier taps. A two of clubs may be a good handy little card sometimes, and able to tackle a king of diamonds, if it is a little trump. Some philosophers get their wisdom with deep thought, and out of ponderous libraries; I pick up my small crumbs of cogitation at a dinner-table; or from Mrs. Mary and Miss Louisa, as they are prattling over their five-o'clock tea.

Well, yesterday at dinner, Jucundus was good enough to tell me a story about myself, which he had heard from a lady of his acquaintance, to whom I send my best compliments. The tale is this. At nine o'clock on the evening of the 31st of November last, just before sunset, I was seen leaving No. 96 Abbey Road, St. John's Wood, leading two little children by the hand, one of them in a nankeen pelisse, and the other having a mole on the third finger of his left hand (she thinks it was the third finger, but is quite sure it was the left hand). Thence I walked with them to Charles Boroughbridge's, pork and sausage man, No. 29 Upper Theresa Road. Here, whilst I left the little girl innocently eating a polony in the front shop, I and Boroughbridge retired with the boy into the back parlour, where Mrs. Boroughbridge was playing cribbage. She put up the cards and boxes, took out a chopper and a napkin, and we cut the little boy's little throat (which he bore with great pluck and resolution), and made him into sausage-meat by the aid of Purkis's excellent sausage-machine. The little girl at first could not understand her brother's absence, but under the pretence of taking her to see Mr. Fechter in *Hamlet*, I led her down to the New River at Sadler's Wells, where a body of a child in a nankeen pelisse was subsequently found, and has never been recognised to the present day. And this Mrs. Lynx can aver, because she saw the whole transaction with her own eyes, as she told Mr. Jucundus.

I have altered the little details of the anecdote somewhat. But this story is, I vow and declare, as true as Mrs. Lynx's. Gracious goodness! how do lies begin? What are the averages of lying? Is the same amount of lies told about every man, and do we pretty much all tell the same amount of lies? Is the average greater in Ireland than in Scotland, or *vice versâ*—among women than among men? Is this a lie I am telling now? If I am talking about you, the odds are, perhaps, that it is. I look back at some which have been told about me, and speculate on them with thanks and wonder. Dear friends have told them of me, have told them to me of myself. Have they not to and of you, dear friend? A friend of mine was dining at a large dinner of clergymen, and a story, as true as the sausage story above given, was told regarding me, by one of those reverend divines in whose frocks sit some anile chatterboxes, as any man who knows this world knows. They take the privilege of their gown. They cabal, and tattle, and hiss, and cackle comminations under their breath. I say the old women of the other sex are not more talkative or more mischievous than some of these. "Such a man ought not to be spoken to," says Gobemouche, narrating the story—and such a story! "And I am surprised he is admitted into society at all." Yes, dear Gobemouche, but the story wasn't true; and I had no more done the wicked deed in question than I had run away with the Queen of Sheba.

I have always longed to know what that story was (or what collection of histories), which a lady had in her mind to whom a servant of mine applied for a place, when I was breaking up my establishment once, and going abroad. Brown went with a very good character from us, which, indeed, she fully deserved after several years' faithful service. But when Mrs. Jones read the name of the person out of whose employment Brown came, "That is quite sufficient," says Mrs. Jones. "You may go. I will never take a servant out of *that* house." Ah, Mrs. Jones, how I should like to know what that crime was, or what that series of villainies, which made you determine never to take a servant out of my house. Do you believe in the story of the little boy and the sausages? Have you swallowed that little minced infant? Have you devoured that young Polonius? Upon my word you have maw enough. We somehow greedily gobble down all stories in which the characters of our friends are chopped up, and believe wrong of them without inquiry. In a late serial work written by this hand, I remember making some pathetic remarks about our propensity to believe ill of our neighbours—and I remember the remarks, not because they were valuable, or novel, or ingenious, but because, within three days after they had appeared in print, the moralist who wrote them, walking home with a friend, heard a story about another friend, which story he straightway believed, and which story was scarcely more true than that sausage fable which is here set down. *O mea culpa, mea maxima culpa!* But though the preacher trips, shall not the doctrine be good? Yea, brethren! Here be the rods. Look you, here are the scourges. Choose me a nice long, swishing, buddy one, light and well-poised in the handle, thick and bushy at the tail. Pick me out a whip-cord thong with some dainty knots in it—and now—we all deserve it—whish, whish, whish! Let us cut into each other all round.

A favourite liar and servant of mine was a man I once had to drive a brougham. He never came to my house, except for orders, and once when he helped to wait at dinner, so clumsily that it was agreed we would dispense with his further efforts. The (job) brougham horse used to look dreadfully lean and tired, and the livery-stable keeper complained that we worked him too hard. Now, it turned out that there was a neighbouring butcher's lady who liked to ride in a brougham; and Tomkins lent her ours, drove her cheerfully to Richmond and Putney, and, I suppose, took out a payment in mutton-chops. We gave this good Tomkins wine and medicine for his family when sick—we supplied him with little comforts and extras which need not now be remembered—and the grateful creature rewarded us by informing some of our tradesmen whom he honoured with his custom, "Mr. Roundabout? Lor' bless you! I carry him up to bed drunk every night in the week." He, Tomkins, being a man of seven stone weight and five feet high; whereas his employer was—but here modesty interferes, and I decline to enter into the avoirdupois question.

Now, what was Tomkins's motive for the utterance and dissemination of these lies? They could further no conceivable end or interest of his own. Had they been true stories, Tomkins's master would, and reasonably, have been still more angry than at the fables. It was but suicidal slander on the part of Tomkins—must come to a discovery—must end in a punishment. The poor wretch had got his place under, as it turned out, a fictitious character. He might have stayed in it, for of course Tomkins had a wife and poor innocent children. He might have had bread, beer, bed, character, coats, coals. He might have nestled in our little island, comfortably sheltered from the storms of life; but we were compelled to cast him out, and send him driving, lonely, perishing, tossing, starving, to sea—to drown. To drown? There be other modes of death whereby rogues die. Good-bye, Tomkins. And so the night-cap is put on, and the bolt is drawn for poor T.

Suppose we were to invite volunteers amongst our respected readers to send in little statements of the lies which they know have been told about themselves: what a heap of correspondence, what an exaggeration of malignities, what a crackling bonfire of incendiary falsehoods, might we not gather together! And a lie once set going, having the breath of life breathed into it by the father of lying, and ordered to run its diabolical little course, lives with a prodigious vitality. You say, "Magna est veritas et prævalebit." Psha! Great lies are as great as great truths, and prevail constantly, and day after day. Take an instance or two out of my own little budget. I sit near a gentleman at dinner, and the conversation turns upon a certain anonymous literary performance which at the time is amusing the town. "Oh," says the gentleman, "everybody knows who wrote that paper: it is Momus's." I was a young author at the time, perhaps proud of my bantling: "I beg your pardon," I say, "it was written by your humble servant." "Indeed!" was all that the man replied, and he shrugged his shoulders, turned his back, and talked to his other neighbour. I never heard sarcastic incredulity more finely conveyed than by that "indeed." "Impudent liar," the gentleman's face said, as clear as face could speak. Where was Magna Veritas, and how did she prevail then? She lifted up her voice, she made her appeal, and she was kicked out of court. In New York I read a newspaper criticism one day (by an exile from our shores who has taken up his abode in the Western Republic), commenting upon a letter of mine which had appeared in a contemporary volume, and wherein it was stated that the writer was a lad in such and such a year, and in point of fact, I was, at the period spoken of, nineteen years of age. "Falsehood, Mr. Roundabout," says the noble critic: "you were then not a lad; you were then six-and-twenty years of age." You see he knew better than papa and mamma and parish register. It was easier for him to think and say I lied, on a two-penny matter connected with my own affairs, than to imagine he was mistaken. Years ago, in a time when we were very mad wags, Arcturus and myself met a gentleman from China who knew the language. We began to speak Chinese against him. We said we were born in China. We were two to one. We spoke the mandarin dialect with perfect fluency. We had the company with us; as in the old old days, the squeak of the real pig was voted not to be so natural as the squeak of the sham pig. O Arcturus, the sham pig squeaks in our streets now to the applause of multitudes, and the reak porker grunts unheeded in his sty!

I once talked for some little time with an amiable lady: it was for the first time; and I saw an expression of surprise on her kind face which said as plainly as face could say, "Sir, do you know that up to this moment I have had a certain opinion of you, and that I begin to think I have been mistaken or misled?" I not only know that she had heard evil reports of me, but I know who told her—one of those acute fellows, my dear brethren, of whom we spoke in a previous sermon, who has found me out—found out actions which I never did, found out thoughts and sayings which I never spoke, and judged me accordingly. Ah, my lad! have I found *you* out? *O risum teneatis*. Perhaps the person I am accusing is no more guilty than I.

How comes it that the evil which men say spreads so widely and lasts so long, whilst our good kind words don't seem somehow to take root, and bear blossom? Is it that in the stony hearts of mankind these pretty flowers can't find a place to grow? Certain it is that scandal is good brisk talk, whereas praise of one's neighbour is by no means lively hearing. An acquaintance grilled, scored, devilled, and served with mustard and cayenne pepper, excites the appetite; whereas a slice of cold friend with currant jelly is but a sickly unrelishing meat.

Now, such being the case, my dear worthy Mrs. Candour, in whom I know there are a hundred good and generous qualities: it being perfectly clear that the good things which we say of our neighbours don't fructify, but somehow perish in the ground where they are dropped, whilst the evil words are wafted by all the winds of scandal, take root in all soils, and flourish amazingly—seeing, I say, that this conversation does not give us a fair chance, suppose we give up censoriousness altogether, and decline uttering our opinions about Brown, Jones, and Robinson, (and Mesdames B., J., and R.) at all. We may be mistaken about every one of them, as, please goodness, those anecdote-mongers against whom I have uttered my meek protest have been mistaken about me. We need not go to the extent of saying that Mrs. Manning was an amiable creature much misunderstood; and Jack Thurtell a gallant unfortunate fellow, not near so black as he was painted; but we will try and avoid personalities altogether in talk, won't we? We will range the fields of science, dear madam, and communicate to each other the pleasing results of our studies. We will, if you please, examine the infinitesimal wonders of nature through the microscope. We will cultivate entomology. We will sit with our arms round each other's waists on the *pons asinorum*, and see the stream of mathematics flow beneath. We will take refuge in cards, and play at "beggar my neighbour," not abuse my neighbour. We will go to the Zoölogical Gardens and talk freely about the gorilla and his kindred, but not talk about people who can talk in their turn. Suppose we praise the High Church? we offend the Low Church. The Broad Church? High and Low are both offended. What do you think of Lord Derby as a politician? And what is your opinion of Lord Palmerston? If you please, will you play me those lovely variations of "In a cottage near a wood"? It is a charming air (you know it in French, I suppose? *Ah! te dirai-je, maman?*) and was a favourite with poor Marie Antoinette. I say "poor," because I have a right to speak with pity of a sovereign who was renowned for so much beauty and so much misfortune. But as for giving any opinion on her conduct, saying that she was good or bad, or indifferent, goodness forbid! We have agreed we will not be censorious. Let us have a game at cards—at *écarté*, if you please. You deal. I ask for cards. I lead the deuce of clubs. . . .

What? there is no deuce! Deuce take it! What? People *will* go on talking about their neighbours, and won't have their mouths stopped by cards, or ever so much microscopes and aquariums? Ah, my poor dear Mrs. Candour, I agree with you. By the way, did you ever see anything like Lady Godiva Trotter's dress last night? People *will* go on chattering, although we hold our tongues; and, after all, my good soul, what will their scandal matter a hundred years hence?

SMALL–BEER CHRONICLE

NOT long since, at a certain banquet, I had the good fortune to sit by Doctor Polymathesis, who knows everything, and who, about the time when the claret made its appearance, mentioned that old dictum of the grumbling Oxford don, that "ALL CLARET *would be port if it could!*" Imbibing a bumper of one or the other not ungratefully, I thought to myself, "Here, surely, Mr. Roundabout, is a good text for one of your reverence's sermons." Let us apply to the human race, dear brethren, what is here said of the vintages of Portugal and Gascony, and we shall have no difficulty in perceiving how many clarets aspire to be ports in their way; how most men and women of our acquaintance, how we ourselves, are Aquitanians giving ourselves Lusitanian airs; how we wish to have credit for being stronger, braver, more beautiful, more worthy than we really are.

Nay, the beginning of this hypocrisy—a desire to excel, a desire to be hearty, fruity, generous, strength-imparting—is a virtuous and noble ambition; and it is most difficult for a man in his own case, or his neighbour's, to say at what point this ambition transgresses the boundary of virtue, and becomes vanity, pretence, and self-seeking. You are a poor man, let us say, showing a bold face to adverse fortune, and wearing a confident aspect. Your purse is very narrow, but you owe no man a penny; your means are scanty, but your wife's gown is decent; your old coat well brushed; your children at a good school; you grumble to no one; ask favours of no one; truckle to no neighbours on account of their superior rank, or (a worse, and a meaner and a more common crime still) envy none for their better fortune. To all outward appearances you are as well to do as your neighbours, who have thrice your income. There may be in this case some little mixture of pretension in your life and behaviour. You certainly *do* put on a smiling face whilst fortune is pinching you. Your wife and girls, so smart and neat at evening parties, are cutting, patching, and cobbling all day to make both ends of life's haberdashery meet. You give a friend a bottle of wine on occasion, but are content yourself with a glass of whisky-and-water. You avoid a cab, saying that of all things you like to walk home after dinner (which you know, my good friend, is a fib). I grant you that in this scheme of life there does enter ever so little hypocrisy; that this claret is loaded, as it were; but your desire to *portify* yourself is amiable, is pardonable, is perhaps honourable: and were there no other hypocrisies than yours in the world we should be a set of worthy fellows; and sermonisers, moralisers, satirisers would have to hold their tongues and go to some other trade to get a living.

But you know you *will* step over that boundary line of virtue and modesty, into the district where humbug and vanity begin, and there the moraliser catches you and makes an example of you. For instance, in a certain novel in another place my friend Mr. Talbot Twysden is mentioned—a man whom you and I know to be a wretched ordinaire, but who persists in treating himself as if he was the finest '20 port. In our Britain there are hundreds of men like him; for ever striving to swell beyond their natural size, to strain beyond their natural strength, to step beyond their natural stride. Search, search within your own waistcoats, dear brethren—*you* know in your hearts, which of your ordinaire qualities you would pass off, and fain consider as first-rate port. And why not you yourself, Mr. Preacher? says the congregation. Dearly beloved, neither in nor out of this pulpit do I profess to be bigger, or cleverer, or wiser, or better than any of you. A short while since, a certain Reviewer announced that I gave myself great pretensions as a philosopher. I a philosopher! I advance pretensions! My dear Saturday friend, And you? Don't you teach everything to everybody? and punish the naughty boys if they don't learn as you bid them? You teach politics to Lord John and Mr. Gladstone. You teach poets how to write; painters, how to paint; gentlemen, manners; and opera-dancers, how to pirouette. I was not a little amused of late by an instance of the modesty of our Saturday friend, who, more Athenian than the Athenians, and *à propos* of a Greek book by a Greek author, sat down and gravely showed the Greek gentleman how to write his own language.

No, I do not, as far as I know, try to be port at all; but offer in these presents, a sound genuine ordinaire, at 18*s*. per doz. let us say, grown on my own hillside, and offered *de bon cœur* to those who will sit down under my *tonnelle*, and have a half-hour's drink and gossip. It is none of your hot porto, my friend. I know there is much better and stronger liquor elsewhere. Some pronounce it sour; some say it is thin; some that it has woefully lost its flavour. This may or may not be true. There are good and bad years; years that surprise everybody; years of which the produce is small and bad, or rich and plentiful. But if my tap is not genuine it is naught, and no man should give himself the trouble to drink it. I do not even say that I would be port if I could; knowing that port (by which I would imply much stronger, deeper, richer, and more durable liquor than my vineyard can furnish) is not relished by all palates, or suitable to all heads. We will assume then, dear brother, that you and I are tolerably modest people; and, ourselves being thus out of the question, proceed to show how pretentious our neighbours are, and how very many of them would be port if they could.

Have you never seen a small man from college placed amongst great folk, and giving himself the airs of a man of fashion? He goes back to his common room with fond reminiscences of Ermine Castle or Strawberry Hall. He writes to the dear Countess to say that dear Lord Lollypop is getting on very well at Saint Boniface, and that the accident which he met with in a scuffle with an inebriated bargeman only showed his spirit and honour, and will not permanently disfigure his Lordship's nose. He gets his clothes from dear Lollypop's London tailor, and wears a mauve or magenta tie when he rides out to see the hounds. A love of fashionable people is a weakness, I do not say of all, but of some tutors. Witness that Eton tutor t'other day, who intimated that in Cornhill we could not understand the perfect purity, delicacy, and refinement of those genteel families who sent their sons to Eton. O usher, *mon ami!* Old Sam Johnson, who, too, had been an usher in his early life, kept a little of that weakness always. Suppose Goldsmith had knocked him up at three in the morning and proposed a boat to Greenwich, as Topham Beauclerc and his friend did, would he have said, "What, my boy, are you for a frolic? I'm with you!" and gone and put on his clothes? Rather he would have pitched poor Goldsmith downstairs. He would have liked to be port if he could. Of course *we* wouldn't. Our opinion of the Portugal grape is known. It grows very high, and is very sour, and we don't go for that kind of grape at all.

"I was walking with Mr. Fox"—and sure this anecdote comes very pat after the grapes—"I was walking with Mr. Fox in the Louvre," says Benjamin West (*apud* some paper I have just been reading), "and I remarked how many people turned round to look at *me*. This shows the respect of the French for the fine arts." This is a curious instance of a very small claret indeed, which imagined itself to be port of the strongest body. There are not many instances of a faith so deep, so simple, so satisfactory as this. I have met many who would like to be port; but with few of the Gascon sort, who absolutely believed they *were* port. George III.

believed in West's port, and thought Reynolds's overrated stuff. When I saw West's pictures at Philadelphia, I looked at them with astonishment and awe. Hide, blushing glory, hide your head under your old nightcap. O immortality! is this the end of you? Did any of you, my dear brethren, ever try and read "Blackmore's Poems," or the "Epics of Baour-Lormian," or the "Henriade," or—what shall we say?—Pollok's "Course of Time"? They were thought to be more lasting than brass by some people, and where are they now? And *our* masterpieces of literature—*our* ports—that if not immortal, at any rate are to last their fifty, their hundred years—oh, sirs, don't you think a very small cellar will hold them?

Those poor people in brass, on pedestals, hectoring about Trafalgar Square and that neighbourhood, don't you think many of them —apart even from the ridiculous execution—cut rather a ridiculous figure, and that we are too eager to set up our ordinaire heroism and talent for port? A Duke of Wellington or two I will grant, though even of these idols a moderate supply will be sufficient. Some years ago a famous and witty French critic was in London, with whom I walked the streets. I am ashamed to say that I informed him (being in hopes that he was about to write some papers regarding the manners and customs of this country) that all the statues he saw represented the Duke of Wellington. That on the arch opposite Apsley House? the Duke in a cloak, and cocked-hat, on horseback. That behind Apsley House in an airy fig-leaf costume? the Duke again. That in Cockspur Street? the Duke with a pigtail—and so on. I showed him an army of Dukes. There are many bronze heroes who after a few years look already as foolish, awkward, and out of place as a man, say at Shoolbred's or Swan & Edgar's. For example, those three Grenadiers in Pall Mall, who have been up only a few months, don't you pity those unhappy household troops, who have to stand frowning and looking fierce there; and think they would like to step down and go to barracks? That they fought very bravely there is no doubt; but so did the Russians fight very bravely; and the French fight very bravely; and so did Colonel Jones and the 99th, and Colonel Brown and the 100th; and I say again that ordinaire should not give itself port airs, and that an honest ordinaire would blush to be found swaggering so. I am sure if you could consult the Duke of York, who is impaled on his column between the two clubs, and ask his late Royal Highness whether he thought he ought to remain there, he would say no. A brave worthy man, not a braggart or boaster, to be put upon that heroic perch must be painful to him. Lord George Bentinck, I suppose, being in the midst of the family park in Cavendish Square, may conceive that he has a right to remain in his place. But look at William of Cumberland, with his hat cocked over his eye, prancing behind Lord George on his Roman-nosed charger: he, depend on it, would be for getting off his horse if he had the permission. He did not hesitate about trifles, as we know; but he was a very truth-telling and honourable soldier; and as for heroic rank and statuesque dignity, I would wager a dozen of '20 Port against a bottle of pure and sound Bordeaux, at 18*s.* per dozen (bottles included), that he never would think of claiming any such absurd distinction. They have got a statue of Thomas Moore at Dublin, I hear. Is he on horseback? Some men should have, say, a fifty years' lease of glory. After a while some gentleman now in brass should go to the melting furnace, and reappear in some other gentleman's shape. Lately I saw that Melville column rising over Edinburgh; come, good men and true, don't you feel a little awkward and uneasy when you walk under it? Who was this to stand in heroic places? and is yon the man whom Scotchmen most delight to honour? I must own deferentially that there is a tendency in North Britain to over-esteem its heroes. Scotch ale is very good and strong, but it is not stronger than all the other beer in the world, as some Scottish patriots would insist. When there has been a war, and stout old Sandy Sansculotte returns home from India or the Crimea, what a bagpiping, shouting, hurraying, and self-glorification takes place round about him! You would fancy, to hear M'Orator after dinner, that the Scotch had fought all the battles, killed all the Russians, Indians rebels, or what not. In Cupar-Fife, there's a little inn called the "Battle of Waterloo," and what do you think the sign is? (I speak from memory, to be sure.) "The Battle of Waterloo" is one broad Scotchman laying about him with a broadsword. Yes, yes, my dear Mac, you are wise, you are good, you are clever, you are handsome, you are brave, you are rich, &c.; but so is Jones over the border. Scotch salmon is good, but there are other good fish in the sea. I once heard a Scotchman lecture on poetry in London. Of course the pieces he selected were chiefly by

Scottish authors, and Walter Scott was his favourite poet. I whispered to my neighbour, who was a Scotchman (by the way, the audience were almost all Scotch, and the room was All-Macs—I beg your pardon, but I couldn't help it, I really couldn't help it)—"The professor has said the best poet was a Scotchman: I wager that he will say the worst poet was a Scotchman too." And sure enough that worst poet, when he made his appearance, was a Northern Briton.

And as we are talking of bragging, and I am on my travels, can I forget one mighty republic—one—two mighty republics, where people are notoriously fond of passing off their claret for port? I am very glad, for the sake of a kind friend, that there is a great and influential party in the United, and I trust, in the Confederate States,[1] who believe that Catawba wine is better than the best champagne. Opposite that famous old White House at Washington, whereof I shall ever have a grateful memory, they have set up an equestrian statue of General Jackson, by a self-taught American artist of no inconsiderable genius and skill. At an evening party a member of Congress seized me in a corner of the room, and asked me if I did not think this was *the finest equestrian statue in the world?* How was I to deal with this plain question, put to me in a corner? I was bound to reply, and accordingly said that I did *not* think it was the finest statue in the world. "Well, sir," says the member of Congress, "but you must remember that Mr. M—— had never seen a statue when he made this!" I suggested that to see other statues might do Mr. M—— no harm. Nor was any man more willing to own his defects, or more modest regarding his merits, than the sculptor himself, whom I met subsequently. But oh! what a charming article there was in a Washington paper next day about the impertinence of criticism and offensive tone of arrogance which Englishmen adopted towards men and works of genius in America! "Who was this man, who," &c. &c.? The Washington writer was angry because I would not accept this American claret as the finest port-wine in the world. Ah me! It is about blood and not wine that the quarrel now is, and who shall foretell its end?

How much claret that would be port if it could is handed about in every society! In the House of Commons what small-beer ora-

[1] Written in July 1861.

tors try to pass for strong! Stay: have I a spite against any one? It is a fact that the wife of the Member for Bungay has left off asking me and Mrs. Roundabout to her evening-parties. Now is the time to have a slap at him. I will say that he was always over-rated, and that now he is lamentably falling off even from what he has been. I will back the Member for Stoke Poges against him; and show that the dashing young Member for Islington is a far sounder man than either. Have I any little literary animosities? Of course not. Men of letters never have. Otherwise, how I could serve out a competitor here, make a face over his works, and show that his would-be port is very meagre ordinaire indeed! Nonsense, man! Why so squeamish? Do they spare *you*? Now you have the whip in your hand, won't you lay on? You used to be a pretty whip enough as a young man, and liked it too. Is there no enemy who would be the better for a little thonging? No. I have militated in former times, not without glory; but I grow peaceable as I grow old. And if I have a literary enemy, why, he will probably write a book ere long, and then it will be *his* turn, and my favourite review will be down upon him.

My brethren, these sermons are professedly short; for I have that opinion of my dear congregation, which leads me to think that were I to preach at great length they would yawn, stamp, make noises, and perhaps go straightway out of church; and yet with this text I protest I could go on for hours. What multitudes of men, what multitudes of women, my dears, pass off their ordinaire for port, their small-beer for strong! In literature, in politics, in the army, the navy, the church, at the bar, in the world, what an immense quantity of cheap liquor is made to do service for better sorts! Ask Serjeant Roland his opinion of Oliver Q. C. "Ordinaire, my good fellow, ordinaire, with a port-wine label!" Ask Oliver his opinion of Roland. "Never was a man so overrated by the world and by himself." Ask Tweedledumski his opinion of Tweedle-deestein's performance. "A quack, my tear sir; an ignoramus, I geef you my vort. He gombose an opera! He is not fit to make dance a bear!" Ask Paddington and Buckmister, those two "swells" of fashion, what they think of each other. They are notorious ordinaire. You and I remember when they passed for very small wine, and now how high and mighty they have become. What do you say to Tomkins's sermons? Ordinaire trying to go down as orthodox port, and very meagre ordinaire too! To Hopkins's historical works?—to Pumkins's poetry? Ordinaire, ordinaire again—thin, feeble, overrated; and so down the whole list. And when we have done discussing our men friends, have we not all the women? Do these not advance absurd pretensions? Do these never give themselves airs? With feeble brains, don't they often set up to be *esprits forts?* Don't they pretend to be women of fashion, and cut their betters? Don't they try and pass off their ordinary-looking girls as beauties of the first order? Every man in his circle knows women who give themselves airs, and to whom we can apply the port-wine simile.

Come, my friends. Here is enough of ordinaire and port for to-day. My bottle has run out. Will anybody have any more? Let us go upstairs, and get a cup of tea from the ladies.

OGRES

I DARESAY the reader has remarked that the upright and independent vowel, which stands in the vowel-list between E and O, has formed the subject of the main part of these essays. How does that vowel feel this morning?—fresh, good-humoured, and lively? The Roundabout lines, which fall from this pen, are correspondingly brisk and cheerful. Has anything, on the contrary, disagreed with the vowel? Has its rest been disturbed, or was yesterday's dinner too good, or yesterday's wine not good enough? Under such circumstances, a darkling misanthropic tinge, no doubt, is cast upon the paper. The jokes, if attempted, are elaborate and dreary. The bitter temper breaks out. That sneering manner is adopted, which you know, and which exhibits itself so especially when the writer is speaking about women. A moody carelessness comes over him. He sees no good in any body or thing: and treats gentlemen, ladies, history, and things in general, with a like gloomy flippancy. Agreed. When the vowel in question is in that mood, if you like airy gaiety and tender gushing benevolence—if you want to be satisfied with yourself and the rest of your fellow-beings; I recommend you, my dear creature, to go to some other shop in Cornhill, or turn to some other article. There are moods in the mind of the vowel of which we are speaking, when it is ill-conditioned and captious. Who always keeps good health and good humour? Do not philosophers grumble? Are not sages sometimes out of temper? and do not angel-women go off in tantrums? To-day my mood is dark. I scowl as I dip my pen in the inkstand.

Here is the day come round—for everything here is done with the utmost regularity:—intellectual labour, sixteen hours; meals, thirty-two minutes; exercise, a hundred and forty-eight minutes; conversation with the family, chiefly literary, and about the house-keeping, one hour and four minutes; sleep, three hours and fifteen minutes (at the end of the month, when the Magazine is complete, I own I take eight minutes more); and the rest for the toilette and the world. Well, I say, the *Roundabout Paper Day* being come, and the subject long since settled in my mind, an excellent subject—a most telling, lively, and popular subject—I go to breakfast determined to finish the meal in $9\frac{3}{4}$ minutes, as usual, and then retire to my desk and work, when—oh, provoking!—here in the paper is the very subject treated on which I was going to write! Yesterday another paper which I saw treated it—and of course, as I need not tell you, spoiled it. Last Saturday, another paper had an article on the subject; perhaps you may guess what it was—but I won't tell you. Only this is true, my favourite subject, which was about to make the best paper we have had for a long time; my bird, my game that I was going to shoot and serve up with such a delicate sauce, has been found by other sportsmen; and pop, pop, pop, a half-dozen of guns have banged at it, mangled it, and brought it down.

"And can't you take some other text?" say you. All this is mighty well. But if you have set your heart on a certain dish for dinner, be it cold boiled veal, or what you will, and they bring you turtle and venison, don't you feel disappointed? During your walk you have been making up your mind that that cold meat, with moderation and a pickle, will be a very sufficient dinner: you have accustomed your thoughts to it; and here, in place of it, is a turkey, surrounded by coarse sausages, or a reeking pigeon-pie, or a fulsome roast pig. I have known many a good and kind man made furiously angry by such a *contretemps*. I have known him lose his temper, call his wife and servants names, and a whole household made miserable. If, then, as is notoriously the case, it is too dangerous to baulk a man about his dinner, how much more about his article! I came to my meal with an ogre-like appetite and gusto.

Fee, faw, fum! Wife, where is that tender little princekin? Have you trussed him, and did you stuff him nicely, and have you taken care to baste him, and do him, not too brown, as I told you? Quick! I am hungry! I begin to whet my knife, to roll my eyes about, and roar and clap my huge chest like a gorilla; and then my poor Ogrina has to tell me that the little princes have all run away, whilst she was in the kitchen, making the paste to bake them in! I pause in the description. I won't condescend to report the bad language, which you know must ensue, when an ogre, whose mind is ill-regulated, and whose habits of self-indulgence are notorious, finds himself disappointed of his greedy hopes. What treatment of his wife, what abuse and brutal behaviour to his children, who, though ogrillons, are children! My dears, you may fancy, and need not ask my delicate pen to describe, the language and behaviour of a vulgar, coarse, greedy, large man with an immense mouth and teeth, which are too frequently employed in the gobbling and crunching of raw man's meat.

And in this circuitous way you see I have reached my present subject, which is, Ogres. You fancy they are dead or only fictitious characters—mythical representatives of strength, cruelty, stupidity, and lust for blood? Though they had seven-leagued boots, you remember all sorts of little whipping-snapping Tom Thumbs used to elude and outrun them. They were so stupid that they gave in to the most shallow abuscades and artifices: witness that well-known ogre, who, because Jack cut open the hasty-pudding, instantly ripped open his own stupid waistcoat and interior. They were cruel, brutal, disgusting, with their sharpened teeth, immense knives, and roaring voices! but they always ended by being overcome by little Tom Thumbkins, or some other smart little champion.

Yes; they were conquered in the end there is no doubt. They plunged headlong (and uttering the most frightful bad language) into some pit where Jack came with his smart *couteau de chasse*, and whipped their brutal heads off. They would be going to devour maidens,

> "But ever when it seemed
> Their need was at the sorest,
> A knight, in armour bright,
> Came riding through the forest."

And down, after a combat, would go the brutal persecutor, with a lance through his midriff. Yes, I say, this is very true and well. But you remember that round the ogre's cave the ground was covered, for hundreds and hundreds of yards, *with the bones of the victims* whom he had lured into the castle. Many knights and maids came to him and perished under his knife and teeth. Were dragons the same as ogres? monsters dwelling in caverns, whence they rushed, attired in plate armour, wielding pikes and torches, and destroying stray passengers who passed by their lair? Monsters, brutes, rapacious tyrants, ruffians, as they were, doubtless they ended by being overcome. But, before they were destroyed, they did a deal of mischief. The bones round their caves were countless. They had sent many brave souls to Hades, before their own fled, howling out of their rascal carcasses, to the same place of gloom.

There is no greater mistake than to suppose that fairies, champions, distressed damsels, and by consequence ogres, have ceased to exist. It may not be *ogreable* to them (pardon the horrible pleasantry, but as I am writing in the solitude of my chamber, I am grinding my teeth—yelling, roaring, and cursing—brandishing my scissors and paper-cutter and as it were have become an ogre). I say there is no greater mistake than to suppose that ogres have ceased to exist. We all *know* ogres. Their caverns are round us, and about us. There are the castles of several ogres within a mile of the spot where I write. I think some of them suspect I am an ogre myself. I am not, but I know they are. I visit them. I don't mean to say that they take a cold roast prince out of the cupboard, and have a cannibal feast before *me*. But I see the bones lying about the roads to their houses, and in the areas and gardens. Politeness, of course, prevents me from making any remarks: but I know them well enough. One of the ways to know 'em is to watch the scared looks of the ogres' wives and children. They lead an awful life. They are present at dreadful cruelties. In their excesses those ogres will stab about and kill not only strangers who happen to call in and ask a night's lodging, but they will outrage, murder, and chop up their own kin. We all know ogres, I say, and have been in their dens often. It is not necessary that ogres who ask you to dine should offer their guests the *peculiar dish* which they like. They cannot always get a Tom Thumb family. They eat mutton and beef too; and I dare say even go out to tea, and invite you to drink it. But

I tell you there are numbers of them going about in the world. And now you have my word for it, and this little hint, it is quite curious what an interest society may be made to have for you by your determining to find out the ogres you meet there.

What does the man mean? says Mrs. Downright, to whom a joke is a very grave thing. I mean, madam, that in the company assembled in your genteel drawing-room, who bow here and there, and smirk in white neck-cloths, you receive men who elbow through life successfully enough, but who are ogres in private: men wicked, false, rapacious, flattering; cruel hectors at home, smiling courtiers abroad; causing wives, children, servants, parents, to tremble before them, and smiling and bowing, as they bid strangers welcome into their castles. I say, there are men who have crunched the bones of victim after victim; in whose closets lie skeletons picked frightfully clean. When these ogres come out into the world, you don't suppose they show their knives, and their great teeth? A neat simple white neckcloth, a merry rather obsequious manner, a cadaverous look, perhaps, now and again, and a rather dreadful grin; but I know ogres very considerably respected: and when you hint to such and such a man, "My dear sir, Mr. Sharpus, whom you appear to like, is, I assure you, a most dreadful cannibal;" the gentleman cries, "Oh, psha, nonsense! Daresay not so black as he is painted. Daresay not worse than his neighbours." We condone everything in this country—private treason, falsehood, flattery, cruelty at home, roguery, and double-dealing. What! Do you mean to say in your acquaintance you don't know ogres guilty of countless crimes of fraud and force, and that knowing them you don't shake hands with them; dine with them at your table; and meet them at their own? Depend upon it, in the time when there were real live ogres, in real caverns or castles, gobbling up real knights and virgins, when they went into the world—the neighbouring market-town, let us say, or earl's castle—though their nature and reputation were pretty well known, their notorious foibles were never alluded to. You would say, "What, Blunderbore, my boy! How do you do? How well and fresh you look! What's the receipt you have for keeping so young and rosy?" And your wife would softly ask after Mrs. Blunderbore and the dear children. Or it would be, "My dear Humguffin! try that pork. It is home-bred, home-fed, and, I promise you, tender. Tell me if you think it is as good as

yours? John, a glass of burgundy to Colonel Humguffin!" You
don't suppose there would be any unpleasant allusions to disagreeable home-reports regarding Humguffin's manner of furnishing
his larder? I say we all of us know ogres. We shake hands and dine
with ogres. And if inconvenient moralists tell us we are cowards
for our pains, we turn round with a *tu quoque*, or say that we
don't meddle with other folks' affairs; that people are much less
black than they are painted, and so on. What! Won't half the
county go to Ogreham Castle? Won't some of the clergy say grace
at dinner? Won't the mothers bring their daughters to dance with
the young Rawheads? And if Lady Ogreham happens to die—I
won't say to go the way of all flesh, that is too revolting—I say if
Ogreham is a widower, do you aver, on your conscience and honour,
that mothers will not be found to offer their young girls to supply
the lamented lady's place? How stale this misanthropy is! Something must have disagreed with this cynic. Yes, my good woman.
I daresay you would like to call another subject. Yes, my fine
fellow; ogre at home, supple as a dancing-master abroad, and shaking in thy pumps, and wearing a horrible grin of sham gaiety to
conceal thy terror, lest I should point thee out:—thou art prosperous and honoured, art thou? I say thou hast been a tyrant and
a robber. Thou hast plundered the poor. Thou hast bullied the
weak. Thou hast laid violent hands on the goods of the innocent
and confiding. Thou hast made a prey of the meek and gentle who
asked for thy protection. Thou hast been hard to thy kinsfolk,
and cruel to thy family. Go, monster! Ah, when shall little Jack
come and drill daylight through thy wicked cannibal carcass? I
see the ogre pass on, bowing right and left to the company; and he
gives a dreadful sidelong glance of suspicion as he is talking to my
Lord Bishop in the corner there.

Ogres in our days need not be giants at all. In former times,
and in children's books, where it is necessary to paint your moral
in such large letters that there can be no mistake about it, ogres
are made with that enormous mouth and *ratelier* which you know
of, and with which they can swallow down a baby, almost without
using that great knife which they always carry. They are too
cunning nowadays. They go about in society, slim, small, quietly
dressed, and showing no especially great appetite. In my own
young days there used to be play ogres—men who would devour

a young fellow in one sitting, and leave him without a bit of flesh
on his bones. They were quiet gentlemanlike-looking people. They
got the young fellow into their cave. Champagne, pâté-de-foie-gras,
and numberless good things, were handed about; and then, having
eaten, the young man was devoured in his turn. I believe these
card and dice ogres have died away almost as entirely as the hasty-
pudding giants whom Tom Thumb overcame. Now, there are
ogres in City courts who lure you into their dens. About our
Cornish mines I am told there are many most plausible ogres, who
tempt you into their caverns and pick your bones there. In a
certain newspaper there used to be lately a whole column of advertisements from ogres who would put on the most plausible,
nay, piteous appearance, in order to inveigle their victims. You
would read, "A tradesman, established for seventy years in the
City, and known and much respected by Messrs. N. M. Rothschild
and Baring Brothers, has pressing need for three pounds until
next Saturday. He can give security for half a million, and forty
thousand pounds will be given for the use of the loan," and so on;
or, "An influential body of capitalists are about to establish a
company, of which the business will be enormous and the profits
proportionately prodigious. They will require a SECRETARY, of
good address and appearance, at a salary of two thousand per
annum. He need not be able to write, but address and manners
are absolutely necessary. As a mark of confidence in the company,
he will have to deposit," &c.; or, "A young widow (of pleasing
manners and appearance) who has a pressing necessity for four
pounds ten for three weeks, offers her Erard's grand piano valued
at three hundred guineas; a diamond cross of eight hundred pounds;
and board and lodging in her elegant villa near Banbury Cross,
with the best references and society, in return for the loan." I
suspect these people are ogres. There are ogres and ogres. Polyphe-
mus was a great, tall, one-eyed, notorious ogre, fetching his victims
out of a hole, and gobbling them up one after another. There could
be no mistake about him. But so were the Sirens ogres—pretty
blue-eyed things, peeping at you coaxingly from out of the water,
and singing their melodious wheedles. And the bones round their
caves were more numerous than the ribs, skulls, and thigh-bones
round the cavern of hulking Polypheme.

To the castle-gates of some of these monsters up rides the dapper champion of the pen; puffs boldly upon the horn which hangs by the chain; enters the hall resolutely, and challenges the big tyrant sulking within. We defy him to combat, the enormous roaring ruffian! We give him a meeting on the green plain before his castle. Green? No wonder it should be green: it is manured with human bones. After a few graceful wheels and curvets, we take our ground. We stoop over our saddle. 'Tis but to kiss the locket of our lady-love's hair. And now the vizor is up: the lance is in rest (Gillott's iron is the point for me). A touch of the spur in the gallant sides of Pegasus, and we gallop at the great brute.

"Cut off his ugly head, Flibbertigibbet, my squire!" And who are these who pour out of the castle? the imprisoned maidens, the maltreated widows, the poor old hoary grandfathers, who have been locked up in the dungeons these scores and scores of years, writh-ing under the tyranny of that ruffian! Ah, ye knights of the pen! May honour be your shield, and truth tip your lances! Be gentle to all gentle people. Be modest to women. Be tender to children. And as for the Ogre Humbug, out sword and have at him.

A MISSISSIPPI BUBBLE

THE group of dusky children of the captivity on the next page is copied out of a little sketch-book which I carried in many a roundabout journey, and will point a moral as well as any other sketch in the volume. The drawing was made in a country where there was such hospitality, friendship, kindness, shown to the humble designer, that his eyes do not care to look out for faults, or his pen to note them. How they sang; how they laughed and grinned; how they scraped, bowed, and complimented you and each other, those negroes of the cities of the Southern parts of the then United States! My business kept me in the towns; I was but in one negro-plantation village, and there were only women and little children, the men being out afield. But there was plenty of cheerfulness in the huts, under the great trees—I speak of what I saw—and amidst the dusky bondsmen of the cities. I witnessed a curious gaiety; heard amongst the black folk endless singing, shouting, and laughter; and saw on holidays black gentle-men and ladies arrayed in such splendour and comfort as freeborn workmen in our towns seldom exhibit. What a grin and bow that dark gentleman performed, who was the porter at the colonel's, when he said, "You write your name, mas'r, else I will forgot." I am not going into the slavery question; I am not an advocate for "the institution," as I know, madam, by that angry toss of your head, you are about to declare me to be. For domestic purposes, my dear lady, it seemed to me about the dearest institution that can be devised. In a house in a Southern city you will find fifteen negroes doing the work which John, the cook, the housemaid, and the help, do perfectly in your own comfortable London house. And these fifteen negroes are the pick of a family of some eighty or ninety: twenty are too sick, or too old for work, let us say; twenty too clumsy: twenty are too young, and have to be nursed and watched by ten more.[1] And master has to maintain the immense crew to do the work of half-a-dozen willing hands. No, no; let Mitchell, the exile from poor dear enslaved Ireland, wish for a gang of "fat niggers"; I would as soon you should make me a present of a score of Bengal elephants, when I need but a single stout horse to pull my brougham.

How hospitable they were, those Southern men! In the North itself the welcome was not kinder, as I, who have eaten Northern and Southern salt, can testify. As for New Orleans, in spring-time, —just when the orchards were flushing over with peach-blossoms, and the sweet herbs came to flavour the juleps—it seemed to me the city of the world where you can eat and drink the most and suffer the least. At Bordeaux itself, claret is not better to drink than at New Orleans. It was all good—believe an expert Robert— from the half-dollar Médoc of the public hotel table, to the private gentleman's choicest wine. Claret is, somehow, good in that gifted place at dinner, at supper, and at breakfast in the morning. It is good: it is superabundant—and there is nothing to pay. Find me speaking ill of such a country! When I do, *pone me pigris campis:* smother me in a desert, or let Mississippi or Garonne drown me! At that comfortable tavern on Pontchartrain we had a *bouillabaisse* than which a better was never eaten at Marseilles: and not the least headache in the morning, I give you my word; on the contrary, you only wake with a sweet refreshing thirst for claret and

---

[1] This was an account given by a gentleman at Richmond of his establishment. Six European servants would have kept his house and stables well. "His farm," he said, "barely sufficed to maintain the negroes residing on it."

water. They say there is fever there in the autumn: but not in the spring-time, when the peach-blossoms blush over the orchards, and the sweet herbs come to flavour the juleps.

I was bound from New Orleans to Saint Louis; and our walk was constantly on the Levee, whence we could see a hundred of those huge white Mississippi steamers at their moorings in the river: "Look," said my friend Lochlomond to me, as we stood one day on the quay—"look at that post! Look at that coffee-house behind it! Sir, last year a steamer blew up in the river yonder, just where you see those men pulling off in a boat. By that post where you are standing a mule was cut in two by a fragment of the burst machinery, and a bit of the chimney-stove in that first-floor window of the coffee-house killed a negro who was cleaning knives in the top room!" I looked at the post, at the coffee-house window, at the steamer in which I was going to embark, at my friend, with a pleasing interest not divested of melancholy. Yesterday it was the mule, thinks I, who was cut in two: it may be *cras mihi*. Why, in the same little sketch-book there is a drawing of an Alabama river steamer which blew up on the very next voyage after that in which your humble servant was on board! Had I but waited another week, I might have—— These incidents give a queer zest to the voyage down the life-stream in America. When our huge, tall, white, pasteboard castle of a steamer began to work up stream, every limb in her creaked, and groaned, and quivered, so that you might fancy she would burst right off. Would she hold together, or would she split into ten millions of shivers? O my home and children! Would your humble servant's body be cut in two across yonder chain on the Levee, or be precipitated into yonder first-floor, so as to damage the chest of a black man cleaning boots at the window? The black man is safe for me, thank goodness. But you see the little accident *might* have happened. It has happened; and if to a mule, why not to a more docile animal? On our journey up the Mississippi, I give you my honour we were on fire three times, and burned our cook-room down. The deck at night was a great firework—the chimney spouted myriads of stars, which fell blackening on our garments, sparkling on to the deck, or gleaming into the mighty stream through which we laboured—the mighty yellow stream with all its snags.

How I kept up my courage through these dangers shall now be

narrated. The excellent landlord of the "Saint Charles Hotel," when I was going away, begged me to accept two bottles of the very finest Cognac, with his compliments; and I found them in my state-room with my luggage. Lochlomond came to see me off, and, as he squeezed my hand at parting, "Roundabout," says he, "the wine mayn't be very good on board, so I have brought a dozen-case of the Médoc which you liked;" and we grasped together the hands of friendship and farewell. Whose boat is this pulling up to the ship? It is our friend Glenlivat, who gave us the dinner on Lake Pontchartrain. "Roundabout," says he, "we have tried to do what we could for you, my boy; and it has been done *de bon cœur*" (I detect a kind tremulousness in the good fellow's voice as he speaks). "I say—hem!—the a—the wine isn't too good on board, so I've brought you a dozen of Médoc for your voyage, you know. And God bless you; and when I come to London in May I shall come and see you. Hallo! here's Johnson come to see you off, too!"

As I am a miserable sinner, when Johnson grasped my hand, he said, "Mr. Roundabout, you can't be sure of the wine on board these steamers, so I thought I would bring you a little case of that light claret which you liked at my house." *Et de trois!* No wonder I could face the Mississippi with so much courage supplied to me! Where are you, honest friends, who gave me of your kindness and your cheer? May I be considerably boiled, blown up, and snagged, if I speak hard words of you. May claret turn sour ere I do!

Mounting the stream it chanced that we had very few passengers. How far is the famous city of Memphis from New Orleans? I do not mean the Egyptian Memphis, but the American Memphis, from which to the American Cairo we slowly toiled up the river— to the American Cairo at the confluence of the Ohio and Mississippi rivers. And at Cairo we parted company from the boat, and from some famous and gifted fellow-passengers who joined us at Memphis, and whose pictures we had seen in many cities of the South. I do not give the names of these remarkable people, unless, by some wondrous chance, in inventing a name I should light upon that real one which some of them bore; but if you please I will say that our fellow-passengers whom we took in at Memphis were no less personages than the Vermont Giant and the famous Bearded Lady of Kentucky and her son. Their pictures I had seen in many cities through which I travelled with my own little performance. I think the Vermont Giant was a trifle taller in his pictures than he was in life (being represented in the former as, at least, some two storeys high); but the lady's prodigious beard received no more than justice at the hands of the painter; that portion of it which I saw being really most black, rich, and curly—I say the portion of beard, for this modest or prudent woman kept I don't know how much of the beard covered up with a red handkerchief, from which I suppose it only emerged when she went to bed, or when she exhibited it professionally.

The Giant, I must think, was an overrated giant. I have known gentlemen, not in the profession, better made, and I should say taller, than the Vermont gentleman. A strange feeling I used to have at meals; when, on looking round our little society, I saw the Giant, the Bearded Lady of Kentucky, the little Bearded Boy of three years old, the Captain (this I *think;* but at this distance of time I would not like to make the statement on affidavit), and the three other passengers, all with their knives in their mouths making play at the dinner—a strange feeling I say it was, and as though I was in a castle of ogres. But, after all, why so squeamish? A few scores of years back, the finest gentlemen and ladies of Europe did the like. Belinda ate with her knife; and Saccharissa had only that weapon, or a two-pronged fork, or a spoon, for her peas. Have you ever looked at Gilray's print of the Prince of Wales, a languid voluptuary, retiring after his meal, and noted the toothpick which he uses? . . . You are right, madam; I own that the subject is revolting and terrible. I will not pursue it. Only—allow that a gentleman, in a shaky steamboat, on a dangerous river, in a far-off country, which caught fire three times during the voyage—(of course I mean the steamboat, not the country)—seeing a giant, a voracious supercargo, a bearded lady, and a little boy, not three years of age, with a chin already quite black and curly, all plying their victuals down their throats with their knives—allow, madam, that in such a company a man had a right to feel a little nervous. I don't know whether you have ever remarked the Indian jugglers swallowing their knives, or seen, as I have, a whole table of people performing the same trick; but if you look at their eyes when they do it, I assure you there is a roll in them which is dreadful.

Apart from this usage, which they practise in common with many thousand most estimable citizens, the Vermont gentleman, and the Kentucky whiskered lady—or did I say the reverse?—whichever you like, my dear sir—were quite quiet, modest, unassuming people. She sat working with her needle, if I remember right. He, I suppose, slept in the great cabin, which was seventy feet long at the least, nor, I am bound to say, did I hear in the night any snores or roars, such as you would fancy ought to accompany the sleep of ogres. Nay, this giant had quite a small appetite (unless, to be sure, he went forward and ate a sheep or two in private with his horrid knife—oh, the dreadful thought; but in *public*, I say, he had quite a delicate appetite), and was also a teetotaler. I don't remember to have heard the lady's voice, though I might, not unnaturally, have been curious to hear it. Was her voice a deep, rich, magnificent bass; or was it soft, fluty, and mild? I shall never know now. Even if she comes to this country, I shall never go and see her. I *have* seen her, and for nothing.

You would have fancied that as, after all, we were only some half-dozen on board, she might have dispensed with her red handkerchief, and talked, and eaten her dinner in comfort: but in covering her chin there was a kind of modesty. That beard was her profession: that beard brought the public to see her: out of her business she wished to put that beard aside as it were: as a barrister would wish to put off his wig. I know some who carry theirs into private life, and who mistake you and me for jury boxes when they address us: but these are not your modest barristers, not your true gentlemen.

Well, I own I respected the lady for the modesty with which, her public business over, she retired into private life. She respected her life, and her beard. That beard having done its day's work, she puts it away in a handkerchief; and becomes, as far as in her lies, a private ordinary person. All public men and women of good sense, I should think, have this modesty. When, for instance, in my small way, poor Mrs. Brown comes simpering up to me, with her album in one hand, a pen in the other, and says, "Ho, ho, dear Mr. Roundabout, write us one of your amusing," &c. &c., my beard drops behind my handkerchief instantly. Why am I to wag my chin and grin for Mrs. Brown's good pleasure? My dear madam, I have been making faces all day. It is my profession. I do my comic business with the greatest pains, seriousness, and trouble: and with it make, I hope, a not dishonest livelihood. If you ask Monsieur Blondin to tea, you don't have a rope stretched from your garret window to the opposite side of the square, and request Monsieur to take his tea out on the centre of the rope? I lay my hand on this waistcoat, and declare that not once in the course of our voyage together did I allow the Kentucky Giant to suppose I was speculating on his stature, or the Bearded Lady to surmise that I wished to peep under the handkerchief which muffled the lower part of her face.

"And the more fool you," says some cynic. (Faugh, those cynics, I hate 'em!) Don't you know, sir, that a man of genius is pleased to have his genius recognised; that a beauty likes to be admired; that an actor likes to be applauded; that stout old Wellington himself was pleased and smiled when the people cheered him as he passed? Suppose you had paid some respectful elegant compliment to that lady? Suppose you had asked that giant if, for once, he would take anything at the liquor-bar? you might have learned a great deal of curious knowledge regarding giants and bearded ladies, about whom you evidently now know very little. There was that little boy of three years old, with a fine beard already, and his little legs and arms as seen out of his little frock, covered with a dark down. What a queer little capering satyr! He was quite good-natured, childish, rather solemn. He had a little Norval dress, I remember: the drollest little Norval.

I have said the B. L. had another child. Now this was a little girl of some six years old as fair and as smooth of skin, dear madam, as your own darling cherubs. She wandered about the great cabin quite melancholy. No one seemed to care for her. All the family affections were centred on Master Esau yonder. His little beard was beginning to be a little fortune already, whereas Miss Rosalba was of no good to the family. No one would pay a cent to see *her* little fair face. No wonder the poor little maid was melancholy. As I looked at her, I seemed to walk more and more in a fairy tale, and more and more in a cavern of ogres. Was this a little foundling whom they had picked up in some forest, where lie the picked bones of the queen her tender mother, and the tough old defunct monarch her father? No. Doubtless they were quite good-natured people, these. I don't believe they were unkind to the little girl without the moustaches. It may have been only my fancy that she repined because she had a cheek no more bearded than a rose's.

Would you wish your own daughter, madam, to have a smooth cheek, a modest air, and a gentle feminine behaviour, or to be—I won't say a whiskered prodigy, like this Bearded Lady of Kentucky—but a masculine wonder, a virago, a female personage of more than female strength, courage, wisdom? Some authors, who shall be nameless, are, I know, accused of depicting the most feeble, brainless, namby-pamby heroines, for ever whimpering tears and prattling commonplaces. *You* would have the heroine of your novel so beautiful that she should charm the captain (or hero, whoever he may be) with her appearance; surprise and confound the bishop with her learning; outride the squire and get the brush, and, when he fell from his horse, whip out a lancet and bleed him; rescue from fever and death the poor cottager's family whom the doctor had given up; make twenty-one at the butts with the rifle, when the poor captain only scored eighteen; give him twenty in fifty at billiards and beat him; and draw tears from the professional Italian people by her exquisite performance (of voice and violoncello) in the evening;—I say, if a novelist would be popular with ladies—the great novel-readers of the world—this is the sort of heroine who would carry him through half-a-dozen editions. Suppose I had asked that Bearded Lady to sing? Confess, now, miss, you would not have been displeased if I had told you that she had a voice like Lablache, only ever so much lower.

My dear, you would like to be a heroine? You would like to travel in triumphal caravans; to see your effigy placarded on city walls; to have your levées attended by admiring crowds, all crying out, "Was there ever such a wonder of a woman?" You would like admiration? Consider the tax you pay for it. You would be alone were you eminent. Were you so distinguished from your neighbours—I will not say by a beard and whiskers, that were odious—but by a great and remarkable intellectual superiority—would you, do you think, be any the happier? Consider envy. Consider solitude. Consider the jealousy and torture of mind which this Kentucky lady must feel, suppose she should hear that there is, let us say, a Missouri prodigy, with a beard larger than hers. Consider how she is separated from her kind by the possession of that wonder of a beard. When that beard grows grey, how lonely she will be, the poor old thing! If it falls off, the public admiration falls off too; and how she will miss it—the compliments of the trumpeters, the admiration of the crowd, the gilded progress of the car. I see an old woman alone in a decrepit old caravan, with cobwebs on the knocker, with a blistered ensign flapping idly over the door. Would you like to be that deserted person? Ah, Chloe! To be good, to be simple, to be modest, to be loved, be thy lot. Be thankful thou art not taller, nor stronger, nor richer, nor wiser than the rest of the world!

DE FINIBUS

WHEN Swift was in love with Stella, and despatching her a letter from London thrice a month, by the Irish packet, you may remember how he would begin Letter No. xxiii., we will say, on the very day when xxii. had been sent away, stealing out of the coffee-house or the assembly so as to be able to prattle with his dear; "never letting go her kind hand, as it were," as some commentator or other has said in speaking of the Dean and his amour. When Mr. Johnson, walking to Dodsley's, and touching the posts in Pall Mall as he walked, forgot to pat the head of one of them, he went back and imposed his hands on it,—impelled I know not by what superstition. I have this I hope not dangerous mania too. As soon as a piece of work is out of hand, and before going to sleep, I like to begin another; it may be to write only half-a-dozen lines: but that is something towards Number the Next. The printer's boy has not yet reached Green Arbour Court with the copy. Those people who were alive half-an-hour since, Pendennis, Clive Newcome, and (what do you call him? what was the name of the last hero? I remember now!) Philip Firmin, have hardly drunk their glass of wine, and the mammas have only this minute got the children's cloaks on, and have been bowed out of my premises—and here I come back to the study again: *tamen usque recurro.* How lonely it looks now all these people are gone! My dear good friends, some folk are utterly tired of you, and say, "What a poverty of friends the man has! He is always asking us to meet those Pendennises, Newcomes, and so forth. Why does he not introduce us to some new characters? Why is he not thrilling like Twostars, learned and profound like Threestars, exquisitely humorous and human like Four-stars? Why, finally, is he not somebody else?" My good people, it is not only impossible to please you all, but it is absurd to try. The dish which one man devours, another dislikes. Is the dinner of to-day not to your taste? Let us hope to-morrow's entertainment will be more agreeable. * * * I resume my original subject. What an odd, pleasant, humorous, melancholy feeling it is to sit in the study alone and quiet, now all these people are gone who have been boarding and lodging with me for twenty months! They have interrupted my rest: they have plagued me at all sorts of minutes: they have thrust themselves upon me when I was ill, or wished to be idle, and I have growled out a "Be hanged to you, can't you leave me alone now?" Once or twice they have prevented my going out to dinner. Many and many a time they have prevented my coming home, because I knew they were there waiting in the study, and a plague take them, and I have left home and family, and gone to dine at the Club, and told nobody where I went. They have bored me, those people. They have plagued me at all sorts of uncomfortable hours. They have made such a disturbance in my mind and house, that sometimes I have hardly known what was going on in my family and scarcely have heard what my neighbour said to me. They are gone at last, and you would expect me to be at ease? Far from it. I should almost be glad if Woolcomb would walk in and talk to me; or Twysden reappear, take his place in that chair opposite me, and begin one of his tremendous stories.

Madmen, you know, see visions, hold conversations with, even draw the likeness of, people invisible to you and me. Is this making of people out of fancy madness? and are novel-writers at all entitled to strait-waistcoats? I often forget people's names in life; and in my own stories contritely own that I make dreadful blunders regarding them; but I declare, my dear sir, with respect to the personages introduced into your humble servant's fables, I know the people utterly—I know the sound of their voices. A gentleman came in to see me the other day, who was so like the picture of Philip Firmin in Mr. Walker's charming drawings in the *Cornhill Magazine* that he was quite a curiosity to me. The same eyes, beard, shoulders, just as you have seen them from month to month. Well, he is not like the Philip Firmin in my mind. Asleep, asleep in the grave, lies the bold, the generous, the reckless, the tender-hearted creature whom I have made to pass through those adventures which have just been brought to an end. It is years since I heard the laughter ringing, or saw the bright blue eyes. When I knew him both were young. I become young as I think of him. And this morning he was alive again in this room, ready to laugh, to fight, to weep. As I write, do you know, it is the grey of evening; the house is quiet; everybody is out; the room is getting a little dark, and I look rather wistfully up from the paper with perhaps ever so little fancy that HE MAY COME IN.——No? No movement. No grey shade, growing more palpable, out of which at last look the well-known eyes. No, the printer came and took him away with the last page of the proofs. And with the printer's boy did the whole cortège of ghosts flit away, invisible! Ha! stay! what is this? Angels and ministers of grace! The door opens, and a dark form—enters, bearing a black—a black suit of clothes. It is John. He says it is time to dress for dinner.

· · · · · ·

Every man who has had his German tutor, and has been coached through the famous "Faust" of Goethe (thou wert my instructor, good old Weissenborn, and these eyes beheld the great master himself in dear little Weimar town!) has read those charming verses which are prefixed to the drama, in which the poet reverts to the time when his work was first composed, and recalls the friends now departed, who once listened to his song. The dear shadows rise up around him, he says; he lives in the past again. It is to-day which appears vague and visionary. We humbler writers cannot create Fausts, or raise up monumental works that shall endure for all ages; but our books are diaries, in which our own feelings must of necessity be set down. As we look to the page written last month, or ten years ago, we remember the day and its events; the child ill, mayhap, in the adjoining room, and the doubts and fears which racked the brain as it still pursued its work; the dear old friend who read the commencement of the tale, and whose gentle hand shall be laid in ours no more. I own for my part that, in reading pages which this hand penned formerly, I often lose sight of the text under my eyes. It is not the words I see; but that past day; that bygone page of life's history; that tragedy, comedy it may be, which our little home company was enacting; that merry-making which we shared; that funeral which we followed; that bitter bitter grief which we buried.

And, such being the state of my mind, I pray gentle readers to deal kindly with their humble servant's manifold shortcomings, blunders, and slips of memory. As sure as I read a page of my own composition, I find a fault or two, half-a-dozen. Jones is called Brown. Brown, who is dead, is brought to life. Aghast, and months after the number was printed, I saw that I had called Philip Firmin, Clive Newcome. Now Clive Newcome is the hero of another story by the reader's most obedient writer. The two men are as different in my mind's eye, as—as Lord Palmerston and Mr. Disraeli let us say. But there is that blunder at page 990, line 76, volume 84 of the *Cornhill Magazine*, and it is past mending; and I wish in my life I had made no worse blunders or errors than that which is hereby acknowledged.

Another Finis written. Another mile-stone passed on this journey from birth to the next world. Sure it is a subject for solemn cogitation. Shall we continue this story-telling business and be voluble to the end of our age? Will it not be presently time, O prattler, to hold your tongue, and let younger people speak? I have a friend, a painter, who, like other persons who shall be nameless, is growing old. He has never painted with such laborious finish as his works now show. This master is still the most humble and diligent of scholars. Of Art, his mistress, he is always an eager reverent pupil. In his calling, in yours, in mine, industry and humility will help and comfort us. A word with you. In a pretty large experience I have not found the men who write books superior in wit or learning to those who don't write at all. In regard of mere information, non-writers must often be superior to writers. You don't expect a lawyer in full practice to be conversant with all kinds of literature; he is too busy with his law; and so a writer is commonly too busy with his own books to be able to bestow attention on the works of other people. After a day's work (in which I have been depicting, let us say, the agonies of Louisa on parting with the Captain, or the atrocious behaviour of the wicked Marquis to Lady Emily) I march to the Club, proposing to improve my mind and keep myself "posted up," as the Americans phrase it, in the literature of the day. And what happens? Given, a walk after luncheon, a pleasing book, and a most comfortable arm-chair by the fire, and you know the rest. A doze ensues. Pleasing book drops suddenly, is picked up once with an air of some confusion, is laid presently softly in lap: head falls on comfortable arm-chair cushion; eyes close: soft nasal music is heard. Am I telling Club secrets? Of afternoons, after lunch, I say, scores of sensible fogies have a doze. Perhaps I have fallen asleep over that very book to which "Finis" has just been written. "And if the writer sleeps, what happens to the readers?" says Jones, coming down upon me with his lightning wit. What? You *did* sleep over it? And a very good thing too. These eyes have more than once seen a friend dozing over pages which this hand has written. There is a vignette somewhere in one of my books of a friend so caught napping with "Pendennis," or the "Newcomes," in his lap; and if a writer can give you a sweet, sooth-ing, harmless sleep, has he not done you a kindness? So is the author who excites and interests you worthy of your thanks and benedictions. I am troubled with fever and ague, that seize me at odd intervals and prostrate me for a day. There is cold fit, for which, I am thankful to say, hot brandy-and-water is prescribed; and this induces hot fit, and so on. In one or two of these fits I have read novels with the most fearful contentment of mind. Once on the Mississippi, it was my dearly beloved "Jacob Faithful:" once, at Frankfort O. M., the delightful "Vingt Ans Après" of Monsieur Dumas: once, at Tunbridge Wells, the thrilling "Woman in White": and these books gave me amusement from morning till sunset. I remember those ague fits with a great deal of pleasure and gratitude. Think of a whole day in bed, and a good novel for a companion! No cares: no remorse about idleness: no visitors: and the Woman in White or the Chevalier d'Artagnan to tell me stories from dawn to night! "Please, ma'am, my master's compli-ments, and can he have the third volume?" (This message was sent to an astonished friend and neighbour who lent me, volume by volume, the "W. in W.") How do you like your novels? I like mine strong, "hot with," and no mistake; no love-making: no observations about society: little dialogue, except where the char-acters are bullying each other: plenty of fighting: and a villain in the cupboard, who is to suffer tortures just before Finis. I don't like your melancholy Finis. I never read the history of a con-sumptive heroine twice. If I might give a short hint to an impartial writer (as the *Examiner* used to say in old days), it would be to act, *not* à la mode le pays de Pole (I think that was the phraseology) but *always* to give quarter. In the story of Philip, just come to an end, I have the permission of the author to state that he was going to drown the two villains of the piece—a certain Doctor F—— and a certain Mr. T. H—— on board the "President," or some other tragic ship—but you see I relented. I pictured to myself Firmin's ghastly face amid the crowd of shuddering people on that reeling deck in the lonely ocean and thought, "Thou ghastly lying wretch, thou shalt not be drowned; thou shalt have a fever only; a knowledge of thy danger; and a chance—ever so small a chance—of repentance." I wonder whether he *did* repent when he found himself in the yellow-fever, in Virginia? The probability is, he fancied that his son had injured him very much, and forgave him on his death-bed. Do you imagine there is a great deal of genuine right-down remorse in the world? Don't people rather find excuses which make their minds easy; endeavour to prove to themselves that they have been lamentably belied and misunderstood; and try and forgive the persecutors who *will* present that bill when it is due; and not bear malice against the cruel ruffian who takes them to the police-office for stealing the spoons? Years ago I had a quarrel with a certain well-known person (I believed a statement regarding him which his friends imparted to me, and which turned out to be quite incorrect). To his dying day that quarrel was never quite made up. I said to his brother, "Why is your brother's soul still dark against me? It is I who ought to be angry and unforgiving: for I was in the wrong." In the region which they now inhabit (for Finis has been set to the volumes of the lives of both here below), if they take any cognisance of our squabbles, and tittle-tattles, and gossips on earth here, I hope they admit that my little error was not of a nature unpardonable. If you have never committed a worse, my good sir, surely the score against you will not be heavy. Ha, *dilectissimi fratres!* It is in regard of sins *not* found out that we may say or sing (in an undertone in a most penitent and lugubrious minor key), "Miserere nobis miseris peccatoribus."

Among the sins of commission which novel-writers not seldom perpetrate, is the sin of grandiloquence, or tall-talking, against which, for my part, I will offer up a special *libera me*. This is the sin of schoolmasters, governesses, critics, sermoners, and instructors of young or old people. Nay (for I am making a clean breast, and liberating my soul), perhaps of all the novel-spinners now extant, the present speaker is the most addicted to preaching. Does he not stop perpetually in his story and begin to preach to you? When he ought to be engaged with business, is he not for ever taking the Muse by the sleeve, and plaguing her with some of his cynical sermons? I cry *peccavi* loudly and heartily. I tell you I would like to be able to write a story which should show no egotism whatever—in which there should be no reflections, no cynicism, no vulgarity (and so forth), but an incident in every other page, a villain, a battle, a mystery in every chapter. I should like to be able to feed a reader so spicily as to leave him hungering and thirsting for more at the end of every monthly meal.

Alexandre Dumas describes himself, when inventing the plan of a work, as lying silent on his back for two whole days on the deck of a yacht in a Mediterranean port. At the end of the two days he arose and called for dinner. In those two days he had built his plot. He had moulded a mighty clay, to be cast presently in perennial brass. The chapters, the characters, the incidents, the combinations were all arranged in the artist's brain ere he set a pen to paper. My Pegasus won't fly, so as to let me survey the field below me. He has no wings, he is blind of one eye certainly; he is restive, stubborn, slow; crops a hedge when he ought to be galloping, or gallops when he ought to be quiet. He never will show off when I want him. Sometimes he goes at a pace which surprises me. Sometimes, when I most wish him to make the running, the brute turns restive, and I am obliged to let him take his own time. I wonder do other novel-writers experience this fatalism? They *must* go a certain way, in spite of themselves. I have been surprised at the observations made by some of my characters. It seems as if an occult Power was moving the pen. The personage does or says something, and I ask, How the dickens did he come to think of that? Every man has remarked in dreams, the vast dramatic power which is sometimes evinced; I won't say the surprising power, for nothing does surprise you in dreams. But those strange characters you meet make instant observations of which you never can have thought previously. In like manner, the imagination foretells things. We spake anon of the inflated style of some writers. What also if there is an *afflated* style,—when a writer is like a Pythoness on her oracle tripod, and mighty words, words which he cannot help, come blowing, and bellowing, and whistling, and moaning through the speaking pipes of his bodily organ? I have told you it was a very queer shock to me the other day when, with a letter of introduction in his hand, the artist's (not my) Philip Firmin walked into this room, and sat down in the chair opposite. In the novel of "Pendennis," written ten years ago, there is an account of a certain Costigan, whom I had invented (as I suppose authors invent their personages out of scraps, heel-taps, odds and ends of characters). I was smoking in a tavern parlour one night—and this Costigan came into the room alive—the very man:—the most remarkable resemblance of the printed sketches of the man, of the rude drawings in which I had depicted him. He had the same little coat, the same battered hat, cocked on one eye, the same twinkle in that eye. "Sir," said I, knowing him to be an old friend whom I had met in unknown regions, "Sir," I said, "may I offer you a glass of brandy-and-water?" "*Bedad, ye may*," says he, "*and I'll sing ye a song tu.*" Of course he spoke with an Irish brogue. Of course he had been in the army. In ten minutes he pulled out an Army Agent's account, whereon his name was written. A few months after we read of him in a police-court. How had I come to know him, to divine him? Nothing shall convince me that I have not seen that man in the world of spirits. In the world of spirits and water I know I did: but that is a mere quibble of words. I was not surprised when he spoke in an Irish brogue. I had had cognisance of him before somehow. Who has not felt that little shock which arises when a person, a place, some words in a book (there is always a collocation) present themselves to you, and you know that you have before met the same person, words, scene, and so forth?

They used to call the good Sir Walter the "Wizard of the North." What if some writer should appear who can write so *enchantingly* that he shall be able to call into actual life the people whom he invents? What if Mignon, and Margaret, and Goetz von Berlichingen are alive now (though I don't say they are visible), and Dugald Dalgetty and Ivanhoe were to step in at that open window by the little garden yonder? Suppose Uncas and our noble old Leather-stocking were to glide silently in? Suppose Athos, Porthos, and Aramis should enter with a noiseless swagger, curling their moustaches? And dearest Amelia Booth, on Uncle Toby's arm; and Tittlebat Titmouse, with his hair dyed green; and all the Crummles company of comedians, with the Gil Blas troop; and Sir Roger de Coverley; and the greatest of all crazy gentlemen, the Knight of La Mancha, with his blessed squire? I say to you, I look rather wistfully towards the window, musing upon these people. Were any of them to enter, I think I should not be very much frightened. Dear old friends, what pleasant hours I have had with them! We do not see each other very often, but when we do, we are ever happy to meet. I had a capital half-hour with Jacob Faithful last night; when the last sheet was corrected, when "Finis," had been written, and the printer's boy, with the copy, was safe in Green Arbour Court.

So you are gone, little printer's boy, with the last scratches and corrections on the proof, and a fine flourish by way of Finis at the story's end. The last corrections? I say those last corrections seem never to be finished. A plague upon the weeds! Every day, when I walk in my own little literary garden-plot, I spy some, and should like to have a spud, and root them out. Those idle words, neighbour, are past remedy. That turning back to the old pages produces anything but elation of mind. Would you not pay a pretty fine to be able to cancel some of them? Oh, the sad old pages, the dull old pages! Oh, the cares, the *ennui*, the squabbles, the repetitions, the old conversations over and over again! But now and again a kind thought is recalled, and now and again a dear memory. Yet a few chapters more, and then the last: after which, behold Finis itself come to an end, and the Infinite begun.

ON SOME CARP AT SANS SOUCI

WE have lately made the acquaintance of an old lady of ninety, who has passed the last twenty-five years of her old life in a great metropolitan establishment, the workhouse, namely, of the parish of Saint Lazarus. Stay—twenty-three or four years ago, she came out once, and thought to earn a little money by hop-picking; but being overworked, and having to lie out at night, she got a palsy which has incapacitated her from all further labour, and has caused her poor old limbs to shake ever since.

An illustration of that dismal proverb which tells us how poverty makes us acquainted with strange bedfellows, this poor old shaking body has to lay herself down every night in her workhouse bed by the side of some other old woman with whom she may or may not agree. She herself can't be a very pleasant bedfellow, poor thing! with her shaking old limbs and cold feet. She lies awake a deal of the night, to be sure, not thinking of the happy old times, for hers never were happy; but sleepless with aches, and agues, and rheumatism of old age. "The gentleman gave me brandy-and-water," she said, her old voice shaking with rapture at the thought. I never had a great love for Queen Charlotte, but I like her better now from what this old lady told me. The Queen, who loved snuff herself, has left a legacy of snuff to certain poorhouses; and in her watchful nights this poor woman takes a pinch of Queen Charlotte's snuff, "and it do comfort me, sir, that it do!" *Pulveris exigui munus.* Here is a forlorn aged creature, shaking with palsy, with no soul among the great struggling multitude of mankind to care for her, not quite trampled out of life, but passed and forgotten in the rush, made a little happy and soothed in her hours of unrest by this penny legacy. Let me think as I write. (The next month's sermon, thank goodness! is safe to press.) This discourse will appear at the season when I have read that wassail-bowls make their appearance; at the season of pantomime, turkey and sausages, plum-puddings, jollifications for schoolboys; Christmas bills, and reminiscences more or less sad and sweet for elders. If we oldsters are not merry, we shall be having a semblance of merriment. We shall see the young folk laughing round the holly-bush. We shall pass the bottle round cosily as we sit by the fire. That old thing will have a sort of festival too. Beef, beer, and pudding will be served to her for that day also. Christmas falls on a Thursday. Friday is the workhouse day for coming out. Mary, remember that old Goody Twoshoes has her invitation for Friday, 26th December! Ninety is she, poor old soul? Ah! what a bonny face to catch under the mistletoe! "Yes, ninety, sir," she says, "and my mother was a hundred, and my grandmother was a hundred and two."

Herself ninety, her mother a hundred, her grandmother a hundred and two? What a queer calculation!

Ninety! Very good, granny: you were born then in 1772.

Your mother, we will say, was twenty-seven when you were born, and was born therefore in 1745.

Your grandmother was thirty when her daughter was born, and was born therefore in 1715.

We will begin with the present granny first. My good old creature, you can't of course remember, but that little gentleman for whom your mother was laundress in the Temple was the ingenious Mr. Goldsmith, author of a "History of England," the "Vicar of Wakefield," and many diverting pieces. You were brought almost an infant to his chambers in Brick Court, and he gave you some sugar-candy, for the Doctor was always good to children. That gentleman who well-nigh smothered you by sitting down on you as you lay in a chair asleep was the learned Mr. S. Johnson, whose history of "Rasselas" you have never read, my poor soul; and whose tragedy of "Irene" I don't believe any man in these kingdoms ever perused. That tipsy Scotch gentleman who used to come to the chambers sometimes, and at whom everybody laughed, wrote a more amusing book than any of the scholars, your Mr. Burke and your Mr. Johnson, and your Doctor Goldsmith. Your father often took him home in a chair to his lodgings; and has done as much for Parson Sterne in Bond Street, the famous wit. Of course, my good creature, you remember the Gordon Riots, and crying, "No Popery!" before Mr. Langdale's house, the Popish distiller's, and that bonny fire of my Lord Mansfield's books in Bloomsbury Square? Bless us, what a heap of illuminations you have seen! For the glorious victory over the Americans at Breed's Hill; for the peace in 1814, and the beautiful Chinese bridge in Saint James's Park; for the coronation of His Majesty, whom you recollect as Prince of Wales, Goody, don't you? Yes; and you went in a procession of laundresses to pay your respects to his good lady, the injured Queen of England, at Brandenburg House; and you remember your mother told you how she was taken to see the Scotch lords executed at the Tower. And as for your grandmother, she was born five months after the battle of Malplaquet, she was; where her poor father was killed, fighting like a bold Briton for the Queen. With the help of a "Wade's Chronology," I can make out ever so queer a history for you, my poor old body, and a pedigree as authentic as many in the peerage-books.

Peerage-books and pedigrees? What does she know about them? Battles and victories, treasons, kings, and beheadings, literary gentlemen, and the like, what have they ever been to her? Granny, did you ever hear of General Wolfe? Your mother may have seen him embark, and your father may have carried a musket under him. Your grandmother may have cried huzza for Marlborough; but what is the Prince Duke to you, and did you ever so much as hear tell of his name? How many hundred or thousand of years had that toad lived who was in the coal at the defunct Exhibition?—and yet he was not a bit better informed than toads seven or eight hundred years younger.

"Don't talk to me your nonsense about Exhibitions, and Prince Dukes, and toads in coals, or coals in toads, or what is it?" says Granny. "I know there was a good Queen Charlotte, for she left me snuff; and it comforts me of a night when I lie awake."

To me there is something very touching in the notion of that little pinch of comfort doled out to Granny, and gratefully inhaled by her in the darkness. Don't you remember what traditions there used to be of chests of plate, bulses of diamonds, laces of inestimable value, sent out of the country privately by the old Queen, to enrich certain relations in M-ckl-nb-rg Str-l-tz? Not all the treasure went. *Non omnis moritur.* A poor old palsied thing at midnight is made happy sometimes as she lifts her shaking old hand to her nose. Gliding noiselessly among the beds where lie the poor creatures huddled in their cheerless dormitory, I fancy an old ghost with a snuff-box that does not creak. "There, Goody, take of my rappee. You will not sneeze, and I shall not say 'God bless you.' But you will think kindly of old Queen Charlotte, won't you? Ah! I had a many troubles, a many troubles. I was a prisoner almost as much as you are. I had to eat boiled mutton every day: *entre nous*, I abominated it. But I never complained. I swallowed it. I made the best of a hard life. We have all our burdens to bear. But hark! I hear the cock-crow, and snuff the morning air." And with this the Royal ghost vanishes up the chimney—if there be a chimney in that dismal harem, where poor old Twoshoes and her companions pass their nights—their dreary nights, their restless nights, their cold long nights, shared in what glum companionship, illumined by what a feeble taper!

"Did I understand you, my good Twoshoes, to say that your mother was seven-and-twenty years old when you were born, and that she married your esteemed father when she herself was twenty-five? 1745, then, was the date of your dear mother's birth. I dare

say her father was absent in the Low Countries, with His Royal
Highness the Duke of Cumberland, under whom he had the honour
of carrying a halberd at the famous engagement of Fontenoy—
or if not there, he may have been at Preston Pans, under General
Sir John Cope, when the wild Highlanders broke through all the
laws of discipline and the English lines; and, being on the spot,
did he see the famous ghost which didn't appear to Colonel Gardiner
of the Dragoons?   My good creature, is it possible you don't remember that Doctor Swift, Sir Robert Walpole (my Lord Orford,
as you justly say), old Sarah Marlborough, and little Mr. Pope
of Twitnam, died in the year of your birth?   What a wretched
memory you have!   What? haven't they a library, and the commonest books of reference at the old convent of Saint Lazarus, where
you dwell?"

"Convent of Saint Lazarus, Prince William, Doctor Swift,
Atossa, and Mr. Pope of Twitnam!   What is the gentleman talking
about?" says old Goody, with a "Ho! ho!" and a laugh like an old
parrot—you know they live to be as old as Methuselah, parrots
do, and a parrot of a hundred is comparrotively young (ho! ho! ho!).
Yes, and likewise carp live to an immense old age.   Some which
Frederick the Great fed at Sans Souci are there now, with great
humps of blue mould on their old backs; and they could tell all
sorts of queer stories, if they chose to speak—but they are very
silent, carp are—of their nature *peu communicatives*.   Oh! what
has been thy long life, old Goody, but a dole of bread and
water and a perch on a cage; a dreary swim round and round a
Lethe of a pond?   What are Rossbach or Jena to those mouldy ones?
and do they know it is a grandchild of England who brings bread to
feed them?

No! Those Sans Souci carp may live to be a thousand years old
and have nothing to tell but that one day is like another; and the
history of friend Goody Twoshoes has not much more variety
than theirs.   Hard labour, hard fare, hard bed, numbing cold all
night, and gnawing hunger most days.   That is her lot.   Is it lawful
in my prayers to say, "Thank Heaven, I am not as one of these"?
If I were eighty, would I like to feel the hunger always gnawing,
gnawing? to have to get up and make a bow when Mr. Bumble
the beadle entered the common room?   To have to listen to
Miss Prim, who came to give me her ideas of the next world?   If I

were eighty, I own I should not like to have to sleep with another gentleman of my own age, gouty, a bad sleeper, kicking in his old dreams, and snoring; to march down my vale of years at word of command, accommodating my tottering old steps to those of the other prisoners in my dingy hopeless old gang; to hold out a trembling hand for a sickly pittance of gruel, and say, "Thank you, ma'am," to Miss Prim when she has done reading her sermon. John! when Goody Twoshoes comes next Friday, I desire she may not be disturbed by theological controversies. You have a very fair voice, and I heard you and the maids singing a hymn very sweetly the other night, and was thankful that our humble household should be in such harmony. Poor old Twoshoes is so old and toothless and quaky, that she can't sing a bit; but don't be giving yourself airs over her, because she can't sing and you can. Make her comfortable at our kitchen hearth. Set that old kettle to sing by our hob. Warm her old stomach with nut-brown ale and a toast laid in the fire. Be kind to the poor old schoolgirl of ninety, who has had leave to come out for a day of Christmas holiday. Shall there be many more Christmases for thee? Think of the ninety she has seen already; the fourscore and ten cold, cheerless, nipping New Years!

If you were in her place, would you like to have a remembrance of better early days, when you were young, and happy, and loving, perhaps; or would you prefer to have no past on which your mind could rest? About the year 1788, Goody, were your cheeks rosy, and your eyes bright, and did some young fellow in powder and a pigtail look in them? We may grow old, but to us some stories never are old. On a sudden they rise up, not dead, but living— not forgotten, but freshly remembered. The eyes gleam on us as they used to do. The dear voice thrills in our hearts. The rapture of the meeting, the terrible terrible parting, again and again the tragedy is acted over. Yesterday, in the street, I saw a pair of eyes so like two which used to brighten at my coming once, that the whole past came back as I walked lonely, in the rush of the Strand, and I was young again in the midst of joys and sorrows, alike sweet and sad, alike sacred and fondly remembered.

If I tell a tale out of school, will any harm come to my old schoolgirl? Once, a lady gave her a half-sovereign, which was a source of great pain and anxiety to Goody Twoshoes. She sewed it away

in her old stays somewhere, thinking here at least was a safe investment—(*vestis*—a vest—an investment,—pardon me, thou poor
old thing, but I cannot help the pleasantry). And what do you
think? Another *pensionnaire* of the establishment cut the coin
out of Goody's stays—*an old woman who went upon two crutches!*
Faugh, the old witch! What? Violence amongst these toothless,
tottering, trembling, feeble ones? Robbery amongst the penniless?
Dogs coming and snatching Lazarus's crumbs out of his lap? Ah,
how indignant Goody was as she told the story! To that pond at
Potsdam where the carp live for hundreds of hundreds of years,
with hunches of blue mould on their back, I dare say the little
Prince and Princess of Preussen-Britannien come sometimes with
crumbs and cakes to feed the mouldy ones. Those eyes may have
goggled from beneath the weeds at Napoleon's jackboots; they
have seen Frederick's lean shanks reflected in their pool; and perhaps Monsieur de Voltaire has fed them—and now, for a crumb
of biscuit they will fight, push, hustle, rob, squabble, gobble, re-
lapsing into their tranquillity when the ignoble struggle is over.
Sans souci, indeed! It is mighty well writing "Sans souci" over
the gate; but where is the gate through which Care has not slipped?
She perches on the shoulders of the sentry in the sentry-box: she
whispers the porter sleeping in his arm-chair: she glides up the
staircase, and lies down between the king and queen in their bed-
royal: this very night I dare say she will perch upon poor old Goody
Twoshoes's meagre bolster, and whisper, "Will the gentleman and
those ladies ask me again? No, no; they will forget poor old Twoshoes." Goody! For shame of yourself! Do not be cynical. Do
not mistrust your fellow-creatures. What? Has the Christmas
morning dawned upon thee ninety times? For fourscore and ten
years has it been thy lot to totter on this earth, hungry and obscure?
Peace and goodwill to thee, let us say at this Christmas season.
Come, drink, eat, rest awhile at our hearth, thou poor old pilgrim!
And of the bread which God's bounty gives us, I pray, brother
reader, we may not forget to set aside a part for those noble and
silent poor, from whose innocent hands war has torn the means
of labour. Enough! As I hope for beef at Christmas, I vow a note
shall be sent to Saint Lazarus Union House, in which Mr. Roundabout requests the honour of Mrs. Twoshoes's company on Friday,
26th December.

AUTOUR DE MON CHAPEAU

NEVER have I seen a more noble tragic face. In the centre of the forehead there was a great furrow of care, towards which the brows rose piteously. What a deep solemn grief in the eyes! They looked blankly at the object before them, but through it, as it were, and into the grief beyond. In moments of pain, have you not looked at some indifferent object so? It mingles dumbly with your grief, and remains afterwards connected with it in your mind. It may be some indifferent thing—a book which you were reading at the time when you received her farewell letter (how well you remember the paragraph afterwards—the shape of the words, and their position on the page); the words you were writing when your mother came in, and said it was all over— she was MARRIED—Emily married—to that insignificant little rival at whom you have laughed a hundred times in her company. Well, well; my friend and reader, whoe'er you be—old man or young, wife or maiden—you have had your grief-pang. Boy, you have lain awake the first night at school, and thought of home. Worse still, man, you have parted from the dear ones with bursting heart: and, lonely boy, recall the bolstering an unfeeling comrade gave you; and, lonely man, just torn from your children—their little tokens of affection yet in your pocket—pacing the deck at evening in the midst of the roaring ocean, you can remember how you were told that supper was ready, and how you went down to the cabin and had brandy-and-water and biscuit. You remember the taste of them. Yes; for ever. You took them whilst you and your Grief were sitting together, and your Grief clutched you round the soul. Serpent, how you have writhed round me, and bitten me! Remorse, Remembrance, &c., come in the night season, and I feel you gnawing, gnawing! . . . I tell you that man's face was like Laocoön's (which, by the way, I always think overrated. The real head is at Brussels, at the Duke Daremberg's, not at Rome).

That man! What man? That man of whom I said that his magnificent countenance exhibited the noblest tragic woe. He was not of European blood. He was handsome, but not of European beauty. His face white—not of a northern whiteness; his eyes protruding somewhat, and rolling in their grief. Those eyes had seen the Orient sun, and his beak was the eagle's. His lips were full. The beard, curling round them, was unkempt and tawny. The locks were of a deep deep coppery red. The hands, swart and powerful, accustomed to the rough grasp of the wares in which he dealt, seemed unused to the flimsy artifices of the bath. He came from the Wilderness, and its sands were on his robe, his cheek, his tattered sandal, and the hardy foot it covered.

And his grief—whence came his sorrow? I will tell you. He bore it in his hand. He had evidently just concluded the compact by which it became his. His business was that of a purchaser of domestic raiment. At early dawn—nay, at what hour when the city is alive—do we not all hear the nasal cry of "Clo"? In Paris, *Habits, Galons, Marchand d'habits*, is the twanging signal with which the wandering merchant makes his presence known. It was in Paris I saw this man. Where else have I not seen him? In the Roman Ghetto—at the Gate of David, in his fathers' once imperial city. The man I mean was an itinerant vendor and purchaser of wardrobes—what you call an—— Enough! You know his name.

On his left shoulder hung his bag; and he held in that hand a white hat, which I am sure he had just purchased, and which was the cause of the grief which smote his noble features. Of course I cannot particularise the sum, but he had given too much for that hat. He felt he might have got the thing for less money. It was not the amount, I am sure; it was the principle involved. He had given fourpence (let us say) for that which threepence would have purchased. He had been done: and a manly shame was upon him, that he, whose energy, acuteness, experience, point of honour, should have made him the victor in any mercantile duel in which he should engage, had been overcome by a porter's wife, who very likely sold him the old hat, or by a student who was tired of it. I can understand his grief. Do I seem to be speaking of it in a disrespectful or flippant way? Then you mistake me. He had been outwitted. He had desired, coaxed, schemed, haggled, got what he wanted, and now found he had paid too much for his bargain. You don't suppose I would ask you to laugh at that man's grief? It is you, clumsy cynic, who are disposed to sneer, whilst it may be tears of genuine sympathy are trickling down this nose of mine. What do you mean by laughing? If you saw a wounded soldier on the field of battle, would you laugh? If you saw a ewe robbed of her lamb, would you laugh, you brute? It is you who are the cynic, and have no feeling: and you sneer because that grief is unintelligible to you which touches my finer sensibility. The OLD CLOTHES'-MAN had been defeated in one of the daily battles of his most interesting, chequered, adventurous life.

Have you ever figured to yourself what such a life must be? The pursuit and conquest of twopence must be the most eager and fascinating of occupations. We might all engage in that business if we would. Do not whist-players, for example, toil, and think, and lose their temper over sixpenny points? They bring study, natural genius, long forethought, memory, and careful historical experience to bear upon their favourite labour. Don't tell me that it is the sixpenny points, and five shillings the rub, which keeps them for hours over their painted pasteboard. It is the desire to conquer. Hours pass by. Night glooms. Dawn, it may be, rises unheeded; and they sit calling for fresh cards at the "Portland," or the "Union," while waning candles splutter in the sockets, and languid waiters snooze in the ante-room. Sol rises. Jones has lost four pounds: Brown has won two; Robinson lurks away to his family house and (mayhap indignant) Mrs. R. Hours of evening, night, morning, have passed away whilst they have been waging this sixpenny battle. What is the loss of four pounds to Jones, the gain of two to Brown? B. is, perhaps, so rich that two pounds more or less are as naught to him; J. is so hopelessly involved that to win four pounds cannot benefit his creditors, or alter his condition; but they play for that stake: they put forward their best energies: they ruff, finesse (what are the technical words, and how do I know?). It is but a sixpenny game if you like; but they want to win it. So as regards my friend yonder with the hat. He stakes his money: he wishes to win the game, not the hat merely. I am not prepared to say that he is not inspired by a noble ambition. Cæsar wished to be first in a village. If first of a hundred yokels, why not first of two? And my friend the old-clothes'-man wishes to win his game, as well as to turn his little sixpence.

Suppose in the game of life—and it is but a twopenny game after all—you are equally eager of winning. Shall you be ashamed of your ambition, or glory in it? There are games, too, which are becoming to particular periods of life. I remember in the days of our youth, when my friend Arthur Bowler was an eminent cricketer.

Slim, swift, strong, well-built, he presented a goodly appearance on the ground in his flannel uniform. *Militâsti non sine gloria*, Bowler my boy! Hush! We tell no tales. Mum is the word. Yonder comes Charley his son. Now Charley his son has taken the field, and is famous among the eleven of his school. Bowler senior, with his capacious waistcoat, &c., waddling after a ball, would present an absurd object, whereas it does the eyes good to see Bowler junior scouring the plain—a young exemplar of joyful health, vigour, activity. The old boy wisely contents himself with amusements more becoming his age and waist; takes his sober ride; visits his farm soberly—busies himself about his pigs, his ploughing, his peaches, or what not. Very small *routinier* amusements interest him; and (thank goodness!) nature provides very kindly for kindly-disposed fogies. We relish those things which we scorn in our lusty youth. I see the young folk of an evening kindling and glowing over their delicious novels. I look up and watch the eager eye flashing down the page, being, for my part, perfectly contented with my twaddling old volume of "Howell's Letters," or the *Gentleman's Magazine*. I am actually arrived at such a calm frame of mind that I like batter-pudding. I never should have believed it possible; but it is so. Yet a little while, and I may relish water-gruel. It will be the age of *mon lait de poule et mon bonnet de nuit*. And then—the cotton extinguisher is pulled over the old noddle, and the little flame of life is popped out.

Don't you know elderly people who make learned notes in Army Lists, Peerages, and the like? This is the batter-pudding, water-gruel of old age. The worn-out old digestion does not care for stronger food. Formerly it could swallow twelve hours' tough reading, and digest an encyclopædia.

If I had children to educate, I would, at ten or twelve years of age, have a professor, or professoress of whist for them, and cause them to be well grounded in that great and useful game. You cannot learn it well when you are old, any more than you can learn dancing or billiards. In our house at home we youngsters did not play whist because we were dear obedient children, and the elders said playing at cards was "a waste of time." A waste of time, my good people! *Allons!* What do elderly home-keeping people do of a night after dinner? Darby gets his newspaper; my dear Joan her *Missionary Magazine* or her volume of Cumming's Sermons—and

don't you know what ensues? Over the arm of Darby's arm-chair
the paper flutters to the ground unheeded, and he performs the
trumpet obbligato *que vous savez* on his old nose. My dear old Joan's
head nods over her sermon (awakening though the doctrine may
be). Ding, ding, ding; can that be ten o'clock? It is time to send
the servants to bed, my dear—and to bed master and mistress go
too. But they have not wasted their time playing at cards. Oh,
no! I belong to a club where there is whist of a night; and not a
little amusing is it to hear Brown speak of Thompson's play, and
vice versâ. But there is one man—Greatorex let us call him—who
is the acknowledged captain and primus of all the whist-players.
We all secretly admire him. I, for my part, watch him in private
life, hearken to what he says, note what he orders for dinner, and
have that feeling of awe for him that I used to have as a boy for
the cock of the school. Not play at whist? "Quelle triste vieillesse
vous vous préparez!" were the words of the great and good Bishop
of Autun. I can't. It is too late now. Too late! too late! Ah!
humiliating confession! That joy might have been clutched, but
the life-stream has swept us by it—the swift life-stream rushing to
the nearing sea. Too late! too late! Twentystone, my boy! when
you read in the papers "Valse à deux temps," and all the fashionable dances taught to adults by "Miss Lightfoots," don't you feel
that you would like to go in and learn? Ah, it is too late! You have
passed the *choreas*, Master Twentystone, and the young people are
dancing without you.

I don't believe much of what my Lord Byron the poet says; but
when he wrote, "So, for a good old gentlemanly vice, I think I shall
put up with avarice," I think his Lordship meant what he wrote,
and if he practised what he preached, shall not quarrel with him.
As an occupation in declining years, I declare I think saving is
useful, amusing, and not unbecoming. It must be a perpetual
amusement. It is a game that can be played by day, by night, at
home and abroad, and at which you must win in the long run.
I am tired and want a cab. The fare to my house, say, is two
shillings. The cabman will naturally want half-a-crown. I pull
out my book. I show him the distance is exactly three miles and
fifteen hundred and ninety yards. I offer him my card—my winning
card. As he retires with the two shillings, blaspheming inwardly,
every curse is a compliment to my skill. I have played him and

beat him; and a sixpence is my spoil and just reward. This is a game, by the way, which women play far more cleverly than we do. But what an interest it imparts to life! During the whole drive home I know I shall have my game at the journey's end; am sure of my hand, and shall beat my adversary. Or I can play in another way. I won't have a cab at all, I will wait for the omnibus: I will be one of the damp fourteen in that steaming vehicle. I will wait about in the rain for an hour, and 'bus after 'bus shall pass, but I will not be beat. I *will* have a place, and get it at length, with my boots wet through, and an umbrella dripping between my legs. I have a rheumatism, a cold, a sore throat, a sulky evening,—a doctor's bill to-morrow perhaps? Yes, but I have won my game, and am gainer of a shilling on this rubber.

If you play this game all through life it is wonderful what daily interest it has, and amusing occupation. For instance, my wife goes to sleep after dinner over her volume of sermons. As soon as the dear soul is sound asleep, I advance softly and puff out her candle. Her pure dreams will be all the happier without that light; and, say she sleeps an hour, there is a penny gained.

As for clothes, *parbleu!* there is not much money to be saved in clothes, for the fact is, as a man advances in life—as he becomes an *Ancient Briton* (mark the pleasantry)—he goes without clothes. When my tailor proposes something in the way of a change of raiment, I laugh in his face. My blue coat and brass buttons will last these ten years. It is seedy? What then? I don't want to charm anybody in particular. You say that my clothes are shabby? What do I care? When I wished to look well in somebody's eyes, the matter may have been different. But now, when I receive my bill of £10 (let us say) at the year's end, and contrast it with old tailor's reckonings, I feel that I have played the game with master tailor, and beat him; and my old clothes are a token of the victory.

I do not like to give servants board-wages, though they are cheaper than household bills: but I know they save out of board-wages, and so beat me. This shows that it is not the money but the game which interests me. So about wine. I have it good and dear. I will trouble you to tell me where to get it good and cheap. You may as well give me the address of a shop where I can buy meat for fourpence a pound, or sovereigns for fifteen shillings apiece. At the game of auctions, docks, shy wine-merchants, depend on it there is *no* winning; and I would as soon think of buying jewellery at an auction in Fleet Street as of purchasing wine from one of your dreadful needy wine-agents such as infest every man's door. Grudge myself good wine? As soon grudge my horse corn. *Merci!* that would be a very losing game indeed, and your humble servant has no relish for such.

But in the very pursuit of saving there must be a hundred harmless delights and pleasures which we who are careless necessarily forego. What do you know about the natural history of your household? Upon your honour and conscience, do you know the price of a pound of butter? Can you say what sugar costs, and how much your family consumes and ought to consume? How much lard do you use in your house? As I think on these subjects I own I hang down the head of shame. I suppose for a moment that you, who are reading this, are a middle-aged gentleman, and paterfamilias. Can you answer the above questions? You know, sir, you cannot. Now turn round, lay down the book, and suddenly ask Mrs. Jones and your daughters if *they* can answer? They cannot. They look at one another. They pretend they can answer. They can tell you the plot and principal characters of the last novel. Some of them know something about history, geology, and so forth. But of the natural history of home—*Nichts*, and for shame on you all! *Honnis soyez!* For shame on you? for shame on us!

In the early morning I hear a sort of call or *jodel* under my window, and know 'tis the matutinal milkman leaving his can at my gate. O household gods! have I lived all these years and don't know the price or the quantity of the milk which is delivered in that can? Why don't I know? As I live, if I live till to-morrow morning, as soon as I hear the call of Lactantius, I will dash out upon him. How many cows? How much milk, on an average, all the year round? What rent? What cost of food and dairy servants? What loss of animals, and average cost of purchase? If I interested myself properly about my pint (or hogshead, whatever it be) of milk, all this knowledge would ensue; all this additional interest in life. What is this talk of my friend Mr. Lewes, about objects at the seaside, and so forth? [1] Objects at the seaside? Objects at the area-bell: objects before my nose: objects which the butcher brings me in his tray: which the cook dresses and puts down before me,

[1] "Seaside Studies." By G. H. Lewes.

and over which I say grace! My daily life is surrounded with objects which ought to interest me. The pudding I eat (or refuse, that is neither here nor there; and, between ourselves, what I have said about batter-pudding, may be taken *cum grano*—we are not come to *that* yet, except for the sake of argument or illustration) —the pudding, I say, on my plate, the eggs that made it, the fire that cooked it, the tablecloth on which it is laid, and so forth—are each and all of these objects a knowledge of which I may acquire— a knowledge of the cost and production of which I might advantageously learn? To the man who *does* know these things, I say the interest of life is prodigiously increased. The milkman becomes a study to him; the baker a being he curiously and tenderly examines. Go, Lewes, and clap a hideous sea-anemone into a glass: I will put a cabman under mine, and make a vivisection of a butcher. O Lares, Penates, and gentle household gods, teach me to sympathise with all that comes within my doors! Give me an interest in the butcher's book. Let me look forward to the ensuing number of the grocer's account with eagerness. It seems ungrateful to my kitchen-chimney not to know the cost of sweeping it; and I trust that many a man who reads this, and muses on it, will feel, like the writer, ashamed of himself, and hang down his head humbly.

Now, if to this household game you could add a little money interest, the amusement would be increased far beyond the mere money value, as a game at cards for sixpence is better than a rubber for nothing. If you can interest yourself about sixpence, all life is invested with a new excitement. From sunrise to sleeping you can always be playing that game—with butcher, baker, coal-merchant, cabman, omnibus-man—nay, diamond-merchant and stockbroker. You can bargain for a guinea over the price of a diamond necklace, or for a sixteenth per cent. in a transaction at the Stock Exchange. We all know men who have this faculty who are not ungenerous with their money. They give it on great occasions. They are more able to help than you and I who spend ours, and say to poor Prodigal who comes to us out at elbow, "My dear fellow, I should have been delighted: but I have already anticipated my quarter, and am going to ask Screwby if he can do anything for me."

In this delightful, wholesome, ever-novel twopenny game, there is a danger of excess, as there is in every other pastime or occupation

of life. If you grow too eager for your twopence, the acquisition
or the loss of it may affect your peace of mind, and peace of mind
is better than any amount of twopences. My friend the old clothes'-
man, whose agonies over the hat have led to this rambling disquisition, has, I very much fear, by a too eager pursuit of small
profits disturbed the equanimity of a mind that ought to be easy
and happy. "Had I stood out," he thinks, "I might have had the
hat for threepence," and he doubts whether, having given fourpence for it, he will ever get back his money. My good Shadrach,
if you go through life passionately deploring the irrevocable, and
allow yesterday's transactions to embitter the cheerfulness of to-day
and to-morrow—as lief walk down to the Seine, souse in, hats, body,
clothes-bag and all, and put an end to your sorrow and sordid cares.
Before and since Mr. Franklin wrote his pretty apologue of the
Whistle, have we not all made bargains of which we repented, and
coveted and acquired objects for which we have paid too dearly?
Who has not purchased his hat in some market or other? There
is General M'Clellan's cocked-hat for example: I dare say he was
eager enough to wear it, and he has learned that it is by no means
cheerful wear. There were the military beavers of Messeigneurs of
Orleans; [1] they wore them gallantly in the face of battle; but I
suspect they were glad enough to pitch them into the James River
and come home in mufti. Ah, *mes amis! à chacun son shako!* I was
looking at a bishop the other day, and thinking, "My right reverend lord, that broad-brim and rosette must bind your great
broad forehead very tightly, and give you many a headache. A
good easy wideawake were better for you, and I would like to see
that honest face with a cutty-pipe in the middle of it." There is
my Lord Mayor. My once dear lord, my kind friend, when your
two years' reign was over, did you not jump for joy and fling your
chapeau-bras out of window: and hasn't *that* hat cost you a pretty
bit of money? There, in a splendid travelling chariot, in the sweetest
bonnet, all trimmed with orange-blossoms and Chantilly lace, sits
my Lady Rosa, with old Lord Snowden by her side. Ah, Rosa!
what a price have you paid for that hat which you wear; and is
your Ladyship's coronet not purchased too dear? Enough of hats.
Sir, or Madam, I take off mine, and salute you with profound respect.

[1] Two cadets of the House of Orleans who served as volunteers under General
M'Clellan in his campaign against Richmond.

ON A MEDAL OF GEORGE THE FOURTH

BEFORE me lies a coin bearing the image and superscription of King George the Fourth, and of the nominal value of two-and-sixpence. But an official friend at a neighbouring turnpike says the piece is hopelessly bad; and a chemist tested it, returning a like unfavourable opinion. A cabman, who had brought me from a Club, left it with the Club porter, appealing to the gent who gave it a pore cabby, at ever so much o'clock of a rainy night, which he hoped he would give him another. I have taken that cabman at his word. He has been provided with a sound coin. The bad piece is on the table before me, and shall have a hole drilled through it, as soon as this essay is written, by a loyal subject who does not desire to deface the Sovereign's image, but to protest against the rascal who has taken his name in vain. *Fid. Def.* indeed! Is this what you call defending the faith? You dare to forge your Sovereign's name, and pass your scoundrel pewter as his silver? I wonder who you are, wretch and most consummate trickster? This forgery is so complete that even now I am deceived by it— I can't see the difference between the base and sterling metal. Perhaps this piece is a little lighter;—I don't know. A little softer:— is it? I have not bitten it; not being a connoisseur in the tasting of pewter or silver. I take the word of three honest men, though it goes against me; and though I have given two-and-sixpence worth of honest consideration for the counter, I shall not attempt to implicate anybody else in my misfortune, or transfer my ill-luck to a deluded neighbour.

I say the imitation is so curiously successful, the stamping, milling of the edges, lettering, and so forth, are so neat, that even now, when my eyes are open, I cannot see the cheat. How did those experts, the cabman, the pikeman, and tradesman, come to find it out? How do they happen to be more familiar with pewter and silver than I am? You see, I put out of the question another point which I might argue without fear of defeat, namely, the cabman's statement that I gave him this bad piece of money. Suppose every cabman who took a shilling fare were to drive away and return presently with a bad coin and an assertion that I had given it to him! This would be absurd and mischievous; an encouragement of vice amongst men who already are subject to temptations. Being *homo*,

I think if I were a cabman myself, I might sometimes stretch a furlong or two in my calculation of distance. But don't come *twice*, my man, and tell me I have given you a bad half-crown. No, no! I have paid once like a gentleman, and once is enough. For instance, during the Exhibition time I was stopped by an old countrywoman in black, with a huge umbrella, who, bursting into tears, said to me "Master, be this the way to Harlow, in Essex?" "This the way to Harlow? This is the way to Exeter, my good lady, and you will arrive there if you walk about 170 miles in your present direction," I answered courteously, replying to the old creature. Then she fell a-sobbing as though her old heart would break. She had a daughter a-dying at Harlow. She had walked already "vifty-dree mile that day." Tears stopped the rest of her discourse, so artless, genuine, and abundant that—I own the truth—I gave her, in I believe genuine silver, a piece of the exact size of that coin which forms the subject of this essay. Well. About a month since, near to the very spot where I had met my old woman, I was accosted by a person in black, a person in a large draggled cap, a person with a huge umbrella, who was beginning, "I say, Master, can you tell me if this be the way to Har——" but here she stopped. Her eyes goggled wildly. She started from me, as Macbeth turned from Macduff. She would not engage with me. It was my old friend of Harlow, in Essex. I dare say she has informed many other people of her daughter's illness, and her anxiety to be put upon the right way to Harlow. Not long since a very gentlemanlike man, Major Delamere let us call him (I like the title of Major very much), requested to see me, named a dead gentleman who he said had been our mutual friend, and on the strength of this mutual acquaintance, begged me to cash his cheque for five pounds!

It is these things, my dear sir, which serve to make a man cynical. I do conscientiously believe that had I cashed the Major's cheque there would have been a difficulty about payment on the part of the respected bankers on whom he drew. On your honour and conscience, do you think that old widow who was walking from Tunbridge Wells to Harlow had a daughter ill, and was an honest woman at all? The daughter couldn't always, you see, be being ill, and her mother on her way to her dear child through Hyde Park. In the same way some habitual sneerers may be inclined to hint that the cabman's story was an invention—or at any rate, choose to ride off (so to speak) on the doubt. No. My opinion, I own, is unfavourable as regards the widow from Tunbridge Wells, and Major Delamere; but, believing the cabman was honest, I am glad to think he was not injured by the reader's most humble servant.

What a queer exciting life this rogue's march must be: this attempt of the bad half-crowns to get into circulation! Had my distinguished friend the Major knocked at many doors that morning, before operating on mine? The sport must be something akin to the pleasure of tiger or elephant hunting. What ingenuity the sportsman must have in tracing his prey—what daring and caution in coming upon him! What coolness in facing the angry animal (for, after all, a man on whom you draw a cheque *à bout portant* will be angry). What a delicious thrill of triumph, if you can bring him down! If I have money at the bankers, and draw for a portion of it over the counter, that is mere prose—any dolt can do that. But, having no balance, say I drive up in a cab, present a cheque at Coutts's, and, receiving the amount, drive off? What a glorious morning's sport that has been! How superior in excitement to the common transactions of everyday life! . . . I must tell a story; it is against myself, I know, but it *will* out, and perhaps my mind will be the easier.

More than twenty years ago, in an island remarkable for its verdure, I met four or five times one of the most agreeable companions with whom I passed a night. I heard that evil times had come upon this gentleman; and, overtaking him in a road near my own house one evening, I asked him to come home to dinner. In two days, he was at my door again. At breakfast-time was this second appearance. He was in a cab (of course he was in a cab; they always are, these unfortunate, these courageous men). To deny myself was absurd. My friend could see me over the parlour blinds, surrounded by my family, and cheerfully partaking of the morning meal. Might he have a word with me? and can you imagine its purport? By the most provoking delay, his uncle the admiral not being able to come to town till Friday—would I cash him a cheque? I need not say it would be paid on Saturday without fail. I tell you that man went away with money in his pocket, and I regret to add that his gallant relative has not *come to town yet!*

Laying down the pen, and sinking back in my chair, here, perhaps, I fall into a five minutes' reverie, and think of one, two, three, half-a-dozen cases in which I have been content to accept that sham promissory coin in return for sterling money advanced. Not a reader, whatever his age, but could tell a like story. I vow and believe there are men of fifty, who will dine well to-day, who have not paid their school debts yet, and who have not taken up their long-protested promises to pay. Tom, Dick, Harry, my boys, I owe you no grudge, and rather relish that wince with which you will read these meek lines and say, "He means me." Poor Jack in Hades! Do you remember a certain pecuniary transaction, and a little sum of money you borrowed "until the meeting of Parliament"? Parliament met often in your lifetime: Parliament has met since: but I think I should scarce be more surprised if your ghost glided into the room now, and laid down the amount of our little account, than I should have been if you had paid me in your lifetime with the actual acceptances of the Bank of England. You asked to borrow, but you never intended to pay. I would as soon have believed that a promissory note of Sir John Falstaff (accepted by Messrs. Bardolph and Nym, and payable in Aldgate), would be as sure to find payment, as that note of the departed—nay, lamented—Jack Thriftless.

He who borrows, meaning to pay, is quite a different person from the individual here described. Many—most, I hope—took Jack's promise for what it was worth—and quite well knew that when he said, "Lend me," he meant, "Give me" twenty pounds. "Give me change for this half-crown," said Jack; "I know it's a pewter piece;" and you gave him the change in honest silver, and pocketed the counterfeit gravely.

What a queer consciousness that must be which accompanies such a man in his sleeping, in his waking, in his walk through life, by his fireside with his children round him! "For what we are going to receive," &c.—he says grace before his dinner. "My dears! Shall I help you to some mutton? I robbed the butcher of the meat. I don't intend to pay him. Johnson my boy, a glass of champagne? Very good, isn't it? Not too sweet. Forty-six. I get it from So-and-so, whom I intend to cheat." As eagles go forth and bring home to their eaglets the lamb or the pavid kid, I say there are men who live and victual their nests by plunder. We all know highway robbers in white neckcloths, domestic bandits, marauders, passers of bad coin. What was yonder cheque which Major Delamere proposed I should cash but a piece of bad money? What was Jack Thriftless's promise to pay? Having got his booty, I fancy Jack or the Major returning home, and wife and children gathering round about him. Poor wife and children! They respect papa very likely. They don't know he is false coin. Maybe the wife has a dreadful inkling of the truth, and, sickening, tries to hide it from the daughters and sons. Maybe she is an accomplice: herself a brazen forgery. If Turpin and Jack Sheppard were married, very likely Mesdames Sheppard and Turpin did not know, at first, what their husbands' real profession was, and fancied, when the men left home in the morning, they only went away to follow some regular and honourable business. Then a suspicion of the truth may have come: then a dreadful revelation; and presently we have the guilty pair robbing together, or passing forged money each on his own account. You know Doctor Dodd? I wonder whether his wife knows that he is a forger and scoundrel? Has she had any of the plunder, think you, and were the darling children's new dresses bought with it? The Doctor's sermon last Sunday was certainly charming, and we all cried. Ah, my poor Dodd! Whilst he is preaching most beautifully, pocket-handkerchief in hand, he is peering over the pulpit cushions, looking out piteously for Messrs. Peachum and Lockit from the police-office. By Doctor Dodd you understand I would typify the rogue of respectable exterior, not committed to gaol yet, but not undiscovered. We all know one or two such. This very sermon perhaps will be read by some, or more likely—for depend upon it, your solemn hypocritic scoundrels don't care much for light literature—more likely, I say, this discourse will be read by some of their wives, who think, "Ah mercy! does that horrible cynical wretch know how my poor husband blacked my eye, or abstracted mamma's silver teapot, or forced me to write So-and-so's name on that piece of stamped paper, or what not?" My good creature, I am not angry with *you*. If your husband has broken your nose, you will vow that he had authority over your person, and a right to demolish any part of it: if he has conveyed away your mamma's teapot, you will say that she gave it to him at your marriage, and it was very ugly, and what not? if he takes your aunt's watch, and you love him, you will carry it ere long to the pawnbroker's, and perjure yourself—oh, how you will perjure yourself—in the witness-box! I know this is a degrading view of woman's noble nature, her exalted mission, and so forth, and so forth. I know you will say this is bad morality. Is it? Do you, or do you not, expect your womankind to stick by you for better or for worse? Say I have committed a forgery, and the officers come in search of me, is my wife, Mrs. Dodd, to show them into the dining-room and say, "Pray step in, gentlemen! My husband has just come home from church. That bill with my Lord Chesterfield's acceptance, I am bound to own, was never written by his Lordship, and the signature is in the Doctor's handwriting." I say, would any man of sense or honour, or fine feeling, praise his wife for telling the truth under such circumstances? Suppose she made a fine grimace, and said, "Most painful as my position is, most deeply as I feel for my William, yet truth must prevail, and I deeply lament to state that the beloved partner of my life *did* commit the flagitious act with which he is charged, and is at this present moment located in the two-pair back, up the chimney, whither it is my duty to lead you." Why, even Dodd himself, who was one of the greatest humbugs who ever lived, would not have had the face to say that he approved of his wife telling the truth in such a case. Would you have had Flora Macdonald beckon the officers, saying, "This way, gentlemen! You will find the Young Chevalier asleep in that cavern"? Or don't you prefer her to be *splendide mendax*, and ready at all risks to save him? If ever I lead a rebellion, and my women betray me, may I be hanged but I will not forgive them: and if ever I steal a teapot, and *my* women don't stand up for me, pass the article under their shawls, whisk down the street with it, outbluster the policeman, and utter any amount of fibs before Mr. Beak, those being are not what I take them to be, and— for a fortune—I won't give them so much as a bad half-crown.

Is conscious guilt a source of unmixed pain to the bosom which harbours it? Has not your criminal, on the contrary, an excitement, an enjoyment within quite unknown to you and me who never did anything wrong in our lives? The housebreaker must snatch a fearful joy as he walks unchallenged by the policeman with his sack full of spoons and tankards. Do not cracksmen, when assembled together, entertain themselves with stories of glorious old burglaries which they or bygone heroes have committed? But that my age is mature and my habits formed, I should really just like to try a little criminality. Fancy passing a forged bill to your banker; calling on a friend and sweeping his sideboard of plate, his hall of umbrellas and coats; and then going home to dress for dinner, say—and to meet a bishop, a judge, and a police magistrate or so, and talk more morally than any man at table! How I should chuckle (as my host's spoons clinked softly in my pocket) whilst I was uttering some noble speech about virtue, duty, charity! I wonder do we meet garotters in society? In an average tea-party, now, how many returned convicts are there? Does John Footman, when he asks permission to go and spend the evening with some friends, pass his time in thuggee; waylay and strangle an old gentleman or two; let himself into your house, with the house-key of course, and appear as usual with the shaving-water when you ring your bell in the morning? The very possibility of such a suspicion invests John with a new and romantic interest in my mind. Behind the grave politeness of his countenance I try and read the lurking treason. Full of this pleasing subject, I have been talking thief-stories with a neighbour. The neighbour tells me how some friends of hers used to keep a jewel-box under a bed in their room; and, going into the room, they thought they heard a noise under the bed. They had the courage to look. The cook was under the bed— under the bed with the jewel-box. Of course she said she had come for purposes connected with her business; but this was absurd. A cook under a bed is not there for professional purposes. A relation of mine had a box containing diamonds under her bed, which diamonds she told me were to be mine. Mine! One day, at dinner-time, between the entrées and the roast, a cab drove away from my relative's house containing the box wherein lay the diamonds. John laid the dessert, brought the coffee, waited all the evening— and oh, how frightened he was when he came to learn that his mistress's box had been conveyed out of her own room, and it contained diamonds—"Law bless us, did it now?" I wonder whether John's subsequent career has been prosperous? Perhaps the gentlemen from Bow Street were all in the wrong when they agreed in suspecting John as the author of the robbery. His noble nature was hurt at the suspicion. You conceive he would not like to remain in a family where they were mean enough to suspect him of stealing a jewel-box out of a bedroom—and the injured man and my relatives soon parted. But, inclining (with my usual cynicism) to think that he did steal the valuables, think of his life for the

month or two whilst he still remains in the service! He shows the
officers over the house, agrees with them that the *coup* must have
been made by persons familiar with it; gives them every assistance;
pities his master and mistress with a manly compassion; points out
what a cruel misfortune it is to himself as an honest man, with
his living to get and his family to provide for, that this suspicion
should fall on him. Finally, he takes leave of his place, with a deep
though natural melancholy that he had ever accepted it. What's
a thousand pounds to gentlefolks? A loss certainly, but they will
live as well without the diamonds as with them. But to John his
Hhhonour was worth more than diamonds, his Hhonour was.
Whohever is to give him back his character? Who is to prevent
hanyone from saying, "Ho yes. This is the footman which was in
the family where the diamonds was stole"? &c.

I wonder has John prospered in life subsequently? If he is
innocent, he does not interest me in the least. The interest of the
case lies in John's behaviour supposing him to be guilty. Imagine
the smiling face, the daily service, the orderly performance of duty,
whilst within John is suffering pangs lest discovery should overtake
him. Every bell of the door which he is obliged to open may bring
a police-officer. The accomplices may peach. What an exciting
life John's must have been for a while. And now, years and years
after, when pursuit has long ceased, and detection is impossible,
does he ever revert to the little transaction? Is it possible those
diamonds cost a thousand pounds? What a rogue the fence must
have been who only gave him so and so! And I pleasingly picture
to myself an old ex-footman and an ancient receiver of stolen goods
meeting and talking over this matter, which dates from times so
early that her present Majesty's fair image could only just have
begun to be coined or forged.

I choose to take John at the time when his little peccadillo is
suspected, perhaps, but when there is no specific charge of robbery
against him. He is not yet convicted: he is not even on his trial;
how then can we venture to say he is guilty? Now think what scores
of men and women walk the world in a like predicament; and what
false coin passes current! Pinchbeck strives to pass off his history
as sound coin. He knows it is only base metal, washed over with
a thin varnish of learning. Poluphloisbos puts his sermons in circulation: sounding brass, lacquered over with white metal, and

marked with the stamp and image of piety. What say you to Drawcansir's reputation as a military commander? to Tibbs's pretensions to be a fine gentleman? to Sapphira's claims as a poetess, or Rodoessa's as a beauty? His bravery, his piety, high birth, genius, beauty—each of these deceivers would palm his falsehood on us, and have us accept his forgeries as sterling coin. And we talk here, please to observe, of weaknesses rather than crimes. Some of us have more serious things to hide than a yellow cheek behind a raddle of rouge, or a white poll under a wig of jetty curls. You know, neighbour, there are not only false teeth in this world, but false tongues: and some make up a bust and an appearance of strength with padding, cotton, and what not? while another kind of artist tries to take you in by wearing under his waistcoat, and perpetually thumping, an immense sham heart. Dear sir, may yours and mine be found, at the right time, of the proper size and in the right place.

And what has this to do with half-crowns, good or bad? Ah, friend! may our coin, battered and clipped, and defaced though it be, be proved to be Sterling Silver on the day of the Great Assay!

THACKERAY 473

SMITH

Alexander Smith (*1830–1867*), *poet and essayist, was born
at Kilmarnock, in Ayrshire; he spent the early years of his life in
Paisley and Glasgow, where he went to school; he learned his father's
trade—that of a designer of patterns for lace-work—but he abandoned
it at the first opportunity. Drifting into literature, his early verses
were printed in a Glasgow paper; later, he was introduced to London
periodicals. In 1853, his first volume of poems was published; it
was received with more favor than were subsequent ones. He became
secretary at the University of Edinburgh, and in 1857 married Flora
Macdonald, of Skye, akin to the Scottish heroine. Overwork and anxiety
to provide for his family brought about his death at an early age.*

*Popular as his early poetry was, he could not earn much from it,
and eked out a small salary by contributing to all sorts of publications.
Much of his best prose is contained in "Dreamthorp," a volume of
essays, mostly new, which appeared in 1863. Other contributions
were gathered together by his friend, Proctor Alexander, in a posthumous volume, entitled "Last Leaves" (1868). The former book, with
selections from the latter, has been edited for the World's Classics
(Oxford) by Hugh Walker, who connects Smith with the group which
includes Lamb, the Thackeray of the "Roundabout Papers," and
Stevenson. Mr. Walker might also have added "Ik. Marvel," and
perhaps Hawthorne, for his "quiet, fanciful quaintness" is not unmixed with melancholy, and his humor is shaded by "a certain medi-
tativeness of spirit." He is not without suggestions, at times, of De
Quincey, in certain moods; his charm, and the quality of his imagination, must be obvious.*

SMITH

DREAMTHORP

IT matters not to relate how or when I became a denizen of Dreamthorp; it will be sufficient to say that I am not a born native, but that I came to reside in it a good while ago now. The several towns and villages in which, in my time, I have pitched a tent did not please, for one obscure reason or another: this one was too large, t'other too small; but when, on a summer evening about the hour of eight, I first beheld Dreamthorp, with its westward-looking windows painted by sunset, its children playing in the single straggling street, the mothers knitting at the open doors, the fathers standing about in long white blouses, chatting or smoking; the great tower of the ruined castle rising high into the rosy air, with a whole troop of swallows—by distance made as small as gnats—skimming about its rents and fissures;—when I first beheld all this, I felt instinctively that my knapsack might be taken off my shoulders, that my tired feet might wander no more, that at last, on the planet, I had found a home. From that evening I have dwelt here, and the only journey I am like now to make, is the very inconsiderable one, so far at least as distance is concerned, from the house in which I live to the graveyard beside the ruined castle. There, with the former inhabitants of the place, I trust to sleep quietly enough, and nature will draw over our heads her coverlet of green sod, and tenderly tuck us in, as a mother her sleeping ones, so that no sound from the world shall ever reach us, and no sorrow trouble us any more.

The village stands far inland; and the streams that trot through the soft green valleys all about have as little knowledge of the sea, as the three-years' child of the storms and passions of manhood. The surrounding country is smooth and green, full of undulations; and pleasant country roads strike through it in every direction, bound for distant towns and villages, yet in no hurry to reach them.

On these roads the lark in summer is continually heard; nests are plentiful in the hedges and dry ditches; and on the grassy banks, and at the feet of the bowed dikes, the blue-eyed speedwell smiles its benison on the passing wayfarer. On these roads you may walk for a year and encounter nothing more remarkable than the country cart, troops of tawny children from the woods, laden with primroses, and at long intervals—for people in this district live to a ripe age—a black funeral creeping in from some remote hamlet; and to this last the people reverently doff their hats and stand aside. Death does not walk about here often, but when he does, he receives as much respect as the squire himself. Everything round one is unhurried, quiet, moss-grown, and orderly. Season follows in the track of season, and one year can hardly be distinguished from another. Time should be measured here by the silent dial, rather than by the ticking clock, or by the chimes of the church. Dreamthorp can boast of a respectable antiquity, and in it the trade of the builder is unknown. Ever since I remember, not a single stone has been laid on the top of another. The castle, inhabited now by jackdaws and starlings, is old; the chapel which adjoins it is older still; and the lake behind both, and in which their shadows sleep, is, I suppose, as old as Adam. A fountain in the market-place, all mouths and faces and curious arabesques—as dry, however, as the castle moat—has a tradition connected with it; and a great noble riding through the street one day several hundred years ago, was shot from a window by a man whom he had injured. The death of this noble is the chief link which connects the place with authentic history. The houses are old, and remote dates may yet be deciphered on the stones above the doors; the apple-trees are mossed and ancient; countless generations of sparrows have bred in the thatched roofs, and thereon have chirped out their lives. In every room of the place men have been born, men have died. On Dreamthorp centuries have fallen, and have left no more trace than have last winter's snowflakes. This commonplace sequence and flowing on of life is immeasurably affecting. That winter morning when Charles lost his head in front of the banqueting-hall of his own palace, the icicles hung from the eaves of the houses here, and the clown kicked the snow-balls from his clouted shoon, and thought but of his supper when, at three o'clock, the red sun set in the purple mist. On that Sunday in June while Waterloo was going on, the gossips, after morning service, stood on the country roads discussing agricultural prospects, without the slightest suspicion that the day passing over their heads would be a famous one in the calendar. Battles have been fought, kings have died, history has transacted itself; but, all unheeding and untouched, Dreamthorp has watched apple-trees redden, and wheat ripen, and smoked its pipe, and quaffed its mug of beer, and rejoiced over its newborn children, and with proper solemnity carried its dead to the churchyard. As I gaze on the village of my adoption, I think of many things very far removed, and seem to get closer to them. The last setting sun that Shakespeare saw reddened the windows here, and struck warmly on the faces of the hinds coming home from the fields. The mighty storm that raged while Cromwell lay a-dying made all the oak-woods groan round about here, and tore the thatch from the very roofs I gaze upon. When I think of this, I can almost, so to speak, lay my hand on Shakespeare and on Cromwell. These poor walls were contemporaries of both, and I find something affecting in the thought. The mere soil is, of course, far older than either, but *it* does not touch one in the same way. A wall is the creation of a human hand, the soil is not.

This place suits my whim, and I like it better year after year. As with everything else, since I began to love it I find it gradually growing beautiful. Dreamthorp—a castle, a chapel, a lake, a straggling strip of gray houses, with a blue film of smoke over all— lies embosomed in emerald. Summer, with its daisies, runs up to every cottage door. From the little height where I am now sitting, I see it beneath me. Nothing could be more peaceful. The wind and the birds fly over it. A passing sunbeam makes brilliant a white gable-end, and brings out the colours of the blossomed apple-tree beyond, and disappears. I see figures in the street, but hear them not. The hands on the church clock seem always pointing to one hour. Time has fallen asleep in the afternoon sunshine. I make a frame of my fingers, and look at my picture. On the walls of the next Academy's Exhibition will hang nothing half so beautiful!

My village is, I think, a special favourite of summer's. Every window-sill in it she touches with colour and fragrance; everywhere she wakens the drowsy murmurs of the hives; every place she scents with apple-blossom. Traces of her hand are to be seen on the weir beside the ruined mill; and even the canal, along which the barges come and go, has a great white water-lily asleep on its olive-coloured face. Never was velvet on a monarch's robe so gorgeous as the green mosses that beruff the roofs of farm and cottage, when the sunbeam slants on them and goes. The old road out towards the common, and the hoary dikes that might have been built in the reign of Alfred, have not been forgotten by the generous adorning season; for every fissure has its mossy cushion, and the old blocks themselves are washed by the loveliest gray-green lichens in the world, and the large loose stones lying on the ground have gathered to themselves the peacefulest mossy coverings. Some of these have not been disturbed for a century. Summer has adorned my village as gaily, and taken as much pleasure in the task, as the people of old, when Elizabeth was queen, took in the adornment of the May-pole against a summer festival. And, just think, not only Dreamthorp, but every English village she has made beautiful after one fashion or another—making vivid green the hill slope on which straggling white Welsh hamlets hang right opposite the sea; drowning in apple-blossom the red Sussex ones in the fat valley. And think, once more, every spear of grass in England she has touched with a livelier green; the crest of every bird she has burnished; every old wall between the four seas has received her mossy and licheny attentions; every nook in every forest she has sown with pale flowers, every marsh she has dashed with the fires of the marigold. And in the wonderful night the moon knows, she hands—the planet on which so many millions of us fight, and sin, and agonise, and die—a sphere of glow-worm light.

Having discoursed so long about Dreamthorp, it is but fair that I should now introduce you to her lions. These are, for the most part, of a commonplace kind; and I am afraid that, if you wish to find romance in them, you must bring it with you. I might speak of the old church-tower, or of the church-yard beneath it, in which the village holds its dead, each resting-place marked by a simple stone, on which is inscribed the name and age of the sleeper, and a Scripture text beneath, in which live our hopes of immortality. But, on the whole, perhaps it will be better to begin with the canal, which wears on its olive-coloured face the big white water-lily already chronicled. Such a secluded place is Dreamthorp that the railway does not come near, and the canal is the only thing that connects it with the world. It stands high, and from it the undulating country may be seen stretching away into the gray of distance, with hills and woods, and stains of smoke which mark the sites of villages. Every now and then a horse comes staggering along the towing-path, trailing a sleepy barge filled with merchandise. A quiet, indolent life these barge-men lead in the summer days. One lies stretched at his length on the sun-heated plank; his comrade sits smoking in the little dog-hutch, which I suppose he calls a cabin. Silently they come and go; silently the wooden bridge lifts to let them through. The horse stops at the bridge-house for a drink, and there I like to talk a little with the men. They serve instead of a newspaper, and retail with great willingness the news they have picked up in their progress from town to town. I am told they sometimes marvel who the old gentleman is who accosts them from beneath a huge umbrella in the sun, and that they think him either very wise or very foolish. Not in the least unnatural! We are great friends, I believe— evidence of which they occasionally exhibit by requesting me to disburse a trifle for drink-money. This canal is a great haunt of mine of an evening. The water hardly invites one to bathe in it, and a delicate stomach might suspect the flavour of the eels caught therein; yet, to my thinking, it is not in the least destitute of beauty. A barge trailing up through it in the sunset is a pretty sight; and the heavenly crimsons and purples sleep quite lovingly upon its glossy ripples. Nor does the evening star disdain it, for as I walk along I see it mirrored therein as clearly as in the waters of the Mediterranean itself.

The old castle and chapel already alluded to are, perhaps, to a stranger, the points of attraction in Dreamthorp. Back from the houses is the lake, on the green sloping banks of which, with broken windows and tombs, the ruins stand. As it is noon, and the weather is warm, let us go and sit on a turret. Here, on these very steps, as old ballads tell, a queen sat once, day after day, looking south-ward for the light of returning spears. I bethink me that yesterday, no further gone, I went to visit a consumptive shoemaker; seated here I can single out his very house, nay, the very window of the room in which he is lying. On that straw roof might the raven alight, and flap his sable wings. There, at this moment, is the supreme tragedy being enacted. A woman is weeping there, and little children are looking on with a sore bewilderment. Before nightfall the poor peaked face of the bowed artisan will have gathered its ineffable peace, and the widow will be led away from the bedside by the tenderness of neighbours, and the cries of the orphan brood will be stilled. And yet this present indubitable suffering and loss does not touch me like the sorrow of the woman of the ballad, the phantom probably of a minstrel's brain. The shoemaker will be forgotten—I shall be forgotten; and long after visitors will sit here and look out on the landscape and murmur the simple lines. But why do death and dying obtrude themselves at the present moment? On the turret opposite, about the distance of a gunshot, is as pretty a sight as eye could wish to see. Two young people, strangers apparently, have come to visit the ruin. Neither the ballad queen, nor the shoemaker down yonder, whose respirations are getting shorter and shorter, touches them in the least. They are merry and happy, and the graybeard turret has not the heart to thrust a foolish moral upon them. They would not thank him if he did, I daresay. Perhaps they could not understand him. Time enough! Twenty years hence they will be able to sit down at his feet, and count griefs with him, and tell him tale for tale. Human hearts get ruinous in so much less time than stone walls and towers. See, the young man has thrown himself down at the girl's feet on a little space of grass. In her scarlet cloak she looks like a blossom springing out of a crevice on the ruined steps. He gives her a flower, and she bows her face down over it almost to her knees. What did the flower say? Is it to hide a blush? He looks delighted; and I almost fancy I see a proud colour on his brow. As I gaze, these young people make for me a perfect idyl. The generous, ungrudging sun, the melancholy ruin, decked, like mad Lear, with flowers and ivies of forgetfulness and grief, and between them, sweet and evanescent, human truth and love!

Love!—does it yet walk the world, or is it imprisoned in poems and romances? Has not the circulating library become the sole home of the passion? Is love not become the exclusive property of novelists and playwrights, to be used by them only for professional purposes? Surely, if the men I see are lovers, or ever have been lovers, they would be nobler than they are. The knowledge that he is beloved should—*must* make a man tender, gentle, upright, pure. While yet a youngster in a jacket, I can remember falling desperately in love with a young lady several years my senior—after the fashion of youngsters in jackets. Could I have fibbed in these days? Could I have betrayed a comrade? Could I have stolen eggs or callow young from the nest? Could I have stood quietly by and seen the weak or the maimed bullied? Nay, verily! In these absurd days she lighted up the whole world for me. To sit in the same room with her was like the happiness of perpetual holiday; when she asked me to run a message for her, or to do any, the slightest, service for her, I felt as if a patent of nobility were conferred on me. I kept my passion to myself, like a cake, and nibbled it in private. Juliet was several years my senior, and had a lover—was, in point of fact, actually engaged; and, in looking back, I can remember I was too much in love to feel the slightest twinge of jealousy. I remember also seeing Romeo for the first time, and thinking him a greater man than Cæsar or Napoleon. The worth I credited him with, the cleverness, the goodness, the everything! He awed me by his manner and bearing. He accepted that girl's love coolly and as a matter of course: it put him no more about than a crown and sceptre puts about a king. What I would have given my life to possess—being only fourteen, it was not much to part with after all—he wore lightly, as he wore his gloves or his cane. It did not seem a bit too good for him. His self-possession appalled me. If I had seen him take the sun out of the sky, and put it into his breeches' pocket, I don't think I should have been in the least degree surprised. Well, years after, when I had discarded my passion with my jacket, I have assisted this middle-aged Romeo home from a roystering wine-party, and heard him hiccup out his marital annoyances, with the strangest remembrances of old times, and the strangest deductions therefrom. Did that man with the idiotic laugh and the blurred utterance ever love? Was he ever capable of loving? I protest I have my doubts. But where are my young people? Gone! So it is always. We begin to moralise and look wise, and Beauty, who is something of a coquette, and of an exacting turn of mind, and likes attentions, gets disgusted with our wisdom or our stupidity, and goes off in a huff. Let the baggage go!

The ruined chapel adjoins the ruined castle on which I am now sitting and is evidently a building of much older date. It is a mere shell now. It is quite roofless, ivy covers it in part; the stone tracery of the great western window is yet intact, but the coloured glass is gone with the splendid vestments of the abbot, the fuming incense, the chanting choirs, and the patient, sad-eyed monks, who muttered *Aves*, shrived guilt, and illuminated missals. Time was when this place breathed actual benedictions, and was a home of active peace. At present it is visited only by the stranger, and delights but the antiquary. The village people have so little respect for it, that they do not even consider it haunted. There are several tombs in the interior bearing knights' escutcheons, which time has sadly defaced. The dust you stand upon is noble. Earls have been brought here in dinted mail from battle, and earls' wives from the pangs of child-bearing. The last trumpet will break the slumber of a right honourable company. One of the tombs—the most perfect of all in point of preservation—I look at often, and try to conjecture what it commemorates. With all my fancies, I can get no further than the old story of love and death. There, on the slab, the white figures sleep; marble hands, folded in prayer, on marble breasts. And I like to think that he was brave, she beautiful; that although the monument is worn by time, and sullied by the stains of the weather, the qualities which it commemorates—husbandly and wifely affection, courtesy, courage, knightly scorn of wrong and falsehood, meekness, penitence, charity—are existing yet somewhere, recognisable by each other. The man who in this world can keep the whiteness of his soul, is not likely to lose it in any other.

In summer I spend a good deal of time floating about the lake. The landing-place to which my boat is tethered is ruinous, like the chapel and palace, and my embarkation causes quite a stir in the sleepy little village. Small boys leave their games and mud-pies, and gather round in silence; they have seen me get off a hundred times, but their interest in the matter seems always new. Not unfrequently an idle cobbler, in red nightcap and leathern apron, leans on a broken stile, and honours my proceedings with his attention. I shoot off, and the human knot dissolves. The lake contains three islands, each with a solitary tree, and on these islands the swans breed. I feed the birds daily with bits of bread. See, one comes gliding towards me, with superbly arched neck, to receive its customary alms! How wildly beautiful its motions! How haughtily it begs! The green pasture lands run down to the edge of the water, and into it in the afternoons the red kine wade and stand knee-deep in their shadows, surrounded by troops of flies. Patiently the honest creatures abide the attacks of their tormentors. Now one swishes itself with its tail—now its neighbour flaps a huge ear. I draw my oars alongside, and let my boat float at its own will. The soft blue heavenly abysses, the wandering streams of vapour, the long beaches of rippled cloud, are glassed and repeated in the lake. Dreamthorp is silent as a picture, the voices of the children are mute; and the smoke from the houses, the blue pillars all sloping in one angle, float upward as if in sleep. Grave and stern the old castle rises from its emerald banks, which long ago came down to the lake in terrace on terrace, gay with fruits and flowers, and with stone nymph and satyrs hid in every nook. Silent and empty enough to-day! A flock of daws suddenly bursts out from a turret, and round and round they wheel, as if in panic. Has some great scandal exploded? Has a conspiracy been discovered? Has a revolution broken out? The excitement has subsided, and one of them, perched on the old banner-staff, chatters confidentially to himself, as he, sideways, eyes the world beneath him. Floating about thus, time passes swiftly, for, before I know where I am, the kine have withdrawn from the lake to couch on the herbage, while one on a little height is lowing for the milkmaid and her pails. Along the road I see the labourers coming home for supper, while the sun setting behind me makes the village windows blaze; and so I take out my oars, and pull leisurely through waters faintly flushed with evening colours.

I do not think that Mr. Buckle could have written his "History of Civilisation" in Dreamthorp, because in it books, conversation, and the other appurtenances of intellectual life, are not to be procured. I am acquainted with birds, and the building of nests—with wild-flowers, and the seasons in which they blow—but with the big world far away, with what men and women are thinking, and doing, and saying, I am acquainted only through the *Times*, and the occasional magazine or review, sent by friends whom I have not looked upon for years, but by whom, it seems, I am not yet forgotten. The village has but few intellectual wants, and the intellectual supply is strictly measured by the demand. Still there is something. Down in the village, and opposite the curiously-carved fountain, is a schoolroom which can accommodate a couple of hundred people on a pinch. There are our public meetings held. Musical entertainments have been given there by a single performer. In that schoolroom last winter an American biologist terrified the villagers, and, to their simple understandings, mingled up the next world with this. Now and again some rare bird of an itinerant lecturer covers dead walls with posters, yellow and blue, and to that schoolroom we flock to hear him. His rounded periods the eloquent gentleman devolves amidst a respectful silence. His audience do not understand him, but they see that the clergyman does, and the doctor does; and so they are content, and look as attentive and wise as possible. Then, in connexion with the school-room, there is a public library, where books are exchanged once a month. This library is a kind of Greenwich Hospital for disabled novels and romances. Each of these books has been in the wars; some are unquestionable antiques. The tears of three generations have fallen upon their dusky pages. The heroes and the heroines are of another age than ours. Sir Charles Grandison is standing with his hat under his arm. Tom Jones plops from the tree into the water, to the infinite distress of Sophia. Moses comes home from market with his stock of shagreen spectacles. Lovers, warriors, and villains—as dead to the present generation of readers as Cambyses—are weeping, fighting, and intriguing. These books, tattered and torn as they are, are read with delight to-day. The viands are celestial if set forth on a dingy tablecloth. The gaps and chasms which occur in pathetic or perilous chapters are felt to be personal calamities. It is with a certain feeling of tenderness that I look upon these books; I think of the dead fingers that have turned over the leaves, of the dead eyes that have travelled along the lines. An old novel has a history of its own. When fresh and new, and before it had breathed its secret, it lay on my lady's table. She killed the weary day with it, and when night came it was placed beneath her pillow. At the sea-side a couple of foolish heads have bent over it, hands have touched and tingled, and it has heard vows and protestations as passionate as any its pages contained. Coming down in the world, Cinderella in the kitchen has blubbered over it by the light of a surreptitious candle, conceiving herself the while the magnificent Georgiana, and Lord Mordaunt, Georgiana's lover, the pot-boy round the corner. Tied up with many a dingy brother, the auctioneer knocks the bundle down to the bidder of a few pence, and it finds its way to the quiet cove of some village library, where with some difficulty—as if from want of teeth, and with numerous interruptions—as if from lack of memory, it tells its old stories, and wakes tears, and blushes, and laughter as of yore. Thus it spends its age, and in a few years it will become unintelligible, and then, in the dust-bin, like poor human mortals in the grave, it will rest from all its labours. It is impossible to estimate the benefit which such books have conferred. How often have they loosed the chain of circumstance! What unfamiliar tears—what unfamiliar laughter they have caused! What chivalry and tenderness they have infused into rustic loves! Of what weary hours they have cheated and beguiled their readers! The big, solemn history-books are in excellent preservation; the story-books are defaced and frayed, and their out-of-elbows condition is their pride, and the best justification of their existence. They are tashed, as roses are, by being eagerly handled and smelt. I observe, too, that the most ancient romances are not in every case the most severely worn. It is the pace that tells in horses, men, and books. There are Nestors wonderfully hale; there are juveniles in a state of dilapidation. One of the youngest books, "The Old Curiosity Shop," is absolutely falling to pieces. That book, like Italy, is possessor of the fatal gift; but happily, in its case, everything can be rectified by a new edition. We have buried warriors and poets, princes and queens, but no one of these was followed to the grave by sincerer mourners than was little Nell.

Besides the itinerant lecturer, and the permanent library, we have the Sunday sermon. These sum up the intellectual aids and furtherances of the whole place. We have a church and a chapel, and I attend both. The Dreamthorp people are Dissenters, for the most part; why, I never could understand; because dissent implies a certain intellectual effort. But Dissenters they are, and Dissenters they are likely to remain. In an ungainly building, filled with hard gaunt pews, without an organ, without a touch of colour in the windows, with nothing to stir the imagination or the devotional sense, the simple people worship. On Sunday, they are put upon a diet of spiritual bread-and-water. Personally, I should desire more generous food. But the labouring people listen attentively, till once they fall asleep, and they wake up to receive the benediction with a feeling of having done their duty. They know they ought to go to chapel, and they go. I go likewise, from habit, although I have long ago lost the power of following a discourse. In my pew, and whilst the clergyman is going on, I think of the strangest things—of the tree at the window, of the congregation of the dead outside, of the wheat-fields and the corn-fields beyond and all around. And the odd thing is, that it is during sermon only that my mind flies off at a tangent and busies itself with things removed from the place and the circumstances. Whenever it is finished fancy returns from her wanderings, and I am alive to the objects around me. The clergyman knows my humour, and is good Christian enough to forgive me; and he smiles good-humouredly when I ask him to let me have the chapel keys, that I may enter, when in the mood, and preach a sermon to myself. To my mind, an empty chapel is impressive; a crowded one, comparatively a commonplace affair. Alone, I could choose my own text, and my silent discourse would not be without its practical applications.

An idle life I live in this place, as the world counts it; but then I have the satisfaction of differing from the world as to the meaning of idleness. A windmill twirling its arms all day is admirable only when there is corn to grind. Twirling its arms for the mere barren pleasure of twirling them, or for the sake of looking busy, does not deserve any rapturous pæan of praise. I must be made happy after my own fashion, not after the fashion of other people. Here I can live as I please, here I can throw the reins on the neck of my whim. Here I play with my own thoughts; here I ripen for the grave.

ON THE WRITING OF ESSAYS

I HAVE already described my environments and my mode of life, and out of both I contrive to extract a very tolerable amount of satisfaction. Love in a cottage, with a broken window to let in the rain, is not my idea of comfort; no more is Dignity, walking forth richly clad, to whom every head uncovers, every knee grows supple. Bruin in winter-time fondly sucking his own paws, loses flesh; and love, feeding upon itself, dies of inanition.

Take the candle of death in your hand, and walk through the stately galleries of the world, and their splendid furniture and array are as the tinsel armour and pasteboard goblets of a penny theatre; fame is but an inscription on a grave, and glory the melancholy blazon on a coffin-lid. We argue fiercely about happiness. One insists that she is found in the cottage which the hawthorn shades. Another that she is a lady of fashion, and treads on cloth of gold. Wisdom, listening to both, shakes a white head, and considers that "a good deal may be said on both sides."

There is a wise saying to the effect that "a man can eat no more than he can hold." Every man gets about the same satisfaction out of life. Mr. Suddlechops, the barber of Seven Dials, is as happy as Alexander at the head of his legions. The business of the one is to depopulate kingdoms, the business of the other to reap beards seven days old; but their relative positions do not affect the question. The one works with razors and soap-lather, the other with battle-cries and well-greaved Greeks. The one of a Saturday night counts up his shabby gains and grumbles; the other on *his* Saturday night sits down and weeps for other worlds to conquer. The pence to Mr. Suddlechops are as important as are the worlds to Alexander. Every condition of life has its peculiar advantages, and wisdom points these out and is contented with them. The varlet who sang—

> A king cannot swagger
> Or get drunk like a beggar,
> Nor be half so happy as I——

had the soul of a philosopher in him. The harshness of the parlour is revenged at night in the servants' hall. The coarse rich man rates his domestic, but there is a thought in the domestic's brain, docile and respectful as he looks, which makes the matter equal, which would madden the rich man if he knew it—make him wince as with a shrewdest twinge of hereditary gout. For insult and degradation are not without their peculiar solaces. You may spit upon Shylock's gaberdine, but the day comes when he demands his pound of flesh; every blow, every insult, not without a certain satisfaction, he adds to the account running up against you in the day-book and ledger of his hate—which at the proper time he will ask you to discharge. Every way we look we see even-handed nature administering her laws of compensation. Grandeur has a heavy tax to pay. The usurper rolls along like a god, surrounded by his guards. He dazzles the crowd—all very fine; but look beneath his splendid trappings and you see a shirt of mail, and beneath *that* a heart cowering in terror of an air-drawn dagger. Whom did the memory of Austerlitz most keenly sting? The beaten emperors? or the mighty Napoleon, dying like an untended watchfire on St. Helena?

Giddy people may think the life I lead here staid and humdrum, but they are mistaken. It is true, I hear no concerts, save those in which the thrushes are performers in the spring mornings. I see no pictures, save those painted on the wide sky-canvas with the colours of sunrise and sunset. I attend neither rout nor ball; I have no deeper dissipation than the tea-table; I hear no more exciting scandal than quiet village gossip. Yet I enjoy my concerts more than I would the great London ones. I like the pictures I see, and think them better painted, too, than those which adorn the walls of the Royal Academy; and the village gossip is more after my turn of mind than the scandals that convulse the clubs. It is wonderful how the whole world reflects itself in the simple village life. The people around me are full of their own affairs and interests; were they of imperial magnitude, they could not be excited more strongly. Farmer Worthy is anxious about the next market; the likelihood of a fall in the price of butter and eggs hardly allows him to sleep o' nights. The village doctor—happily we have only one—skirrs hither and thither in his gig, as if man could neither die nor be born without his assistance. He is continually standing on the confines of existence, welcoming the new comer, bidding farewell to the goer-away. And the robustious fellow who sits at the head of the table when the Jolly Swillers meet at the Blue Lion on Wednesday evenings is a great politician, sound of lung metal, and wields the village in the taproom, as my Lord Palmerston wields the nation in the House. His listeners think him a wiser personage than the Premier, and he is inclined to lean to that opinion himself. I find everything here that other men find in the big world. London is but a magnified Dreamthorp.

And just as the Rev. Mr. White took note of the ongoings of the seasons in and around Hampshire Selborne, watched the colonies of the rooks in the tall elms, looked after the swallows in the cottage and rectory eaves, played the affectionate spy on the private lives of chaffinch and hedge-sparrow, was eavesdropper to the solitary cuckoo; so here I keep eye and ear open; take note of man, woman, and child; find many a pregnant text imbedded in the commonplace of village life; and, out of what I see and hear, weave in my own room my essays as solitarily as the spider weaves his web in the darkened corner. The essay, as a literary form, resembles the lyric, in so far as it is moulded by some central mood— whimsical, serious, or satirical. Give the mood, and the essay, from the first sentence to the last, grows around it as the cocoon grows around the silkworm. The essay-writer is a chartered libertine, and a law unto himself. A quick ear and eye, an ability to discern the infinite suggestiveness of common things, a brooding meditative spirit, are all that the essayist requires to start business with. Jaques, in "As You Like It," had the makings of a charming essayist. It is not the essayist's duty to inform, to build pathways through metaphysical morasses, to cancel abuses, any more than it is the duty of the poet to do these things. Incidentally he may do something in that way, just as the poet may, but it is not his duty, and should not be expected of him. Sky-larks are primarily created to sing, although a whole choir of them may be baked in pies and brought to table; they were born to make music, although they may incidentally stay the pangs of vulgar hunger. The essayist is a kind of poet in prose, and if questioned harshly as to his uses, he might be unable to render a better apology for his existence than a flower might. The essay should be pure literature as the poem is pure literature. The essayist wears a lance, but he cares more for the sharpness of its point than for the pennon that flutters on it, than for the banner of the captain under whom he serves. He plays with death as Hamlet plays with Yorick's skull, and he reads the morals—strangely stern, often, for such fragrant lodging—which are folded up in the bosoms of roses. He has no pride, and is deficient in a sense of the congruity and fitness of things. He lifts a pebble from the ground, and puts it aside more carefully than any gem; and on a nail in a cottage-door he will hang the mantle of his thought, heavily brocaded with the gold of rhetoric. He finds his way into the Elysian Fields through portals the most shabby and commonplace.

The essayist plays with his subject, now in whimsical, now in grave, now in melancholy mood. He lies upon the idle grassy bank, like Jaques, letting the world flow past him, and from this thing and the other he extracts his mirth and his moralities. His main gift is an eye to discover the suggestiveness of common things; to find a sermon in the most unpromising texts. Beyond the vital hint, the first step, his discourses are not beholden to their titles. Let him take up the most trivial subject, and it will lead him away to the great questions over which the serious imagination loves to brood—fortune, mutability, death—just as inevitably as the runnel, trickling among the summer hills, on which sheep are bleating, leads you to the sea; or as, turning down the first street you come to in the city, you are led finally, albeit by many an intricacy, out into the open country, with its waste places and its woods, where you are lost in a sense of strangeness and solitariness. The world is to the meditative man what the mulberry plant is to the silkworm. The essay-writer has no lack of subject-matter. He has the day that is passing over his head; and, if unsatisfied with that, he has the world's six thousand years to depasture his gay or serious humour upon. I idle away my time here, and I am finding new subjects every hour. Everything I see or hear is an essay in bud. The world is everywhere whispering essays, and one need only be the world's amanuensis. The proverbial expression which last evening the clown dropped as he trudged homeward to supper, the light of the setting sun on his face, expands before me to a dozen pages. The coffin of the pauper, which to-day I saw carried carelessly along, is as good a subject as the funeral procession of an emperor. Craped drum and banner add nothing to death; penury and disrespect take nothing away. Incontinently my thought moves like a slow-paced hearse with sable nodding plumes. Two rustic lovers, whispering between the darkening hedges, is as potent to project my mind into the tender passion as if I had seen Romeo touch the cheek of Juliet in the moonlight garden. Seeing a curly-headed child asleep in the sunshine before a cottage-door is sufficient excuse for a discourse on childhood; quite as good as if I had seen infant Cain asleep in the lap of Eve with Adam looking on. A lark cannot rise to heaven without raising as many thoughts as there are notes in its song. Dawn cannot pour its white light on my village without starting from their dim lair a hundred reminiscences; nor can sunset burn above yonder trees in the west without attracting to itself the melancholy of a lifetime. When spring unfolds her green leaves I would be provoked to indite an essay on hope and youth, were it not that it is already writ in the carols of the birds; and I might be tempted in autumn to improve the occasion, were it not for the rustle of the withered leaves as I walk through the woods. Compared with that simple music, the saddest-cadenced words have but a shallow meaning.

The essayist who feeds his thoughts upon the segment of the world which surrounds him cannot avoid being an egotist; but then his egotism is not unpleasing. If he be without taint of boastfulness, of self-sufficiency, of hungry vanity, the world will not press the charge home. If a man discourses continually of his wines, his plate, his titled acquaintances, the number and quality of his horses, his men-servants and maid-servants, he must discourse very skilfully indeed if he escapes being called a coxcomb. If a man speaks of death—tells you that the idea of it continually haunts him, that he has the most insatiable curiosity as to death and dying, that his thought mines in churchyards like a "demon-mole" —no one is specially offended, and that this is a dull fellow is the hardest thing likely to be said of him. Only, the egotism that over-crows you is offensive, that exalts trifles and takes pleasure in them, that suggests superiority in matters of equipage and furniture; and the egotism is offensive, because it runs counter to and jostles your self-complacency. The egotism which rises no higher than the grave is of a solitary and a hermit kind—it crosses no man's path, it disturbs no man's *amour propre*. You may offend a man if you say you are as rich as he, as wise as he, as handsome as he. You offend no man if you tell him that, like him, you have to die. The king, in his crown and coronation robes, will allow the beggar to claim that relationship with him. To have to die is a distinction of which no man is proud. The speaking about one's self is not necessarily offensive. A modest, truthful man speaks better about himself than about anything else, and on that subject his speech is likely to be most profitable to his hearers. Certainly, there is no subject with which he is better acquainted, and on which he has a better title to be heard. And it is this egotism, this perpetual reference to self, in which the charm of the essayist resides. If a man is worth knowing at all, he is worth knowing well. The essayist gives you his thoughts, and lets you know, in addition, how he came by them. He has nothing to conceal; he throws open his doors and windows, and lets him enter who will. You like to walk round peculiar or important men as you like to walk round a building, to view it from different points and in different lights. Of the essayist, when his mood is communicative, you obtain a full picture. You are made his contemporary and familiar friend. You enter into his humours and his seriousness. You are made heir of his whims, prejudices, and playfulness. You walk through the whole nature of him, as you walk through the streets of Pompeii, looking into the interior of stately mansions, reading the satirical scribblings on the walls. And the essayist's habit of not only giving you his thoughts, but telling you how he came by them, is interesting, because it shews you by what alchemy the ruder world becomes transmuted into the finer. We like to know the lineage of ideas, just as we like to know the lineage of great earls and swift race-horses. We like to know that the discovery of the law of gravitation was born of the fall of an apple in an English garden on a summer afternoon. Essays written after this fashion are racy of the soil in which they grow, as you taste the lava in the vines grown on the slopes of Etna, they say. There is a healthy Gascon flavour in Montaigne's Essays; and Charles Lamb's are scented with the primroses of Covent Garden.

The essayist does not usually appear early in the literary history of a country: he comes naturally after the poet and the chronicler. His habit of mind is leisurely; he does not write from any special stress of passionate impulse; he does not create material so much as he comments upon material already existing. It is essential for him that books should have been written, and that they should, at least to some extent, have been read and digested. He is usually full of allusions and references, and these his reader must be able to follow and understand. And in this literary walk, as in most others, the giants came first: Montaigne and Lord Bacon were our earliest essayists, and, as yet, they are our best. In point of style, these essays are different from anything that could now be produced. Not only is the thinking different—the manner of setting forth the thinking is different also. We despair of reaching the thought, we despair equally of reaching the language. We can no more bring back their turns of sentence than we can bring back their tournaments. Montaigne, in his serious moods, has a curiously rich and intricate eloquence; and Bacon's sentence bends beneath the weight of his thought, like a branch beneath the weight of its fruit. Bacon seems to have written his essays with Shakespeare's pen. There is a certain want of ease about the old writers which has an irresistible charm. The language flows like a stream over a pebbled bed, with propulsion, eddy, and sweet recoil—the pebbles, if retarding movement, giving ring and dimple to the surface, and breaking the whole into babbling music. There is a ceremoniousness in the mental habits of these ancients. Their intellectual garniture is picturesque, like the garniture of their bodies. Their thoughts are courtly and high mannered. A singular analogy exists between the personal attire of a period and its written style. The peaked beard, the starched collar, the quilted doublet, have their correspondence in the high sentence and elaborate ornament (worked upon the thought like figures upon tapestry) of Sidney and Spenser. In Pope's day men wore rapiers, and their weapons they carried with them into literature, and frequently unsheathed them too. They knew how to stab to the heart with an epigram. Style went out with the men who wore knee-breeches and buckles in their shoes. We write more easily now; but in our easy writing there is ever a taint of flippancy: our writing is to theirs, what shooting-coat and wideawake are to doublet and plumed hat.

Montaigne and Bacon are our earliest and greatest essayists, and likeness and unlikeness exist between the men. Bacon was constitutionally the graver nature. He writes like one on whom presses the weight of affairs, and he approaches a subject always on its serious side. He does not play with it fantastically. He lives amongst great ideas, as with great nobles, with whom he dare not be too familiar. In the tone of his mind there is ever something imperial. When he writes on building, he speaks of a palace with spacious entrances, and courts, and banqueting-halls; when he writes on gardens, he speaks of alleys and mounts, waste places and fountains, of a garden "which is indeed prince-like." To read over his table of contents, is like reading over a roll of peers' names. We have, taking them as they stand, essays treating *Of Great Place, Of Boldness, Of Goodness and Goodness of Nature, Of Nobility, Of Seditions and Troubles, Of Atheism, Of Superstition, Of Travel, Of Empire, Of Counsel*—a book plainly to lie in the closets of statesmen and princes, and designed to nurture the noblest natures. Bacon always seems to write with his ermine on. Montaigne was different from all this. His table of contents reads in comparison like a medley, or a catalogue of an auction. He was quite as wise as Bacon; he could look through men quite as clearly, and search them quite as narrowly; certain of his moods were quite as serious, and in one corner of his heart he kept a yet profounder melancholy; but he was volatile, a humourist, and a gossip. He could be dignified enough on great occasions, but dignity and great occasions bored him. He could stand in the presence with propriety enough, but then he got out of the presence as rapidly as possible. When, in the thirty-eighth year of his age, he—somewhat world-weary, and with more scars on his heart than he cared to discover—retired to his château, he placed his library "in the great tower overlooking the entrance to the court," and over the central rafter he inscribed in large letters the device—"I DO NOT UNDERSTAND; I PAUSE; I EXAMINE." When he began to write his Essays he had no great desire to shine as an author; he wrote simply to relieve teeming heart and brain. The best method to lay the spectres of the mind is to commit them to paper. Speaking of the Essays, he says, "This book has a domestic and private object. It is intended for the use of my relations and friends; so that, when they have lost me, which they will soon do, they may find in it some features of my condition and humours; and by this means keep up more completely, and in a more lively manner, the knowledge they have of me." In his Essays he meant to portray himself, his habits, his modes of thought, his opinions, what fruit of wisdom he had gathered from experience sweet and bitter; and the task he has executed with wonderful fidelity. He does not make himself a hero. Cromwell would have his warts painted; and Montaigne paints his, and paints them too with a certain fondness. He is perfectly tolerant of himself and of everybody else. Whatever be the subject, the writing flows on easy, equable, self-satisfied, almost always with a personal anecdote floating on the surface. Each event of his past life he considers a fact of nature; creditable or the reverse, there it is; sometimes to be speculated upon, not in the least to be regretted. If it is worth nothing else, it may be made the subject of an essay, or, at least, be useful as an illustration. We have not only his thoughts, we see also how and from what they arose. When he presents you with a bouquet, you notice that the flowers have been plucked up by the roots, and to the roots a portion of the soil still adheres. On his daily life his Essays grew like lichens upon rocks. If a thing is useful to him, he is not squeamish as to where he picks it up. In his eyes there is nothing common or unclean; and he accepts a favour as willingly from a beggar as from a prince. When it serves his purpose, he quotes a tavern catch, or the smart saying of a kitchen wench, with as much relish as the fine sentiment of a classical poet, or the gallant *bon mot* of a king. Everything is important which relates to himself. That his moustache, if stroked with his perfumed glove, or handkerchief, will retain the odour a whole day, is related with as much gravity as the loss of a battle, or the march of a desolating plague. Montaigne, in his grave passages, reaches an eloquence intricate and highly wrought; but then his moods are Protean, and he is constantly alternating his stateliness with familiarity, anecdote, humour, coarseness. His Essays are like a mythological landscape—you hear the pipe of Pan in the distance, the naked goddess moves past, the satyr leers from the thicket. At the core of him profoundly melancholy, and consumed by a hunger for truth, he stands like Prospero in the enchanted island, and he has Ariel and Caliban to do his behests and run his errands. Sudden alternations are very characteristic of him. Whatever he says suggests its opposite. He laughs at himself and his reader. He builds his castle of cards for the mere pleasure of knocking it down again. He is ever unexpected and surprising. And with this curious mental activity, this play and linked dance of discordant elements, his page is alive and restless, like the constant flicker of light and shadow in a mass of foliage which the wind is stirring.

Montaigne is avowedly an egotist; and by those who are inclined to make this a matter of reproach, it should be remembered that the value of egotism depends entirely on the egotist. If the egotist is weak, his egotism is worthless. If the egotist is strong, acute, full of distinctive character, his egotism is precious, and remains a possession of the race. If Shakespeare had left personal revelations, how we should value them! if, indeed, he has not in some sense left them—if the tragedies and comedies are not personal revelations altogether—the multiform nature of the man rushing toward the sun at once in Falstaff, Hamlet, and Romeo. But calling Montaigne an egotist does not go a great way to decipher him. No writer takes the reader so much into his confidence, and no one so entirely escapes the penalty of confidence. He tells us everything about himself, we think; and when all is told, it is astonishing how little we really know. The esplanades of Montaigne's palace are thoroughfares, men from every European country rub clothes there, but somewhere in the building there is a secret room in which the master sits, of which no one but himself wears the key. We read in the Essays about his wife, his daughter, his daughter's governess, of his cook, of his page, "who was never found guilty of telling the truth," of his library, the Gascon harvest outside his château, his habits of composition, his favourite speculations; but somehow the man himself is constantly eluding us. His daughter's governess, his page, the ripening Gascon fields, are never introduced for their own sakes; they are employed to illustrate and set off the subject on which he happens to be writing. A brawl in his own kitchen he does not consider worthy of being specially set down, but he has seen and heard everything; it comes in his way when travelling in some remote region, and accordingly it finds a place. He is the frankest, most outspoken of writers; and that very frankness and outspokenness puts the reader off his guard. If you wish to preserve your secret, wrap it up in frankness. The Essays are full of this trick. The frankness is as well simulated as the grape-branches of the Grecian artist which the birds flew towards and pecked. When Montaigne retreats, he does so like a skilful general, leaving his fires burning. In other ways, too, he is an adept in putting his reader out. He discourses with the utmost gravity, but you suspect mockery or banter in his tones. He is serious with the most trifling subjects, and he trifles with the most serious. "He broods eternally over his own thought," but who can tell what his thought may be for the nonce? He is of all writers the most vagrant, surprising, and, to many minds, illogical. His sequences are not the sequences of other men. His writings are as full of transformations as a pantomime or a fairy tale. His arid wastes lead up to glittering palaces, his banqueting-halls end in a dog-hutch. He begins an essay about trivialities, and the conclusion is in the other world. And the peculiar character of his writing, like the peculiar character of all writing which is worth anything, arises from constitutional turn of mind. He is constantly playing at fast and loose with himself and his reader. He mocks and scorns his deeper nature; and, like Shakespeare in

"Hamlet," says his deepest things in a jesting way. When he is gayest, be sure there is a serious design in his gaiety. Singularly shrewd and penetrating—sad, not only from sensibility of exquisite nerve and tissue, but from meditation, and an eye that pierced the surfaces of things—fond of pleasure, yet strangely fascinated by death—sceptical, yet clinging to what the Church taught and believed—lazily possessed by a high ideal of life, yet unable to reach it, careless perhaps often to strive after it, and with no very high opinion of his own goodness, or of the goodness of his fellows—and with all these serious elements, an element of humour mobile as flame, which assumed a variety of forms, now pure fun, now mischievous banter, now blistering scorn—humour in all its shapes, carelessly exercised on himself and his readers—with all this variety, complexity, riot, and contradiction almost of intellectual forces within, Montaigne wrote his bewildering Essays—with the exception of Rabelais, the greatest modern Frenchman—the creator of a distinct literary form, and to whom, down even to our day, even in point of subject-matter, every essayist has been more or less indebted.

Bacon is the greatest of the serious and stately essayists—Montaigne the greatest of the garrulous and communicative. The one gives you his thoughts on Death, Travel, Government, and the like, and lets you make the best of them; the other gives you his on the same subjects, but he wraps them up in personal gossip and reminiscence. With the last it is never Death or Travel alone; it is always Death one-fourth, and Montaigne three-fourths; or Travel one-fourth, and Montaigne three-fourths. He pours his thought into the water of gossip, and gives you to drink. He gilds his pill always, and he always gilds it with himself. The general characteristics of his Essays have been indicated, and it is worth while inquiring what they teach, what positive good they have done, and why for three centuries they have charmed, and still continue to charm.

The Essays contain a philosophy of life, which is not specially high, yet which is certain to find acceptance more or less with men who have passed out beyond the glow of youth, and who have made trial of the actual world. The essence of his philosophy is a kind of cynical common sense. He will risk nothing in life; he will keep to the beaten track; he will not let passion blind or enslave him; he will gather around him what good he can, and will therewith endeavour to be content. He will be, as far as possible, self-sustained; he will not risk his happiness in the hands of man, or of woman either. He is shy of friendship, he fears love, for he knows that both are dangerous. He knows that life is full of bitters, and he holds it wisdom that a man should console himself, as far as possible, with its sweets, the principal of which are peace, travel, leisure, and the writing of essays. He values obtainable Gascon bread and cheese more than the unobtainable stars. He thinks crying for the moon the foolishest thing in the world. He will remain where he is. He will not deny that a new world may exist beyond the sunset, but he knows that to reach the new world there is a troublesome Atlantic to cross; and he is not in the least certain that, putting aside the chance of being drowned on the way, he will be one whit happier in the new world than he is in the old. For his part he will embark with no Columbus. He feels that life is but a sad thing at best; but as he has little hope of making it better, he accepts it, and will not make it worse by murmuring. When the chain galls him, he can at least revenge himself by making jests on it. He will temper the despotism of nature by epigrams. He has read Æsop's fable, and is the last man in the world to relinquish the shabbiest substance to grasp at the finest shadow.

Of nothing under the sun was Montaigne quite certain, except that every man—whatever his station—might travel farther and fare worse; and that the playing with his own thoughts, in the shape of essay-writing, was the most harmless of amusements. His practical acquiescence in things does not promise much fruit, save to himself; yet in virtue of it he became one of the forces of the world—a very visible agent in bringing about the Europe which surrounds us to-day. He lived in the midst of the French religious wars. The rulers of his country were execrable Christians, but most orthodox Catholics. The burning of heretics was a public amusement, and the court ladies sat out the play. On the queen-mother and on her miserable son lay all the blood of the St. Bartholomew. The country was torn asunder; everywhere was battle, murder, pillage, and such woeful partings as Mr. Millais has represented in his incomparable picture. To the solitary humorous essayist this state of things was hateful. He was a good Catholic in his easy way; he attended divine service regularly; he crossed himself when he yawned. He conformed in practice to every rule of the Church; but if orthodox in these matters, he was daring in speculation. There was nothing he was not bold enough to question. He waged war after his peculiar fashion with every form of superstition. He worked under the foundations of priestcraft. But while serving the Reformed cause, he had no sympathy with Reformers. If they would but remain quiet, but keep their peculiar notions to themselves, France would rest! That a man should go to the stake for an opinion, was as incomprehensible to him as that a priest or king should send him there for an opinion. He thought the persecuted and the persecutors fools about equally matched. He was easy-tempered and humane—in the hunting-field, he could not bear the cry of a dying hare with composure—martyr-burning had consequently no attraction for such a man. His scepticism came into play, his melancholy humour, his sense of the illimitable which surrounds man's life, and which mocks, defeats, flings back his thought upon himself. Man is here, he said, with bounded powers, with limited knowledge, with an unknown behind, an unknown in front, assured of nothing but that he was born, and that he must die; why then, in Heaven's name should he burn his fellow for a difference of opinion in the matter of surplices, or as to the proper fashion of conducting devotion? Out of his scepticism and merciful disposition grew, in that fiercely intolerant age, the idea of toleration, of which he was the apostle. Widely read, charming every one by his wit and wisdom, his influence spread from mind to mind, and assisted in bringing about the change which has taken place in European thought. His ideas, perhaps, did not spring from the highest sources. He was no ascetic, he loved pleasure, he was tolerant of everything except cruelty; but on that account we should not grudge him his meed. It is in this indirect way that great writers take their place among the forces of the world. In the long run, genius and wit side with the right cause. And the man fighting against wrong to-day is assisted, in a greater degree than perhaps he is himself aware, by the sarcasm of this writer, the metaphor of that, the song of the other, although the writers themselves professed indifference, or were even counted as belonging to the enemy.

Montaigne's hold on his readers arises from many causes. There is his frank and curious self-delineation; *that* interests, because it is the revelation of a very peculiar nature. Then there is the positive value of separate thoughts imbedded in his strange whimsicality and humour. Lastly, there is the perennial charm of style, which is never a separate quality, but rather the amalgam and issue of all the mental and moral qualities in a man's possession, and which bears the same relation to these that light bears to the mingled elements that make up the orb of the sun. And style, after all, rather than thought, is the immortal thing in literature. In literature, the charm of style is indefinable, yet all-subduing, just as fine manners are in social life. In reality, it is not of so much consequence what you say, as how you say it. Memorable sentences are memorable on account of some single irradiating word. "But Shadwell never *deviates* into sense," for instance. Young Roscius, in his provincial barn, will repeat you the great soliloquy of Hamlet, and although every word may be given with tolerable correctness, you find it just as commonplace as himself; the great actor speaks it, and you "read Shakespeare as by a flash of lightning." And it is in Montaigne's style, in the strange freaks and turnings of his thought, his constant surprises, his curious alternations of humour and melancholy, his careless, familiar form of address, and the grace with which everything is done, that his charm lies, and which makes the hundredth perusal of him as pleasant as the first.

And on style depends the success of the essayist. Montaigne said the most familiar things in the finest way. Goldsmith could not be termed a thinker; but everything he touched he brightened, as after a month of dry weather, the shower brightens the dusty shrubbery of a suburban villa. The world is not so much in need of new thoughts as that when thought grows old and worn with usage it should, like current coin, be called in, and, from the mint of genius, reissued fresh and new. Love is an old story enough, but in every generation it is re-born, in the downcast eyes and blushes of young maidens. And so, although he fluttered in Eden, Cupid is young to-day. If Montaigne had lived in Dreamthorp, as I am now living, had he written essays as I am now writing them, his English Essays would have been as good as his Gascon ones. Looking on, the country cart would not for nothing have passed him on the road to market, the setting sun would be arrested in its splendid colours, the idle chimes of the church would be translated into a thoughtful music. As it is, the village life goes on, and there is no result. My sentences are not much more brilliant than the speeches of the clowns; in my book there is little more life than there is in the market-place on the days when there is no market.

ON DEATH AND THE FEAR OF DYING

LET me curiously analyse eternal farewells, and the last pressures of loving hands. Let me smile at faces bewept, and the nodding plumes and slow paces of funerals. Let me write down brave heroical sentences—sentences that defy death, as brazen Goliath the hosts of Israel.

"When death waits for us is uncertain; let us everywhere look for him. The premeditation of death is the premeditation of liberty; who has learnt to die, has forgot to serve. There is nothing of evil in life for him who rightly comprehends that death is no evil; to know how to die delivers us from all subjection and constraint. *Paulus Æmilius* answered him whom the miserable *king of Macedon*, his prisoner, sent to entreat him that he would not lead him in his triumph, '*Let him make that request to himself.*' In truth, in all things, if nature do not help a little, it is very hard for art and industry to perform anything to purpose. I am, in my own nature, not melancholy, but thoughtful; and there is nothing I have more continually entertained myself withal than the imaginations of death, even in the gayest and most wanton time of my age. In the company of ladies, and in the height of mirth, some have perhaps thought me possessed of some jealousy, or meditating upon the uncertainty of some imagined hope, whilst I was entertaining myself with the remembrance of some one surprised a few days before with a burning fever, of which he died, returning from an entertainment like this, with his head full of idle fancies of love and jollity, as mine was then; and for aught I knew, the same destiny was attending me. Yet did not this thought wrinkle my forehead any more than any other." . . . " 'Why doest thou fear this last day? It contributes no more to thy destruction than every one of the rest. The last step is not the cause of lassitude, it does but confer it. Every day travels toward death; the last only arrives at it.' These are the good lessons our mother nature teaches. I have often considered with myself whence it should proceed, that in war the image of death—whether we look upon it as to our own particular danger, or that of another—should, without comparison, appear less dreadful than at home in our own houses (for if it were not so, it would be an army of whining milksops), and that being still in all places the same, there should be, notwithstanding, much more assurance in peasants and the meaner sort of people, than others of better quality and education; and I do verily believe, that it is those terrible ceremonies and preparations wherewith we set it out, that more terrify us than the thing itself; a new, quite contrary way of living, the cries of mothers, wives, and children, the visits of astonished and affected friends, the attendance of pale and blubbered servants, a dark room set round with burning tapers, our beds environed with physicians and divines; in fine, nothing but ghostliness and horror round about us, render it so formidable, that a man almost fancies himself dead and buried already. Children are afraid even of those they love best, and are best acquainted with, when disguised in a vizor, and so are we; the vizor must be removed as well from things as persons; which being taken away, we shall find nothing underneath but the very same death that a mean servant, or a poor chambermaid, died a day or two ago, without any manner of apprehension or concern." [1]

"Men feare *death* as children feare to goe in the darke; and as that natural feare in children is increased with tales, so is the other. Certainly the contemplation of *death* as the *wages of sinne*, and passage to another world, is holy and religious; but the feare of it as a tribute due unto nature, is weake. Yet in religious meditations there is sometimes mixture of vanitie and of superstition. You shal reade in some of the friars' books of *mortification*, that a man should thinke unto himself what the paine is if he have but his finger-end pressed or tortured; and thereby imagine what the paines of *death* are when the whole body is corrupted and dissolved; when many times *death* passeth with lesse paine than the torture of a Lemme. For the most vitall parts are not the quickest of sense. Groanes and convulsions, and a discoloured face, and friends weeping, and blackes and obsequies, and the like, shew *death* terrible. It is worthy the observing, that there is no passion in the minde of man so weake but it mates and masters the feare of *death;* and therefore death is no such terrible enemy when a man hath so many

[1] Montaigne.

attendants about him that can winne the combat of him. *Revenge* triumphs over *death*, *love* subjects it, *honour* aspireth to it, *griefe* fleeth to it, *feare* pre-occupieth it; nay, we read, after *Otho* the emperour had slaine himselfe, *pitty*, (which is the tenderest of affections,) provoked many to die, out of meer compassion to their soveraigne, and as the truest sort of followers. . . . It is as naturall to die as to be borne; and to a little infant, perhaps, the one is as painfull as the other. He that dies in an earnest pursuit is like one that is wounded in hot blood, who for the time scarce feels the hurt; and, therefore, a minde fixt and bent upon somewhat that is good, doth avert the sadness of *death*. But above all, believe it, the sweetest canticle is, *Nunc Dimittis*, when a man hath obtained worthy ends and expectations. Death hath this also; that it openeth the gate to good fame, and extinguisheth envie." [1]

These sentences of the great essayists are brave and ineffectual as Leonidas and his Greeks. Death cares very little for sarcasm or trope; hurl at him a javelin or a rose, it is all one. We build around ourselves ramparts of stoical maxims, edifying to witness, but when the terror comes these yield as the knots of river flags to the shoulder of Behemoth.

Death is terrible only in presence. When distant, or supposed to be distant, we can call him hard or tender names, nay, even poke our poor fun at him. *Mr. Punch*, on one occasion, when he wished to ridicule the useful-information leanings of a certain periodical publication, quoted from its pages the sentence, "Man is mortal," and people were found to grin broadly over the exquisite stroke of humour. Certainly the words, and the fact they contain, are trite enough. Utter the sentence gravely in any company, and you are certain to provoke laughter. And yet some subtle recognition of the fact of death runs constantly through the warp and woof of the most ordinary human existence. And this recognition does not always terrify. The spectre has the most cunning disguises, and often when near us we are unaware of the fact of proximity. Unsuspected, this idea of death lurks in the sweetness of music; it has something to do with the pleasure with which we behold the vapours of morning; it comes between the passionate lips of lovers; it lives in the thrill of kisses. "An inch deeper, and you will find the emperor." Probe joy to its last fibre, and you will

[1] Bacon.

find death. And it is the most merciful of all the merciful provisions of nature, that a haunting sense of insecurity should deepen the enjoyment of what we have secured; that the pleasure of our warm day and its activities should to some extent arise from a vague consciousness of the waste night which environs it, in which no arm is raised, in which no voice is ever heard. Death is the ugly fact which nature has to hide, and she hides it well. Human life were otherwise an impossibility. The pantomime runs on merrily enough; but when once Harlequin lifts his vizor, Columbine disappears, the jest is frozen on the Clown's lips, and the hand of the filching Pantaloon is arrested in the act. Wherever death looks, *there* is silence and trembling. But although on every man he will one day or another look, he is coy of revealing himself till the appointed time. He makes his approaches like an Indian warrior, under covers and ambushes. We have our parts to play, and he remains hooded till they are played out. We are agitated by our passions, we busily pursue our ambitions, we are acquiring money or reputation, and all at once, in the centre of our desires, we discover the "Shadow feared of man." And so nature fools the poor human mortal evermore. When she means to be deadly, she dresses her face in smiles; when she selects a victim, she sends him a poisoned rose. There is no pleasure, no shape of good fortune, no form of glory in which death has not hid himself, and waited silently for his prey.

And death is the most ordinary thing in the world. It is as common as births; it is of more frequent occurrence than marriages and the attainment of majorities. But the difference between death and other forms of human experience lies in this, that we can gain no information about it. The dead man is wise, but he is silent. We cannot wring his secret from him. We cannot interpret the ineffable calm which gathers on the rigid face. As a consequence, when our thought rests on death we are smitten with isolation and loneliness. We are without company on the dark road; and we have advanced so far upon it that we cannot hear the voices of our friends. It is in this sense of loneliness, this consciousness of identity and nothing more, that the terror of dying consists. And yet, compared to that road, the most populous thoroughfare of London or Pekin is a desert. What enumerator will take for us the census of the dead? And this matter of death and dying, like most things else in the world, may be exaggerated by our own fears and hopes. Death, terrible to look forward to, may be pleasant even to look back at. Could we be admitted to the happy fields, and hear the conversations which blessed spirits hold, one might discover that to conquer death a man has but to die; that by that act terror is softened into familiarity, and that the remembrance of death becomes but as the remembrance of yesterday. To these fortunate ones death may be but a date, and dying a subject fruitful in comparisons, a matter on which experiences may be serenely compared. Meantime, however, *we* have not yet reached that measureless content, and death scares, piques, tantalises, as mind and nerve are built. Situated as we are, knowing that it is inevitable, we cannot keep our thoughts from resting on it curiously, at times. Nothing interests us so much. The Highland seer pretended that he could see the winding-sheet high upon the breast of the man for whom death was waiting. Could we behold any such visible sign, the man who bore it, no matter where he stood—even if he were a slave watching Cæsar pass—would usurp every eye. At the coronation of a king, the wearing of *that* order would dim royal robe, quench the sparkle of the diadem, and turn to vanity the herald's cry. Death makes the meanest beggar august, and that augustness would assert itself in the presence of a king. And it is this curiosity with regard to everything related to death and dying which makes us treasure up the last sayings of great men, and attempt to wring out of them tangible meanings. Was Goethe's "Light—light, more light!" a prayer, or a statement of spiritual experience, or simply an utterance of the fact that the room in which he lay was filling with the last twilight? In consonance with our own natures we interpret it the one way or the other—*he* is beyond our questioning. For the same reason it is that men take interest in executions—from Charles I on the scaffold at Whitehall, to Porteous in the Grass-market execrated by the mob. These men are not dulled by disease, they are not delirious with fever; they look death in the face, and what in these circumstances they say and do has the strangest fascination for us.

What does the murderer think when his eyes are for ever blinded by the accursed nightcap? In what form did thought condense itself between the gleam of the lifted axe and the rolling of King Charles's head in the sawdust? This kind of speculation may be morbid, but it is not necessarily so. All extremes of human experience touch us; and we have all the deepest personal interest in the experience of death. Out of all we know about dying we strive to clutch something which may break its solitariness, and relieve us by a touch of companionship.

To denude death of its terrible associations were a vain attempt. The atmosphere is always cold around an iceberg. In the contemplation of dying the spirit may not flinch, but pulse and heart, colour and articulation, are always cowards. No philosophy will teach them bravery in the stern presence. And yet there are considerations which rob death of its ghastliness, and help to reconcile us to it. The thoughtful happiness of a human being is complex, and in certain moved moments, which, after they have gone, we can recognise to have been our happiest, some subtle thought of death has been curiously intermixed. And this subtle intermixture it is which gives the happy moment its character—which makes the difference between the gladness of a child, resident in mere animal health and impulse, and too volatile to be remembered, and the serious joy of a man, which looks before and after, and takes in both this world and the next. Speaking broadly, it may be said that it is from some obscure recognition of the fact of death that life draws its final sweetness. An obscure, haunting recognition, of course; for if more than that, if the thought becomes palpable, defined, and present, it swallows up everything. The howling of the winter wind outside increases the warm satisfaction of a man in bed; but this satisfaction is succeeded by quite another feeling when the wind grows into a tempest, and threatens to blow the house down. And this remote recognition of death may exist almost constantly in a man's mind, and give to his life keener zest and relish. His lights may burn the brighter for it, and his wines taste sweeter. For it is on the tapestry of a dim ground that the figures come out in the boldest relief and the brightest colour.

If we were to live here always, with no other care than how to feed, clothe, and house ourselves, life would be a very sorry business. It is immeasurably heightened by the solemnity of death. The brutes die even as we; but it is our knowledge that we have to die which makes us human. If nature cunningly hides death, and so permits us to play out our little games, it is easily seen that our knowing it to be inevitable, that to every one of us it will come one

day or another, is a wonderful spur to action. We really do work
while it is called to-day, because the night cometh when no man
can work. We may not expect it soon—it may not have sent us a
single *avant-courier*—yet we all know that every day brings it
nearer. On the supposition that we were to live here always, there
would be little inducement to exertion. But, having some work at
heart, the knowledge that we may be, any day, finally interrupted,
is an incentive to diligence. We naturally desire to have it completed, or at least far advanced toward completion, before that
final interruption takes place. And knowing that his existence here
is limited, a man's workings have reference to others rather than
to himself, and thereby into his nature comes a new influx of
nobility. If a man plants a tree, he knows that other hands than
his will gather the fruit; and when he plants it, he thinks quite as
much of those other hands as of his own. Thus to the poet there is
the dearer life after life; and posterity's single laurel leaf is valued
more than a multitude of contemporary bays. Even the man immersed in money-making does not make money so much for himself as for those who may come after him. Riches in noble natures
have a double sweetness. The possessor enjoys his wealth, and he
heightens that enjoyment by an imaginative entrance into the
pleasure which his son or his nephew may derive from it when he is
away, or the high uses to which he may turn it. Seeing that we have
no perpetual lease of life and its adjuncts, we do not live for ourselves. And thus it is that death, which we are accustomed to
consider an evil, really acts for us the friendliest part, and takes
away the commonplace of existence. My life, and your life, flowing on thus day by day, is a vapid enough piece of business; but
when we think that it must *close*, a multitude of considerations,
not connected with ourselves, but with others, rush in, and va-
pidity vanishes at once. Life, if it were to flow on for ever and *thus*,
would stagnate and rot. The hopes, and fears, and regrets, which
move and trouble it, keep it fresh and healthy, as the sea is kept
alive by the trouble of its tides. In a tolerably comfortable world,
where death is not, it is difficult to see from what quarter these
healthful fears, regrets, and hopes could come. As it is, there are
agitations and sufferings in our lots enough; but we must remember that it is on account of these sufferings and agitations that we
become creatures breathing thoughtful breath. As has already been

said, death takes away the commonplace of life. And positively, when one looks on the thousand and one poor, foolish, ignoble faces of this world, and listens to the chatter as poor and foolish as the faces, one, in order to have any proper respect for them, is forced to remember that solemnity of death, which is silently waiting. The foolishest person will look grand enough one day. The features are poor now, but the hottest tears and the most passionate embraces will not seem out of place *then*. If you wish to make a man look noble, your best course is to kill him. What superiority he may have inherited from his race, what superiority nature may have personally gifted him with, comes out in death. The passions which agitate, distort, and change, are gone away for ever, and the features settle back into a marble calm, which is the man's truest image. Then the most affected look sincere, the most volatile serious—all noble, more or less. And nature will not be surprised into disclosures. The man stretched out there may have been voluble as a swallow, but now—when he could speak to some purpose—neither pyramid nor sphinx holds a secret more tenaciously.

Consider, then, how the sense of impermanence brightens beauty and elevates happiness. Melancholy is always attendant on beauty, and that melancholy brings out its keenness as the dark-green corrugated leaf brings out the wan loveliness of the primrose. The spectator enjoys the beauty, but his knowledge that *it* is fleeting, and that *he* is fleeting, adds a pathetic something to it; and by that something the beautiful object and the gazer are alike raised.

Everything is sweetened by risk. The pleasant emotion is mixed and deepened by a sense of mortality. Those lovers who have never encountered the possibility of last embraces and farewells are novices in the passion. Sunset affects us more powerfully than sunrise, simply because it *is* a setting sun, and suggests a thousand analogies. A mother is never happier than when her eyes fill over her sleeping child, never does she kiss it more fondly, never does she pray for it more fervently; and yet there is more in her heart than visible red cheek and yellow curl; possession and bereavement are strangely mingled in the exquisite maternal mood, the one heightening the other. All great joys are serious; and emotion must be measured by its complexity and the deepness of its reach. A musician may draw pretty notes enough from a single key, but the richest music is that in which the whole force of the instrument is employed, in the production of which every key is vibrating; and, although full of solemn touches and majestic tones, the final effect may be exuberant and gay. Pleasures which rise beyond the mere gratification of the senses are dependent for their exquisiteness on the number and variety of the thoughts which they evoke. And that joy is the greatest which, while felt to be joy, can include the thought of death and clothe itself with that crowning pathos. And in the minds of thoughtful persons every joy does, more or less, with that crowning pathos clothe itself.

In life there is nothing more unexpected and surprising than the arrivals and departures of pleasure. If we find it in one place to-day, it is vain to seek it there to-morrow. You cannot lay a trap for it. It will fall into no ambuscade, concert it ever so cunningly. Pleasure has no logic; it never treads in its own footsteps. Into our commonplace existence it comes with a surprise, like a pure white swan from the airy void into the ordinary village lake; and just as the swan, for no reason that can be discovered, lifts itself on its wings and betakes itself to the void again, *it* leaves us, and our sole possession is its memory. And it is characteristic of pleasure that we can never recognise it to be pleasure till after it is gone. Happiness never lays its finger on its pulse. If we attempt to steal a glimpse of its features it disappears. It is a gleam of unreckoned gold. From the nature of the case, our happiness, such as in its degree it has been, lives in memory. We have not the voice itself; we have only its echo. We are never happy; we can only remember that we were so once. And while in the very heart and structure of the happy moment there lurked an obscure consciousness of death, the memory in which past happiness dwells is always a regretful memory. This is why the tritest utterance about the past, youth, early love, and the like, has always about it an indefinable flavour of poetry, which pleases and affects. In the wake of a ship there is always a melancholy splendour. The finest set of verses of our modern time describes how the poet gazed on the "happy autumn fields," and remembered the "days that were no more." After all, a man's real possession is his memory. In nothing else is he rich, in nothing else is he poor.

In our warm imaginative youth, death is far removed from us, and attains thereby a certain picturesqueness. The grim thought stands in the ideal world as a ruin stands in a blooming landscape.

The thought of death sheds a pathetic charm over everything then. The young man cools himself with a thought of the winding-sheet and the charnel, as the heated dancer cools himself on the balcony with the night-air. The young imagination plays with the idea of death, makes a toy of it, just as a child plays with edge-tools till once it cuts its fingers. The most lugubrious poetry is written by very young and tolerably comfortable persons. When a man's mood becomes really serious he has little taste for such foolery. The man who has a grave or two in his heart, does not need to haunt churchyards. The young poet uses death as an antithe-sis; and when he shocks his reader by some flippant use of it in that way, he considers he has written something mightily fine. In his gloomiest mood he is most insincere, most pretentious. The older and wiser poet avoids the subject as he does the memory of pain; or when he does refer to it, he does so in a reverential manner, and with some sense of its solemnity and of the magnitude of its issues. It was in that year of revelry, 1814, and while undressing from balls, that Lord Byron wrote his "Lara," as he informs us. Dis-robing, and haunted, in all probability, by eyes in whose light he was happy enough, the spoiled young man, who then affected death-pallors, and wished the world to believe that he felt his richest wines powdered with the dust of graves—of which wine, notwithstanding, he frequently took more than was good for him—wrote,

> That sleep the loveliest, since it dreams the least.

The sleep referred to being death. This was meant to take away the reader's breath; and after performing the feat, Byron betook himself to his pillow with a sense of supreme cleverness. Contrast with this Shakespeare's far out-looking and thought-heavy lines—lines which, under the same image, represent death—

> To die—to sleep;—
> To sleep! perchance to dream;—ay, there's the rub;
> For in that sleep of death what dreams may come!

And you see at once how a man's notions of death and dying are deepened by a wider experience. Middle age may fear death quite as little as youth fears it; but it has learned seriousness, and it has no heart to poke fun at the lean ribs, or to call it fond names like a lover, or to stick a primrose in its grinning chaps, and draw a strange pleasure from the irrelevancy.

The man who has reached thirty, feels at times as if he had come out of a great battle. Comrade after comrade has fallen; his own life seems to have been charmed. And knowing how it fared with his friends—perfect health one day, a catarrh the next, blinds drawn down, silence in the house, blubbered faces of widow and orphans, intimation of the event in the newspapers, with a request that friends will accept of it, the day after—a man, as he draws near middle age, begins to suspect every transient indisposition; to be careful of being caught in a shower, to shudder at sitting in wet shoes; he feels his pulse, he anxiously peruses his face in a mirror, he becomes critical as to the colour of his tongue. In early life illness is a luxury, and draws out toward the sufferer curious and delicious tendernesses, which are felt to be a full over-payment of pain and weakness; then there is the pleasant period of convalescence, when one tastes a core and marrow of delight in meats, drinks, sleep, silence; the bunch of newly-plucked flowers on the table, the sedulous attentions and patient forbearance of nurses and friends. Later in life, when one occupies a post, and is in discharge of duties which are accumulating against recovery, illness and convalescence cease to be luxuries. Illness is felt to be a cruel interruption of the ordinary course of things, and the sick person is harassed by a sense of the loss of time and the loss of strength. He is placed *hors de combat;* all the while he is conscious that the battle is going on around him, and he feels his temporary withdrawal a misfortune. Of course, unless a man is very unhappily circumstanced, he has in his later illnesses all the love, patience, and attention which sweetened his earlier ones; but then he cannot rest in them, and accept them as before as compensation in full. The world is ever with him; through his interests and his affections he has meshed himself in an intricate net-work of relationships and other dependences, and a fatal issue—which in such cases is ever on the cards—would destroy all these, and bring about more serious matters than the shedding of tears. In a man's earlier illnesses, too, he had not only no such definite future to work out, he had a stronger spring of life and hope; he was rich in time, and could wait; and lying in his chamber now, he cannot help remembering that, as Mr. Thackeray expresses it, there comes at last an illness to which there may be no convalescence. What if that illness be already come? And so there is nothing left for him, but to bear the rod with patience, and to exercise a humble faith in the Ruler of all. If he recovers, some half-dozen people will be made happy; if he does not recover, the same number of people will be made miserable for a little while, and, during the next two or three days, acquaintances will meet in the street—"You've heard of poor So-and-so? Very sudden! Who would have thought it? Expect to meet you at ——'s on Thursday. Good-bye." And so the end. Your death and my death are mainly of importance to ourselves. The black plumes will be stripped off our hearses within the hour; tears will dry, hurt hearts close again, our graves grow level with the churchyard, and although we are away, the world wags on. It does not miss us; and those who are near us, when the first strangeness of vacancy wears off, will not miss us much either.

We are curious as to death-beds and death-bed sayings; we wish to know how the matter stands; how the whole thing looks to the dying. Unhappily—perhaps, on the whole, happily—we can gather no information from these. The dying are nearly as reticent as the dead. The inferences we draw from the circumstances of death, the pallor, the sob, the glazing eye, are just as likely to mislead us as not. Manfred exclaims, "Old man, 'tis not so difficult to die!" Sterling wrote Carlyle "that it was all very strange, yet not so strange as it seemed to the lookers on." And so, perhaps, on the whole it is. The world has lasted six thousand years now, and, with the exception of those at present alive, the millions who have breathed upon it—splendid emperors, horny-fisted clowns, little children in whom thought has never stirred—*have* died, and what they have done, we also shall be able to do. It may not be so difficult, may not be so terrible, as our fears whisper. The dead keep their secrets, and in a little while we shall be as wise as they—and as taciturn.

A LARK'S FLIGHT

RIGHTLY or wrongly, during the last twenty or thirty years a strong feeling has grown up in the public mind against the principle, and a still stronger feeling against the practice, of capital punishments. Many people who will admit that the execution of the murderer may be, abstractly considered, just enough, sincerely doubt whether such execution be expedient, and are in their own minds perfectly certain that it cannot fail to demoralise the spectators. In consequence of this, executions have become rare; and it is quite clear that many scoundrels, well worthy of the noose, contrive to escape it. When, on the occasion of a wretch being turned off, the spectators are few, it is remarked by the newspapers that the mob is beginning to lose its proverbial cruelty, and to be stirred by humane pulses; when they are numerous, and especially when girls and women form a majority, the circumstance is noticed and deplored. It is plain enough that, if the newspaper considered such an exhibition beneficial, it would not lament over a few thousand eager witnesses: if the sermon be edifying, you cannot have too large a congregation; if you teach a moral lesson in a grand, impressive way, it is difficult to see how you can have too many pupils. Of course, neither the justice nor the expediency of capital punishments falls to be discussed here. This, however, may be said, that the popular feeling against them may not be so admirable a proof of enlightenment as many believe. It is true that the spectacle is painful, horrible; but in pain and horror there is often hidden a certain salutariness, and the repulsion of which we are conscious is as likely to arise from debilitation of public nerve, as from a higher reach of public feeling. To my own thinking, it is out of this pain and hatefulness that an execution becomes invested with an ideal grandeur. It is sheer horror to all concerned—sheriffs, halbertmen, chaplain, spectators, Jack Ketch, and culprit; but out of all this, and towering behind the vulgar and hideous accessories of the scaffold, gleams the majesty of implacable law. When every other fine morning a dozen cut-purses were hanged at Tyburn, and when such sights did not run very strongly against the popular current, the spectacle *was* vulgar, and could be of use only to the possible cut-purses congregated around the foot of the scaffold. Now, when the law has become so far merciful; when the punishment of death is reserved for the murderer; when he can be condemned only on the clearest evidence; when, as the days draw slowly on to doom, the frightful event impending over one stricken wretch throws its shadow over the heart of every man, woman, and child in the great city; and when the official persons whose duty it is to see the letter of the law carried out perform that duty at the expense of personal pain, a public execution is not vulgar, it becomes positively sublime. It is dreadful, of course; but its dreadfulness melts into pure awfulness. The attention is taken off the criminal, and is lost in a sense of the grandeur of justice; and the spectator who beholds an execution, solely as it appears to the eye, without recognition of the idea which towers behind it, must be a very unspiritual and unimaginative spectator indeed.

It is taken for granted that the spectators of public executions—the artisans and country people who take up their stations overnight as close to the barriers as possible, and the wealthier classes who occupy hired windows and employ opera-glasses—are merely drawn together by a morbid relish for horrible sights. He is a bold man who will stand forward as the advocate of such persons—so completely is the popular mind made up as to their tastes and motives. It is not disputed that the large body of the mob, and of the occupants of windows, have been drawn together by an appetite for excitement; but it is quite possible that many come there from an impulse altogether different. Just consider the nature of the expected sight—a man in tolerable health probably, in possession of all his faculties, perfectly able to realise his position, conscious that for him this world and the next are so near that only a few seconds divide them—such a man stands in the seeing of several thousand eyes. He is so peculiarly circumstanced, so utterly lonely—hearing the tolling of his own death-bell, yet living, wearing the mourning clothes for his own funeral—that he holds the multitude together by a shuddering fascination. The sight is a peculiar one, you must admit, and every peculiarity has its attractions. Your volcano is more attractive than your ordinary mountain. Then consider the unappeasable curiosity as to death which haunts every human being, and how pathetic that curiosity is, in so far as it suggests our own ignorance and helplessness, and we see at once that people *may* flock to public executions for other purposes than the gratification of morbid tastes: that they would pluck if they could some little knowledge of what death is; that imaginatively they attempt to reach to it, to touch and handle it through an experience which is not their own. It is some obscure desire of this kind, a movement of curiosity not altogether ignoble, but in some degree pathetic; some rude attempt of the imagination to wrest from the death of the criminal information as to the

great secret in which each is profoundly interested, which draws
around the scaffold people from the country harvest-fields, and
from the streets and alleys of the town. Nothing interests men so
much as death. Age cannot wither it, nor custom stale it. "A
greater crowd would come to see me hanged," Cromwell is reported to have said when the populace came forth on a public
occasion. The Lord Protector was right in a sense of which, perhaps, at the moment he was not aware. Death is greater than
official position. When a man has to die, he may safely dispense
with stars and ribbands. He is invested with a greater dignity
than is held in the gift of kings. A greater crowd *would* have
gathered to see Cromwell hanged, but the compliment would
have been paid to death rather than to Cromwell. Never were the
motions of Charles I so scrutinised as when he stood for a few
moments on the scaffold that winter morning at Whitehall. King
Louis was no great orator usually, but when on January 2, 1793,
he attempted to speak a few words in the Place de la Revolution,
it was found necessary to drown his voice in a harsh roll of soldiers'
drums. Not without a meaning do people come forth to see men
die. We stand in the valley, they on the hill-top, and on their
faces strikes the light of the other world, and from some sign or
signal of theirs we attempt to discover or extract a hint of what it
is all like.

To be publicly put to death, for whatever reason, must ever be
a serious matter. It is always bitter, but there are degrees in its
bitterness. It is easy to die like Stephen with an opened heaven
above you, crowded with angel faces. It is easy to die like Balmerino
with a chivalrous sigh for the White Rose, and an audible "God
bless King James." Such men die for a cause in which they glory,
and are supported thereby; they are conducted to the portals of
the next world by the angels, Faith, Pity, Admiration. But it is
not easy to die in expiation of a crime like murder, which engirdles
you with trembling and horror even in the loneliest places, which
cuts you off from the sympathies of your kind, which reduces the
universe to two elements—a sense of personal identity, and a
memory of guilt. In so dying, there must be inconceivable bitterness; a man can have no other support than what strength he may
pluck from despair, or from the iron with which nature may have
originally braced heart and nerve. Yet, taken as a whole, criminals

on the scaffold comport themselves creditably. They look Death in the face when he wears his cruellest aspect, and if they flinch somewhat, they can at least bear to look. I believe that, for the criminal, execution within the prison walls, with no witnesses save some half-dozen official persons, would be infinitely more terrible than execution in the presence of a curious, glaring mob. The daylight and the publicity are alien elements, which wean the man a little from himself. He steadies his dizzy brain on the crowd beneath and around him. He has his last part to play, and his manhood rallies to play well. Nay, so subtly is vanity inter-twined with our motives, the noblest and the most ignoble, that I can fancy a poor wretch with the noose dangling at his ear, and with barely five minutes to live, soothed somewhat with the idea that his firmness and composure will earn him the approbation, perhaps the pity, of the spectators. He would take with him, if he could, the good opinion of his fellows. This composure of criminals puzzles one. Have they looked at death so long and closely, that familiarity has robbed it of terror? Has life treated them so harshly, that they are tolerably well pleased to be quit of it on any terms? Or is the whole thing mere blind stupor and delirium, in which thought is paralysed, and the man an automaton? Speculation is useless. The fact remains that criminals for the most part die well and bravely. It is said that the championship of England was to be decided at some little distance from London on the morning of the day on which Thurtell was executed, and that, when he came out on the scaffold, he inquired privily of the executioner if the result had yet become known. Jack Ketch was not aware, and Thurtell expressed his regret that the ceremony in which he was chief actor should take place so inconveniently early in the day. Think of a poor Thurtell forced to take his long journey an hour, perhaps, before the arrival of intelligence so important.

More than twenty years ago I saw two men executed, and the impression then made remains fresh to this day. For this there were many reasons. The deed for which the men suffered created an immense sensation. They were hanged on the spot where the murder was committed—on a rising ground, some four miles north-east of the city; and as an attempt at rescue was apprehended, there was a considerable display of military force on the occasion. And when, in the dead silence of thousands, the criminals stood beneath the halters, an incident occurred, quite natural and slight in itself, but when taken in connexion with the business then proceeding, so unutterably tragic, so overwhelming in its pathetic suggestion of contrast, that the feeling of it has never departed, and never will. At the time, too, I speak of, I was very young; the world was like a die newly cut, whose every impression is fresh and vivid.

While the railway which connects two northern capitals was being built, two brothers from Ireland, named Doolan, were engaged upon it in the capacity of navvies. For some fault or negligence, one of the brothers was dismissed by the overseer—a Mr. Green—of that particular portion of the line on which they were employed. The dismissed brother went off in search of work, and the brother who remained—Dennis was the Christian name of him—brooded over this supposed wrong, and in his dull, twilighted brain revolved projects of vengeance. He did not absolutely mean to take Green's life, but he meant to thrash him to within an inch of it. Dennis, anxious to thrash Green, but not quite seeing his way to it, opened his mind one afternoon, when work was over, to his friends—fellow-Irishmen and navvies—Messrs. Redding and Hickie. These took up Doolan's wrong as their own, and that evening, by the dull light of a bothy fire, they held a rude parliament, discussing ways and means of revenge. It was arranged that Green should be thrashed—the amount of thrashing left an open question, to be decided, unhappily, when the blood was up and the cinder of rage blown into a flame. Hickie's spirit was found not to be a mounting one, and it was arranged that the active partners in the game should be Doolan and Redding. Doolan, as the aggrieved party, was to strike the first blow, and Redding, as the aggrieved party's particular friend, asked and obtained permission to strike the second. The main conspirators, with a fine regard for the feelings of the weaker Hickie, allowed him to provide the weapons of assault—so that by some slight filament of aid he might connect himself with the good cause. The unambitious Hickie at once applied himself to his duty. He went out, and in due time returned with two sufficient iron pokers. The weapons were examined, approved of, and carefully laid aside. Doolan, Redding, and Hickie ate their suppers, and retired to their several couches to sleep, peacefully enough no doubt. About the same time, too, Green, the English overseer, threw down his weary limbs, and entered on his last sleep—little dreaming what the morning had in store for him.

Uprose the sun, and uprose Doolan and Redding, and dressed, and thrust each his sufficient iron poker up the sleeve of his blouse, and went forth. They took up their station on a temporary wooden bridge which spanned the line, and waited there. Across the bridge, as was expected, did Green ultimately come. He gave them good morning; asked, "why they were loafing about?" received no very pertinent answer, perhaps did not care to receive one; whistled— the unsuspecting man!—thrust his hands into his breeches pockets, turned his back on them, and leaned over the railing of the bridge, inspecting the progress of the works beneath. The temptation was really too great. What could wild Irish flesh and blood do? In a moment out from the sleeve of Doolan's blouse came the hidden poker, and the first blow was struck, bringing Green to the ground. The friendly Redding, who had bargained for the second, and who, naturally enough, was in fear of being cut out altogether, jumped on the prostrate man, and fulfilled his share of the bargain with a will. It was Redding it was supposed who sped the unhappy Green. They overdid their work—like young authors—giving many more blows than were sufficient, and then fled. The works, of course, were that morning in consternation. Redding and Hickie were, if I remember rightly, apprehended in the course of the day. Doolan got off, leaving no trace of his whereabouts.

These particulars were all learned subsequently. The first intimation which we schoolboys received of anything unusual having occurred, was the sight of a detachment of soldiers with fixed bayonets, trousers rolled up over muddy boots, marching past the front of the Cathedral hurriedly home to barracks. This was a circumstance somewhat unusual. We had, of course, frequently seen a couple of soldiers trudging along with sloped muskets, and that cruel glitter of steel which no one of us could look upon quite unmoved; but in such cases, the deserter walking between them in his shirt-sleeves, his pinioned hands covered from public gaze by the loose folds of his great-coat, explained everything. But from the hurried march of these mud-splashed men nothing could be gathered, and we were left to speculate upon its meaning. Gradually, however, before the evening fell, the rumour of a murder having been committed spread through the city, and with that I instinctively connected the apparition of the file of muddy soldiers. Next day, murder was in every mouth. My schoolfellows talked of it to the detriment of their lessons; it flavoured the tobacco of the fustian artizan as he smoked to work after breakfast; it walked on 'Change amongst the merchants. It was known that two of the persons implicated had been captured, but that the other, and guiltiest, was still at large; and in a few days out on every piece of boarding and blank wall came the "Hue and cry"—describing Doolan like a photograph, to the colour and cut of his whiskers, and offering £100 as reward for his apprehension, or for such information as would lead to his apprehension—like a silent, implacable bloodhound following close on the track of the murderer. This terrible broad-sheet I read, was certain that *he* had read it also, and fancy ran riot over the ghastly fact. For him no hope, no rest, no peace, no touch of hands gentler than the hangman's; all the world is after him like a roaring prairie of flame! I thought of Doolan, weary, foot-sore, heart-sore, entering some quiet village of an evening; and to quench his thirst, going up to the public well, around which the gossips are talking, and hearing that they were talking of *him;* and seeing from the well itself, IT glaring upon him, as if conscious of his presence, with a hundred eyes of vengeance. I thought of him asleep in out-houses, and starting up in wild dreams of the policeman's hand upon his shoulder fifty times ere morning. He had committed the crime of Cain, and the weird of Cain he had to endure. But yesterday innocent, how unimportant; to-day bloody-handed, the whole world is talking of him, and everything he touches, the very bed he sleeps on, steals from him his secret, and is eager to betray.

Doolan was finally captured in Liverpool, and in the Spring Assize the three men were brought to trial. The jury found them guilty, but recommended Hickie to mercy on account of some weakness of mind on his part. Sentence was, of course, pronounced with the usual solemnities. They were set apart to die; and when snug abed o' nights—for imagination is most mightily moved by contrast—I crept into their desolate hearts, and tasted a misery which was not my own. As already said, Hickie was recommended to mercy, and the recommendation was ultimately in the proper quarter given effect to.

The evening before the execution has arrived, and the reader has now to imagine the early May sunset falling pleasantly on the outskirts of the city. The houses looking out upon an open square or space, have little plots of garden-ground in their fronts, in which mahogany-coloured wall-flowers and mealy auriculas are growing. The side of this square, along which the City Road stretches northward, is occupied by a blind asylum, a brick building, the bricks painted red and picked out with white, after the tidy English fashion, and a high white cemetery wall, over which peers the spire of the Gothic Cathedral; and beyond that, on the other side of the ravine, rising out of a populous city of the dead, a stone John Knox looks down on the Cathedral, a Bible clutched in his outstretched and menacing hand. On all this the May sunset is striking, dressing everything in its warm, pleasant pink, lingering in the tufts of foliage that nestle around the asylum, and dipping the building itself one half in light, one half in tender shade. This open space or square is an excellent place for the games of us boys, and "Prisoners' Base" is being carried out with as much earnestness as the business of life now by those of us who are left. The girls, too, have their games of a quiet kind, which we hold in huge scorn and contempt. In two files, linked arm-in-arm, they alternately dance towards each other and then retire, singing the while, in their clear, girlish treble, verses, the meaning and pertinence of which time has worn away—

> The Campsie Duke's a-riding, a-riding, a-riding,

being the oft-recurring "owercome" or refrain. All this is going on in the pleasant sunset light, when by the apparition of certain waggons coming up from the city, piled high with blocks and beams, and guarded by a dozen dragoons, on whose brazen helmets the sunset danced, every game is dismembered, and we are in a moment a mere mixed mob of boys and girls, flocking around to stare and wonder. Just at this place something went wrong with one of the waggon wheels, and the procession came to a stop. A crowd collected, and we heard some of the grown-up people say that the scaffold was being carried out for the ceremony of to-morrow. Then, more intensely than ever, one realised the condition of the doomed men. *We* were at our happy games in the sunset, *they* were entering on their last night on earth. After hammering and delay the wheel was put to rights, the sunset died out, waggons and dragoons got into motion and disappeared; and all the night through, whether awake or asleep, I saw the torches burning, and heard the hammers clinking, and witnessed as clearly as if I had been an onlooker, the horrid structure rising, till it stood complete, with a huge cross-beam from which two empty halters hung, in the early morning light.

Next morning the whole city was in commotion. Whether the authorities were apprehensive that a rescue would be attempted, or were anxious merely to strike terror into the hundreds of wild Irishry engaged on the railway, I cannot say; in any case, there was a display of military force quite unusual. The carriage in which the criminals—Catholics both—and their attendant priests were seated, was guarded by soldiers with fixed bayonets; indeed, the whole regiment then lying in the city was massed in front and behind, with a cold, frightful glitter of steel. Besides the foot soldiers, there were dragoons, and two pieces of cannon; a whole little army, in fact. With a slenderer force battles have been won which have made a mark in history. What did the prisoners think of their strange importance, and of the tramp and hurly-burly all around? When the procession moved out of the city, it seemed to draw with it almost the entire population; and when once the country roads were reached, the crowd spread over the fields on either side, ruthlessly treading down the tender wheat braid. I got a glimpse of the doomed, blanched faces which had haunted me so long, at the turn of the road, where, for the first time, the black cross-beam with its empty halters first became visible to them. Both turned and regarded it with a long, steady look; that done, they again bent their heads attentively to the words of the clergyman. I suppose in that long, eager, fascinated gaze they practically *died*—that for them death had no additional bitterness. When the mound was reached on which the scaffold stood, there was immense confusion. Around it a wide space was kept clear by the military; the cannon were placed in position; out flashed the swords of the dragoons; beneath and around on every side was the crowd. Between two brass helmets I could see the scaffold clearly enough, and when in a little while the men, bareheaded and with their attendants, appeared upon it, the surging crowd became stiffened with fear and awe. And now it was that the incident so simple, so natural, so much in the ordinary course of things, and yet so frightful in its tragic suggestions, took place. Be it remembered that the season was early May, that the day was fine, that the wheat-fields were clothing themselves in the green of the young crop, and that around the scaffold, standing on a sunny mound, a wide space was kept clear. When the men appeared beneath the beam, each under his proper halter, there was a dead silence—every one was gazing too intently to whisper to his neighbour even. Just then, out of the grassy space at the foot of the scaffold, in the dead silence audible to all, a lark rose from the side of its nest, and went singing upward in its happy flight. O heaven! how did that song translate itself into dying ears? Did it bring in one wild burning moment father, and mother, and poor Irish cabin, and prayers said at bed-time, and the smell of turf fires, and innocent sweethearting, and rising and setting suns? Did it—but the dragoon's horse has become restive, and his brass helmet bobs up and down and blots everything; and there is a sharp sound, and I feel the great crowd heave and swing, and hear it torn by a sharp shiver of pity, and the men whom I saw so near but a moment ago are at immeasurable distance, and have solved the great enigma—and the lark has not yet finished his flight: you can see and hear him yonder in the fringe of a white May cloud.

This ghastly lark's flight, when the circumstances are taken into consideration, is, I am inclined to think, more terrible than anything of the same kind which I have encountered in books. The artistic uses of contrast as background and accompaniment, are well known to nature and the poets. Joy is continually worked on sorrow, sorrow on joy; riot is framed in peace, peace in riot. Lear and the Fool always go together. Trafalgar is being fought while Napoleon is sitting on horseback watching the Austrian army laying down its arms at Ulm. In Hood's poem, it is when looking on the released schoolboys at their games that Eugene Aram remembers he is a murderer. And these two poor Irish labourers could not die without hearing a lark singing in their ears. It is Nature's fashion. She never quite goes along with us. She is sombre at weddings, sunny at funerals, and she frowns on ninety-nine out of a hundred pic-nics.

There is a stronger element of terror in this incident of the lark than in any story of a similar kind I can remember.

A good story is told of an Irish gentleman—still known in London society—who inherited the family estates and the family banshee. The estates he lost—no uncommon circumstance in the history of Irish gentlemen,—but the banshee, who expected no favours, stuck to him in his adversity, and crossed the channel with him, making herself known only on occasions of deathbeds and sharp family misfortunes. This gentleman had an ear, and, seated one night at the opera, the *keen*—heard once or twice before on memorable occasions—thrilled through the din of the orchestra and the passion of the singers. He hurried home of course, found his immediate family well, but on the morrow a telegram arrived with the announcement of a brother's death. Surely of all superstitions that is the most imposing which makes the other world interested in the events which befall our mortal lot. For the mere pomp and pride of it, your ghost is worth a dozen retainers, and it is entirely inexpensive. The peculiarity and supernatural work of this story lies in the idea of the old wail piercing through the sweet entanglement of stringed instruments and extinguishing Grisi. Modern circumstances and luxury crack, as it were, and reveal for a moment misty and aboriginal time big with portent. There is a ridiculous Scotch story in which one gruesome touch lives. A clergyman's female servant was seated in the kitchen one Saturday night reading the Scriptures, when she was somewhat startled by hearing at the door the tap and voice of her sweetheart. Not expecting him, and the hour being somewhat late, she opened it in astonishment, and was still more astonished to hear him on entering abuse Scripture-reading. He behaved altogether in an unprecedented manner, and in many ways terrified the poor girl. Ultimately he knelt before her, and laid his head on her lap. You can fancy her consternation when glancing down she discovered that, *instead of hair, the head was covered with the moss of the moorland*. By a sacred name she adjured him to tell who he was, and in a moment the figure was gone. It was the Fiend, of course—diminished sadly since Milton saw him bridge chaos—fallen from worlds to kitchen-wenches. But just think how in the story, in half-pity, in half-terror, the popular feeling of homelessness, of being outcast, of being unsheltered as waste and desert places, had incarnated itself in that strange covering of the head. It is a true supernatural touch. One other story I have heard in the misty Hebrides: A Skye gentleman was riding along an empty moorland road. All at once, as if it had sprung from the ground, the empty road was crowded by a funeral procession. Instinctively he drew his horse to a side to let it pass, which it did without sound of voice, without tread of foot. Then he knew it was an apparition. Staring on it, he knew every person who either bore the corpse or who walked behind as mourners. There were the neighbouring proprietors at whose houses he dined, there were the members of his own kirk-session, there were the men to whom he was wont to give good-morning when he met them on the road or at market. Unable to discover his own image in the throng, he was inwardly marvelling whose funeral it *could* be, when the troop of spectres vanished, and the road was empty as before. Then, remembering that the coffin had an invisible occupant, he cried out, "It is my funeral!" and, with all his strength taken out of him, rode home to die. All these stories have their own touches of terror; yet I am inclined to think that my lark rising from the scaffold foot, and singing to two such auditors, is more terrible than any one of them.

CHRISTMAS

OVER the dial-face of the year, on which the hours are months, the apex resting in sunshine, the base in withered leaves and snows, the finger of time does not travel with the same rapidity. Slowly it creeps up from snow to sunshine; when it has gained the summit it seems almost to rest for a little; rapidly it rushes down from sunshine to the snow. Judging from my own feelings, the distance from January to June is greater than from June to January—the period from Christmas to Midsummer seems longer than the period from Midsummer to Christmas. This feeling arises, I should fancy, from the preponderance of *light* on that half of the dial on which the finger seems to be travelling upwards, compared with the half on which it seems to be travelling downwards. This light to the eye, the mind translates into time. Summer days are long, often wearisomely so. The long-lighted days are bracketed together by a little bar of twilight, in which but a star or two find time to twinkle. Usually one has less occupation in summer than in winter, and the surplusage of summer light, a stage too large for the play, wearies, oppresses, sometimes appals.

From the sense of time we can only shelter ourselves by occupation; and when occupation ceases while yet some three or four hours of light remain, the burden falls down, and is often greater than we can bear. Personally, I have a certain morbid fear of those endless summer twilights. A space of light stretching from half-past 2 a.m. to 11 p.m. affects me with a sense of infinity, of horrid sameness, just as the sea or the desert would do. I feel that for too long a period I am under the eye of a taskmaster. Twilight is always in itself, or at least in its suggestions, melancholy; and these midsummer twilights are so long, they pass through such series of lovely change, they are throughout so mournfully beautiful, that in the brain they beget strange thoughts, and in the heart strange feelings. We see too much of the sky, and the long, lovely, pathetic, lingering evening light, with its suggestions of eternity and death, which one cannot for the soul of one put into words, is somewhat too much for the comfort of a sensitive human mortal. The day dies, and makes no apology for being such an unconscionable time in dying; and all the while it colours our thoughts with its own solemnity. There is no relief from this kind of thing at midsummer. You cannot close your shutters and light your candles; that in the tone of mind which circumstances superinduce would be brutality. You cannot take Pickwick to the window and read it by the dying light; that is profanation. If you have a friend with you, you can't talk; the hour makes you silent. You are driven in on your self-consciousness. The long light wearies the eye, a sense of time disturbs and saddens the spirit; and that is the reason, I think, that one half of the year seems so much longer than the other half; that on the dial-plate whose hours are months, the restless finger *seems* to move more slowly when travelling upward from autumn leaves and snow to light, than when it is travelling downward from light to snow and withered leaves.

Of all the seasons of the year, I like winter best. That peculiar burden of time I have been speaking of, does not affect me now. The day is short, and I can fill it with work; when evening comes, I have my lighted room and my books. Should black care haunt me, I throw it off the scent in Spenser's forests, or seek refuge from it among Shakespeare's men and women, who are by far the best company I have met with, or am like to meet with, on earth. I am sitting at this present moment with my curtains drawn; the cheerful fire is winking at all the furniture in the room, and from every leg and arm the furniture is winking to the fire in return. I put off the outer world with my greatcoat and boots, and put on contentment and idleness with my slippers. On the hearth-rug, Pepper, coiled in a shaggy ball, is asleep in the ruddy light and heat. An imaginative sense of the cold outside increases my present comfort—just as one never hugs one's own good luck so affectionately as when listening to the relation of some horrible misfortune which has overtaken others. Winter has fallen on Dreamthorp, and it looks as pretty when covered with snow, as when covered with apple blossom. Outside, the ground is hard as iron; and over the low dark hill, lo! the tender radiance that precedes the morn. Every window in the little village has its light, and to the traveller coming on, enveloped in his breath, the whole place shines like a congregation of glow-worms. A pleasant enough sight to him if his home be there! At this present season, the canal is not such a pleasant promenade as it was in summer. The barges come and go as usual, but at this time I do not envy the bargemen quite so much. The horse comes smoking along; the tarpaulin which covers the merchandise is sprinkled with hoar frost; and the helmsman, smoking his short pipe for the mere heat of it, cowers over a few red cinders contained in a framework of iron. The labour of the poor fellows will soon be over for a time; for if this frost continues, the canal will be sheathed in a night, and next day stones will be thrown upon it, and a daring urchin venturing upon it will go souse head over heels, and run home with his teeth in a chatter; and the day after, the lake beneath the old castle will be sheeted, and the next, the villagers will be sliding on its gleaming face from ruddy dawn at nine to ruddy eve at three; and hours later, skaters yet unsatisfied will be moving ghost-like in the gloom—now one, now another, shooting on sounding irons into a clear space of frosty light, chasing the moon, or the flying image of a star! Happy youths leaning against the frosty wind!

I am a Christian I hope, although far from a muscular one—consequently I cannot join the skaters on the lake. The floor of ice, with the people upon it, will be but a picture to me. And, in truth, it is in its pictorial aspect that I chiefly love the bleak season. As an artist, winter can match summer any day. The heavy, feathery flakes have been falling all the night through, we shall suppose,

and when you get up in the morning the world is draped in white.
What a sight it is! It is the world you knew, but yet a different
one. The familiar look has gone, and another has taken its place;
and a not unpleasant puzzlement arises in your mind, born of the
patent and the remembered aspect. It reminds you of a friend who
has been suddenly placed in new circumstances, in whom there is
much that you recognise, and much that is entirely strange. How
purely, divinely white when the last snow-flake has just fallen!
How exquisite and virginal the repose! It touches you like some
perfection of music. And winter does not work only on a broad
scale; he is careful in trifles. Pluck a single ivy leaf from the old
wall, and see what a jeweller he is! How he has silvered over the
dark-green reticulations with his frosts! The faggot which the
Tramp gathers for his fire is thicklier incrusted with gems than
ever was sceptre of the Moguls. Go into the woods, and behold
on the black boughs his glories of pearl and diamond—pendent
splendours that, smitten by the noon-ray, melt into tears and fall
but to congeal into splendours again. Nor does he work in black
and white alone. He has on his palette more gorgeous colours than
those in which swim the summer setting suns; and with these, about
three o'clock, he begins to adorn his west, sticking his red hot ball
of a sun in the very midst; and a couple of hours later, when the
orb has fallen, and the flaming crimson has mellowed into liquid
orange, you can see the black skeletons of trees scribbled upon the
melancholy glory. Nor need I speak of the magnificence of a winter
midnight, when space, sombre blue, crowded with star and planet,
"burnished by the frost" is glittering like the harness of an arch-
angel full panoplied against a battle day.

For years and years now I have watched the seasons come and
go around Dreamthorp, and each in its turn interests me as if I
saw it for the first time. But the other week it seems that I saw
the grain ripen; then by day a motley crew of reapers were in the
fields, and at night a big red moon looked down upon the stooks
of oats and barley; then in mighty wains the plenteous harvest
came swaying home, leaving a largess on the roads for every bird;
then the round, yellow, comfortable-looking stacks stood around
the farm-houses, hiding them to the chimneys; then the woods
reddened, the beech hedges became russet, and every puff of wind
made rustle the withered leaves; then the sunset came before the

early dark, and in the east lay banks of bleak pink vapour, which are ever a prophecy of cold; then out of a low dingy heaven came all day, thick and silent, the whirling snow;—and so by exquisite succession of sight and sound have I been taken from the top of the year to the bottom of it, from midsummer, with its unreaped harvests, to the night on which I am sitting here—Christmas 1862.

Sitting here, I incontinently find myself holding a levee of departed Christmas nights. Silently, and without special call, into my study of imagination come these apparitions, clad in snowy mantles, brooched and gemmed with frosts. Their numbers I do not care to count, for I know they are the numbers of my years. The visages of two or three are sad enough, but on the whole 'tis a congregation of jolly ghosts. The nostrils of my memory are assailed by a faint odour of plum-pudding and burnt brandy. I hear a sound as of light music, a whisk of women's dresses whirled round in dance, a click as of glasses pledged by friends. Before one of these apparitions is a mound, as of a new-made grave, on which the snow is lying. I know, I know! Drape thyself not in white like the others, but in mourning stole of crape; and instead of dance music, let there haunt around thee the service for the dead! I know that sprig of Mistletoe, O Spirit in the midst! Under it I swung the girl I loved—girl no more now than I am boy—and kissed her spite of blush and pretty shriek. And thou, too, with fragrant trencher in hand, over which blue tongues of flame are playing, do I know—most ancient apparition of them all. I remember thy reigning night. Back to very days of childhood am I taken by thy ghostly raisins simmering in a ghostly brandy flame. Where now the merry boys and girls that thrust their fingers in thy blaze? And now, when I think of it, thee also would I drape in black raiment, around thee also would I make the burial service murmur.

Men hold the anniversaries of their birth, of their marriage, of the birth of their first-born, and they hold—although they spread no feast, and ask no friends to assist—many another anniversary besides. On many a day in every year does a man remember what took place on that self-same day in some former year, and chews the sweet or bitter herb of memory, as the case may be. Could I ever hope to write a decent Essay, I should like to write one "On the Revisiting of Places." It is strange how important the poorest human being is to himself! how he likes to double back on his experiences, to stand on the place he has stood before, to meet himself face to face as it were! I go to the great city in which my early life was spent, and I love to indulge myself in this whim. The only thing I care about is that portion of the city which is connected with myself. I don't think this passion of reminiscence is debased by the slightest taint of vanity. The lamp-post, under the light of which in the winter rain there was a parting so many years ago, I contemplate with the most curious interest. I stare on the windows of the houses in which I once lived, with a feeling which I should find difficult to express in words. I think of the life I led there, of the good and the bad news that came, of the sister who died, of the brother who was born; and were it at all possible, I should like to knock at the once familiar door, and look at the old walls—which could speak to me so strangely—once again. To revisit that city is like walking away back with my yesterdays. I startle myself with myself at the corners of streets, I confront forgotten bits of myself at the entrance to houses. In windows which to another man would seem blank and meaningless, I find personal poems too deep to be ever turned into rhymes—more pathetic, mayhap, than I have ever found on printed page. The spot of ground on which a man has stood is for ever interesting to him. Every experience is an anchor holding him the more firmly to existence. It is for this reason that we hold our sacred days, silent and solitary anniversaries of joy and bitterness, renewing ourselves thereby, going back upon ourselves, living over again the memorable experience. The full yellow moon of next September will gather into itself the light of the full yellow moons of Septembers long ago. In this Christmas night all the other Christmas nights of my life live. How warm, breathing, full of myself is the year 1862, now almost gone! How bare, cheerless, unknown, the year 1863, about to come in! It stretches before me in imagination like some great, gaunt untenanted ruin of a Colosseum, in which no footstep falls, no voice is heard; and by this night year its naked chambers and windows, three hundred and sixty-five in number, will be clothed all over, and hidden by myself as if with covering ivies. Looking forward into an empty year strikes one with a certain awe, because one finds therein no recognition. The years behind have a friendly aspect, and they are warmed by the fires we have kindled, and all their echoes are the echoes of our own voices.

This, then, is Christmas 1862. Everything is silent in Dream-thorp. The smith's hammer reposes beside the anvil. The weaver's flying shuttle is at rest. Through the clear wintry sunshine the bells this morning rang from the gray church tower amid the leafless elms, and up the walk the villagers trooped in their best dresses and their best faces—the latter a little reddened by the sharp wind: mere redness in the middle aged; in the maids, wonderful bloom to the eyes of their lovers—and took their places decently in the ancient pews. The clerk read the beautiful prayers of our Church, which seem more beautiful at Christmas than at any other period. For that very feeling which breaks down at this time the barriers which custom, birth, or wealth have erected between man and man, strikes down the barrier of time which intervenes between the worshipper of to-day and the great body of worshippers who are at rest in their graves. On such a day as this, hearing these prayers, we feel a kinship with the devout generations who heard them long ago. The devout lips of the Christian dead murmured the responses which we now murmur; along this road of prayer did their thoughts of our innumerable dead, our brothers and sisters in faith and hope, approach the Maker, even as ours at present approach Him. Prayers over, the clergyman—who is no Boanerges, or Chrysostom, golden-mouthed, but a loving, genial-hearted, pious man, the whole extent of his life from boyhood until now, full of charity and kindly deeds, as autumn fields with heavy wheaten ears; the clergyman, I say—for the sentence is becoming unwieldy on my hands, and one must double back to secure connexion—read out in that silvery voice of his, which is sweeter than any music to my ear, those chapters of the New Testament that deal with the birth of the Saviour. And the red-faced rustic congregation hung on the good man's voice as he spoke of the Infant brought forth in a manger, of the shining angels that appeared in mid-air to the shepherds, of the miraculous star that took its station in the sky, and of the wise men who came from afar and laid their gifts of frankincense and myrrh at the feet of the Child. With the story every one was familiar, but on that day, and backed by the per-suasive melody of the reader's voice, it seemed to all quite new—at least, they listened attentively as if it were. The discourse that followed possessed no remarkable thoughts; it dealt simply with the goodness of the Maker of heaven and earth, and the shortness of time, with the duties of thankfulness and charity to the poor; and I am persuaded that every one who heard returned to his house in a better frame of mind. And so the service remitted us all to our own homes, to what roast-beef and plum-pudding slender means permitted, to gatherings around cheerful fires, to half-pleasant, half-sad remembrances of the dead and the absent.

From sermon I have returned like the others, and it is my purpose to hold Christmas alone. I have no one with me at table, and my own thoughts must be my Christmas guests. Sitting here, it is pleasant to think how much kindly feeling exists this present night in England. By imagination I can taste of every table, pledge every toast, silently join in every roar of merriment. I become a sort of universal guest. With what propriety is this jovial season placed amid dismal December rains and snows! How one pities the unhappy Australians, with whom everything is turned topsy-turvy, and who hold Christmas at midsummer! The face of Christmas glows all the brighter for the cold. The heart warms as the frost increases. Estrangements which have embittered the whole year, melt in to-night's hospitable smile. There are warmer hand-shakings on this night than during the by-past twelve months. Friend lives in the mind of friend. There is more charity at this time than at any other. You get up at midnight and toss your spare coppers to the half-benumbed musicians whiffling beneath your windows, although at any other time you would consider their performance a nuisance, and call angrily for the police. Poverty, and scanty clothing, and fireless grates, come home at this season to the bosoms of the rich, and they give of their abundance. The very red-breast of the woods enjoys his Christmas feast. Good feeling incarnates itself in plum-pudding. The Master's words, "The poor ye have always with you," wear at this time a deep significance. For at least one night on each year over all Christendom there is brotherhood. And good men, sitting amongst their families, or by a solitary fire like me, when they remember the light that shone over the poor clowns huddling on the Bethlehem plains eighteen hundred years ago, the apparition of shining angels overhead, the song "Peace on earth and goodwill toward men," which for the first time hallowed the midnight air,—pray for that strain's fulfilment, that battle and strife may vex the nations no more, that not only on Christmas-eve, but the whole year round, men shall be brethren, owning one Father in heaven.

Although suggested by the season, and by a solitary dinner, it is not my purpose to indulge in personal reminiscence and talk. Let all that pass. This is Christmas-day, the anniversary of the world's greatest event. To one day all the early world looked forward; to the same day the later world looks back. That day holds time together. Isaiah, standing on the peaks of prophecy, looked across ruined empires and the desolations of many centuries, and saw on the horizon the new star arise, and was glad. On this night eighteen hundred years ago, Jove was discrowned, the Pagan heaven emptied of its divinities, and Olympus left to the solitude of its snows. On this night, so many hundred years bygone, the despairing voice was heard shrieking on the Ægean, "Pan is dead, great Pan is dead!" On this night, according to the fine reverence of the poets, all things that blast and blight are powerless, disarmed by sweet influences:—

> Some say that ever 'gainst the season comes
> Wherein our Saviour's birth is celebrated
> The bird of dawning singeth all night long;
> And then they say no spirit dare stir abroad;
> The nights are wholesome; then no planets strike;
> No fairy takes, nor witch hath power to charm:
> So hallow'd and so gracious is the time.

The flight of the pagan mythology before the new faith has been a favourite subject with the poets; and it has been my custom for many seasons to read Milton's "Hymn to the Nativity" on the evening of Christmas Day. The bass of heaven's deep organ seems to blow in the lines, and slowly and with many echoes the strain melts into silence. To my ear the lines sound like the full-voiced choir and the rolling organ of a cathedral, when the afternoon light streaming through the painted windows fills the place with solemn colours and masses of gorgeous gloom. To-night I shall float my lonely hours away on music:—

> The oracles are dumb,
> No voice or hideous hum
> Runs through the archèd roof in words deceiving:
> Apollo from his shrine
> Can no more divine

With hollow shriek the steep of Delphos leaving.
  No nightly trance or breathèd spell
Inspires the pale-eyed priest from the prophetic cell.

      The lonely mountains o'er,
      And the resounding shore,
  A voice of weeping heard and loud lament:
      From haunted spring, and dale
      Edged with poplars pale,
  The parting genius is with sighing sent:
    With flower-enwoven tresses torn
The nymphs in twilight shades of tangled thickets mourn.

      Peor and Baalim
      Forsake their temples dim
  With that twice-batter'd god of Palestine;
      And moonèd Ashtaroth,
      Heaven's queen and mother both,
  Now sits not girt with tapers' holy shine!
    The Lybic Hammon shrinks his horn,
In vain the Tyrian maids their wounded Thammuz mourn.

      And sullen Moloch, fled,
      Hath left in shadows dread
  His burning idol, all of blackest hue:
      In vain with cymbals' ring
      They call the grisly king
  In dismal dance about the furnace blue:
    The brutish gods of Nile as fast,
Isis, and Orus, and the dog Anubis haste.

      He feels from Juda's land
      The dreaded Infant's hand,
  The rays of Bethlehem blind his dusky eyne:
      Nor all the gods beside
      Dare longer there abide,
  Not Typhon huge ending in snaky twine.
    Our Babe to shew His Godhead true
Can in His swaddling bands control the damnèd crew.

These verses, as if loath to die, linger with a certain persistence
in mind and ear. This is the "mighty line" which critics talk about!
And just as in an infant's face you may discern the rudiments of
the future man, so in the glorious hymn may be traced the more
majestic lineaments of the "Paradise Lost."

Strangely enough, the next noblest dirge for the unrealmed divinities which I can call to remembrance, and at the same time the most eloquent celebration of the new power and prophecy of its triumph, has been uttered by Shelley, who cannot in any sense be termed a Christian poet. It is one of the choruses in "Hellas," and perhaps had he lived longer amongst us, it would have been the prelude to higher strains. Of this I am certain, that before his death the mind of that brilliant genius was rapidly changing—that for him the Cross was gathering attractions round it—that the wall which he complained had been built up between his heart and his intellect was being broken down, and that rays of a strange splendour were already streaming upon him through the interstices. What a contrast between the darkened glory of "Queen Mab"— of which in after-life he was ashamed, both as a literary work and as an expression of opinion—and the intense, clear, lyrical light of this triumphant poem!—

> A power from the unknown God,
>   A Promethean conqueror came:
> Like a triumphal path he trod
>   The thorns of death and shame.
>   A mortal shape to him
>   Was like the vapour dim
> Which the orient planet animates with light.
>   Hell, sin, and slavery came
>   Like bloodhounds mild and tame,
> Nor prey'd until their lord had taken flight.
>   The moon of Mahomet
>   Arose, and it shall set;
> While blazon'd, as on heaven's immortal noon,
>   The Cross leads generations on.
>
> Swift as the radiant shapes of sleep,
>   From one whose dreams are paradise,
> Fly, when the fond wretch wakes to weep,
>   And day peers forth with her blank eyes:
>   So fleet, so faint, so fair,
>   The powers of earth and air
> Fled from the folding-star of Bethlehem.
>   Apollo, Pan, and Love,
>   And even Olympian Jove,
> Grew weak, for killing Truth had glared on them.
>   Our hills, and seas, and streams,
>   Dispeopled of their dreams,
> Their waters turn'd to blood, their dew to tears,
>   Wail'd for the golden years.

For my own part, I cannot read these lines without emotion—not so much for their beauty as for the change in the writer's mind which they suggest. The self-sacrifice which lies at the centre of Christianity should have touched this man more deeply than almost any other. That it was beginning to touch and mould him, I verily believe. He died and made *that* sign. Of what music did that storm in Spezia Bay rob the world!

"The Cross leads generations on." Believing as I do that my own personal decease is not more certain than that our religion will subdue the world, I own that it is with a somewhat saddened heart that I pass my thoughts around the globe, and consider how distant is yet that triumph. There are the realms on which the Crescent beams, the monstrous many-headed gods of India, the Chinaman's heathenism, the African's devil-rites. These are, to a large extent, principalities and powers of darkness with which our religion has never been brought into collision, save at trivial and far-separated points, and in these cases the attack has never been made in strength. But what of our own Europe—the home of philosophy, of poetry, and painting? Europe, which has produced Greece, and Rome, and England's centuries of glory; which has been illumined by the fires of martyrdom; which has heard a Luther preach; which has listened to Dante's "mystic unfathomable song"; to which Milton has opened the door of heaven—what of it? And what, too, of that younger America, starting in its career with all our good things, and enfranchised of many of our evils? Did not the December sun now shining look down on thousands slaughtered at Fredericksburg, in a most mad, most incomprehensible quarrel? And is not the public air which European nations breathe at this moment, as it has been for several years back, charged with thunder? Despots are plotting, ships are building, man's ingenuity is bent, as it never was bent before, on the invention and improvement of instruments of death; Europe is bristling with five millions of bayonets: and this is the condition of a world for which the Son of God died eighteen hundred and sixty-two years ago! There is no mystery of Providence so inscrutable as this; and yet, is not the very sense of its mournfulness a proof that the spirit of Christianity is living in the minds of men? For, of a verity, military glory is becoming in our best thoughts a bloody rag, and conquest the first in the catalogue of mighty crimes, and a throned tyrant, with armies, and treasures, and the cheers of millions rising up like a cloud of incense around him, but a mark for the thunderbolt of Almighty God—in reality poorer than Lazarus stretched at the gate of Dives. Besides, all these things are getting themselves to some extent mitigated. Florence Nightingale—for the first time in the history of the world—walks through the Scutari hospitals, and "poor, noble, wounded, and sick men," to use her Majesty's tender phrases, kiss her shadow as it falls on them. The Emperor Napoleon does not make war to employ his armies, or to consolidate his power; he does so for the sake of an "idea" more or less generous and disinterested. The soul of mankind would revolt at the blunt, naked truth; and the taciturn emperor knows this, as he knows most things. This imperial hypocrisy, like every other hypocrisy, is a homage which vice pays to virtue. There cannot be a doubt that when the political crimes of kings and governments, the sores that fester in the heart of society, and all "the burden of the unintelligible world," weigh heaviest on the mind, we have to thank Christianity for it. That pure light makes visible the darkness. The Sermon on the Mount makes the morality of the nations ghastly. The Divine love makes human hate stand out in dark relief. This sadness, in the essence of it nobler than any joy, is the heritage of the Christian. An ancient Roman could not have felt so. Everything runs on smoothly enough so long as Jove wields the thunder. But Venus, Mars, and Minerva are far behind us now; the Cross is before us; and self-denial and sorrow for sin, and the remembrance of the poor, and the cleansing of our own hearts, are duties incumbent upon every one of us. If the Christian is less happy than the pagan, and at times I think he is so, it arises from the reproach of the Christian's unreached ideal, and from the stings of his finer and more scrupulous conscience. His whole moral organisation is finer, and he must pay the noble penalty of finer organisations.

Once again, for the purpose of taking away all solitariness of feeling, and of connecting myself, albeit only in fancy, with the proper gladness of the time, let me think of the comfortable family dinners now being drawn to a close, of the good wishes uttered, and the presents made, quite valueless in themselves, yet felt to be invaluable from the feelings from which they spring; of the little children, by sweetmeats lapped in Elysium; and of the pantomime, pleasantest Christmas sight of all, with the pit a sea of grinning delight, the boxes a tier of beaming juvenility, the galleries, piled up to the far-receding roof, a mass of happy laughter which a clown's joke brings down in mighty avalanches. In the pit, sober people relax themselves, and suck oranges, and quaff ginger-pop; in the boxes, Miss, gazing through her curls, thinks the Fairy Prince the prettiest creature she ever beheld, and Master, that to be a clown must be the pinnacle of human happiness; while up in the galleries the hard literal world is for an hour sponged out and obliterated; the chimney-sweep forgets, in his delight when the policeman comes to grief, the harsh call of his master, and Cinderella, when the demons are foiled, and the long-parted lovers meet and embrace in a paradise of light and pink gauze, the grates that must be scrubbed to-morrow. All bands and trappings of toil are for one hour loosened by the hands of imaginative sympathy. What happiness a single theatre can contain! And those of maturer years, or of more meditative temperament, sitting at the pantomime, can extract out of the shifting scenes meanings suitable to themselves; for the pantomime is a symbol or adumbration of human life. Have we not all known Harlequin, who rules the roast, and has the pretty Columbine to himself? Do we not all know that rogue of a clown with his peculating fingers, who brazens out of every scrape, and who conquers the world by good humour and ready wit? And have we not seen Pantaloons not a few, whose fate it is to get all the kicks and lose all the halfpence, to fall through all the trap-doors, break their shins over all the barrows, and be for ever captured by the policeman, while the true pilferer, the clown, makes his escape with the booty in his possession? Methinks I know the realities of which these things are but the shadows; have met with them in business, have sat with them at dinner. But to-night no such notions as these intrude; and when the torrent of fun, and transformation, and practical joking which rushed out of the beautiful fairy world, is in the beautiful fairy world gathered up again, the high-heaped happiness of the theatre will disperse itself, and the Christmas pantomime will be a pleasant memory the whole year through. Thousands on thousands of people are having their midriffs tickled at this moment; in fancy I see their lighted faces, in memory I hear their mirth.

By this time I should think every Christmas dinner at Dreamthorp or elsewhere has come to an end. Even now in the great cities the theatres will be dispersing. The clown has wiped the paint off his face. Harlequin has laid aside his wand, and divested himself of his glittering raiment; Pantaloon, after refreshing himself with a pint of porter, is rubbing his aching joints; and Columbine, wrapped up in a shawl, and with sleepy eyelids, has gone home in a cab. Soon, in the great theatre, the lights will be put out, and the empty stage will be left to ghosts. Hark! midnight from the church tower vibrates through the frosty air. I look out on the brilliant heaven, and see a milky way of powdery splendour wandering through it, and clusters and knots of stars and planets shining serenely in the blue frosty spaces; and the armed apparition of Orion, his spear pointing away into immeasurable space, gleaming overhead; and the familiar constellation of the Plough dipping down into the west; and I think when I go in again that there is one Christmas the less between me and my grave.

MEN OF LETTERS

MR. HAZLITT has written many pleasant essays, but none pleasanter than that entitled "My First Acquaintance with Poets," which, in the edition edited by his son, opens the *Winterslow* series. It relates almost entirely to Coleridge; containing sketches of his personal appearance, fragments of his conversation, and is filled with a young man's generous enthusiasm, belief, admiration, as with sunrise. He had met Coleridge, walked with him, talked with him, and the high intellectual experience not only made him better acquainted with his own spirit and its folded powers, but—as is ever the case with such spiritual encounters—it touched and illuminated the dead outer world. The road between Wem and Shrewsbury was familiar enough to Hazlitt, but as the twain passed along it on that winter day, it became etherialised, poetic—wonderful, as if leading across the Delectable Mountains to the Golden City, whose gleam is discernible on the horizon. The milestones were mute with attention, the pines upon the hill had ears for the stranger as he passed. Eloquence made the red leaves rustle on the oak; made the depth of heaven seem as if swept by a breath of spring; and when the evening star appeared, Hazlitt saw it as Adam did while in Paradise and but one day old. "As we passed along," writes the essayist, "between Wem and Shrewsbury, and I eyed the blue hill tops seen through the wintry branches, or the red, rustling leaves of the sturdy oak-trees by the wayside, a sound was in my ears as of a syren's song. I was stunned, startled with it as from deep sleep; but I had no notion that I should ever be able to express my admiration to others in motley imagery or quaint allusion, till the light of his genius shone into my soul, like the sun's rays glittering in the puddles of the road. I was at that time dumb, inarticulate, helpless, like a worm by the wayside, crushed, bleeding, lifeless; but now, bursting from the deadly bands that bound them, my ideas float on winged words, and as they expand their plumes, catch the golden light of other years. My soul has indeed remained in its original bondage, dark, obscure, with longings infinite and unsatisfied; my heart, shut up in the prison-house of this rude clay, has never found, nor will it ever find, a heart to speak to; but that my understanding also did not remain dumb and brutish, or at length found a language to express itself, I owe to Coleridge." Time and sorrow, personal ambition thwarted and fruitlessly driven back on itself, hopes for the world defeated and unrealised, changed the enthusiastic youth into a petulant, unsocial man; yet ever as he remembered that meeting and his wintry walk from Wem to Shrewsbury the early glow came back, and again a "sound was in his ears as of a syren's song."

We are not all hero-worshippers like Hazlitt, but most of us are so to a large extent. A large proportion of mankind feel a quite peculiar interest in famous writers. They like to read about them, to know what they said on this or the other occasion, what sort of house they inhabited, what fashion of dress they wore, if they liked any particular dish for dinner, what kind of women they fell in love with, and whether their domestic atmosphere was stormy or the reverse. Concerning such men no bit of information is too trifling; everything helps to make out the mental image we have dimly formed for ourselves. And this kind of interest is heightened by the artistic way in which time occasionally groups them. The race is gregarious; they are visible to us in clumps like primroses; they are brought into neighbourhood and flash light on each other like gems in a diadem. We think of the wild geniuses who came up from the universities to London in the dawn

of the English drama. Greene, Nash, Marlowe—our first professional men of letters—how they cracked their satirical whips, how
they brawled in taverns, how pinched they were at times, how,
when they possessed money, they flung it from them as if it were
poison, with what fierce speed they wrote, how they shook the
stage. Then we think of the "Mermaid" in session, with Shakespeare's bland, oval face, the light of a smile spread over it, and
Ben Jonson's truculent visage, and Beaumont and Fletcher sitting
together in their beautiful friendship, and fancy as best we can the
drollery, the repartee, the sage sentences, the lightning gleams of
wit, the thunder-peals of laughter.

> What things have we seen
> Done at the Mermaid! Heard words that have been
> So nimble, and so full of subtle flame,
> As if that every one from whence they came
> Had meant to put his whole soul in a jest,
> And had resolved to live a fool the rest
> Of his dull life.

Then there is the "Literary Club," with Johnson, and Garrick,
and Burke, and Reynolds, and Goldsmith sitting in perpetuity in
Boswell. The Doctor has been talking there for a hundred years,
and there will he talk for many a hundred more. And we of another generation, and with other things to think about, can enter
any night we please, and hear what is going on. Then we have
the swarthy ploughman from Ayrshire sitting at Lord Monboddo's
with Dr. Blair, Dugald Stewart, Henry Mackenzie, and the rest.
These went into the presence of the wonderful rustic thoughtlessly
enough, and now they cannot return even if they would. They
are defrauded of oblivion. Not yet have they tasted forgetfulness
and the grave. The day may come when Burns shall be forgotten,
but till that day arrives—and the eastern sky as yet gives no token
of its approach—*him* they must attend as satellites the sun, as
courtiers their king. Then there are the Lakers—Wordsworth,
Coleridge, Southey, De Quincey burdened with his tremendous
dream, Wilson in his splendid youth. What talk, what argument,
what readings of lyrical and other ballads, what contempt of critics,
what a hail of fine things! Then there is Charles Lamb's room in
Inner Temple Lane, the hush of a whist table in one corner, the
host stuttering puns as he deals the cards; and sitting round about,

Hunt, whose every sentence is flavoured with the hawthorn and the primrose, and Hazlitt maddened by Waterloo and St. Helena, and Godwin with his wild theories, and Kemble with his Roman look. And before the morning comes, and Lamb stutters yet more thickly—for there is a slight flavour of punch in the apartment— what talk there has been of Hogarth's prints, of Izaak Walton, of the old dramatists, of Sir Thomas Browne's "Urn Burial," with Elia's quaint humour breaking through every interstice, and flowering in every fissure and cranny of the conversation! One likes to think of these social gatherings of wits and geniuses; they are more interesting than conclaves of kings or convocations of bishops. One would like to have been the waiter at the "Mermaid," and to have stood behind Shakespeare's chair. What was that functionary's opinion of his guests? Did he listen and become witty by infection? or did he, when his task was over, retire unconcernedly to chalk up the tavern score? One envies somewhat the damsel who brought Lamb the spirit-case and the hot water. I think of these meetings, and, in lack of companionship, frame for myself imaginary conversations—not so brilliant, of course, as Mr. Landor's, but yet sufficient to make pleasant for me the twilight hour while the lamp is yet unlit, and my solitary room is filled with the ruddy lights and shadows of the fire.

Of human notabilities men of letters are the most interesting, and this arises mainly from their outspokenness as a class. The writer makes himself known in a way that no other man makes himself known. The distinguished engineer may be as great a man as the distinguished writer, but as a rule we know little about him. We see him invent a locomotive, or bridge a strait, but there our knowledge stops; we look at the engine, we walk across the bridge, we admire the ingenuity of the one, we are grateful for the conveniency of the other, but to our apprehensions the engineer is undeciphered all the while. Doubtless he reveals himself in his work as the poet reveals himself in his song, but then this revelation is made in a tongue unknown to the majority. After all, we do not feel that we get nearer him. The man of letters, on the other hand, is outspoken, he takes you into his confidence, he keeps no secret from you. Be you beggar, be you king, you are welcome. He is no respecter of persons. He gives without reserve his fancies, his wit, his wisdom; he makes you a present of all that the painful or the happy years have brought him. The writer makes his reader heir in full. Men of letters are a peculiar class. They are never commonplace or prosaic—at least those of them that mankind care for. They are airy, wise, gloomy, melodious spirits. They give us the language we speak, they furnish the subjects of our best talk. They are full of generous impulses and sentiments, and keep the world young. They have said fine things on every phase of human experience. The air is full of their voices. Their books are the world's holiday and playground, and into these neither care, nor the dun, nor despondency can follow the enfranchised man. Men of letters forerun science as the morning star the dawn. Nothing has been invented, nothing has been achieved, but has gleamed a bright-coloured Utopia in the eyes of one or the other of these men. Several centuries before the Great Exhibition of 1851 rose in Hyde Park, a wondrous hall of glass stood, radiant in sunlight, in the verse of Chaucer. The electric telegraph is not so swift as the flight of Puck. We have not yet realised the hippogriff of Ariosto. Just consider what a world this would be if ruled by the best thoughts of men of letters! Ignorance would die at once, war would cease, taxation would be lightened, not only every Frenchman, but every man in the world, would have his hen in the pot. May would not marry January. The race of lawyers and physicians would be extinct. Fancy a world, the affairs of which are directed by Goethe's wisdom and Goldsmith's heart! In such a case methinks the millennium were already come. Books are a finer world within the world. With books are connected all my desires and aspirations. When I go to my long sleep, on a book will my head be pillowed. I care for no other fashion of greatness. I'd as lief not be remembered at all as remembered in connexion with anything else. I would rather be Charles Lamb than Charles XII. I would rather be remembered by a song than by a victory. I would rather build a fine sonnet than have built St. Paul's. I would rather be the discoverer of a new image than the discoverer of a new planet. Fine phrases I value more than bank-notes. I have ear for no other harmony than the harmony of words. To be occasionally quoted is the only fame I care for.

But what of the literary life? How fares it with the men whose days and nights are devoted to the writing of books? We know the famous men of letters, we give them the highest place in our regards;

we crown them with laurels so thickly that we hide the furrows on their foreheads. Yet we must remember that there are men of letters who have been equally sanguine, equally ardent, who have pursued perfection equally unselfishly, but who have failed to make themselves famous. We know the ships that come with streaming pennons into the immortal ports; we know but little of the ships that have gone on fire on the way thither—that have gone down at sea. Even with successful men we cannot know precisely how matters have gone. We read the fine raptures of the poet, but we do not know into what kind of being he relapses when the inspiration is over, any more than, seeing and hearing the lark shrilling at the gate of heaven, we know with what effort it has climbed thither, or into what kind of nest it must descend. The lark is not always singing; no more is the poet. The lark is only interesting *while* singing, at other times it is but a plain brown bird. We may not be able to recognise the poet when he doffs his singing robes; he may then sink to the level of his admirers. We laugh at the fancies of the humorist, but he may have written his brilliant things in a dismal enough mood. The writer is not continually dwelling amongst the roses and lilies of life, he is not continually uttering generous sentiments, and saying fine things. On him, as on his brethren, the world presses with its prosaic needs. He has to make love and marry, and run the usual matrimonial risks. The income-tax collector visits him as well as others. Around his head at Christmas-times drives a snowstorm of bills. He must keep the wolf from the door, and he has only his goose-quills to confront it with. And here it is, having to deal with alien powers, that his special temperament comes into play, and may work him evil. Wit is not worldly wisdom. A man gazing on the stars is proverbially at the mercy of the puddles on the road. A man may be able to disentangle intricate problems, be able to recall the past, and yet be cozened by an ordinary knave. The finest expression will not liquidate a butcher's account. If Apollo puts his name to a bill, he must meet it when it becomes due, or go into the *Gazette*. Armies are not always cheering on the heights which they have won; there are forced marches, occasional shortness of provisions, bivouacs on muddy plains, driving in of pickets, and the like, although these inglorious items are forgotten when we read the roll of victories inscribed on their banners. The books of the great writer are only portions of the great writer. His life acts on his writings; his writings react on his life. His life may impoverish his books; his books may impoverish his life. Apollo's

> Branch that might have grown full straight,

may have the worm of a vulgar misery gnawing at its roots. The heat of inspiration may be subtracted from the household fire; and those who sit by it may be the colder in consequence. A man may put all his good things in his books, and leave none for his life, just as a man may expend his fortune on a splendid dress, and carry a pang of hunger beneath it.

There are few less exhilarating books than the biographies of men of letters, and of artists generally; and this arises from the pictures of comparative defeat which, in almost every instance, such books contain. In these books we see failure more or less— seldom clear, victorious effort. If the art is exquisite, the marble is flawed; if the marble is pure, there is defect in art. There is always something lacking in the poem; there is always irremediable defect in the picture. In the biography we see persistent, passionate effort, and almost constant repulse. If, on the whole, victory is gained, one wing of the army has been thrown into confusion. In the life of a successful farmer, for instance, one feels nothing of this kind; his year flows on harmoniously, fortunately: through ploughing, seed-time, growth of grain, the yellowing of it beneath meek autumn suns and big autumn moons, the cutting of it down, riotous harvest-home, final sale, and large balance at the banker's. From the point of view of almost unvarying success the farmer's life becomes beautiful, poetic. Everything is an aid and help to him. Nature puts her shoulder to his wheel. He takes the winds, the clouds, the sunbeams, the rolling stars into partnership, and, asking no dividend, they let him retain the entire profits. As a rule, the lives of men of letters do not flow on in this successful way. In their case there is always either defect in the soil or defect in the husbandry. Like the Old Guard at Waterloo, they are fighting bravely on a lost field. In literary biography there is always an element of tragedy, and the love we bear the dead is mingled with pity. Of course the life of a man of letters is more perilous than the life of a farmer; more perilous than almost any other kind of life which it is given a human being to conduct. It is more difficult to obtain the mastery over spiritual ways and means than over material ones, and he must command *both*. Properly to conduct his life he must not only take large crops off his fields, he must also leave in his fields the capacity of producing large crops. It is easy to drive in your chariot two horses of one breed; not so easy when the one is of terrestrial stock, the other of celestial; in every respect different—in colour, temper, and pace.

At the outset of his career, the man of letters is confronted by the fact that he must live. The obtaining of a livelihood is preliminary to everything else. Poets and cobblers are placed on the same level so far. If the writer can barter MSS. for sufficient coin, he may proceed to develop himself; if he cannot so barter it, there is a speedy end of himself, and of his development also. Literature has become a profession; but it is in several respects different from the professions by which other human beings earn their bread. The man of letters, unlike the clergyman, the physician, or the lawyer, has to undergo no special preliminary training for his work, and while engaged in it, unlike the professional persons named, he has no accredited status. Of course, to earn any success, he must start with as much special knowledge, with as much dexterity in his craft, as your ordinary physician; but then he is not recognised till once he is successful. When a man takes a physician's degree, he has done something; when a man betakes himself to literary pursuits, he has done nothing—till once he is lucky enough to make his mark. There is no special preliminary training for men of letters, and, as a consequence, their ranks are recruited from the vagrant talent of the world. Men that break loose from the professions, who stray from the beaten tracks of life, take refuge in literature. In it are to be found doctors, lawyers, clergymen, and the motley nation of Bohemians. Any one possessed of a nimble brain, a quire of paper, a steel pen, and ink-bottle, can start business. Any one who chooses may enter the lists, and no questions are asked concerning his antecedents. The battle is won by sheer strength of brain. From all this it comes that the man of letters has usually a history of his own: his individuality is more pronounced than the individuality of other men; he has been knocked about by passion and circumstance. All his life he has had a dislike for iron rules and commonplace maxims. There is something of the gipsy in his nature. He is to some extent eccentric, and he indulges his eccentricity. And the misfortunes of men of letters—the vulgar and patent misfortunes, I mean— arise mainly from the want of harmony between their impulsiveness and volatility, and the staid unmercurial world with which they are brought into conflict. They are unconventional in a world of conventions; they are fanciful, and are constantly misunderstood in prosaic relations. They are wise enough in their books, for there they are sovereigns, and can shape everything to their own likings; out of their books, they are not unfrequently extremely foolish, for they exist then in the territory of an alien power, and are constantly knocking their heads against existing orders of things. Men of letters take prosaic men out of themselves; but they are weak where the prosaic men are strong. They have their own way in the world of ideas, prosaic men in the world of facts. From his practical errors the writer learns something, if not always humility and amendment. A memorial flower grows on every spot where he has come to grief; and the chasm he cannot overleap he bridges with a rainbow.

But the man of letters has not only to live, he has to develop himself; and his earning of money and his intellectual development should proceed simultaneously and in proportionate degrees. Herein lies the main difficulty of the literary life. Out of his thought the man must bring fire, food, clothing; and fire, food, clothing must in their turns subserve thought. It is necessary, for the proper conduct of such a life, that while the balance at the banker's increases, intellectual resource should increase at the same ratio. Progress should not be made in the faculty of expression alone— progress at the same time should be made in thought; for thought is the material on which expression feeds. Should sufficient advance not be made in this last direction, in a short time the man feels that he has expressed himself—that now he can only more or less dexterously repeat himself—more or less prettily become his own echo. It is comparatively easy to acquire facility in writing; but it is an evil thing for the man of letters when such facility is the only thing he has acquired—when it has been, perhaps, the only thing he has striven to acquire. Such miscalculation of ways and means suggests vulgarity of aspiration, and a fatal material taint. In the life in which this error has been committed there can be no proper harmony, no satisfaction, no spontaneous delight in effort. The man does not create—he is only desperately keeping up appearances. He has at once become "a base mechanical," and his successes are not much higher than the successes of the acrobat or the rope-dancer. This want of proper relationship between resources of expression and resources of thought, or subject-matter for expression, is common enough, and some slight suspicion of it flashes across the mind at times in reading even the best authors. It lies at the bottom of every catastrophe in the literary life. Frequently a man's first book is good, and all his after productions but faint and yet fainter reverberations of the first. The men who act thus are in the long run deserted like worked-out mines. A man reaches his limits as to thought long before he reaches his limits as to expression; and a haunting suspicion of this is one of the peculiar bitters of the literary life. Hazlitt tells us that, after one of his early interviews with Coleridge, he sat down to his Essay on the Natural Disinterestedness of the Human Mind. "I sat down to the task shortly afterwards for the twentieth time, got new pens and paper, determined to make clean work of it, wrote a few sentences in the skeleton style of a mathematical demonstration, stopped half-way down the second page, and, after trying in vain to pump up any words, images, notions, apprehensions, facts, or observations, from that gulf of abstraction in which I had plunged myself for four or five years preceding, gave up the attempt as labour in vain, and shed tears of hopeless despondency on the blank unfinished paper. I can write fast enough now. Am I better than I was then? oh no! One truth discovered, one pang of regret at not being able to express it, is worth all the fluency and flippancy in the world." This regretful looking back to the past, when emotions were keen and sharp, and when thought wore the novel dress of a stranger, and this dissatisfaction with the acquirements of the present, is common enough with the man of letters. The years have come and gone, and he is conscious that he is not intrinsically richer—he has only learned to assort and display his riches to advantage. His wares have neither increased in quantity nor improved in quality—he has only procured a window in a leading thoroughfare. He can catch his butterflies more cunningly, he can pin them on his cards more skilfully, but their wings are fingered and tawdry compared with the time when they winnowed before him in the sunshine over the meadows of youth. This species of regret is peculiar to the class of which I am speaking, and they often discern failure in what the world counts success. The veteran does not look back to the time when he was in the awkward squad; the accountant does not sigh over the time when he was bewildered by the mysteries of double-entry. And the reason is obvious. The dexterity which time and practice have brought to the soldier and the accountant is pure gain: the dexterity of expression which time and practice have brought to the writer is gain too, in its way, but not quite so pure. It may have been cultivated and brought to its degree of excellence at the expense of higher things. The man of letters lives by thought and expression, and his two powers may not be perfectly balanced. And, putting aside its effect on the reader, and through that, on the writer's pecuniary prosperity, the tragedy of want of equipoise lies in this. When the writer expresses his thought, it is immediately dead to him, however life-giving it may be to others; he pauses midway in his career, he looks back over his uttered past— brown desert to him, in which there is no sustenance—he looks forward to the green *un*uttered future, and beholding its narrow limits, knows it is all that he can call his own—on that vivid strip he must pasture his intellectual life.

Is the literary life, on the whole, a happy one? Granted that the writer is productive, that he possesses abundance of material, that he has secured the ear of the world, one is inclined to fancy that no life could be happier. Such a man seems to live on the finest of the wheat. If a poet, he is continually singing; if a novelist, he is supreme in his ideal world; if a humorist, everything smiles back upon his smile; if an essayist, he is continually saying the wisest, most memorable things. He breathes habitually the serener air which ordinary mortals can only at intervals respire, and in their happiest moments. Such conceptions of great writers are to some extent erroneous. Through the medium of their books we know them only in their active mental states—in their triumphs; we do not see them when sluggishness has succeeded the effort which was delight. The statue does not come to her white limbs all at once. It is the bronze wrestler, not the flesh-and-blood one, that stands for ever over a fallen adversary with the pride of victory on his face. Of the labour, the weariness, the self-distrust, the utter despondency of the great writer, we know nothing. Then, for the

attainment of mere happiness or contentment, any high faculty
of imagination is a questionable help. Of course imagination lights
the torch of joy, it deepens the carmine on the sleek cheek of the
girl, it makes wine sparkle, makes music speak, gives rays to the
rising sun. But in all its supreme sweetnesses there is a perilous
admixture of deceit, which is suspected even at the moment when
the senses tingle keenliest. And it must be remembered that this
potent faculty can darken as well as brighten. It is the very soul
of pain. While the trumpets are blowing in Ambition's ear, it
whispers of the grave. It drapes Death in austere solemnities, and
surrounds him with a gloomy court of terrors. The life of the
imaginative man is never a commonplace one: his lights are brighter,
his glooms are darker, than the lights and glooms of the vulgar.
His ecstasies are as restless as his pains. The great writer has this
perilous faculty in excess; and through it he will, as a matter of
course, draw out of the atmosphere of circumstance surrounding
him the keenness of pleasure and pain. To my own notion, the
best gifts of the gods are neither the most glittering nor the most
admired. These gifts I take to be, a moderate ambition, a taste
for repose with circumstances favourable thereto, a certain mild-
ness of passion, an even-beating pulse, an even-beating heart.
I do not consider heroes and celebrated persons the happiest of
mankind. I do not envy Alexander the shouting of his armies,
nor Dante his laurel wreath. Even were I able, I would not purchase these at the prices the poet and the warrior paid. So far,
then, as great writers—great poets, especially—are of imagination
all compact—a peculiarity of mental constitution which makes a
man go shares with every one he is brought into contact with;
which makes him enter into Romeo's rapture when he touches
Juliet's cheek among cypresses silvered by the Verona moonlight,
and the stupor of the blinded and pinioned wretch on the scaffold
before the bolt is drawn—so far as this special gift goes, I do not
think the great poet—and by virtue of it he *is* a poet—is likely to
be happier than your more ordinary mortal. On the whole, perhaps,
it is the great readers rather than the great writers who are entirely to be envied. They pluck the fruits, and are spared the
trouble of rearing them. Prometheus filched fire from heaven, and
had for reward the crag of Caucasus, the chain, the vulture; while
they for whom he stole it cook their suppers upon it, stretch out

benumbed hands towards it, and see its light reflected in their children's faces. They are comfortable: he, roofed by the keen crystals of the stars, groans above.

Trifles make up the happiness or the misery of mortal life. The majority of men slip into their graves without having encountered on their way thither any signal catastrophe or exaltation of fortune or feeling. Collect a thousand ignited sticks into a heap, and you have a bonfire which may be seen over three counties. If, during thirty years, the annoyances connected with shirt-buttons found missing when you are hurriedly dressing for dinner, were gathered into a mass and endured at once, it would be misery equal to a public execution. If, from the same space of time, all the little titillations of a man's vanity were gathered into one lump of honey and enjoyed at once, the pleasure of being crowned would not perhaps be much greater. If the equanimity of an ordinary man be at the mercy of trifles, how much more will the equanimity of the man of letters, who is usually the most sensitive of the race, and whose peculiar avocation makes sad work with the fine tissues of the nerves. Literary composition is, I take it, with the exception of the crank, in which there is neither hope nor result, the most exhausting to which a human being can apply himself. Just consider the situation. Here is your man of letters, tender-hearted as Cowper, who would not count upon his list of friends the man who tramples heedlessly upon a worm; as light of sleep and abhorrent of noise as Beattie, who denounces chanticleer for his lusty proclamation of morning to his own and the neighbouring farmyards in terms that would be unmeasured if applied to Nero; as alive to blame as Byron, who declared that the praise of the greatest of the race could not take the sting from the censure of the meanest. Fancy the sufferings of a creature so built and strung in a world which creaks so vilely on its hinges as this! Will such a man confront a dun with an imperturbable countenance? Will he throw himself back in his chair and smile blandly when his chamber is lanced through and through by the notes of a street bagpiper? When his harassed brain should be solaced by music, will he listen patiently to stupid remarks? I fear not. The man of letters suffers keenlier than people suspect from sharp, cruel noises, from witless observations, from social misconceptions of him of every kind, from hard utilitarian wisdom, and from his own good things going to the grave unrecognised and unhonoured. And, forced to live by his pen, to extract from his brain bread and beer, clothing, lodging, and income tax, I am not surprised that he is oftentimes nervous, querulous, impatient. Thinking of these things, I do not wonder at Hazlitt's spleen, at Charles Lamb's punch, at Coleridge's opium. I think of the days spent in writing, and of the nights which repeat the day in dream, and in which there is no refreshment. I think of the brain which must be worked out at length: of Scott, when the wand of the enchanter was broken, writing poor romances; of Southey sitting vacantly in his library, and drawing a feeble satisfaction from the faces of his books. And for the man of letters there is more than the mere labour: he writes his book, and has frequently the mortification of seeing it neglected or torn to pieces. Above all men, he longs for sympathy, recognition, applause. He respects his fellow-creature, because he beholds in him a possible reader. To write a book, to send it forth to the world and the critics, is to a sensitive person like plunging mother-naked into tropic waters where sharks abound. It is true that, like death, the terror of criticism lives most in apprehension; still, to have been frequently criticised, and to be constantly liable to it, are disagreeable items in a man's life. Most men endure criticism with commendable fortitude, just as most criminals when under the drop conduct themselves with calmness. They bleed, but they bleed inwardly. To be flayed in the *Saturday Review*, for instance—a whole amused public looking on—is far from pleasant; and, after the operation, the ordinary annoyances of life probably magnify themselves into tortures. The grasshopper becomes a burden. Touch a flayed man ever so lightly, and with ever so kindly an intention, and he is sure to wince. The skin of the man of letters is peculiarly sensitive to the bite of the critical mosquito; and he lives in a climate in which such mosquitoes swarm. He is seldom stabbed to the heart—he is often killed by pin-pricks.

But, to leave palisade and outwork, and come to the interior of the citadel, it may be said that great writers, although they must ever remain shining objects of regard to us, are not exempted from ordinary limitations and conditions. They are cabined, cribbed, confined, even as their more prosaic brethren. It is in the nature of every man to be endued with that he works in.

Thus, in course of time, the merchant becomes bound up in his ventures and his ledger; an indefinable flavour of the pharmacopœia lingers about the physician; the bombazin and horsehair of the lawyer eat into his soul—his experiences are docqueted in a clerkly hand, bound together with red tape, and put away in professional pigeon-holes. A man naturally becomes leavened by the profession which he has adopted. He thinks, speaks, and dreams "shop," as the colloquial phrase has it. Men of letters are affected by their profession just as merchants, physicians, and lawyers are. In course of time the inner man becomes stained with ink, like blotting-paper. The agriculturist talks constantly of bullocks—the man of letters constantly of books. The printing-press seems constantly in his immediate neighbourhood. He is stretched on the rack of an unfavourable review—he is lapped in the Elysium of a new edition. The narrowing effect of a profession is in every man a defect, albeit an inevitable one. Byron, who had a larger amount of common sense than any poet of his day, tells us, in "Beppo,"

> One hates an author that's *all author;* fellows
> In foolscap uniforms turn'd up with ink.

And his lordship's "hate" in the matter is understandable enough. In his own day, Scott and himself were almost the only distinguished authors who were not "all authors," just as Mr. Helps and Sir Edward Bulwer Lytton are almost the only representatives of the class in ours. This professional taint not only resides in the writer, impairing his fulness and completion; it flows out of him into his work, and impairs it also. It is the professional character which authorship has assumed which has taken individuality and personal flavour from so much of our writing, and prevented to a large extent the production of enduring books. Our writing is done too hurriedly, and to serve a purpose too immediate. Literature is not so much an art as a manufacture. There is a demand, and too many crops are taken off the soil; it is never allowed to lie fallow, and to nourish itself in peacefulness and silence. When so many cups are to be filled, too much water is certain to be put into the teapot. Letters have become a profession, and probably of all professions it is, in the long run, the least conducive to personal happiness. It is the most precarious. In it, above all others, to be weak is to be miserable. It is the least mechanical, consequently the most exhausting; and in its higher walks it deals with a man's most vital material—utilises his emotions, trades on his faculties of love and imagination, uses for its own purposes the human heart by which he lives. These things a man requires for himself; and when they are in a large proportion transported to an ideal world, they make the ideal world all the more brilliant and furnished, and leave his ordinary existence all the more arid and commonplace. You cannot spend money and have it; you cannot use emotion and possess it. The poet who sings loudly of love and love's delights, may in the ordinary intercourse of life be all the colder for his singing. The man who has been moved while describing an imaginary death-bed to-day, is all the more likely to be unmoved while standing by his friend's grave to-morrow. Shakespeare, after emerging from the moonlight in the Verona orchard, and Romeo and Juliet's silvery interchange of vows, was, I fear me, not marvellously enamoured of the autumn on Ann Hathaway's cheek. It is in some such way as this that a man's books may impoverish his life; that the fire and heat of his genius may make his hearth all the colder. From considerations like these, one can explain satisfactorily enough to one's self the domestic misadventures of men of letters—of poets especially. We know the poets only in their books; their wives know them out of them. Their wives see the other side of the moon; and we have been made pretty well aware how they have appreciated *that*.

The man engaged in the writing of books is tempted to make such writing the be-all and end-all of his existence—to grow his literature out of his history, experience, or observation, as the gardener grows out of soils brought from a distance the plants which he intends to exhibit. The cup of life foams fiercely over into first books; materials for the second, third, and fourth must be carefully sought for. The man of letters, as time passes on and the professional impulse works deeper, ceases to regard the world with a single eye. The man slowly merges into the artist. He values new emotions and experiences, because he can turn these into artistic shapes. He plucks "copy" from rising and setting suns. He sees marketable pathos in his friend's death-bed. He carries the peal of his daughter's marriage-bells into his sentences or his rhymes; and in these the music sounds sweeter to him than in the sunshine and the wind. If originally of a meditative, introspective mood, his profession can hardly fail to confirm and deepen his peculiar temperament. He begins to feel his own pulse curiously, and for a purpose. As a spy in the service of literature, he lives in the world and its concerns. Out of everything he seeks thoughts and images, as out of everything the bee seeks wax and honey. A curious instance of this mode of looking at things occurs in Goethe's "Letters from Italy," with whom, indeed, it was a fashion, and who helped himself out of the teeming world to more effect than any man of his time:

"From Botzen to Trent the stage is nine leagues, and runs through a valley which constantly increases in fertility. All that merely struggles into vegetation on the higher mountains has here more strength and vitality. The sun shines with warmth, and there is once more belief in a Deity.

"A poor woman cried out to me to take her child into my vehicle, as the soil was burning its feet. I did her this service out of honour to the strong light of Heaven. The child was strangely decked out, *but I could get nothing from it in any way.*"

It is clear that out of all this the reader gains; but I cannot help thinking that for the writer it tends to destroy entire and simple living—all hearty and final enjoyment in life. Joy and sorrow, death and marriage, the comic circumstance and the tragic, what befalls him, what he observes, what he is brought into contact with, do not affect him as they affect other men; they are secrets to be rifled, stones to be built with, clays to be moulded into artistic shape. In giving emotional material artistic form, there is indisputably a certain noble pleasure; but it is of a solitary and severe complexion, and takes a man out of the circle and sympathies of his fellows. I do not say that this kind of life makes a man selfish, but it often makes him *seem* so; and the results of this seeming, on friendship and the domestic relationships, for instance, are as baleful as if selfishness really existed. The peculiar temptation which besets men of letters, the curious playing with thought and emotion, the tendency to analyse and take everything to pieces, has two results, and neither aids his happiness nor even his literary success. On the one hand, and in relation to the social relations, it gives him somewhat of an icy aspect, and so breaks the spring and eagerness of affectionate response. For the best affection is shy, reticent, undemonstrative, and needs to be drawn out by its like. If unrecognised like an acquaintance on the street, it passes by, making no sign, and is for the time being a stranger. On the other hand, the desire to say a fine thing about a phenomenon, whether natural or moral, prevents a man from reaching the inmost core of the phenomenon. Entrance into these matters will never be obtained by the most sedulous seeking. The man who has found an entrance cannot tell how he came there, and he will never find his way back again by the same road. From this law arise all the dreary conceits and artifices of the poets; it is through the operation of the same law that many of our simple songs and ballads are inexpressibly affecting, because in them there is no consciousness of authorship; emotion and utterance are twin-born, consentaneous—like sorrow and tears, a blow and its pain, a kiss and its thrill. When a man is happy, every effort to express his happiness mars its completeness. I am not happy at all unless I am happier than I know. When the tide is full there is silence in channel and creek. The silence of the lover when he clasps the maid is better than the passionate murmur of the song which celebrates her charms. If to be near the rose makes the nightingale tipsy with delight, what must it be to be the rose herself? One feeling of the "wild joys of living—the leaping from rock to rock," is better than the "muscular-Christianity" literature which our time has produced. I am afraid that the profession of letters interferes with the elemental feelings of life; and I am afraid, too, that in the majority of cases this interference is not justified by its results. The entireness and simplicity of life is flawed by the intrusion of an inquisitive element, and this inquisitive element never yet found anything which was much worth the finding. Men live by the primal energies of love, faith, imagination; and happily it is not given to every one to *live*, in the pecuniary sense, by the artistic utilisation and sale of these. You cannot make ideas; they must come unsought if they come at all.

From pastoral graves extracting thoughts divine

is a profitable occupation enough, if you stumble on the little churchyard covered over with silence, and folded among the hills. If you go to the churchyard with intent to procure thoughts, as you go into the woods to gather anemones, you are wasting your time. Thoughts must come naturally, like wild flowers; they cannot be forced in a hotbed—even although aided by the leaf-mould of your past—like exotics. And it is the misfortune of men of letters of our day that they cannot afford to wait for this natural flowering of thought, but are driven to the forcing process, with the results which were to be expected.

AN ESSAY ON AN OLD SUBJECT

THE discovery of a grey hair when you are brushing out your whiskers of a morning—first fallen flake of the coming snows of age—is a disagreeable thing; so is the intimation from your old friend and comrade that his eldest daughter is about to be married; so are flying twinges of gout, shortness of breath on the hill-side, the fact that even the moderate use of your friend's wines at dinner upsets you. These things are disagreeable, because they tell you that you are no longer young—that you have passed through youth, are now in middle age, and faring onward to the shadows in which somewhere a grave is hid.

Thirty is the age of the gods; and the first grey hair informs you that you are at least ten or twelve years older than that. Apollo is never middle-aged, but you are. Olympus lies several years behind you; you have lived for more than half your natural term; and you know the road which lies before you is very different from that which lies behind. You have yourself changed. In the present man of forty-two you can barely recognise the boy of nineteen that once was. Hope sang on the sunny slope of life's hill as you ascended; she is busily singing the old song in the ears of a new generation, but you have passed out of the reach of her voice. You have tried your strength; you have learned precisely what you can do; you have thrown the hammer so often that you know to an inch how far you *can* throw it—at least you are a great fool if you do not. The world, too, has been looking on, and has made up its mind about you. It has appraised you as an auctioneer appraises an estate or the furniture of a house. "Once you served Prince Florizel and wore three pile," but the brave days of campaigning are over. What to you are canzonets and love-songs? The mighty passion is vapid and second-hand. Cupid will never more flutter rosily over your head; at most he will only flutter in an uninspired fashion above the head of your daughter-in-law. You have sailed round the world, seen all its wonders, and come home again, and must adorn your dwelling, as best you can, with the rare things you have picked up on the way. At life's table you have tasted of every dish except the Covered One, and of that you will have your share by and by. The road over which you are fated to march is more than half traversed, and at every onward stage the scenery is certain to become more sombre, and in due time the twilight will fall. To you, on your onward journey, there will be little to astonish, little to delight. The Interpreter's House is behind where you first read the poets; so is also the House Beautiful with the Three Damsels, where you first learned to love. As you pass onward you are attended by your henchman Memory, who may be either the cheerfullest or gloomiest of companions. You have come up out of the sweet-smelling valley flowers; you are now on the broken granite, seamed and wrinkled with dried up water-courses; and before you, striking you full in the face, is the broad disc of the solitary setting sun.

One does not like to be an old fogy, and still less perhaps does one like to own to being one. You may remember when you were the youngest person in every company into which you entered, and how it pleased you to think how precociously clever you were, and how opulent in Time. You were introduced to the great Mr Blank—at least twenty years older than yourself—and could not help thinking how much greater you would be than Mr Blank by the time you reached his age. But pleasant as it is to be the youngest member of every company, that pleasure does not last for ever. As years pass on you do not quite develop into the genius you expected; and the new generation makes its appearance and pushes you from your stool. You make the disagreeable discovery that there is a younger man of promise in the world than even you; then the one younger man becomes a dozen younger men; then younger men come flowing in like waves; and before you know where you are, by this impertinent younger generation—fellows who were barely breeched when you won your first fame—you are shouldered into Old Fogydom, and your staid ways are laughed at, perhaps, by the irreverent scoundrels into the bargain. There is nothing more wonderful in youth than this wealth in Time. It is only a Rothschild who can indulge in the amusement of tossing a sovereign to a beggar. It is only a young man who can dream

and build castles in the air. What are twenty years to a young
fellow of twenty? An ample air-built stage for his pomps and
triumphal processions. What are twenty years to a middle-aged
man of forty-five? The falling of the curtain, the covering up of
the empty boxes, the screwing out of the gas, and the counting of
the money taken at the doors, with the notion, perhaps, that the
performance was rather a poor thing. It is with a feeling curiously
compounded of pity and envy that one listens to young men talking of what they are going to do. They will light their torches at
the sun! They will regenerate the world! They will abolish war,
and hand in the Millennium! What pictures they will paint!
What poems they will write! One knows while one listens how it
will all end. But it is Nature's way; she is always sending on her
young generations full of hope. The Atlantic roller bursts in harmless foam among the shingle and driftwood at your feet, but the
next, nothing daunted by the fate of its predecessor, comes on
with threatening crest, as if to carry everything before it. And so
it will be for ever and ever. The world could not get on else. My
experience is of use only to myself. I cannot bequeath it to my
son as I can my cash. Every human being must start untrammelled
and work out the problem for himself. For a couple of thousand
years now the preacher has been crying out *Vanitas vanitatum*,
but no young man takes him at his word. The blooming apple
must grate in the young man's teeth before he owns that it is dust
and ashes. Young people will take nothing on hearsay. I remember,
when a lad, of Todd's *Student's Manual* falling into my hands. I
perused therein a solemn warning against novel reading. Nor did
the reverend compiler speak without authority. He stated that he
had read the works of Fielding, Smollett, Sir Walter Scott, American
Cooper, James, and the rest, and he laid his hand on his heart and
assured his young friends that in each of these works, even the
best of them, were subtle snares and gilded baits for the soul.
These books they were adjured to avoid, as they would a pestilence
or a raging fire. It was this alarming passage in the transatlantic
Divine's treatise that first made a novel reader of me. I was not
content to accept his experience: I must see for myself. Every
one must begin at the beginning; and it is just as well. If a new
generation were starting with the wisdom of its elders, what would
be the consequence? Would there be any love-making twenty

years after? Would there be any fine extravagance? Would there
be any lending of money? Would there be any noble friendships
such as that of Damon and Pythias, or of David and Jonathan,
or even of our own Beaumont and Fletcher, who had purse, wardrobe, and genius in common? It is extremely doubtful. *Vanitas
vanitatum* is a bad doctrine to begin life with. For the plant Experience to be of any worth, a man must grow it for himself.

The man of forty-five or thereby is compelled to own, if he sits
down to think about it, that existence is very different from what
it was twenty years previously. His life is more than half spent,
to begin with. He is like one who has spent seven hundred and
fifty pounds of his original patrimony of a thousand. Then from
his life there has departed that "wild freshness of morning" which
Tom Moore sang about. In his onward journey he is not likely to
encounter anything absolutely new. He has already conjugated
every tense of the verb To Be. He has been in love twice or thrice.
He has been married—only once, let us trust. In all probability
he is the father of a fine family of children. He has been ill, and
he has recovered; he has experienced triumph and failure; he has
known what it is to have money in his purse, and what it is to
want money in his purse. Sometimes he has been a debtor, sometimes he has been a creditor. He has stood by the brink of half a
dozen graves, and heard the clod falling on the coffin-lid. All this
he has experienced; the only new thing before him is death, and
even to that he has at various times approximated. Life has lost
most of its unexpectedness, its zest, its novelty, and has become
like a worn shoe or a thread-bare doublet. To him there is no new
thing under the sun. But then this growing old is a gradual process;
and zest, sparkle, and novelty are not essential to happiness. The
man who has reached five-and-forty has learned what a pleasure
there is in customariness and use and wont—in having everything
around him familiar, tried, confidential. Life may have become
humdrum, but his tastes have become humdrum too. Novelty
annoys him, the intrusion of an unfamiliar object puts him out.
A pair of newly embroidered slippers would be much more ornamental than the well-worn articles which lie warming for him before the library fire; but then he cannot get his feet into them so
easily. He is contented with his old friends—a new friend would
break the charm of the old familiar faces. He loves the hedgerows,

and the fields, and the brook, and the bridge which he sees every day, and he would not exchange them for Alps and glaciers. By the time a man has reached forty-five he lies as comfortably in his habits as the silkworm in its cocoon. On the whole, I take it that middle age is a happier period than youth. In the entire circle of the year there are no days so delightful as those of a fine October, when the trees are bare to the mild heavens, and the red leaves bestrew the road, and you can feel the breath of winter, morning and evening—no days so calm, so tenderly solemn, and with such a reverent meekness in the air. The lyrical upburst of the lark at such a time would be incongruous. The only sounds suitable to the season are the rusty caw of the homeward-sliding rook—the creaking of the wain returning empty from the farm-yard. There is an "unrest, which men miscall delight," and of that "unrest" youth is, for the most part, composed. From this middle age is free. The setting suns of youth are crimson and gold; the setting suns of middle age

> Do take a sober colouring from an eye
> That hath kept watch o'er man's mortality.

Youth is the slave of beautiful faces, and fine eyes, and silver-sweet voices—they distract, madden, alarm. To middle age women are but the gracefullest statues, the loveliest poems. They delight but hurt not; they awake no passion, they heighten no pulse. And the imaginative man of middle age possesses after a fashion all the passionate turbulence, all the keen delights, of his earlier days. They are not dead—they are dwelling in the antechamber of Memory, awaiting his call; and when they *are* called they wear an ethereal something which is not their own. The Muses are the daughters of Memory: youth is the time to love, but middle age the period at which the best love-poetry is written. And middle age too—the early period of it, when a man is master of his instruments, and knows what he can do—is the best season of intellectual activity. The playful capering flames of a newly kindled fire is a pretty sight, but not nearly so effective—any housewife will tell you—as when the flames are gone, and the whole mass of fuel has become caked into a sober redness that emits a steady glow. There is nothing good in this world which time does not improve. A silver wedding is better than the voice of the Epithalamium; and the most beautiful face that ever was, is made yet more beautiful when there is laid upon it the reverence of silver hairs.

There is a certain even-handed justice in Time; and for what he takes away he gives us something in return. He robs us of elasticity of limb and spirit, and in its place he brings tranquillity and repose—the mild autumnal weather of the soul. He takes away Hope, but he gives us Memory. And the settled, unfluctuating atmosphere of middle age is no bad exchange for the stormful emotions, the passionate crises and suspenses of the earlier day. The constitutional melancholy of the middle-aged man is a dim background on which the pale flowers of life are brought out in the tenderest relief. Youth is the time for action, middle age for thought. In youth we hurriedly crop the herbage; in middle age, in a sheltered place, we chew the ruminative cud. In youth, red-handed, red-ankled, with songs and shoutings, we gather in the grapes; in middle age, under our own fig-tree, or in quiet gossip with a friend, we drink the wine free of all turbid lees. Youth is a lyrical poet, middle age a quiet essayist, fond of recounting experiences, and of appending a moral to every incident. In youth the world is strange and unfamiliar, novel and exciting, everything wears the face and garb of a stranger; in middle age the world is covered over with reminiscence as with a garment: it is made homely with usage, it is made sacred with graves. The middle-aged man can go nowhere without treading the mark of his own footsteps; and in middle age, too, provided the man has been a good and an ordinarily happy one, along with this mental tranquillity there comes a corresponding sweetness of the moral atmosphere. He has seen the good and the evil that are in the world, the ups and the downs, the almost general desire of the men and the women therein to do the right thing if they could but see how; and he has learned to be uncensorious, humane,—to attribute the best motives to every action, and to be chary of imputing a sweeping and cruel blame. He has a quiet smile for the vainglorious boast, a feeling of respect for shabby-genteel virtues, a pity for the thread-bare garments proudly worn, and for the napless hat glazed into more than pristine brilliancy from frequent brushing after rain. He would not be satirical for the world. He has no finger of scorn to point at anything under the sun. He has a hearty "Amen" for every good wish, and in the worst cases he leans to a verdict of Not Proven. And along with this pleasant blandness and charity, a certain grave, serious humour, "a smile on the lip and a tear in the eye," is noticeable frequently in middle-aged persons—a phase of humour peculiar to that period of life, as the chrysanthemum to December. Pity lies at the bottom of it, just as pity lies, unsuspected, at the bottom of love. Perhaps this special quality of humour—with its sadness of tenderness, its mirth with the heart-ache, its gaiety growing out of deepest serious-ness, like a crocus on a child's grave—never approaches more closely to perfection than in some passages of Mr Hawthorne's writings, who was a middle-aged man from earliest boyhood. And although middle-aged persons have lost the actual possession of youth, yet in virtue of this humour they can comprehend it, see all round it, enter imaginatively into every sweet and bitter of it. They wear the key Memory at their girdles, and they can open every door in the chamber of youth. And it is also in virtue of this peculiar humour that—Mr Dickens's *Little Nell* to the contrary—it is only middle-aged persons who can, either as poets or artists, create for us a child. There is no more beautiful thing on earth than an old man's love for his granddaughter; more beautiful even—from the absence of all suspicion of direct personal bias or interest—than his love for his own daughter; and it is only the meditative, sad-hearted, middle-aged man who can creep into the heart of a child and interpret it, and show forth the new nature to us in the subtle cross-lights of contrast and suggestion. Imagi-natively thus, the wrinkles of age become the dimples of infancy. Wordsworth was not a very young man when he held the colloquy with the little maid who insisted, in her childish logic, that she was one of seven. Mr Hawthorne was not a young man when he painted "Pearl" by the side of the brook in the forest; and he was middle-aged and more when he drew "Pansie," the most ex-quisite child that lives in English words. And when speaking of middle age, of its peculiar tranquillity and humour, why not tell of its peculiar beauty as well? Men and women make their own beauty or their own ugliness. Sir Edward Bulwer Lytton speaks in one of his novels of a man "who was uglier than he had any business to be;" and, if we could but read it, every human being carries his life in his face, and is good-looking or the reverse as that life has been good or evil. On our features the fine chisels of thought and emotion are eternally at work. Beauty is not the monopoly of blooming young men, and of white and pink maids. There is a slow-growing beauty which only comes to perfection in old age. Grace belongs to no period of life, and goodness improves the longer it exists. I have seen sweeter smiles on a lip of seventy than I ever saw on a lip of seventeen. There is the beauty of youth, and there is also the beauty of holiness—a beauty much more seldom met, and more frequently found in the arm-chair by the fire, with grandchildren around its knee, than in the ball-room or the promenade. Husband and wife, who have fought the world side by side, who have made common stock of joy and sorrow, and aged together, are not unfrequently found curiously alike in personal appearance, and in pitch and tone of voice— just as twin pebbles on the beach, exposed to the same tidal influences, are each other's *alter ego*. *He* has gained a feminine something which brings his manhood into full relief. *She* has gained a masculine something which acts as a foil to her womanhood. Beautiful are they in life, these pale winter roses, and in death they shall not be divided. When Death comes, he will pluck not one, but both.

And in any case, to the old man, when the world becomes trite, the triteness arises not so much from a cessation as from a transference of interest. What is taken from this world is given to the next. The glory is in the east in the morning, it is in the west in the afternoon, and when it is dark the splendour is irradiating the realm of the under-world. He would only follow.

ON DREAMS AND DREAMING

IN dealing with the curious phenomenon of Dreaming, the materialists and spiritualists are, as usual, in extremes: the one class regarding the phenomenon as mainly the result of indigestion, the other as one of the proofs of the immortality of the soul. In this matter it may be prudent to steer a middle course. One thing is certain, that whatever be the cause, the substance of a dream, whether it be beautiful or ghastly, depends entirely upon the dreamer. All men dream, just as all men live; but the dreams of men are as different as are their lives. You require opium and

Coleridge combined before you arrive at *Kubla Khan:* few men have extracted such terrors from a pork chop as Fuseli. Every man has his own fashion of dreaming, just as every man has his own opinions, conceptions, and way of looking at things. While asleep a man does not in the least lose his personality. Dreams are the most curious *asides* and soliloquies of the soul. When a man recollects his dream, it is like meeting the ghost of himself. Dreams often surprise us into the strangest self-knowledge. If a man wishes to know his own secret opinion of himself, he had better take cognizance of his dreams. A coward is never brave in his dream, the gross man is never pure, the untruthful man lies and knows he is lying. Dreaming is the truest confessional, and often the sharpest penance. In sleep the will is quiescent, and dreaming is like the talking in the ranks when the men are standing at ease, and the eye of the inspecting officer is absent for the nonce; it is like the chatting of the domestics round the kitchen-fire of the castle after the lord and the lady have retired—incoherent babblement for the most part; but the men in the ranks say things that the commanding officer might ponder on occasion, and the gossiping servants in the comfortable firelight downstairs, commenting on the events of the day, give their opinions on this thing and the other which has happened, and criticise not unfrequently the conduct of the master and mistress. You feel your pulse when you wish to arrive at the secret of your bodily health; pay attention to your dreams if you wish to arrive at the secret of your health, morally and spiritually.

All men dream, and the most common experience of the phenomenon is the sort of double existence which it entails. The life of the night is usually very different from the life of the day. And these strange spectres and shapes of slumber do not perish; they live in some obscure ante-room or limbo of memory, and reappear at times in the most singular fashion. Most people have been startled by this reappearance. Something of importance to you has happened quite new, quite unexpected; you are sitting in a strange railway-station waiting for the train; you have gone to see a friend in a distant part of the country, and in your solitary evening stroll you come on a pool of water, with three pollard willows, such as you see in old engravings, growing beside it, and above the willows an orange sunset through which a string of rooks are flying; and all at once this new thing which has happened wears the face of an old experience; the strange railway-station becomes familiar; and the pool, the willows, the sunset with the undulating line of rooks, seem to have been witnessed *not* for the first time. This curious feeling is gone almost as swiftly as it has come; but you are perplexed with the sense of a double identity, with the emergence as of a former existence. The feeling alluded to is so swift and intangible that often you cannot arrest it; you cannot pin it down for inspection as you would a butterfly on a card; but when you *can*, you find that what has startled you with familiarity is simply a vagrant dream—that from the obscure limbo of the memory some occult law of association has called a wandering wraith of sleep, and that for a moment it has flitted betwixt you and the sunshine of consciousness, dimming it as it flits.

One thing is worthy of remark, that in dreaming, in that reverie of the consciousness, men are usually a good deal cleverer than when they are awake. You may not be much of a Shakespeare in your waking moments, but you attain to something of his faculty when your head is on the pillow. In dreams, whatever latent dramatic power you may possess awakes, and is at work. The dreamer brings far-separated people together, he arranges them in groups, he connects them by the subtlest films of interest; and the man who is in the habit of taking cognizance of his dreams soon learns that the phantoms of men and women whom he has once known, and who revisit him in slumber, are more life-like images— talking more consistently, and exhibiting certain little characteristics and personal traits which had never been to him the subject of conscious thought—than those he is accustomed to deal with during his waking hours. And then the strange persons and events one does dream about on occasions,—persons long dead, localities known in childhood, and never seen since; events which happened to yourself or to others, and which seem to have faded out of remembrance as completely as the breath of yesterday has faded from the face of the mirror. But these things have not so faded. There is a "Lost Office" in the memory, where all the waifs and strays of experience are taken care of. Word and act; the evil deed and the good one; the fair woman's face which was the starlight of your boyhood; the large white moon that rose over the harvest-fields in the September in which you were in love; the thrush that sang out in the garden betwixt light and dark of summer dawn, when the pressure of a hand at parting the night before kept you awake,— all these things, which you suppose to have perished as utterly as the clothes you wore thirty years ago, have no more perished than you have yourself. Memory deals with these things as a photographer deals with his negatives; she does not destroy them, she simply places them aside, for future use, mayhap. If you are a dreamer, you will know this. And in dreams the imagination does not always deal with experience; it frequently goes beyond that, and guesses at matters of which it cannot have any positive knowledge. There is no more common terror in dreams than that of falling over a precipice; and most dreamers are aware that in so dreaming they have felt the air *cold*, as they cut through it, in their swift rush earthwards. This, of course, cannot be matter of experience, as those who have been so precipitated are placed conclusively out of court. But it is curious that the dreamer should so feel; that the swift imagination should not only vividly realise the descent itself, but in unimportant accessory of the descent—the chilliness of the swiftly-severed air—as well. And then the all-absorbing fact of Death exercises an intolerable fascination over many a dreaming brain. A man dreamed once that he, along with sixteen others, had been captured on a field of battle, and that, by a refinement of cruelty, they were to be shot singly. It so happened that the dreamer was the seventeenth. The sixteenth man knelt, the levelled muskets spat fire, crackled, and he fell forward on his face. The dreamer was then conscious of the most burning feeling of envy of the dead man—he *had* died, he *was* dead; he who was but a few yards distant a second ago, was now removed to an immeasurable distance; he had gained his rest. And when the dreamer's turn came to kneel, and when the muskets of the platoon converged upon him, he found himself marvelling whether, between the time the bullets struck and the loss of sensation, he could interject the thought, "This is death." Of death this man knew nothing; but even in the dream of sleep his imagination could not help playing curiously with the idea, and attempting to realise it; and in his waking moments he could not have realised it so thoroughly. Altogether this vividness of the imagination in dreams is something to which nothing exactly corresponds in the waking state. A Scotch schoolboy dreams that he is being chased by the Foul Fiend, and as he flies along, he hears behind him a hard and a soft sound alternately; and this does not surprise him, because he knows perfectly that the hard sound is the clang of the cloven hoof on the roadway. In thus unconsciously working the tradition of the cloven hoof into the body of his impression, the Scotch schoolboy has become a John Bunyan for the time being, and is far beyond his normal state of imaginative activity. If you are aroused from sleep by hearing your own name called, you start up in bed with an impression so vivid that you fancy the sound is yet lingering in your ears. I once heard a friend, and one not specially fanciful usually, tell how he had been one night tormented by the strangest vision. He was asleep, and on a curtain of darkness there hung before him a beautiful female face; and this face, as if keeping time with the ticks of the watch under his pillow, the beating of his pulse, the systole and diastole of his heart, was alternately beautiful—and a skull. There, on the curtain of darkness, the apparition throbbed in regular and dreadful change. And this strange and regularly recurring antithesis of beauty and horror, with the spiritual meaning and significance under it—for the loveliest face that ever poet sang, or painter painted, or lover kissed, is but a skull beclothed with flesh: we are all naked under our clothes, we are all skeletons under our flesh—was as much out of my prosaic friend's usual way of thinking as crown, sceptre, and robe of state are out of a day labourer's way of life. He was a good deal astonished at his dream, and I, with my perhaps super-subtle interpretation of it, was a good deal astonished that he should have had *such* a dream. But the truth seems to be, that when the will is asleep the imagination awakes and plays. The most prosaic creature is a poet when he dreams. Every dreamer is, for the time being, in possession of the lamp of Aladdin—the world is ductile to be shaped as fancy wills. And this vividness of impression in dream—the realisation of strange situations, the recalling of dead persons—is not only singular, as showing the potency of imagination, which, perhaps unsuspectingly, we all possess—but out of the chaos of dreams a man may now and again extract a curious self-knowledge. The dreamer's belief in his dream is usually intense, and I suppose the man who fancied himself the seventeenth man to be shot, and who saw the muskets of the silent platoon converging upon him, felt very much as the poor mutineer does, who, seated on his coffin, sees the same thing of a raw morning; and from his dream he might discover, to some extent, how nature has steeled his nerves, how he might comport himself in deadly crises. In dreams, better often than in waking moments, a man finds out, as has been said, the private opinion he entertains of himself; and in dreams, too, when placed in circumstances outside of his actual experience, and which, in all probability, will never be evolved in actual experience, he becomes in some sense his own inspecting officer, and reviews his own qualities. Through dreaming, a man is dual—he is actor and spectator: and in dreaming, he is never a hypocrite; the coward never by any possibility can dream that he is brave, the liar never that he is truthful; the falsest man awake is sincere when he dreams.

Looking into a dream is like looking into the interior of a watch; you see the processes at work by which results are obtained. A man thus becomes his own eavesdropper, he plays the spy on himself. Hope and fear, and the other passions, are all active, but then activity is uncontrolled by the will, and in remembering dreams one has the somewhat peculiar feeling of being one's own spiritual anatomist. And as the dreaming brain concerns itself mainly with the ideas which stir the waking one, and as dreams are ruled by no known logic, conform to no recognisable laws of sequence, are stopped in career by no pale or limit, it is not in the least surprising that in remote unscientific periods these wild guesses of the spirit and bodyings forth of its secret wishes and expectations should have been credited with prevision. Even people in the present day, if any superstitious tincture runs in the blood, or if they are endowed with fineness of imaginative perception, find it hard to shake off the old belief. For, come how it may, dreams, in point of fact, often *do* read the future. We do not know what subtle lines of communication may radiate between spirit and spirit. If, a century ago, a man had sent a message from London to Edinburgh in ten minutes, he would have been looked upon as the blackest of magicians; now such messages cost only a couple of shillings, and are matters of daily commerce. That a man in London should speak to a man in Edinburgh was just as astonishing and incredible to all practical minds a century ago, as that spirit should speak with spirit is incredible to the same minds at the present day. But the apparent prevision of dreams falls, of course, to be explained on quite other grounds than that of some supposed spiritual telegraphy. The dreaming brain is continually busying itself with the objects of fear or desire, and that it should occasionally make a lucky guess is not an unlikely circumstance. Suppose a man is a candidate for some office or post which he covets, the chances are that, while the bestowal of the post is yet in abeyance, he will dream either that he has obtained it, or that he has lost it; and should his dream jump with the ultimate result, he at once concludes it to have been prophetic. Suppose a man has a near relative at an Indian station, that for a couple of mails, contrary to custom, he has received no letter, and that he dreams a ship is bearing on through a sea of moonlight with the dead body of his friend on board (a result, as regards the friend, certainly on the cards, and a dream, as regards himself, not in the least improbable —on the contrary, most likely and natural, should his interest in his friend be great), and that it proves true that the friend has died—it would be difficult to convince the man that his dream had not something of prophecy in it. If dreams are not fulfilled, they are naturally forgotten; if fulfilled, they are just as naturally remembered. That dreams, working continually in the stuff of daily hope and fear, giving palpable shape and image to desire and dread, should sometimes be found to forestall the future fact, is not in the least a matter for wonder. Such coincidences are as certain to occur, by the law of chances, as that a penny, if tossed up a hundred times, will come down heads a certain number of times. What concerns the dreamers more are the hopes and fears, the desires and aversions with which the dreaming fancy works; looking into these he may gain some information concerning himself not easily obtainable otherwise.

WINTER

TO town and country Winter comes alike, but to each he comes in different fashion. To the villager, he stretches a bold frosty hand; to the townsman, a clammy one. To the villager, he comes wrapt in cold clear air; to the townsman, in yellow fogs, through which the gas-lamps blear at noon. To the villager, he brings snow on the bare trees, frosty spangles on the roadways, exquisite silver chasings and adornments to the ivies on the walls, tumults of voices and noises of skating-irons, smouldering orange sunsets that distain the snows, make brazen the window panes, and fire even the icicles at the cottage eaves. To the townsman, he brings influenzas, secret slides on unlighted pavements, showers of snowballs from irreverent urchins, damp feet, avalanches from the roofs of houses six storeys high, cab fares wofully begrudged, universal slush. Winter is like a Red Indian, noble in his forests and solitudes, deteriorated by cities and civilisation. The signs of his approach are different in the town and in the village. To a certain northern city, whose spires fret my sky-line of a morning, his proximity is made known by the departure of the last tourist and the arrival of the first student; by brown papers taken from windows in fashionable streets and squares; by the reassembling of schools and academies; and by advertisements in the newspapers relative to the opening of the University. By these signs, rather than by the cawing of uneasy rooks, or the whirling away of the last red leaf, the inhabitants know that the stern season is at hand; a salvo of inaugural addresses announces that he is in their midst, and the reappearance of lawyers in the long-deserted halls of the Parliament House, is regarded as a prophecy of snow. In that famous northern city, winter is disagreeable, as in other cities. Lawyers, doctors, and professors tumble out of bed, and shave by gas-light. The entire population catches cold, and the clergymen are coughed down on Sundays. The falling snow covers the pavements—except the spaces in front of the bakers' shops, which are wet, and black, and steaming; in due time it makes dumb the streets, muffling every sound of wheel and hoof; it slips its moorings, and hangs in icicles and avalanches from the roofs of houses, but it does not appear in any perfection; it has lost all purity, and is dingy as a city sparrow. It is regarded as a nuisance; shopkeepers scrape it from their doors, deft scavengers build it in mounds along the streets; in a couple of days thaw sets in, and from roof, and eave, and cornice, from window-sill, gargoyle, and spout, there is a universal sound of weeping, like that which was heard in the old Norse world, when gods and men lamented the death of Balder the Beautiful. On frosty mornings, cab-horses, whose shoes are never sharpened in preparation, although the previous night every star was sparkling like steel, are tumbling on the hilly streets, and the fare gesticulates from the window, and one man holds down the head of the terrified animal, whose breath is like a wreath of incense, and the driver, clothed in a drab great-coat, with a comforter up to his nose, is busy with the girths, and small boys gather round, and attempt to blow some warmth into their benumbed fingers. Up from the sea comes a wicked *harr*, shedding disastrous twilight; church spires are visible half way up and disappear; the lights in shops are yellow smears on the darkness; at crossings, vehicles burst on you in a moment, and in another moment are swallowed up; and on the obscure pavement all ties of relationship and acquaintanceship are dissolved. Men are strangers for the time being; without a sinking of the heart, debtor brushes clothes with creditor; and with never a thrill Romeo steps off the pavement to let Juliet pass, quite unconscious that his divinity is near. Even on the more favourable days there is little to please one in a wintry city; over head the smoke hangs heavily and lazily; for an hour or so a small uninteresting sun is stuck on the murky sky, like a red wafer on a dirty letter, and the setting is accomplished as rapidly as possible, and without any attempt at pomp. The south-west will not even turn out a corporal's guard to present arms to such a visitor. The townsman does not care for Winter, although he may care for what Winter brings—the long lighted evenings in which he can read or work, the lectures, the dinner-parties, the concerts, the theatres, and, if very young, the sprig of mistletoe stuck under the chandelier of a Christmas night.

But in this quiet place—distant but a few miles from the city of which I have been speaking—Winter is as pleasant as summer in her prime. To this village, Winter sends other *avant-couriers* than the taking down of brown paper from the windows of great houses, or the advertisement of college sessions. The rooks gathering in the coloured woods was one sign; the ploughing of the wheat-fields was another. The reddening of the beech hedges told me Winter was on his way. The Robin hopping along the shrubbery walks in his search for crumbs—remembering well they were scattered there last year—told me he was at hand. The rime of a morning on the old walls outside told me he was already come. One could feel the impalpable presence in the crisp air, in the clear blue distance with the Castle and city spires etched upon it, in the stillness broken only by the rustle of a withered leaf, in the bright yet sobered sunlight, in the quickened current of the blood as one

walked. Sated whilom with foliage, in my rambles my eye delights
in naked branches, and I please myself with noting how many
objects become visible at this season which summer had kept
secret; ragged nests high up in trees, houses and farm-buildings
standing amongst woods, bridges, and fences, and the devious
courses of streams. These things are lost and buried in the leafiness
of summer, and are only to be recognised now, as truths are discerned in age which youth never guesses of. When I return, the
sunset is burning away behind the stripes of ancient pines that
stand on the scarped bank above the stream, making their bronzed
trunks yet more red—yet more dark their undecaying verdure.
And by the last gleam on the distant hills, I notice that their
crests are hoary. Snow, then, has already come, and will be with
us anon.

Winter in the country, without snow, is like a summer without
the rose. Snow is Winter's specialty, its crowning glory, its last
exquisite grace. Snow comes naturally in Winter, as foliage comes
in summer; but although one may have been familiar with it during forty seasons, it always takes one with a certain pleased surprise and sense of strangeness. In each Winter the falling of the
first snow-flake is an event; it lays hold of the imagination. A
child does not ordinarily take notice of the coming of leaves and
flowers, but it will sit at a window for an hour, watching the
descent of the dazzling apparition, with odd thoughts and fancies
in the little brain. Snow attracts the child as the plumage of some
rare and foreign bird would. The most prosaic of mortals, when
he comes downstairs of a morning, and finds a new soft, white
world, instead of the hard familiar black one, is conscious of some
obscure feeling of pleasure, the springs of which he might find it
difficult to explain. I do not care much for snow in town; but in
the country it is ever a marvel: it wipes out all boundary lines
and distinctions between fields; it clothes the skeletons of trees
with a pure wonder; through the strangely transfigured landscape
the streams run black as ink and without a sound; and over all,
the cold blue frosty heaven smiles as if in very pleasure at its work.
On such a day, how windless and composed the atmosphere, how
bright the frosty sunlight, from what a distance comes a shout or
the rusty caw of a rook! "Earth hath not anything to show more
fair." And somehow the season seems to infuse a spirit of jollity

into everything. As I walk about I fancy the men I meet look ruddier and healthier; that they talk in louder and cheerier tones; that their chests heave with a sincerer laughter. They are more charitable, I know. Winter binds "earth-born companions and fellow-mortals" together, from man to red-breast; and interior domestic life takes a new charm from the strange pallor outside. The good creature Fire feels exhilarated, and licks with its pliant tongue, as if pleased and flattered. Sofa and slippers become luxuries. The tea-urn purrs like a fondled cat. In those long warm-lighted evenings, books communicate more of their inmost souls than they do in summer; and a moment's glance at the village church-roof, sparkling to the frosty moon, adds warmth to fleecy blankets, and a depth to repose.

The white flakes are coming at last! Stretch out your hand— the meteor falls into it lighter than a rose-leaf, and is in a moment a tear. It is as fragile as beautiful. How innocent in appearance the new-fallen snow, the surface of which a descending leaf would dimple almost! and yet there is nothing fiercer, deadlier, crueller, more treacherous. On wild uplands and moors it covers roads and landmarks, and makes the wanderer travel hopeless miles till he sinks down exhausted; it steeps his senses in a pleasing stupor, till he fancies he sees the light of his far-off dwelling, and hears the voices of his children, who will be orphans before the morn; it smites him on the mouth and face as he dies, and then covers him up, softly as with kisses, tenderly as with eiderdown, like a sleek-white murderer as it is. In alliance with the demon of wind, it will drift and spin along the mountain-sides, and in a couple of hours a hundred sheep and their shepherd are smothered in a corry on Ben Nevis. Welded by frost into an avalanche, it slides from its dizzy hold, and falls on an Alpine village, crushing it to powder. A snowflake is weak in itself, but in multitudes it is omnipotent. These terrible crystals have stayed the marches of conquerors and broken the strength of empires. The innumerous flakes flying forth on the Russian wind are deadlier than bullets; they bite more bitterly than Cossack lances. In front, behind, on every side, for leagues and leagues they fall in the dim twilight, flinging themselves in front of the weary soldier's foot, clogging the wheels of cannon, making the banner an icy sheet, stilling the drum that beats the charge. O, weary soldiers of the Empire, eyes that saw the sun of Austerlitz, hearts that love Napoleon—to this grim battle with Winter, Lodi and Arcola were holiday parades! The Loire will murmur from antique town to town, through pleasant summer lands of France, till it rests in the Spanish sea; vines stretched from pole to pole will glow in setting suns; girls will dance at village festivals; but for you, never more the murmuring river, nor the ripening grape, nor the dancing girl's waist and smile. For you the deadly snow-kisses, the sleep and the dreams that bring death, the dreadful embalming of frosts, potent as the spices that preserve Pharaoh.

At home, Winter is a terrible despot; but like the wild Goths which he nurtured, he becomes more civilised as he travels South. Like a travelled man of the world, he adapts himself to the countries in which he sojourns. The ice, which is misery at Labrador, is luxury at Naples. In our country we know Winter chiefly in his mild and fanciful moods. In England he is artist and adorner. He brightens the bloom on the cheeks of girls; he breathes the quaintest forests on our bedroom windows; he beards cottage eaves with icicles; he makes the lake a floor on which the skater may disport himself; he fires the south-west with sober sunsets; he gives star and planet a metallic lustre. But with all these pleasant qualities and obliging graces, he wears here, as at home, the old heart. Have you not seen him in our own streets pinch cruelly a poor child scantily clad? Do we not know how he maltreats the desolate widow and the unemployed artisan? Do we not hear of him in savage mood killing outright poor homeless wretches whom he has discovered asleep on stairs or in deserted cellars? Here, as I have said, he is partially civilised, but at home he is a despot; there he piles the iceberg that sails southward to crush ships; there he pinches the starved wolf; there he makes the Esquimaux shiver through all his furs. And the Arctic voyagers whom he takes prisoner and locks up in his immeasurable dungeons of snow and ice, *they* know what a Giant Despair he is; and friends at home who wait and wait, and to whom no news ever comes, know it too.

There is one more good thing about Winter—he brings Christmas. Through the bleak December the thought of the coming festival is pleasant—like the reflection of a fire on our faces. We taste the cake before it is baked, and when it is actually before us we find that it is none the worse for the fond handling of imagination. Christmas-day is the pleasantest day in the whole year. On that day we think tenderly of distant friends; we strive to forgive injuries—to close accounts with ourselves and the world—to begin the new year with a white leaf, and a trust that the chapter of life about to be written will contain more notable entries, a fairer sprinkling of good actions, fewer erasures made in blushes, and fewer ugly blots than some of the earlier ones. And to make Christmas perfect, the ground should be covered and the trees draped with snow; the bleak world outside should make us enjoy all the more keenly the comforts we possess; and, above all, it should make us remember the poor and the needy; for a charitable deed is the best close of any chapter of our lives, and the best promise, too, for the record about to be begun.

We are accustomed to consider Winter the grave of the year, but it is not so in reality. In the stripped trees, the mute birds, the disconsolate gardens, the frosty ground, there is only an apparent cessation of Nature's activities. Winter is a pause in music, but during the pause the musicians are privately tuning their strings, to prepare for the coming outburst. When the curtain falls on one piece at the theatre, the people are busy behind the scenes making arrangements for that which is to follow. Winter is such a pause, such a fall of the curtain. Under ground, beneath snow and frost, next spring and summer are secretly getting ready. The roses which young ladies will gather six months hence for hair or bosom, are already in hand. In Nature there is no such thing as paralysis. Each thing flows into the other, as movement into movement in graceful dances; Nature's colours blend in imperceptible gradation; all her notes are sequacious. I go out to my garden and notice that when the last leaves have fallen off my lilac and currant-bushes, like performers at the side-wings waiting their turn to come on, the new buds are all ready. To-day I beheld great knobs of buds on a horse-chestnut of mine, liquored over with an oily exudation which glittered in the sunlight. In my plants, the life which in June and July was exuberant in blossom and odour, has withdrawn to the root, where it lies *perdue*, taking counsel with itself regarding the course of action to be adopted next season. The spring of 1864 is even now under-ground, and the first snows will hardly have melted till it will peep out timorously in snowdrops;

then, bolder grown, will burst in crocuses, holding up their coloured lamps; then, by fine gradations, the floral year will reach its noon, the rose; then, by fine gradations, it will die in a sunset of hollyhocks and tiger-lilies; and so we come again to withered leaves and falling snows.

GEORGE ELIOT
MARY ANN (EVANS) CROSS

MARY ANN (EVANS) CROSS, *better known by her pen-name "George Eliot" (1819–1880), was born in Chilvers Coton, Warwickshire. After schooling at Attleborough, Nuneaton, and Coventry, she returned home at her mother's death (1836) to take care of her father's house. When her father died in 1849, she travelled with friends on the Continent, becoming assistant-editor of the "Westminster Review" on her return to England. She did some translating from the German, met many literary people, including George Henry Lewes; in 1854 her union with him began, both regarding it as a legal marriage, though his insane wife was still living. After a period of travel, they settled in Richmond, where she did more translating and wrote reviews. With Mr. Lewes's encouragement, she tried her hand at fiction, and to shorter stories novels succeeded: "Adam Bede" (1859) was the first of many, which won her recognition from other novelists and the larger public. She travelled frequently on the Continent with Mr. Lewes, and had just finished a collection of miscellaneous essays when Mr. Lewes died; she edited and collected his writings. "The Impressions of Theophrastus Such" appeared in 1879; the next year she married John Walter Cross, an old friend of Mr. Lewes and herself, and died eight months later after a short illness.*

As a novelist, her power of character-portrayal is noteworthy for its vividness and insight; she is somewhat inclined to preach, and shows a tendency to pessimism, but she is not without humor. Her essays are full of common-sense, and delightful satire.

GEORGE ELIOT

HOW WE ENCOURAGE RESEARCH

THE serene and beneficent goddess Truth, like other deities whose disposition has been too hastily inferred from that of the men who have invoked them, can hardly be well pleased with much of the worship paid to her even in this milder age, when the stake and the rack have ceased to form part of her ritual. Some cruelties still pass for service done in her honour: no thumb-screw is used, no iron boot, no scorching of flesh; but plenty of controversial bruising, laceration, and even lifelong maiming. Less than formerly; but so long as this sort of truth-worship has the sanction of a public that can often understand nothing in a controversy except personal sarcasm or slanderous ridicule, it is likely to continue. The sufferings of its victims are often as little regarded as those of the sacrificial pig offered in old time, with what we now regard as a sad miscalculation of effects.

One such victim is my old acquaintance Merman.

Twenty years ago Merman was a young man of promise, a conveyancer with a practice which had certainly budded, but, like Aaron's rod, seemed not destined to proceed further in that marvellous activity. Meanwhile he occupied himself in miscellaneous periodical writing and in a multifarious study of moral and physical science. What chiefly attracted him in all subjects were the vexed questions which have the advantage of not admitting the decisive proof or disproof that renders many ingenious arguments superannuated. Not that Merman had a wrangling disposition: he put all his doubts, queries, and paradoxes deferentially, contended without unpleasant heat and only with a sonorous eagerness against the personality of Homer, expressed himself civilly though firmly on the origin of language, and had tact enough to drop at the right moment such subjects as the ultimate reduction of all the so-called elementary substances, his own total scepticism concern-

578

ing Manetho's chronology, or even the relation between the magnetic condition of the earth and the outbreak of revolutionary tendencies. Such flexibility was naturally much helped by his amiable feeling toward woman, whose nervous system, he was convinced, would not bear the continuous strain of difficult topics; and also by his willingness to contribute a song whenever the same desultory charmer proposed music. Indeed his tastes were domestic enough to beguile him into marriage when his resources were still very moderate and partly uncertain. His friends wished that so ingenious and agreeable a fellow might have more prosperity than they ventured to hope for him, their chief regret on his account being that he did not concentrate his talent and leave off forming opinions on at least half-a-dozen of the subjects over which he scattered his attention, especially now that he had married a "nice little woman" (the generic name for acquaintances' wives when they are not markedly disagreeable). He could not, they observed, want all his various knowledge and Laputan ideas for his periodical writing which brought him most of his bread, and he would do well to use his talents in getting a specialty that would fit him for a post. Perhaps these well-disposed persons were a little rash in presuming that fitness for a post would be the surest ground for getting it; and on the whole, in now looking back on their wishes for Merman, their chief satisfaction must be that those wishes did not contribute to the actual result.

For in an evil hour Merman did concentrate himself. He had for many years taken into his interest the comparative history of the ancient civilisations, but it had not preoccupied him so as to narrow his generous attention to everything else. One sleepless night, however (his wife has more than once narrated to me the details of an event memorable to her as the beginning of sorrows), after spending some hours over the epoch-making work of Grampus, a new idea seized him with regard to the possible connection of certain symbolic monuments common to widely scattered races. Merman started up in bed. The night was cold, and the sudden withdrawal of warmth made his wife first dream of a snowball, and then cry—

"What is the matter, Proteus?"

"A great matter, Julia. That fellow Grampus, whose book is

cried up as a revelation, is all wrong about the Magicodumbras and the Zuzumotzis, and I have got hold of the right clew."

"Good gracious! does it matter so much? Don't drag the clothes, dear."

"It signifies this, Julia, that if I am right I shall set the world right; I shall regenerate history; I shall win the mind of Europe to a new view of social origins; I shall bruise the head of many superstitions."

"Oh no, dear, don't go too far into things. Lie down again. You have been dreaming. What are the Madicojumbras and Zuzitotzums? I never heard you talk of them before. What use can it be troubling yourself about such things?"

"That is the way, Julia—that is the way wives alienate their husbands, and make any hearth pleasanter to him than his own!"

"What *do* you mean, Proteus?"

"Why, if a woman will not try to understand her husband's ideas, or at least to believe that they are of more value than she can understand—if she is to join anybody who happens to be against him, and suppose he is a fool because others contradict him—there is an end of our happiness. That is all I have to say."

"Oh no, Proteus, dear. I do believe what you say is right. That is my only guide. I am sure I never have any opinions in any other way: I mean about subjects. Of course there are many little things that would tease you, that you like me to judge of for myself. I know I said once that I did not want you to sing 'Oh ruddier than the cherry,' because it was not in your voice. But I cannot remember ever differing from you about *subjects*. I never in my life thought any one cleverer than you."

Julia Merman was really a "nice little woman," not one of the stately Dians sometimes spoken of in those terms. Her black *silhouette* had a very infantine aspect, but she had discernment and wisdom enough to act on the strong hint of that memorable conversation, never again giving her husband the slightest ground for suspecting that she thought treasonably of his ideas in relation to the Magicodumbras and Zuzumotzis, or in the least relaxed her faith in his infallibility because Europe was not also convinced of it. It was well for her that she did not increase her troubles in this way; but to do her justice, what she was chiefly anxious about was to avoid increasing her husband's troubles.

Not that these were great in the beginning. In the first development and writing out of his scheme, Merman had a more intense
kind of intellectual pleasure than he had ever known before. His
face became more radiant, his general view of human prospects
more cheerful. Foreseeing that truth as presented by himself
would win the recognition of his contemporaries, he excused with
much liberality their rather rough treatment of other theorists
whose basis was less perfect. His own periodical criticisms had
never before been so amiable: he was sorry for that unlucky majority whom the spirit of the age, or some other prompting more
definite and local, compelled to write without any particular
ideas. The possession of an original theory which has not yet been
assailed must certainly sweeten the temper of a man who is not
beforehand ill-natured. And Merman was the reverse of ill-natured.

But the hour of publication came; and to half-a-dozen persons,
described as the learned world of two hemispheres, it became
known that Grampus was attacked. This might have been a small
matter; for who or what on earth that is good for anything is not
assailed by ignorance, stupidity, or malice—and sometimes even
by just objection? But on examination it appeared that the attack
might possibly be held damaging, unless the ignorance of the
author were well exposed and his pretended facts shown to be
chimeras of that remarkably hideous kind begotten by imperfect
learning on the more feminine element of original incapacity.
Grampus himself did not immediately cut open the volume which
Merman had been careful to send him, not without a very lively
and shifting conception of the possible effects which the explosive
gift might produce on the too eminent scholar—effects that must
certainly have set in on the third day from the despatch of the
parcel. But in point of fact Grampus knew nothing of the book
until his friend Lord Narwhal sent him an American newspaper
containing a spirited article by the well-known Professor Sperm N.
Whale which was rather equivocal in its bearing, the passages
quoted from Merman being of rather a telling sort, and the paragraphs which seemed to blow defiance being unaccountably feeble,
coming from so distinguished a Cetacean. Then, by another post,
arrived letters from Butzkopf and Dugong, both men whose signa-
tures were familiar to the Teutonic world in the *Selten-erscheinende
Monat-schrift* or Hayrick for the insertion of Split Hairs, asking

their Master whether he meant to take up the combat, because, in the contrary case, both were ready.

Thus America and Germany were roused, though England was still drowsy, and it seemed time now for Grampus to find Merman's book under the heap and cut it open. For his own part he was perfectly at ease about his system; but this is a world in which the truth requires defence, and specious falsehood must be met with exposure. Grampus having once looked through the book, no longer wanted any urging to write the most crushing of replies. This, and nothing less than this, was due from him to the cause of sound inquiry; and the punishment would cost him little pains. In three weeks from that time the palpitating Merman saw his book announced in the programme of the leading Review. No need for Grampus to put his signature. Who else had his vast yet microscopic knowledge, who else his power of epithet? This article in which Merman was pilloried and as good as mutilated—for he was shown to have neither ear nor nose for the subtleties of philological and archæological study—was much read and more talked of, not because of any interest in the system of Grampus, or any precise conception of the danger attending lax views of the Magicodumbras and Zuzumotzis, but because the sharp epigrams with which the victim was lacerated, and the soaring fountains of acrid mud which were shot upward and poured over the fresh wounds, were found amusing in recital. A favourite passage was one in which a certain kind of sciolist was described as a creature of the Walrus kind, having a phantasmal resemblance to higher animals when seen by ignorant minds in the twilight, dabbling or hobbling in first one element and then the other, without parts or organs suited to either, in fact one of Nature's impostors who could not be said to have any artful pretences, since a congenital incompetence to all precision of aim and movement made their every action a pretence—just as a being born in doeskin gloves would necessarily pass a judgment on surfaces, but we all know what his judgment would be worth. In drawing-room circles, and for the immediate hour, this ingenious comparison was as damaging as the showing up of Merman's mistakes and the mere smattering of linguistic and historical knowledge which he had presumed to be a sufficient basis for theorising; but the more learned cited his blunders aside to each other and laughed the laugh of the initiated. In fact, Merman's was a remarkable case of sudden notoriety. In London drums and clubs he was spoken of abundantly as one who had written ridiculously about the Magicodumbras and Zuzumotzis: the leaders of conversation, whether Christians, Jews, infidels, or of any other confession except the confession of ignorance, pronouncing him shallow and indiscreet if not presumptuous and absurd. He was heard of at Warsaw, and even Paris took knowledge of him. M. Cachalot had not read either Grampus or Merman, but he heard of their dispute in time to insert a paragraph upon it in his brilliant work, *L'orient au point de vue actuel*, in which he was dispassionate enough to speak of Grampus as possessing a *coup d'œil presque français* in matters of historical interpretation, and of Merman as nevertheless an objector *qui mérite d'être connu*. M. Porpesse, also, availing himself of M. Cachalot's knowledge, reproduced it in an article with certain additions, which it is only fair to distinguish as his own, implying that the vigorous English of Grampus was not always as correct as a Frenchman could desire, while Merman's objections were more sophistical than solid. Presently, indeed, there appeared an able *extrait* of Grampus's article in the valuable *Rapporteur scientifique et historique*, and Merman's mistakes were thus brought under the notice of certain Frenchmen who are among the masters of those who know on oriental subjects. In a word, Merman, though not extensively read, was extensively read about.

Meanwhile, how did he like it? Perhaps nobody, except his wife, for a moment reflected on that. An amused society considered that he was severely punished, but did not take the trouble to imagine his sensations; indeed this would have been a difficulty for persons less sensitive and excitable than Merman himself. Perhaps that popular comparison of the Walrus had truth enough to bite and blister on thorough application, even if exultant ignorance had not applauded it. But it is well known that the walrus, though not in the least a malignant animal, if allowed to display its remarkably plain person and blundering performances at ease in any element it chooses, becomes desperately savage and musters alarming auxiliaries when attacked or hurt. In this characteristic, at least, Merman resembled the walrus. And now he concentrated himself with a vengeance. That his counter-theory was fundamentally the right one he had a genuine conviction, whatever collateral

mistakes he might have committed; and his bread would not cease
to be bitter to him until he had convinced his contemporaries that
Grampus had used his minute learning as a dust-cloud to hide
sophistical evasions—that, in fact, minute learning was an obstacle
to clear-sighted judgment, more especially with regard to the
Magicodumbras and Zuzumotzis, and that the best preparation
in this matter was a wide survey of history, and a diversified observation of men. Still, Merman was resolved to muster all the
learning within his reach, and he wandered day and night through
many wildernesses of German print, he tried compendious methods
of learning oriental tongues, and, so to speak, getting at the marrow
of languages independently of the bones, for the chance of finding
details to corroborate his own views, or possibly even to detect
Grampus in some oversight or textual tampering. All other work
was neglected: rare clients were sent away and amazed editors
found this maniac indifferent to his chance of getting book-parcels
from them. It was many months before Merman had satisfied
himself that he was strong enough to face round upon his adversary. But at last he had prepared sixty condensed pages of eager
argument which seemed to him worthy to rank with the best models
of controversial writing. He had acknowledged his mistakes, but
he had restated his theory so as to show that it was left intact in
spite of them; and he had even found cases in which Ziphius, Mi-
crops, Scrag Whale the explorer, and other Cetaceans of unanswerable authority, were decidedly at issue with Grampus. Especially
a passage cited by this last from that greatest of fossils Megalo-
saurus was demonstrated by Merman to be capable of three different interpretations, all preferable to that chosen by Grampus,
who took the words in their most literal sense; for, 1°, the incomparable Saurian, alike unequalled in close observation and far-
glancing comprehensiveness, might have meant those words
ironically; 2°, *motzis* was probably a false reading for *potzis*, in
which case its bearing was reversed; and 3°, it is known that in the
age of the Saurians there were conceptions about the *motzis* which
entirely remove it from the category of things comprehensible in
an age when Saurians run ridiculously small: all which views were
godfathered by names quite fit to be ranked with that of Grampus.
In fine, Merman wound up his rejoinder by sincerely thanking the
eminent adversary without whose fierce assault he might not have

undertaken a revision in the course of which he had met with unexpected and striking confirmations of his own fundamental views.
Evidently Merman's anger was at white heat.

The rejoinder being complete, all that remained was to find a
suitable medium for its publication. This was not so easy. Distinguished mediums would not lend themselves to contradictions
of Grampus, or if they would, Merman's article was too long and
too abstruse, while he would not consent to leave anything out of
an article which had no superfluities; for all this happened years
ago when the world was at a different stage. At last, however, he
got his rejoinder printed, and not on hard terms, since the medium,
in every sense modest, did not ask him to pay for its insertion.

But if Merman expected to call out Grampus again, he was
mistaken. Everybody felt it too absurd that Merman should
undertake to correct Grampus in matters of erudition, and an
eminent man has something else to do than to refute a petty objector twice over. What was essential had been done: the public
had been enabled to form a true judgment of Merman's incapacity,
the Magicodumbras and Zuzumotzis were but subsidiary elements
in Grampus's system, and Merman might now be dealt with by
younger members of the master's school. But he had at least the
satisfaction of finding that he had raised a discussion which would
not be let die. The followers of Grampus took it up with an ardour
and industry of research worthy of their exemplar. Butzkopf
made it the subject of an elaborate *Einleitung* to his important
work, *Die Bedeutung des Ægyptischen Labyrinthes;* and Dugong, in
a remarkable address which he delivered to a learned society in
Central Europe, introduced Merman's theory with so much power
of sarcasm that it became a theme of more or less derisive allusion
to men of many tongues. Merman with his Magicodumbras and
Zuzumotzis was on the way to become a proverb, being used il-
lustratively by many able journalists who took those names of
questionable things to be Merman's own invention, "than which,"
said one of the graver guides, "we can recall few more melancholy
examples of speculative aberration." Naturally the subject passed
into popular literature, and figured very commonly in advertised
programmes. The fluent Loligo, the formidable Shark, and a
younger member of his remarkable family known as S. Catulus,
made a special reputation by their numerous articles, eloquent,

lively, or abusive, all on the same theme, under titles ingeniously varied, alliterative, sonorous, or boldly fanciful; such as "Moments with Mr Merman," "Mr Merman and the Magicodumbras," "Greenland Grampus and Proteus Merman," "Grampian Heights and their Climbers, or the New Excelsior." They tossed him on short sentences; they swathed him in paragraphs of winding imagery; they found him at once a mere plagiarist and a theoriser of unexampled perversity, ridiculously wrong about *potzis* and ignorant of Pali; they hinted, indeed, at certain things which to their knowledge he had silently brooded over in his boyhood, and seemed tolerably well assured that this preposterous attempt to gainsay an incomparable Cetacean of world-wide fame had its origin in a peculiar mixture of bitterness and eccentricity which, rightly estimated and seen in its definite proportions, would furnish the best key to his argumentation. All alike were sorry for Merman's lack of sound learning, but how could their readers be sorry? Sound learning would not have been amusing; and as it was, Merman was made to furnish these readers with amusement at no expense of trouble on their part. Even burlesque writers looked into his book to see where it could be made use of, and those who did not know him were desirous of meeting him at dinner as one likely to feed their comic vein.

On the other hand, he made a serious figure in sermons under the name of "Some" or "Others" who had attempted presumptuously to scale eminences too high and arduous for human ability, and had given an example of ignominious failure edifying to the humble Christian.

All this might be very advantageous for able persons whose superfluous fund of expression needed a paying investment, but the effect on Merman himself was unhappily not so transient as the busy writing and speaking of which he had become the occasion. His certainty that he was right naturally got stronger in proportion as the spirit of resistance was stimulated. The scorn and unfairness with which he felt himself to have been treated by those really competent to appreciate his ideas had galled him and made a chronic sore; and the exultant chorus of the incompetent seemed a pouring of vinegar on his wound. His brain became a registry of the foolish and ignorant objections made against him, and of continually amplified answers to these objections. Unable to get his answers printed, he had recourse to that more primitive mode of publication, oral transmission or button-holding, now generally regarded as a troublesome survival, and the once pleasant, flexible Merman was on the way to be shunned as a bore. His interest in new acquaintances turned chiefly on the possibility that they would care about the Magicodumbras and Zuzumotzis; that they would listen to his complaints and exposures of unfairness, and not only accept copies of what he had written on the subject, but send him appreciative letters in acknowledgment. Repeated disappointment of such hopes tended to embitter him, and not the less because after a while the fashion of mentioning him died out, allusions to his theory were less understood, and people could only pretend to remember it. And all the while Merman was perfectly sure that his very opponents who had knowledge enough to be capable judges were aware that his book, whatever errors of statement they might detect in it, had served as a sort of divining rod, pointing out hidden sources of historical interpretation; nay, his jealous examination discerned in a new work by Grampus himself a certain shifting of ground which—so poor Merman declared—was the sign of an intention gradually to appropriate the views of the man he had attempted to brand as an ignorant impostor.

And Julia? And the housekeeping?—the rent, food, and clothing, which controversy can hardly supply unless it be of the kind that serves as a recommendation to certain posts. Controversial pamphlets have been known to earn large plums; but nothing of the sort could be expected from unpractical heresies about the Magicodumbras and Zuzumotzis. Painfully the contrary. Merman's reputation as a sober thinker, a safe writer, a sound lawyer, was irretrievably injured: the distractions of controversy had caused him to neglect useful editorial connections, and indeed his dwindling care for miscellaneous subjects made his contributions too dull to be desirable. Even if he could now have given a new turn to his concentration, and applied his talents so as to be ready to show himself an exceptionally qualified lawyer, he would only have been like an architect in competition, too late with his superior plans: he would not have had an opportunity of showing his qualification. He was thrown out of the course. The small capital which had filled up deficiencies of income was almost exhausted, and Julia, in the effort to make supplies equal to wants, had to use much ingenuity in diminishing the wants. The brave and affectionate woman whose small outline, so unimpressive against an illuminated background, held within it a good share of feminine heroism, did her best to keep up the charm of home and soothe her husband's excitement; parting with the best jewel among her wedding presents in order to pay rent, without ever hinting to her husband that this sad result had come of his undertaking to convince people who only laughed at him. She was a resigned little creature, and reflected that some husbands took to drinking and other to forgery: hers had only taken to the Magicodumbras and Zuzumotzis, and was not unkind—only a little more indifferent to her and the two children than she had ever expected he would be, his mind being eaten up with "subjects," and constantly a little angry, not with her, but with everybody else, especially those who were celebrated.

This was the sad truth. Merman felt himself ill used by the world, and thought very much worse of the world in consequence. The gall of his adversaries' ink had been sucked into his system and ran in his blood. He was still in the prime of life, but his mind was aged by that eager monotonous construction which comes of feverish excitement on a single topic and uses up the intellectual strength.

Merman had never been a rich man, but he was now conspicuously poor, and in need of the friends who had power or interest which he believed they could exert on his behalf. Their omitting or declining to give this help could not seem to him so clearly as to them an inevitable consequence of his having become impracticable, or at least of his passing for a man whose views were not likely to be safe and sober. Each friend in turn offended him, though unwillingly, and was suspected of wishing to shake him off. It was not altogether so; but poor Merman's society had undeniably ceased to be attractive, and it was difficult to help him. At last the pressure of want urged him to try for a post far beneath his earlier prospects, and he gained it. He holds it still, for he has no vices, and his domestic life has kept up a sweetening current of motive around and within him. Nevertheless, the bitter flavour mingling itself with all topics, the premature weariness and withering, are irrevocably there. It is as if he had gone through a disease which alters what we call the constitution. He has long ceased to talk eagerly of the ideas which possess him, or to attempt making proselytes. The dial has moved onward, and he himself sees many of his former guesses in a new light. On the other hand, he has seen what he foreboded, that the main idea which was at the root of his too rash theorising has been adopted by Grampus and received with general respect, no reference being heard to the ridiculous figure this important conception made when ushered in by the incompetent "Others."

Now and then, on rare occasions, when a sympathetic *tête-à-tête* has restored some of his old expansiveness, he will tell a companion in a railway carriage, or other place of meeting favourable to autobiographical confidences, what has been the course of things in his particular case, as an example of the justice to be expected of the world. The companion usually allows for the bitterness of a disappointed man, and is secretly disinclined to believe that Grampus was to blame.

A MAN SURPRISED AT HIS ORIGINALITY

AMONG the many acute sayings of La Rochefoucauld, there is hardly one more acute than this: "La plus grande ambition n'en a pas la moindre apparence lorsqu'elle se rencontre dans une impossibilité absolue d'arriver où elle aspire." Some of us might do well to use this hint in our treatment of acquaintances and friends from whom we are expecting gratitude because we are so very kind in thinking of them, inviting them, and even listening to what they say—considering how insignificant they must feel themselves to be. We are often fallaciously confident in supposing that our friend's state of mind is appropriate to our moderate estimate of his importance: almost as if we imagined the humble mollusc (so useful as an illustration) to have a sense of his own exceeding softness and low place in the scale of being. Your mollusc, on the contrary, is inwardly objecting to every other grade of solid rather than to himself. Accustomed to observe what we think an unwarrantable conceit exhibiting itself in ridiculous pretensions and forwardness to play the lion's part, in obvious self-complacency and loud peremptoriness, we are not on the alert to detect the egoistic claims of a more exorbitant kind often hidden under an apparent neutrality or an acquiescence in being put out of the question.

Thoughts of this kind occurred to me yesterday when I saw the name of Lentulus in the obituary. The majority of his acquaintances, I imagine, have always thought of him as a man justly unpretending and as nobody's rival; but some of them have perhaps been struck with surprise at his reserve in praising the work of his contemporaries, and have now and then felt themselves in need of a key to his remarks on men of celebrity in various departments. He was a man of fair position, deriving his income from a business in which he did nothing, at leisure to frequent clubs and at ease in giving dinners; well-looking, polite, and generally acceptable in society as a part of what we may call its bread-crumb—the neutral basis needful for the plums and spice. Why, then, did he speak of the modern Maro or the modern Flaccus with a peculiarity in his tone of assent to other people's praise which might almost have led you to suppose that the eminent poet had borrowed money of him and showed an indisposition to repay? He had no criticism to offer, no sign of objection more specific than a slight cough, a scarcely perceptible pause before assenting, and an air of self-control in his utterance—as if certain considerations had determined him not to inform against the so-called poet, who to his knowledge was a mere versifier. If you had questioned him closely, he would perhaps have confessed that he did think something better might be done in the way of Eclogues and Georgics, or of Odes and Epodes, and that to his mind poetry was something very different from what had hitherto been known under that name.

For my own part, being of a superstitious nature, given readily to imagine alarming causes, I immediately, on first getting these mystic hints from Lentulus, concluded that he held a number of entirely original poems, or at the very least a revolutionary treatise on poetics, in that melancholy manuscript state to which works excelling all that is ever printed are necessarily condemned; and I was long timid in speaking of the poets when he was present. For what might not Lentulus have done, or be profoundly aware of, that would make my ignorant impressions ridiculous? One cannot well be sure of the negative in such a case, except through certain positives that bear witness to it; and those witnesses are not always to be got hold of. But time wearing on, I perceived that the attitude of Lentulus toward the philosophers was essentially the same as his attitude toward the poets; nay, there was something so much more decided in his mode of closing his mouth after brief speech on the former, there was such an air of rapt consciousness in his private hints as to his conviction that all thinking hitherto had been an elaborate mistake, and as to his own power of conceiving a sound basis for a lasting superstructure, that I began to believe less in the poetical stores, and to infer that the line of Lentulus lay rather in the rational criticism of our beliefs and in systematic construction. In this case I did not figure to myself the existence of formidable manuscripts ready for the press; for great thinkers are known to carry their theories growing within their minds long before committing them to paper, and the ideas which made a new passion for them when their locks were jet or auburn, remain perilously unwritten, an inwardly developing condition of their successive selves, until the locks are grey or scanty. I only meditated improvingly on the way in which a man of exceptional faculties, and even carrying within him some of that fierce refiner's fire which is to purge away the dross of human error, may move about in society totally unrecognised, regarded as a person whose opinion is superfluous, and only rising into a power in emergencies of threatened black-balling. Imagine a Descartes or a Locke being recognised for nothing more than a good fellow and a perfect gentleman—what a painful view does such a picture suggest of impenetrable dulness in the society around them!

I would at all times rather be reduced to a cheaper estimate of a particular person, if by that means I can get a more cheerful view of my fellow-men generally; and I confess that in a certain curiosity which led me to cultivate Lentulus's acquaintance, my hope leaned to the discovery that he was a less remarkable man than he had seemed to imply. It would have been a grief to discover that he was bitter or malicious, but by finding him to be neither a mighty poet, nor a revolutionary poetical critic, nor an epoch-making philosopher, my admiration for the poets and thinkers whom he rated so low would recover all its buoyancy, and I should not be left to trust to that very suspicious sort of merit which constitutes an exception in the history of mankind, and recommends itself as the total abolitionist of all previous claims on our confidence. You are not greatly surprised at the infirm logic of the coachman who would persuade you to engage him by insisting that any other would be sure to rob you in the matter of hay and corn, thus demanding a difficult belief in him as the sole exception from the frailties of his calling; but it is rather astonishing that the wholesale decriers of mankind and its performances should be even more unwary in their reasoning than the coachman, since each of them not merely confides in your regarding himself as an exception, but overlooks the almost certain fact that you are wondering whether he inwardly excepts *you*. Now, conscious of entertaining some common opinions which seemed to fall under the mildly intimated but sweeping ban of Lentulus, my self-complacency was a little concerned.

Hence I deliberately attempted to draw out Lentulus in private dialogue, for it is the reverse of injury to a man to offer him that hearing which he seems to have found nowhere else. And for whatever purposes silence may be equal to gold, it cannot be safely taken as an indication of specific ideas. I sought to know why Lentulus was more than indifferent to the poets, and what was that new poetry which he had either written or, as to its principles, distinctly conceived. But I presently found that he knew very little of any particular poet, and had a general notion of poetry as the use of artificial language to express unreal sentiments: he instanced "The Giaour," "Lalla Rookh," "The Pleasures of Hope," and "Ruin seize thee, ruthless King;" adding, "and plenty more." On my observing that he probably preferred a larger, simpler style, he emphatically assented. "Have you not," said I, "written something of that order?" "No; but I often compose as I go along. I see how things might be written as fine as Ossian, only with true ideas. The world has no notion what poetry will be."

It was impossible to disprove this, and I am always glad to believe that the poverty of our imagination is no measure of the world's resources. Our posterity will no doubt get fuel in ways that we are unable to devise for them. But what this conversation persuaded me of was, that the birth with which the mind of Lentulus was pregnant could not be poetry, though I did not question that he composed as he went along, and that the exercise was accompanied with a great sense of power. This is a frequent experience in dreams, and much of our waking experience is but a dream in the daylight. Nay, for what I saw, the compositions might be fairly classed as Ossianic. But I was satisfied that Lentulus could not disturb my grateful admiration for the poets of all ages by eclipsing them, or by putting them under a new electric light of criticism.

Still, he had himself thrown the chief emphasis of his protest and his consciousness of corrective illumination on the philosophic thinking of our race, and his tone in assuring me that everything which had been done in that way was wrong—that Plato, Robert Owen, and Dr Tuffle, who wrote in the "Regulator," were all equally mistaken—gave my superstitious nature a thrill of anxiety. After what had passed about the poets, it did not seem likely that Lentulus had all systems by heart; but who could say he had not seized that thread which may somewhere hang out loosely from the web of things and be the clue of unravelment? We need not go far to learn that a prophet is not made by erudition. Lentulus at least had not the bias of a school; and if it turned out that he was in agreement with any celebrated thinker, ancient or modern, the agreement would have the value of an undesigned coincidence not due to forgotten reading. It was therefore with renewed curiosity that I engaged him on this large subject—the universal erroneousness of thinking up to the period when Lentulus began that process. And here I found him more copious than on the theme of poetry. He admitted that he did contemplate writing down his thoughts, but his difficulty was their abundance. Apparently he was like the wood-cutter entering the thick forest and saying, "Where shall I begin?" The same obstacle appeared in a minor degree to cling about his verbal exposition, and accounted perhaps for his rather helter-skelter choice of remarks bearing on the number of unaddressed letters sent to the post-office; on what logic really is, as tending to support the buoyancy of human mediums and mahogany tables; on the probability of all miracles under all religions when explained by hidden laws, and my unreasonableness in supposing that their profuse occurrence at half a guinea an hour in recent times was anything more than a coincidence; on the haphazard way in which marriages are determined—showing the baselessness of social and moral schemes; and on his expectation that he should offend the scientific world when he told them what he thought of electricity as an agent.

No man's appearance could be graver or more gentleman-like than that of Lentulus as we walked along the Mall while he delivered these observations, understood by himself to have a regenerative bearing on human society. His wristbands and black gloves, his hat and nicely clipped hair, his laudable moderation in beard, and his evident discrimination in choosing his tailor, all seemed to excuse the prevalent estimate of him as a man untainted with heterodoxy, and likely to be so unencumbered with opinions that he would always be useful as an assenting and admiring listener. Men of science seeing him at their lectures doubtless flattered themselves that he came to learn from them; the philosophic ornaments of our time, expounding some of their luminous ideas in the social circle, took the meditative gaze of Lentulus for one of surprise not unmixed with a just reverence at such close reasoning towards so novel a conclusion; and those who are called men of the world considered him a good fellow who might be asked to vote for a friend of their own and would have no troublesome notions to make him unaccommodating. You perceive how very much they were all mistaken, except in qualifying him as a good fellow.

This Lentulus certainly was, in the sense of being free from envy, hatred, and malice; and such freedom was all the more remarkable an indication of native benignity, because of his gaseous, illimitably expansive conceit. Yes, conceit; for that his enormous and contentedly ignorant confidence in his own rambling thoughts was usually clad in a decent silence, is no reason why it should be less strictly called by the name directly implying a complacent self-estimate unwarranted by performance. Nay, the total privacy in which he enjoyed his consciousness of inspiration was the very condition of its undisturbed placid nourishment and gigantic growth. Your audibly arrogant man exposes himself to tests: in attempting to make an impression on others he may possibly (not always) be made to feel his own lack of definiteness; and the demand for definiteness is to all of us a needful check on vague depreciation of what others do, and vague ecstatic trust in our own superior ability. But Lentulus was at once so unreceptive, and so little gifted with the power of displaying his miscellaneous deficiency of information, that there was really nothing to hinder his astonishment at the spontaneous crop of ideas which his mind secretly yielded. If it occurred to him that there were more meanings than one for the word "motive," since it sometimes means the end aimed at, and sometimes the feeling that prompted the aiming, and that the word "cause" was also of changeable import, he was naturally struck with the truth of his own perception, and was convinced that if this vein were well followed out much might be made of it. Men were evidently in the wrong about cause and effect, else why was society in the confused state we behold? And as to motive, Lentulus felt that when he came to write down his views he should look deeply into this kind of subject and show up thereby the anomalies of our social institutions; meanwhile the various aspects of "motive" and "cause" flitted about among the motley crowd of ideas which he regarded as original, and pregnant with reformative efficacy. For his unaffected goodwill made him regard all his insight as only valuable because it tended toward reform.

The respectable man had got into his illusory maze of discoveries by letting go that clue of conformity in his thinking which he had kept fast hold of in his tailoring and manners. He regarded heterodoxy as a power in itself, and took his inacquaintance with doctrines for a creative dissidence. But his epitaph needs not to be a melancholy one. His benevolent disposition was more effective for good than his silent presumption for harm. He might have been mischievous but for the lack of words: instead of being astonished at his inspirations in private, he might have clad his addled originalities, disjointed commonplaces, blind denials, and balloon-like conclusions, in that mighty sort of language which would have made a new Koran for a knot of followers. I mean no disrespect to the ancient Koran, but one would not desire the roc to lay more eggs and give us a whole wing-flapping brood to soar and make twilight.

Peace be with Lentulus, for he has left us in peace. Blessed is the man who, having nothing to say, abstains from giving us wordy evidence of the fact—from calling on us to look through a heap of millet-seed in order to be sure that there is no pearl in it.

A TOO DEFERENTIAL MAN

A LITTLE unpremediated insincerity must be indulged under the stress of social intercourse. The talk even of an honest man must often represent merely his wish to be inoffensive or agreeable rather than his genuine opinion or feeling on the matter in hand. His thought, if uttered, might be wounding; or he has not the ability to utter it with exactness, and snatches at a loose paraphrase; or he has really no genuine thought on the question, and is driven to fill up the vacancy by borrowing the remarks in vogue. These are the winds and currents we have all to steer amongst, and they are often too strong for our truthfulness or our wit. Let us not bear too hardly on each other for this common incidental frailty, or think that we rise superior to it by dropping all considerateness and deference.

But there are studious, deliberate forms of insincerity which it is fair to be impatient with: Hinze's, for example. From his name you might suppose him to be German: in fact, his family is Alsatian, but has been settled in England for more than one generation. He is the superlatively deferential man, and walks about with murmured wonder at the wisdom and discernment of everybody who talks to him. He cultivates the low-toned *tête-à-tête*, keeping his hat carefully in his hand and often stroking it, while he smiles with downcast eyes, as if to relieve his feelings under the pressure of the remarkable conversation which it is his honour to enjoy at the present moment. I confess to some rage on hearing him yesterday talking to Felicia, who is certainly a clever woman, and, without any unusual desire to show her cleverness, occasionally says something of her own or makes an allusion which is not quite common. Still, it must happen to her as to every one else to speak of many subjects on which the best things were said long ago, and in conversation with a person who has been newly introduced those well-worn themes naturally recur as a further development of salutations and preliminary media of understanding, such as pipes, chocolate, or mastic-chewing, which serve to confirm the impression that our new acquaintance is on a civilised footing and has enough regard for formulas to save us from shocking outbursts of individualism, to which we are always exposed with the tamest bear or baboon. Considered purely as a matter of information, it cannot any longer be important for us to learn that a British subject included in the last census holds Shakespeare to be supreme in the presentation of character; still, it is as admissible for any one to make this statement about himself as to rub his hands and tell you the air is brisk, if only he will let it fall as a matter of course, with a parenthetic lightness, and not announce his adhesion to a commonplace with an emphatic insistence, as if it were a proof of singular insight. We mortals should chiefly like to talk to each other out of goodwill and fellowship, not for the sake of hearing revelations or being stimulated by witticisms; and I have usually found that it is the rather dull person who appears to be disgusted with his contemporaries because they are not always strikingly original, and to satisfy whom the party at a country house should have included the prophet Isaiah, Plato, Francis Bacon, and Voltaire. It is always your heaviest bore who is astonished at the tameness of modern celebrities: naturally; for a little of his company has reduced them to a state of flaccid fatigue. It is right and meet that there should be an abundant utterance of good sound commonplaces. Part of an agreeable talker's charm is that he lets them fall continually with no more than their due emphasis. Giving a pleasant voice to what we are all well assured of, makes a sort of wholesome air for more special and dubious remark to move in.

Hence it seemed to me far from unbecoming in Felicia that in her first dialogue with Hinze, previously quite a stranger to her, her observations were those of an ordinarily refined and well-educated woman on standard subjects, and might have been printed in a manual of polite topics and creditable opinions. She had no desire to astonish a man of whom she had heard nothing particular. It was all the more exasperating to see and hear Hinze's reception of her well-bred conformities. Felicia's acquaintances know her as the suitable wife of a distinguished man, a sensible, vivacious, kindly-disposed woman, helping her husband with graceful apologies written and spoken, and making her receptions agreeable to all comers. But you would have imagined that Hinze had been prepared by general report to regard this introduction to her as an opportunity comparable to an audience of the Delphic Sibyl. When she had delivered herself on the changes in Italian travel, on the difficulty of reading Ariosto in these busy times, on the want of equilibrium in French political affairs, and on the pre-eminence of German music, he would know what to think. Felicia was evidently embarrassed by his reverent wonder, and, in dread lest she should seem to be playing the oracle, became somewhat confused, stumbling on her answers rather than choosing them. But this made no difference to Hinze's rapt attention and subdued eagerness of inquiry. He continued to put large questions, bending his head slightly that his eyes might be a little lifted in awaiting her reply.

"What, may I ask, is your opinion as to the state of Art in England?"

"Oh," said Felicia, with a light deprecatory laugh, "I think it suffers from two diseases—bad taste in the patrons, and want of inspiration in the artists."

"That is true indeed," said Hinze, in an undertone of deep conviction. "You have put your finger with strict accuracy on the causes of decline. To a cultivated taste like yours this must be particularly painful."

"I did not say there was actual decline," said Felicia, with a touch of *brusquerie*. "I don't set myself up as the great personage whom nothing can please."

"That would be too severe a misfortune for others," says my complimentary ape. "You approve, perhaps, of Rosemary's 'Babes in the Wood,' as something fresh and *naïve* in sculpture?"

"I think it enchanting."

"Does he know that? Or *will* you permit me to tell him?"

"Heaven forbid! It would be an impertinence in me to praise a work of his—to pronounce on its quality; and that I happen to like it can be of no consequence to him."

Here was an occasion for Hinze to smile down on his hat and stroke it—Felicia's ignorance that her praise was inestimable being peculiarly noteworthy to an observer of mankind. Presently he was quite sure that her favourite author was Shakespeare, and wished to know what she thought of Hamlet's madness. When she had quoted Wilhelm Meister on this point, and had afterward testified that "Lear" was beyond adequate presentation, that "Julius Cæsar" was an effective acting play, and that a poet may know a good deal about human nature while knowing little of geography, Hinze appeared so impressed with the plenitude of these revelations that he recapitulated them, weaving them together with threads of compliment—"As you very justly observed;" and—"It is most true, as you say;" and—"It were well if others noted what you have remarked."

Some listeners, incautious in their epithets, would have called Hinze an "ass." For my part, I would never insult that intelligent and unpretending animal who no doubt brays with perfect simplicity and substantial meaning to those acquainted with his idiom, and if he feigns more submission than he feels, has weighty reasons for doing so—I would never, I say, insult that historic and ill-appreciated animal, the ass, by giving his name to a man whose continuous pretence is so shallow in its motive, so unexcused by any sharp appetite as this of Hinze's.

But perhaps you would say that his adulatory manner was originally adopted under strong promptings of self-interest, and that his absurdly over-acted deference to persons from whom he expects no patronage is the unreflecting persistence of habit—just as those who live with the deaf will shout to everybody else.

And you might indeed imagine that in talking to Tulpian, who has considerable interest at his disposal, Hinze had a desired appointment in his mind. Tulpian is appealed to on innumerable subjects, and if he is unwilling to express himself on any one of them, says so with instructive copiousness: he is much listened to, and his utterances are registered and reported with more or less exactitude. But I think he has no other listener who comports himself as Hinze does—who, figuratively speaking, carries about a small spoon ready to pick up any dusty crumb of opinion that the eloquent man may have let drop. Tulpian, with reverence be it said, has some rather absurd notions, such as a mind of large discourse often finds room for: they slip about among his higher conceptions and multitudinous acquirements like disreputable characters at a national celebration in some vast cathedral, where to the ardent soul all is glorified by rainbow light and grand associations: any vulgar detective knows them for what they are. But Hinze is especially fervid in his desire to hear Tulpian dilate on his crotchets, and is rather troublesome to bystanders in asking them whether they have read the various fugitive writings in which these crotchets have been published. If an expert is explaining some matter on which you desire to know the evidence, Hinze teases you with Tulpian's guesses, and asks the expert what he thinks of them.

In general, Hinze delights in the citation of opinions, and would hardly remark that the sun shone without an air of respectful appeal or fervid adhesion. The "Iliad," one sees, would impress him little if it were not for what Mr Fugleman has lately said about it; and if you mention an image or sentiment in Chaucer he seems not to heed the bearing of your reference, but immediately tells you that Mr Hautboy, too, regards Chaucer as a poet of the first order, and he is delighted to find that two such judges as you and Hautboy are at one.

What is the reason of all this subdued ecstasy, moving about, hat in hand, with well-dressed hair and attitudes of unimpeachable correctness? Some persons conscious of sagacity decide at once that Hinze knows what he is about in flattering Tulpian, and has a carefully appraised end to serve though they may not see it. They are misled by the common mistake of supposing that men's behaviour, whether habitual or occasional, is chiefly determined by a distinctly conceived motive, a definite object to be gained or a definite evil to be avoided. The truth is, that, the primitive wants of nature once tolerably satisfied, the majority of mankind, even in a civilised life full of solicitations, are with difficulty aroused to the distinct conception of an object towards which they will direct their actions with careful adaptation, and it is yet rarer to find one who can persist in the systematic pursuit of such an end. Few lives are shaped, few characters formed, by the contemplation of definite consequences seen from a distance and made the goal of continuous effort or the beacon of a constantly avoided danger: such control by foresight, such vivid picturing and practical logic are the distinction of exceptionally strong natures; but society is chiefly made up of human beings whose daily acts are all performed either in unreflecting obedience to custom and routine or from immediate promptings of thought or feeling to execute an immediate purpose. They pay their poor-rates, give their vote in affairs political or parochial, wear a certain amount of starch, hinder boys from tormenting the helpless, and spend money on tedious observances called pleasures, without mentally adjusting these practices to their own well-understood interest or to the general, ultimate welfare of the human race; and when they fall into

ungraceful compliment, excessive smiling, or other luckless efforts
of complaisant behaviour, these are but the tricks or habits gradually formed under the successive promptings of a wish to be agreeable, stimulated day by day without any widening resources for
gratifying the wish. It does not in the least follow that they are
seeking by studied hypocrisy to get something for themselves.
And so with Hinze's deferential bearing, complimentary parenthe-
ses, and worshipful tones, which seem to some like the over-acting
of a part in a comedy. He expects no appointment or other ap-
preciable gain through Tulpian's favour; he has no doubleness
toward Felicia; there is no sneering or backbiting obverse to his
ecstatic admiration. He is very well off in the world, and cherishes
no unsatisfied ambition that could feed design and direct flattery.
As you perceive, he has had the education and other advantages
of a gentleman without being conscious of marked result, such as a
decided preference for any particular ideas or functions: his mind
is furnished as hotels are, with everything for occasional and
transient use. But one cannot be an Englishman and gentleman
in general: it is in the nature of things that one must have an
individuality, though it may be of an often-repeated type. As
Hinze in growing to maturity had grown into a particular form and
expression of person, so he necessarily gathered a manner and
frame of speech which made him additionally recognisable. His
nature is not tuned to the pitch of a genuine direct admiration,
only to an attitudinising deference which does not fatigue itself
with the formation of real judgments. All human achievement
must be wrought down to this spoon-meat—this mixture of other
persons' washy opinions and his own flux of reverence for what is
third-hand, before Hinze can find a relish for it.

He has no more leading characteristic than the desire to stand
well with those who are justly distinguished; he has no base ad-
mirations, and you may know by his entire presentation of himself,
from the management of his hat to the angle at which he keeps his
right foot, that he aspires to correctness. Desiring to behave
becomingly and also to make a figure in dialogue, he is only like
the bad artist whose picture is a failure. We may pity these ill-
gifted strivers, but not pretend that their works are pleasant to
behold. A man is bound to know something of his own weight
and muscular dexterity, and the puny athlete is called foolish

before he is seen to be thrown. Hinze has not the stuff in him to be at once agreeably conversational and sincere, and he has got himself up to be at all events agreeably conversational. Notwithstanding this deliberateness of intention in his talk he is unconscious of falsity, for he has not enough of deep and lasting impression to find a contrast or diversity between his words and his thoughts. He is not fairly to be called a hypocrite, but I have already confessed to the more exasperation at his make-believe reverence, because it has no deep hunger to excuse it.

ONLY TEMPER

WHAT is temper? Its primary meaning, the proportion and mode in which qualities are mingled, is much neglected in popular speech, yet even here the word often carries a reference to an habitual state or general tendency of the organism in distinction from what are held to be specific virtues and vices. As people confess to bad memory without expecting to sink in mental reputation, so we hear a man declared to have a bad temper and yet glorified as the possessor of every high quality. When he errs or in any way commits himself, his temper is accused, not his character, and it is understood that but for a brutal bearish mood he is kindness itself. If he kicks small animals, swears violently at a servant who mistakes orders, or is grossly rude to his wife, it is remarked apologetically that these things mean nothing —they are all temper.

Certainly there is a limit to this form of apology, and the forgery of a bill, or the ordering of goods without any prospect of paying for them, has never been set down to an unfortunate habit of sulkiness or of irascibility. But on the whole there is a peculiar exercise of indulgence towards the manifestations of bad temper which tends to encourage them, so that we are in danger of having among us a number of virtuous persons who conduct themselves detestably, just as we have hysterical patients who, with sound organs, are apparently labouring under many sorts of organic disease. Let it be admitted, however, that a man may be "a good fellow" and yet have a bad temper, so bad that we recognise his merits with reluctance, and are inclined to resent his occasionally amiable behaviour as an unfair demand on our admiration.

Touchwood is that kind of good fellow. He is by turns insolent, quarrelsome, repulsively haughty to innocent people who approach him with respect, neglectful of his friends, angry in the face of legitimate demands, procrastinating in the fulfilment of such demands, prompted to rude words and harsh looks by a moody disgust with his fellow-men in general—and yet, as everybody will assure you, the soul of honour, a steadfast friend, a defender of the oppressed, an affectionate-hearted creature. Pity that, after a certain experience of his moods, his intimacy becomes insupportable! A man who uses his balmorals to tread on your toes with much frequency and an unmistakeable emphasis may prove a fast friend in adversity, but meanwhile your adversity has not arrived and your toes are tender. The daily sneer or growl at your remarks is not to be made amends for by a possible eulogy or defence of your understanding against depreciators who may not present themselves, and on an occasion which may never arise. I cannot submit to a chronic state of blue and green bruise as a form of insurance against an accident.

Touchwood's bad temper is of the contradicting pugnacious sort. He is the honourable gentleman in opposition, whatever proposal or proposition may be broached, and when others join him he secretly damns their superfluous agreement, quickly discovering that his way of stating the case is not exactly theirs. An invitation or any sign of expectation throws him into an attitude of refusal. Ask his concurrence in a benevolent measure: he will not decline to give it, because he has a real sympathy with good aims; but he complies resentfully, though where he is let alone he will do much more than any one would have thought of asking for. No man would shrink with greater sensitiveness from the imputation of not paying his debts, yet when a bill is sent in with any promptitude he is inclined to make the tradesman wait for the money he is in such a hurry to get. One sees that this antagonistic temper must be much relieved by finding a particular object, and that its worst moments must be those where the mood is that of vague resistence, there being nothing specific to oppose. Touchwood is never so little engaging as when he comes down to breakfast with a cloud on his brow, after parting from you the night before with an affectionate effusiveness at the end of a confidential conversation which has assured you of mutual understanding. Impossible that you can have committed any offence. If mice have disturbed him, that is not your fault; but, nevertheless, your cheerful greeting had better not convey any reference to the weather, else it will be met by a sneer which, taking you unawares, may give you a crushing sense that you make a poor figure with your cheerfulness, which was not asked for. Some daring person perhaps introduces another topic, and uses the delicate flattery of appealing to Touchwood for his opinion, the topic being included in his favourite studies. An indistinct muttering, with a look at the carving-knife in reply, teaches that daring person how ill he has chosen a market for his deference. If Touchwood's behaviour affects you very closely you had better break your leg in the course of the day: his bad temper will then vanish at once: he will take a painful journey on your behalf; he will sit up with you night after night; he will do all the work of your department so as to save you from any loss in consequence of your accident; he will be even uniformly tender to you till you are well on your legs again, when he will some fine morning insult you without provocation, and make you wish that his generous goodness to you had not closed your lips against retort.

It is not always necessary that a friend should break his leg for Touchwood to feel compunction and endeavour to make amends for his bearishness or insolence. He becomes spontaneously conscious that he has misbehaved, and he is not only ashamed of himself, but has the better prompting to try and heal any wound he has inflicted. Unhappily the habit of being offensive "without meaning it" leads usually to a way of making amends which the injured person cannot but regard as a being amiable without meaning it. The kindnesses, the complimentary indications or assurances, are apt to appear in the light of a penance adjusted to the foregoing lapses, and by the very contrast they offer call up a keener memory of the wrong they atone for. They are not a spontaneous prompting of goodwill, but an elaborate compensation. And, in fact, Dion's atoning friendliness has a ring of artificiality. Because he formerly disguised his good feeling towards you he now expresses more than he quite feels. It is in vain. Having made you extremely uncomfortable last week he has absolutely diminished his power of making you happy to-day: he struggles against this result by excessive effort, but he has taught you to observe his fitfulness rather than to be warmed by his episodic show of regard.

I suspect that many persons who have an uncertain, incalculable temper flatter themselves that it enhances their fascination; but perhaps they are under the prior mistake of exaggerating the charm which they suppose to be thus strengthened; in any case they will do well not to trust in the attractions of caprice and moodiness for a long continuance or for close intercourse. A pretty woman may fan the flame of distant adorers by harassing them, but if she lets one of them make her his wife, the point of view from which he will look at her poutings and tossings and mysterious inability to be pleased will be seriously altered. And if slavery to a pretty woman, which seems among the least conditional forms of abject service, will not bear too great a strain from her bad temper even though her beauty remain the same, it is clear that a man whose claims lie in his high character or high performances had need impress us very constantly with his peculiar value and indispensableness, if he is to test our patience by an uncertainty of temper which leaves us absolutely without grounds for guessing how he will receive our persons or humbly advanced opinions, or what line he will take on any but the most momentous occasions.

For it is among the repulsive effects of this bad temper, which is supposed to be compatible with shining virtues, that it is apt to determine a man's sudden adhesion to an opinion, whether on a personal or impersonal matter, without leaving him time to consider his grounds. The adhesion is sudden and momentary, but it either forms a precedent for his line of thought and action, or it is presently seen to have been inconsistent with his true mind. This determination of partisanship by temper has its worst effects in the career of the public man, who is always in danger of getting so enthralled by his own words that he looks into facts and questions not to get rectifying knowledge, but to get evidence that will justify his actual attitude which was assumed under an impulse dependent on something else than knowledge. There has been plenty of insistence on the evil of swearing by the words of a master, and having the judgment uniformly controlled by a "He said it;" but a much worse woe to befall a man is to have every judgment controlled by an "I said it"—to make a divinity of his own short-sightedness or passion-led aberration and explain the world in its honour. There is hardly a more pitiable degradation than this for a man of high gifts. Hence I cannot join with those who wish that Touchwood, being young enough to enter on public life, should get elected for Parliament and use his excellent abilities to serve his country in that conspicuous manner. For hitherto, in the less momentous incidents of private life, his capricious temper has only produced the minor evil of inconsistency, and he is even greatly at ease in contradicting himself, provided he can contradict you, and disappoint any smiling expectation you may have shown that the impressions you are uttering are likely to meet with his sympathy, considering that the day before he himself gave you the example which your mind is following. He is at least free from those fetters of self-justification which are the curse of parliamentary speaking, and what I rather desire for him is that he should produce the great book which he is generally pronounced capable of writing, and put his best self imperturbably on record for the advantage of society; because I should then have steady ground for bearing with his diurnal incalculableness, and could fix my gratitude as by a strong staple to that unvarying monumental service. Unhappily, Touchwood's great powers have been only so far manifested as to be believed in, not demonstrated. Everybody rates them highly, and thinks that whatever he chose to do would be done in a first-rate manner. Is it his love of disappointing complacent expectancy which has gone so far as to keep up this lamentable negation, and made him resolve not to write the comprehensive work which he would have written if nobody had expected it of him?

One can see that if Touchwood were to become a public man and take to frequent speaking on platforms or from his seat in the House, it would hardly be possible for him to maintain much integrity of opinion, or to avoid courses of partisanship which a healthy public sentiment would stamp with discredit. Say that he were endowed with the purest honesty, it would inevitably be dragged captive by this mysterious, Protean bad temper. There would be the fatal public necessity of justifying oratorical Temper which had got on its legs in its bitter mood and made insulting imputations, or of keeping up some decent show of consistency with opinions vented out of Temper's contradictoriness. And words would have to be followed up by acts of adhesion.

Certainly if a bad-tempered man can be admirably virtuous, he must be so under extreme difficulties. I doubt the possibility that a high order of character can coexist with a temper like Touchwood's. For it is of the nature of such temper to interrupt the formation of healthy mental habits, which depend on a growing harmony between perception, conviction, and impulse. There may be good feelings, good deeds—for a human nature may pack endless varieties and blessed inconsistencies in its windings—but it is essential to what is worthy to be called high character, that it may be safely calculated on, and that its qualities shall have taken the form of principles or laws habitually, if not perfectly, obeyed.

If a man frequently passes unjust judgments, takes up false attitudes, intermits his acts of kindness with rude behaviour or cruel words, and falls into the consequent vulgar error of supposing that he can make amends by laboured agreeableness, I cannot consider such courses any the less ugly because they are ascribed to "temper." Especially I object to the assumption that his having a fundamentally good disposition is either an apology or a compensation for his bad behaviour. If his temper yesterday made him lash the horses, upset the curricle and cause a breakage in my rib, I feel it no compensation that to-day he vows he will drive me anywhere in the gentlest manner any day as long as he lives. Yesterday was what it was, my rib is paining me, it is not a main object of my life to be driven by Touchwood—and I have no confidence in his lifelong gentleness. The utmost form of placability I am capable of is to try and remember his better deeds already performed, and, mindful of my own offences, to bear him no malice. But I cannot accept his amends.

If the bad-tempered man wants to apologise he had need to do it on a large public scale, make some beneficent discovery, produce some stimulating work of genius, invent some powerful process—prove himself such a good to contemporary multitudes and future generations, as to make the discomfort he causes his friends and acquaintances a vanishing quality, a trifle even in their own estimate.

A POLITICAL MOLECULE

THE most arrant denier must admit that a man often furthers larger ends than he is conscious of, and that while he is transacting his particular affairs with the narrow pertinacity of a respectable ant, he subserves an economy larger than any purpose of his own. Society is happily not dependent for the growth of fellowship on the small minority already endowed with comprehensive sympathy: any molecule of the body politic, working towards his own interest in an orderly way gets his understanding more or less penetrated with the fact that his interest is included in that of a large number. I have watched several political molecules being educated in this way by the nature of things into a faint feeling of fraternity. But at this moment I am thinking of Spike, an elector who voted on the side of Progress though he was not inwardly attached to it under that name. For abstractions are deities having many specific names, local habitations, and forms of activity, and so get a multitude of devout servants who care no more for them under their highest titles than the celebrated person who, putting with forcible brevity a view of human motives now much insisted on, asked what Posterity had done for him that he should care for Posterity? To many minds, even among the ancients (thought by some to have been invariably poetical) the goddess of wisdom was doubtless worshipped simply as the patroness of spinning and weaving. Now spinning and weaving from a manufacturing, wholesale point of view, was the chief form under which Spike from early years had unconsciously been a devotee of Progress.

He was a political molecule of the most gentlemanlike appearance, not less than six feet high, and showing the utmost nicety in the care of his person and equipment. His umbrella was especially remarkable for its neatness, though perhaps he swung it unduly in walking. His complexion was fresh, his eyes small, bright, and twinkling. He was seen to great advantage in a hat and great-coat —garments frequently fatal to the impressiveness of shorter figures; but when he was uncovered in the drawing-room, it was impossible not to observe that his head shelved off too rapidly from the eyebrows towards the crown, and that his length of limb seemed to have used up his mind so as to cause an air of abstraction from conversational topics. He appeared, indeed, to be preoccupied with a sense of his exquisite cleanliness, clapped his hands together and rubbed them frequently, straightened his back, and even opened his mouth and closed it again with a slight snap, apparently for no other purpose than the confirmation to himself of his own powers in that line. These are innocent exercises, but they are not such as give weight to a man's personality. Sometimes Spike's mind, emerging from its preoccupation, burst forth in a remark delivered with smiling zest; as, that he did like to see gravel walks well rolled, or that a lady should always wear the best jewellery, or that a bride was a most interesting object; but finding these ideas received rather coldly, he would relapse into abstraction, draw up his back, wrinkle his brows longitudinally, and seem to regard society, even including gravel walks, jewellery, and brides, as essentially a poor affair. Indeed his habit of mind was desponding, and he took melancholy views as to the possible extent of human pleasure and the value of existence. Especially after he had made his fortune in the cotton manufacture, and had thus attained the chief object of his ambition—the object which had engaged his talent for order and persevering application. For his easy leisure caused him much *ennui*. He was abstemious, and had none of those temptations to sensual excess which fill up a man's time first with indulgence and then with the process of getting well from its effects. He had not, indeed, exhausted the sources of knowledge, but here again his notions of human pleasure were narrowed by his want of appetite; for though he seemed rather surprised at the consideration that Alfred the Great was a Catholic, or that apart from the Ten Commandments any conception of moral conduct had occurred to mankind, he was not simulated to further inquiries on these remote matters. Yet he aspired to what he regarded as intellectual society, willingly entertained beneficed clergymen, and bought the books he heard spoken of, arranging them carefully on the shelves of what he called his library, and occasionally sitting alone in the same room with them. But some minds seem well glazed by nature against the admission of knowledge, and Spike's was one of them. It was not, however, entirely so with regard to politics. He had had a strong opinion about the Reform Bill, and saw clearly that the large trading towns ought to send members. Portraits of the Reform heroes hung framed and glazed in his library: he prided himself on being a Liberal. In this last particular, as well as in not giving benefactions and not making loans without interest, he showed unquestionable firmness. On the Repeal of the Corn Laws, again, he was thoroughly convinced. His mind was expansive toward foreign markets, and his imagination could see that the people from whom we took corn might be able to take the cotton goods which they had hitherto dispensed with. On his conduct in these political concerns, his wife, otherwise influential as a woman who belonged to a family with a title in it, and who had condescended in marrying him, could gain no hold: she had to blush a little at what was called her husband's "radicalism"—an epithet which was a very unfair impeachment of Spike, who never went to the root of anything. But he understood his own trading affairs, and in this way became a genuine, constant political element. If he had been born a little later he could have been accepted as an eligible member of Parliament, and if he had belonged to a high family he might have done for a member of the Government. Perhaps his indifference to "views" would have passed for administrative judiciousness, and he would have been so generally silent that he must often have been silent in the right place. But this is empty speculation: there is no warrant for saying what Spike would have been and known so as to have made a calculable political element, if he had not been educated by having to manage his trade. A small mind trained to useful occupation for the satisfying of private need becomes a representative of genuine class-needs. Spike objected to certain items of legislation because they hampered his own trade, but his neighbours' trade was hampered by the same causes; and though he would have been simply selfish in a question of light or water between himself and a fellow-townsman, his need for a change in legislation, being shared by all his neighbours in trade, ceased to be simply selfish, and raised him to a sense of common injury and common benefit. True, if the law could have been changed for the benefit of his particular business, leaving the cotton trade in general in a sorry condition while he prospered, Spike might not have thought that result intolerably unjust; but the nature of things did not allow of such a result being contemplated as possible; it allowed of an enlarged market for Spike only through the enlargement of his neighbours' market, and the Possible is always the ultimate master of our efforts and desires. Spike was obliged to contemplate a general benefit, and thus became public-spirited in spite of himself. Or rather, the nature of things transmuted his active egoism into a demand for a public benefit.

Certainly, if Spike had been born a marquis he could not have had the same chance of being useful as a political element. But he might have had the same appearance, have been equally null in conversation, sceptical as to the reality of pleasure, and destitute of historical knowledge; perhaps even dimly disliking Jesuitism as a quality in Catholic minds, or regarding Bacon as the inventor of physical science. The depths of middle-aged gentlemen's ignorance will never be known, for want of public examinations in this branch.

A HALF–BREED

AN early deep-seated love to which we become faithless has its unfailing Nemesis, if only in that division of soul which narrows all newer joys by the intrusion of regret and the established presentiment of change. I refer not merely to the love of a person, but to the love of ideas, practical beliefs, and social habits. And faithlessness here means not a gradual conversion dependent on enlarged knowledge, but a yielding to seductive circumstance; not a conviction that the original choice was a mistake, but a subjection to incidents that flatter a growing desire. In this sort of love it is the forsaker who has the melancholy lot; for an abandoned belief may be more effectively vengeful than Dido. The child of a wandering tribe, caught young and trained to polite life, if he feels an hereditary yearning can run away to the old wilds and get his nature into tune. But there is no such recovery possible to the man who remembers what he once believed without being convinced that he was in error, who feels within him unsatisfied stirrings toward old beloved habits and intimacies from which he has far receded without conscious justification or unwavering sense of superior attractiveness in the new. This involuntary renegade has his character hopelessly jangled and out of tune. He is like an organ with its stops in the lawless condition of obtruding themselves without method, so that hearers are amazed by the most unexpected transitions—the trumpet breaking in on the flute, and the oböe confounding both.

Hence the lot of Mixtus affects me pathetically, notwithstanding that he spends his growing wealth with liberality and manifest enjoyment. To most observers he appears to be simply one of the fortunate and also sharp commercial men who began with meaning to be rich, and have become what they meant to be: a man never taken to be well-born, but surprisingly better informed than the well-born usually are, and distinguished among ordinary commercial magnates by a personal kindness which prompts him not only to help the suffering in a material way through his wealth, but also by direct ministration of his own; yet with all this, diffusing, as it were, the odour of a man delightedly conscious of his wealth as an equivalent for the other social distinctions of rank and intellect which he can thus admire without envying. Hardly one among those superficial observers can suspect that he aims or has ever aimed at being a writer; still less can they imagine that his mind is often moved by strong currents of regret and of the most unworldly sympathies from the memories of a youthful time when his chosen associates were men and women whose only distinction was a religious, a philanthropic, or an intellectual enthusiasm, when the lady on whose words his attention most hung was a writer of minor religious literature, when he was a visitor and exhorter of the poor in the alleys of a great provincial town, and when he attended the lectures given specially to young men by Mr Apollos, the eloquent congregational preacher, who had studied in Germany and had liberal advanced views then far beyond the ordinary teaching of his sect. At that time Mixtus thought himself a young man of socially reforming ideas, of religious principles and religious yearnings. It was within his prospects also to be rich, but he looked forward to a use of his riches chiefly for reforming and religious purposes. His opinions were of a strongly democratic stamp, except that even then, belonging to the class of employers, he was opposed to all demands in the employed that would restrict the expansiveness of trade. He was the most democratic in relation to the unreasonable privileges of the aristocracy and landed interest; and he had also a religious sense of brotherhood with the poor. Altogether, he was a sincerely benevolent young man, interested in ideas, and renouncing personal ease for the sake of study, religious communion, and good works. If you had known him then, you would have expected him to marry a highly serious and perhaps literary woman, sharing his benevolent and religious habits, and likely to encourage his studies—a woman who along with himself would play a distinguished part in one of the most enlightened religious circles of a great provincial capital.

How is it that Mixtus finds himself in a London mansion, and in society totally unlike that which made the ideal of his younger years? And whom *did* he marry?

Why, he married Scintilla, who fascinated him, as she had fascinated others, by her prettiness, her liveliness, and her music. It is a common enough case, that of a man being suddenly captivated by a woman nearly the opposite of his ideal; or if not wholly captivated, at least effectively captured by a combination of circumstances along with an unwarily manifested inclination which might otherwise have been transient. Mixtus was captivated and then captured on the worldly side of his disposition, which had been always growing and flourishing side by side with his philanthropic and religious tastes. He had ability in business, and he had early meant to be rich; also, he was getting rich, and the taste for such success was naturally growing with the pleasure of rewarded exertion. It was during a business sojourn in London that he met Scintilla, who, though without fortune, associated with families of Greek merchants living in a style of splendour, and with artists patronised by such wealthy entertainers. Mixtus on this occasion became familiar with a world in which wealth seemed the key to a more brilliant sort of dominance than that of a religious patron in the provincial circles of X. Would it not be possible to unite the two kinds of sway? A man bent on the most useful ends might, *with a fortune large enough,* make morality magnificent, and recommend religious principle by showing it in combination with the best kind ot house and the most liberal of tables; also with a wife whose graces, wit, and accomplishments gave a finish sometimes lacking even to establishments got up with that unhesitating worldliness to which high cost is a sufficient reason. Enough.

Mixtus married Scintilla. Now this lively lady knew nothing of Nonconformists, except that they were unfashionable: she did not distinguish one conventicle from another, and Mr Apollos with his enlightened interpretations seemed to her as heavy a bore, if not quite so ridiculous, as Mr Johns could have been with his solemn twang at the Baptist chapel in the lowest suburbs, or as a local preacher among the Methodists. In general, people who appeared seriously to believe in any sort of doctrine, whether religious, social, or philosophical, seemed rather absurd to Scintilla. Ten to one these theoretic people pronounced oddly, had some reason or other for saying that the most agreeable things were wrong, wore objectionable clothes, and wanted you to subscribe to something. They were probably ignorant of art and music, did not understand *badinage*, and, in fact, could talk of nothing amusing. In Scintilla's eyes the majority of persons were ridiculous and deplorably wanting in that keen perception of what was good taste, with which she herself was blessed by nature and education; but the people understood to be religious or otherwise theoretic, were the most ridiculous of all, without being proportionately amusing and invitable.

Did Mixtus not discover this view of Scintilla's before their marriage? Or did he allow her to remain in ignorance of habits and opinions which had made half the occupation of his youth?

When a man is inclined to marry a particular woman, and has made any committal of himself, this woman's opinions, however different from his own, are readily regarded as part of her pretty ways, especially if they are merely negative; as, for example, that she does not insist on the Trinity, or on the rightfulness or expediency of church rates, but simply regards her lover's troubling himself in disputation on these heads as stuff and nonsense. The man feels his own superior strength, and is sure that marriage will make no difference to him on the subjects about which he is in earnest. And to laugh at men's affairs is a woman's privilege, tending to enliven the domestic hearth. If Scintilla had no liking for the best sort of nonconformity, she was without any troublesome bias toward Episcopacy, Anglicanism, and early sacraments, and was quite contented not to go to church.

As to Scintilla's acquaintance with her lover's tastes on these subjects, she was equally convinced on her side that a husband's queer ways while he was a bachelor would be easily laughed out of him when he had married an adroit woman. Mixtus, she felt, was an excellent creature, quite likable, who was getting rich; and Scintilla meant to have all the advantages of a rich man's wife. She was not in the least a wicked woman; she was simply a pretty animal of the ape kind, with an aptitude for certain accomplishments which education had made the most of.

But we have seen what has been the result to poor Mixtus. He has become richer even than he dreamed of being, has a little palace in London, and entertains with splendour the half-aristocratic, professional, and artistic society which he is proud to think select. This society regards him as a clever fellow in his particular branch, seeing that he has become a considerable capitalist, and as a man desirable to have on the list of one's acquaintance. But from every other point of view Mixtus finds himself personally submerged: what he happens to think is not felt by his esteemed guests to be of any consequence, and what he used to think with the ardour of conviction he now hardly ever expresses. He is transplanted, and the sap within him has long been diverted into other than the old lines of vigorous growth. How could he speak to the artist Crespi or to Sir Hong Kong Bantam about the enlarged doctrine of Mr Apollos? How could he mention to them his former efforts toward evangelising the inhabitants of the X. alleys? And his references to his historical and geographical studies towards a survey of possible markets for English products are received with an air of ironical suspicion by many of his political friends, who take his pretension to give advice concerning the Amazon, the Euphrates, and the Niger as equivalent to the currier's wide views on the applicability of leather. He can only make a figure through his genial hospitality. It is in vain that he buys the best pictures and statues of the best artists. Nobody will call him a judge in art. If his pictures and statues are well chosen it is generally thought that Scintilla told him what to buy; and yet Scintilla in other connections is spoken of as having only a superficial and often questionable taste. Mixtus, it is decided, is a good fellow, not ignorant— no, really having a good deal of knowledge as well as sense, but not easy to classify otherwise than as a rich man. He has consequently become a little uncertain to as his own point of view, and in his most unreserved moments of friendly intercourse, even when speaking to listeners whom he thinks likely to sympathise with the earlier part of his career, he presents himself in all his various aspects and feels himself in turn what he has been, what he is, and what others take him to be (for this last status is what we must all more or less accept). He will recover with some glow of enthusiasm the vision of his old associates, the particular limit he was once accustomed to trace of freedom in religious speculation, and his old ideal of a worthy life; but he will presently pass to the argument that money is the only means by which you can get what is best worth having in the world, and will arrive at the exclamation "Give me money!" with the tone and gesture of a man who both feels and knows. Then if one of his audience, not having money, remarks that a man may have made up his mind to do without money because he prefers something else, Mixtus is with him immediately, cordially concurring in the supreme value of mind and genius, which indeed make his own chief delight, in that he is able to entertain the admirable possessors of these attributes at his own table, though not himself reckoned among them. Yet, he will proceed to observe, there was a time when he sacrificed his sleep to study, and even now amid the press of business he from time to time thinks of taking up the manuscripts which he hopes some day to complete, and is always increasing his collection of valuable works bearing on his favourite topics. And it is true that he has read much in certain directions, and can remember what he has read; he knows the history and theories of colonisation, and the social condition of countries that do not at present consume a sufficiently large share of our products and manufactures. He continues his early habit of regarding the spread of Christianity as a great result of our commercial intercourse with black, brown, and yellow populations; but this is an idea not spoken of in the sort of fashionable society that Scintilla collects round her husband's table, and Mixtus now philosophically reflects that the cause must come before the effect, and that the thing to be directly striven for is the commercial intercourse, not excluding a little war if that also should prove needful as a pioneer of Christianity. He has long been wont to feel bashful about his former religion; as if it were an old attachment having consequences which he did not abandon but kept in decent privacy, his avowed objects and actual position being incompatible with their public acknowledgment.

There is the same kind of fluctuation in his aspect toward social questions and duties. He has not lost the kindness that used to make him a benefactor and succourer of the needy, and he is still liberal in helping forward the clever and industrious; but in his active superintendence of commercial undertakings he has contracted more and more of the bitterness which capitalists and employers often feel to be a reasonable mood toward obstructive proletaries. Hence many who have occasionally met him when trade questions were being discussed, conclude him to be indistinguishable from the ordinary run of moneyed and money-getting men. Indeed, hardly any of his acquaintances know what Mixtus really is, considered as a whole—nor does Mixtus himself know it.

DEBASING THE MORAL CURRENCY

"IL ne faut pas mettre un ridicule où il n'y en a point: c'est se gâter le goût, c'est corrompre son jugement et celui des autres. Mais le ridicule qui est quelque part, il faut l'y voir, l'en tirer avec grâce et d'une manière qui plaise et qui instruise."

I am fond of quoting this passage from La Bruyère, because the subject is one where I like to show a Frenchman on my side, to save my sentiments from being set down to my peculiar dulness and deficient sense of the ludicrous, and also that they may profit by that enhancement of ideas when presented in a foreign tongue, that glamour of unfamiliarity conferring a dignity on the foreign names of very common things, of which even a philosopher like Dugald Stewart confesses the influence. I remember hearing a fervid woman attempt to recite in English the narrative of a begging Frenchman who described the violent death of his father in the July days. The narrative had impressed her, through the mists of her flushed anxiety to understand it, as something quite grandly pathetic; but finding the facts turn out meagre, and her audience cold, she broke off, saying, "It sounded so much finer in French— *j'ai vu le sang de mon père*, and so on—I wish I could repeat it in French." This was a pardonable illusion in an old-fashioned lady who had not received the polyglot education of the present day; but I observe that even now much nonsense and bad taste win admiring acceptance solely by virtue of the French language, and one may fairly desire that what seems a just discrimination should profit by the fashionable prejudice in favor of La Bruyère's idiom. But I wish he had added that the habit of dragging the ludicrous into topics where the chief interest is of a different or even opposite kind is a sign not of endowment, but of deficiency. The art of spoiling is within reach of the dullest faculty: the coarsest clown with a hammer in his hand might chip the nose off every statue and bust in the Vatican, and stand grinning at the effect of his work. Because wit is an exquisite product of high powers, we are not therefore forced to admit the sadly confused inference of the monotonous jester that he is establishing his superiority over every less facetious person, and over every topic on which he is ignorant or insensible, by being uneasy until he has distorted it in the small cracked mirror which he carries about with him as a joking apparatus. Some high authority is needed to give many worthy and timid persons the freedom of muscular repose under the growing demand on them to laugh when they have no other reason than the peril of being taken for dullards; still more to inspire them with the courage to say that they object to the theatrical spoiling for themselves and their children of all affecting themes, all the grander deeds and aims of men, by burlesque associations adapted to the taste of rich fish-mongers in the stalls and their assistants in the gallery. The English people in the present generation are falsely reputed to know Shakespeare (as, by some innocent persons, the Florentine mule-drivers are believed to have known the *Divina Commedia*, not, perhaps, excluding all the subtle discourses in the *Purgatorio* and *Paradiso*); but there seems a clear prospect that in the coming generation he will be known to them through burlesques, and that his plays will find a new life as pantomimes. A bottle-nosed Lear will come on with a monstrous corpulence from which he will frantically dance himself free during the midnight storm; Rosalind and Celia will join in a grotesque ballet with shepherds and shepherdesses; Ophelia in fleshings and a voluminous brevity of grenadine will dance through the mad scene, finishing with the famous "attitude of the scissors" in the arms of Laertes; and all the speeches in "Hamlet" will be so ingeniously parodied that the originals will be reduced to a mere *memoria technica* of the improver's puns—premonitory signs of a hideous millennium, in which the lion will have to lie down with the lascivious monkeys whom (if we may trust Pliny) his soul naturally abhors.

I have been amazed to find that some artists whose own works have the ideal stamp, are quite insensible to the damaging tendency of the burlesquing spirit which ranges to and fro and up and down on the earth, seeing no reason (except a precarious censorship) why it should not appropriate every sacred, heroic, and pathetic theme which serves to make up the treasure of human admiration, hope, and love. One would have thought that their own half-despairing efforts to invest in worthy outward shape the vague inward impressions of sublimity, and the consciousness of an implicit ideal in the commonest scenes, might have made them susceptible of some disgust or alarm at a species of burlesque which is likely to render their compositions no better than a dissolving view, where every noble form is seen melting into its preposterous caricature. It used to be imagined of the unhappy medieval Jews that they parodied Calvary by crucifying dogs; if they had been guilty they would at least have had the excuse of the hatred and rage begotten by persecution. Are we on the way to a parody which shall have no other excuse than the reckless search after fodder for degraded appetites—after the pay to be earned by pasturing Circe's herd where they may defile every monument of that growing life which should have kept them human?

The world seems to me well supplied with what is genuinely ridiculous: wit and humour may play as harmlessly or beneficently round the changing facets of egoism, absurdity, and vice, as the sunshine over the rippling sea or the dewy meadows. Why should we make our delicious sense of the ludicrous, with its invigorating shocks of laughter and its irrepressible smiles which are the outglow of an inward radiation as gentle and cheering as the warmth of morning, flourish like a brigand on the robbery of our mental wealth?—or let it take its exercise as a madman might, if allowed a free nightly promenade, by drawing the populace with bonfires which leave some venerable structure a blackened ruin or send a scorching smoke across the portraits of the past, at which we once looked with a loving recognition of fellowship, and disfigure them into butts of mockery?—nay, worse—use it to degrade the healthy appetites and affections of our nature as they are seen to be degraded in insane patients whose system, all out of joint, finds matter for screaming laughter in mere topsy-turvy, makes every passion preposterous or obscene, and turns the hard-won order of life into a second chaos hideous enough to make one wail that the first was ever thrilled with light?

This is what I call debasing the moral currency: lowering the value of every inspiring fact and tradition so that it will command less and less of the spiritual products, the generous motives which sustain the charm and elevation of our social existence—the something besides bread by which man saves his soul alive. The bread-winner of the family may demand more and more coppery shillings, or assignats, or greenbacks for his day's work, and so get the needful quantum of food; but let that moral currency be emptied of its value—let a greedy buffoonery debase all historic beauty, majesty, and pathos, and the more you heap upon the desecrated symbols the greater will be the lack of the ennobling emotions which subdue the tyranny of suffering, and make ambition one with social virtue.

And yet, it seems, parents will put into the hands of their children ridiculous parodies (perhaps with more ridiculous "illustrations") of the poems which stirred their own tenderness or filial piety, and carry them to make their first acquaintance with great men, great works, or solemn crises through the medium of some miscellaneous burlesque which, with its idiotic puns and farcical attitudes, will remain among their primary associations, and reduce them throughout their time of studious preparation for life to the moral imbecility of an inward giggle at what might have stimulated their high emulation or fed the fountains of compassion, trust, and constancy. One wonders where these parents have deposited that stock of morally educating stimuli which is to be independent of poetic tradition, and to subsist in spite of the finest images being degraded and the finest words of genius being poisoned as with some befooling drug.

Will fine wit, will exquisite humour prosper the more through this turning of all things indiscriminately into food for a gluttonous laughter, an idle craving without sense of flavours? On the contrary. That delightful power which La Bruyère points to—"le ridicule qui est quelque part, il faut l'y voir, l'en tirer avec grâce et d'une manière qui plaise et qui instruise"—depends on a discrimination only compatible with the varied sensibilities which give sympathetic insight, and with the justice of perception which is another name for grave knowledge. Such a result is no more to be expected from faculties on the strain to find some small hook by which they may attach the lowest incongruity to the most momentous subject, than it is to be expected of a sharper, watching for gulls in a great political assemblage, that he will notice the blundering logic of partisan speakers, or season his observation with the salt of historical parallels. But after all our psychological teaching, and in the midst of our zeal for education, we are still, most of us, at the stage of believing that mental powers and habits have somehow, not perhaps in the general statement, but in any particular case, a kind of spiritual glaze against conditions which we are continually applying to them. We soak our children in habits of contempt and exultant gibing, and yet are confident that—as Clarissa one day said to me—"We can always teach them to be reverent in the right place, you know." And doubtless if she were to take her boys to see a burlesque Socrates, with swollen legs, dying in the utterance of cockney puns, and were to hang up a sketch of this comic scene among their bedroom prints, she would think this preparation not at all to the prejudice of their emotions on hearing their tutor read that narrative of the *Apology* which has been consecrated by the reverent gratitude of ages. This is the impoverishment that threatens our posterity:—a new Famine, a meagre fiend with lewd grin and clumsy hoof, is breathing a moral mildew over the harvest of our human sentiments. These are the most delicate elements of our too easily perishable civilisation. And here again I like to quote a French testimony. Sainte Beuve, referring to a time of insurrectionary disturbance, says: "Rien de plus prompt à baisser que la civilisation dans des crises comme celle-ci; on perd en trois semaines le résultat de plusieurs siècles. La civilisation, la *vie* est une chose apprise et inventée, qu'on le sache bien: '*Inventas aut qui vitam excoluere per artes.*' Les hommes après quelques années de paix oublient trop cette verité: ils arrivent à croire que la *culture* est chose innée, qu'elle est la même chose que la *nature*. La sauvagerie est toujours là à deux pas, et, dès qu'on lâche pied, elle recommence." We have been severely enough taught (if we were willing to learn) that our civilisation, considered as a splendid material fabric, is helplessly in peril without the spiritual police of sentiments or ideal feelings. And it is this invisible police which we had need, as a community, strive to maintain in efficient force. How if a dangerous "Swing" were sometimes disguised in a versatile entertainer devoted to the amusement of mixed audiences? And I confess that sometimes when I see a certain style of young lady, who checks our tender admiration with rouge and henna and all the blazonry of an extravagant expenditure, with slang and bold *brusquerie* intended to signify her emancipated view of things, and with cynical mockery which she mistakes for penetration, I am sorely tempted to hiss out *"Pétroleuse!"* It is a small matter to have our palaces set aflame compared with the misery of having our sense of a noble womanhood, which is the inspiration of a purifying shame, the promise of life-penetrating affection, stained and blotted out by images of repulsiveness. These things come—not of higher education, but—of dull ignorance fostered into pertness by the greedy vulgarity which reverses Peter's visionary lesson and learns to call all things common and unclean. It comes of debasing the moral currency.

The Tirynthians, according to an ancient story reported by Athenæus, becoming conscious that their trick of laughter at everything and nothing was making them unfit for the conduct of serious affairs, appealed to the Delphic oracle for some means of cure. The god prescribed a peculiar form of sacrifice, which would be effective if they could carry it through without laughing. They did their best; but the flimsy joke of a boy upset their unaccustomed gravity, and in this way the oracle taught them that even the gods could not prescribe a quick cure for a long vitiation, or give power and dignity to a people who in a crisis of the public well-being were at the mercy of a poor jest.

THE WASP CREDITED WITH THE HONEYCOMB

NO man, I imagine, would object more strongly than Euphorion to communistic principles in relation to material property, but with regard to property in ideas he entertains such principles willingly, and is disposed to treat the distinction between Mine and Thine in original authorship as egoistic, narrowing, and low. I have known him, indeed, insist, at some expense of erudition on the prior right of an ancient, a medieval, or an eighteenth century writer to be credited with a view or statement lately advanced with some show of originality; and this championship seems to imply a nicety of conscience towards the dead. He is evidently unwilling that his neighbours should get more credit than is due to them, and in this way he appears to recognise a certain proprietorship even in spiritual production. But perhaps it is no real inconsistency that, with regard to many instances of modern origination, it is his habit to talk with a Gallic largeness and refer to the universe: he expatiates on the diffusive nature of intellectual products, free and all-embracing as the liberal air; on the infinitesimal smallness of individual origination compared with the massive inheritance of thought on which every new generation enters; on that growing preparation for every epoch through which certain ideas or modes of view are said to be in the air, and, still more metaphorically speaking, to be inevitably absorbed, so that every one may be excused for not knowing how he got them. Above all, he insists on the proper subordination of the irritable self, the mere vehicle of an idea or combination which, being produced by the sum total of the human race, must belong to that multiple entity, from the accomplished lecturer or populariser who transmits it, to the remotest generation of Fuegians or Hottentots, however indifferent these may be to the superiority of their right above that of the eminently perishable dyspeptic author.

One may admit that such considerations carry a profound truth to be even religiously contemplated, and yet object all the more to the mode in which Euphorion seems to apply them. I protest against the use of these majestic conceptions to do the dirty work of unscrupulosity, and justify the non-payment of conscious debts which cannot be defined or enforced by the law. Especially since it is observable that the large views as to intellectual property which can apparently reconcile an able person to the use of lately borrowed ideas as if they were his own, when this spoliation is favoured by the public darkness, never hinder him from joining in the zealous tribute of recognition and applause to those warriors of Truth whose triumphal arches are seen in the public ways, those conquerors whose battles and "annexations" even the carpenters and bricklayers know by name. Surely the acknowledgment of a mental debt which will not be immediately detected, and may never be asserted, is a case to which the traditional susceptibility to "debts of honour" would be suitably transferred. There is no massive public opinion that can be expected to tell on these relations of thinkers and investigators—relations to be thoroughly understood and felt only by those who are interested in the life of ideas and acquainted with their history. To lay false claim to an invention or discovery which has an immediate market value; to vamp up a professedly new book of reference by stealing from the pages of one already produced at the cost of much labour and material; to copy somebody else's poem and send the manuscript to a magazine, or hand it about among friends as an original "effusion;" to deliver an elegant extract from a known writer as a piece of improvised eloquence:—these are the limits within which the dishonest pretence of originality is likely to get hissed or hooted and bring more or less shame on the culprit. It is not necessary to understand the merit of a performance, or even to spell with any comfortable confidence, in order to perceive at once that such pretences are not respectable. But the difference between these vulgar frauds, these devices of ridiculous jays whose ill-secured plumes are seen falling off them as they run, and the quiet appropriation of other people's philosophic or scientific ideas, can hardly be held to lie in their moral quality unless we take impunity as our criterion. The pitiable jays had no presumption in their favour and foolishly fronted an alert incredulity; but Euphorion, the accomplished theorist, has an audience who expect much of him, and take it as the most natural thing in the world that every unusual view which he presents anonymously should be due solely to his ingenuity. His borrowings are no incongruous feathers awkwardly stuck on; they have an appropriateness which makes them seem an answer to anticipation, like the return phrases of a melody. Certainly one cannot help the ignorant conclusions of polite society, and there are perhaps fashionable persons who, if a speaker has occasion to explain what the occiput is, will consider that he has lately discovered that curiously named portion of the animal frame: one cannot give a genealogical introduction to every long-stored item of fact or conjecture that may happen to be a revelation for the large class of persons who are understood to judge soundly on a small basis of knowledge. But Euphorion would be very sorry to have it supposed that he is unacquainted with the history of ideas, and sometimes carries even into minutiæ the evidence of his exact registration of names in connection with quotable phrases or suggestions: I can therefore only explain the apparent infirmity of his memory in cases of larger "conveyance" by supposing that he is accustomed by the very association of largeness to range them at once under those grand laws of the universe in the light of which Mine and Thine disappear and are resolved into Everybody's or Nobody's, and one man's particular obligations to another melt untraceably into the obligations of the earth to the solar system in general.

Euphorion himself, if a particular omission of acknowledgment were brought home to him, would probably take a narrower ground of explanation. It was a lapse of memory; or it did not occur to him as necessary in this case to mention a name, the source being well known—or (since this seems usually to act as a strong reason for mention) he rather abstained from adducing the name because it might injure the excellent matter advanced, just as an obscure trade-mark casts discredit on a good commodity, and even on the retailer who has furnished himself from a quarter not likely to be esteemed first-rate. No doubt this last is a genuine and frequent reason for the non-acknowledgment of indebtedness to what one may call impersonal as well as personal sources: even an American editor of school classics whose own English could not pass for more than a syntactical shoddy of the cheapest sort, felt it unfavourable to his reputation for sound learning that he should be obliged to the Penny Cyclopædia, and disguised his references to it under contractions in which *Us. Knowl.* took the place of the low word *Penny*. Works of this convenient stamp, easily obtained and well nourished with matter, are felt to be like rich but unfashionable relations who are visited and received in privacy, and whose capital is used or inherited without any ostentatious insistence on their names and places of abode. As to memory, it is known that this frail faculty naturally lets drop the facts which are less flattering to our self-love—when it does not retain them carefully as subjects not to be approached, marshy spots with a warning flag over them. But it is always interesting to bring forward eminent names, such as Patricius or Scaliger, Euler or Lagrange, Bopp or Humboldt. To know exactly what has been drawn from them is erudition and heightens our own influence, which seems advantageous to mankind; whereas to cite an author whose ideas may pass as higher currency under our own signature can have no object except the contradictory one of throwing the illumination over his figure when it is important to be seen oneself. All these reasons must weigh considerably with those speculative persons who have to ask themselves whether or not Universal Utilitarianism requires that in the particular instance before them they should injure a man who has been of service to them, and rob a fellow-workman of the credit which is due to him.

After all, however, it must be admitted that hardly any accusation is more difficult to prove, and more liable to be false, than that of a plagiarism which is the conscious theft of ideas and deliberate reproduction of them as original. The arguments on the side of acquittal are obvious and strong:—the inevitable coincidences of contemporary thinking; and our continual experience of finding notions turning up in our minds without any label on them to tell us whence they came; so that if we are in the habit of expecting much from our own capacity we accept them at once as a new inspiration. Then, in relation to the elder authors, there is the difficulty first of learning and then of remembering exactly what has been wrought into the backward tapestry of the world's history, together with the fact that ideas acquired long ago reappear as the sequence of an awakened interest or a line of inquiry which is really new in us, whence it is conceivable that if we were ancients some of us might be offering grateful hecatombs by mistake, and proving our honesty in a ruinously expensive manner. On the other hand, the evidence on which plagiarism is concluded is often of a kind which, though much trusted in questions of erudition and historical criticism, is apt to lead us injuriously astray in our daily judgments, especially of the resentful, condemnatory sort. How Pythagoras came by his ideas, whether St Paul was acquainted with all the Greek poets, what Tacitus must have known by hearsay and systematically ignored, are points on which a false persuasion of knowledge is less damaging to justice and charity than an erroneous confidence, supported by reasoning fundamentally similar, of my neighbour's blameworthy behaviour in a case where I am personally concerned. No premises require closer scrutiny than those which lead to the constantly echoed conclusion, "He must have known," or "He must have read." I marvel that this facility of belief on the side of knowledge can subsist under the daily demonstration that the easiest of all things to the human mind is *not* to know and *not* to read. To praise, to blame, to shout, grin, or hiss, where others shout, grin, or hiss— these are native tendencies; but to know and to read are artificial, hard accomplishments, concerning which the only safe supposition is, that as little of them has been done as the case admits. An author, keenly conscious of having written, can hardly help imagining his condition of lively interest to be shared by others, just as we are all apt to suppose that the chill or heat we are conscious of must be general, or even to think that our sons and daughters, our pet schemes, and our quarrelling correspondence, are themes to which intelligent persons will listen long without weariness. But if the ardent author happen to be alive to practical teaching he will soon learn to divide the larger part of the enlightened public into those who have not read him and think it necessary to tell him so when they meet him in polite society, and those who have equally abstained from reading him, but wish to conceal this negation, and speak of his "incomparable works" with that trust in testimony which always has its cheering side.

Hence it is worse than foolish to entertain silent suspicions of plagiarism, still more to give them voice, when they are founded on a construction of probabilities which a little more attention to everyday occurrences as a guide in reasoning would show us to be really worthless, considered as proof. The length to which one man's memory can go in letting drop associations that are vital to another can hardly find a limit. It is not to be supposed that a person desirous to make an agreeable impression on you would deliberately choose to insist to you, with some rhetorical sharpness, on an argument which you were the first to elaborate in public; yet any one who listens may overhear such instances of oblivious-ness. You naturally remember your peculiar connection with your acquaintance's judicious views; but why should *he?* Your father-hood, which is an intense feeling to you, is only an additional fact of meagre interest for him to remember; and a sense of obligation to the particular living fellow-struggler who has helped us in our thinking, is not yet a form of memory the want of which is felt to be disgraceful or derogatory, unless it is taken to be a want of polite instruction, or causes the missing of a cockade on a day of celebration. In our suspicions of plagiarism we must recognise, as the first weighty probability, that what we who feel injured remember best is precisely what is least likely to enter lastingly into the memory of our neighbours. But it is fair to maintain that the neighbour who borrows your property, loses it for a while, and when it turns up again forgets your connection with it and counts it his own, shows himself so much the feebler in grasp and rectitude of mind. Some absent persons cannot remember the state of wear in their own hats and umbrellas, and have no mental check to tell them that they have carried home a fellow-visitor's more recent purchase: they may be excellent householders, far removed from the suspicion of low devices, but one wishes them a more correct perception, and a more wary sense that a neighbour's umbrella may be newer than their own.

True, some persons are so constituted that the very excellence of an idea seems to them a convincing reason that it must be, if not solely, yet especially theirs. It fits in so beautifully with their general wisdom, it lies implicitly in so many of their manifested opinions, that if they have not yet expressed it (because of pre-occupation) it is clearly a part of their indigenous produce, and is proved by their immediate eloquent promulgation of it to belong more naturally and appropriately to them than to the person who seemed first to have alighted on it, and who sinks in their all-originating consciousness to that low kind of entity, a second cause. This is not lunacy, nor pretence, but a genuine state of mind very effective in practice, and often carrying the public with it, so that the poor Columbus is found to be a very faulty adventurer, and the continent is named after Amerigo. Lighter examples of this instinctive appropriation are constantly met with among brilliant talkers. Aquila is too agreeable and amusing for any one who is not himself bent on display to be angry at his conversational rapine —his habit of darting down on every morsel of booty that other birds may hold in their beaks, with an innocent air, as if it were all intended for his use, and honestly counted on by him as a tribute in kind. Hardly any man, I imagine, can have had less trouble in gathering a showy stock of information than Aquila. On close inquiry you would probably find that he had not read one epoch-making book of modern times, for he has a career which obliges him to much correspondence and other official work, and he is too fond of being in company to spend his leisure moments in study; but to his quick eye, ear, and tongue, a few predatory excursions in conversation where there are instructed persons, gradually furnish surprisingly clever modes of statement and allusion on the dominant topic. When he first adopts a subject he necessarily falls into mistakes, and it is interesting to watch his gradual progress into fuller information and better nourished irony, without his ever needing to admit that he has made a blunder or to appear conscious of correction. Suppose, for example, he had incautiously founded some ingenious remarks on a hasty reckoning that nine thirteens made a hundred and two, and the insignificant Bantam, hitherto silent, seemed to spoil the flow of ideas by stating that the product could not be taken as less than a hundred and seventeen, Aquila would glide on in the most graceful manner from a repetition of his previous remark to the continuation—"All this is on the supposition that a hundred and two were all that could be got out of nine thirteens; but as all the world knows that nine thirteens will yield," &c.—proceeding straightway into a new train of ingenious consequences, and causing Bantam to be regarded by all present as one of those slow persons who take irony for ignorance, and who would warn the weasel to keep awake. How should a small-eyed, feebly crowing mortal like him be quicker in arithmetic than the keen-faced forcible Aquila, in whom universal knowledge is easily credible? Looked into closely, the conclusion from a man's profile, voice, and fluency to his certainty in multiplication beyond the twelves, seems to show a confused notion of the way in which very common things are connected; but it is on such false correlations that men found half their inferences about each other, and high places of trust may sometimes be held on no better foundation.

It is a commonplace that words, writings, measures, and performances in general, have qualities assigned them not by a direct judgment on the performances themselves, but by a presumption of what they are likely to be, considering who is the performer. We all notice in our neighbours this reference to names as guides in criticism, and all furnish illustrations of it in our own practice; for, check ourselves as we will, the first impression from any sort of work must depend on a previous attitude of mind, and this will constantly be determined by the influences of a name. But that our prior confidence or want of confidence in given names is made up of judgments just as hollow as the consequent praise or blame they are taken to warrant, is less commonly perceived, though there is a conspicuous indication of it in the surprise or disappointment often manifested in the disclosure of an authorship about which everybody has been making wrong guesses. No doubt if it had been discovered who wrote the "Vestiges," many an ingenious structure of probabilities would have been spoiled, and some disgust might have been felt for a real author who made comparatively so shabby an appearance of likelihood. It is this foolish trust in prepossessions, founded on spurious evidence, which makes a medium of encouragement for those who, happening to have the ear of the public, give other people's ideas the advantage of appearing under their own well-received name, while any remonstrance from the real producer becomes an unwelcome disturbance of complacency with each person who has paid complimentary tributes in the wrong place.

Hardly any kind of false reasoning is more ludicrous than this on the probabilities of origination. It would be amusing to catechise the guessers as to their exact reasons for thinking their guess "likely:" why Hoopoe of John's has fixed on Toucan of Magdalen; why Shrike attributes its peculiar style to Buzzard, who has not hitherto been known as a writer; why the fair Columba thinks it must belong to the reverend Merula; and why they are all alike disturbed in their previous judgment of its value by finding that it really came from Skunk, whom they had either not thought of at all, or thought of as belonging to a species excluded by the nature of the case. Clearly they were all wrong in their notion of the specific conditions, which lay unexpectedly in the small Skunk, and in him alone—in spite of his education nobody knows where, in spite of somebody's knowing his uncles and cousins, and in spite of nobody's knowing that he was cleverer than they thought him.

Such guesses remind one of a fabulist's imaginary council of animals assembled to consider what sort of creature had constructed a honeycomb found and much tasted by Bruin and other epicures. The speakers all started from the probability that the maker was a bird, because this was the quarter from which a wondrous nest might be expected; for the animals at that time, knowing little of their own history, would have rejected as inconceivable the notion that a nest could be made by a fish; and as to the insects, they were not willingly received in society and their ways were little known. Several complimentary presumptions were expressed that the honeycomb was due to one or the other admired and popular bird, and there was much fluttering on the part of the Nightingale and Swallow, neither of whom gave a positive denial, their confusion perhaps extending to their sense of identity; but the Owl hissed at this folly, arguing from his particular knowledge that the animal which produced honey must be the Musk-rat, the wondrous nature of whose secretions required no proof; and, in the powerful logical procedure of the Owl, from musk to honey was but a step. Some disturbance arose hereupon, for the Musk-rat began to make himself obtrusive, believing in the Owl's opinion of his powers, and feeling that he could have produced the honey if he had thought of it; until an experimental Butcher-bird proposed to anatomise him as a help to decision. The hubbub increased, the opponents of the Musk-rat inquiring who his ancestors were; until a diversion was created by an able discourse of the Macaw on structures generally, which he classified so as to include the honeycomb, entering into so much admirable exposition that there was a prevalent sense of the honeycomb having probably been produced by one who understood it so well. But Bruin, who had probably eaten too much to listen with edification, grumbled in his low kind of language, that "Fine words butter no parsnips," by which he meant to say that there was no new honey forthcoming.

Perhaps the audience generally was beginning to tire, when the Fox entered with his snout dreadfully swollen, and reported that the beneficent originator in question was the Wasp, which he had found much smeared with undoubted honey, having applied his nose to it—whence indeed the able insect, perhaps justifiably irritated at what might seem a sign of scepticism, had stung him with some severity, an infliction Reynard could hardly regret, since the swelling of a snout normally so delicate would corroborate his statement, and satisfy the assembly that he had really found the honey-creating genius.

The Fox's admitted acuteness, combined with the visible swelling, were taken as undeniable evidence, and the revelation undoubtedly met a general desire for information on a point of interest. Nevertheless, there was a murmur the reverse of delighted, and the feelings of some eminent animals were too strong for them: the Orang-outang's jaw dropped so as seriously to impair the vigour of his expression, the edifying Pelican screamed and flapped her wings, the Owl hissed again, the Macaw became loudly incoherent, and the Gibbon gave his hysterical laugh; while the Hyæna, after indulging in a more splenetic guffaw, agitated the question whether it would not be better to hush up the whole affair, instead of giving public recognition to an insect whose produce, it was now plain, had been much over-estimated. But this narrow-spirited motion was negatived by the sweet-toothed majority. A complimentary deputation to the Wasp was resolved on, and there was a confident hope that this diplomatic measure would tell on the production of honey.

DISEASES OF SMALL AUTHORSHIP

PARTICULAR callings, it is known, encourage particular diseases. There is a painter's colic: the Sheffield grinder falls a victim to the inhalation of steel dust: clergymen so often have a certain kind of sore throat that this otherwise secular ailment gets named after them. And perhaps, if we were to inquire, we should find a similar relation between certain moral ailments and these various occupations, though here in the case of clergymen there would be specific differences: the poor curate, equally with the rector, is liable to clergyman's sore throat, but he would probably be found free from the chronic moral ailments encouraged by the possession of glebe and those higher chances of preferment which follow on having a good position already. On the other hand, the poor curate might have severe attacks of calculating expectancy concerning parishioners' turkeys, cheeses, and fat geese, or of uneasy rivalry for the donations of clerical charities.

Authors are so miscellaneous a class that their personified diseases, physical and moral, might include the whole procession of human disorders, led by dyspepsia and ending in madness—the awful Dumb Show of a world-historic tragedy. Take a large enough area of human life and all comedy melts into tragedy, like the Fool's part by the side of Lear. The chief scenes get filled with erring heroes, guileful usurpers, persecuted discoverers, dying deliverers: everywhere the protagonist has a part pregnant with doom. The comedy sinks to an accessory, and if there are loud laughs they seem a convulsive transition from sobs; or if the comedy is touched with a gentle lovingness, the panoramic scene is one where

> "Sadness is a kind of mirth,
> So mingled as if mirth did make us sad
> And sadness merry." [1]

But I did not set out on the wide survey that would carry me into tragedy, and in fact had nothing more serious in my mind

[1] Two Noble Kinsmen.

than certain small chronic ailments that come of small authorship. I was thinking principally of Vorticella, who flourished in my youth not only as a portly lady walking in silk attire, but also as the authoress of a book entitled "The Channel Islands, with Notes and an Appendix." I would by no means make it a reproach to her that she wrote no more than one book; on the contrary, her stopping there seems to me a laudable example. What one would have wished, after experience, was that she had refrained from producing even that single volume, and thus from giving her self-importance a troublesome kind of double incorporation which became oppressive to her acquaintances, and set up in herself one of those slight chronic forms of disease to which I have just referred. She lived in the considerable provincial town of Pumpiter, which had its own newspaper press, with the usual divisions of political partisanship and the usual varieties of literary criticism— the florid and allusive, the *staccato* and peremptory, the clairvoyant and prophetic, the safe and pattern-phrased, or what one might call "the many-a-long-day style."

Vorticella, being the wife of an important townsman, had naturally the satisfaction of seeing "The Channel Islands" reviewed by all the organs of Pumpiter opinion, and their articles or paragraphs held as naturally the opening pages in the elegantly bound album prepared by her for the reception of "critical opinions." This ornamental volume lay on a special table in her drawing-room, close to the still more gorgeously bound work of which it was the significant effect, and every guest was allowed the privilege of reading what had been said of the authoress and her work in the "Pumpiter Gazette and Literary Watchman," the "Pumpshire Post," the "Church Clock," the "Independent Monitor," and the lively but judicious publication known as the "Medley Pie;" to be followed up, if he chose, by the instructive perusal of the strikingly confirmatory judgments, sometimes concurrent in the very phrases, of journals from the most distant counties—as the "Latchgate Argus," the "Penllwy Universe," the "Cockaleekie Advertiser," the "Goodwin Sands Opinion," and the "Land's End Times."

I had friends in Pumpiter and occasionally paid a long visit there. When I called on Vorticella, who had a cousinship with my hosts, she had to excuse herself because a message claimed her attention for eight or ten minutes, and handing me the album of critical opinions said, with a certain emphasis which, considering my youth, was highly complimentary, that she would really like me to read what I should find there. This seemed a permissive politeness which I could not feel to be an oppression, and I ran my eyes over the dozen pages, each with a strip or islet of newspaper in the centre, with that freedom of mind (in my case meaning freedom to forget) which would be a perilous way of preparing for examination. This *ad libitum* perusal had its interest for me. The private truth being that I had not read "The Channel Islands," I was amazed at the variety of matter which the volume must contain to have impressed these different judges with the writer's surpassing capacity to handle almost all branches of inquiry and all forms of presentation. In Jersey she had shown herself an historian, in Guernsey a poetess, in Alderney a political economist, and in Sark a humorist. There were sketches of character scattered through the pages which might put our "fictionists" to the blush; the style was eloquent and racy, studded with gems of felicitous remark; and the moral spirit throughout was so superior that, said one, "the recording angel" (who is not supposed to take account of literature as such) "would assuredly set down the work as a deed of religion." The force of this eulogy on the part of several reviewers was much heightened by the incidental evidence of their fastidious and severe taste, which seemed to suffer considerably from the imperfections of our chief writers, even the dead and canonised: one afflicted them with the smell of oil, another lacked erudition and attempted (though vainly) to dazzle them with trivial conceits, one wanted to be more philosophical than nature had made him, another in attempting to be comic produced the melancholy effect of a half-starved Merry-Andrew; while one and all, from the author of the "Areopagitica" downwards, had faults of style which must have made an able hand in the "Latchgate Argus" shake the many-glanced head belonging thereto with a smile of compassionate disapproval. Not so the authoress of "The Channel Islands;" Vorticella and Shakespeare were allowed to be faultless. I gathered that no blemishes were observable in the work of this accomplished writer, and the repeated information that she was "second to none" seemed after this superfluous. Her thick octavo —notes, appendix and all—was unflagging from beginning to end; and the "Land's End Times," using a rather dangerous rhetorical

figure, recommended you not to take up the volume unless you had
leisure to finish it at a sitting. It had given one writer more pleasure
than he had had for many a long day—a sentence which had a
melancholy resonance, suggesting a life of studious languor such
as all previous achievements of the human mind failed to stimulate
into enjoyment. I think the collection of critical opinions wound
up with this sentence, and I had turned back to look at the litho-
graphed sketch of the authoress which fronted the first page of the
album, when the fair original re-entered and I laid down the volume on its appropriate table.

"Well, what do you think of them?" said Vorticella, with an emphasis which had some significance unperceived by me. "I know
you are a great student. Give me *your* opinion of these opinions."

"They must be very gratifying to you," I answered with a little
confusion, for I perceived that I might easily mistake my footing,
and I began to have a presentiment of an examination for which
I was by no means crammed.

"On the whole—yes," said Vorticella, in a tone of concession.
"A few of the notices are written with some pains, but not one
of them has really grappled with the chief idea in the appendix. I
don't know whether you have studied political economy, but you
saw what I said on page 398 about the Jersey fisheries?"

I bowed—I confess it—with the mean hope that this movement
in the nape of my neck would be taken as sufficient proof that I
had read, marked, and learned. I do not forgive myself for this
pantomimic falsehood, but I was young and morally timorous, and
Vorticella's personality had an effect on me something like that of
a powerful mesmeriser when he directs all his ten fingers toward
your eyes, as unpleasantly visible ducts for the invisible stream. I
felt a great power of contempt in her, if I did not come up to her
expectations.

"Well," she resumed, "you observe that not one of them has
taken up that argument. But I hope I convinced you about the
drag-nets?"

Here was a judgment on me. Orientally speaking, I had lifted
up my foot on the steep descent of falsity and was compelled to set
it down on a lower level. "I should think you must be right," said
I, inwardly resolving that on the next topic I would tell the truth.

"I *know* that I am right," said Vorticella. "The fact is that no critic in this town is fit to meddle with such subjects, unless it be Volvox, and he, with all his command of language, is very superficial. It is Volvox who writes in the 'Monitor.' I hope you noticed how he contradicts himself?"

My resolution, helped by the equivalence of dangers, stoutly prevailed, and I said, "No."

"No! I am surprised. He is the only one who finds fault with me. He is a Dissenter, you know. The 'Monitor' is the Dissenters' organ, but my husband has been so useful to them in municipal affairs that they would not venture to run my book down; they feel obliged to tell the truth about me. Still Volvox betrays himself. After praising me for my penetration and accuracy, he presently says I have allowed myself to be imposed upon and have let my active imagination run away with me. That is like his dissenting impertinence. Active my imagination may be, but I have it under control. Little Vibrio, who writes the playful notice in the 'Medley Pie,' has a clever hit at Volvox in that passage about the steeplechase of imagination, where the loser wants to make it appear that the winner was only run away with. But if you did not notice Volvox's self-contradiction you would not see the point," added Vorticella, with rather a chilling intonation. "Or perhaps you did not read the 'Medley Pie' notice? That is a pity. Do take up the book again. Vibrio is a poor little tippling creature, but, as Mr. Carlyle would say, he has an eye, and he is always lively."

I did take up the book again, and read as demanded.

"It is very ingenious," said I, really appreciating the difficulty of being lively in this connection: it seemed even more wonderful than that a Vibrio should have an eye.

"You are probably surprised to see no notices from the London press," said Vorticella. "I have one—a very remarkable one. But I reserve it until the others have spoken, and then I shall introduce it to wind up. I shall have them reprinted, of course, and inserted in future copies. This from the 'Candelabrum' is only eight lines in length, but full of venom. It calls my style dull and pompous. I think that will tell its own tale, placed after the other critiques."

"People's impressions are so different," said I. "Some persons find 'Don Quixote' dull."

"Yes," said Vorticella, in emphatic chest tones, "dulness is a matter of opinion; but pompous! That I never was and never could be. Perhaps he means that my matter is too important for his taste; and I have no objection to *that*. I did not intend to be trivial. I should just like to read you that passage about the drag-nets, because I could make it clearer to you."

A second (less ornamental) copy was at her elbow and was already opened, when to my great relief another guest was announced, and I was able to take my leave without seeming to run away from "The Channel Islands," though not without being compelled to carry with me the loan of "the marked copy," which I was to find advantageous in a re-perusal of the appendix, and was only requested to return before my departure from Pumpiter. Looking into the volume now with some curiosity, I found it a very ordinary combination of the commonplace and ambitious, one of those books which one might imagine to have been written under the old Grub Street coercion of hunger and thirst, if they were not known beforehand to be the gratuitous productions of ladies and gentlemen whose circumstances might be called altogether easy, but for an uneasy vanity that happened to have been directed toward authorship. Its importance was that of a polypus, tumour, fungus, or other erratic outgrowth, noxious and disfiguring in its effect on the individual organism which nourishes it. Poor Vorticella might not have been more wearisome on a visit than the majority of her neighbours, but for this disease of magnified self-importance belonging to small authorship. I understand that the chronic complaint of "The Channel Islands" never left her. As the years went on, and the publication tended to vanish in the distance for her neighbours' memory, she was still bent on dragging it to the foreground, and her chief interest in new acquaintances was the possibility of lending them her book, entering into all details concerning it, and requesting them to read her album of "critical opinions." This really made her more tiresome than Gregarina, whose distinction was that she had had cholera, and who did not feel herself in her true position with strangers until they knew it.

My experience with Vorticella led me for a time into the false supposition that this sort of fungous disfiguration, which makes Self disagreeably larger, was most common to the female sex; but I presently found that here too the male could assert his superiority and show a more vigorous boredom. I have known a man with a single pamphlet containing an assurance that somebody else was wrong, together with a few approved quotations, produce a more powerful effect of shuddering at his approach than ever Vorticella did with her varied octavo volume, including notes and appendix. Males of more than one nation recur to my memory who produced from their pocket on the slightest encouragement a small pink or buff duodecimo pamphlet, wrapped in silver paper, as a present held ready for an intelligent reader. "A mode of propagandism," you remark in excuse; "they wished to spread some useful corrective doctrine." Not necessarily: the indoctrination aimed at was perhaps to convince you of their own talents by the sample of an "Ode on Shakespeare's Birthday," or a translation from Horace.

Vorticella may pair off with Monas, who had also written his one book—"Here and There; or, a Trip from Truro to Transylvania"—and not only carried it in his portmanteau when he went on visits, but took the earliest opportunity of depositing it in the drawing-room, and afterward would enter to look for it, as if under pressure of a need for reference, begging the lady of the house to tell him whether she had seen "a small volume bound in red." One hostess at last ordered it to be carried into his bedroom to save his time; but it presently reappeared in his hands, and was again left with inserted slips of paper on the drawing-room table.

Depend upon it, vanity is human, native alike to men and women; only in the male it is of denser texture, less volatile, so that it less immediately informs you of its presence, but is more massive and capable of knocking you down if you come into collision with it; while in women vanity lays by its small revenges as in a needle-case always at hand. The difference is in muscle and finger-tips, in traditional habits and mental perspective, rather than in the original appetite of vanity. It is an approved method now to explain ourselves by a reference to the races as little like us as possible, which leads me to observe that in Fiji the men use the most elaborate hair-dressing, and that wherever tattooing is in vogue the male expects to carry off the prize of admiration for pattern and workmanship. Arguing analogically, and looking for this tendency of the Fijian or Hawaian male in the eminent European, we must suppose that it exhibits itself under the forms of civilised apparel; and it would be a great mistake to estimate passionate effort by the effect it produces on our perception or understanding. It is conceivable that a man may have concentrated no less will and expectation on his wristbands, gaiters, and the shape of his hat-brim, or an appearance which impresses you as that of the modern "swell," than the Ojibbeway on an ornamentation which seems to us much more elaborate. In what concerns the search for admiration at least, it is not true that the effect is equal to the cause and resembles it. The cause of a flat curl on the masculine forehead, such as might be seen when George the Fourth was king, must have been widely different in quality and intensity from the impression made by that small scroll of hair on the organ of the beholder. Merely to maintain an attitude and gait which I notice in certain club men, and especially an inflation of the chest accompanying very small remarks, there goes, I am convinced, an expenditure of psychical energy little appreciated by the multitude—a mental vision of Self and deeply impressed beholders, which is quite without antitype in what we call the effect produced by that hidden process.

No! there is no need to admit that women would carry away the prize of vanity in a competition where differences of custom were fairly considered. A man cannot show his vanity in a tight skirt which forces him to walk sideways down the staircase; but let the match be between the respective vanities of largest beard and tightest skirt, and here too the battle would be to the strong.

MORAL SWINDLERS

IT is a familiar example of irony in the degradation of words that "what a man is worth" has come to mean how much money he possesses; but there seems a deeper and more melancholy irony in the shrunken meaning that popular or polite speech assigns to "morality" and "morals." The poor part these words are made to play recalls the fate of those pagan divinities who, after being understood to rule the powers of the air and the destinies of men, came down to the level of insignificant demons, or were even made a farcical show for the amusement of the multitude.

Talking to Melissa in a time of commercial trouble, I found her disposed to speak pathetically of the disgrace which had fallen on Sir Gavial Mantrap, because of his conduct in relation to the Eocene

Mines, and to other companies ingeniously devised by him for the punishment of ignorance in people of small means: a disgrace by which the poor titled gentleman was actually reduced to live in comparative obscurity on his wife's settlement of one or two hundred thousand in the consols.

"Surely your pity is misapplied," said I, rather dubiously, for I like the comfort of trusting that a correct moral judgment is the strong point in woman (seeing that she has a majority of about a million in our islands), and I imagined that Melissa might have some unexpressed grounds for her opinion. "I should have thought you would rather be sorry for Mantrap's victims—the widows, spinsters, and hard-working fathers whom his unscrupulous haste to make himself rich has cheated of all their savings, while he is eating well, lying softly, and after impudently justifying himself before the public, is perhaps joining in the General Confession with a sense that he is an acceptable object in the sight of God, though decent men refuse to meet him.

"Oh, all that about the Companies, I know, was most unfortunate. In commerce people are led to do so many things, and he might not know exactly how everything would turn out. But Sir Gavial made a good use of his money, and he is a thoroughly *moral* man."

"What do you mean by a thoroughly moral man?" said I.

"Oh, I suppose every one means the same by that," said Melissa, with a slight air of rebuke. "Sir Gavial is an excellent family man— quite blameless there; and so charitable round his place at Tiptop. Very different from Mr Barabbas, whose life, my husband tells me, is most objectionable, with actresses and that sort of thing. I think a man's morals should make a difference to us. I'm not sorry for Mr Barabbas, but *I am* sorry for Sir Gavial Mantrap."

I will not repeat my answer to Melissa, for I fear it was offensively brusque, my opinion being that Sir Gavial was the more pernicious scoundrel of the two, since his name for virtue served as an effective part of a swindling apparatus; and perhaps I hinted that to call such a man moral showed rather a silly notion of human affairs. In fact, I had an angry wish to be instructive, and Melissa, as will sometimes happen, noticed my anger without appropriating my instruction, for I have since heard that she speaks of me as rather violent-tempered, and not over strict in my views of morality.

I wish that this narrow use of words which are wanted in their full meaning were confined to women like Melissa. Seeing that Morality and Morals under their *alias* of Ethics are the subject of voluminous discussion, and their true basis a pressing matter of dispute—seeing that the most famous book ever written on Ethics, and forming a chief study in our colleges, allies ethical with political science or that which treats of the constitution and prosperity of States, one might expect that educated men would find reason to avoid a perversion of language which lends itself to no wider view of life than that of village gossips. Yet I find even respectable historians of our own and foreign countries, after showing that a king was treacherous, rapacious, and ready to sanction gross breaches in the administration of justice, end by praising him for his pure moral character, by which one must suppose them to mean that he was not lewd nor debauched, not the European twin of the typical Indian potentate whom Macaulay describes as passing his life in chewing bang and fondling dancing-girls. And since we are sometimes told of such maleficent kings that they were religious, we arrive at the curious result that the most serious wide-reaching duties of man lie quite outside both Morality and Religion—the one of these consisting in not keeping mistresses (and perhaps not drinking too much), and the other in certain ritual and spiritual transactions with God which can be carried on equally well side by side with the basest conduct toward men. With such a classification as this it is no wonder, considering the strong reaction of language on thought, that many minds, dizzy with indigestion of recent science and philosophy, are far to seek for the grounds of social duty, and without entertaining any private intention of committing a perjury which would ruin an innocent man, or seeking gain by supplying bad preserved meats to our navy, feel themselves speculatively obliged to inquire why they should not do so, and are inclined to measure their intellectual subtlety by their dissatisfaction with all answers to this "Why?" It is of little use to theorise in ethics while our habitual phraseology stamps the larger part of our social duties as something that lies aloof from the deepest needs and affections of our nature. The informal definitions of popular language are the only medium through which theory really affects the mass of minds even among the nominally educated; and when a man whose business hours, the solid part of every day, are spent in an unscrupulous course of public or private action which has every calculable chance of causing widespread injury and misery, can be called moral because he comes home to dine with his wife and children and cherishes the happiness of his own hearth, the augury is not good for the use of high ethical and theological disputation.

Not for one moment would one willingly lose sight of the truth that the relation of the sexes and the primary ties of kinship are the deepest roots of human wellbeing, but to make them by themselves the equivalent of morality is verbally to cut off the channels of feeling through which they are the feeders of that wellbeing. They are the original fountains of a sensibility to the claims of others, which is the bond of societies; but being necessarily in the first instance a private good, there is always the danger that individual selfishness will see in them only the best part of its own gain; just as knowledge, navigation, commerce, and all the conditions which are of a nature to awaken men's consciousness of their mutual dependence and to make the world one great society, are the occasions of selfish, unfair action, of war and oppression, so long as the public conscience or chief force of feeling and opinion is not uniform and strong enough in its insistence on what is demanded by the general welfare. And among the influences that must retard a right public judgment, the degradation of words which involve praise and blame will be reckoned worth protesting against by every mature observer. To rob words of half their meaning, while they retain their dignity as qualifications, is like allowing to men who have lost half their faculties the same high and perilous command which they won in their time of vigour; or like selling food and seeds after fraudulently abstracting their best virtues: in each case what ought to be beneficiently strong is fatally enfeebled, if not empoisoned. Until we have altered our dictionaries and have found some other word than *morality* to stand in popular use for the duties of man to man, let us refuse to accept as moral the contractor who enriches himself by using large machinery to make pasteboard soles pass as leather for the feet of unhappy conscripts fighting at miserable odds against invaders: let us rather call him a miscreant, though he were the tenderest, most faithful of husbands, and contend that his own experience of home happiness makes his reckless infliction of suffering on others all the more atrocious. Let us refuse to accept as moral any political leader who should allow his conduct in relation to great issues to be determined by egoistic passion, and boldly say that he would be less immoral even though he were as lax in his personal habits as Sir Robert Walpole, if at the same time his sense of the public welfare were supreme in his mind, quelling all pettier impulses beneath a magnanimous impartiality. And though we were to find among that class of journalists who live by recklessly reporting injurious rumours, insinuating the blackest motives in opponents, descanting at large and with an air of infallibility on dreams which they both find and interpret, and stimulating bad feeling between nations by abusive writing which is as empty of real conviction as the rage of a pantomime king, and would be ludicrous if its effects did not make it appear diabolical—though we were to find among these a man who was benignancy itself in his own circle, a healer of private differences, a soother in private calamities, let us pronounce him nevertheless flagrantly immoral, a root of hideous cancer in the commonwealth, turning the channels of instruction into feeders of social and political disease.

In opposite ways one sees bad effects likely to be encouraged by this narrow use of the word *morals*, shutting out from its meaning half those actions of a man's life which tell momentously on the wellbeing of his fellow-citizens, and on the preparation of a future for the children growing up around him. Thoroughness of workmanship, care in the execution of every task undertaken, as if it were the acceptance of a trust which it would be a breach of faith not to discharge well, is a form of duty so momentous that if it were to die out from the feeling and practice of a people, all reforms of institutions would be helpless to create national prosperity and national happiness. Do we desire to see public spirit penetrating all classes of the community and affecting every man's conduct, so that he shall make neither the saving of his soul nor any other private saving an excuse for indifference to the general welfare? Well and good. But the sort of public spirit that scamps its breadwinning work, whether with the trowel, the pen, or the overseeing brain, that it may hurry to scenes of political or social agitation, would be as baleful a gift to our people as any malignant demon could devise. One best part of educational training is that which comes through special knowledge and manipulative or other skill, with its usual accompaniment of delight, in relation to work which is the daily bread-winning occupation—which is a man's contribution to the effective wealth of society in return for what he takes as his own share. But this duty of doing one's proper work well, and taking care that every product of one's labour shall be genuinely what it pretends to be, is not only left out of morals in popular speech, it is very little insisted on by public teachers, at least in the only effective way—by tracing the continuous effects of ill-done work. Some of them seem to be still hopeful that it will follow as a necessary consequence from week-day services, ecclesiastical decoration, and improved hymn-books; others apparently trust to descanting on self-culture in general, or to raising a general sense of faulty circumstances; and meanwhile lax, make-shift work, from the high conspicuous kind to the average and obscure, is allowed to pass unstamped with the disgrace of immorality, though there is not a member of society who is not daily suffering from it materially and spiritually, and though it is the fatal cause that must degrade our national rank and our commerce in spite of all open markets and discovery of available coal-seams.

I suppose one may take the popular misuse of the words Morality and Morals as some excuse for certain absurdities which are occasional fashions in speech and writing—certain old lay-figures, as ugly as the queerest Asiatic idol, which at different periods get propped into loftiness, and attired in magnificent Venetian drapery, so that whether they have a human face or not is of little consequence. One is, the notion that there is a radical, irreconcilable opposition between intellect and morality. I do not mean the simple statement of fact, which everybody knows, that remarkably able men have had very faulty morals, and have outraged public feeling even at its ordinary standard; but the supposition that the ablest intellect, the highest genius, will see through morality as a sort of twaddle for bibs and tuckers, a doctrine of dulness, a mere incident in human stupidity. We begin to understand the acceptance of this foolishness by considering that we live in a society where we may hear a treacherous monarch, or a malignant and lying politician, or a man who uses either official or literary power as an instrument of his private partiality or hatred, or a manufacturer who devises the falsification of wares, or a trader who deals in virtueless seed-grains, praised or compassionated because of his excellent morals. Clearly if morality meant no more than such decencies as are practiced by these poisonous members of society, it would be possible to say, without suspicion of light-headedness, that morality lay aloof from the grand stream of human affairs, as a small channel fed by the stream and not missed from it. While this form of nonsense is conveyed in the popular use of words, there must be plenty of well-dressed ignorance at leisure to run through a box of books, which will feel itself initiated in the freemasonry of intellect by a view of life which might take for a Shakespearean motto—

> "Fair is foul and foul is fair,
> Hover through the fog and filthy air"—

and will find itself easily provided with striking conversation by the rule of reversing all the judgments on good and evil which have come to be the calendar and clock-work of society. But let our habitual talk give morals their full meaning as the conduct which, in every human relation, would follow from the fullest knowledge and the fullest sympathy—a meaning perpetually corrected and enriched by a more thorough appreciation of dependence in things, and a finer sensibility to both physical and spiritual fact—and this ridiculous ascription of superlative power to minds which have no effective awe-inspiring vision of the human lot, no response of understanding to the connection between duty and the material processes by which the world is kept habitable for cultivated man, will be tacitly discredited without any need to cite the immortal names that all are obliged to take as the measure of intellectual rank and highly-charged genius.

Suppose a Frenchman—I mean no disrespect to the great French nation, for all nations are afflicted with their peculiar parasitic growths, which are lazy, hungry forms, usually characterised by a disproportionate swallowing apparatus: suppose a Parisian who should shuffle down the Boulevard with a soul ignorant of the gravest cares and the deepest tenderness of manhood, and a frame more or less fevered by debauchery, mentally polishing into utmost refinement of phrase and rhythm verses which were an enlargement on that Shakespearean motto, and worthy of the most expensive title to be furnished by the vendors of such antithetic ware as *Les marguerites de l'Enfer*, or *Les délices de Béelzébuth*. This supposed personage might probably enough regard his negation of those moral sensibilities which make half the warp and woof of human history, his indifference to the hard thinking and hard handiwork of life, to which he owed even his own gauzy mental garments with their spangles of poor paradox, as the royalty of genius, for we are used to witness such self-crowning in many forms of mental alienation; but he would not, I think, be taken, even by his own generation, as a living proof that there can exist such a combination as that of moral stupidity and trivial emphasis of personal indulgence with the large yet finely discriminating vision which marks the intellectual masters of our kind. Doubtless there are many sorts of transfiguration, and a man who has come to be worthy of all gratitude and reverence may have had his swinish period, wallowing in ugly places; but suppose it had been handed down to us that Sophocles or Virgil had at one time made himself scandalous in this way: the works which have consecrated their memory for our admiration and gratitude are not a glorifying of swinishness, but an artistic incorporation of the highest sentiment known to their age.

All these may seem to be wide reasons for objecting to Melissa's pity for Sir Gavial Mantrap on the ground of his good morals; but their connection will not be obscure to any one who has taken pains to observe the links uniting the scattered signs of our social development.

STEVENSON

ROBERT LOUIS STEVENSON (1850–1894), *novelist, poet, essayist, was born at Edinburgh. His health was bad from childhood, and his schooling was frequently interrupted by illness or trips abroad with his father. Entering Edinburgh University in 1867, he thought of following in his father's footsteps as an engineer; his health was not equal to the preparation for this profession, and he tried law, was called to the Bar, but never practiced. He had written from childhood, and when his health broke down, he travelled, met many literary men in London. As his condition improved, he contributed essays and short stories to the periodicals. Frequent trips in search of health interrupted his labors, but he was able to work at intervals—at Davos, the Riviera, the South of England, Saranac, and finally the South Seas, where his health improved, he produced the novels, stories, and essays which reflect nothing of his illness and suffering. Death brought a sudden end to his career in 1894.*

A conscious artist, his style shows no evidence of the care he devoted to it. Romantic, he has a moral aim; his fertile imagination and his understanding of childhood keep his writing ever fresh; his essays are serious but never heavy, and his humor is pervasive.

STEVENSON

AN OLD SCOTS GARDENER

I THINK I might almost have said the last: somewhere, indeed, in the uttermost glens of the Lammermuir or among the south-western hills there may yet linger a decrepit representative of this by-gone good fellowship; but as far as actual experience goes, I have only met one man in my life who might fitly be quoted in the same breath with Andrew Fairservice—though without his vices. He was a man whose very presence could impart a savour of quaint antiquity to the baldest and most modern flower-plots. There was a dignity about his tall stooping form, and an earnestness in his wrinkled face, that recalled Don Quixote; but a Don Quixote who had come through the training of the Covenant, and been nourished in his youth on *Walker's Lives* and *The Hind let Loose*.

Now, as I could not bear to let such a man pass away with no sketch preserved of his old-fashioned virtues, I hope the reader will take this as an excuse for the present paper, and judge as kindly as he can the infirmities of my description. To me, who find it so difficult to tell the little that I know, he stands essentially as a *genius loci*. It is impossible to separate his spare form and old straw hat from the garden in the lap of the hill, with its rocks overgrown with clematis, its shadowy walks, and the splendid breadth of champaign that one saw from the north-west corner. The garden and gardener seem part and parcel of each other. When I take him from his right surroundings and try to make him appear for me on paper, he looks unreal and phantasmal: the best that I can say may convey some notion to those that never saw him, but to me it will be ever impotent.

The first time that I saw him, I fancy Robert was pretty old already: he had certainly begun to use his years as a stalking-horse. Latterly he was beyond all the impudences of logic, considering a reference to the parish register worth all the reasons in the world. *"I am old and well stricken in years,"* he was wont to say; and I never found any one bold enough to answer the argument. Apart from this vantage that he kept over all who were not yet octogenarian, he had some other drawbacks as a gardener. He shrank the very place he cultivated. The dignity and reduced gentility of his appearance made the small garden cut a sorry figure. He was full of tales of greater situations in his younger days. He spoke of castles and parks with a humbling familiarity. He told of places where under-gardeners had trembled at his looks, where there were meres and swanneries, labyrinths of walk and wildernesses of sad shrubbery in his control, till you could not help feeling that it was condescension on his part to dress your humbler garden plots. You were thrown at once into an invidious position. You felt that you were profiting by the needs of dignity, and that his poverty and not his will consented to your vulgar rule. Involuntarily you compared yourself with the swineherd that made Alfred watch his cakes, or some bloated citizen who may have given his sons and his condescension to the fallen Dionysius. Nor were the disagreeables purely fanciful and metaphysical, for the sway that he exercised over your feelings he extended to your garden, and, through the garden, to your diet. He would trim a hedge, throw away a favourite plant, or fill the most favoured and fertile section of the garden with a vegetable that none of us could eat, in supreme contempt for our opinion. If you asked him to send you in one of your own artichokes, *"That I wull, mem,"* he would say, *"with pleasure, for it is mair blessed to give than to receive."* Ay, and even when, by extra twisting of the screw, we prevailed on him to prefer our commands to his own inclination, and he went away, stately and sad, professing that *"our wull was his pleasure,"* but yet reminding us that he would do it *"with feelin's"*—even then, I say, the triumphant master felt humbled in his triumph, felt that he ruled on sufferance only, that he was taking a mean advantage of the other's low estate, and that the whole scene had been one of those "slights that patient merit of the unworthy takes."

In flowers his taste was old-fashioned and catholic; affecting sunflowers and dahlias, wall-flowers and roses, and holding in supreme aversion whatsoever was fantastic, new-fashioned or wild. There was one exception to this sweeping ban. Foxgloves, though undoubtedly guilty on the last count, he not only spared, but loved; and when the shrubbery was being thinned, he stayed his hand and dexterously manipulated his bill in order to save every stately stem. In boyhood, as he told me once, speaking in that tone that only actors and the old-fashioned common folk can use nowadays, his heart grew "*proud*" within him when he came on a burn-course among the braes of Manor that shone purple with their graceful trophies; and not all his apprenticeship and practice for so many years of precise gardening had banished these boyish recollections from his heart. Indeed, he was a man keenly alive to the beauty of all that was bygone. He abounded in old stories of his boyhood, and kept pious account of all his former pleasures; and when he went (on a holiday) to visit one of the fabled great places of the earth where he had served before, he came back full of little pre-Raphaelite reminiscences that showed real passion for the past, such as might have shaken hands with Hazlitt or Jean-Jacques.

But however his sympathy with his old feelings might affect his liking for the foxgloves, the very truth was that he scorned all flowers together. They were but garnishings, childish toys, trifling ornaments for ladies' chimney-shelves. It was towards his cauliflowers and peas and cabbage that his heart grew warm. His preference for the more useful growths was such that cabbages were found invading the flower-plots, and an outpost of savoys was once discovered in the centre of the lawn. He would prelect over some thriving plant with wonderful enthusiasm, piling reminiscence on reminiscence of former and perhaps yet finer specimens. Yet even then he did not let the credit leave himself. He had, indeed, raised "*finer o' them*"; but it seemed that no one else had been favoured with a like success. All other gardeners, in fact, were mere foils to his own superior attainments; and he would recount, with perfect soberness of voice and visage, how so and so had wondered, and such another could scarcely give credit to his eyes. Nor was it with his rivals only that he parted praise and blame. If you remarked how well a plant was looking, he would gravely touch his hat and thank you with solemn unction; all credit in the matter falling to him. If, on the other hand, you called his attention to some back-going vegetable, he would quote Scripture: "*Paul may plant and Apollos may water*"; all blame being left to Providence, on the score of deficient rain or untimely frosts.

There was one thing in the garden that shared his preference with his favourite cabbages and rhubarb, and that other was the bee-hive. Their sound, their industry, perhaps their sweet product also, had taken hold of his imagination and heart, whether by way of memory or no I cannot say, although perhaps the bees too were linked to him by some recollection of Manor braes and his country childhood. Nevertheless, he was too chary of his personal safety or (let me rather say) his personal dignity to mingle in any active office towards them. But he could stand by while one of the contemned rivals did the work for him, and protest that it was quite safe in spite of his own considerate distance and the cries of the distressed assistant. In regard to bees, he was rather a man of word than deed, and some of his most striking sentences had the bees for text. "*They are indeed wonderfu' creatures, mem*," he said once. "*They just mind me o' what the Queen of Sheba said to Solomon—and I think she said it wi' a sigh—'The half of it hath not been told unto me.'*"

As far as the Bible goes, he was deeply read. Like the old Covenanters, of whom he was the worthy representative, his mouth was full of sacred quotations; it was the book that he had studied most and thought upon most deeply. To many people in his station the Bible, and perhaps Burns, are the only books of any vital literary merit that they read, feeding themselves, for the rest, on the draff of country newspapers, and the very instructive but not very palatable pabulum of some cheap educational series. This was Robert's position. All day long he had dreamed of the Hebrew stories, and his head had been full of Hebrew poetry and Gospel ethics; until they had struck deep root into his heart, and the very expressions had become a part of him; so that he rarely spoke without some antique idiom or Scripture mannerism that gave a raciness to the merest trivialities of talk. But the influence of the Bible did not stop here. There was more in Robert than quaint phrase and ready store of reference. He was imbued with a spirit of peace and love: he interposed between man and wife: he threw himself between the angry, touching his hat the while with all the ceremony of an usher: he protected the birds from everybody but himself, seeing, I suppose, a great difference between official execution and wanton sport. His mistress telling him one day to put some ferns into his master's particular corner, and adding, "Though, indeed, Robert, he doesn't deserve them, for he wouldn't help me to gather them," "*Eh, mem*," replies Robert, "*but I wouldnae say that, for I think he's just a most deservin' gentleman.*" Again, two of our friends, who were on intimate terms, and accustomed to use language to each other somewhat without the bounds of the parliamentary, happened to differ about the position of a seat in the garden. The discussion, as was usual when these two were at it, soon waxed tolerably insulting on both sides. Every one accustomed to such controversies several times a day was quietly enjoying this prize-fight of somewhat abusive wit—every one but Robert, to whom the perfect good faith of the whole quarrel seemed unquestionable, and who, after having waited till his conscience would suffer him to wait no more, and till he expected every moment that the disputants would fall to blows, cut suddenly in with tones of almost tearful entreaty: "*Eh, but, gentlemen, I wad hae nae mair words about it!*" One thing was noticeable about Robert's religion: it was neither dogmatic nor sectarian. He never expatiated (at least, in my hearing) on the doctrines of his creed, and he never condemned anybody else. I have no doubt that he held all Roman Catholics, Atheists, and Mahometans as considerably out of it; I don't believe he had any sympathy for Prelacy; and the natural feelings of man must have made him a little sore about Free-Churchism; but at least, he never talked about these views, never grew controversially noisy, and never openly aspersed the belief or practice of anybody. Now all this is not generally characteristic of Scots piety; Scots sects being churches militant with a vengeance, and Scots believers perpetual crusaders the one against the other, and missionaries the one to the other. Perhaps Robert's originally tender heart was what made the difference; or, perhaps, his solitary and pleasant labour among fruits and flowers had taught him a more sunshiny creed than those whose work is among the tares of fallen humanity; and the soft influences of the garden had entered deep into his spirit,

"Annihilating all that's made
To a green thought in a green shade."

But I could go on for ever chronicling his golden sayings or telling of his innocent and living piety. I had meant to tell of his cottage, with the German pipe hung reverently above the fire, and the shell box that he had made for his son, and of which he would say pathetically: *"He was real pleased wi' it at first, but I think he's got a kind o' tired o' it now"*—the son being then a man of about forty. But I will let all these pass. *"'Tis more significant: he's dead."* The earth, that he had digged so much in his life, was dug out by another for himself; and the flowers that he had tended drew their life still from him, but in a new and nearer way. A bird flew about the open grave, as if it too wished to honour the obsequies of one who had so often quoted Scripture in favour of its kind: "Are not two sparrows sold for one farthing? and yet not one of them falleth to the ground."

Yes, he is dead. But the kings did not rise in the place of death to greet him "with taunting proverbs" as they rose to greet the haughty Babylonian; for in his life he was lowly, and a peacemaker, and a servant of God.

ORDERED SOUTH

BY a curious irony of fate, the places to which we are sent when health deserts us are often singularly beautiful. Often, too, they are places we have visited in former years, or seen briefly in passing by, and kept ever afterward in pious memory; and we please ourselves with the fancy that we shall repeat many vivid and pleasurable sensations, and take up again the thread of our enjoyment in the same spirit as we let it fall. We shall now have an opportunity of finishing many pleasant excursions, inter-rupted of yore before our curiosity was fully satisfied. It may be that we have kept in mind, during all these years, the recollection of some valley into which we have just looked down for a moment before we lost sight of it in the disorder of the hills; it may be that we have lain awake at night, and agreeably tantalised ourselves with the thought of corners we had never turned, or summits we had all but climbed: we shall now be able, as we tell ourselves, to complete all these unfinished pleasures, and pass beyond the barriers that confined our recollections.

The promise is so great, and we are all so easily led away when hope and memory are both in one story, that I dare say the sick man is not very inconsolable when he receives sentence of banish-ment, and is inclined to regard his ill-health as not the least fortunate accident of his life. Nor is he immediately undeceived. The stir and speed of the journey, and the restlessness that goes to bed with him as he tries to sleep between two days of noisy progress, fever him, and stimulate his dull nerves into something of their old quickness and sensibility. And so he can enjoy the faint autumnal splendour of the landscape, as he sees hill and plain, vineyard and forest, clad in one wonderful glory of fairy gold, which the first great winds of winter will transmute, as in the fable, into withered leaves. And so too he can enjoy the admirable brevity and simplicity of such little glimpses of country and country ways as flash upon him through the windows of the train; little glimpses that have a character all their own; sights seen as a travelling swallow might see them from the wing, or Iris as she went abroad over the land on some Olympian errand. Here and there, indeed, a few children huzzah and wave their hands to the express; but for the most part, it is an interruption too brief and isolated to attract much notice; the sheep do not cease from browsing; a girl sits balanced on the projecting tiller of a canal-boat, so precariously that it seems as if a fly or the splash of a leaping fish would be enough to overthrow the dainty equilibrium, and yet all these hundreds of tons of coal and wood and iron have been precipitated roaring past her very ear, and there is not a start, not a tremor, not a turn of the averted head, to indicate that she has been even conscious of its passage. Herein, I think, lies the chief attraction of railway travel. The speed is so easy, and the train disturbs so little the scenes through which it takes us, that our heart becomes full of the placidity and stillness of the country; and while the body is borne forward in the flying chain of carriages, the thoughts alight, as the humour moves them, at unfrequented stations; they make haste up the poplar alley that leads towards the town; they are left behind with the signalman as, shading his eyes with his hand, he watches the long train sweep away into the golden distance.

Moreover, there is still before the invalid the shock of wonder and delight with which he will learn that he has passed the indefinable line that separates South from North. And this is an uncertain moment; for sometimes the consciousness is forced upon him early, on the occasion of some slight association, a colour, a flower, or a scent; and sometimes not until, one fine morning, he wakes up with the southern sunshine peeping through the *persiennes*, and the southern patois confusedly audible below the windows. Whether it come early or late, however, this pleasure will not end with the anticipation, as do so many others of the same family. It will leave him wider awake than it found him, and give a new significance to all he may see for many days to come. There is something in the mere name of the South that carries enthusiasm along with it. At the sound of the word, he pricks up his ears; he becomes as anxious to seek out beauties and to get by heart the permanent lines and character of the landscape, as if he had been told that it was all his own—an estate out of which he had been kept unjustly, and which he was now to receive in free and full possession. Even those who have never been there before feel as if they had been; and everybody goes comparing, and seeking for the familiar, and finding it with such ecstasies of recognition, that one would think they were coming home after a weary absence, instead of travelling hourly farther abroad.

It is only after he is fairly arrived and settled down in his chosen corner, that the invalid begins to understand the change that has befallen him. Everything about him is as he had remembered, or as he had anticipated. Here, at his feet, under his eyes, are the olive gardens and the blue sea. Nothing can change the eternal magnificence of form of the naked Alps behind Mentone; nothing, not even the crude curves of the railway, can utterly deform the suavity of contour of one bay after another along the whole reach of the Riviera. And of all this, he has only a cold head knowledge that is divorced from enjoyment. He recognises with his intelligence that this thing and that thing is beautiful, while in his heart of hearts he has to confess that it is not beautiful for him. It is in vain that he spurs his discouraged spirit; in vain that he chooses out points of view, and stands there, looking with all his eyes, and waiting for some return of the pleasure that he remembers in other days, as the sick folk may have awaited the coming of the angel at the pool of Bethesda. He is like an enthusiast leading about with him a stolid, indifferent tourist. There is some one by who is out of sympathy with the scene, and is not moved up to the measure of the occasion; and that some one is himself. The world is disenchanted for him. He seems to himself to touch things with muffled hands, and to see them through a veil. His life becomes a palsied fumbling after notes that are silent when he has found and struck them. He cannot recognise that this phlegmatic and un-impressionable body with which he now goes burthened, is the same that he knew heretofore so quick and delicate and alive.

He is tempted to lay the blame on the very softness and amenity of the climate, and to fancy that in the rigours of the winter at home, these dead emotions would revive and flourish. A longing for the brightness and silence of fallen snow seizes him at such times. He is homesick for the hale rough weather; for the tracery of the frost upon his window-panes at morning, the reluctant descent of the first flakes, and the white roofs relieved against the sombre sky. And yet the stuff of which these yearnings are made is of the flimsiest: if but the thermometer fall a little below its ordinary Mediterranean level, or a wind come down from the snow-clad Alps behind, the spirit of his fancies changes upon the instant, and many a doleful vignette of the grim wintry streets at home returns to him, and begins to haunt his memory. The hopeless, huddled attitude of tramps in doorways; the flinching gait of bare-foot children on the icy pavement; the sheen of the rainy streets towards afternoon; the meagre anatomy of the poor defined by the clinging of wet garments; the high canorous note of the North-easter on days when the very houses seem to stiffen with cold: these, and such as these, crowd back upon him, and mockingly substitute themselves for the fanciful winter scenes with which he had pleased himself awhile before. He cannot be glad enough that he is where he is. If only the others could be there also; if only those tramps could lie down for a little in the sunshine, and those children warm their feet, this once, upon a kindlier earth; if only there were no cold anywhere, and no nakedness, and no hunger; if only it were as well with all men as it is with him!

For it is not altogether ill with the invalid, after all. If it is only rarely that anything penetrates vividly into his numbed spirit, yet, when anything does, it brings with it a joy that is all the more poignant for its very rarity. There is something pathetic in these occasional returns of a glad activity of heart. In his lowest hours he will be stirred and awakened by many such; and they will spring perhaps from very trivial sources; as a friend once said to me, the "spirit of delight" comes often on small wings. For the pleasure that we take in beautiful nature is essentially capricious.

It comes sometimes when we least look for it; and sometimes, when we expect it most certainly, it leaves us to gape joylessly for days together, in the very home-land of the beautiful. We may have passed a place a thousand times and one; and on the thousand and second it will be transfigured, and stand forth in a certain splendour of reality from the dull circle of surroundings; so that we see it "with a child's first pleasure," as Wordsworth saw the daffodils by the lake-side. And if this falls out capriciously with the healthy, how much more so with the invalid. Some day he will find his first violet, and be lost in pleasant wonder, by what alchemy the cold earth of the clods, and the vapid air and rain, can be transmuted into colour so rich and odour so touchingly sweet. Or perhaps he may see a group of washerwomen relieved, on a spit of shingle, against the blue sea, or a meeting of flower-gatherers in the tempered daylight of an olive garden; and something significant or monumental in the grouping, something in the harmony of faint colour that is always characteristic of the dress of these southern women, will come home to him unexpectedly, and awake in him that satisfaction with which we tell ourselves that we are the richer by one more beautiful experience. Or it may be something even slighter: as when the opulence of the sunshine, which somehow gets lost and fails to produce its effect on the large scale, is suddenly revealed to him by the chance isolation—as he changes the position of his sunshade—of a yard or two of road-way with its stones and weeds. And then, there is no end to the infinite variety of the olive yards themselves. Even the colour is indeterminate and continually shifting: now you would say it was green, now grey, now blue; now tree stands above tree, like "cloud on cloud," massed into filmy indistinctness; and now, at the wind's will, the whole sea of foliage is shaken and broken up with little momentary silverings and shadows. But every one sees the world in his own way. To some the glad moment may have arrived on other provocations; and their recollection may be most vivid of the stately gait of women carrying burthens on their heads; of tropical effects with canes and naked rock and sunlight; of the relief of cypresses; of the troubled, busy-looking groups of sea-pines, that seem always as if they were being wielded and swept together by a whirlwind; of the air coming, laden with virginal perfumes, over the myrtles and the scented underwood; of the empurpled hills standing up, solemn and sharp, out of the green-gold air of the east at evening.

There go many elements, without doubt, to the making of one such moment of intense perception; and it is on the happy agreement of these many elements, on the harmonious vibration of many nerves, that the whole delight of the moment must depend. Who can forget how, when he has chanced upon some attitude of complete restfulness, after long uneasy rolling to and fro on grass or heather, the whole fashion of the landscape has been changed for him, as though the sun had just broken forth, or a great artist had only then completed, by some cunning touch, the composition of the picture? And not only a change of posture—a snatch of perfume, the sudden singing of a bird, the freshness of some pulse of air from an invisible sea, the light shadow of a travelling cloud, the merest nothing that sends a little shiver along the most infinitesimal nerve of a man's body—not one of the least of these but has a hand somehow in the general effect, and brings some refinement of its own into the character of the pleasure we feel.

And if the external conditions are thus varied and subtle, even more so are those within our own bodies. No man can find out the world, says Solomon, from beginning to end, because the world is in his heart; and so it is impossible for any of us to understand, from beginning to end, that agreement of harmonious circumstances that creates in us the highest pleasure of admiration, precisely because some of these circumstances are hidden from us for ever in the constitution of our own bodies. After we have reckoned up all that we can see or hear or feel, there still remains to be taken into account some sensibility more delicate than usual in the nerves affected, or some exquisite refinement in the architecture of the brain, which is indeed to the sense of the beautiful as the eye or the ear to the sense of hearing or sight. We admire splendid views and great pictures; and yet what is truly admirable is rather the mind within us, that gathers together these scattered details for its delight, and makes out of certain colours, certain distributions of graduated light and darkness, that intelligible whole which alone we call a picture or a view. Hazlitt, relating in one of his essays how he went on foot from one great man's house to another's in search of works of art, begins suddenly to triumph over these noble and wealthy owners, because he was more capable of enjoying their costly possessions than they were; because they had paid the money and he had received the pleasure. And the occasion is a fair one for self-complacency. While the one man was working to be able to buy the picture, the other was working to be able to enjoy the picture. An inherited aptitude will have been diligently improved in either case; only the one man has made for himself a fortune, and the other has made for himself a living spirit. It is a fair occasion for self-complacency, I repeat, when the event shows a man to have chosen the better part, and laid out his life more wisely, in the long run, than those who have credit for most wisdom. And yet even this is not a good unmixed; and like all other possessions, although in a less degree, the possession of a brain that has been thus improved and cultivated, and made into the prime organ of a man's enjoyment, brings with it certain inevitable cares and disappointments. The happiness of such an one comes to depend greatly upon those fine shades of sensation that heighten and harmonise the coarser elements of beauty. And thus a degree of nervous prostration, that to other men would be hardly disagreeable, is enough to overthrow for him the whole fabric of his life, to take, except at rare moments, the edge off his pleasures, and to meet him wherever he goes with failure, and the sense of want, and disenchantment of the world and life.

It is not in such numbness of spirit only that the life of the invalid resembles a premature old age. Those excursions that he had promised himself to finish, prove too long or too arduous for his feeble body; and the barrier-hills are as impassible as ever. Many a white town that sits far out on the promontory, many a comely fold of wood on the mountain-side, beckons and allures his imagination day after day, and is yet as inaccessible to his feet as the clefts and gorges of the clouds. The sense of distance grows upon him wonderfully; and after some feverish efforts and the fretful uneasiness of the first few days, he falls contentedly in with the restrictions of his weakness. His narrow round becomes pleasant and familiar to him as the cell to a contented prisoner. Just as he has fallen already out of the mid race of active life, he now falls out of the little eddy that circulates in the shallow waters of the sanatorium. He sees the country people come and go about their everyday affairs, the foreigners stream out in goodly pleasure parties; the stir of man's activity is all about him, as he suns him-

self inertly in some sheltered corner; and he looks on with a patriarchal impersonality of interest, such as a man may feel when he
pictures to himself the fortunes of his remote descendants, or the
robust old age of the oak he has planted over-night.

In this falling aside, in this quietude and desertion of other men,
there is no inharmonious prelude to the last quietude and desertion
of the grave; in this dulness of the senses there is a gentle preparation for the final insensibility of death. And to him the idea of
mortality comes in a shape less violent and harsh than is its wont,
less as an abrupt catastrophe than as a thing of infinitesimal gradation, and the last step on a long decline of way. As we turn to
and fro in bed, and every moment the movements grow feebler
and smaller and the attitude more restful and easy, until sleep
overtakes us at a stride and we move no more, so desire after
desire leaves him; day by day his strength decreases, and the circle
of his activity grows ever narrower; and he feels, if he is to be thus
tenderly weaned from the passion of life, thus gradually inducted
into the slumber of death, that when at last the end comes, it will
come quietly and fitly. If anything is to reconcile poor spirits to
the coming of the last enemy, surely it should be such a mild approach as this; not to hale us forth with violence, but to persuade
us from a place we have no further pleasure in. It is not so much,
indeed, death that approaches as life that withdraws and withers
up from round about him. He has outlived his own usefulness,
and almost his own enjoyment; and if there is to be no recovery;
if never again will he be young and strong and passionate, if the
actual present shall be to him always like a thing read in a book or
remembered out of the far-away past; if, in fact, this be veritably
nightfall, he will not wish greatly for the continuance of a twilight
that only strains and disappoints the eyes, but steadfastly await
the perfect darkness. He will pray for Medea: when she comes,
let her either rejuvenate or slay.

And yet the ties that still attach him to the world are many
and kindly. The sight of children has a significance for him such
as it may have for the aged also, but not for others. If he has
been used to feel humanely, and to look upon life somewhat more
widely than from the narrow loophole of personal pleasure and
advancement, it is strange how small a portion of his thoughts will
be changed or embittered by this proximity of death. He knows

that already, in English counties, the sower follows the ploughman up the face of the field, and the rooks follow the sower; and he knows also that he may not live to go home again and see the corn spring and ripen, and be cut down at last, and brought home with gladness. And yet the future of this harvest, the continuance of drought or the coming of rain unseasonably, touch him as sensibly as ever. For he has long been used to wait with interest the issue of events in which his own concern was nothing; and to be joyful in a plenty, and sorrowful for a famine, that did not increase or diminish, by one half loaf, the equable sufficiency of his own supply. Thus there remain unaltered all the disinterested hopes for mankind and a better future which have been the solace and inspiration of his life. These he has set beyond the reach of any fate that only menaces himself; and it makes small difference whether he die five thousand years, or five thousand and fifty years, before the good epoch for which he faithfully labours. He has not deceived himself; he has known from the beginning that he followed the pillar of fire and cloud, only to perish himself in the wilderness, and that it was reserved for others to enter joyfully into possession of the land. And so, as everything grows greyer and quieter about him, and slopes towards extinction, these unfaded visions accompany his sad decline, and follow him, with friendly voices and hopeful words, into the very vestibule of death. The desire of love or of fame scarcely moved him, in his days of health, more strongly than these generous aspirations move him now; and so life is carried forward beyond life, and a vista kept open for the eyes of hope, even when his hands grope already on the face of the impassable.

Lastly, he is bound tenderly to life by the thought of his friends; or shall we not say rather, that by their thought for him, by their unchangeable solicitude and love, he remains woven into the very stuff of life, beyond the power of bodily dissolution to undo? In a thousand ways will he survive and be perpetuated. Much of Étienne de la Boëtie survived during all the years in which Montaigne continued to converse with him on the pages of the ever-delightful essays. Much of what was truly Goethe was dead already when he revisited places that knew him no more, and found no better consolation than the promise of his own verses, that soon he too would be at rest. Indeed, when we think of what it is that we most seek and cherish, and find most pride and pleasure in calling ours, it will sometimes seem to us as if our friends, at our decease, would suffer loss more truly than ourselves. As a monarch who should care more for the outlying colonies he knows on the map or through the report of his vicegerents, than for the trunk of his empire under his eyes at home, are we not more concerned about the shadowy life that we have in the hearts of others, and that portion in their thoughts and fancies which, in a certain far-away sense, belongs to us, than about the real knot of our identity—that central metropolis of self, of which alone we are immediately aware—or the diligent service of arteries and veins and infinitesimal activity of ganglia, which we know (as we know a proposition in Euclid) to be the source and substance of the whole? At the death of every one whom we love, some fair and honourable portion of our existence falls away, and we are dislodged from one of these dear provinces; and they are not, perhaps, the most fortunate who survive a long series of such impoverishments, till their life and influence narrow gradually into the meagre limit of their own spirits, and Death, when he comes at last, can destroy them at one blow.

NOTE.—To this essay I must in honesty append a word or two of qualification; for this is one of the points on which a slightly greater age teaches us a slightly different wisdom:

A youth delights in generalities, and keeps loose from particular obligations; he jogs on the footpath way, himself pursuing butterflies, but courteously lending his applause to the advance of the human species and the coming of the kingdom of justice and love. As he grows older, he begins to think more narrowly of man's action in the general, and perhaps more arrogantly of his own in the particular. He has not that same unspeakable trust in what he would have done had he been spared, seeing finally that that would have been little; but he has a far higher notion of the blank that he will make by dying. A young man feels himself one too many in the world; his is a painful situation; he has no calling; no obvious utility; no ties, but to his parents, and these he is sure to disregard. I do not think that a proper allowance has been made for this true cause of suffering in youth; but by the mere fact of a prolonged existence, we outgrow either the fact or else the feeling. Either we become so callously accustomed to our own useless figure in the world, or else—and this, thank God, in the majority of cases—we so collect about us the interest or the love of our fellows, so multiply our effective part in the affairs of life, that we need to entertain no longer the question of our right to be.

And so in the majority of cases, a man who fancies himself dying, will get cold comfort from the very youthful view expressed in this essay. He, as a living man, has some to help, some to love, some to correct; it may be, some to punish.

These duties cling, not upon humanity, but upon the man himself. It is he, not another, who is one woman's son and a second woman's husband and a third woman's father. That life which began so small, has now grown, with a myriad filaments, into the lives of others. It is not indispensable; another will take the place and shoulder the discharged responsibility; but the better the man and the nobler his purposes, the more will he be tempted to regret the extinction of his powers and the deletion of his personality. To have lived a generation, is not only to have grown at home in that perplexing medium, but to have assumed innumerable duties. To die at such an age, has, for all but the entirely base, something of the air of a betrayal. A man does not only reflect upon what he might have done in a future that is never to be his; but beholding himself so early a deserter from the fight, he eats his heart for the good he might have done already. To have been so useless and now to lose all hope of being useful any more—there it is that death and memory assail him. And even if mankind shall go on, founding heroic cities, practising heroic virtues, rising steadily from strength to strength; even if his work shall be fulfilled, his friends consoled, his wife remarried by a better than he; how shall this alter, in one jot, his estimation of a career which was his only business in this world, which was so fitfully pursued, and which is now so ineffectively to end?

AN APOLOGY FOR IDLERS

"BOSWELL: We grow weary when idle.

"JOHNSON: That is, sir, because others being busy, we want company; but if we were idle, there would be no growing weary; we should all entertain one another."

JUST now, when every one is bound, under pain of a decree in absence convicting them of *lèse*-respectability, to enter on some lucrative profession, and labour therein with something not far short of enthusiasm, a cry from the opposite party who are content when they have enough, and like to look on and enjoy in the meanwhile, savours a little of bravado and gasconade. And yet this should not be. Idleness so called, which does not consist in doing nothing, but in doing a great deal not recognised in the dogmatic formularies of the ruling class, has as good a right to state its position as industry itself. It is admitted that the presence of people who refuse to enter in the great handicap race for sixpenny pieces, is at once an insult and a disenchantment for those who do. A fine fellow (as we see so many) takes his determination, votes for the sixpences, and in the emphatic Americanism, "goes for" them. And while such an one is ploughing distressfully up the road, it is not hard to understand his resentment, when he perceives cool persons in the meadows by the wayside, lying with a handkerchief over their ears and a glass at their elbow. Alexander is touched in a very delicate place by the disregard of Diogenes. Where was the glory of having taken Rome for these tumultuous barbarians, who poured into the Senate house, and found the Fathers sitting silent and unmoved by their success? It is a sore thing to have laboured along and scaled the arduous hilltops, and when all is done, find humanity indifferent to your achievement. Hence physicists condemn the unphysical; financiers have only a superficial toleration for those who know little of stocks; literary persons despise the unlettered; and people of all pursuits combine to disparage those who have none.

But though this is one difficulty of the subject, it is not the greatest. You could not be put in prison for speaking against industry, but you can be sent to Coventry for speaking like a fool. The greatest difficulty with most subjects is to do them well; therefore, please to remember this is an apology. It is certain that much may be judiciously argued in favor of diligence; only there is something to be said against it, and that is what, on the present occasion, I have to say. To state one argument is not necessarily to be deaf to all others, and that a man has written a book of travels in Montenegro, is no reason why he should never have been to Richmond.

It is surely beyond a doubt that people should be a good deal idle in youth. For though here and there a Lord Macaulay may escape from school honours with all his wits about him, most boys pay so dear for their medals that they never afterwards have a shot in their locker, and begin the world bankrupt. And the same holds true during all the time a lad is educating himself, or suffering others to educate him. It must have been a very foolish old gentleman who addressed Johnson at Oxford in these words: "Young man, ply your book diligently now, and acquire a stock of knowledge; for when years come upon you, you will find that poring upon books will be but an irksome task." The old gentleman seems to have been unaware that many other things besides reading grow irksome, and not a few become impossible, by the time a man has to use spectacles and cannot walk without a stick. Books are good enough in their own way, but they are a mighty bloodless substitute for life. It seems a pity to sit, like the Lady of

Shalott, peering into a mirror, with your back turned on all the bustle and glamour of reality. And if a man reads very hard, as the old anecdote reminds us, he will have little time for thoughts.

If you look back on your own education, I am sure it will not be the full, vivid, instructive hours of truantry that you regret; you would rather cancel some lack-lustre periods between sleep and waking in the class. For my own part, I have attended a good many lectures in my time. I still remember that the spinning of a top is a case of Kinetic Stability. I still remember that Emphyteusis is not a disease, nor Stillicide a crime. But though I would not willingly part with such scraps of science, I do not set the same store by them as by certain other odds and ends that I came by in the open street while I was playing truant. This is not the moment to dilate on that mighty place of education, which was the favourite school of Dickens and of Balzac, and turns out yearly many inglorious masters in the Science of the Aspects of Life. Suffice it to say this: if a lad does not learn in the streets, it is because he has no faculty of learning. Nor is the truant always in the streets, for if he prefers, he may go out by the gardened suburbs into the country. He may pitch on some tuft of lilacs over a burn, and smoke innumerable pipes to the tune of the water on the stones. A bird will sing in the thicket. And there he may fall into a vein of kindly thought, and see things in a new perspective. Why, if this be not education, what is? We may conceive Mr. Worldly Wiseman accosting such an one, and the conversation that should thereupon ensue:—

"How, now, young fellow, what dost thou here?"

"Truly, sir, I take mine ease."

"Is not this the hour of the class? and should'st thou not be plying thy Book with diligence, to the end thou mayest obtain knowledge?"

"Nay, but thus also I follow after Learning, by your leave."

"Learning, quotha! After what fashion, I pray thee? Is it mathematics?"

"No, to be sure."

"Is it metaphysics?"

"Nor that."

"Is it some language?"

"Nay, it is no language."

"Is it a trade?"

"Nor a trade neither."

"Why, then, what is't?"

"Indeed, sir, as a time may soon come for me to go upon Pilgrimage, I am desirous to note what is commonly done by persons in my case, and where are the ugliest Sloughs and Thickets on the Road; as also, what manner of Staff is of the best service. Moreover, I lie here, by this water, to learn by root-of-heart a lesson which my master teaches me to call Peace, or Contentment."

Hereupon Mr. Worldly Wiseman was much commoved with passion, and shaking his cane with a very threatful countenance, broke forth upon this wise: "Learning, quotha!" said he; "I would have all such rogues scourged by the Hangman!"

And so he would go his way, ruffling out his cravat with a crackle of starch, like a turkey when it spreads its feathers.

Now this, of Mr. Wiseman's, is the common opinion. A fact is not called a fact, but a piece of gossip, if it does not fall into one of your scholastic categories. An inquiry must be in some acknowledged direction, with a name to go by; or else you are not inquiring at all, only lounging; and the workhouse is too good for you. It is supposed that all knowledge is at the bottom of a well, or the far end of a telescope. Sainte-Beuve, as he grew older, came to regard all experience as a single great book, in which to study for a few years ere we go hence; and it seemed all one to him whether you should read in Chapter xx., which is the differential calculus, or in Chapter xxxix., which is hearing the band play in the gardens. As a matter of fact, an intelligent person, looking out of his eyes and hearkening in his ears, with a smile on his face all the time, will get more true education than many another in a life of heroic vigils. There is certainly some chill and arid knowledge to be found upon the summits of formal and laborious science; but it is all round about you, and for the trouble of looking, that you will acquire the warm and palpitating facts of life. While others are filling their memory with a lumber of words, one-half of which they will forget before the week be out, your truant may learn some really useful art: to play the fiddle, to know a good cigar, or to speak with ease and opportunity to all varieties of men. Many who have "plied their book diligently," and know all about some one branch or another of accepted lore, come out of the study with an ancient and owl-like demeanour, and prove dry, stockish, and dyspeptic in all the better and brighter parts of life. Many make a large fortune, who remain underbred and pathetically stupid to the last. And meantime there goes the idler, who began life along with them—by your leave, a different picture. He has had time to take care of his health and his spirits; he has been a great deal in the open air, which is the most salutary of all things for both body and mind; and if he has never read the great Book in very recondite places, he has dipped into it and skimmed it over to excellent purpose. Might not the student afford some Hebrew roots, and the business man some of his half-crowns, for a share of the idler's knowledge of life at large, and Art of Living? Nay, and the idler has another and more important quality than these. I mean his wisdom. He who has much looked on at the childish satisfaction of other people in their hobbies, will regard his own with only a very ironical indulgence. He will not be heard among the dogmatists. He will have a great and cool allowance for all sorts of people and opinions. If he finds no out-of-the-way truths, he will identify himself with no very burning falsehood. His way takes him along a by-road, not much frequented, but very even and pleasant, which is called Commonplace Lane, and leads to the Belvedere of Common-sense. Thence he shall command an agreeable, if no very noble prospect; and while others behold the East and West, the Devil and the Sunrise, he will be contentedly aware of a sort of morning hour upon all sublunary things, with an army of shadows running speedily and in many different directions into the great daylight of Eternity. The shadows and the generations, the shrill doctors and the plangent wars, go by into ultimate silence and emptiness; but underneath all this, a man may see, out of the Belvedere windows, much green and peaceful landscape; many firelit parlours; good people laughing, drinking, and making love as they did before the Flood or the French Revolution; and the old shepherd telling his tale under the hawthorn.

Extreme *busyness*, whether at school or college, kirk or market, is a symptom of deficient vitality; and a faculty for idleness implies a catholic appetite and a strong sense of personal identity. There is a sort of dead-alive, hackneyed people about, who are scarcely conscious of living except in the exercise of some conventional occupation. Bring these fellows into the country, or set them aboard ship, and you will see how they pine for their desk or their study. They have no curiosity: they cannot give themselves over to random provocations; they do not take pleasure in the exercise of their faculties for its own sake; and unless Necessity lays about them with a stick, they will even stand still. It is no good speaking to such folk: they *cannot* be idle, their nature is not generous enough; and they pass those hours in a sort of coma, which are not dedicated to furious moiling in the gold-mill. When they do not require to go to the office, when they are not hungry and have no mind to drink, the whole breathing world is a blank to them. If they have to wait an hour or so for a train, they fall into a stupid trance with their eyes open. To see them, you would suppose there was nothing to look at and no one to speak with; you would imagine they were paralysed or alienated; and yet very possibly they are hard workers in their own way, and have good eyesight for a flaw in a deed or a turn of the market. They have been to school and college, but all the time they had their eye on the medal; they have gone about in the world and mixed with clever people, but all the time they were thinking of their own affairs. As if a man's soul were not too small to begin with, they have dwarfed and narrowed theirs by a life of all work and no play; until here they are at forty, with a listless attention, a mind vacant of all material of amusement, and not one thought to rub against another while they wait for the train. Before he was breeched, he might have clambered on the boxes; when he was twenty, he would have stared at the girls; but now the pipe is smoked out, the snuffbox empty, and my gentleman sits bolt upright upon a bench, with lamentable eyes. This does not appeal to me as being Success in Life.

But it is not only the person himself who suffers from his busy habits, but his wife and children, his friends and relations, and down to the very people he sits with in a railway carriage or an omnibus. Perpetual devotion to what a man calls his business is only to be sustained by perpetual neglect of many other things. And it is not by any means certain that a man's business is the most important thing he has to do. To an impartial estimate it will seem clear that many of the wisest, most virtuous, and most beneficent parts that are to be played upon the Theatre of Life are filled by gratuitous performers, and pass, among the world at large, as phases of

idleness. For in that Theatre, not only the walking gentlemen,
singing chambermaids, and diligent fiddlers in the orchestra, but
those who look on and clap their hands from the benches, do really
play a part and fulfil important offices toward the general result.
You are no doubt very dependent on the care of your lawyer and
stockbroker, of the guards and signalmen who convey you rapidly
from place to place, and the policemen who walk the streets for
your protection; but is there not a thought of gratitude in your
heart for certain other benefactors who set you smiling when they
fall in your way, or season your dinner with good company?
Colonel Newcome helped to lose his friend's money; Fred Bayham
had an ugly trick of borrowing shirts; and yet they were better
people to fall among than Mr. Barnes. And though Falstaff was
neither sober nor very honest, I think I could name one or two
long-faced Barabbases whom the world could better have done
without. Hazlitt mentions that he was more sensible of obligation
to Northcote, who had never done him anything he could call a
service, than to his whole circle of ostentatious friends; for he
thought a good companion emphatically the greatest benefactor.
I know there are people in the world who cannot feel grateful unless the favour has been done them at the cost of pain and difficulty.
But this is a churlish disposition. A man may send you six sheets
of letter-paper covered with the most entertaining gossip, or you
may pass half an hour pleasantly, perhaps profitably, over an
article of his; do you think the service would be greater, if he had
made the manuscript in his heart's blood, like a compact with the
devil? Do you really fancy you should be more beholden to your
correspondent, if he had been damning you all the while for your
importunity? Pleasures are more beneficial than duties because,
like the quality of mercy, they are not strained, and they are twice
blest. There must always be two to a kiss, and there may be a
score in a jest; but wherever there is an element of sacrifice, the
favour is conferred with pain, and, among generous people, received
with confusion. There is no duty we so much underrate as the
duty of being happy. By being happy, we sow anonymous benefits
upon the world, which remain unknown even to ourselves, or when
they are disclosed, surprise nobody so much as the benefactor.
The other day, a ragged, barefoot boy ran down the street after a
marble, with so jolly an air that he set every one he passed into a

good-humour; one of these persons, who had been delivered from more than usually black thoughts, stopped the little fellow and gave him some money with this remark: "You see what sometimes comes of looking pleased." If he had looked pleased before, he had now to look both pleased and mystified. For my part, I justify this encouragement of smiling rather than tearful children; I do not wish to pay for tears anywhere but upon the stage; but I am prepared to deal largely in the opposite commodity. A happy man or woman is a better thing to find than a five-pound note. He or she is a radiating focus of good-will; and their entrance into a room is as though another candle had been lighted. We need not care whether they could prove the forty-seventh proposition; they do a better thing than that, they practically demonstrate the great Theorem of the Livableness of Life. Consequently, if a person cannot be happy without remaining idle, idle he should remain. It is a revolutionary precept; but thanks to hunger and the workhouse, one not easily to be abused; and within practical limits, it is one of the most incontestable truths in the whole Body of Morality. Look at one of your industrious fellows for a moment, I beseech you. He sows hurry and reaps indigestion; he puts a vast deal of activity out to interest, and receives a large measure of nervous derangement in return. Either he absents himself entirely from all fellowship, and lives a recluse in a garret, with carpet slippers and a leaden inkpot; or he comes among people swiftly and bitterly, in a contraction of his whole nervous system, to discharge some temper before he returns to work. I do not care how much or how well he works, this fellow is an evil feature in other people's lives. They would be happier if he were dead. They could easier do without his services in the Circumlocution Office, than they can tolerate his fractious spirits. He poisons life at the well-head. It is better to be beggared out of hand by a scapegrace nephew, than daily hag-ridden by a peevish uncle.

And what, in God's name, is all this pother about? For what cause do they embitter their own and other people's lives? That a man should publish three or thirty articles a year, that he should finish or not finish his great allegorical picture, are questions of little interest to the world. The ranks of life are full; and although a thousand fall, there are always some to go into the breach. When they told Joan of Arc she should be at home minding women's work, she answered there were plenty to spin and wash. And so, even with your own rare gifts! When nature is "so careless of the single life," why should we coddle ourselves into the fancy that our own is of exceptional importance? Suppose Shakespeare had been knocked on the head some dark night in Sir Thomas Lucy's preserves, the world would have wagged on better or worse, the pitcher gone to the well, the scythe to the corn, and the student to his book; and no one been any the wiser of the loss. There are not many works extant, if you look the alternative all over, which are worth the price of a pound of tobacco to a man of limited means. This is a sobering reflection for the proudest of our earthly vanities. Even a tobacconist may, upon consideration, find no great cause for personal vainglory in the phrase; for although tobacco is an admirable sedative, the qualities necessary for retailing it are neither rare nor precious in themselves. Alas and alas! you may take it how you will, but the services of no single individual are indispensable. Atlas was just a gentleman with a protracted nightmare! And yet you see merchants who go and labour themselves into a great fortune and thence into the bankruptcy court; scribblers who keep scribbling at little articles until their temper is a cross to all who come about them, as though Pharaoh should set the Israelites to make a pin instead of a pyramid; and fine young men who work themselves into a decline, and are driven off in a hearse with white plumes upon it. Would you not suppose these persons had been whispered, by the Master of the Ceremonies, the promise of some momentous destiny? and that this lukewarm bullet on which they play their farces was the bull's-eye and centrepoint of all the universe? And yet it is not so. The ends for which they give away their priceless youth, for all they know, may be chimerical or hurtful; the glory and riches they expect may never come, or may find them indifferent; and they and the world they inhabit are so inconsiderable that the mind freezes at the thought.

CRABBED AGE AND YOUTH

"You know my mother now and then argues very notably; always very warmly at least. I happen often to differ from her; and we both think so well of our own arguments, that we very seldom are so happy as to convince one another. A pretty common case, I believe, in all *vehement* debatings. She says, I am *too witty;* Anglicè, *too pert;* I, that she is *too wise;* that is to say, being likewise put into English, *not so young as she has been.*"—Miss Howe to Miss Harlowe, *Clarissa*, vol. ii. Letter xiii.

THERE is a strong feeling in favour of cowardly and prudential proverbs. The sentiments of a man while he is full of ardour and hope are to be received, it is supposed, with some qualification. But when the same person has ignominiously failed and begins to eat up his words, he should be listened to like an oracle. Most of our pocket wisdom is conceived for the use of mediocre people, to discourage them from ambitious attempts, and generally console them in their mediocrity. And since mediocre people constitute the bulk of humanity, this is no doubt very properly so. But it does not follow that the one sort of proposition is any less true than the other, or that Icarus is not to be more praised, and perhaps more envied, than Mr. Samuel Budgett the Successful Merchant. The one is dead, to be sure, while the other is still in his counting-house counting out his money; and doubtless this is a consideration. But we have, on the other hand, some bold and magnanimous sayings common to high races and natures, which set forth the advantage of the losing side, and proclaim it better to be a dead lion than a living dog. It is difficult to fancy how the mediocrities reconcile such sayings with their proverbs. According to the latter, every lad who goes to sea is an egregious ass; never to forget your umbrella through a long life would seem a higher and wiser flight of achievement than to go smiling to the stake; and so long as you are a bit of a coward and inflexible in money matters, you fulfil the whole duty of man.

It is a still more difficult consideration for our average men, that while all their teachers, from Solomon down to Benjamin Franklin and the ungodly Binney, have inculcated the same ideal of manners, caution, and respectability, those characters in history who have most notoriously flown in the face of such precepts are spoken of in hyperbolical terms of praise, and honoured with public monuments in the streets of our commercial centres. This is very bewildering to the moral sense. You have Joan of Arc, who left a humble but honest and reputable livelihood under the eyes of her parents, to go a-colonelling, in the company of rowdy soldiers, against the enemies of France; surely a melancholy example for one's daughters! And then you have Columbus, who may have pioneered America, but, when all is said, was a most imprudent navigator. His life is not the kind of thing one would like to put into the hands of young people; rather, one would do one's utmost to keep it from their knowledge, as a red flag of adventure and disintegrating influence in life. The time would fail me if I were to recite all the big names in history whose exploits are perfectly irrational and even shocking to the business mind. The incongruity is speaking; and I imagine it must engender among the mediocrities a very peculiar attitude towards the nobler and showier sides of national life. They will read of the Charge of Balaclava in much the same spirit as they assist at a performance of the *Lyons Mail*. Persons of substance take in the *Times* and sit composedly in pit or boxes according to the degree of their prosperity in business. As for the generals who go galloping up and down among bombshells in absurd cocked hats—as for the actors who raddle their faces and demean themselves for hire upon the stage—they must belong, thank God! to a different order of beings, whom we watch as we watch the clouds careering in the windy, bottomless inane, or read about like characters in ancient and rather fabulous annals. Our offspring would no more think of copying their behaviour, let us hope, than of doffing their clothes and painting themselves blue in consequence of certain admissions in the first chapter of their school history of England.

Discredited as they are in practice, the cowardly proverbs hold their own in theory; and it is another instance of the same spirit, that the opinions of old men about life have been accepted as final. All sorts of allowances are made for the illusions of youth; and none, or almost none, for the disenchantments of age. It is held to be a good taunt, and somehow or other to clinch the question logically, when an old gentleman waggles his head and says: "Ah, so I thought when I was your age." It is not thought an answer at all, if the young man retorts: "My venerable sir, so I shall most probably think when I am yours." And yet the one is as good as the other: pass for pass, tit for tat, a Roland for an Oliver.

"Opinion in good men," says Milton, "is but knowledge in the making." All opinions, properly so called, are stages on the road to truth. It does not follow that a man will travel any further; but if he has really considered the world and drawn a conclusion, he has travelled as far. This does not apply to formulæ got by rote, which are stages on the road to nowhere but second childhood and the grave. To have a catchword in your mouth is not the same thing as to hold an opinion; still less is it the same thing as to have made one for yourself. There are too many of these catchwords in the world for people to rap out upon you like an oath and by way of an argument. They have a currency as intellectual counters; and many respectable persons pay their way with nothing else. They seem to stand for vague bodies of theory in the background. The imputed virtue of folios full of knockdown arguments is supposed to reside in them, just as some of the majesty of the British Empire dwells in the constable's truncheon. They are used in pure superstition, as old clodhoppers spoil Latin by way of an exorcism. And yet they are vastly serviceable for checking unprofitable discussion and stopping the mouths of babes and sucklings. And when a young man comes to a certain stage of intellectual growth, the examination of these counters forms a gymnastic at once amusing and fortifying to the mind.

Because I have reached Paris, I am not ashamed of having passed through Newhaven and Dieppe. They were very good places to pass through, and I am none the less at my destination. All my old opinions were only stages on the way to the one I now hold, as itself is only a stage on the way to something else. I am no more abashed at having been a red-hot Socialist with a panacea of my own than at having been a sucking infant. Doubtless the world is quite right in a million ways; but you have to be kicked about a little to convince you of the fact. And in the meanwhile you must do something, be something, believe something. It is not possible to keep the mind in a state of accurate balance and blank; and even if you could do so, instead of coming ultimately to the right conclusion, you would be very apt to remain in a state of balance and blank to perpetuity. Even in quite intermediate stages, a dash of enthusiasm is not a thing to be ashamed of in the retrospect: if St. Paul had not been a very zealous Pharisee, he would have been a colder Christian. For my part, I look back to the time when

I was a Socialist with something like regret. I have convinced myself (for the moment) that we had better leave these great changes to what we call great blind forces; their blindness being so much more perspicacious than the little, peering, partial eyesight of men. I seem to see that my own scheme would not answer; and all the other schemes I ever heard propounded would depress some elements of goodness just as much as they encouraged others. Now I know that in thus turning Conservative with years, I am going through the normal cycle of change and travelling in the common orbit of men's opinions. I submit to this, as I would submit to gout or grey hair, as a concomitant of growing age or else of failing animal heat; but I do not acknowledge that it is necessarily a change for the better—I dare say it is deplorably for the worse. I have no choice in the business, and can no more resist this tendency of my mind than I could prevent my body from beginning to totter and decay. If I am spared (as the phrase runs) I shall doubtless outlive some troublesome desires; but I am in no hurry about that; nor, when the time comes, shall I plume myself on the immunity. Just in the same way, I do not greatly pride myself on having outlived my belief in the fairy tales of Socialism. Old people have faults of their own; they tend to become cowardly, niggardly, and suspicious. Whether from the growth of experience or the decline of animal heat, I see that age leads to these and certain other faults; and it follows, of course, that while in one sense I hope I am journeying toward the truth, in another I am undubitably posting toward these forms and sources of error.

As we go catching and catching at this or that corner of knowledge, now getting a foresight of generous possibilities, now chilled with a glimpse of prudence, we may compare the headlong course of our years to a swift torrent in which a man is carried away; now he is dashed against a boulder, now he grapples for a moment to a trailing spray; at the end, he is hurled out and overwhelmed in a dark and bottomless ocean. We have no more than glimpses and touches; we are torn away from our theories; we are spun round and round and shown this or the other view of life, until only fools or knaves can hold to their opinions. We take a sight at a condition in life, and say we have studied it; our most elaborate view is no more than an impression. If we had breathing space, we should take the occasion to modify and adjust; but at this breakneck hurry, we are no sooner boys than we are adult, no sooner in love than married or jilted, no sooner one age than we begin to be another, and no sooner in the fulness of our manhood than we begin to decline towards the grave. It is in vain to seek for consistency or expect clear and stable views in a medium so perturbed and fleeting. This is no cabinet science, in which things are tested to a scruple; we theorise with a pistol to our head; we are confronted with a new set of conditions on which we have not only to pass a judgment, but to take action, before the hour is at an end. And we cannot even regard ourselves as a constant; in this flux of things, our identity itself seems in a perpetual variation; and not infrequently we find our own disguise the strangest in the masquerade. In the course of time, we grow to love things we hated and hate things we loved. Milton is not so dull as he once was, nor perhaps Ainsworth so amusing. It is decidedly harder to climb trees, and not nearly so hard to sit still. There is no use pretending; even the thrice royal game of hide and seek has somehow lost in zest. All our attributes are modified or changed; and it will be a poor account of us if our views do not modify and change in a proportion. To hold the same views at forty as we held at twenty is to have been stupefied for a score of years, and take rank, not as a prophet, but as an unteachable brat, well birched and none the wiser. It is as if a ship captain should sail to India from the port of London; and having brought a chart of the Thames on deck at his first setting out, should obstinately use no other for the whole voyage.

And mark you, it would be no less foolish to begin at Gravesend with a chart of the Red Sea. *Si Jeunesse savait, si Vieillesse pouvait*, is a very pretty sentiment, but not necessarily right. In five cases out of ten, it is not so much that the young people do not know, as that they do not choose. There is something irreverent in the speculation, but perhaps the want of power has more to do with the wise resolutions of age than we are always willing to admit. It would be an instructive experiment to make an old man young again and leave him all his *savoir*. I scarcely think he would put his money in the Savings Bank after all; I doubt if he would be such an admirable son as we are led to expect; and as for his conduct in love, I believe firmly he would out-Herod Herod, and put the whole of his new compeers to the blush. Prudence is a wooden

Juggernaut, before whom Benjamin Franklin walks with the portly air of a high priest, and after whom dances many a successful merchant in the character of Atys. But it is not a deity to cultivate in youth. If a man lives to any considerable age, it cannot be denied that he laments his imprudences, but I notice he often laments his youth a deal more bitterly and with a more genuine intonation.

It is customary to say that age should be considered, because it comes last. It seems just as much to the point, that youth comes first. And the scale fairly kicks the beam, if you go on to add that age, in a majority of cases, never comes at all. Disease and accident make short work of even the most prosperous persons; death costs nothing, and the expense of a headstone is an inconsiderable trifle to the happy heir. To be suddenly snuffed out in the middle of ambitious schemes, is tragical enough at best; but when a man has been grudging himself his own life in the meanwhile, and saving up everything for the festival that was never to be, it becomes that hysterically moving sort of tragedy which lies on the confines of farce. The victim is dead—and he has cunningly overreached himself: a combination of calamities none the less absurd for being grim. To husband a favorite claret until the batch turns sour, is not at all an artful stroke of policy; and how much more with a whole cellar—a whole bodily existence! People may lay down their lives with cheerfulness in the sure expectation of a blessed immortality; but that is a different affair from giving up youth with all its admirable pleasures, in the hope of a better quality of gruel in a more than problematical, nay, more than improbable, old age. We should not compliment a hungry man, who should refuse a whole dinner and reserve all his appetite for the dessert, before he knew whether there was to be any dessert or not. If there be such a thing as imprudence in the world, we surely have it here. We sail in leaky bottoms and on great and perilous waters; and to take a cue from the dolorous old naval ballad, we have heard the mermaidens singing, and know that we shall never see dry land any more. Old and young, we are all on our last cruise. If there is a fill of tobacco among the crew, for God's sake pass it round, and let us have a pipe before we go!

Indeed, by the report of our elders, this nervous preparation for old age is only trouble thrown away. We fall on guard, and after all it is a friend who comes to meet us. After the sun is down and the west faded, the heavens begin to fill with shining stars. So, as we grow old, a sort of equable jog-trot of feeling is substituted for the violent ups and downs of passion and disgust; the same influence that restrains our hopes, quiets our apprehensions; if the pleasures are less intense, the troubles are milder and more tolerable; and in a word, this period for which we are asked to hoard up everything as for a time of famine, is, in its own right, the richest, easiest, and happiest of life. Nay, by managing its own work and following its own happy inspiration, youth is doing the best it can to endow the leisure of age. A full, busy youth is your only prelude to a self-contained and independent age; and the muff inevitably develops into the bore. There are not many Dr. Johnsons, to set forth upon their first romantic voyage at sixty-four. If we wish to scale Mont Blanc or visit a thieves' kitchen in the East End, to go down in a diving dress or up in a balloon, we must be about it while we are still young. It will not do to delay until we are clogged with prudence and limping with rheumatism, and people begin to ask us, "What does Gravity out of bed?" Youth is the time to go flashing from one end of the world to the other both in mind and body; to try the manners of different nations; to hear the chimes at midnight; to see sunrise in town and country; to be converted at a revival; to circumnavigate the metaphysics, write halting verses, run a mile to see a fire, and wait all day long in the theatre to applaud *Hernani*. There is some meaning in the old theory about wild oats; and a man who has not had his green-sickness and got done with it for good, is as little to be depended on as an unvaccinated infant. "It is extraordinary," says Lord Beaconsfield, one of the brightest and best preserved of youths up to the date of his last novel,[1] "it is extraordinary how hourly and how violently change the feelings of an inexperienced young man." And this mobility is a special talent entrusted to his care; a sort of indestructible virginity; a magic armour, with which he can pass unhurt through great dangers and come unbedaubed out of the miriest passages. Let him voyage, speculate, see all that he can, do all that he may; his soul has as many lives as a cat, he will live in all weathers, and never be a half-penny the worse. Those who go to the devil in youth, with

[1] *Lothair*.

anything like a fair chance, were probably little worth saving from
the first; they must have been feeble fellows—creatures made of
putty and pack-thread, without steel or fire, anger or true joyful-
ness, in their composition; we may sympathise with their parents,
but there is not much cause to go into mourning for themselves;
for to be quite honest, the weak brother is the worst of mankind.

When the old man waggles his head and says, "Ah, so I thought
when I was your age," he has proved the youth's case. Doubtless,
whether from growth of experience or decline of animal heat, he
thinks so no longer; but he thought so while he was young; and all
men have thought so while they were young, since there was dew
in the morning or hawthorn in May; and here is another young
man adding his vote to those of previous generations and rivetting
another link to the chain of testimony. It is as natural and as right
for a young man to be imprudent and exaggerated, to live in
swoops and circles, and beat about his cage like any other wild
thing newly captured, as it is for old men to turn grey, or mothers
to love their offspring, or heroes to die for something worthier than
their lives.

By way of an apologue for the aged, when they feel more than
usually tempted to offer their advice, let me recommend the following little tale. A child who had been remarkably fond of toys
(and in particular of lead soldiers) found himself growing to the
level of acknowledged boyhood without any abatement of this
childish taste. He was thirteen; already he had been taunted for
dallying overlong about the playbox; he had to blush if he was
found among his lead soldiers; the shades of the prison-house were
closing about him with a vengeance. There is nothing more difficult than to put the thoughts of children into the language of their
elders; but this is the effect of his meditations at this juncture:
"Plainly," he said, "I must give up my playthings, in the meanwhile, since I am not in a position to secure myself against idle
jeers. At the same time, I am sure that playthings are the very
pick of life; all people give them up out of the same pusillanimous
respect for those who are a little older; and if they do not return
to them as soon as they can, it is only because they grow stupid
and forget. I shall be wiser; I shall conform for a little to the ways
of their foolish world; but so soon as I have made enough money,
I shall retire and shut myself up among my playthings until the

day I die." Nay, as he was passing in the train along the Esterel
mountains between Cannes and Fréjus, he remarked a pretty
house in an orange garden at the angle of a bay, and decided that
this should be his Happy Valley. Astrea Redux; childhood was to
come again! The idea has an air of simple nobility to me, not unworthy of Cincinnatus. And yet, as the reader has probably anticipated, it is never likely to be carried into effect. There was a worm
in the bud, a fatal error in the premises. Childhood must pass
away, and then youth, as surely as age approaches. The true wisdom is to be always seasonable, and to change with a good grace
in changing circumstances. To love playthings well as a child,
to lead an adventurous and honourable youth, and to settle, when
the time arrives, into a green and smiling age, is to be a good artist
in life and deserve well of yourself and your neighbour.

You need repent none of your youthful vagaries. They may
have been over the score on one side, just as those of age are probably over the score on the other. But they had a point; they not
only befitted your age and expressed its attitude and passions,
but they had a relation to what was outside of you, and implied
criticisms on the existing state of things, which you need not allow
to have been undeserved, because you now see that they were
partial. All error, not merely verbal, is a strong way of stating
that the current truth is incomplete. The follies of youth have a
basis in sound reason, just as much as the embarrassing questions
put by babes and sucklings. Their most antisocial acts indicate
the defects of our society. When the torrent sweeps the man
against a boulder, you must expect him to scream, and you need
not be surprised if the scream is sometimes a theory. Shelley,
chafing at the Church of England, discovered the cure of all evils
in universal atheism. Generous lads, irritated at the injustices of
society, see nothing for it but the abolishment of everything and
Kingdom Come of anarchy. Shelley was a young fool; so are these
cock-sparrow revolutionaries. But it is better to be a fool than
to be dead. It is better to emit a scream in the shape of a theory
than to be entirely insensible to the jars and incongruities of life
and take everything as it comes in a forlorn stupidity. Some
people swallow the universe like a pill; they travel on through the
world like smiling images pushed from behind. For God's sake
give me the young man who has brains enough to make a fool of

himself! As for the others, the irony of facts shall take it out of their hands, and make fools of them in downright earnest, ere the farce be over. There shall be such a mopping and a mowing at the last day, and such blushing and confusion of countenance for all those who have been wise in their own esteem, and have not learnt the rough lessons that youth hands on to age. If we are indeed here to perfect and complete our own natures, and grow larger, stronger, and more sympathetic against some nobler career in the future, we had all best bestir ourselves to the utmost while we have the time. To equip a dull, respectable person with wings would be but to make a parody of an angel.

In short, if youth is not quite right in its opinions, there is a strong probability that age is not much more so. Undying hope is co-ruler of the human bosom with infallible credulity. A man finds he has been wrong at every preceding stage of his career, only to deduce the astonishing conclusion that he is at last entirely right. Mankind, after centuries of failure, are still upon the eve of a thoroughly constitutional millennium. Since we have explored the maze so long without result, it follows, for poor human reason, that we cannot have to explore much longer; close by must be the centre, with a champagne luncheon and a piece of ornamental water. How if there were no centre at all, but just one alley after another, and the whole world a labyrinth without end or issue?

I overheard the other day a scrap of conversation, which I take the liberty to reproduce. "What I advance is true," said one. "But not the whole truth," answered the other. "Sir," returned the first (and it seemed to me there was a smack of Dr. Johnson in the speech), "Sir, there is no such thing as the whole truth!" Indeed, there is nothing so evident in life as that there are two sides to a question. History is one long illustration. The forces of nature are engaged, day by day, in cudgelling it into our backward intelligences. We never pause for a moment's consideration, but we admit it as an axiom. An enthusiast sways humanity exactly by disregarding this great truth, and dinning it into our ears that this or that question has only one possible solution; and your enthusiast is a fine florid fellow, dominates things for awhile and shakes the world out of a doze; but when once he is gone, an army of quiet and uninfluential people set to work to remind us of the other side and demolish the generous imposture. While Calvin is putting everybody exactly right in his *Institutes*, and hot-headed Knox is thundering in the pulpit, Montaigne is already looking at the other side in his library in Perigord, and predicting that they will find as much to quarrel about in the Bible as they had found already in the Church. Age may have one side, but assuredly Youth has the other. There is nothing more certain than that both are right, except perhaps that both are wrong. Let them agree to differ; for who knows but what agreeing to differ may not be a form of agreement rather than a form of difference?

I suppose it is written that any one who sets up for a bit of a philosopher must contradict himself to his very face. For here have I fairly talked myself into thinking that we have the whole thing before us at last; that there is no answer to the mystery, except that there are as many as you please; that there is no centre to the maze because, like the famous sphere, its centre is everywhere; and that agreeing to differ with every ceremony of politeness, is the only "one undisturbed song of pure content" to which we are ever likely to lend our musical voices.

ÆS TRIPLEX

THE changes wrought by death are in themselves so sharp and final, and so terrible and melancholy in their consequences, that the thing stands alone in man's experience, and has no parallel upon earth. It outdoes all other accidents because it is the last of them. Sometimes it leaps suddenly upon its victims like a Thug; sometimes it lays a regular siege and creeps upon their citadel during a score of years. And when the business is done, there is sore havoc made in other people's lives, and a pin knocked out by which many subsidiary friendships hung together. There are empty chairs, solitary walks, and single beds at night. Again, in taking away our friends, death does not take them away utterly, but leaves behind a mocking, tragical, and soon intolerable residue, which must be hurriedly concealed. Hence a whole chapter of sights and customs striking to the mind, from the pyramids of Egypt to the gibbets and dule trees of mediæval Europe. The poorest persons have a bit of pageant going towards the tomb; memorial stones are set up over the least memorable; and, in order to preserve some show of respect for what remains of our old loves and friendships, we must accompany it with much grimly ludicrous ceremonial, and the hired undertaker parades before the door. All this, and much more of the same sort, accompanied by the eloquence of poets, has gone a great way to put humanity in error; nay, in many philosophies the error has been embodied and laid down with every circumstance of logic; although in real life the bustle and swiftness, in leaving people little time to think, have not left them time enough to go dangerously wrong in practice.

As a matter of fact, although few things are spoken of with more fearful whisperings than this prospect of death, few have less influence on conduct under healthy circumstances. We have all heard of cities in South America built upon the side of fiery mountains, and how, even in this tremendous neighbourhood, the inhabitants are not a jot more impressed by the solemnity of mortal conditions than if they were delving gardens in the greenest corner of England. There are serenades and suppers and much gallantry among the myrtles overhead; and meanwhile the foundation shudders underfoot, the bowels of the mountain growl, and at any moment living ruin may leap sky-high into the moonlight, and tumble man and his merry-making in the dust. In the eyes of very young people, and very dull old ones, there is something indescribably reckless and desperate in such a picture. It seems not credible that respectable married people, with umbrellas, should find appetite for a bit of supper within quite a long distance of a fiery mountain; ordinary life begins to smell of high-handed debauch when it is carried on so close to a catastrophe; and even cheese and salad, it seems, could hardly be relished in such circumstances without something like a defiance of the Creator. It should be a place for nobody but hermits dwelling in prayer and maceration, or mere born-devils drowning care in a perpetual carouse.

And yet, when one comes to think upon it calmly, the situation of these South American citizens forms only a very pale figure for the state of ordinary mankind. This world itself, travelling blindly and swiftly in over-crowded space, among a million other worlds travelling blindly and swiftly in contrary directions, may very well come by a knock that would set it into explosion like a penny squib. And what, pathologically looked at, is the human body with all its organs, but a mere bagful of petards? The least of these is as dangerous to the whole economy as the ship's powder-magazine to the ship; and with every breath we breathe, and every meal we eat, we are putting one or more of them in peril. If we clung as devotedly as some philosophers pretend we do to the abstract idea of life, or were half as frightened as they make out we are, for the subversive accident that ends it all, the trumpets might sound by the hour and no one would follow them into battle— the blue-peter might fly at the truck, but who would climb into a sea-going ship? Think (if these philosophers were right) with what a preparation of spirit we should affront the daily peril of the dinner-table: a deadlier spot than any battle-field in history, where the far greater proportion of our ancestors have miserably left their bones! What woman would ever be lured into marriage, so much more dangerous than the wildest sea? And what would it be to grow old? For, after a certain distance, every step we take in life we find the ice growing thinner below our feet, and all around us and behind us we see our contemporaries going through. By the time a man gets well into the seventies, his continued exist- ence is a mere miracle; and when he lays his old bones in bed for the night, there is an overwhelming probability that he will never see the day. Do the old men mind it, as a matter of fact? Why, no. They were never merrier; they have their grog at night, and tell the raciest stories; they hear of the death of people about their own age, or even younger, not as if it was a grisly warning, but with a simple childlike pleasure at having outlived some one else; and when a draught might puff them out like a guttering candle, or a bit of a stumble shatter them like so much glass, their old hearts keep sound and unaffrighted, and they go on, bubbling with laughter, through years of man's age compared to which the valley at Balaclava was as safe and peaceful as a village cricket-green on Sunday. It may fairly be questioned (if we look to the peril only) whether it was a much more daring feat for Curtius to plunge into the gulf, than for any old gentleman of ninety to doff his clothes and clamber into bed.

Indeed, it is a memorable subject for consideration, with what unconcern and gaiety mankind pricks on along the Valley of the Shadow of Death. The whole way is one wilderness of snares, and the end of it, for those who fear the last pinch, is irrevocable ruin. And yet we go spinning through it all, like a party for the Derby. Perhaps the reader remembers one of the humourous devices of the deified Caligula: how he encouraged a vast concourse of holiday-makers on to his bridge over Baiæ bay; and when they were in the height of their enjoyment, turned loose the Prætorian guards among the company, and had them tossed into the sea. This is no bad miniature of the dealings of nature with the transitory race of man. Only, what a chequered picnic we have of it, even while it lasts! and into what great waters, not to be crossed by any swimmer, God's pale Prætorian throws us over in the end!

We live the time that a match flickers; we pop the cork of a ginger-beer bottle, and the earthquake swallows us on the instant. Is it not odd, is it not incongruous, is it not, in the highest sense of human speech, incredible, that we should think so highly of the ginger-beer, and regard so little the devouring earthquake? The love of Life and the fear of Death are two famous phrases that grow harder to understand the more we think about them. It is a well-known fact that an immense proportion of boat accidents would never happen if people held the sheet in their hands instead of making it fast; and yet, unless it be some martinet of a professional mariner or some landsman with shattered nerves, every one of God's creatures makes it fast. A strange instance of man's unconcern and brazen boldness in the face of death!

We confound ourselves with metaphysical phrases, which we import into daily talk with noble inappropriateness. We have no idea of what death is, apart from its circumstances and some of its consequences to others; and although we have some experience of living, there is not a man on earth who has flown so high into abstraction as to have any practical guess at the meaning of the word *life*. All literature, from Job and Omar Khayyam to Thomas Carlyle or Walt Whitman, is but an attempt to look upon the human state with such largeness of view as shall enable us to rise from the consideration of living to the Definition of Life. And our sages give us about the best satisfaction in their power when they say that it is a vapour, or a show, or made out of the same stuff with dreams. Philosophy, in its more rigid sense, has been at the same work for ages; and after a myriad bald heads have wagged over the problem, and piles of words have been heaped one upon another into dry and cloudy volumes without end, philosophy has the honour of laying before us, with modest pride, her contribution toward the subject: that life is a Permanent Possibility of Sensation. Truly a fine result! A man may very well love beef, or hunt-ing, or a woman; but surely, surely, not a Permanent Possibility of Sensation! He may be afraid of a precipice, or a dentist, or a large enemy with a club, or even an undertaker's man; but not certainly of abstract death. We may trick with the word life in its dozen senses until we are weary of tricking; we may argue in terms of all the philosophies on earth, but one fact remains true throughout—that we do not love life, in the sense that we are greatly preoccupied about its conservation; that we do not, properly speaking, love life at all, but living. Into the views of the least careful there will enter some degree of providence; no man's eyes are fixed entirely on the passing hour; but although we have some anticipation of good health, good weather, wine, active employment, love, and self-approval, the sum of these anticipations does not amount to anything like a general view of life's possibilities and issues; nor are those who cherish them most vividly, at all the most scrupulous of their personal safety. To be deeply interested in the accidents of our existence, to enjoy keenly the mixed texture of human experience, rather leads a man to disregard precautions, and risk his neck against a straw. For surely the love of living is stronger in an Alpine climber roping over a peril, or a hunter riding merrily at a stiff fence, than in a creature who lives upon a diet and walks a measured distance in the interest of his constitution.

There is a great deal of very vile nonsense talked upon both sides of the matter: tearing divines reducing life to the dimensions of a mere funeral procession, so short as to be hardly decent; and melancholy unbelievers yearning for the tomb as if it were a world too far away. Both sides must feel a little ashamed of their perform-ances now and again when they draw in their chairs to dinner. Indeed, a good meal and a bottle of wine is an answer to most standard works upon the question. When a man's heart warms to his viands, he forgets a great deal of sophistry, and soars into a rosy zone of contemplation. Death may be knocking at the door, like the Commander's statue; we have something else in hand, thank God, and let him knock. Passing bells are ringing all the world over. All the world over, and every hour, some one is part-ing company with all his aches and ecstacies. For us also the trap is laid. But we are so fond of life that we have no leisure to enter-tain the terror of death. It is a honeymoon with us all through, and none of the longest. Small blame to us if we give our whole hearts to this glowing bride of ours, to the appetites, to honour, to the hungry curiosity of the mind, to the pleasure of the eyes in nature, and the pride of our own nimble bodies.

We all of us appreciate the sensations; but as for caring about the Permanence of the Possibility, a man's head is generally very bald, and his senses very dull, before he comes to that. Whether we regard life as a lane leading to a dead wall—a mere bag's end, as the French say—or whether we think of it as a vestibule or gymnasium, where we wait our turn and prepare our faculties for some more noble destiny; whether we thunder in a pulpit, or pule in little atheistic poetry-books, about its vanity and brevity; whether we look justly for years of health and vigour, or are about to mount into a Bath-chair, as a step towards the hearse; in each and all of these views and situations there is but one conclusion possible: that a man should stop his ears against paralysing terror, and run the race that is set before him with a single mind. No one surely could have recoiled with more heartache and terror from the thought of death than our respected lexicographer; and yet we know how little it affected his conduct, how wisely and boldly he walked, and in what a fresh and lively vein he spoke of life. Already an old man, he ventured on his Highland tour; and his heart, bound with triple brass, did not recoil before twenty-seven individual cups of tea. As courage and intelligence are the two qualities best worth a good man's cultivation, so it is the first part of intelligence to recognise our precarious estate in life, and the first part of courage to be not at all abashed before the fact. A frank and somewhat headlong carriage, not looking too anxiously before, not dallying in maudlin regret over the past, stamps the man who is well armoured for this world.

And not only well armoured for himself, but a good friend and a good citizen to boot. We do not go to cowards for tender dealing; there is nothing so cruel as panic; the man who has least fear for his own carcass, has most time to consider others. That eminent chemist who took his walks abroad in tin shoes, and subsisted wholly upon tepid milk, had all his work cut out for him in considerate dealings with his own digestion. So soon as prudence has begun to grow up in the brain, like a dismal fungus, it finds its first expression in a paralysis of generous acts. The victim begins to shrink spiritually; he develops a fancy for parlours with a regulated temperature, and takes his morality on the principle of tin shoes and tepid milk. The care of one important body or soul becomes so engrossing, that all the noises of the outer world begin to come thin and faint into the parlour with the regulated temperature; and the tin shoes go equably forward over blood and rain. To be overwise is to ossify; and the scruple-monger ends by standing stockstill. Now the man who has his heart on his sleeve, and a good whirling weathercock of a brain, who reckons his life as a thing to be dashingly used and cheerfully hazarded, makes a very different acquaintance of the world, keeps all his pulses going true and fast, and gathers impetus as he runs, until, if he be running toward anything better than wildfire, he may shoot up and become a constellation in the end. Lord look after his health; Lord have a care of his soul, says he; and he has at the key of the position, and swashes through incongruity and peril toward his aim. Death is on all sides of him with pointed batteries, as he is on all sides of all of us; unfortunate surprises gird him round; mimmouthed friends and relations hold up their hands in quite a little elegiacal synod about his path: and what cares he for all this? Being a true lover of living, a fellow with something pushing and spontaneous in his inside, he must, like any other soldier, in any other stirring, deadly warfare, push on at his best pace until he touch the goal. "A peerage or Westminster Abbey!" cried Nelson in his bright, boyish, heroic manner. These are great incentives; not for any of these, but for the plain satisfaction of living, of being about their business in some sort or other, do the brave, serviceable men of every nation tread down the nettle danger, and pass flyingly over all the stumbling-blocks of prudence. Think of the heroism of Johnson, think of that superb indifference to mortal limitation that set him upon his dictionary, and carried him through triumphantly until the end! Who, if he were wisely considerate of things at large, would ever embark upon any work much more considerable than a halfpenny post card? Who would project a serial novel, after Thackeray and Dickens had each fallen in midcourse? Who would find heart enough to begin to live, if he dallied with the consideration of death?

And, after all, what sorry and pitiful quibbling all this is! To forego all the issues of living in a parlour with the regulated temperature—as if that were not to die a hundred times over, and for ten years at a stretch! As if it were not to die in one's own lifetime, and without even the sad immunities of death! As if it were not to die, and yet be the patient spectators of our own pitiable change! The Permanent Possibility is preserved, but the sensations carefully held at arm's length, as if one kept a photographic plate in a dark chamber. It is better to lose health like a spendthrift than to waste it like a miser. It is better to live and be done with it, than to die daily in the sickroom. By all means begin your folio; even if the doctor does not give you a year, even if he hesitates about a month, make one brave push and see what can be accomplished in a week. It is not only in finished undertakings that we ought to honour useful labour. A spirit goes out of the man who means execution, which outlives the most untimely ending. All who have meant good work with their whole hearts, have done good work, although they may die before they have the time to sign it. Every heart that has beat strong and cheerfully has left a hopeful impulse behind it in the world, and bettered the tradition of mankind. And even if death catch people, like an open pitfall, and in mid-career, laying out vast projects, and planning monstrous foundations, flushed with hope, and their mouths full of boastful language, they should be at once tripped up and silenced: is there not something brave and spirited in such a termination? and does not life go down with a better grace, foaming in full body over a precipice, than miserably straggling to an end in sandy deltas? When the Greeks made their fine saying that those whom the gods love die young, I cannot help believing they had this sort of death also in their eye. For surely, at whatever age it overtake the man, this is to die young. Death has not been suffered to take so much as an illusion from his heart. In the hot-fit of life, a-tiptoe on the highest point of being, he passes at a bound on to the other side. The noise of the mallet and chisel is scarcely quenched, the trumpets are hardly done blowing, when, trailing with him clouds of glory, this happy-starred, full-blooded spirit shoots into the spiritual land.

EL DORADO

IT seems as if a great deal were attainable in a world where there are so many marriages and decisive battles, and where we all, at certain hours of the day, and with great gusto and despatch, stow a portion of victuals finally and irretrievably into the bag which contains us. And it would seem also, on a hasty view, that the attainment of as much as possible was the one goal of man's contentious life. And yet, as regards the spirit, this is but a semblance. We live in an ascending scale when we live happily, one thing leading to another in an endless series. There is always a new horizon for onward-looking men, and although we dwell on a small planet, immersed in petty business and not enduring beyond a brief period of years, we are so constituted that our hopes are inaccessible, like stars, and the term of hoping is prolonged until the term of life. To be truly happy is a question of how we begin and not of how we end, of what we want and not of what we have. An aspiration is a joy forever, a possession as solid as a landed estate, a fortune which we can never exhaust and which gives us year by year a revenue of pleasurable activity. To have many of these is to be spiritually rich. Life is only a very dull and ill-directed theatre unless we have some interests in the piece; and to those who have neither art nor science, the world is a mere arrangement of colours, or a rough footway where they may very well break their shins. It is in virtue of his own desires and curiosities that any man continues to exist with even patience, that he is charmed by the look of things and people, and that he wakens every morning with a renewed appetite for work and pleasure. Desire and curiosity are the two eyes through which he sees the world in the most enchanted colours: it is they that make women beautiful or fossils interesting: and the man may squander his estate and come to beggary, but if he keeps these two amulets he is still rich in the possibilities of pleasure. Suppose he could take one meal so compact and comprehensive that he should never hunger any more; suppose him, at a glance, to take in all the features of the world and allay the desire for knowledge; suppose him to do the like in any province of experience—would not that man be in a poor way for amusement ever after?

One who goes touring on foot with a single volume in his knapsack reads with circumspection, pausing often to reflect, and often laying the book down to contemplate the landscape or the prints in the inn parlour; for he fears to come to an end of his entertainment, and be left companionless on the last stages of his journey. A young fellow recently finished the works of Thomas Carlyle, winding up, if we remember aright, with the ten notebooks upon Frederick the Great. "What!" cried the young fellow, in consternation, "is there no more Carlyle? Am I left to the daily papers?" A more celebrated instance is that of Alexander, who wept bitterly because he had no more worlds to subdue. And when Gibbon had finished the *Decline and Fall*, he had only a few moments of joy; and it was with a "sober melancholy" that he parted from his labours.

Happily we all shoot at the moon with ineffectual arrows; our hopes are set on inaccessible El Dorado; we come to an end of nothing here below. Interests are only plucked up to sow themselves again, like mustard. You would think, when the child was born, there would be an end to trouble; and yet it is only the beginning of fresh anxieties; and when you have seen it through its teething and its education, and at last its marriage, alas! it is only to have new fears, new quivering sensibilities, with every day; and the health of your children's children grows as touching a concern as that of your own. Again, when you have married your wife, you would think you were got upon a hilltop, and might begin to go downward by an easy slope. But you have only ended courting to begin marriage. Falling in love and winning love are often difficult tasks to overbearing and rebellious spirits; but to keep in love is also a business of some importance, to which both man and wife must bring kindness and good-will. The true love story commences at the altar, when there lies before the married pair a most beautiful contest of wisdom and generosity, and a life-long struggle towards an unattainable ideal. Unattainable? Ay, surely unattainable, from the very fact that they are two instead of one.

"Of making books there is no end," complained the Preacher; and did not perceive how highly he was praising letters as an occupation. There is no end, indeed, to making books or experiments, or to travel, or to gathering wealth. Problem gives rise to problem. We may study for ever, and we are never as learned as we would. We have never made a statue worthy of our dreams.

And when we have discovered a continent, or crossed a chain of mountains, it is only to find another ocean or another plain upon the further side. In the infinite universe there is room for our swiftest diligence and to spare. It is not like the works of Carlyle, which can be read to an end. Even in a corner of it, in a private park, or in the neighbourhood of a single hamlet, the weather and the seasons keep so deftly changing that although we walk there for a lifetime there will be always something new to startle and delight us.

There is only one wish realisable on the earth; only one thing that can be perfectly attained: Death. And from a variety of circumstances we have no one to tell us whether it be worth attaining.

A strange picture we make on our way to our chimæras, ceaselessly marching, grudging ourselves the time for rest; indefatigable, adventurous pioneers. It is true that we shall never reach the goal; it is even more than probable that there is no such place; and if we lived for centuries and were endowed with the powers of a god, we should find ourselves not much nearer what we wanted at the end. O toiling hands of mortals! O unwearied feet, travelling ye know not whither! Soon, soon, it seems to you, you must come forth on some conspicuous hilltop, and but a little way further, against the setting sun, descry the spires of El Dorado. Little do ye know your own blessedness; for to travel hopefully is a better thing than to arrive, and the true success is to labour.

THE FOREIGNER AT HOME

"This is no my ain house;
I ken by the biggin' o't."

TWO recent books,[1] one by Mr. Grant White on England, one on France by the diabolically clever Mr. Hillebrand, may well have set people thinking on the divisions of races and nations. Such thoughts should arise with particular congruity and force to inhabitants of that United Kingdom, peopled from so many different stocks, babbling so many different dialects, and offering in its extent such singular contrasts, from the busiest overpopulation to the unkindliest desert, from the Black Country to

[1] 1881.

the Moor of Rannoch. It is not only when we cross the seas that we go abroad; there are foreign parts of England; and the race that has conquered so wide an empire has not yet managed to assimilate the islands whence she sprang. Ireland, Wales, and the Scottish mountains still cling, in part, to their old Gaelic speech. It was but the other day that English triumphed in Cornwall, and they still show in Mousehole, on St. Michael's Bay, the house of the last Cornish-speaking woman. English itself, which will now frank the traveller through the most of North America, through the greater South Sea Islands, in India, along much of the coast of Africa, and in the ports of China and Japan, is still to be heard, in its home country, in half a hundred varying stages of transition. You may go all over the States, and—setting aside the actual intrusion and influence of foreigners, negro, French, or Chinese—you shall scarce meet with so marked a difference of accent as in the forty miles between Edinburgh and Glasgow, or of dialect as in the hundred miles between Edinburgh and Aberdeen. Book English has gone round the world, but at home we still preserve the racy idioms of our fathers, and every county, in some parts every dale, has its own quality of speech, vocal or verbal. In like manner, local custom and prejudice, even local religion and local law, linger on into the latter end of the nineteenth century—*imperia in imperio*, foreign things at home.

In spite of these promptings to reflection, ignorance of his neighbours is the character of the typical John Bull. His is a domineering nature, steady in fight, imperious to command, but neither curious nor quick about the life of others. In French colonies, and still more in the Dutch, I have read that there is an immediate and lively contact between the dominant and the dominated race, that a certain sympathy is begotten, or at the least a transfusion of prejudices, making life easier for both. But the Englishman sits apart, bursting with pride and ignorance. He figures among his vassals in the hour of peace with the same disdainful air that led him on to victory. A passing enthusiasm for some foreign art or fashion may deceive the world; it cannot impose upon his intimates. He may be amused by a foreigner as by a monkey, but he will never condescend to study him with any patience. Miss Bird, an authoress with whom I profess myself in love, declares all the viands of Japan to be uneatable—a staggering pretension. So, when the Prince of Wales's marriage was celebrated at Mentone by a dinner to the Mentonese, it was proposed to give them solid English fare—roast beef and plum pudding, and no tomfoolery. Here we have either pole of the Britannic folly. We will not eat the food of any foreigner; nor, when we have the chance, will we suffer him to eat of it himself. The same spirit inspired Miss Bird's American missionaries, who had come thousands of miles to change the faith of Japan, and openly professed their ignorance of the religions they were trying to supplant.

I quote an American in this connection without scruple. Uncle Sam is better than John Bull, but he is tarred with the English stick. For Mr. Grant White the States are the New England States and nothing more. He wonders at the amount of drinking in London; let him try San Francisco. He wittily reproves English ignorance as to the status of women in America; but has he not himself forgotten Wyoming? The name Yankee, of which he is so tenacious, is used over the most of the great Union as a term of reproach. The Yankee States, of which he is so staunch a subject, are but a drop in the bucket. And we find in his book a vast virgin ignorance of the life and prospects of America; every view partial, parochial, not raised to the horizon; the moral feeling proper, at the largest, to a clique of States; and the whole scope and atmosphere not American, but merely Yankee. I will go far beyond him in reprobating the assumption and the incivility of my countryfolk to their cousins from beyond the sea; I grill in my blood over the silly rudeness of our newspaper articles; and I do not know where to look when I find myself in company with an American and see my countrymen unbending to him as to a performing dog. But in the case of Mr. Grant White example were better than precept. Wyoming is, after all, more readily accessible to Mr. White than Boston to the English, and the New England self-sufficiency no better justified than the Britannic.

It is so, perhaps, in all countries; perhaps in all, men are most ignorant of the foreigners at home. John Bull is ignorant of the States; he is probably ignorant of India; but considering his opportunities, he is far from ignorant of countries nearer his own door. There is one country, for instance—its frontier not so far from London, its people closely akin, its language the same in all essentials with the English—of which I will go bail he knows nothing.

His ignorance of the sister kingdom cannot be described; it can only be illustrated by anecdote. I once travelled with a man of plausible manners and good intelligence—a University man, as the phrase goes—a man, besides, who had taken his degree in life and knew a thing or two about the age we live in. We were deep in talk, whirling between Peterborough and London; among other things, he began to describe some piece of legal injustice he had recently encountered, and I observed in my innocence that things were not so in Scotland. "I beg your pardon," said he, "this is a matter of law." He had never heard of the Scots law; nor did he choose to be informed. The law was the same for the whole country, he told me roundly; every child knew that. At last, to settle matters, I explained to him that I was a member of a Scottish legal body, and had stood the brunt of an examination in the very law in question. Thereupon he looked me for a moment full in the face and dropped the conversation. This is a monstrous instance, if you like, but it does not stand alone in the experience of Scots.

England and Scotland differ, indeed, in law, in history, in religion, in education, and in the very look of nature and men's faces, not always widely, but always trenchantly. Many particulars that struck Mr. Grant White, a Yankee, struck me, a Scot, no less forcibly; he and I felt ourselves foreigners on many common provocations. A Scotsman may tramp the better part of Europe and the United States, and never again receive so vivid an impression of foreign travel and strange lands and manners as on his first excursion into England. The change from a hilly to a level country strikes him with delighted wonder. Along the flat horizon there arise the frequent venerable towers of churches. He sees at the end of airy vistas the revolution of the windmill sails. He may go where he pleases in the future; he may see Alps, and Pyramids, and lions; but it will be hard to beat the pleasure of that moment. There are, indeed, few merrier spectacles than that of many windmills bickering together in a fresh breeze over a woody country; their halting alacrity of movement, their pleasant business, making bread all day with uncouth gesticulations, their air, gigantically human, as of a creature half alive, put a spirit of romance into the tamest landscape. When the Scottish child sees them first he falls immediately in love; and from that time forward windmills keep turning in his dreams. And so, in their degree, with every feature of the life and landscape. The warm, habitable age of towns and hamlets, the green, settled, ancient look of the country; the lush hedgerows, stiles, and privy pathways in the fields; the sluggish, brimming rivers; chalk and smock-frocks; chimes of bells and the rapid, pertly-sounding English speech—they are all new to the curiosity; they are all set to English airs in the child's story that he tells himself at night. The sharp edge of novelty wears off; the feeling is scotched, but I doubt whether it is ever killed. Rather it keeps returning, ever the more rarely and strangely, and even in scenes to which you have been long accustomed suddenly awakes and gives a relish to enjoyment or heightens the sense of isolation.

One thing especially continues unfamiliar to the Scotsman's eye—the domestic architecture, the look of streets and buildings; the quaint, venerable age of many, and the thin walls and warm colouring of all. We have, in Scotland, far fewer ancient buildings, above all in country places; and those that we have are all of hewn or harled masonry. Wood has been sparingly used in their construction; the window-frames are sunken in the wall, not flat to the front, as in England; the roofs are steeper-pitched; even a hill farm will have a massy, square, cold and permanent appearance. English houses, in comparison, have the look of cardboard toys, such as a puff might shatter. And to this the Scotsman never becomes used. His eye can never rest consciously on one of these brick houses— rickles of brick, as he might call them—or on one of these flat-chested streets, but he is instantly reminded where he is, and instantly travels back in fancy to his home. "This is no my ain house; I ken by the biggin' o't." And yet perhaps it is his own, bought with his own money, the key of it long polished in his pocket; but it has not yet, and never will be, thoroughly adopted by his imagination; nor does he cease to remember that, in the whole length and breadth of his native country, there was no building even distantly resembling it.

But it is not alone in scenery and architecture that we count England foreign. The constitution of society, the very pillars of the empire, surprise and even pain us. The dull, neglected peasant, sunk in matter, insolent, gross and servile, makes a startling contrast with our own long-legged, long-headed, thoughtful, Bible-quoting ploughman. A week or two in such a place as Suffolk leaves the Scotsman gasping. It seems incredible that within the boundaries of his own island a class should have been thus forgotten. Even the educated and intelligent, who hold our own opinions and speak in our own words, yet seem to hold them with a difference or from another reason, and to speak on all things with less interest and conviction. The first shock of English society is like a cold plunge. It is possible that the Scot comes looking for too much, and to be sure his first experiment will be in the wrong direction. Yet surely his complaint is grounded; surely the speech of Englishmen is too often lacking in generous ardour, the better part of the man too often withheld from the social commerce, and the contact of mind with mind evaded as with terror. A Scottish peasant will talk more liberally out of his own experience. He will not put you by with conversational counters and small jests; he will give you the best of himself, like one interested in life and man's chief end. A Scotsman is vain, interested in himself and others, eager for sympathy, setting forth his thoughts and experience in the best light. The egoism of the Englishman is self-contained. He does not seek to proselytise. He takes no interest in Scotland or the Scots, and, what is the unkindest cut of all, he does not care to justify his indifference. Give him the wages of going on and being an Englishman, that is all he asks; and in the meantime, while you continue to associate, he would rather not be reminded of your baser origin. Compared with the grand, tree-like self-sufficiency of his demeanour, the vanity and curiosity of the Scot seem uneasy, vulgar, and immodest. That you should continually try to establish human and serious relations, that you should actually feel an interest in John Bull, and desire and invite a return of interest from him, may argue something more awake and lively in your mind, but it still puts you in the attitude of a suitor and a poor relation. Thus even the lowest class of the educated English towers over a Scotsman by the head and shoulders.

Different indeed is the atmosphere in which Scottish and English youth begin to look about them, come to themselves in life, and gather up those first apprehensions which are the material of future thought and, to a great extent, the rule of future conduct. I have been to school in both countries, and I found, in the boys of the North, something at once rougher and more tender, at once more reserve and more expansion, a greater habitual distance

chequered by glimpses of a nearer intimacy, and on the whole
wider extremes of temperament and sensibility. The boy of the
South seems more wholesome, but less thoughtful; he gives himself
to games as to a business, striving to excel, but is not readily transported by imagination; the type remains with me as cleaner in
mind and body, more active, fonder of eating, endowed with a
lesser and a less romantic sense of life and of the future, and more
immersed in present circumstances. And certainly, for one thing,
English boys are younger for their age. Sabbath observance makes
a series of grim, and perhaps serviceable, pauses in the tenor of
Scottish boyhood—days of great stillness and solitude for the
rebellious mind, when in the dearth of books and play, and in the
intervals of studying the Shorter Catechism, the intellect and
senses prey upon and test each other. The typical English Sunday,
with the huge midday dinner and the plethoric afternoon, leads
perhaps to different results. About the very cradle of the Scot
there goes a hum of metaphysical divinity; and the whole of two
divergent systems is summed up, not merely speciously, in the two
first questions of the rival catechisms, the English tritely inquiring,
"What is your name?" the Scottish striking at the very roots of
life with, "What is the chief end of man?" and answering nobly,
if obscurely, "To glorify God and to enjoy Him for ever." I do
not wish to make an idol of the Shorter Catechism; but the fact
of such a question being asked opens to us Scots a great field of
speculation; and the fact that it is asked of all of us, from the peer
to the ploughboy, binds us more nearly together. No Englishman
of Byron's age, character and history, would have had patience
for long theological discussions on the way to fight for Greece;
but the daft Gordon blood and the Aberdonian schooldays kept
their influence to the end. We have spoken of the material conditions; nor need much more be said of these: of the land lying everywhere more exposed, of the wind always louder and bleaker,
of the black, roaring winters, of the gloom of high-lying, old stone
cities, imminent on the windy seaboard; compared with the level
streets, the warm colouring of the brick, the domestic quaintness
of the architecture, among which English children begin to grow up
and come to themselves in life. As the stage of the University
approaches, the contrast becomes more express. The English lad
goes to Oxford or Cambridge; there, in an ideal world of gardens,

to lead a semi-scenic life, costumed, disciplined and drilled by proctors. Nor is this to be regarded merely as a stage of education; it is a piece of privilege besides, and a step that separates him further from the bulk of his compatriots. At an earlier age the Scottish lad begins his greatly different experience of crowded class-rooms, of a gaunt quadrangle, of a bell hourly booming over the traffic of the city to recall him from the public-house where he has been lunching, or the streets where he has been wandering fancy-free. His college life has little of restraint, and nothing of necessary gentility. He will find no quiet clique of the exclusive, studious and cultured; no rotten borough of the arts. All classes rub shoulders on the greasy benches. The raffish young gentleman in gloves must measure his scholarship with the plain, clownish laddie from the parish school. They separate, at the session's end, one to smoke cigars about a watering-place, the other to resume the labours of the field beside his peasant family. The first muster of a college class in Scotland is a scene of curious and painful interest; so many lads, fresh from the heather, hang round the stove in cloddish embarrassment, ruffled by the presence of their smarter comrades, and afraid of the sound of their own rustic voices. It was in these early days, I think, that Professor Blackie won the affection of his pupils, putting these uncouth, umbrageous students at their ease with ready human geniality. Thus, at least, we have a healthy democratic atmosphere to breathe in while at work; even when there is no cordiality there is always a juxtaposition of the different classes, and in the competition of study the intellectual power of each is plainly demonstrated to the other. Our tasks ended, we of the North go forth as freemen into the humming, lamplit city. At five o'clock you may see the last of us hiving from the college gates, in the glare of the shop windows, under the green glimmer of the winter sunset. The frost tingles in our blood, no proctor lies in wait to intercept us; till the bell sounds again, we are the masters of the world; and some portion of our lives is always Saturday, *la trêve de Dieu.*

Nor must we omit the sense of the nature of his country and his country's history gradually growing in the child's mind from story and from observation. A Scottish child hears much of shipwreck, outlying iron skerries, pitiless breakers, and great sea-lights; much of the heathery mountains, wild clans, and hunted Covenanters. Breaths come to him in song of the distant Cheviots and the ring of foraying hoofs. He glories in his hard-fisted forefathers, of the iron girdle and the handful of oatmeal, who rode so swiftly and lived so sparely on their raids. Poverty, ill-luck, enterprise, and constant resolution are the fibres of the legend of his country's history. The heroes and kings of Scotland have been tragically fated; the most marking incidents in Scottish history—Flodden, Darien, or the Forty-five—were still either failures or defeats; and the fall of Wallace and the repeated reverses of the Bruce combine with the very smallness of the country to teach rather a moral than a material criterion for life. Britain is altogether small, the mere taproot of her extended empire; Scotland, again, which alone the Scottish boy adopts in his imagination, is but a little part of that, and avowedly cold, sterile and unpopulous. It is not so for nothing. I once seemed to have perceived in an American boy a greater readiness of sympathy for lands that are great, and rich, and growing, like his own. It proved to be quite otherwise; a mere dumb piece of boyish romance, that I had lacked penetration to divine. But the error serves the purpose of my argument; for I am sure, at least, that the heart of young Scotland will be always touched more nearly by paucity of number and Spartan poverty of life.

So we may argue, and yet the difference is not explained. That Shorter Catechism which I took as being so typical of Scotland, was yet composed in the city of Westminster. The division of races is more sharply marked within the borders of Scotland itself than between the countries. Galloway and Buchan, Lothian and Lochaber, are like foreign parts; yet you may choose a man from any of them, and, ten to one, he shall prove to have the headmark of a Scot. A century and a half ago the Highlander wore a different costume, spoke a different language, worshipped in another church, held different morals, and obeyed a different social constitution from his fellow-countrymen either of the South or North. Even the English, it is recorded, did not loathe the Highlander and the Highland costume as they were loathed by the remainder of the Scots. Yet the Highlander felt himself a Scot. He would willingly raid into the Scottish lowlands; but his courage failed him at the border, and he regarded England as a perilous, unhomely land. When the Black Watch, after years of foreign service, returned to Scotland, veterans leaped out and kissed the earth at Port Patrick. They had been in Ireland, stationed among men of their own race and language, where they were well liked and treated with affection; but it was the soil of Galloway that they kissed at the extreme end of the hostile lowlands, among a people who did not understand their speech, and who had hated, harried, and hanged them since the dawn of history. Last, and perhaps most curious, the sons of chieftains were often educated on the continent of Europe. They went abroad speaking Gaelic; they returned speaking, not English, but the broad dialect of Scotland. Now, what idea had they in their minds when they thus, in thought, identified themselves with their ancestral enemies? What was the sense in which they were Scottish and not English, or Scottish and not Irish? Can a bare name be thus influential on the minds and affections of men, and a political aggregation blind them to the nature of facts? The story of the Austrian Empire would seem to answer, No; the far more galling business of Ireland clenches the negative from nearer home. Is it common education, common morals, a common language or a common faith, that join men into nations? There were practically none of these in the case we are considering.

The fact remains: in spite of the difference of blood and language, the Lowlander feels himself the sentimental countryman of the Highlander. When they meet abroad, they fall upon each other's neck in spirit; even at home there is a kind of clannish intimacy in their talk. But from his compatriot in the South the Lowlander stands consciously apart. He has had a different training; he obeys different laws; he makes his will in other terms, is otherwise divorced and married; his eyes are not at home in an English landscape or with English houses; his ear continues to remark the English speech; and even though his tongue acquire the Southern knack, he will still have a strong Scots accent of the mind.

OLD MORTALITY

I

THERE is a certain graveyard, looked upon on the one side by a prison, on the other by the windows of a quiet hotel; below, under a steep cliff, it beholds the traffic of many lines of rail, and the scream of the engine and the shock of meeting buffers mount to it all day long. The aisles are lined with the inclosed sepulchres of families, door beyond door, like houses in a street; and in the morning the shadow of the prison turrets, and of many tall memorials, falls upon the graves. There, in the hot fits of youth, I came to be unhappy. Pleasant incidents are woven with my memory of the place. I here made friends with a certain plain old gentleman, a visitor on sunny mornings, gravely cheerful, who, with one eye upon the place that awaited him, chirped about his youth like winter sparrows; a beautiful housemaid of the hotel once, for some days together, dumbly flirted with me from a window and kept my wild heart flying; and once—she possibly remembers—the wise Eugenia followed me to that austere inclosure. Her hair came down, and in the shelter of the tomb my trembling fingers helped her to repair the braid. But for the most part I went there solitary and, with irrevocable emotion, pored on the names of the forgotten. Name after name, and to each the conventional attributions and the idle dates: a regiment of the unknown that had been the joy of mothers, and had thrilled with the illusions of youth, and at last, in the dim sick-room, wrestled with the pangs of old mortality. In that whole crew of the silenced there was but one of whom my fancy had received a picture; and he, with his comely, florid countenance, bewigged and habited in scarlet, and in his day combining fame and popularity, stood forth, like a taunt, among that company of phantom appellations. It was then possible to leave behind us something more explicit than these severe, monotonous and lying epitaphs; and the thing left, the memory of a painted picture and what we call the immortality of a name, was hardly more desirable than mere oblivion. Even David Hume, as he lay composed beneath that "circular idea," was fainter than a dream; and when the housemaid, broom in hand, smiled and beckoned from the open window, the fame of that bewigged philosopher melted like a raindrop in the sea.

And yet in soberness I cared as little for the housemaid as for David Hume. The interests of youth are rarely frank; his passions, like Noah's dove, come home to roost. The fire, sensibility, and volume of his own nature, that is all that he has learned to recognise. The tumultuary and grey tide of life, the empire of routine, the unrejoicing faces of his elders, fill him with contemptuous surprise; there also he seems to walk among the tombs of spirits; and it is only in the course of years, and after much rubbing with his fellow-men, that he begins by glimpses to see himself from without and his fellows from within: to know his own for one among the thousand undenoted countenances in the city street, and to divine in others the throb of human agony and hope. In the meantime he will avoid the hospital doors, the pale faces, the cripple, the sweet whiff of chloroform—for there, on the most thoughtless, the pains of others are burned home; but he will continue to walk, in a divine self-pity, the aisles of the forgotten graveyard. The length of man's life, which is endless to the brave and busy, is scorned by his ambitious thought. He cannot bear to have come for so little, and to go again so wholly. He cannot bear, above all, in that brief scene, to be still idle, and by way of cure, neglects the little that he has to do. The parable of the talent is the brief epitome of youth. To believe in immortality is one thing, but it is first needful to believe in life. Denunciatory preachers seem not to suspect that they may be taken gravely and in evil part; that young men may come to think of time as of a moment, and with the pride of Satan wave back the inadequate gift. Yet here is a true peril; this it is that sets them to pace the graveyard alleys and to read, with strange extremes of pity and derision, the memorials of the dead.

Books were the proper remedy: books of vivid human import, forcing upon their minds the issues, pleasures, busyness, importance and immediacy of that life in which they stand; books of smiling or heroic temper, to excite or to console; books of a large design, shadowing the complexity of that game of consequences to which we all sit down, the hanger-back not least. But the average sermon flees the point, disporting itself in that eternity of which we know, and need to know, so little; avoiding the bright, crowded, and momentous fields of life where destiny awaits us. Upon the average book a writer may be silent; he may set it down to his ill-hap that when his own youth was in the acrid fermentation, he should have

fallen and fed upon the cheerless fields of Obermann. Yet to
Mr. Arnold, who led him to these pastures, he still bears a
grudge. The day is perhaps not far off when people will begin
to count *Moll Flanders*, ay, or *The Country Wife*, more wholesome and more pious diet than these guide-books to consistent
egoism.

But the most inhuman of boys soon wearies of the inhumanity
of Obermann. And even while I still continued to be a haunter
of the graveyard, I began insensibly to turn my attention to the
grave-diggers, and was weaned out of myself to observe the conduct of visitors. This was day-spring indeed, to a lad in such great
darkness. Not that I began to see men, or try to see them, from
within, nor to learn charity and modesty and justice from the sight;
but still stared at them externally from the prison windows of my
affectation. Once I remember to have observed two working-
women with a baby halting by a grave; there was something
monumental in the grouping, one upright carrying the child,
the other with bowed face crouching by her side. A wreath
of immortelles under a glass dome had thus attracted them; and,
drawing near I overheard their judgment on that wonder. "Eh!
what extravagance!" To a youth afflicted with the callosity
of sentiment, this quaint and pregnant saying appeared merely
base.

My acquaintance with grave-diggers, considering its length, was
unremarkable. One indeed, whom I found plying his spade in the
red evening, high above Allan Water and in the shadow of Dunblane
Cathedral, told me of his acquaintance with the birds that still
attended on his labours; how some would even perch about him,
waiting for their prey; and in a true Sexton's Calendar, how the
species varied with the season of the year. But this was the very
poetry of the profession. The others whom I knew were somewhat
dry. A faint flavour of the gardener hung about them, but sophisticated and disbloomed. They had engagements to keep, not alone
with the deliberate series of the seasons, but with mankind's clocks
and hour-long measurement of time. And thus there was no leisure
for the relishing pinch, or the hour-long gossip, foot on spade.
They were men wrapped up in their grim business; they liked well
to open long-closed family vaults, blowing in the key and throwing
wide the grating; and they carried in their minds a calendar of

names and dates. It would be "in fifty-twa" that such a tomb was last opened for "Miss Jemimy." It was thus they spoke of their past patients—familiarly but not without respect, like old family servants. Here is indeed a servant, whom we forget that we possess; who does not wait at the bright table, or run at the bell's summons, but patiently smokes his pipe beside the mortuary fire, and in his faithful memory notches the burials of our race. To suspect Shakespeare in his maturity of a superficial touch savours of paradox, yet he was surely in error when he attributed insensibility to the digger of the grave. But perhaps it is on Hamlet that the charge should lie; or perhaps the English sexton differs from the Scottish. The "goodman delver," reckoning up his years of office, might have at least suggested other thoughts. It is a pride common among sextons. A cabinet-maker does not count his cabinets, nor even an author his volumes, save when they stare upon him from the shelves; but the grave-digger numbers his graves. He would indeed be something different from human if his solitary open-air and tragic labours left not a broad mark upon his mind. There, in his tranquil aisle, apart from city clamour, among the cats and robins and the ancient effigies and legends of the tomb, he waits the continual passage of his contemporaries, falling like minute drops into eternity. As they fall, he counts them; and this enumeration, which was at first perhaps appalling to his soul, in the process of years and by the kindly influence of habit grows to be his pride and pleasure. There are many common stories telling how he piques himself on crowded cemeteries. But I will rather tell of the old grave-digger of Monkton, to whose unsuffering bedside the minister was summoned. He dwelt in a cottage built into the wall of the churchyard; and through a bull's-eye pane above his bed he could see, as he lay dying, the rank grasses and the upright and recumbent stones. Dr. Laurie was, I think, a Moderate: 'tis certain, at least, that he took a very Roman view of deathbed dispositions; for he told the old man that he had lived beyond man's natural years, that his life had been easy and reputable, that his family had all grown up and been a credit to his care, and that it now behoved him unregretfully to gird his loins and follow the majority. The grave-digger heard him out; then he raised himself upon one elbow, and with the other hand pointed through the window to the scene of his life-long labours. "Doctor," he said, "I ha'e laid three hunner and fowerscore in that kirkyaird; an it had been His wull," indicating Heaven, "I would ha'e likit weel to ha'e made out the fower hunner." But it was not to be; this tragedian of the fifth act had now another part to play; and the time had come when others were to gird and carry him.

II

I would fain strike a note that should be more heroical; but the ground of all youth's suffering, solitude, hysteria, and haunting of the grave, is nothing else than naked, ignorant selfishness. It is himself that he sees dead; those are his virtues that are forgotten; his is the vague epitaph. Pity him but the more, if pity be your cue; for where a man is all pride, vanity, and personal aspiration, he goes through fire unshielded. In every part and corner of our life, to lose oneself is to be gainer; to forget oneself is to be happy; and this poor, laughable and tragic fool has not yet learned the rudiments; himself, giant Prometheus, is still ironed on the peaks of Caucasus. But by-and-by his truant interests will leave that tortured body, slip abroad, and gather flowers. Then shall death appear before him in an altered guise; no longer as a doom peculiar to himself, whether fate's crowning injustice or his own last vengeance upon those who fail to value him; but now as a power that wounds him far more tenderly, not without solemn compensations, taking and giving, bereaving and yet storing up.

The first step for all is to learn to the dregs our own ignoble fallibility. When we have fallen through storey after storey of our vanity and aspiration, and sit rueful among the ruins, then it is that we begin to measure the stature of our friends: how they stand between us and our own contempt, believing in our best; how, linking us with others, and still spreading wide the influential circle, they weave us in and in with the fabric of contemporary life; and to what petty size they dwarf the virtues and the vices that appeared gigantic in our youth. So that at the last, when such a pin falls out—when there vanishes in the least breath of time one of those rich magazines of life on which we drew for our supply—when he who had first dawned upon us as a face among the faces of the city, and, still growing, came to bulk on our regard with those clear features of the loved and living man, falls in a

breath to memory and shadow, there falls along with him a whole
wing of the palace of our life.

III

One such face I now remember; one such blank some half a dozen
of us labour to dissemble. In his youth he was most beautiful in
person, most serene and genial by disposition; full of racy words
and quaint thoughts. Laughter attended on his coming. He had
the air of a great gentleman, jovial and royal with his equals, and
to the poorest student gentle and attentive. Power seemed to
reside in him exhaustless; we saw him stoop to play with us, but
held him marked for higher destinies; we loved his notice; and I
have rarely had my pride more gratified than when he sat at my
father's table, my acknowledged friend. So he walked among us,
both hands full of gifts, carrying with nonchalance the seeds of a
most influential life.

The powers and the ground of friendship is a mystery; but,
looking back, I can discern that, in part, we loved the thing he
was, for some shadow of what he was to be. For with all his beauty,
power, breeding, urbanity and mirth, there was in those days
something soulless in our friend. He would astonish us by sallies,
witty, innocent and inhumane; and by a misapplied Johnsonian
pleasantry, demolish honest sentiment. I can still see and hear
him, as he went his way along the lamplit streets, *Là ci darem la
mano* on his lips, a noble figure of a youth, but following vanity
and incredulous of good; and sure enough, somewhere on the high
seas of life, with his health, his hopes, his patrimony and his self-
respect, miserably went down.

From this disaster, like a spent swimmer, he came desperately
ashore, bankrupt of money and consideration; creeping to the
family he had deserted; with broken wing, never more to rise.
But in his face there was a light of knowledge that was new to it.
Of the wounds of his body he was never healed; died of them
gradually, with clear-eyed resignation; of his wounded pride, we
knew only from his silence. He returned to that city where he had
lorded it in his ambitious youth; lived there alone, seeing few;
striving to retrieve the irretrievable; at times still grappling with
that mortal frailty that had brought him down; still joying in his
friend's successes; his laugh still ready but with kindlier music;

and over all his thoughts the shadow of that unalterable law which he had disavowed and which had brought him low. Lastly, when his bodily evils had quite disabled him, he lay a great while dying, still without complaint, still finding interests; to his last step gentle, urbane and with the will to smile.

The tale of this great failure is, to those who remained true to him, the tale of a success. In his youth he took thought for no one but himself; when he came ashore again, his whole armada lost, he seemed to think of none but others. Such was his tenderness for others, such his instinct of fine courtesy and pride, that of that impure passion of remorse he never breathed a syllable; even regret was rare with him, and pointed with a jest. You would not have dreamed, if you had known him then, that this was that great failure, that beacon to young men, over whose fall a whole society had hissed and pointed fingers. Often have we gone to him, red-hot with our own hopeful sorrows, railing on the rose-leaves in our princely bed of life, and he would patiently give ear and wisely counsel; and it was only upon some return of our own thoughts that we were reminded what manner of man this was to whom we disembosomed: a man, by his own fault, ruined; shut out of the garden of his gifts; his whole city of hope both ploughed and salted; silently awaiting the deliverer. Then something took us by the throat; and to see him there, so gentle, patient, brave and pious, oppressed but not cast down, sorrow was so swallowed up in admiration that we could not dare to pity him. Even if the old fault flashed out again, it but awoke our wonder that, in that lost battle, he should have still the energy to fight. He had gone to ruin with a kind of kingly *abandon*, like one who condescended; but once ruined, with the lights all out, he fought as for a kingdom. Most men, finding themselves the authors of their own disgrace, rail the louder against God or destiny. Most men, when they repent, oblige their friends to share the bitterness of that repentance. But he had held an inquest and passed sentence: *mene, mene;* and condemned himself to smiling silence. He had given trouble enough; had earned misfortune amply, and foregone the right to murmur.

Thus was our old comrade, like Samson, careless in his days of strength; but on the coming of adversity, and when that strength was gone that had betrayed him—"for our strength is weakness"—

he began to blossom and bring forth. Well, now, he is out of the fight: the burthen that he bore thrown down before the great deliverer. We

> " in the vast cathedral leave him;
> God accept him,
> Christ receive him! "

IV

If we go now and look on these innumerable epitaphs, the pathos and the irony are strangely fled. They do not stand merely to the dead, these foolish monuments; they are pillars and legends set up to glorify the difficult but not desperate life of man. This ground is hallowed by the heroes of defeat.

I see the indifferent pass before my friend's last resting-place; pause, with a shrug of pity, marvelling that so rich an argosy had sunk. A pity, now that he is done with suffering, a pity most uncalled for, and an ignorant wonder. Before those who loved him, his memory shines like a reproach; they honour him for silent lessons; they cherish his example; and in what remains before them of their toil, fear to be unworthy of the dead. For this proud man was one of those who prospered in the valley of humiliation— of whom Bunyan wrote that, "Though Christian had the hard hap to meet in the valley with Apollyon, yet I must tell you, that in former times men have met with angels here; have found pearls here; and have in this place found the words of life."

A GOSSIP ON A NOVEL OF DUMAS'S

THE books that we re-read the oftenest are not always those that we admire the most; we choose and we revisit them for many and various reasons, as we choose and revisit human friends. One or two of Scott's novels, Shakespeare, Molière, Montaigne, *The Egoist*, and the *Vicomte de Bragelonne*, form the inner circle of my intimates. Behind these comes a good troop of dear acquaintances; *The Pilgrim's Progress* in the front rank, *The Bible in Spain* not far behind. There are besides a certain number that look at me with reproach as I pass them by on my shelves: books that I once thumbed and studied: houses which were once like home to me, but where I now rarely visit. I am on these sad terms (and blush to confess it) with Wordsworth, Horace, Burns and Hazlitt. Last of all, there is the class of book that has its hour of brilliancy—glows, sings, charms, and then fades again into insignificance until the fit return. Chief of those who thus smile and frown on me by turns, I must name Virgil and Herrick, who, were they but

"Their sometime selves the same throughout the year,"

must have stood in the first company with the six names of my continual literary intimates. To these six, incongruous as they seem, I have long been faithful, and hope to be faithful to the day of death. I have never read the whole of Montaigne, but I do not like to be long without reading some of him, and my delight in what I do read never lessens. Of Shakespeare I have read all but *Richard III., Henry VI., Titus Andronicus,* and *All's Well that Ends Well;* and these, having already made all suitable endeavour, I now know that I shall never read—to make up for which unfaithfulness I could read much of the rest for ever. Of Molière— surely the next greatest name of Christendom—I could tell a very similar story; but in a little corner of a little essay these princes are too much out of place, and I prefer to pay my fealty and pass on. How often I have read *Guy Mannering, Rob Roy,* or *Redgauntlet,* I have no means of guessing, having begun young. But it is either four or five times that I have read *The Egoist,* and either five or six that I have read the *Vicomte de Bragelonne.*

Some, who would accept the others, may wonder that I should have spent so much of this brief life of ours over a work so little famous as the last. And, indeed, I am surprised myself; not at my own devotion, but the coldness of the world. My acquaintance with the *Vicomte* began, somewhat indirectly, in the year of grace 1863, when I had the advantage of studying certain illustrated dessert plates in a hotel at Nice. The name of d'Artagnan in the legends I already saluted like an old friend, for I had met it the year before in a work of Miss Yonge's. My first perusal was in one of those pirated editions that swarmed at that time out of Brussels, and ran to such a troop of neat and dwarfish volumes. I understood but little of the merits of the book; my strongest memory is of the execution of d'Eyméric and Lyodot—a strange testimony to the dulness of a boy, who could enjoy the rough-

and-tumble in the Place de Grève, and forget d'Artagnan's visits to the two financiers. My next reading was in winter-time, when I lived alone upon the Pentlands. I would return in the early night from one of my patrols with the shepherd; a friendly face would meet me in the door, a friendly retriever scurry upstairs to fetch my slippers; and I would sit down with the *Vicomte* for a long, silent, solitary lamp-light evening by the fire. And yet I know not why I call it silent, when it was enlivened with such a clatter of horseshoes, and such a rattle of musketry, and such a stir of talk; or why I call those evenings solitary in which I gained so many friends. I would rise from my book and pull the blind aside, and see the snow and the glittering hollies chequer a Scottish garden, and the winter moonlight brighten the white hills. Thence I would turn again to that crowded and sunny field of life in which it was so easy to forget myself, my cares, and my surroundings: a place busy as a city, bright as a theatre, thronged with memorable faces, and sounding with delightful speech. I carried the thread of that epic into my slumbers, I woke with it unbroken, I rejoiced to plunge into the book again at breakfast, it was with a pang that I must lay it down and turn to my own labours; for no part of the world has ever seemed to me so charming as these pages, and not even my friends are quite so real, perhaps quite so dear, as d'Artagnan.

Since then I have been going to and fro at very brief intervals in my favourite book; and I have now just risen from my last (let me call it my fifth) perusal, having liked it better and admired it more seriously than ever. Perhaps I have a sense of ownership, being so well known in these six volumes. Perhaps I think that d'Artagnan delights to have me read of him, and Louis Quatorze is gratified, and Fouquet throws me a look, and Aramis, although he knows I do not love him, yet plays to me with his best graces, as to an old patron of the show. Perhaps, if I am not careful, something may befall me like what befell George IV. about the battle of Waterloo, and I may come to fancy the *Vicomte* one of the first, and Heaven knows the best, of my own works. At least, I avow myself a partisan; and when I compare the popularity of the *Vicomte* with that of *Monte Cristo*, or its own elder brother, the *Trois Mousquetaires*, I confess I am both pained and puzzled.

To those who have already made acquaintance with the titular hero in the pages of *Vingt Ans Après*, perhaps the name may act as a deterrent. A man might well stand back if he supposed he were to follow, for six volumes, so well-conducted, so fine-spoken, and withal so dreary a cavalier as Bragelonne. But the fear is idle. I may be said to have passed the best years of my life in these six volumes, and my acquaintance with Raoul has never gone beyond a bow; and when he, who has so long pretended to be alive, is at last suffered to pretend to be dead, I am sometimes reminded of a saying in an earlier volume: "*Enfin, dit Miss Stewart*"—and it was of Bragelonne she spoke—"*enfin il a fait quelque chose: c'est, ma foi! bien heureux.*" I am reminded of it, as I say; and the next moment, when Athos dies of his death, and my dear d'Artagnan bursts into his storm of sobbing, I can but deplore my flippancy.

Or perhaps it is La Vallière that the reader of *Vingt Ans Après* is inclined to flee. Well, he is right there too, though not so right. Louise is no success. Her creator has spared no pains; she is well meant, not ill designed, sometimes has a word that rings out true; sometimes, if only for a breath, she may even engage our sympathies. But I have never envied the King his triumph. And so far from pitying Bragelonne for his defeat, I could wish him no worse (not for lack of malice, but imagination) than to be wedded to that lady. Madame enchants me; I can forgive that royal minx her most serious offences; I can thrill and soften with the King on that memorable occasion when he goes to upbraid and remains to flirt; and when it comes to the "*Allons, aimez-moi donc,*" it is my heart that melts in the bosom of de Guiche. Not so with Louise. Readers cannot fail to have remarked that what an author tells us of the beauty or the charm of his creatures goes for nought; that we know instantly better; that the heroine cannot open her mouth but what, all in a moment, the fine phrases of preparation fall from round her like the robes from Cinderella, and she stands before us, self-betrayed, as a poor, ugly, sickly wench, or perhaps a strapping market-woman. Authors, at least, know it well; a heroine will too often start the trick of "getting ugly"; and no disease is more difficult to cure. I said authors; but indeed I had a side eye to one author in particular, with whose works I am very well acquainted, though I cannot read them, and who has spent many vigils in this cause, sitting beside his ailing puppets and (like a

magician) wearying his art to restore them to youth and beauty.
There are others who ride too high for these misfortunes. Who
doubts the loveliness of Rosalind? Arden itself was not more
lovely. Who ever questioned the perennial charm of Rose Jocelyn,
Lucy Desborough, or Clara Middleton? fair women with fair
names, the daughters of George Meredith. Elizabeth Bennet
has but to speak, and I am at her knees. Ah! these are the creators
of desirable women. They would never have fallen in the mud
with Dumas and poor La Vallière. It is my only consolation that
not one of all of them, except the first, could have plucked at the
moustache of d'Artagnan.

Or perhaps, again, a proportion of readers stumble at the threshold. In so vast a mansion there were sure to be back stairs and
kitchen offices where no one would delight to linger; but it was at
least unhappy that the vestibule should be so badly lighted; and
until, in the seventeenth chapter, d'Artagnan sets off to seek
his friends, I must confess, the book goes heavily enough. But,
from thenceforward, what a feast is spread! Monk kidnapped;
d'Artagnan enriched; Mazarin's death; the ever delectable adventure of Belle Isle, wherein Aramis outwits d'Artagnan, with
its epilogue (vol. v. chap. xxviii.), where d'Artagnan regains the
moral superiority; the love adventures of Fontainebleau, with
St. Aignan's story of the dryad and the business of de Guiche, de
Wardes, and Manicamp; Aramis made general of the Jesuits;
Aramis at the Bastille; the night talk in the forest of Sénart; Belle
Isle again, with the death of Porthos; and last, but not least, the
taming of d'Artagnan the untamable, under the lash of the young
King. What other novel has such epic variety and nobility of incident? often, if you will, impossible; often of the order of an Arabian
story; and yet all based in human nature. For if you come to that,
what novel has more human nature? not studied with the microscope, but seen largely, in plain daylight, with the natural eye?
What novel has more good sense, and gaiety, and wit, and unflagging, admirable literary skill? Good souls, I suppose, must sometimes read it in the blackguard travesty of a translation. But there
is no style so untranslatable; light as a whipped trifle, strong as
silk; wordy like a village tale; pat like a general's dispatch; with
every fault, yet never tedious; with no merit, yet inimitably right.
And, once more, to make an end of commendations, what novel

is inspired with a more unstrained or a more wholesome morality?

Yes; in spite of Miss Yonge, who introduced me to the name of d'Artagnan only to dissuade me from a nearer knowledge of the man, I have to add morality. There is no quite good book without a good morality; but the world is wide, and so are morals. Out of two people who have dipped into Sir Richard Burton's *Thousand and One Nights*, one shall have been offended by the animal details; another to whom these were harmless, perhaps even pleasing, shall yet have been shocked in his turn by the rascality and cruelty of all the characters. Of two readers, again, one shall have been pained by the morality of a religious memoir, one by that of the *Vicomte de Bragelonne*. And the point is that neither need be wrong. We shall always shock each other both in life and art; we cannot get the sun into our pictures, nor the abstract right (if there be such a thing) into our books; enough if, in the one, there glimmer some hint of the great light that blinds us from heaven; enough if, in the other, there shine, even upon foul details, a spirit of magnanimity. I would scarce send to the *Vicomte* a reader who was in quest of what we may call puritan morality. The ventri-potent mulatto, the great eater, worker, earner and waster, the man of much and witty laughter, the man of the great heart and alas! of the doubtful honesty, is a figure not yet clearly set before the world; he still awaits a sober and yet genial portrait; but with whatever art that may be touched, and whatever indulgence, it will not be the portrait of a precisian. Dumas was certainly not thinking of himself, but of Planchet, when he put into the mouth of d'Artagnan's old servant this excellent profession: "*Monsieur, j'étais une de ces bonnes pâtes d'hommes que Dieu a fait pour s'animer pendant un certain temps et pour trouver bonnes toutes choses qui accompagnent leur séjour sur la terre.*" He was thinking, as I say, of Planchet, to whom the words are aptly fitted; but they were fitted also to Planchet's creator; and perhaps this struck him as he wrote, for observe what follows: "*D'Artagnan s'assit alors près de la fenêtre, et, cette philosophie de Planchet lui ayant paru solide, il y rêva.*" In a man who finds all things good, you will scarce expect much zeal for negative virtues: the active alone will have a charm for him; abstinence, however wise, however kind, will always seem to such a judge entirely mean and partly impious. So with Dumas. Chastity is not near his heart; nor yet, to his own sore cost, that virtue of frugality which is the armour of the artist. Now, in the *Vicomte*, he had much to do with the contest of Fouquet and Colbert. Historic justice should be all upon the side of Colbert, of official honesty, and fiscal competence. And Dumas knew it well: three times at least he shows his knowledge; once it is but flashed upon us and received with the laughter of Fouquet himself, in the jesting controversy in the gardens of Saint Mandé; once it is touched on by Aramis in the forest of Sénart; in the end, it is set before us clearly in one dignified speech of the triumphant Colbert. But in Fouquet, the waster, the lover of good cheer and wit and art, the swift transactor of much business, "*l'homme de bruit, l'homme de plaisir, l'homme qui n'est que parce que les autres sont*," Dumas saw something of himself and drew the figure the more tenderly. It is to me even touching to see how he insists on Fouquet's honour; not seeing, you might think, that unflawed honour is impossible to spendthrifts; but rather, perhaps, in the light of his own life, seeing it too well, and clinging the more to what was left. Honour can survive a wound; it can live and thrive without a member. The man rebounds from his disgrace; he begins fresh foundations on the ruins of the old; and when his sword is broken, he will do valiantly with his dagger. So it is with Fouquet in the book; so it was with Dumas on the battlefield of life.

To cling to what is left of any damaged quality is virtue in the man; but perhaps to sing its praises is scarcely to be called morality in the writer. And it is elsewhere, it is in the character of d'Artagnan, that we must look for that spirit of morality, which is one of the chief merits of the book, makes one of the main joys of its perusal, and sets it high above more popular rivals. Athos, with the coming of years, has declined too much into the preacher, and the preacher of a sapless creed; but d'Artagnan has mellowed into a man so witty, rough, kind and upright, that he takes the heart by storm. There is nothing of the copybook about his virtues, nothing of the drawing-room in his fine, natural civility; he will sail near the wind; he is no district visitor—no Wesley or Robespierre; his conscience is void of all refinement whether for good or evil; but the whole man rings true like a good sovereign. Readers who have approached the *Vicomte*, not across country, but by the legitimate, five-volumed avenue of the *Mousquetaires* and *Vingt Ans Après*, will not have forgotten d'Artagnan's ungentlemanly and perfectly improbable trick upon Milady. What a pleasure it is, then, what a reward, and how agreeable a lesson, to see the old captain humble himself to the son of the man whom he had personated! Here, and throughout, if I am to choose virtues for myself or my friends, let me choose the virtues of d'Artagnan. I do not say there is no character as well drawn in Shakespeare; I do say there is none that I love so wholly. There are many spiritual eyes that seem to spy upon our actions—eyes of the dead and the absent, whom we imagine to behold us in our most private hours, and whom we fear and scruple to offend: our witnesses and judges. And among these, even if you should think me childish, I must count my d'Artagnan—not d'Artagnan of the memoirs whom Thackeray pretended to prefer—a preference, I take the freedom of saying, in which he stands alone; not the d'Artagnan of flesh and blood, but him of the ink and paper; not Nature's, but Dumas's. And this is the particular crown and triumph of the artist—not to be true merely, but to be lovable; not simply to convince, but to enchant.

There is yet another point in the *Vicomte* which I find incomparable. I can recall no other work of the imagination in which the end of life is represented with so nice a tact. I was asked the other day if Dumas made me laugh or cry. Well, in this my late fifth reading of the *Vicomte*, I did laugh once at the small Coquelin de Volière business, and was perhaps a thought surprised at having done so: to make up for it, I smiled continually. But for tears, I do not know. If you put a pistol to my throat, I must own the tale trips upon a very airy foot—within a measurable distance of unreality; and for those who like the big guns to be discharged and the great passions to appear authentically, it may even seem inadequate from first to last. Not so to me; I cannot count that a poor dinner, or a poor book, where I meet with those I love; and, above all, in this last volume, I find a singular charm of spirit. It breathes a pleasant and a tonic sadness, always brave, never hysterical. Upon the crowded, noisy life of this long tale, evening gradually falls; and the lights are extinguished, and the heroes pass away one by one. One by one they go, and not a regret embitters their departure; the young succeed them in their places, Louis Quatorze is swelling larger and shining broader, another generation and another France dawn on the horizon; but for us and these old men whom we have loved so long the inevitable end draws near and is welcome. To read this well is to anticipate experience. Ah, if only when these hours of the long shadows fall for us in reality and not in figure, we may hope to face them with a mind as quiet!

But my paper is running out; the siege guns are firing on the Dutch frontier; and I must say adieu for the fifth time to my old comrade fallen on the field of glory. *Adieu*—rather *au revoir!* Yet a sixth time, dearest d'Artagnan, we shall kidnap Monk and take horse together for Belle Isle.

THOMPSON

FRANCIS THOMPSON (*1859–1907*), *poet and essayist, was born at Preston.   A Catholic, he studied at Ushaw College, with thoughts of entering the priesthood; at the age of seventeen, he began the study of medicine at Manchester, following his father's wish.   After six years, he gave up a study repugnant to him, having failed his examinations for a degree.   He went to London in 1885, supporting himself by various odd jobs; suffering from neuralgia, he fell a prey to the opium habit, and became destitute.   He began to write poetry, which was accepted by various periodicals, and his first volume of verse appeared in 1893.   His health was ruined by opium, and he was given treatment to break the habit; while undergoing this treatment, he continued to write.   From 1893 to 1897, he lived in Wales; later he returned to London, where he died of consumption in 1907.*

Best known as a poet, and for his essay on "Shelley," he wrote other papers, chiefly on literary subjects.   He says much in a few words, and his judgment is as sound as his phrasing is memorable.   The intrusion of that form of modesty—or egoism—known to-day as an "inferiority complex," is perhaps the result of his struggles against poverty and ill-health.   Fortunately it is rare.   Some of his writing is colored by his religious views, but he is in no sense a propagandist; even in his prose, he shows his poetic mind.

THOMPSON

THE WAY OF IMPERFECTION

OVID, with the possible exception of Catullus, is the most modern-minded of Latin poets. It is therefore with delight that we first encounter his dictum, so essentially modern, so opposed to the æsthetic feeling of the ancient world, *decentiorem esse faciem in quâ aliquis nævus esset*. It was a dictum borne out by his own practice, a practice at heart essentially romantic rather than classic; and there can therefore be little wonder that the saying was scouted by his contemporaries as an eccentricity of genius. The dominant cult of classicism was the worship of perfection, and the Goth was its iconoclast. Then at length literature reposed in the beneficent and quickening shadow of imperfection, which gave us for consummate product Shakespeare, in whom greatness and imperfection reached their height. Since him, however, there has been a gradual decline from imperfection. Milton, at his most typical, was far too perfect; Pope was ruined by his quest for the quality; and if Dryden partially escaped, it was because of the rich faultiness with which Nature had endowed him. The stand made by the poets of the early part of the nineteenth century was only temporarily successful; and now [1889], we suppose, no thoughtful person can contemplate without alarm the hold which the renascent principle has gained over the contemporary mind. Unless some voice be raised in timely protest, we feel that English art (in its widest sense) must soon dwindle to the extinction of unendurable excellence.

Over the whole contemporary mind is the trail of this serpent perfection. It even affects the realm of colour, where it begets cloying, enervating harmonies, destitute of those stimulating contrasts by which the great colourists threw into relief the general agreement of their hues. It leads in poetry to the love of miniature finish, and *that* in turn (because minute finish is most completely attainable in short poems) leads to the tyranny of sonnet, ballade, rondeau, triolet, and their kind. The principle leads again to æstheticism; which is simply the aspiration for a hot-house seclusion of beauty in a world which Nature has tempered by bracing gusts of ugliness.

The most nobly conceived character in assuming *vraisemblance* takes up a certain quantity of imperfection; it is its water of crystallization: expel this, and far from securing, as the artist fondly deems, a more perfect crystal, the character falls to powder. We by no means desire those improbable incongruities which, frequent enough in actual life, should in art be confined to comedy. But even incongruities may find their place in serious art, if they be artistic incongruities, not too glaring or suggestive of unlikelihood; incongruities which are felt by the reader to have a whimsical hidden keeping with the congruities of the character, which enhance the consent of the general qualities by an artistically modulated dissent; which just lend, and no more than lend, the ratifying seal of Nature to the dominating regularities of characterization.

From the neglect of all this have come the hero and heroine; and among all prevalent types of heroine, *the* worst is one apparently founded on Pope's famous dictum,

Most women have no characters at all—

a dictum which we should denounce with scorn, if so acute an observer as De Quincey did not stagger us by defending it. He defends it to attack Pope. Pope (says De Quincey) did not see that what he advances as a reproach against women constitutes the very beauty of them. It is the absence of any definite character which enables their character to be moulded by others: and it is this soft plasticity which renders them such charming companions as wives. We should be inclined to say that the feminine characteristic which De Quincey considered plasticity was rather elasticity. Now the most elastic substance in Nature is probably ivory. What are the odds, you subtle, paradoxical, delightful ghost of delicate thought, what *are* the odds on your moulding a billiard ball?

Does anyone believe in Patient Grizzel? Still more, does anyone believe in the Nut-brown Maid? Yet their descendants infest literature, from Spenser to Dickens and Tennyson, from Una to Enid; made tolerable in the poem only by their ideal surroundings.

The dream of "a perfect woman nobly planned" underlies the thing; albeit Wordsworth goes on to show that his "perfect woman" had her little failings. Shakespeare was not afraid to touch with such failings his finest heroines; he knew that these defects serve only to enhance the large nobilities of character, as the tender imperfections and wayward wilfulnesses of individual rose-petals enhance the prevalent symmetry of the rose. His most consummate woman, Imogen, possesses her little naturalizing traits. Take the situation where she is confronted with her husband's order for her murder. What the Patient Grizzel heroine would have done we all know. She would have behaved with unimpeachable resignation, and prepared for death with a pathos ordered according to the best canons of art. What does this glorious Imogen do? Why (and we publicly thank Heaven for it), after the first paroxysm of weeping, which makes the blank verse sob, she bursts into a fit of thoroughly feminine and altogether charming jealousy. A perfect woman indeed, for she is imperfect! Imogen, however, it may be urged, is not a Patient Grizzel. Take, then, Desdemona, who is. That is to say, Desdemona represents the type in nature which Patient Grizzel misrepresents. Mark now the difference in treatment. Shakespeare knew that these gentle, affectionate, yielding, all-submissive and all-suffering dispositions are founded on weakness, and accordingly he gave Desdemona the defects of her qualities. He would have no perfection in *his* characters. Rather than face the anger of the man whom she so passionately loves, Desdemona will lie—a slight lie, but one to which the ideal distortion of her would never be allowed to yield. Yet the weakness but makes Shakespeare's lady more credible, more piteous, perhaps even more lovable.

From the later developments of contemporary fiction the faultless hero and heroine have, we admit, relievingly disappeared. So much good has been wrought by the craze for "human documents." But alas! the disease expelled, who will expel the medicine? And the hydra perfection merely shoots up a new head. It is now a desire for the perfect reproduction of Nature, uninterfered with by the writer's ideals or sympathies; so that we have novelists who stand coldly aloof from their characters, and exhibit them with passionless countenance. We all admire the representations which result: "How beautifully drawn! how exactly like Nature!" Yes, beautifully drawn; but they do not live. They resemble the mask in *Phaedrus*—a cunning semblance, *at animam non habet*. This attitude of the novelist is fatal to artistic illusion: his personages do not move us because they do not move him. Partridge believed in the ghost because "the little man on the stage was more frightened than I"; and in novel-reading we are all Partridges, we only believe in the novelist's creations when he shows us that he believes in them himself. Finally, this pestilence attacks in literature the form no less than the essence, the integuments even more than the vitals. Hence arises the dominant belief that mannerism is vicious; and accordingly critics have erected the ideal of a style stripped of everything special or peculiar, a style which should be to thought what light is to the sun. Now this pure white light of style is as impossible as undesirable; it *must* be splintered into colour by the refracting media of the individual mind, and humanity will always prefer the colour. Theoretically we ought to have no mannerisms; practically we cannot help having them, and without them style would be flavourless—"faultily faultless, icily regular, splendidly null." Men will not drink distilled water; it is entirely pure and entirely insipid. The object of writing is to communicate individuality, the object of style adequately to embody that individuality; and since in every individuality worth anything there are characteristic pecularities, these must needs be reproduced in the embodiment. So reproduced we call them mannerisms. They correspond to those little unconscious tricks of voice, manner, gesture, in a friend which are to us the friend himself, and which we would not forgo. It is affected to imitate another's tricks of demeanour: similarly, it is affected to imitate another's mannerisms. We should avoid as far as possible in conversation passing conventionalities of speech, because they are brainless; similarly, we should avoid as far as possible in writing the mannerisms of our age, because they corrupt originality. But in essence, mannerisms—individual mannerisms—are a season of style, and happily unavoidable. It is, for instance, stated in the *Encyclopædia Britannica* that De Quincey is not a manneristic writer; and, so put, the assertion has much truth. Yet he is full of mannerisms, mannerisms which every student lovingly knows, and without which the essayist would not be our very own De Quincey.

We say, therefore: Guard against this seductive principle of perfection. Order yourselves to a wise conformity with that Nature who cannot for the life of her create a brain without making one half of it weaker than the other half, or even a fool without a flaw in his folly; who cannot set a nose straight on a man's face, and whose geometrical drawing would be tittered at by half the pupils of South Kensington. Consider who is the standing modern oracle of perfection, and what resulted from *his* interpretation of it. "Trifles make perfection, and perfection is no trifle." No; it is half a pound of muscle to the square inch—and *that* is no trifle. One satisfactory reflection we have in concluding. Wherever else the reader may be grieved by perfection, this article, at least, is sacred from the accursed thing.

Now, how much of all this do we mean? Hearken, O reader, to an apologue.

Once on a time there was a hypochondriac, who—though his digestion was excellent—believed that his delicate system required a most winnowed choice of viands. His physician, in order to humour him, prescribed a light and carefully varied diet. But the hypochondriac was not satisfied.

"I want to know, Doctor," he said, "how much of this food really contributes to the building up of my system, and how much is waste material!"

"That," observed the sage physician, "I cannot possibly tell you without recondite analysis and nice calculation."

"Then," said the hypochondriac, in a rage, "I will not eat your food. You are an impostor, Sir, and a charlatan, and I believe now your friends who told me that you were a homœopath in disguise."

"My dear Sir," replied the unmoved physician, "if you will eat nothing but what is entire nutriment, you will soon need to consult, not a doctor, but a chameleon. To what purpose are your digestive organs, unless to secrete what is nutritious, and excrete what is innutritious!"

And the moral is—no, the reader shall have a pleasure denied to him in his outraged childhood. He that hath understanding, let him understand.

THE FOURTH ORDER OF HUMANITY

IN the beginning of things came man, sequent to him woman; on woman followed the child, and on the child the doll. It is a climax of development; and the crown of these is the doll.

To the doll's supremacy in beauty woman's self bears testimony, implicit, if unconscious. For ages has she tricked her face in pigment, and her brows in alien hair; her *contours* she has filled to counterfeit roundness, her eyes and lashes tinged: and all in a frustrate essay to compass by Art what in the doll is right of Nature. Even the child exhibits distinct inferiorities. It is full of thwartness and eating and drinking, and selffulness (selfishness were a term too dully immitigate), and a plentiful lack of that repose wherein the doll is nearest to the quiet gods. For my own part, I profess that much acquaintance only increases my consideration for this fourth order of humanity: always excepting the very light-blue-eyed doll, in whose regard there is a certain chill *hauteur* against which my diffidence is not proof.

Consider the life of dolls. At the whim of some *debonair* maternal tyranness, they veer on every wind of mutability; are the sport of imputed moods, suffer qualities over which they have no election,— are sorry or glad, indocile or amiable, at their mistress' whim and mandate; they are visited with stripes, or the soft aspersion of kisses; with love delectably persecuted, or consigned to the element quiet of neglect; exalted to the dimple of their mistress' cheek, or dejected to the servile floor; rent and mutilated, or rocked and murmured over; blamed or petted, be-rated or loved. Nor why it is thus or thus with them, are they any wise witting; wherefore these things should be, they know not at all.

> Consider the life of us—
> Oh, my cousins the dolls!

Some consciousness, I take it, there was; some secret sense of this occult co-rivalry in fate, which withheld me even in childhood from the youthful male's contempt for these short-lived parasites of the nursery. I questioned, with wounded feelings, the straitened feminine intolerance which said to the boy: "Thou shalt not hold a baby; thou shalt not possess a doll." In the matter of babies, I was hopeless to shake the illiberal prejudice; in the matter of dolls,

I essayed to confound it. By eloquence and fine diplomacy I wrung from my sisters a concession of dolls; whence I date my knowledge of the kind.

But ineluctible sex declared itself. I dramatized them, I fell in love with them; I did not father them; intolerance was justified of its children. One in particular I selected, one with surpassing fairness crowned, and bowed before the fourteen inches of her skirt. She was beautiful. She was one of Shakespeare's heroines. She was an amity of inter-removed miracles; all wrangling excellencies at pact in one sole doll; the frontiers of jealous virtues marched in her, yet trespassed not against her peace. I desired for her some worthy name; and asked of my mother: Who was the fairest among living women? Laughingly was I answered that I was a hard questioner, but that perhaps the Empress of the French bore the bell for beauty. Hence, accordingly, my Princess of puppetdom received her style; and at this hour, though she has long since vanished to some realm where all sawdust is wiped for ever from dolls' wounds, I cannot hear that name but the Past touches me with a rigid agglomeration of small china fingers.

But why with childhood and with her should I close the blushing recital of my puppet-loves? Men are but children of a larger growth; and your statue, I warrant me, is but your crescent doll. Wherefore, then, should I leave unmemorized the statue which thralled my youth in a passion such as feminine mortality was skill-less to instigate? Nor at this let any boggle; for *she* was a goddess. Statue I have called her; but indeed she was a bust, a head, a face—and who that saw that face could have thought to regard further? She stood nameless in the gallery of sculptural casts which she strangely deigned to inhabit; but I have since learned that men call her the Vatican Melpomene. Rightly stood she nameless, for Melpomene she never was: never went words of hers from bronzèd lyre in tragic order; never through *her* enspelled lips moaned any syllables of woe. Rather, with her leaf-twined locks, she seemed some strayed Bacchante, indissolubly filmed in secular reverie. The expression which gave her divinity resistless I have always suspected for an accident of the cast; since in frequent engravings of her prototype I never met any such aspect. The secret of this indecipherable significance, I slowly discerned, lurked in the singularly diverse set of the two corners of the mouth;

so that her profile wholly shifted its meaning according as it was
viewed from the right or left. In one corner of her mouth the little
languorous firstling of a smile had gone to sleep; as if she had fallen
a-dream, and forgotten that it was there. The other had drooped,
as of its own listless weight, into a something which guessed at
sadness; guessed, but so as indolent lids are easily grieved by the
pricks of the slate-blue dawn. And on the full countenance those
two expressions blended to a single expression inexpressible; as
if pensiveness had played the Mænad, and now her arms grew
heavy under the cymbals. Thither each evening, as twilight fell,
I stole to meditate and worship the baffling mysteries of her meaning: as twilight fell, and the blank noon surceased arrest upon her
life, and in the vaguening countenance the eyes broke out from
their daylong ambuscade. Eyes of violet blue, drowsed-amorous,
which surveyed me not, but looked ever beyond, where a spell
enfixed them,

Waiting for something, not for me.

And I was content. Content; for by such tenure of unnoticedness
I knew that I held my privilege to worship: had she beheld me,
she would have denied, have contemned my gaze. Between us,
now, are years and tears: but the years waste her not, and the
tears wet her not; neither misses she me or any man. There, I
think, she is standing yet; there, I think, she will stand for ever:
the divinity of an accident, awaiting a divine thing impossible,
which can never come to her, and she knows this not.
    For I reject the vain fable that the ambrosial creature is really
an unspiritual compound of lime, which the gross ignorant call
plaster of Paris. If Paris indeed had to do with her, it was he of
Ida. And for him, perchance, she waits.

A RENEGADE POET ON THE POET

A POET is one who endeavours to make the worst of both
worlds. For he is thought seldom to make provision
for himself in the next life, and 'tis odds if he gets any
in this. The world will have nothing with his writings because
they are not of the world; nor the religious, because they are not
of religion. He is suspect of the worldly, because of his unworldli-

ness, and of the religious for the same reason. For there is a way of the world in religion, no less than in irreligion. Nay, though he should frankly cast in his lot with the profane, he is in no better case with them; for he alone of men, though he travel to the Pit, picks up no company by the way; but has a contrivance to evade Scripture, and find out a narrow road to damnation. Indeed, if the majority of men go to the nether abodes, 'tis the most hopeful argument I know of his salvation; for 'tis inconceivable he should ever do as other men.

Mr. Robert Louis Stevenson does not stick to affirm that the *littérateur* in general is but a poor devil of a fellow, who lives to please, and earns his bread by doing what he likes. Let this mere son of joy, says Mr. Stevenson, sleek down his fine airs before men who are of some use in the world. Yet if religion be useful, so is poetry. For poetry is the teacher of beauty; and without beauty men would soon lose the conception of a God, and exchange God for the devil: as indeed happens at this day among many savages where the worships of ugliness and of the devil flourish together. Whence it was, doubtless, that poetry and religion were of old so united, as is seen in the prophetic books of the Bible. Where men are not kept in mind of beauty they become lower than the beasts; for a dog, I will maintain, is a very tolerable judge of beauty, as appears from the fact that any liberally educated dog does, in a general way, prefer a woman to a man. The instinct of men is against this *renegado* of a Robert Louis. Though Butler justly observes that all men love and admire clothes, but scorn and despise him that made them, 'tis of tailors that he speaks. A *modiste* is held in as fair a reverence as any tradesman; and 'tis evident that the ground of the difference is because a *modiste* has some connexion with art and beauty, but a tailor only with ugliness and utility. There is no utilitarian but will class a soapmaker as a worthy and useful member of the community; yet is there no necessity why a man should use soap. Nay, if necessity be any criterion of usefulness (and surely that is useful which is necessary), the universal practice of mankind will prove poetry to be more useful than soap; since there is no recorded age in which men did not use poetry, but for some odd thousand years the world got on very tolerably well without soap. Look closely into the matter, and there are no people really useful to a man, in the strict utilitarian sense, but butchers and bakers, for they feed man; builders, for they house a man; women, for they help him into the world; and doctors and soldiers, for they help him out of it.

Then, too, this rogue of an R. L. S., I doubt me (plague on him! I cannot get him out of my head), has found writing pretty utilitarian—to himself; and utility begins at home, I take it. Does he not eat and drink romances, and has he not dug up Heaven knows what riches (the adventurer!) in *Treasure Island?* And as for usefulness to other men, since we must have that or be ignoble, it seems—is there no utility in pleasure, pray you, when it makes a man's heart the better for it; as do, I am very certain, sun, and flowers, and Stevensons?

Did we give in to that sad dog of a Robert Louis, we must needs set down the poor useless poet as a son of joy. But the title were an irony more mordant than the title of the hapless ones to whom it likens him. *Filles de joie?* O rather *filles d'amertume!* And if the pleasure they so mournfully purvey were lofty and purging as it is abysmal and corrupting, then would Stevenson's parallel be just; but *then*, too, from ignoble victims they would become noble ministrants. 'Tis a difference which vitiates the whole comparison, O careless player with the toys of the gods! whom we have taken, I warrant me, more gravely than you take your whimsical self in this odd pleasantry!

Like his sad sisters, but with *that* transfiguring distinction, the poet sows in sorrow that men may reap in joy. He serves his pleasure, say you, R. L. S.? 'Tis a strange pleasure, if so it be. He loves his art? No, his art loves *him;* cleaves to him when she has become unwelcome, a very weariness of the flesh. He is the sorry sport of a mischievous convention. The traditions of his craft, fortified by the unreasonable and misguiding lessons of those sages who have ever instructed the poet in the things that make for his better misery, persuade him that he can be no true singer except he slight the world. Wordsworth has taught him a most unnecessary apprehension lest the world should be too much with him; which, to be sure, was very singular in Wordsworth, who never had the world with him till he was come near to going out of it. The poor fool, therefore, devotes assiduous practice to acquiring an art which comes least natural to him of all men; and, after employing a world of pains to scorn the world, is strangely huffed that it should return the compliment in kind. There is left him no better remedy but, having spent his youth in alienating its opinion, to spend his manhood in learning to despise its opinion. And though it be a hard matter to contemn the world, 'tis a yet harder matter to contemn its contempt. I regard the villainous misleaders of poets who have preached up these doctrines as all one for selfish cruelty with those who maintained the tradition of operatic eunuchs; and would have them equally suppressed by Christian sentiment. For they have procured the severance of the one from his kind to gratify their understanding, as of the other to gratify their ear.

MOESTITIAE ENCOMIUM

MARSH, and night. There are sounds; no man shall say what sounds. There are shadows; no man shall say what shadows. There is light; were there not shadow, no man should call it light. The landscape is a sketch blotted in with smoke of Erebus, and grey from the cheek of death: those trees which threaten from the horizon—they are ranked apparitions, no boon of gracious God. The heaven is a blear copy of the land. Athwart the saturnine marsh, runs long, pitilessly straight, ghastly with an inward pallor (for no gleam dwells on it from the sky), the leprous, pined, infernal watercourse; a water for the Plutonian naiads— exhaling cold perturbation. It is a stream, a land, a heaven, pernicious to the heart of man; created only for

> The abhorred estate
> Of empty shades, and disembodied elves.

Over this comes up of a sudden an unlawful moon. My very heart blanches. But a voice which is not the voice of reed, or sedge, or flag, or wind, yet is as the voice of each, says: "Fear not; it is I, whom you know." I know her, this power that has parted from the side of Terror; she is Sadness, and we are companions of old. Yet not here am I most familiar with her presence; far oftener have I found her lurking in the blocked-out, weighty shadows which fall from the tyrannous sun. We love the tyrannous sun she and I.

I know her, for I am of the age, and the age is hers. Alas for the nineteenth century, with so much pleasure, and so little joy; so much learning, and so little wisdom; so much effort, and so

little fruition; so many philosophers, and such little philosophy;
so many seers, and such little vision; so many prophets, and such
little foresight; so many teachers, and such an infinite wild vortex
of doubt! the one divine thing left to us is Sadness. Even our
virtues take her stamp; the intimacy of our loves is born of despair;
our very gentleness to our children is because we know how short
their time. "Eat," we say, "eat, drink, and be merry; for to-morrow
ye are men."

I know her; and praise, knowing. Foolishly we shun this shunless
Sadness; fondly we deem of her as but huntress of men, who is
tender and the bringer of tenderness to those she visits with her
fearful favours. A world without joy were more tolerable than a
world without sorrow. Without sadness where were brotherliness?
For in joy is no brotherliness, but only a boon-companionship.
She is the Spartan sauce which gives gusto to the remainder-viands
of life, the broken meats of love. "The full soul loatheth an honeycomb; but to the hungry soul every bitter thing is sweet." Her
servitors rise in the hierarchy of being: to woman, in particular,
hardly comes the gracious gift of sweetness till her soul has been
excavated by pain. Even a dog in sadness is nearer to the level
and the heart of man. She has her dark *accolade*, her sombre patents
of nobility; but the titles of that abhorred peerage are clemently
and benignly unsuccessive. Our sweetest songs are from her, Shelley
knew; but he needed not to have limited the benefaction by song.
She is not fair, poor Grief; yet in her gift is highest fairness. Love,
says Plato, is unbeautiful: yet Love makes all things beautiful.
And all things take on beauty which pass into the hueless flame of
her aureole. It may chance to one, faring through a wet grey day-
fall, that suddenly from behind him spurts the light of the sinking
sun. Instantly, the far windows of unseen homesteads break into
flash through the rain-smoke, the meads run over with yellow
light, the scattered trees are splashed with saffron. He turns about
towards the fountain of the splendorous surprise—sees but a weeping sundown of pallid and sickly gold. So, throughout humanity,
my eyes discern a mourning loveliness; so I turn expectant—"What,
pale Sorrow? Could all this have been indeed from you? And
give you so much beauty that no dower of it remains for your
own?" Nay, but my vision was unversed when I disvalued her
comeliness, and I looked not with the looking of her lovers.

Nay, but to our weak mortality the extremity of immitigate beauty is inapprehensible save through reflection and dilution. Sorrow is fair with an unmortal fairness, which we see not till it is humanized in the sorrowful. The sweetest smiles I know, her rod draws forth from the rock of an abiding melancholy; the faces which haunt me from canvas attest that *she* prescribed to the painter's hand; of the most beautiful among the sons of men it is recorded that, though many had seen Him weep, no man had seen Him smile. Nor with beauty end her gifts to men. Solomon, who found in knowledge but increase of sorrow, might have found in sorrow increase of knowledge: it is less wisdom that reveals mourning, than mourning that reveals wisdom—as the Hindoo gathers secret things from gazing in the pool of ink. Power is the reward of sadness. It was after the Christ had wept over Jerusalem that He uttered some of His most august words; it was when His soul had been sorrowful even unto death that His enemies fell prostrate before His voice. Who suffers, conquers. The bruised is the breaker. By torture the Indians try their braves; by torture Life, too, tries the elected victors of her untriumphal triumphs, and of cypress is the commemoration on their brows. Sadness the king-maker, *morituri te salutant!*

Come, therefore, O Sadness, fair and froward and tender; dolorous coquette of the Abyss, who claspest them that shun thee, with fierce kisses that hiss against their tears; wraith of the mists of sighs; mermaid of the flood Cocytus, of the waves which are salt with the weeping of the generations; most menacing seductress, whose harp is stringed with lamentations, whose voice is fatal with disastrous prescience; draw me down, merge me, under thy waters of wail! Of thy undesired loveliness am I desirous, for I have looked long on thy countenance, and can forget it not, not the footfalls of thy majesty which still shake the precincts of my heart: under the fringed awnings of the sunsets thou art throned, and *thy* face parts the enfolding pavilions of the Evens; thou art very dear to the heart of Night; thou art mistress of the things unmetable which are dreadful to meted life, mistress of the barren hearth and the barren soul of man, mistress of the weepings of death and of birth; the cry of the bride is thine and the pang of the first kiss, the pain which is mortise to delight, the flowers which trail between the ruined chaps of mortality, the over-

foliaging death which chequers all human suns. Of thy beauty
undesired am I desirous, for knowledge is with thee, and dominion,
and piercing, and healing; thou woundest with a thorn of light;
thou sittest portress by the gates of hearts; and a sceptred quiet
rests regal in thine eyes' sepulchral solitudes, in the tenebrous
desolations of thine eyes.

"The over-foliaging death which chequers all human suns."
Even so. Not by Cocytus is delimited her delimitless realm. For
I have a vision; and the manner of the vision is this. I see the
Angel of life. It (for it may be of either sex) is a mighty grey-
winged Angel, with bowed and hidden face, looking into the river
of life. And sometimes a waver of sunshine rests upon its grey
wings and folded veil, so that I seem to see its face, and to see it
exceeding beautiful; and then again the sunlight fades, and I
dare not attempt to penetrate that veil, for I imagine the countenance exceeding awful. And I see that within its sad drapery the
Angel weeps, and its tears fall into the water of life: but whether
they be tears of joy or sorrow, only its Creator knows, not I. I
have tasted the water of life where the tears of the Angel fell; and
the taste was bitter as brine.

Then, say you, they were tears of sorrow? The tears of joy are
salt, as well as the tears of sorrow. And in that sentence are many
meanings.

POPE

THERE was born in eighteenth century England a pale little
diseased wretch of a boy. Since it was evident that he would
never be fit for any healthy and vigorous trade, and that
he must all his life be sickly and burdensome to himself, and since
it is the usual way of such unhappy beings to add to their unhappi-
ness by their own perversities of choice, he naturally became a
poet. And after living for long in a certain miserable state called
glory, reviled and worshipped and laughed at and courted, despised
by the women he loved, very ill looked after, amid the fear and
malignity of many and the affection of very few, the wizened little
suffering monstrosity died, and was buried in Westminster Abbey,
by way of encouraging others to follow in his footsteps. And
though a large number of others have done so with due and proper
misfortune, in all the melancholy line there is, perhaps, no such

destined a wretch as Alexander Pope. What fame can do to still the cravings of such a poor prodigal of song, in the beggarly raiment of his tattered body, that it did for him. The husks of renown he had in plenty, and had them all his life, as no other poet has had. But Voltaire testified that the author of that famous piece of philosophy, "Whatever is, is right," was the most miserable man he had ever known.

This king of the eighteenth century is still the king of the eighteenth century by general consent. Dryden was a greater poet, *meo judicio*, but he did not represent the eighteenth century so well as Pope. All that was elegant and airy in the polished artificiality of that age reaches its apotheosis in the *Rape of the Lock*. It is Pope's masterpiece, a Watteau in verse. The poetry of manners could no further go than in this boudoir epic, unmatched in any literature. It is useless, I may here say, to renew the old dispute whether Pope was a poet. Call his verse poetry or what you will, it is work in verse which could not have been done in prose, and, of its kind, never equalled. Then the sylph machinery in the *Rape of the Lock* is undoubted work of fancy: the fairyland of powder and patches, *A Midsummer Night's Dream* seen through chocolate-fumes. The *Essay on Man* is naught to us nowadays, as a whole. It has brilliant artificial passages. It has homely aphorisms such as only Pope and Shakespeare could produce— the quintessence of pointed common sense: many of them have passed into the language, and are put down, by three out of five who quote them, to Shakespeare. But, as a piece of reasoning in verse, the *Essay on Man* is utterly inferior to Dryden's *Hind and Panther*. Even that brilliant achievement could not escape the doom which hangs over the didactic poem pure and simple; and certain, therefore, was the fate of the *Essay on Man*.

The *Dunciad* De Quincey ranked even above the *Rape of the Lock*. At my peril I venture to question a judgement backed by all the ages. The superb satire of parts of the poem I admit; I admit the exceedingly fine close, in which Pope touched a height he never touched before or after; I admit the completeness of the scheme. But from that completeness comes the essential defect of the poem. He adapted the scheme from Dryden's *MacFlecknoe*. But Dryden's satire is at once complete and succinct: Pope has built upon the scheme an edifice greater than it will bear; has extended a witty and ingenious idea to a portentous extent at which it ceases to be amusing. The mock solemnity of Dryden's idea becomes a very real and dull solemnity when it is extended to liberal epic proportions. A serious epic is apt to nod, with the force of a Milton behind it; an epic satire fairly goes to sleep. A pleasantry in several books is past a pleasantry. And it is bolstered out with a great deal which is sheer greasy scurrility. The mock-heroic games of the poets are in large part as dully dirty as the waters into which Pope makes them plunge.

If the poem had been half as long, it might have been a master-piece. As it is, unless we are to reckon masterpieces by avoirdupois weight, or to assign undue value to mere symmetry of scheme, I think we must look for Pope's satirical masterpiece elsewhere. Not in the satire on women, where Pope seems hardly to have his heart in his work; but in the imitations from Horace, those generally known as Pope's *Satires*. Here he is at his very best and tersest. They are as brilliant as anything in the *Dunciad*, and they are brilliant right through; the mordant pen never flags. It matters not that they are imitated from Horace. They gain by it: their limits are circumscribed, their lines laid down, and Pope writes the better for having these limits set him, this tissue on which to work. Not a whit does he lose in essential originality: nowhere is he so much himself. It is very different from Horace, say the critics. Surely that is exactly the thing for which to thank poetry and praise Pope. It has not the pleasant urbane good humour of the Horatian spirit. No, it has the spirit of Pope—and satire is the gainer. Horace is the more charming companion; Pope is the greater satirist. In place of an echo of Horace (and no verse translation was ever anything but feeble which attempted merely to echo the original), we have a new spirit in satire; a fine series of English satirical poems, which in their kind are unapproached by the Roman, and in his kind wisely avoid the attempt to approach him. *Satires after Horace* would have been a better title than *Imitations;* for less imitative poems in essence were never written. These and the *Rape of the Lock* are Pope's finest title to fame. The *Elegy on an Unfortunate Lady* has at least one part which shows a pathos little to have been surmised from his later work; and so, perhaps (in a much less degree, I think), have fragments of the once famous *Eloisa to Abelard*. But the *Pastorals*, and the *Windsor Forest*, and the *Ode on St Cecilia's Day*, and other things in which Pope tried the serious or natural vein, are only fit to be remembered with Macpherson's Ossian and the classical enormities of the French painter David.

On the whole, it is as a satirist we must think of him, and the second greatest in the language. The gods are in pairs, male and female; and if Dryden was the Mars of English satire, Pope was the Venus—a very eighteenth century Venus, quite as conspicuous for malice as for elegance. If a woman's satire were informed with genius, and cultivated to the utmost perfection of form by lifelong and exclusive literary practice, one imagines it would be much like Pope's. His style seems to me feminine in what it lacks; the absence of any geniality, any softening humour to abate its mortal thrust. It is feminine in what it has, the malice, the cruel dexterity, the delicate needle point which hardly betrays its light and swift entry, yet stings like a bee. Even in his coarseness—as in the *Dunciad*—Pope appears to me female. It is the coarseness of the fine ladies of that material time, the Lady Maries and the rest of them. Dryden is a rough and thick-natured man, cudgelling his adversaries with coarse speech in the heat and brawl and the bluntness of his sensibilities; a country squire, who is apt at times to use the heavy end of his cutting whip; but when Pope is coarse he is coarse with effort, he goes out of his way to be nasty, in the evident endeavour to imitate a man. It is a girl airing the slang of her schoolboy brother.

The one thing, perhaps, which differentiates him from a woman, and makes it possible to read his verse with a certain pleasure, without that sense of unrelieved cruelty which repels one in much female satire, is his artist's delight in the exercise of his power. You feel that, if there be malice, intent to wound, even spite, yet none of these count for so much with him as the exercise of his superb dexterity in fence. He is like Ortheris fondly patting his rifle after that long shot which knocked over the deserter, in Mr Kipling's story. After all, you reflect, it is fair fight; if his hand was against many men, many men's hands were against him. So you give yourself up to admire the shell-like epigram, the rocketing and dazzling antithesis, the exquisitely deft play of point, by which the little invalid kept in terror his encompassing cloud of enemies—many of them adroit and formidable wits themselves. And you think, also, that the man who was loved by Swift, the professional hater, was not a man without a heart; though he wrote the most finished and brilliant satire in the language.

BACON

FIRST and before all things, Francis Bacon, Lord Verulam, was a great philosopher. In saying this we make no pretension to estimate the value of his philosophy, regarded as an exposition of truth. But it is the acknowledged fact that he is the founder, the *fons et origo*, of that utilitarian school of philosophy which is peculiarly English. We do not say that without him we should have had no Scottish school of philosophy; no Hume, no Bain, no Reid; that without him we should have had no Locke, no John Stuart Mill, no Herbert Spencer—who, though very different from the utilitarian school, is nevertheless essentially English, and could not have arisen without the various English philosophers (whether strictly English or Scottish) who had preceded him. That school was in the air, and was bound to come. It is perhaps only in the case of a Shakespeare that we can say a whole literature—nay, almost a whole nation—would have been different if he had not appeared. But as things have been arranged, the whole temper of the British school of philosophy looks back to Bacon as its starting-point.

Far more, in our opinion, must it be said that the whole of English physical science must acknowledge Bacon as its very Adam and progenitor. Not because Bacon was himself a great physical investigator; but because he first pointed out the aims and the temper of the physical investigator. Cowley stated the truth, with the usual perspicacity of the poet. Bacon did not enter the Promised Land, but he had the vision of it, and pointed the way to it. His whole aim was to start a new philosophical school, which should antithesize the philosophy of the scholastics and the ancients by proceeding from without inwards, instead of from within outwards; from phenomena to essence, not from essence to phenomena. Physical investigation was but a branch of this new departure, as he conceived it. Yet, in laying down this principle, he unwittingly became the patriarch of our modern scientists. Huxley was bred from his loins, and men greater in physical science than Huxley. This, we unhesitatingly aver, seems to us a greater achievement than the authorship of the British school of philosophy. Already there is a reaction towards the recognition of that very scholastic school which Bacon, the philosopher, lived only to destroy and bring into contempt. But there is not, nor ever will be, any reaction from the temper of physical research which he first inculcated. Other views may arise as to the value of the principle he laid down in regard to philosophy. There can be no other view as to the value of the principle he laid down in regard to physical science.

Here, however, we are not concerned with him on these grounds. We are concerned with him solely as one of the explorers in English prose. And here his name is not so great. He wrote many things, including the not very successful attempt to follow the path of Plato and Sir Thomas More, in the *New Atlantis*. But he survives chiefly by his Essays. They mainly show Bacon the chancellor, the courtier, and man of the world. They are full of very shrewd wisdom, of a devious and not over-principled kind. No attempt is there in them at deep truths, such as you might expect from a philosopher. Not truth, but expediency; the truth of self-interest and worldly consideration, is their aim. They show Bacon as an opportunist of the first water, a respectable British Machiavel. If to be a sage in the art of "getting on" constitutes greatness, then, and not otherwise, they are great. As regards their style, they are doubtless what he would himself call very pithy, pregnant, and sententious. The sentences are short, clear, well-knit, unsuperfluous. But there is no attempt at the more complex evolutions of style; and the succession of short barks (so to speak) is apt to get as tiresome as the utterances of a dog, though he barked like the hoariest sage in kenneldom. There is one exception; and that (if we remember rightly) is the first essay in the collection. But though the earliest (or almost the earliest, if our memory should deceive us) in the book, it is stated by editors to be the latest written. We can well believe it. For here Bacon ascends to an altogether higher level in subject-matter; and naturally, therefore, to an altogether higher level in style. In the sustained dignity of its sentences, as in the sustained dignity of its thought, it is altogether worthy of Sir Thomas Browne, and might not unhappily be taken for the work of that later and greater master of prose.

Otherwise, even as regards the terseness and weight of wisdom in individual sentences (the excellence in which Bacon excels), the palm must be given to his philosophical works, in spite of their alien language. For example:

Present justice is in your power; for that which is to come you have no security.

Or again:

Men believe that their reason governs words. But it is also true that words, like the arrows from a Tartar bow, are shot back, and react on the mind.

And yet again (though it is a precept which has its exceptions, in the case of intuitional minds):

Let every student of Nature take this as a fact, that whatever the mind seizes and dwells on with peculiar satisfaction is to be held in suspicion.

Consider also this most practical maxim:

In attempts to improve your character, know what is in your power and what beyond it.

Or finally, the saying in the *De Amicitia*, which we quote in the original language on account of its superior terseness:

Magna civitas, magna solitudo.

It might be a saying from Seneca or St Augustine, so pregnant and sparse in wording is it. And if we have somewhat deprecated the excessive praise usually given to Bacon as a writer of prose, let it be acknowledged that, compared with the average modern writer, he is fine and full of matter indeed. It is only by comparison with the great writers of the seventeenth century that he appears less a master of his art. But then, he preceded them; and perhaps even Sir Thomas Browne learned something from him.

DON QUIXOTE

WAS there ever so strange a book as this *Don Quixote!* To what class shall we assign it? Solitary, singular, it will not be pigeon-holed; your literary entomologists shall ticket it, *genus* and *sub-genus* it, at their peril. It is complex beyond measure. It is a piece of literary duplicity without precedent or succession; nay, duplicity within duplicity, a sword turning all ways, like that which guarded "unpermitted Eden," to quote a cancelled verse of Rossetti's *Love's Nocturn*.

Let not Swift say that he was born to introduce and refine irony. The irony of Cervantes is refined and dangerous beyond the irony of Swift; Swift's is obvious beside it. All irony is double-tongued; but whether it be the irony of Swift, or Swift's predecessors, or Swift's successors, it has this characteristic: that its duplicity is (so to speak) a one-sided duplicity; if you do not take the inner meaning, you read baffled, without pleasure, without admiration, without comprehension. But this strange irony, this grave irony, this broadly-laughing irony, of the strange, grave, humorous Spaniard, delights even those who have not a touch of the ironic in their composition. They laugh at the comic mask, who cannot see the melancholy face behind it. It is the Knight of the Rueful Countenance in the vizard of Sancho Panza; and all laugh, while some few have tears in their laughter. And they know not that their derision is derided; that they are trapped and cozened into jeers; that Cervantes, from behind his mask, beholds their grins with a sardonic smile.

A core of scornful and melancholy protest, set about with a pulp of satire, and outside all a rind of thick burlesque—that is *Don Quixote*. It never "laughed Spain's chivalry away." Chivalry was no more, in a country where it could be written. Where it could be thought an impeachment of idealism, idealism had ceased to be. Against this very state of things its secret but lofty contempt is aimed. Herein lies its curious complexity. Outwardly Cervantes falls in with the waxing materialism of the day, and professes to satirize everything that is chivalrous and ideal. Behind all that, is subtle, suppressed, mordant satire of the material spirit in all its forms: the clownish materialism of the boor; the comfortable materialism of the *bourgeois;* the pedantic materialism of the scholar and the mundane cleric; the idle, luxurious, arrogant materialism of the noble—all agreeing in derisive conceit of superiority to the poor madman who still believes in grave, exalted, heroic ideas of life and duty. Finally, at the deepmost core of the strange and wonderful satire, in which the hidden mockery is so opposite to the seeming mockery, lies a sympathy even to tears with all height and heroism insulated and out of date, mad to the eyes of a purblind world: nay, a bitter confession that such nobility is, indeed, mad and phantasmal, in so much as it imputes its own greatness to a petty and clay-content society. Even Sancho is held up to admiration mixed with smiles, because he has the dim yet tough insight to follow what he does not understand, yet obscurely feels to be worthy of love and following. The author of the heroic *Numantia* a contemner of the lofty and ideal! It could not be. Surely Don Quixote has much of the writer's self; of his poetic discontent with the earthy and money-seeking society around him. There is no true laughter in literature with such a hidden sadness as that of Cervantes.

Yet it is laughter, and not all sad. The man is a humorist, and feels that if the world be full of mournful humour, yet life would go nigh to madness if there were not some honest laughter as well—laughter from the full lungs. Therefore he gives us Sancho—rich, unctuous, Shakespearean humour to the marrow of him. The mockers of the Don, with their practical jests on him, furnish the understanding reader with but pitying and half-reluctant laughter; but the faithful compost of fat and flesh who cleaves to the meagre visionary allows us mirth unstinted and unqualified. Many a touch in this creation of the great Spaniard reminds us of like touches in the greatest of Englishmen. Sancho's blunt rejection of titles, for example: "Don does not belong to me, nor ever did to any of my family: I am called plain Sancho Panza, my father was a Sancho, and my grandfather a Sancho, and they were all Panzas, without any addition of Dons or Donnas." Who does not remember at once the drunken tinker's "What! am I not Christopher Sly?" etc. The two passages are delightfully kindred in style and humour. How like, too, are Sancho's meandering telling of his story at the Duke's table, and Dame Quickly's narrative style, when she recounts Falstaff's promise of marriage! Unadulterated peasant nature both—the same in Spain as in Eastcheap. What more gloriously characteristic than Sancho's rebutting of the charge that he may prove ungrateful in advancement to high station? "Souls like mine are covered four inches thick with the grease of the old Christian."

But enough. With all the inward gravity of his irony, Cervantes has abundantly provided that we need not take his seriousness too seriously: there is laughter even for those who enter deepest into that grave core.

GOLDSMITH'S PROSE

IN the prose style of that delightful poet and universal man of letters, Oliver Goldsmith, the man himself counts for so much that it is impossible to write of one without the other. One can trace the derivations of that style, it is true; one can discern that it owes much to French influence. Style does not come out of the blue, be it ever so native to the man, and however authentic his genius. But when you have recognized its Gallic derivation, that which gives it breath of life, and radiates from it in personal fascination, is Goldsmith himself—the careless Goldsmith, the much-tried Goldsmith, the sweet-natured Goldsmith, the Goldsmith who took his troubles like a happy-go-lucky child: an Irish child withal, bright, emotional, and candid.

Yet all this would not have produced the inexpressibly exhilarating mixture we call Goldsmith, limpid and effervescent, touched with the simplest sentiment, enriched with the most varied experience, unfailing in dexterous grace, had this Irish child not been also a child of the eighteenth century. Into this artificial, unruffled eighteenth century, which made composure not merely an inward ideal but an external law, was born this Celtic child, uttering himself right out with a modern sincerity, and an unconsciousness not often modern. The result, at its best, is a combination of qualities singularly piquant and unreproducible. Born into the nineteenth century with such a temperament, a life so troublous and largely *manqué*, Goldsmith would have had the *weltschmerz* pretty badly. He would have wailed the impossibility of things; he would have taken the bandage from his sores; his gaiety would have been dashed with some eclipse. Born into the eighteenth century, he had no encouragement to the indulgence of world-smart. He kept his sores under decent covering, knowing there was small sympathy for literary groans; he looked neither back nor forward, took the hour as it came, and piped against his troubles if Fate gave him half a chance. That European tour, when, half scholarly impostor, half minstrel, he alternately challenged disputants (not forthcoming) and fluted for a living, is a type of his whole career. The Irishman of that character no longer exists: and if personal dignity gains by his vanishing, the gaiety of nations suffers. No wonder that the dignifiedly Britannic, and a trifle priggish, Johnsonian circle was half scandalized by the advent amongst it of this improvident creature of Nature.

Johnson, sternly moralizing under adversity, meets Goldie piping against it, and shakes his unambrosial wig. Yet it says much for the formidable old Doctor that he seems to have appreciated the simple, sweet-natured genius better than did the rest of his circle. It is the fashion to discredit Boswell's stories of Goldsmith on the ground of envy. Jealous they self-evidently are, but they are too racy of the Goldsmith soil not to be true. The *naïf* vanity is the vanity of a child. One can imagine Goldie breaking his shins in imitating a mountebank—and laugh with kindly amusement. Where talk was supremely valued, he would plunge in, sink or swim. But only that bewigged eighteenth century circle could sneer at him for the harmless weakness. He knew he had the brilliance in him, and pathetically hoped he could teach it to shine at the call of the moment. A little ugly man, slow-tongued and unattractive to women, he sought indemnity for his maimed life in plum-coloured coats, Tokay, and the sorry loves of Covent Garden. "Goldie was wild, sir," and small cause for wonder.

But all that weakness is strength in his charming prose. There was valiance, could the Doctor have seen it, in that clear fountain of gaiety which turned all his misfortunes to brightness and favour. It is his sunny wit and sweet heart which clarifies his style; his lovable humour draws for us perpetual refreshment from the vicissitudes of a life as hard as ever fell to struggling poet. What modern writer is brave child enough to extract sunshine from the recollection of his own darkest hours? A more admirable example you could not have of Goldsmith's prose than that exquisitely sly description of George's search for a living in the *Vicar of Wakefield*. Yet small was the laughter in the experiences which furnished it to poor Goldie; and it was written when he was still struggling for bread. The narrative is saturated with humour as delicate as it is buoyant, and kindly with large good nature towards the very rogues and blockheads who have set their heels on the helpless seeker for bread. The mere technique is that of a master: every sentence deftly shaped, yet easy as the song of a bird; the phrasing unobtrusively perfect, as we have lost the art of perfecting it in our self-conscious age. He had, indeed, the great heritage of eighteenth century prose, which a succession of masters had shaped to the purposes of wit and humour. But he had lightened it, made it nimble and touched it with an artless-seeming grace, as it never was before. This in the very day when Johnson had compelled English prose to the following of his own deep-draughted movement. Yet, by a singular stretch of blind jealousy, Boswell and others accused him of imitating the Gargantuan Doctor!

Perhaps Johnson may have had some influence on his serious and "elevated" style, which is antithetic and not a little rhetorical. Perhaps Johnson, also, taught him compactness of structure and grammatical accuracy, which are invaluable even in his lightest style. But, though he "touched nothing he did not adorn," and was as irresistible in the pathos of poor Olivia as in the humours of Mr. Jenkinson or Miss Carolina Wilhelmina Skeggs, it is as a comedian that one loves him best. That gay humour could pass from demure slyness to the most buoyant farce; and the combination of extravagance with the deftest delicacy is perhaps his most characteristic and felicitous achievement. Beau Tibbs, in the *Citizen of the World*, is farce; but farce which nowadays would pass for comedy. But Beau Tibbs is too great to be displayed in a mere extract; he must be read entire. Why is Goldsmith unknown at the present day by that delightful series of papers? If the cream of his comedy be in the plays and the *Vicar*, yet, for the sake of Beau Tibbs alone, the *Citizen* should be resuscitated. And if this inadequate article sends one fresh reader to those neglected essays, it will not have been written uselessly.

THE POET'S POET

HERE is a poet who is just poetry, and the stuff of poetry; whose narrative—a mere vehicle for his ideas—is a tissue of romantic fancy, careless of manners or character, of interest epic or dramatic. He has been much beloved of poets, and little of that vague entity, the "general reader." Shakespeare had read him much: Milton called him master; he made Cowley a poet two hundred years ago, Keats a poet the other day, and who shall say how many in the illustrious line between? Raleigh and Sidney were his lovers in life; for they also were poets. Raleigh might hail in him a double kinship, as poet and explorer. Was not Spenser indeed a great explorer, among the greatest in that age of adventure, when a man got up in the morning and said, "I have an idea. If you have nothing better to do, let us go continent-hunting." And he that had not found an island or so was accounted a fellow of no spirit.

Well, Spenser for his share rediscovered Poetry; or, at least, made Poetry possible. It is among the strangest of strange things that the early sixteenth century should have lisped and stammered where the fourteenth had sung with full mouth; that where the middle ages had led with Chaucer, it should follow with Skelton; that Surrey, Wyatt, and Spenser's immediate forerunners should doubtfully experiment in an art of which Chaucer had been consummate master. The tongue of Chaucer was changed; the methods of Chaucer held good. Yet the poets were a people of a stammering tongue; their art had gone back to infancy; and things were at such a pass that the egregious Harvey was for setting the English Muses to their *gradus ad Parnassum* and the penning (singing were a misnomer) of obscene horrors styled hexameters, elegiacs, and the like. Then came Spenser, and found again that land of Poetry, more golden than any El Dorado towards which Raleigh ever set his bold-questing keel. He joined hands with Chaucer across the years: even the metre of his earlier poems is Chaucer's. A swarm of adventurers followed their Columbus; and English Poetry was.

For all which, outside the poets, he got little more recognition than he gets now. To a cultured Queen and her Court he cried, in new and unmatched verse, that:

> Fame with golden wings aloft doth fly
> Above the reach of ruinous decay,
> And with brave plumes doth beat the azure sky
> Admired of base-born men from far away:
> Then whoso will with virtuous deeds essay
> To mount to heaven, on Pegasus must ride,
> And with sweet poets' verse be glorified.
>
> For not to have been dipt in Lethe lake
> Could save the son of Thetis from to die;
> But that blind bard did him immortal make
> With verses dipt in dew of Castaly:
> Which made the Eastern Conqueror to cry—
> "O fortunate young man, whose virtue found
> So brave a trump, thy noble acts to sound!"

What deaf adder could withstand such charming? "With verses dipt in dew of Castaly"—can you not hear the delicate dewy drip of that exquisitely musical line?

> Provide, therefore, ye Princes, while ye may,
> That of the Muses ye may honoured be,

exhorted the poet in logical conclusion: and the Princes "provided"—on the cheap. The Cecils and Elizabeths rated their "immortality" a good deal below the pay of a foreign spy.

"Greatest Gloriane," like a many be-rhymed ladies, probably yawned over her *Faëry Queen* and one may be sure never got to the end of it. It would be curious to inquire how many lovers of poetry have read through it or *The Excursion*. The *Faëry Queen* is in truth a poem that no man can read through save as a duty, and in a series of arduous campaigns (so to speak). The later books of it steadily fail in power; but that is not all. The Spenserian stanza, beautiful for a time, in the course of four hundred or so pages becomes a very wearisome and cumbrous narrative form. The repetition of it grows monotonous; it fatigues by the perpetual discontinuity. Spenser himself seems to find it sometimes cumbrous, in the end. You have occasional lines like—

> Until they both do hear what she to them will say.

No, the *Faëry Queen* must not be read on end; it is a poem to linger over and dip into. It is, indeed, as much a series of poems as the *Idylls of the King*. It is not a great poem as its model, Ariosto's *Orlando Furioso*, is a great poem; for Spenser has planned on a scale beyond his physical power of endurance, and its completion would have been only so much superfluous evidence of the fact. Its waning power was not caused by waning genius; for in the same year with the latest books he published his magnificent lyrical poems. But if not a great poem it is great poetry; nay, we might say it contains great poems.

The obvious qualities of it and its author are grown mere truisms. He is princely in fancy rather than imagination. His gift of vision (in a specialized sense of the word) is unapproached. Every one has remarked upon that faculty of seeing visions, and presenting them as before the bodily eye: the *Faëry Queen* is a gallery hung with the rarest tapestries, an endless procession of dream-pictures.

There is no emotion, save the emotion of beauty. Yet incidentally, like the exclamations of a dreaming man, he will utter brief passages of tenderest pathos, or exultant joy:

> Nought is there under heaven's wide hollowness
> That moves more dear compassion of mind,
> Than beauty brought to unworthy wretchedness.

The mournful sweetness of those lines is insurpassable; and they are quintessential Spenser. Yet it is unluckily characteristic of him, too, that he mars half the effect of this perfect passage by not stopping with its completion, but following it with a line which makes an anti-climax, and is too manifestly inserted for rhyme's sake:

> Through envy's snares, or fortune's freaks unkind.

One might almost take that little passage as a text for one's whole disquisition on Spenser. For, after all, it is not in the richly luxuriant descriptive embroidery, or the pictures brushed in with words as with line and colour, which are traditionally quoted by this poet's critics, that the highest Spenser lies. The secret of him is shut in those three lines.

Wherein lies their power? The language is so utterly plain that an uninspired poet would have fallen upon baldness. Yet Spenser is a mine of diction (as was remarked to us by a poet who had worked in that mine). But here he had no need for his gorgeous opulence of diction: a few commonest words, and the spell was worked. It is all a matter of relation: the words take life from each other, and become an organism, as with Coleridge. And it is a matter of music; an integral element in the magic of the passage is its sound. In this necromancy, by which the most elementary words, entering into a secret relation of sense and sound, acquire occult property, Spenser is a master. And that which gives electric life to their relation is the Spenserian subtlety of emotion. Here it is specifically pathos, at another time it is joyous exultation, or again the pleasure of beauty. But behind and underneath all these emotional forms, the central and abiding quality, the essence of his emotion, is peace, and the radiance of peace. The final effect of all, in this and kindred passages, is lyrical.

Yes, lyrical. We are well-nigh minded to write ourselves down arch-heretics, and say that the *Faëry Queen* is a superb error. Spenser, it almost seems to us, was a supreme lyric poet who, by the influence of tradition and example, was allured to spend his strength in narrative poetry, and found his true path only at the close of his literary career. Throughout the *Faëry Queen* he is happy when he drops narration to dream dreams, and touches his serenest height in some brief, casual access of lyric feeling such as we have quoted. And in his last years, before misfortune silenced him, he wrote an all-too-small, precious handful of lyrics, which cover but a few pages, yet are greater than all his "great" poem together, flowing with milk and honey of poetry though it be.

In those grand Platonic *Hymns to Beauty*, in the *Prothalamion* and *Epithalamion*, all his finest qualities are gathered into organic wholes, sublimated by a lyric ardour which is the radiant effluence of central peace. Joy never had such expression as in the *Epithalamion*, so serenely noble that its intensity of joy may almost be missed, as the swift interflux of the blue heaven cheats us with the aspect of perfect calm. To express supreme joy is the most difficult of tasks (as a critic has remarked), far more difficult than to express intense sadness, which is the chosen aim of most modern poetry. Here it is supremely expressed, in connexion with the culminating point of natural joy; and is ennobled by the interfused presence of something loftier and more perfect than joy—that static joy which is peace. How well could we have forgone the full latter half of the *Faëry Queen* for some twenty more of such consummate lyrics! But Spenser found his greatest gift, his truest line of work, all too late, when the night was closing on him wherein no man can work— the night of poverty, ruin, and sorrow-hastened age.

NOTES

LAMB

2 The best text of Lamb's essays is that of the edition by E. V. Lucas (*The Works of Charles and Mary Lamb*), vol. II: *Elia* and the *Last Essays of Elia* (London, 1903); see also the edition with introduction and notes by Alfred Aingier, whose six-volume edition of Lamb appeared between 1883 and 1888. Lamb's essays were collected in 1823 and 1833: of those here printed, the essays to and including "A Bachelor's Complaint" appeared in *Elia*, and the rest in *The Last Essays*. Certain changes made when Lamb printed the essays in book-form are noted by Mr. Lucas.

3 **E. B.**—Lucas records Lamb's "Key" as giving "Edward Burney, half-brother of Miss Burney."

6 **A.** has been identified as William Ayrton, friend of Lamb, who was a well-known musical critic of that day. See note to p. 233.—**Baralipton** is a term in logic. See Webster's Unabridged Dictionary, under *mode* (3, b) fourth figure.

7 **The Enraged Musician** refers to Hogarth's picture, bearing this title (Lucas).

8 **Amabilis insania.** "Delightful ecstasy."—**Mentis** . . . "Very pleasant hallucinations" (Horace).—**Subrusticus pudor.** "Rustic bashfulness" (Cicero). —**Nov**—— Vincent Novello, the organist, a great friend of Lamb's.

9 **Malleus** . . . "The Heretics' Hammer" (the Latin title of a work by Faber, who opposed Luther).—**Marcion, Ebion,** and **Cerinthus** were three early sectarians.—**Gog** and **Magog** (Revelations xx, 7–9) personate all unbelievers.

11 **Zimmermann** (1728–1795), a Swiss physician and philosopher, who wrote *On Solitude* (*Über die Einsamkeit*).

14 **The Levities**—spirits of laughter and fun. —**Ortelius,** a sixteenth-century Dutch geographer.—**Arrowsmith,** an early nineteenth-century cartographer.

15 **The four great monarchies** were the Assyrian, Persian, Grecian, Roman. —**M.,** Thomas Manning, mathematician and traveller.

16   **Norton Falgate**, or Folgate, a street from the end of Bishopsgate Without to Shoreditch. Cf. *London and Its Environs Described* (London, 1761), V, 59; Harben, *A Dictionary of London* (London, 1918), pp. 94 and 443.

17   **Lily** and **Linacre**. The "fathers of English scholarship," friends of More, Erasmus, and Colet, in the early sixteenth century.— **Flori-** and **Spici-legia**. "Anthologies and gleanings," (*lit.* "cullings of flowers," "gleanings of grain").

18   The **Tractate** is Milton's. It was published in 1644.

19   **Mollia** . . . "At the most favorable times" (adapted from Vergil).

22   **Essex Street** was "the headquarters" of Unitarianism. Lamb is here rather speaking of Elia than of himself. His parents had seven children, of whom three lived to grow up.

23   **James and Bridget Elia** are his brother John and his sister Mary.

24   **Domenichino**, an Italian painter of the sixteenth and seventeenth centuries.

26   The three **Carracci** were painters of the Bolognese School; **Giordano** and **Maratti** are minor painters.

27   **Clarkson**, a friend of Lamb's, was an anti-slavery agitator. Lamb's "Key" says the Society was for the Relief of Distrest Sailors (Lucas).

31   **B. F.** is Lamb's friend Barron Field, mentioned in several essays; cf. "Distant Correspondents," and the "very dear friend" in "The Old and the New Schoolmaster." Cf. note to p. 233.

36   **B.——**John Braham, *né* Abraham, a great tenor of the first half of the nineteenth century. Lamb here refers to his singing in Händel's oratorio "Israel in Eygpt" (Lucas).

41   **Rarus hospes**. "An uncommon guest."

44   **C——** is identified by Lucas as Coleridge; "but Lamb may really have said it." —**Dagon**. Lucas refers to Judges xvi, 23 and 1 Samuel, v.—**Hog's Norton**, where pigs eat "organs" (penny-royal), and where, says Lucas, a villager named Pigg played the organ. Lamb refers to an old proverb.

45   **Lucian**, a Greek satirist, wittily attacks even religion. —**C. V. L.,** Charles Valentine le Grice, a schoolfellow of Lamb.

46   **Non** . . . "But that was not the place for such things" (adapted from Horace). —**Horresco referens**. "I shudder at the recollection" (Vergil).

49   **My dear F.** See note to p. 31.

50   Mrs. (Elizabeth) **Rowe** (1674–1737) wrote *Friendship in Death, in Twenty Letters from the Dead to the Living.* —**The Post-Angel** is in Cowley's *Hymn to Light* (Lucas).

53   **Melior lutus,** "Finer clay" (Juvenal); **sol pater,** "father sun."— **The Adventures of Peter Wilkins** (1751) was by Robert Paltock; it long remained popular.

54   **J. W.,** Lamb's friend James White, who died in 1820. (Cf. "The Praise of Chimney-Sweepers.")

56   **Alsatia,** a district near Whitefriars, forming a sanctuary for debtors. —**The Catos of the pit.** Cato was Roman Censor.

61   **Asps or Amphisbænas.** Lucas finds an echo of Milton's line (*P. L.,* x, 524):

> "Scorpion and Asp, and Amphisbæna dire."

69   **Speciosa miracula.** "Shining wonders" (Horace).

74   **Mordecai,** etc. See Esther iii, 2; iv, 1–3; Luke xvi, 20; 1 Kings xiii, 24; Exodus viii, 3, 6; Ecclesiastes x, 1; Matthew vii, 3; Luke x, 42; Proverbs xxvi, 1. **Agathocles's** father was a potter.

75   **Aliquando . . .** "Sometimes he had to be restrained." (Cf. Jonson on Shakespeare.)

79   **These young Grotiuses.** Lucas notes that among the works of Grotius (1583–1645) was *De Jure Belli et Pacis.*

80   **The Convalescent.** Lucas records the fact that Lamb had a severe nervous breakdown after his retirement from the India House; "indeed his health was never sound for long together when he became a free man."

83   **Philoctetes.** The arrows of Hercules, dipped in the poison of the Lernæan hydra, inflicted incurable wounds. They were bequeathed to Philoctetes, who, on the voyage to Troy, wounded himself in the foot with one, and was left on Lemnos by the Greeks. A play by Sophocles tells the story of his being fetched from there by Ulysses and Diomed. —**Tityus,** the giant, covered nine acres when he lay on the ground (Lucas).

88   **Hickman,** the pugilist, is described in Hazlitt's "The Fight"; one of the characters in Richardson's novel, the lover of Miss Bayes, was a Mr. Hickman. —**Tom Brown** (1663–1704) was a satirist.—

89   **Bully Dawson** is mentioned in the *Spectator;* in his youth, Sir Roger kicked Bully Dawson in a public coffee-house, for calling him youngster. —Bernard **Mandeville's** *Fable of the Bees* was, notes Lucas, a favorite book of Lamb's.

92   Lamb wrote to Wordsworth in 1833, when the *Last Essays* was newly out: "I want you in the *Popular Fallacies* to like the 'home that is no home,' and 'rising with the lark.' " The former of these naturally interested Lamb deeply, for it contains a hardly-disguised account of his own struggles with the crowd of loungers and good-natured friends who intruded on his leisure hours, and hindered his reading and writing. There is little to call for a note in these papers. The pun of Swift's criticized—with rare acumen—in the Fallacy "that the worst puns are the best," was on a lady's mantua dragging to the ground a Cremona violin. Swift is said to have quoted Vergil's line—

> "Mantua væ miseræ nimium vicini Cremonæ."
>
> [Mantua, alas! too near unhappy Cremona.]
>
> (Aingier.)

Homely, in England, means " homelike."

94   **It has been prettily said.** Probably by Mary Lamb [in *Poetry for Children* (1809)],—or by Lamb himself. See "The First Tooth" (Lucas).

95   **Much knowledge.** Cf. Ecclesiastes ix, 10: ". . . there is no work, nor device, nor knowledge, nor wisdom, in the grave. . . ."

98   Robert **Merry** (1755–1798) was an affected versifier. Lucas thinks the story of his avoidance of the lady of his first choice was "probably true."

100   **The Imperial forgetter.** Nebuchadnezzar (see Daniel ii).

HUNT

103   There is no standard collection of Hunt's works; a selection of his contributions to the *Indicator, Companion,* and *Seer* was reprinted in 1833, 1850, and reissued in 1865. Perhaps the most easily accessible collection of his essays is that made by Arthur Symons for the Camelot Series (London, 1888); another selection, with illustrations by Brock, was made by the same editor in 1910.

104   **John Buncle,** by Thomas Amory (1691–1788) was published in two volumes, anonymously, 1756–1766. It showed a hero who was married to several wives in quick succession. Hazlitt's essay on this work appeared in the *Examiner,* 17 September 1815; the fame of the novel was largely due to Lamb and Hazlitt.

105   John Manners, **Marquis of Granby** (1721–1770) was an English general, whose popularity is still witnessed by the numerous inns which bear his name. It is perhaps natural that the Old Lady should

PAGE

prefer the heroes of her youth to those of the later age. —John **Wilkes** (1727–1797) politician, publicist, and agitator, founded the *North Briton* (1762). Imprisoned for criticizing George III, he was soon released, and became a popular hero. Expelled from Parliament (1764) and reëlected several times, he was declared ineligible for membership. He served as alderman, sheriff, and (in 1774) as Lord Mayor of London. His meeting with Dr. Johnson, engineered by Boswell, is described in the *Life*.

106 **Southerne's** tragedy *Oroonoko* (1696) was founded on Mrs. Behn's novel (1688).

108 "**Hot cockles**" was one of the old games played at Bracebridge Hall on Christmas Eve. See Irving's *Sketch Book*. See also below, p. 140.

117 **Giulio (Cesare) Cordara** (1704–1785) was an Italian poet and historiographer of the Jesuits.

119 **The Queen of France.** It is told of Eleanor of Aquitaine (1122–1204) that when her husband Louis VII of France shaved his beard, and presented himself before her, she said that while she had consented to endure without complaint the humiliating disdain of the king, she could not continue to live with a man who had no beard on his chin. The quarrel (which most historians lay to other causes) ended in a separation (1152), and Eleanor subsequently married Henry II of England. (See Larousse's *Grand Dictionnaire Universel*, under *barbe*.) —There is doubtless a pun in the misspelling of **Bedreddin Hassan,** who was the son of Noureddin Ali, in the Arabian Nights' story of that name. —**Edward Wortley Montagu** (the son of Lady Mary Wortley Montagu) was born in 1713, and died in 1776. He is the "young Montagu" mentioned by Lamb in "The Praise of Chimney-Sweepers."

135 "**The other**" probably refers to William Hazlitt.

136 **E voi ridete** ("And you can laugh"). A song from Mozart's opera, *Cosi Fan Tutte* (1790).

HAZLITT

146 The Hazlitt selections here have been collated with the editions of A. R. Waller and Arnold Glover, and of P. P. Howe (the Centenary Edition—the *Complete Works of William Hazlitt*—in 21 volumes, not all of which have appeared: London and Toronto, 1930 ff.) which is based on the earlier edition. Both of these are fully annotated. In a few instances I have silently changed Hazlitt's erratic spelling.

The essays here collected may be found in the following volumes of the Waller and Glover edition: In *Table-Talk*, "Character of Cobbett" (also in *The Spirit of the Age*); "On Living to One's-Self;" "On Vulgarity and Affectation;" "On Going a Journey;" "On Familiar Style;" in *The Plain Speaker*, "On Reading Old Books;" in *Fugitive Writings*,—Waller and Glover, volume XI,—"Thoughts on Taste" (the conclusion of this essay did not appear in any periodical, but is taken from the *Sketches and Essays* (collected in 1839), where it was printed "perhaps from MS. or proof "). In Waller and Glover, volume XII, are "Of Persons One Would Wish to Have Seen," "Of the Feeling of Immortality in Youth," and "On a Sun-Dial."

The Howe text has been followed in all of the selections save "Of Nicknames," "Thoughts on Taste," "Of Persons One Would Wish to Have Seen," "Of the Feeling of Immortality in Youth," and "On a Sun-Dial," where I have used the Waller and Glover edition, on which the Howe edition is based.

146   **Hæ nugæ** . . . "These trifles will lead to serious evils" (Horace).

147   Do not confuse **Jacobin** with *Jacobite*.

152   **Causa causæ** . . . "The cause of the cause became the cause of the thing caused."

154   **Stat** . . . "He stands in the shadow of his name."

157   **Nil admirari** is more correctly translated, "To wonder at nothing." Pope quotes Creech's translation of Horace, "Not to admire is all the art I know," but *admire* meant "wonder at" in the eighteenth century. Horace says, "To wonder at nothing is almost the one and only thing which can make and keep a man happy."

157(*n.*)   **Non satis** . . . "It is not enough that poems be pretty; they should convey pleasure."

164   The third paper did not appear in the *Edinburgh* (*New Scots*) *Magazine:* it is reprinted by Waller and Glover from "Sketches and Essays."

171   **William Cobbett** (1766–1835), an English political writer, journalist, and member of Parliament (1832, 1834) was in America from 1792 to 1800.—**Tom Cribb** (1781–1848) was a champion pugilist, retired, when Hazlitt wrote this essay, to the proprietorship of a London public-house.

173   **Caviar,** a delicacy for some people, is not generally liked by the masses, who have not acquired the taste for it. So here, as in *Hamlet*, the word suggests something over the heads of the general

public. —The **Whigs** are the political ancestors of the Liberals, and (Hazlitt thinks) did not understand the radicalism of Cobbett.— **Nunquam** . . . "He never had to be suppressed." (Cf. note, p. 75.)

174 Howe identifies the dash: "Brougham, no doubt." Others query "Coleridge?" —The **Grammar** was *A Grammar of the English Language, in a Series of Letters* (1818).

175 For the **Yanguesian** carriers, see *Don Quixote.*

181 **Lady Morgan** (1783–1859) wrote under her maiden name, Sydney Owenson. She was a popular author of the early nineteenth century. *The Wild Irish Girl* (1806) passed through seven editions in two years. In a recent paper (*P. M. L. A.*, June, 1933), A. Lionel Stevenson suggests that she was the original of Thackeray's Becky Sharp. —In a note to the *Confessions of an English Opium Eater,* De Quincey observes that " '**Anastasius**' was written by the famous and opulent Mr. Hope, and was in 1821 a book both of high reputation and of great influence amongst the leading circles of society." Thomas Hope (1770–1831), merchant-prince, traveller, novelist, and writer on art, produced a treatise *On the Origin and Prospects of Man* which is noticed in Carlyle's "Characteristics." —**Delphine,** title and heroine of a novel (1802) by Madame de Staël, written during her banishment from France by Napoleon I, when she travelled in Italy and Switzerland.—"**Mail-coach copies**" were the earliest —the bulk of the edition followed by slower, cheaper methods of transportation.—**Millar** (1707–1768) was the publisher of Thomson and Fielding.—John **Thurloe** (1616–1668) was Secretary of State from 1653 to 1660; his *State Papers* were edited in 1742.

185 **New Éloïse.** See Hazlitt's essays "On the Character of Rousseau," and "On Going a Journey."

186 The reference in the note is to Lamb. —**Leurre de dupe** ("decoy of the dupe") is, Waller and Glover point out, an expression of Rousseau's.

187 Waller and Glover identify the "**great preacher**" as Edward Irving (1792–1834), on whom De Quincey wrote an essay—see his *London Reminiscences* iv (in Masson's edition, III, 121–126).

188 **Intus** . . . "They are a part of my inmost self." (Persius.)

193 "**Melts down hours to minutes**" is a phrase which Hazlitt uses again in "On a Sun-Dial" (see p. 265, below).

195 **When in Holland.** As Waller and Glover remark, this story of Goldsmith is much exaggerated. They refer to Northcote's *Life of*

Reynolds, Prior's *Life of Goldsmith*, Forster's *Life and Times of Oliver Goldsmith*, and Boswell's *Life of Johnson;* also to Hazlitt's paper "On Common Fame."—The **"celebrated talker"** is tentatively identified as Coleridge by Howe.

196 **"Malbrook"** is the French pronunciation of "Marlborough." The song (dating from c. 1709) became popular in France—the air is that of "We Won't Go Home Until Morning."

197 For L——, Hazlitt's son prints "Lethbridge" in his edition of *Table-Talk;* Howe identifies "the neighbouring Baronet" as Sir Thomas Lethbridge. The line is adapted from Pope.

199 Hazlitt's unhappy married life must have been in the mind of those readers who knew him.

200 **The man in the Hartz Mountains.** The reference is to the mirage of the Brocken.

203(*n.*) **Labentem** . . . "You measure the passage of time by your own heavens."

208 **Janus Weathercock** was one of the pseudonyms of Thomas Griffiths Wainewright (1794–1852), a contributor to the *London Magazine* in 1820 (see Waller and Glover's note).—The **Royal Coburg** Theatre, Waterloo Road, was opened in 1818; later it was named the Victoria Theatre; it was the forerunner of the present "Old Vic." The **Surrey** Theatre was opened in 1810, in the Blackfriars Road; became the Royal Circus, but reverted to its original name under the management of Dibdin in 1819. See, on these early nineteenth-century theatres, E. B. Watson, *Sheridan to Robertson* (Cambridge, Massachusetts, 1926). —**"Ashley's"** is a mispronunciation of "Astley's."

209 **Milanie** was a dancer at the Italian Opera, at this time. The quotation is Wainewright's (Howe).

210 **Servum** . . . "Servile herd of imitators" (Horace).

211 **Odi** . . . "I hate the profane crowd and keep them at a distance" (Horace).

219 In the Paris *Table-Talk,* C—— is printed "Coleridge."

220 **All-Foxden** (near Nether-Stowey, Somersetshire) was where Hazlitt visited Coleridge in 1798; he was there again in 1803. —L—— is Lamb.

221 **Procul** . . . "Far hence, away, ye profane!" (Vergil).

222 **Bonne bouche.** "Sweetmeat," "pleasant morsel." The first and second editions read *bon bouche.*

PAGE

224 Stonehenge is a circle of prehistoric monoliths on Salisbury Plain.

230 For **Tulippomania,** see the *Tatler*, no. 218.

231 Sermo . . . "Speech that creeps on the ground."

233f. B—— is Lamb, at one of whose "Wednesdays" the conversation described is supposed to have taken place. A—— is William Ayrton (1777–1858), the musician; **Captain C.** and **M. C.** are Captain and Martin Burney [the first, James Burney (1750–1821), was with Cook on his third voyage (1776–1779); he retired from the navy in 1784, and devoted himself to literature]. **Miss D**—— has been identified as Mrs. Reynolds, who had been Lamb's schoolmistress; **E**—— is probably Edward Phillips; **J. F**——, Barron Field; **G**——, William Godwin; **H**——, Leigh Hunt.

237 **Cadmuses.** In Greek mythology, Cadmus, a Phœnician prince, slew a dragon, and sowed its teeth; from them sprang armed men, who fought and killed each other, until five were left; with these he is reputed to have founded Thebes. He is also the one who introduced the alphabet into Greece from Phœnicia. (Jason, too, sowed dragon's teeth, which produced armed men, from whom he was saved by Medea.) A "Cadmean victory" is one which ruins victors as well as vanquished.

238 The **Wandering Jew** has been frequently treated in literature: by Quinet, Schlegel, Andersen, Sue, etc., and Doré has illustrated the tale. There are several versions—some calling him a servant of Pilate, named Cartaphilus, who gave Christ a blow when He was led to execution; others, naming him Ahasuerus, a cobbler who refused Christ permission to rest when he passed his house on the way to Golgotha. Both legends agree in the sentence pronounced upon him: "Thou shalt wander on the earth until I return." An Italian story of a Jew named Malchus, who struck Christ with an iron glove, and was condemned to whirl ceaselessly around an underground pillar until the last day, is not to be confused with the others.

240 **Enthusiast** frequently, in the eighteenth and early nineteenth centuries, has the sense of "fanatic."

244 **Mrs. Hutchinson** is, of course, Lucy—not Anne. Her life of her husband (published in 1806) was much admired by Lamb, as were the letters of "the thrice noble **Margaret Newcastle**" (see "The Two Races of Men,"), whose husband, William Cavendish (1592–1676), was created Earl of Newcastle in 1628, and Duke of Newcastle in 1665. Colonel John Hutchinson (1615–1664) was one of the regicides.

246 **That night**—of despotism. Cf. p. 254, below.

251(*n.*) **Monstrum** . . . "Huge monster of a double form." (Cf. Vergil, *Æn.* iii, 658.)

253 **Divinæ** . . . "Particles of divine ether."

259 **The French.** Hazlitt's judgment on the French strikes some observers as superficial, as does De Quincey's estimate of the same nation (see below, p. 269).

259(*n.*) Robert **Bloomfield** (1766–1823), poet and shoemaker, whose best-known poem, *The Farmer's Boy*, appeared in 1800.

261 **Allons** . . . "Come, my son, I am more of a child than you."

262 "**That things should be that are now no more.**" Cf. p. 255. —The title of the **Earl of Windsor** was added to those held by the Marquis of Bute in 1796; this was, then, a new creation—newer, even, than that of the House of Hanover, to which George IV belonged. —**De non apparentibus** . . . "As to things which do not appear, the conclusion is the same as to things which do not exist." (Coke.)

264(*n.*) **Le son** . . . "The sound of bells has always singularly affected me."

266 **Something of the kind.** Probably, suggest Waller and Glover, Hazlitt refers to the sketch of his father in "My First Acquaintance With Poets" (1823).

DE QUINCEY

268 The text is based on *The Collected Writings of Thomas De Quincey*, edited with notes by Professor David Masson, in fourteen volumes (London, 1896–1897); see also the *Works*, in sixteen volumes (Edinburgh, 1862).

In Masson's edition, "Walking Stewart" is to be found in volume III, "On Suicide" in volume VIII, "On the Knocking at the Gate in *Macbeth*," and "Conversation" in volume X, and "Hazlitt" in volume XI.

268 **John Stewart** (1749–1822) led an extraordinary life (see D. N. B., and authorities there cited; also De Quincey's article in *Tait's Magazine* for October, 1840, and Professor Masson's "editorial note" after the two articles in his edition of De Quincey—III, 118–120). He travelled much, and had many adventures; an idea of his character is given in this paper, which is an example of the development of the description of a typical figure into the portrait of an individual. This paper is sometimes printed under the title "Walking

PAGE

Stewart"; it appeared originally in a series of articles contributed by De Quincey to the *London Magazine* under the general title of "Notes from the Pocket-Book of a late Opium-Eater," and was reprinted by Masson from the revised text prepared for the Edinburgh collection of his works (1858) by De Quincey. In an "editorial note" by Masson (III, 118–120) various inaccurate statements by De Quincey are corrected. —Stewart's books are listed in Masson's edition of De Quincey (III, 97, n.) from Lowndes's *Bibliographer's Manual* (Bohn). Most of the books were printed for private distribution only. —**Madame Mara** (*née* Schmeling) (1749–1833) was a German singer; she lost her voice in 1802.

270   **Hyder,** or Haidar, **Ali,** of obscure origin, became the ruler of Mysore in 1759; he usurped the title of Maharaja in 1766, and he died in 1782.

272   The **"memoir"** was, notes Masson, an obituary notice of "Walking Stewart" which appeared in the *London Magazine* for November, 1822.

275   **Crazy.** Hamlet was "but mad north-north-west."

276   **Lampadophoroi.** In Masson's edition this note (of De Quincey's) is inserted: "Lamp or torch bearers, the several parties to an obscure Grecian game. The essential point known to us moderns is that, in running, they passed on to each other a lighted torch, under what conditions, beyond that of keeping the torch burning, is very imperfectly explained. But already this feature of the game, without further details, qualifies the partakers in it to represent symbolically those who, from generation to generation, pass onwards the traditions of gathering knowledge."

278   In Masson's edition, **W——** is expanded: "Wilson of Edinburgh."

280   **Proton pseudos.** "First falsehood." —The final paragraph is subordinated to a footnote in Masson's text. (This paper was signed "X. Y. Z.") Masson records that De Quincey had intended to enlarge it, "but this was not done."

282   **Quoad.** "Regarding," "as far as . . . is concerned." —Masson observes that this passage concerning **Williams** is "a kind of presentiment of De Quincey's subsequent extravaganza called *Murder considered as one of the Fine Arts*," where the butcheries are described in great detail.

285   **Biathanatos,** by John Donne (1573–1631) was published post-

humously in 1644. The author became a clergyman in 1616—having previously led the life of an Elizabethan poet, man of letters and wit. —**Religion** . . . Kant's work ("Religion within the Limits of Mere Reason") was published in 1793. —Cesare Bonesano, Marchese di **Beccaria** (1735–1794) was one of the earliest opponents of the death penalty; his most famous work, *On Crimes and Punishments* (1764), was very influential. Voltaire's *Affaire La Barre* is addressed to Beccaria.

288   **Tædium vitæ.** "Weariness of life."

289(*n.*) The Rev. **George Gilfillan** (1813–1878), a popular writer, published in 1845 a collection of sketches and criticism—later followed by two others—under the title of *A Gallery of Literary Portraits;* the paper on Hazlitt is in the set of notes occasioned by the first volume. (For more details, see Masson's edition of De Quincey, XI, 326–327, n.)

290   John **Foster** (1770–1843) was an essayist who furnished the subject of the paper preceding this one. He was a Baptist minister, whose *Essays, in a Series of Letters* had a high reputation earlier in the century. —**Fallentis semita vitæ,** "The pathway of life which escapes observation" (Horace).

291   Masson thinks this **friend** was "probably Charles Lamb."

294   **Modern Pygmalion.** The proper title, as Masson notes, is *Liber Amoris, or The New Pygmalion* (1823).

300   **Conversation.** Reprinted, from the original in *Tait's Magazine* (October, 1847), "with considerable enlargements," in 1860, in the posthumous (fourteenth) volume of De Quincey's edition of his Collective Writings (Masson). The text is taken from Masson's edition.

303   **Lord Bacon.** Masson refers to "Of Studies," and "Of Friendship," where Bacon shows the benefits of "conference" or conversation. De Quincey here refers directly to the former.

304   **Fioriture.** "Flourishes."

308   **Strumous diathesis.** "A scrofulous condition."

309   The original article in *Tait's Magazine* stopped with the paragraph ending "much arrogance in the talker." The rest is a subsequent addition.

310   **Lâcheté.** "Cowardice."

312   Dr. Isaac **Watts's** "Improvement of the Mind" was published in

1741. —Masson notes the "blundered structure" of the sentence: *"of little practical use;* nor would it ever have been *thought so,"* etc. But the sense is clear.

318   "Parties" for "persons" was in good use early in the nineteenth century, though it is not now. —Baron **William** [Karl Wilhelm] **von Humboldt** (1767–1835) should not be confused with Baron Friedrich Heinrich Alexander von Humboldt (1769–1859), the naturalist.

320   **Unde pedem proferre pudor vetat.** "Whence modesty prevents one from stepping."

DICKENS

324   I have collated the text of Dickens's essays with the rare editions of *Sketches of Young Gentlemen* (London, 1838) and *Sketches of Young Couples* (London, 1840) in the Harvard Library. These papers were not published in periodicals. In most of the collections of Dickens's works, "A Noble Savage" is in *Miscellanies* or *Reprinted Pieces;* the other two papers are found in *The Uncommercial Traveller*—a title used by Dickens in *All the Year Round.*

330   The celebrated **Mr. Thurtell** was the gambler and murderer who was executed in 1824 at the age of thirty for the murder of William Weare. See Thackeray's "On a Hundred Years Hence," and Smith's "A Lark's Flight."

331   **Johnsonian sense.** This might refer either to the *Dictionary* of Dr. Samuel Johnson, or to the "humors" of Ben Jonson's comedy. The distinction in spelling is not always carefully observed.

337   For the history of the **Adelphi Theatre,** a house famous for melodrama, see E. B. Watson's *Sheridan to Robertson, a Study of the Nineteenth-Century London Stage* (Cambridge, Massachusetts, 1926). In 1838, Madame Céleste made her début here in a speaking part, in Bernard's *Saint Mary's Eve;* and Professor Watson cites from the *Theatrical Examiner's* account of this play (p. 357 f.): ". . . O'Smith's breakfast was a splendid thing. . . ."

339   William **Etty** (1787–1849) was an English painter of historical subjects.

341   **Guernsey shirts.** Compare the more modern "jerseys."

356   George **Catlin** (1796–1872) was an American artist and traveller among the American Indians and in Europe. His chief work was

PAGE

Illustrations of the Manners, Customs, and Condition of the North American Indians (1841). His collection of portraits of Indians from life is in the United States National Museum at Washington.

365 For **Aceldama,** see Matthew xxvii, 7–8 ("field of blood").—**Horace Kinch** is not an historical character.

366 **Devoted,** in the older sense of "doomed," "set apart by a vow, for destruction." Cf. Milton's "These wicked tents devoted" (*P. L.* v, 887).

370 **A Plea** was printed in *All the Year Round* under the general title, "New Uncommercial Samples."

THACKERAY

376 The text of the *Roundabout Papers* is that of the Biographical Edition of the *Works,* with introductions by Thackeray's daughter, Anne Ritchie (New York and London, 1903), in volume XI of which they appear. A fully annotated edition of the papers, edited by Professor J. E. Wells, New York, Harcourt, Brace, 1925, may be mentioned.

376 **On a Lazy Idle Boy.** This essay opened the series in the newly-founded *Cornhill Magazine,* of which Thackeray was the first editor. —**Diligence** has a deceptive look to those readers who do not realize that it is here a French noun, meaning "stage-coach." Nor is **gymnasium** our "gym," but a German name for a school something like our "high school," or "preparatory school."

379 **Antar** was an Arabian warrior and poet, who lived just before Mohammed; he was the probable hero of a celebrated romance named for him—perhaps by Asmai (740–830), the preceptor of Haroun-al-Raschid. —**T,** of course, is Thackeray.—John Scott, first Earl of **Eldon** (1751–1838), Lord Chancellor of England.

380 **Ailes-de-pigeon,** an old mode of dressing men's side hair (or wig) in the form of pigeons' wings. —**Gunter's** is a restaurant or tea-room in London; cf. Thackeray's paper "On Ribbons" ("Sir Richard Gunter . . . presiding at the buffet"). —**"The veteran"** is G. P. R. James (1801–1860), author of some seventy-seven works in 198 volumes, including *Richelieu* (1829), *Darnley* (1830), *De l'Orme* (1830). His "two horsemen" will be remembered best (if not solely) through Thackeray's parody "Barbazure," contributed to *Punch.* —The **"ghost-story"** is Bulwer-Lytton's "The Haunted and the Haunters."

381   The **"ordinary"** meal (or *table d'hôte*) served at an inn, at a fixed price.—**Medioque** . . . "from the midst of the fountain of pleasures."—**Amari aliquid,** "something of bitterness." (Lucretius.)

> "Medio de fonte leporum
> Surgit amari aliquid, quod in ipsis floribus angat."
> (*De Rerum Nat.*)

382   [**De mortuis**] **nil nisi bonum:** "[Of the dead], nothing but what is good." According to Plutarch, it was a law of Solon that men must not speak ill of the dead. —**Allibone's** article puts the sale of Irving's works at more than half a million.

384   **To replace her.** With Thackeray's tribute to Irving's faithfulness, compare Irving's "Rural Funerals" (in *The Sketch Book*), especially: "The love which survives the tomb is one of the noblest attributes of the soul . . . who would root out such a sorrow from the heart?"

384(*n.* **1**)   **Two kings of Brentford** were characters in Buckingham's farce, *The Rehearsal,* who appear together and do the same things.

385   Joseph René **Bellot** (1826–1853), a French arctic navigator.

386   **K. K.** (*Kaiserlich-Königlich*). "Imperial and royal." —The **senior wranglers** were honors men at Cambridge, placed in the first class in the mathematical tripos; the first on the list was the "senior wrangler" for that year. The honor was last conferred in 1909.

387   **A cœur ouvert.** "With open heart." —The **"catholic dome in Bloomsbury,"** is, of course, the British Museum Library.

388   The **Athenæum.** A London club.

389   **Tunbridge Toys.** In her introduction (p. xvi), Mrs. Ritchie recalls the writing of this essay: "in the summer of 1860, when we were staying at Tunbridge Wells in an old wooden house. . . . The grandparents were living in the ground-floor sitting-room; we were established overhead. . . ."

393   **Valancour** (cf. Valancourt, in Thackeray's "On a Peal of Bells") is the hero of *The Mysteries of Udolpho* (1794), and **Manfroni** is the villain of Mrs. Radcliffe's romance of that name.—**Thaddeus of Warsaw,** a popular novel by Jane Porter (1803).

394   On **Corinthian Tom and Jerry Hawthorn,** see "De Juventute." Pierce Egan (1772–1849) wrote *Life in London: or the Day and Night Scenes of Jerry Hawthorn and his elegant friend Corinthian Tom,* a selection of sketches giving the sports and amusements of London during the Regency; it was a forerunner of *Pickwick* (cf. Cross, *Development of the English Novel,* 176, 177).

395   **Ovum** and **malum**—the egg and the apple—were the extremes of the Roman dinner; cf. the modern slang "from soup to nuts."—**"I have touched on this subject before"**—see "Thorns in the Cushion."

400   **Tom Bowling,** a character in Smollett's *Roderick Random;* also the hero of Dibdin's song, "Here, a sheer hulk, lies poor Tom Bowling." The name became proverbial for a sailor. Professor Wells refers also to a tale bearing this name, by Captain Frederick Chamier (1839).

403   **Atque sciebat.** "And he knew [that the executioner was waiting for him]." (Cf. Horace.)

406   **Coram populo.** "Before the people."

407   **Siste tandem, carnifex!** "But hold, executioner."—**Jack Ketch,** a notorious executioner in the seventeenth century, gave his name to the public executioner or hangman.—**They talk . . .** Cf. Chaucer's "Murder will out."

410   **"Ktema es aei."** "An eternal possession."—**Dies iræ.** "Day of wrath."

412   **Addison in his nightgown.** Says Holmes (*Professor at the Breakfast-Table,* xii): "Addison gets up a *tableau* and utters an admirable sentiment—or somebody makes the posthumous dying epigram for him." —General Count de **Cambronne** (1770–1842) is said to have exclaimed at Waterloo, "The Guard dies, but does not surrender"— but the sentence is probably apocryphal. —Benjamin Robert **Haydon** (1786–1846) was a noted English historical painter.

413   On the history of the **Sadler's Wells** theatre, see Watson's *Sheridan to Robertson,* esp. pp. 216 ff.

415   **O mea culpa . . .** "My sin, my grievous sin!"—A **stone** is fourteen pounds.

416   **Magna est . . .** "Great is Truth, and she shall prevail." (See 1 Esdras, iv, 41, where the text reads *prævalet*—though it is often quoted in the future.)

417   **O risum teneatis.** "Withhold your laughter" (Horace). —**Marie (de Roux) Manning** (1821–1849) murderess, was hanged with her husband. Her career suggested the character of Mademoiselle Hortense, Lady Dedlock's waiting-woman, in *Bleak House,* to Dickens (see D. N. B.) —**Jack Thurtell** (1794–1824) was a gambler and murderer, who was executed for the murder of William Weare. (Cf. notes to p. 330 and p. 516.)

418   **Lord Derby,** a Tory politician (Prime Minister, 1852, 1858–1859; 1866–1868); **Lord Palmerston,** a Whig politician, was Prime Min-

ister from 1855 to 1865, save for Derby's term. (Cf. "De Finibus.")
—**Ah, te dirai-je,** a folk-song still sung; the words run:

"Ah, vous dirai-je, maman,
Ce qui cause mon tourment?
Papa veut que je raisonne
Comme une grande personne;
Moi, je dis que les bonbons
Valent mieux que la raison."

One can guess why it was a favorite with Marie Antoinette.

420   **Talbot Twysden,** in *The Adventures of Philip.* See "De Finibus,"
below. —**Lord John Russell** (1792–1878) and **William Ewart Gladstone** (1809–1898), Liberal politicians.

421   **Topham Beauclerk** (1739–1780), an English gentleman of refined tastes and charming conversation, the intimate of Dr. Johnson.
—**Charles James Fox** (1749–1806), orator and statesman. —**Benjamin West** (1738–1820), American-born painter, President of the
Royal Academy after Sir Joshua Reynolds. —The **Gascons** are
famous for their boasting.

422   **Sir Richard Blackmore** (1650–1729), poet and physician, wrote
several long dull poems, praised by Addison and Johnson, which are
now forgotten. —**Baour-Lormian** (1770–1854), member of the
Académie Française, 1815; translated Tasso's *Jerusalem Delivered*
(1795); *Ossian* (1801), besides writing many plays, novels, etc.—
Henriade, an epic poem by Voltaire, intended to inspire hatred of
intolerance. —**Robert Pollock** (1789–1827) poet and Scottish Dissenting clergyman, who died of tuberculosis the year *The Course of
Time* was published. The poem was very popular in both England
and America. —**Apsley House,** the residence of the Duke of Wellington, at Hyde Park Corner. Built for Lord Bathurst in 1785, it was
given by the Government to Wellington in 1820. —**Shoolbred's** and
Swan & Edgar's are drapers' shops in London. —Frederick Augustus,
Duke of York, second son of George III (1763–1827), commanded
various unsuccessful expeditions on the Continent, but was made
Field Marshal.

423   **Lord George Bentinck,** second son of the Duke of Portland (1802–
1848), was a sportsman and politician. —**William of Cumberland,**
younger son of George II (1721–1765), an English general, commanded at Fontenoy, Culloden, etc.—**Thomas Moore** (1779–1852),
the poet, was a native of Dublin. —**Henry Dundas, Viscount Melville** (1742–1811), politician. —**Sandy Sansculotte,** because he wore

kilts. In the French Revolution, the Jacobins did not wear knee-breeches—hence the word came to mean "radicals."

424   Almacks, fashionable assembly-rooms, opened in 1765. See "De Juventute." The pun is obvious.

425   I have militated. See below, p. 459 and note.—Serjeant, a barrister of the highest rank, outranking the King's Counsel socially, but professionally inferior to him. Until 1873, they alone could be justices of the Supreme Court. —Q. C., Queen's Counsel. As Professor Wells points out, Rowland, Serjeant, and Oliver, Q. C., opposed each other in the Barnes Newcome divorce suit (*The Newcomes*). "A Roland for an Oliver" is proverbial; the names are those of heroes in French romances.

426   Esprits forts. "Keen (lit. strong) minds, great wits."

428   Couteau de chasse. "Hunting knife."

431   Ratelier. "Set of teeth."

433   Joseph Gillott (1799–1873), English manufacturer of steel pens.— "On the next page." These papers were accompanied with an occasional sketch by the author; these are here omitted, but they may be found in many editions of Thackeray. Note the slightly different text of the opening paragraph in Wells's edition, where the illustration is a vignette.

434   John Mitchell (1815–1875), an Irish revolutionist, banished in 1848, for fourteen years; he escaped from Van Dieman's Land, and went to New York in 1854, returning to Ireland in 1874, after twenty years in America. —"Believe an expert Robert" (*crede experto Roberto*) was a mediæval proverb; here Robert refers to Thackeray himself. [Cf. *Notes and Queries*, 24 May 1930 (clviii) p. 375.]—Pone me . . . "Place me in the desert fields." (Cf. Horace.) —Bouillabaisse, a stew of fish and vegetables, with seasoning, one of the specialties of Marseilles. Thackeray's fondness for it is recorded in his *Ballad of Bouillabaisse*.

435   Cras mihi. "To-morrow my turn."

437   The name Belinda appears in Pope's *Rape of the Lock*, the *Spectator*, and in many Restoration comedies; Saccharissa is in Waller's poems.

439   Charles Blondin (Jean François Gravelet) (1824–1897), French acrobat and tight-rope walker, crossed Niagara on a tight-rope in 1855, 1859, and 1860. He performed frequently at the Crystal Palace, near London. —Young Norval, the hero of Home's tragedy, *Douglas* (1787). —Esau was hairy; see Genesis xxv, 25; xxvii, 23.

PAGE

440 Luigi **Lablache** (1794–1858), an Italian operatic basso. Cf. "De Juventute."

441 **Tamen usque recurro.** "Yet I shall come back." (Cf. Horace.)

443 **Goethe** died in 1832.

444 **Volume 84.** This paper appeared in volume 6 (no. 32)—this passage, on p. 284. *The Adventures of Philip* ends in the same number; *The Small House at Allington* begins in the next.

446 **Ã la mode . . .** "After the Polish fashion." *À la polonaise* would be more idiomatic. —**Doctor F—— and T—— H——.** Firmin and Tufton Hunt were villainous characters in *The Adventures of Philip*. —The **President** was lost in 1841. —**Dilectissimi fratres.** "Most dearly loved brethren." —**Miserere . . .** "Have pity on us, miserable sinners." —**Libera me.** "Deliver me."

448 **Tittlebat Titmouse** is the hero of Samuel Warren's *Ten Thousand a Year.* The other characters are well-known.

450 **Pulveris . . .** "A gift of a little powder (dust)."

451 **Doctor.** Goldsmith's doctor's degree is problematical; he may have received an M. B. from Louvain or Padua, though no date is known.

452 **Non omnis moritur.** "It does not wholly die." (Cf. Horace.)

453 **"Your birth"** should, of course, be "your mother's birth," (for Granny was born in 1772). Pope and Sarah Marlborough died in 1744; Swift and Walpole in 1745.

459 **Militasti . . .** "You fought not without glory." (Cf. Horace.)— **Mon lait de poule . . .** "My egg-nog and nightcap."

460 **Quelle triste vieillesse . . .** "What a sad old age you are preparing for yourself." Talleyrand (1754–1838) was **Bishop of Autun** (1788–1790), resigning under the Revolution. —**Choreas.** "Dancing-school." —**Twentystone,** two hundred and eighty pounds.

464 **Ã chacun sonshako.** "To each his own cap." The French saying is "*à chacun sa chacune,*" "to every Jack his Jill." —The **Lord Mayor's** term is for a year; but Thackeray here refers to William Cubitt chosen for 1860–1861, and reëlected for 1861–1862, because of his "ability and munificence." (Wells.)

467 **Ã bout portant,** "point-blank." (Note the pun on "draw.")

469 Dick **Turpin,** a highwayman executed in 1739, is not to be confused with Archbishop Turpin of Rheims (d. 794). —**Jack Sheppard** (1702–1724) was a famous English robber, generous and popular, who has been made a hero by Defoe and Ainsworth. —**Dr.** William

PAGE

Dodd (1729–1777), clergyman and author, in 1777 forged the name of Lord Chesterfield (his former pupil) to a bond for £4200, and in spite of the efforts of Dr. Johnson and others, was executed in London.

470   **Splendide mendax.** "Magnificently false" (Horace).—**"Beak"** is is still slang for *a magistrate*.

472   **Pinchbeck** (from the name of the inventor) is an alloy used to imitate gold in cheap jewelry.—**Poluphloisbos,** a Homeric epithet, the "loud resounding [sea]."

473   **Drawcansir,** is in *The Rehearsal;* **Tibbs,** a "beau" in *The Citizen of the World.* —**Sapphira** is perhaps suggestive not only of the wife of Ananias (see Acts, v), but of Sappho—for the Biblical Sapphira was no poetess, though she lied. The further suggestion has been made (see *Notes and Queries* for 22 January 1927, p. 71) that there is here also a hint of "blue-stocking" (sapphire), implying that the pretence of poetry in this would-be Sappho is as false as the word of Ananias's wife. Wells derives Rodoessa from the Latin *rodo*, "to gnaw, to slander,"—but there may be a suggestion of the Greek *rhodoessa* ("the rose-coloured lady")—a hint that she uses rouge. See *Notes and Queries* for 20 November 1926 (cli, 371) where Mr. Edward Bensly comments on Thackeray's "playfulness" in making up proper names.

SMITH

475   Mosher of Portland has published an excellent edition of *Dreamthorp* (1913), with an introduction ("Mr. Stevenson's Forerunner") by James Ashcroft Noble. I have also examined the first American edition of *Dreamthorp* (Boston, 1864). The essays from the *Last Leaves* have been collated with the first edition of that volume, edited, with a memoir, by Patrick Proctor Alexander, M. A. (Edinburgh, 1868).

488   **Rev. Gilbert White** (1720–1793), an English naturalist; graduate and Fellow of Oriel College, Oxford; curate at Selborne, he became famous for his *Natural History and Antiquities of Selborne* (1789).

501f.   **When death . . .** The whole essay (I, xix—"That to Philosophize is to Learne How to Die"), from which this extract is taken, may be compared with Smith's. The citation is made by Montaigne from Thales. It is interesting to compare this translation with Florio's.

505   Captain John **Porteous,** an officer of the city guard, was hanged by an angry mob in 1736. See D. N. B., Scott's *Heart of Midlothian,* and his note on the Porteous mob.

512 It may not be so difficult. Compare Sir Thomas Browne's *Religio Medici*, especially part I, section 44: "I am much taken with two verses of Lucan, since I have been able not only, as we do at school, to construe, but understand:

> "'Victurosque Dei celant ut vivere durent,
> Felix esse mori.'
> *[Pharsalia*, iv, 9.]
> "We're all deluded, vainly searching ways
> To make us happy by the length of days;
> For cunningly, to make 's protract this breath,
> The gods conceal the happiness of death."

515 For **Stephen's** death, see Acts vii, 55, 56.—Arthur Elphinstone, sixth and last Lord **Balmerino** (1688–1746), a Jacobite, was taken prisoner at Culloden, tried for treason, and executed on Tower Hill. When he was beheaded, the executioner at the first stroke cut only half through the neck and (we are told) his lordship turned round and grinned at the bungler. (See D. N. B., and Brewer's *Dictionary of Phrase and Fable.*)

516 **Thurtell** is referred to by Dickens ("The Out-and-Out Young Gentleman") and Thackeray ("On a Hundred Years Hence"). See notes to pp. 330 and 417.

523 Giulia **Grisi** (1811–1869), a celebrated Italian soprano, was famed as an opera singer. She sang in London from 1834 to 1861, visited the United States in 1854, and appeared in London again at intervals from 1866 to 1869.

530 **Boanerges** ("The sons of thunder") was an appellation given by Christ to James and John; see Mark iii, 17. The name has been applied to any declamatory orator or preacher.

542 **Charles XII** of Sweden (1682–1718), a celebrated soldier, who invaded Denmark, defeated the Russians, the Saxons and Poles, was defeated by Peter the Great at Pultowa (1709), and was killed at the siege of Frederikshald, Norway.

543 **Go into the Gazette** (an official journal published twice a week containing the names of those receiving honors, of bankrupts, and public notices) as a bankrupt.

550 The **crank** is an instrument of prison discipline: a small wheel revolving in a box filled with gravel. The labor of turning it is severe when there is much gravel in the box.—James **Beattie** (1735–1803), Scottish poet and philosopher, is chiefly remembered for his

PAGE

poem *The Minstrel*, of which the first book was published in 1771 and the second in 1774.

552 Sir Edward Bulwer Lytton (Lord Lytton) (1803–1873) is better known as a novelist and playwright than as an essayist, though he wrote many articles and essays for the periodical press, including the *New Monthly Magazine*, of which he became editor in 1831. —Sir Arthur Helps (1813–1875) was an English historian and essayist, who held various government positions, and enjoyed the confidence of Queen Victoria, who entrusted him with the editorship of the *Speeches and Addresses of the Prince Consort* (1862) and her own *Leaves from the Journal of Our Life in the Highlands* (1868). He is best known for his essays, and for several volumes on *The Conquerors of the New World*, and *The Spanish Conquests in America*, together with various biographies.

558 Remember of. Not now considered good usage. —Todd is John Todd (1800–1873), an American Congregational clergyman and author, whose *Student's Manual* appeared in 1835. For long he was a pastor in Pittsfield, Massachusetts, where he died. —James is G. P. R. James, the "veteran novelist" referred to by Thackeray: cf. above, note to p. 380.

564 John Henry Fuseli (originally Füssli)—a Swiss-English painter and art critic (1741–1825). Blake and other artists owed much to his friendship.

GEORGE ELIOT

578 The text of George Eliot's essays has been collated with that in the Blackwood edition (Edinburgh and London, 1879) which bears the publishers' note: "The Manuscript of this Work was put into our hands towards the close of last year, but the publication has been delayed owing to the domestic affliction of the Author."

581 Selten . . . "Seldom-appearing Monthly."

583 L'Orient . . . "The Orient from the present point-of-view."— Coup d'œil . . . "An almost French way of looking at things."— Qui mérite . . . "Who deserves to be known." —Extrait, "Extract." —Rapporteur . . . "Scientific and Historical Reporter."

585 Einleitung. "Introduction." —Die Bedeutung . . . "The Meaning of the Egyptian Labyrinth."

589 La plus grande . . . "The greatest ambition does not look at all like ambition, when absolutely incapable of attaining its end."

604 Dion. Perhaps a slip; or perhaps a reference to Dion, tyrant of

Syracuse (356 B.C.)—the subject of lives by Plutarch and Nepos, who was unpopular among the luxurious citizens and was murdered by them. He inspired a poem by Wordsworth.

608   **Posterity.** This query was erroneously attributed to Sir Boyle Roche (1743–1807) in a speech in the House of Commons. In *McFingal* (1776), canto ii, John Trumbull (1750–1831) wrote:

> "What has posterity done for us
> That we, lest they their rights should lose
> Should trust our necks to gripe of noose?"

617   **Il ne faut pas . . .** "You must not put ridicule where none exists: this is to spoil your taste and corrupt your judgment and that of others. But where ridicule does exist, you must see it, and bring it out gracefully and in a manner which both pleases and instructs." —**The July days:** the Revolution of 27, 28, and 29 July 1830, by which the government of Charles X and the elder line of the Bourbons was overthrown.—**J'ai vu . . .** "I saw my father's blood."

618   **The lion . . .** See Pliny's *Natural History*, trans. Bostock and Riley (London, 1900), II, 269 (Book VIII, ch. xix): "The only malady to which the lion is subject is loss of appetite; this, however, is cured by putting insults upon him, by means of the pranks of monkeys placed about him, a thing which rouses his anger."

621   **Rien . . .** "Nothing declines more rapidly than civilization in crises like this; in three weeks the result of several centuries is lost. Civilization, *life*, is a thing learned and discovered; bear it in mind.

> Searching wits, of more mechanic parts,
> Who cherished life with new-invented arts.
>   [Vergil.]

Men forget this truth too quickly after several years of peace; they come to think that *culture* is inborn, that it is the same thing as *nature*. Barbarism is always two steps away, and as soon as we give ground, it begins again."—**A dangerous "Swing."** Probably a reference to the agitators of 1830–1831 who signed their letters "Swing" or "Captain Swing," commanding farmers and landed proprietors to abandon threshing-machines and pay higher wages to their laborers, threatening destruction of property if not obeyed. Three "lives" of the fictitious rick-burner "Captain Swing" appeared.

622   **Pétroleuse.** "Fire-brand." The women in the Revolution of 1848 who set fire to public buildings with kerosene oil.

625   **Us[ual] know[ledge].**

PAGE
629 The "Vestiges." Robert Chambers (1802–1871) published anonymously in 1844 the *Vestiges of Creation*, a then revolutionary and startling work, which holds an important place in the history of evolution between Lamarck and Darwin, preparing the way for the *Origin of Species*. The authorship of the *Vestiges* was ascribed to Chambers in 1854; it was first announced in 1884. (See the edition of *Chambers's Encyclopædia* by David Patrick, III, 316.)

645 Les marguerites . . . "The daisies of Hell."—Les délices . . . "The delights of Beëlzebub."

STEVENSON

648 The Stevenson essays are collated with the text of the Biographical Edition (Charles Scribner's Sons) and used with the kind permission of these authorized American publishers of Stevenson. After periodical publication, the essays were collected and printed in book-form: "Crabbed Age and Youth," "An Apology for Idlers," "Æs Triplex," "El Dorado," and "Ordered South" in *Virginibus Puerisque* (1881), and the other four in *Memories and Portraits* (1887).

648 Andrew Fairservice, a character in *Rob Roy*.—Patrick Walker, "the Covenanting hagiographer," was born about 1650, and died about 1745. A rebel, he escaped from Leith tolbooth in 1685, and became a pedlar, vagrant, and gatherer of old stories. He published the lives of several prominent Covenanters; was one of the "irreconcilable zealots known as 'Society men,'" who left their testimony in the *Hind Let Loose*, and his biographies had great chapbook vogue. Sir Walter turned them to good account in *Old Mortality* and *The Heart of Midlothian*. In the notes of the latter book, Scott calls him "Peter Walker." [See Chambers's *Cyclopædia of English Literature*, edited by David Patrick (London and Edinburgh, 1902) II, 101.]—Genius loci. "The spirit of the place."

655 Persiennes. "Blinds."

667 Belvidere, a building commanding a fine prospect, or a place of observation on the top of a house.

672 "The ungodly Binney." Perhaps Thomas Binney (1798–1874), a nonconformist divine, who was best known for his attacks on the Established Church: if he is the one referred to, the adjective may be regarded as ironical, if its meaning is not.

676 Si jeunesse . . . "If Youth knew, if Age could do."

677 The character of Atys. In Phrygian worship, Atys was the beloved of Cybele. The myth is the counterpart of the Greek legend of Aphrodite and Adonis, itself borrowed from the Semitic legend of Tammuz and Ishtar.

680 **Astrea redux.** "Justice returned to lead." Dryden wrote a poem with this title, to celebrate the Restoration of Charles II.

682 **Æs triplex.** "Triple brass." (Horace.)

686 **The Commander's statue.** A statue temporarily endowed with life—see Molière's *Le Festin de Pierre*.

687 The "**respected lexicographer**" is, of course, Dr. Johnson. —Professor Wann suggests that the "**eminent chemist**" is "probably Dr. Joseph Black (1728–1799), Professor of Chemistry at Edinburgh."

688 **Mimmouthed.** "Primly reticent, mim," ("demure, prudish, affectedly modest"). Sc. and Dial. Eng.—**Thackeray and Dickens.** Stevenson, too, left an unfinished novel: *Weir of Hermiston*.

692 **The foreigner.** Scotland "proved a hard mother to Stevenson, and . . . had much to do with making him great, in spite of her terrible weather and sea fogs which nearly killed him, and which finally drove him forever from her shores." Rice, *Stevenson: How to Know Him*, pp. 19 f.

693 **Imperia in imperio.** "Sovereignties within a sovereignty."— Compare Stevenson's character of **John Bull** with Washington Irving's essay, in the *Sketch Book*.

694 **Yankee.** The connotation of *Yankee* has perhaps changed since Stevenson's day. Originally applied to New Englanders, the word during the American Civil War designated the Northerners (used perhaps with contempt by the Southerners); but now it is generally used—even by themselves—to apply to all Americans, without any thought of "reproach."

695 **Sister kingdom.** Compare the Scotsman's comments on England with Lamb's and Thackeray's comments on the Scotch—in "Imperfect Sympathies" and "Small-Beer Chronicle" for instance.

699 **La trêve de Dieu.** "The truce of God." Here, Saturday. In the Middle Ages, the truce forbade wars and brawls at certain seasons, on certain days, in the Church's attempt to lessen feudal brutality.

700 **Darien,** William Patterson's colony in Panama, chartered by the Scottish Parliament in 1695, and abandoned in 1700.

702 Compare "**Old Mortality**" with Hazlitt's "On the Feeling of Immortality in Youth."

707   **Là ci darem la mano,** a song in Mozart's *Don Giovanni*. ("Give me your hand, fair maiden.")

708   **Mene, mene.** See Daniel v, 25, 26. "God hath numbered thy kingdom and finished it."

712   **Enfin . . .** " 'At last,' said Miss Stewart, 'at last he has done something; and that, I swear, is lucky.' "—**Allons . . .** "Come, love me then."

714   **Monsieur . . .** "Sir, I was one of those good bits of mortal clay God made to live for a certain time, and to find good in all things which accompany their sojourn on earth."—**D'Artagnan . . .** "D'Artagnan then sat down near the window, and, this philosophy of Planchet's appearing solid to him, he dreamed about it."

715   **L'homme de bruit . . .** "The man of noise, the man of pleasure, the man who is, only because the others are."

716   **Thackeray pretended . . .** See Thackeray's "On a Peal of Bells": "I think I like d'Artagnan in his own memoirs best."

THOMPSON

719   I am indebted to Wilfrid Meynell, Esq., for permission to use the essays of Francis Thompson, collected in the third volume of his *Works* (London, 1913), and published in America by Scribner.

719   **Decentiorem . . .** "[He thought] that a face on which there was a blemish was more comely."

722   **At animam,** "But it has no soul."

724   **Thwartness.** "Perversity." Murray (O. E. D.) records its use in the sixteenth and seventeenth centuries, noting that the word is "now rare."

729   **Moestitiæ . . .** "Praise of sadness."

731   **Morituri . . .** "Those who are about to die, salute thee."— **Cocytus,** a river of Hades, tributary of the Acheron.

733   **Meo judicio.** "According to my judgment."—**Dryden,** it may be remarked, died in 1700.

738   **Magna civitas . . .** "A great city [is] a great solitude." (Quoted frequently; see Bacon's "Of Friendship.")

743   **The Poet's Poet.** "[Spenser] has always been felt by his country-men to be what Charles Lamb called him, the 'Poet's Poet.' " Leigh Hunt, "Spenser," introducing selections from this poet, in *Imagination and Fancy*.

INDEX

775